T0214496

# Lecture Notes in Computer Science    11662

More information about this series at http://www.springer.com/series/7412

Fakhri Karray · Aurélio Campilho ·
Alfred Yu (Eds.)

# Image Analysis
# and Recognition

16th International Conference, ICIAR 2019
Waterloo, ON, Canada, August 27–29, 2019
Proceedings, Part I

 Springer

*Editors*
Fakhri Karray (iD)
University of Waterloo
Waterloo, ON, Canada

Aurélio Campilho (iD)
University of Porto
Porto, Portugal

Alfred Yu (iD)
University of Waterloo
Waterloo, ON, Canada

ISSN 0302-9743                ISSN 1611-3349   (electronic)
Lecture Notes in Computer Science
ISBN 978-3-030-27201-2        ISBN 978-3-030-27202-9   (eBook)
https://doi.org/10.1007/978-3-030-27202-9

LNCS Sublibrary: SL6 – Image Processing, Computer Vision, Pattern Recognition, and Graphics

This Springer imprint is published by the registered company Springer Nature Switzerland AG
The registered company address is: Gewerbestrasse 11, 6330 Cham, Switzerland

# Preface

ICIAR 2019 was the 16th edition of the series of annual conferences on image analysis and recognition, offering a forum for participants to interact and present their latest research contributions in the theory, methodology, and applications of image analysis and recognition. ICIAR 2019, the International Conference on Image Analysis and Recognition, was held in Waterloo, Ontario, Canada, August 27–29, 2019. ICIAR is organized by AIMI, the Association for Image and Machine Intelligence, a not-for-profit organization registered in Ontario, Canada.

We received a total of 142 papers from 27 countries. Before the review process, all the papers were checked for similarity using a comparison database of scholarly work. The review process was carried out by members of the Program Committee and other reviewers. Each paper was reviewed by at least two reviewers (most articles received three professional reviews), and checked by the conference chairs. A total of 84 papers were finally accepted and appear in these proceedings. We would like to sincerely thank the authors for responding to our call, and to thank the reviewers for the careful evaluation and feedback provided to the authors. It is this collective effort that resulted in the strong conference program and high-quality proceedings.

We were very pleased to include four outstanding keynote talks: "Image Synthesis and Its Growing Role in Medical Imaging" by Professor Jerry Prince of Johns Hopkins University, USA; "Exploiting Data Sparsity and Machine Learning in Medical Imaging" by Professor Michael Insana, of the University of Illinois at Urbana Champaign, USA; "Knowledge Discovery: Can We Do Better than Deep Neural Networks" by Professor Ling Guan of Ryerson University, Toronto, Canada; and "Palmprint Authentication—Research and Development" by Professor David Zhang of Chinese University of Hong Kong (Shenzhen), Hong Kong. We would like to express our gratitude to our distinguished keynote speakers for accepting our invitation to share their vision and recent advances in their areas of expertise.

Besides the standard sessions, the program included five special sessions in the theory and applications of tools of image analysis and recognition:

- Image Analysis and Recognition for Automotive Industry
- Deep Learning on the Edge
- Medical Imaging and Analysis Using Deep Learning and Machine Intelligence
- Adaptive Methods for Ultrasound Beamforming and Motion Estimation
- Signal Processing Techniques for Ultrasound Tissue Characterization and Imaging in Complex Biological Media

We would like to thank the program co-chairs, Dr. Wail Gueaieb, of the University of Ottawa, and Dr. Shady Shehata of YourIKA Inc., who secured a high-quality program, Dr. Mark Crowley of the University of Waterloo and Dr. Chahid Ouali of YourIKA Inc., for helping with the local logistics with precious assistance from Nichola Harrilall, of the Waterloo AI Institute, and Dr. Khaled Hammouda, the publications chair and webmaster of the conference, for maintaining the website, managing the registrations, interacting with the authors, and preparing the proceedings. We are also grateful to Springer's editorial staff, for supporting this publication in the LNCS series. Additionally, we would like to thank the precious sponsorship and support of the Faculty of Engineering, at the University of Waterloo, notably, Dean Pearl Sullivan, the Faculty of Engineering at the University of Porto, the Institute for Systems and Computer Engineering, Technology and Science (INESC TEC), Portugal, the Waterloo AI Institute at the University of Waterloo, the Center for Pattern Analysis and Machine Intelligence at the University of Waterloo, and the Center for Biomedical Engineering Research at INESC TEC. We also appreciate the valuable co-sponsorship of the IEEE Computational Intelligence Society, Waterloo-Kitchener Chapter.

We were very pleased to welcome all the participants to ICIAR 2019. For those who were not able to attend, we hope this publication provides a good overview of the research presented at the conference, and we look forward to meeting you at the next ICIAR conference.

August 2019                                              Fakhri Karray
                                                      Aurélio Campilho
                                                          Alfred Yu

# Organization

## General Chairs

Fakhri Karray — University of Waterloo, Canada
karray@uwaterloo.ca

Aurélio Campilho — University of Porto, Portugal
campilho@fe.up.pt

Alfred Yu — University of Waterloo, Canada
alfred.yu@uwaterloo.ca

## Organizing Committee Chairs

Mark Crowley — University of Waterloo, Canada
mcrowley@uwaterloo.ca

Chahid Ouali — YourIKA Inc., Canada
chahid.ouali@gmail.com

## Program Committee Chairs

Shady Shehata — YourIKA Inc., Canada
shady.h.shehata@gmail.com

Wail Gueaieb — University of Ottawa, Canada
wgueaieb@uottawa.ca

## Industrial Liaison Chair

Alaa Khamis — GM-Canada
alaakhamis@gmail.com

## Publication and Web Chair

Khaled Hammouda — Waterloo, Canada
khaledh@aimiconf.org

## Supported and Co-sponsored by

AIMI – Association for Image and Machine Intelligence

**UNIVERSITY OF WATERLOO**
FACULTY OF ENGINEERING

Faculty of Engineering
University of Waterloo
Canada

CPAMI – Centre for Pattern Analysis and Machine Intelligence
University of Waterloo
Canada

Waterloo AI Institute
Canada

Center for Biomedical Engineering Research
INESC TEC – Institute for Systems and Computer Engineering,
Technology and Science
Portugal

Department of Electrical and Computer Engineering
Faculty of Engineering
University of Porto
Portugal

IEEE Computational Intelligence Society
Kitchener-Waterloo Chapter

# Program Committee

| | |
|---|---|
| J. Alba-Castro | University of Vigo, Spain |
| L. Alexandre | University of Beira Interior, Portugal |
| H. Araujo | University of Coimbra, Portugal |
| G. Azzopardi | University of Groningen, The Netherlands |
| J. Batista | University of Coimbra, Portugal |
| R. Bernardes | University of Coimbra, Portugal |
| H. Bogunovic | Medical University Vienna, Austria |
| J. Boisvert | CNRC, Ottawa, Canada |
| F. Camastra | University of Naples Parthenope, Italy |
| A. Campilho | University of Porto, Portugal |
| C. Carvalho | INESC TEC, Portugal |
| P. Carvalho | INESC TEC, Portugal |
| F. Ciompi | Radboud University Medical Center, The Netherlands |
| A. Cunha | INESC TEC, Portugal |
| J. Debayle | Ecole Nationale Supérieure des Mines de Saint-Etienne (ENSM-SE), France |
| L. Demi | University of Trento, Italy |
| M. Dimiccoli | Institut de Robòtica i Informàtica Industrial (CSIC-UPC), Spain |
| L. Duong | École de Technologie Superieure, Canada |
| M. Ebrahimi | University of Ontario Institute of Technology, Canada |
| A. El Khatib | University of Waterloo, Canada |
| M. El-Sakka | University of Western Ontario, Canada |
| F. Falck | Imperial College London, UK |
| P. Fallavollita | University of Ottawa, Canada |
| J. Fernandez | CNB-CSIC, Spain |
| R. Fisher | University of Edinburgh, UK |
| D. Frejlichowski | West Pomeranian University of Technology, Szczecin, Poland |
| A. Galdran | INESC TEC, Portugal |
| M. García | University of Valladolid, Spain |
| V. Gonzalez-Castro | Universidad de Leon, Spain |
| G. Grossi | University of Milan, Italy |
| W. Gueaieb | University of Ottawa, Canada |
| M. Hassaballah | South Valley University, Egypt |
| F. Karray | University of Waterloo, Canada |
| F. Khalvati | University of Toronto, Canada |
| A. Khamis | General Motors of Canada, Canada |
| Y. Kita | National Institute AIST, Japan |
| R. Kolar | Brno University of Technology, Czech Republic |
| M. Koskela | CSC, IT Center for Science Ltd., Finland |
| A. Kuijper | TU Darmstadt & Fraunhofer IGD, Germany |
| H. Li | University of New Brunswick, Canada |
| J. Lorenzo-Ginori | Universidad Central Marta Abreu de Las Villas, Cuba |

| | |
|---|---|
| A. Wong | University of Waterloo, Canada |
| L. Xu | University of Waterloo, Canada |
| J. Xue | University College London, UK |
| A. Yu | University of Waterloo, Canada |
| P. Zemcik | Brno University of Technology, Czech Republic |
| B. Zhang | University of Macau, SAR China |
| H. Zhou | Queen's University Belfast, UK |
| R. Zwiggelaar | Aberystwyth University, UK |

## Additional Reviewers

| | |
|---|---|
| T. Araújo | INESC TEC, Portugal |
| G. Aresta | INESC TEC, Portugal |
| D. Kumar | University of Waterloo, Canada |
| L. Yu | ASML, USA |

# Contents – Part I

**Image Analysis**

# Contents – Part II

## Applications

## Medical Imaging and Analysis Using Deep Learning and Machine Intelligence

## Image Analysis and Recognition for Automotive Industry

## Adaptive Methods for Ultrasound Beamforming and Motion Estimation

# Image Processing

# Proximal Splitting Networks for Image Restoration

Raied Aljadaany$^{(\boxtimes)}$, Dipan K. Pal$^{(\boxtimes)}$, and Marios Savvides$^{(\boxtimes)}$

CyLab Biometrics Center, Carnegie Mellon University, Pittsburgh, PA, USA
{raljadaa,dipanp,marioss}@andrew.cmu.edu

**Abstract.** Image restoration problems are typically ill-posed requiring the design of suitable priors. These priors are typically hand-designed and are fully instantiated throughout the process. In this paper, we introduce a novel framework for handling inverse problems related to image restoration based on elements from the half quadratic splitting method and proximal operators. Modeling the proximal operator as a convolutional network, we defined an implicit prior on the image space as a *function class* during training. This is in contrast to the common practice in literature of having the prior to be fixed and fully instantiated even during training stages. Further, we allow this proximal operator to be tuned differently for each iteration which greatly increases modeling capacity and allows us to reduce the number of iterations by an order of magnitude as compared to other approaches. Our final network is an end-to-end one whose run time matches the previous fastest algorithms while outperforming them in recovery fidelity on two image restoration tasks. Indeed, we find our approach achieves state-of-the-art results on benchmarks in image denoising and image super resolution while recovering more complex and finer details.

## 1 Introduction

Single image restoration aims to reconstruct a clear image from corrupted measurements. Assume a corrupted image $y$ can be generated via convolving a clear image $x$ with a known linear space-invariant blur kernel $k$. This can be written as:

$$y = k * x + \epsilon \tag{1}$$

where $\epsilon$ is an additive zero-mean white Gaussian noise and $*$ is the convolution operation. The problem of recovering the clean image is an ill-posed inverse problem. One approach to solve it is by assuming some prior (or a set of) on the image space. Thus, the clean image can be approximated by solving the following optimization problem

$$x^* = arg\min_x \|y - k * x\|_2^2 + g(x) \tag{2}$$

---

**Electronic supplementary material** The online version of this chapter (https://doi.org/10.1007/978-3-030-27202-9_1) contains supplementary material, which is available to authorized users.

© Springer Nature Switzerland AG 2019
F. Karray et al. (Eds.): ICIAR 2019, LNCS 11662, pp. 3–17, 2019.
https://doi.org/10.1007/978-3-030-27202-9_1

where $\|.\|_2$ is the $l_2$ norm and $g$ is an operator that defines some prior (e.g $l_1$ norm is used to promote sparsity). A good prior is important to recover a feasible and high-quality solution. Indeed, priors are common in signal and image processing tasks such as inverse problems [1,2] and these communities have spent considerable effort in hand designing suitable priors for signals [3–5].

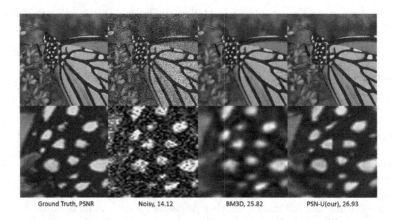

Ground Truth, PSNR        Noisy, 14.12        BM3D, 25.82        PSN-U(our), 26.93

**Fig. 1.** De-noising results of "Fly" (Set12) with Gaussian noise added with $\sigma = 50$. Numbers indicate PSNR. Our algorithm called Proximal-Splitting Network (PSN, U denotes unknown noise level) produces sharper edges in various orientations, an artifact of a powerful learned prior. For illustration, we compare against BM3D [6].

In this work, we build a framework where the image prior is a *function class* during training, rather than a specific instantiation. Parameters of this function are learned which then acts as a fully instantiated prior during testing. This allows for a far more flexible prior which is learned and tuned according to the data. This is somewhat in contrast to what the concept of a prior is in the general machine learning setting where it is usually a specific function (rather a function class). In our application for image restoration, the prior function class is defined to be a deep convolutional network. Such networks have exceptional capacity at modelling complex functions while capturing natural structures in images such as spatial reciprocity through convolutions. A large function class for the prior allows the optimization to model richer statistics within the image space, which leads to better reconstruction performance (as we find in our experiments).

Our reconstruction network takes only two inputs, the corrupted image and the kernel, then it reconstructs the clear image with a single forward pass. The network architecture is designed following a recovery algorithm based on the half quadratic splitting method involving the proximal operator (see Sect. 3). Proximal operators have been successfully applied in many image processing tasks (*e.g.* [7]). They are powerful and can work under more general conditions (e.g don't require differentiability) and are simple to implement and study. Theoretically, the reconstruction process is driven primarily by the half-quadratic splitting method with no trainable parameters. The only need for training arises when the proximal operators in this architecture are modelled using deep networks. This training only helps the network to learn parameters such that the overall pipeline is effective. Our overall framework is flexible and can be applied to almost any image based inverse problem, though in this work we focus on image denoising and image super-resolution.

**Contributions.** We propose a novel framework for image restoration tasks called Proximal Splitting Networks (PSN). Our network architecture is theoretically motivated through the half quadratic splitting method and the proximal operator. Further, we model the proximal operators as deep convolutional networks that result in more flexible signal priors tuned to the data, while requiring a number of iterations an order of magnitude less compared to some previous works. Finally, we demonstrate state-of-the-art results on two image restoration tasks, namely image denoising and image super resolution on multiple standard benchmarks.

## 2 Prior Art

**Priors in Image Restoration.** The design of priors for solving inverse problems has enjoyed a rich history. There have been linear transforms proposed as priors which also assume low energy or sparsity etc [8–10]. However, it has been shown that these approaches fail when the solution space invoked by the assumed prior does not contain good approximations of the real data [11]. There have also been other signal processing methods such as BM3D [6], and those levaraging total variation [12] and dictionary learning [4,11,13] techniques that have been successful in several of these tasks. Proximal operators [14] and half quadratic splitting [12] methods have been useful in a few image recovering algorithms such as [9]. These methods assume hand-designed priors approximated via careful choice of the norm. Although this has provided much success, they are limited in the expressive capacity of the prior which ultimately limits the quality of the solution. In our approach, we *learn* the prior from a function class for our problem during the optimization. Thus our algorithm utilizes a more expressive prior that is informed by data.

**Deep Learning Approaches and Our Generalization.** Deep learning approaches have emerged successful in modelling high level image statistics and thus have excelled at image restoration problems. Some example applications include blind de-convolution [15], super-resolution [16] and de-noising [17]. Though these methods have powerful generalization, it remains unclear as to what the relation between the architecture and the prior used is. In this work however, the network is clearly motivated based on a combination of the proximal operator and half quadratic splitting methods. Further, we show that our network is a generalization of the approaches in [16,17] in the supplementary.

**Deep Learning Approaches Which Learn the Prior.** It is worth mentioning that several approaches have used a proximal gradient decent algorithm

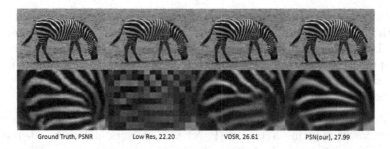

**Fig. 2.** Super-resolution results of "Zebra"(Set14) downsampling (scale) factor X4. Numbers indicate PSNR. Proximal-Splitting Network (PSN) produces much sharper and well-defined edges in various orientations, as artifact of a powerful learned prior. For illustration, we compare against VDSR [16].

[18], ADMM algorithm [19] or a gradient decent method [20] to recover an image where the prior is computed via a deep learning network. Although, these approaches preform well with respect to the reconstruction performance, they inherit important limitations in terms of computation efficiency. Proximal gradient decent, ADMM and gradient decent methods being first order iterative methods with linear or sub-linear convergence rate, typically require many tens of iterations for convergence. Each iteration consists of a forward pass through the network, which emerges as a considerable bottleneck. Our approach addresses this problem by allowing different proximal operators to be learned at every 'iteration'. This increases modelling capacity of the overall network and allows for much lower iterations (an order of magnitude lower in our case).

**Deep Learning Structure Based on Theoretical Approaches.** There are several approaches that employed CNNs for image restoration [21–23] where the structure of the network is driven from a theoretical model for image recovery. In [21], the author proposed the cascade of shrinkage fields for image restoration. CSF can be seen as a ConvNet where the architecture of this network is a cascade of Gaussian conditional random fields [24]. [23] proposed trainable nonlinear reaction diffusion (TNRD) which is a ConvNet that has structure based on nonlinear diffusion models [25]. In [22], the authors proposed GradNet applied to noise-blind deblurring. The architecture of GradNet is motivated by the Majorization-Minimization (MM) algorithm [26]. However, these approaches assume that the prior term is driven from or approximated by Gaussian mixture model [27] which is represented by ConvNet. Our method is free of this assumption.

## 3   Proximal Splitting in Deep Networks

Our main goal is the design of a feed forward neural network for image restoration. For the architecture, we take inspiration from two tools in optimization. The first being the proximal operator which allows for a solution to a problem to be part of some predefined solution space. The second component being the half quadratic splitting technique which allows a sum of objective functions to be solved in alternating sequence using proximal operators. We briefly describe these two components and then utilize them to design our system architecture.

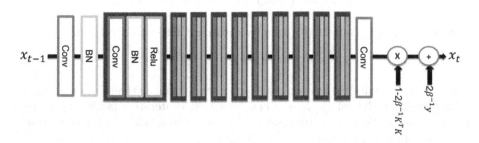

**Fig. 3.** Architecture of a single Proximal Block, the fundamental component of the Proximal Splitting Network (PSN). This block implements a single iteration of the half quadratic splitting method for the constraints in PSN optimization problem (Eq. 12). The block has 10 layers, each being the Convolution, ReLU and Batch Normalization [28] combination. All intermediate layers had 64 channels with $3 \times 3$ convolutions, except the first/last Conv layer with 3/1 channel (RGB/grey-scale).

### 3.1 Proximal Operator

Let $h : R^n \to R$ be a function. The proximal operator of the function $h$ with the parameter $\beta$ is defined as

$$prox_{h,\beta}(x) = arg \min_{z} \beta\|z - x\|_2^2 + h(z) \qquad (3)$$

If the function $h(x)$ is a strong convex function and twice differentiable with respect to $x$ and $\beta$ is large, the proximal operator of the function $h$ converges to a gradient descent step (a proof of this known result is presented in the supplementary). In this case the proximal operator can be approximated as:

$$prox_{h,\beta}(x) \approx x - 2\beta^{-1}\nabla h(x) \qquad (4)$$

### 3.2 Half Quadratic Splitting

Now note that the image recovery optimization problem (Eq. 2) can be rewritten as:

$$x^* = arg \min_{x} f(x) + g(x) \qquad (5)$$

where $f$ is the data fidelity term and $g$ is a function that represents the prior. Depending on this prior $g(x)$, Eq. 5 might be hard to optimize, especially when the prior function is not convex. The half quadratic splitting method [12] restructures this problem (Eq. 5) into a constrained optimization problem by introducing an auxiliary variable $v$. Under this approach, the optimization problem in Eq. 5 is reformulated as:

$$x^*, v^* = arg\min_{x,v} f(x) + g(v), \ s.t. \ v = x \tag{6}$$

The next step is to convert the equality constraint into its Lagrangian.

$$x^*, v^* = arg\min_{x,v} f(x) + g(v) + \beta\|v - x\|_2^2 \tag{7}$$

where $\beta$ is a penalty parameter. As $\beta$ approaches infinity, the solution of Eq. 7 is equivalent to that of Eq. 5, and can be solved in iterative fashion by fixing one variable, updating the other and vice versa. By using the proximal operator, these updating steps become

$$x_t = prox_{f,\beta}(v_t) \quad v_t = prox_{g,\beta}(x_{t-1}) \tag{8}$$

When the image $x$ is fixed, the optimum $v$ can be found through the proximal operator involving $g(z)$ and $\beta$. Clearly, this depends on the prior which is the $g$ function. For instance, if $g(z)$ is $l_1$ norm, the prox operator will be a soft threshold operator which forces the signal to be sparse [9]. However, for real-world image data, the optimal class of functions for $g$ is not known, which by extension makes the prox-operator sub-optimal for recovery. In the following subsection, we will propose an approach to optimize for the prox operator within a predefined search space.

As a final note, recall that since the added noise is assumed to be Gaussian, $f$ is the euclidean distances between the corrupted image and the clean image convolved with a kernel. Thus, $f(x) = \frac{1}{2}\|y - k * x\|_2^2$ which is convex and twice differentiable. This allows the updating step in Eq. 8 for $x$ to be approximated via gradient decent while modifying the proximal operator from Eq. 4:

$$x_t = v_t - 2\beta^{-1}[K^T(Kv_t - y)] \tag{9}$$

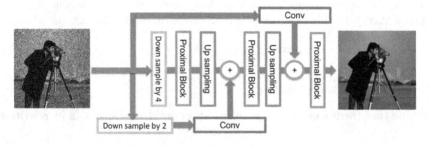

**Fig. 4.** The multi-scale Proximal Splitting Network (PSN) architecture for image restoration tasks. Each Up-sampling block does so by a factor of 2 whereas each Proximal Block has 10 layers (see Fig. 3). The two Conv layers have 1 or 3 channels each (Grey-scale vs. RGB image space) with $3 \times 3$ kernels

where $K$ is the matrix form of the convolution operation with $k$ and $K^T$ is its transpose.

### 3.3 Proximal Splitting Networks

We now develop the core optimization problem which will then yield the Proximal Splitting Network architecture. Our main approach for image recovery is to use the half quadratic splitting method which alternately updates the image $x$ and an auxiliary variable $v$ as in Eq. 8. Thus, for $S$ iterations the optimization procedure becomes

$$v_t = prox_{g,\beta}(x_{t-1}), \quad x_t = v_t - 2\beta^{-1}[K^T(Kv_t - y)] \quad \forall t = 1, \dots, S \qquad (10)$$

Note that the update for $v_t$ still contains a proximal operator depending on the prior $g$. There have been studies such as [18], where the authors replace the proximal operator with a Deep Denoising Network (DnCNN) [17]. Similarly, the authors in [29] use BM3D or the NLM denoiser rather than the proximal operator to update the value of an image. It is also important to note that these studies utilized these denoisers in an iterative fashion *i.e.* the *same* proximal operator with its parameters was used through multiple iterations. Considering that the number of iterations in these studies were significantly high (about 30 for both [18] and [29]) and the fact that every iteration requires a forward pass through a deep network, these methods have large computational bottleneck.

Although these methods work well, there is much to gain from defining a more flexible proximal operator in two ways. First, defining a larger solution space for the proximal operator would allow for the algorithm to choose more fitting operators. Secondly, allowing the proximal operator networks at different stages (iterations) to maintain separate weights allows for each operator to be tuned to the statistics of the estimated image at that stage. This also allows us to keep the number of iterations or stages very small in comparison due to the larger modelling capacity (3 in our experiments, which is an order of magnitude less than previous studies [18,29]). Keeping these in mind, we choose the model for the proximal operator in our formulation to be a deep convolutional network, which introduces desirable inductive biases. These biases themselves act as our 'prior' while providing the optimization a large enough function search space to choose from. The rest of the prior (*i.e.* the actual parameters of the convolutional network) are tuned according to the data. Under this modification, the update step for $v_t$ becomes

$$v_t = \Gamma_\Theta^t(x_{t-1}) \qquad (11)$$

where $\Gamma_\Theta^t$ is a convolutional network for the $t^{th}$ iteration. Note that for every iteration, there is a separate such network. Defining the proximal operator (and the image prior) to be different for every iteration, the final optimization problem becomes

$$\min_\Theta L(x_{gt}, x_S) \quad \text{s.t} \quad v_t = \Gamma_\Theta^t(x_{t-1}), \quad x_t = v_t - 2\beta^{-1}[K^T(Kv_t - y)] \,\forall t = 1, \dots, S \qquad (12)$$

where $x_{gt}$ is the ground truth clean image, $x_S$ is the final estimated image, $S$ is the number of stages (iterations) and $x^0$ is the initial input image. Note that the minimization in this formulation is only on $\Theta$ *i.e.* the parameters of the set of proximal networks $\Gamma_\Theta^t$ $\forall t$. The loss function here can be any suitable function, though we minimize the Euclidean error for this study assuming Gaussian noise. It is important to note a subtle point regarding the recovery framework. The minimization in Eq. 12 only tunes the network $\Gamma_\Theta$ towards the desired task based off the data. However, the core algorithm for reconstruction is still based on Eq. 10 *i.e.* iterations of the half quadratic splitting based reconstruction. It is also useful to observe the interplay between the objective function and the constraints. The first constraint and the loss objective in Eq. 12 work to project the recovered image onto the image space while the second constraint pushes the recovered image to be as close as possible to the corrupted input image. A single iteration over these constraints according to half quadratic splitting, and the proximal network $\Gamma_\Theta$ together result in what we call the Proximal Block as shown in Fig. 3. The Proximal Block is the fundamental component using which the overall network is built (as we describe soon).

**Multi-scale Proximal Splitting Network.** Multi-scale decomposition has been widely applied in many applications, such as edge-aware filtering [30], image blending [31] and semantic segmentation [32]. Multi-scale architecture extensions have also emerged as a standard technique to further improve the performance of deep learning approaches to image recovery tasks such as image de-convolution [15] and image super-resolution [33]. We find that the multi-scaling is useful incorporate it into the Proximal Splitting Network algorithm. These approaches usually require that the output of each intermediate scale stage be the cleaned/processed image at that scale. Complying with this, multi-scaled PSN networks are designed such that the intermediate outputs form a Gaussian pyramid of cleaned images. For better performance, we apply reconstruction fidelity loss functions at each level of the pyramid. This also helps provide stronger gradients for the entire network pipeline, especially the first few layers which are typically harder to train.

**Proximal Splitting Network Architecture for Image Restoration.** Finally, we implement Eq. 12 to arrive at the PSN architecture while utilizing multiple Proximal Blocks in Fig. 4. The number of Proximal Blocks (from Fig. 3) equals the number of stages or iterations for the half-quadratic splitting method (Eq. 12) which we set to be 3 *i.e.* $S = 3$. Recall that this is an order of magnitude lesser than some previous works [18,29]. In Fig. 4, the input image is the corrupted image convolved with the $K^T$ (e.g the input image is the noisy image for image denoising and it is the up sampled image via bi cubic interpolation for image super-resolution in the experiment part) . The down sampling is achieved via bi-cubic down sampling and the up sampling by a de-convolution layer [34]. Through a preliminary grid search, we find that $\beta = 8$ works satisfactorily.

**Table 1.** Denoising PSNR test results of several algorithms on BSD68 with noise levels of $\sigma = \{15, 25, 50\}$. **Bold** numbers denote the highest performing model, whereas *Italics* denotes the second highest. PSN outperforms previous state-of-the-art when the noise level is known, however matches it when it is unknown.

| $\sigma$ | BM3D [6] | WNNM [35] | EPLL [27] | MLP [36] | CSF [21] | TNRD [23] | DnCNN [17] | PSN-K (Ours) | PSN-U (Ours) |
|---|---|---|---|---|---|---|---|---|---|
| 15 | 31.07 | 31.37 | 31.21 | — | 31.24 | 31.42 | *31.61* | **31.70** | *31.60* |
| 25 | 28.57 | 28.83 | 28.68 | 28.96 | 28.74 | 28.92 | *29.16* | **29.27** | *29.17* |
| 50 | 25.62 | 25.87 | 25.67 | 26.03 | — | 25.97 | 26.23 | **26.32** | *26.30* |

**Table 2.** Denoising PSNR results of several algorithms on Set12 with noise levels of $\sigma = \{15, 25, 50\}$. **Bold** numbers denote the highest performing model, whereas *Italics* denotes the second highest. PSN outperforms state-of-the-art for many images.

| | C.Man | House | Pepp | Starf. | Fly | Airpl. | Parrot | Lena | Barb. | Boat | Man | Couple |
|---|---|---|---|---|---|---|---|---|---|---|---|---|
| $\sigma = 15$ | | | | | | | | | | | | |
| BM3D [6] | 31.91 | 34.93 | 32.69 | 31.14 | 31.85 | 31.07 | 31.37 | 34.26 | *33.10* | 32.13 | 31.92 | 32.10 |
| CSF [21] | 31.95 | 34.39 | 32.85 | 31.55 | 32.33 | 31.33 | 31.37 | 34.06 | 31.92 | 32.01 | 32.08 | 31.98 |
| EPLL [27] | 31.85 | 34.17 | 32.64 | 31.13 | 32.10 | 31.19 | 31.42 | 33.93 | 31.38 | 31.93 | 32.00 | 31.93 |
| WNNM [35] | 32.17 | **35.13** | 32.99 | 31.82 | 32.71 | 31.39 | *31.62* | 34.27 | **33.60** | 32.27 | 32.11 | 32.17 |
| TNRD [23] | *32.19* | 34.53 | 33.04 | 31.75 | 32.56 | 31.46 | *31.63* | 34.24 | 32.13 | 32.14 | 32.23 | 32.11 |
| DnCNN [17] | 32.10 | 34.93 | 33.15 | *32.02* | *32.94* | 31.56 | *31.63* | *34.56* | 32.09 | *32.35* | **32.41** | *32.41* |
| PSN-K (Ours) | **32.58** | *35.04* | **33.23** | **32.17** | **33.11** | **31.75** | 31.89 | **34.62** | 32.64 | **32.52** | *32.39* | **32.43** |
| PSN-U (Ours) | 32.04 | 35.03 | *33.21* | 31.94 | *32.93* | *31.61* | *31.62* | *34.56* | 32.49 | *32.41* | 32.37 | **32.43** |
| $\sigma = 25$ | | | | | | | | | | | | |
| BM3D [6] | 29.47 | 32.99 | 30.29 | 28.57 | 29.32 | 28.49 | 28.97 | 32.03 | *30.73* | 29.88 | 29.59 | 29.70 |
| CSF [21] | 29.51 | 32.41 | 30.32 | 28.87 | 29.69 | 28.80 | 28.91 | 31.87 | 28.99 | 29.75 | 29.68 | 29.50 |
| EPLL [27] | 29.21 | 32.14 | 30.12 | 28.48 | 29.35 | 28.66 | 28.96 | 31.58 | 28.53 | 29.64 | 29.57 | 29.46 |
| WNNM [35] | 29.63 | 33.22 | 30.55 | 29.09 | 29.98 | 28.81 | 29.13 | 32.24 | **31.28** | 29.98 | 29.74 | 29.80 |
| TNRD [23] | 29.72 | 32.53 | 30.57 | 29.09 | 29.85 | 28.88 | 29.18 | 32.00 | 29.41 | 29.91 | 29.87 | 29.71 |
| DnCNN [17] | *29.94* | 33.05 | 30.84 | *29.34* | *30.25* | *29.09* | *29.35* | 32.42 | 29.69 | 30.20 | *30.09* | 30.10 |
| PSN-K (Ours) | **30.28** | **33.26** | **31.01** | **29.57** | **30.30** | **29.28** | **29.38** | **32.57** | 30.17 | **30.31** | **30.10** | **30.18** |
| PSN-U (Ours) | 29.79 | *33.23* | *30.90* | 29.30 | 30.17 | 29.06 | 29.25 | *32.45* | 29.94 | *30.25* | 30.05 | *30.12* |
| $\sigma = 50$ | | | | | | | | | | | | |
| BM3D [6] | 26.13 | 29.69 | 26.68 | 25.04 | 25.82 | 25.10 | 25.90 | 29.05 | *27.22* | 26.78 | 26.81 | 26.46 |
| MLP [36] | 26.37 | 29.64 | 26.68 | 25.43 | 26.26 | 25.56 | 26.12 | 29.32 | 25.24 | 27.03 | 27.07 | 26.67 |
| WNNM [35] | 26.45 | *30.33* | 26.95 | 25.44 | 26.32 | 25.42 | 26.14 | 29.25 | **27.79** | 26.97 | 26.95 | 26.64 |
| TNRD [23] | 26.62 | 29.48 | 27.10 | 25.42 | 26.31 | 25.59 | 26.16 | 28.93 | 25.70 | 26.94 | 26.98 | 26.50 |
| DnCNN [17] | *27.03* | 30.02 | *27.39* | *25.72* | *26.83* | *25.89* | 26.48 | *29.38* | 26.38 | *27.23* | **27.23** | 26.09 |
| PSN-K (Ours) | 27.10 | **30.34** | *27.40* | **25.84** | 26.92 | **25.90** | *26.56* | **29.54** | 26.45 | 27.20 | *27.21* | **27.09** |
| PSN-U (Ours) | **27.21** | *30.21* | **27.53** | 25.63 | **26.93** | 25.89 | **26.62** | 29.54 | *26.56* | **27.27** | **27.23** | *27.04* |

# 4 Empirical Evaluation on Image Restoration

We evaluate our proposed approach against state-of-the-art algorithms on standard benchmarks for the tasks of image denoising and image super resolution. For training we use Adam [37] for 50 epochs with a batch size of 128 for all models.

Runtimes for evaluated PSN network are on par with the fastest algorithms while outperforming previous state-of-the-arts (provided in the supplementary).

## 4.1   Image De-noising

Our first task is image denoising where given a noisy image (with a known and unknown level of noise), the task is to output a noiseless version of the image. Image denoising is considered as special case of Eq. 1 where $k$ is a delta function with no shift.

**Experiment:** We train on 400 images of size $180 \times 180$ from the Berkeley Segmentation Dataset (BSD) [38]. We set the patch size as $64 \times 64$, and crop about one million random patches to train. We train four models as described in [17]. Three of these models are trained on images with three different levels of Gaussian noise i.e., $\sigma = 15$, 25 and 50. We refer to these models as PSN-K (Proximal Split Net-Known noise level). The fourth model is trained for blind Gaussian denoising, where no level of $\sigma$ is assumed. For blind Gaussian denoising, we train a single model and set the *range* of the noise level in the training images to be $\sigma \in [0, 60]$. We refer to these models as PSN-U (Unknown noise level). We test on two well known datasets, the Berkeley Segmentation Dataset (BSD68) [39] containing a total of 68 images and Set12 [6] with 12 images with no overlap during training. We compare our approach with several state-of-the-art methods such as BM3D [6], WNNM [35], TRND [23], EPLL [27], DnCNN [17], MLP [36] and CSF [21].

**Results:** Table 1 showcases the testing PSNR results on BSD68. We observe that PSN-K outperforms all other algorithms to obtain a new state-of-the-art on BSD68. However, the noise-blind version (PSN-U) very closely matches the previous state-of-the-art and for $\sigma = 25, 50$ outperform it. Table 2 shows the testing PSNRs for Set12. We find that for most images, PSN-K achieves new state-of-the-arts. The noise-blind model PSN-U also beats the state-of-art on many images in some cases even PSN-K. PSN-U performs particularly well at high levels of noise *i.e.* $\sigma = 50$. Figures 1 and 5 present some qualitative results illustrating the high level of detail PSN recovers. More results are presented in the supplementary.

## 4.2   Image Super-Resolution

Our second task aims to reconstruct a high-resolution image from a single low-resolution image. Image super-resolution is considered as special case of Eq. 1 where $k$ is a bicubic down sampling filter with no added noise.

**Experiment:** For training, we use DIV2K dataset. The dataset consists of 800 training images (2K resolution). The data set is augmented with random horizontal flips and $90°$ rotations. We set the high resolution patch size to be $128 \times 128$. The low res patches are generated via bicubic down sampling of the high resolution patches. We trained a single model for each of three different scales i.e., 2X,

3X and 4X. We test our algorithm on four benchmark datasets. The datasets are Set5 [40], Set14 [41], BSDS100 [42] and URBAN100 [43]. We compare our approach with several state-of-the-art methods such as A+ [44], RFL [45], Self-ExSR [43], SRCNN [46], FSRCNN [47], SCN [48], DRCN [49], LapSRN [33] and VDSR [16] in terms of the PSNR and SSIM metrics as in [16].

**Results:** From Table 3, it is clear that PSN achieves state-of-the-art results both in terms of PSNR and SSIM for all four benchmarks for all scales by a significant margin. This demonstrates the efficacy of the algorithm in application to the image super-resolution problem. Figures 2 and 5 present some qualitative results. Notice that PSN recovers complex structures more clearly. More results are presented in the supplementary.

**Table 3.** The PSNR and SSIM results of several algorithms on four image super resolution benchmarks. PSN outperforms all previous algorithms significantly and consistently (except for the 3X case on Urban100). PSN also outperforms the works of [43–46,48] on all four benchmarks, whose specific results we present in the supplementary due to space constraints.

| Algorithm | Scale | SET5 PSNR/SSIM | SET14 PSNR/SSIM | BSDS100 PSNR/SSIM | URBAN100 PSNR/SSIM |
|---|---|---|---|---|---|
| Bicubic | 2X | 33.69/0.931 | 30.25/0.870 | 29.57/0.844 | 26.89/0.841 |
| FSRCNN [47] | | 37.05/0.956 | 32.66/0.909 | 31.53/0.892 | 29.88/0.902 |
| DRCN [49] | | 37.63/0.959 | 33.06/0.912 | 31.85/0.895 | 30.76/0.914 |
| LapSRN [33] | | 37.52/0.959 | 33.08/0.913 | 31.80/0.895 | 30.41/0.910 |
| DRRN [50] | | 37.74/0.959 | 33.23/0.914 | 32.05/0.897 | 31.23/0.919 |
| VDSR [16] | | 37.53/0.959 | 33.05/0.913 | 31.90/0.896 | 30.77/0.914 |
| PSN (Ours) | | **38.09/0.960** | **33.68/0.919** | **32.33/0.901** | **31.97/0.921** |
| Bicubic | 3X | 30.41/0.869 | 27.55/0.775 | 27.22/0.741 | 24.47/0.737 |
| FSRCNN [47] | | 33.18/0.914 | 29.37/0.824 | 28.53/0.791 | 26.43/0.808 |
| DRCN [49] | | 33.83/0.922 | 29.77/0.832 | 28.80/0.797 | 27.15/0.828 |
| LapSRN [33] | | 33.82/0.922 | 29.87/0.832 | 28.82/0.798 | 27.07/0.828 |
| DRRN [50] | | 34.03/0.924 | 29.96/0.835 | 28.95/0.800 | **27.53**/0.764 |
| VDSR [16] | | 33.67/0.921 | 29.78/0.832 | 28.83/0.799 | 27.14/**0.829** |
| PSN (Ours) | | **34.56/0.927** | **30.14/0.845** | **29.26/0.809** | 27.43/0.757 |
| Bicubic | 4X | 28.43/0.811 | 26.01/0.704 | 25.97/0.670 | 23.15/0.660 |
| FSRCNN [47] | | 30.72/0.866 | 27.61/0.755 | 26.98/0.715 | 24.62/0.728 |
| DRCN [49] | | 31.54/0.884 | 28.03/0.768 | 27.24/0.725 | 25.14/0.752 |
| LapSRN [33] | | 31.54/0.885 | 28.19/0.772 | 27.32/0.727 | 25.21/0.756 |
| DRRN [50] | | 31.68/0.888 | 28.21/0.772 | 27.38/0.728 | 25.44/0.764 |
| VDSR [16] | | 31.35/0.883 | 28.02/0.768 | 27.29/0.726 | 25.18/0.754 |
| PSN (Ours) | | **32.36/0.896** | **28.40/0.786** | **27.73/0.742** | **25.63/0.768** |

# 5   Relationship to Other Algorithms

It is worth mentioning that several approaches have used proximal gradient decent [18], ADMM [19] or a gradient decent method [20] to recover an image where the prior is computed via a deep learning network. Although, these approaches preform well with respect to the reconstruction performance, they inherit important limitations in terms of computation efficiency. Proximal gradient decent, ADMM and gradient decent methods being first order iterative methods with linear or sub-linear convergence rate, typically require many tens of iterations for convergence as in [18]. Indeed, the previous method requires executing the forward-backward algorithm during the testing phase which significantly increases the complexity both in terms of memory and time. Each iteration consists of a forward pass through the deep network where each layer signifies a single iteration, which emerges as a considerable bottleneck. Our approach addresses this problem by allowing *different* proximal operator networks to be learned at every 'iteration'. This increases modelling capacity of the overall network and allows for much lower iterations (an order of magnitude lower in our case, *i.e.* 3 as opposed around 30 in [18]). Moreover, both [18] and [19] fail to converge at 4X for super-resolution where our approach achieved the state-of-the-art results. Further, our approach doesn't require a high dimension hyper-parameter grid search as in [18,19]. Finally, unlike both these approaches, we adapt a multi scale architecture to improve the performance of the proposed approach.

**Fig. 5.** The first row shows the de-noising results of "Airpl." (Set12) compared against BM3D [6] with added Gaussian noise ($\sigma = 50$). The second row illustrates the super-resolution output of "Comic" (Set14) compared against VDSR [16] with a down-sampling (scale) factor of 4. PSN recovers finer details and more complex structures than the baselines.

# 6  Conclusion

We proposed a theoretically motivated novel deep architecture for image recovery, inspired from the half quadratic algorithm and utilizing the proximal operator. Extensive experiments in image denoising and image super resolution demonstrated the proposed Proximal Splitting Network is effective and achieves a new state-of-the-art on both tasks. Furthermore, the proposed framework is flexible and can be potentially applied to other tasks such as image in-painting and compressed sensing, which are left to be explored in future work.

# References

1. Mallat, S.: A Wavelet Tour of Signal Processing: The Sparse Way. Academic Press, Burlington (2008)
2. Kim, K.I., Kwon, Y.: Single-image super-resolution using sparse regression and natural image prior. IEEE Trans. Pattern Anal. Mach. Intell. **32**(6), 1127–1133 (2010)
3. Antonini, M., Barlaud, M., Mathieu, P., Daubechies, I.: Image coding using wavelet transform. IEEE Trans. Image Process. **1**(2), 205–220 (1992)
4. Rubinstein, R., Bruckstein, A.M., Elad, M.: Dictionaries for sparse representation modeling. Proc. IEEE **98**(6), 1045–1057 (2010)
5. Sun, J., Xu, Z., Shum, H.-Y.: Image super-resolution using gradient profile prior. In: IEEE Conference on Computer Vision and Pattern Recognition, CVPR 2008, pp. 1–8. IEEE (2008)
6. Dabov, K., Foi, A., Katkovnik, V., Egiazarian, K.: Image denoising by sparse 3-D transform-domain collaborative filtering. IEEE Trans. Image Process. **16**(8), 2080–2095 (2007)
7. Nikolova, M., Ng, M.K.: Analysis of half-quadratic minimization methods for signal and image recovery. SIAM J. Sci. Comput. **27**(3), 937–966 (2005)
8. Hoeher, P., Kaiser, S., Robertson, P.: Two-dimensional pilot-symbol-aided channel estimation by Wiener filtering. In: 1997 IEEE International Conference on Acoustics, Speech, and Signal Processing, ICASSP 1997, vol. 3, pp. 1845–1848. IEEE (1997)
9. Beck, A., Teboulle, M.: A fast iterative shrinkage-thresholding algorithm for linear inverse problems. SIAM J. Imaging Sci. **2**(1), 183–202 (2009)
10. Altintaç, A., et al.: 1988 index IEEE transactions on antennas and propagation (1988)
11. Elad, M., Aharon, M.: Image denoising via sparse and redundant representations over learned dictionaries. IEEE Trans. Image Process. **15**(12), 3736–3745 (2006)
12. Wang, Y., Yang, J., Yin, W., Zhang, Y.: A new alternating minimization algorithm for total variation image reconstruction. SIAM J. Imaging Sci. **1**(3), 248–272 (2008)
13. Tosic, I., Frossard, P.: Dictionary learning. IEEE Signal Process. Magaz. **28**(2), 27–38 (2011)
14. Parikh, N., Boyd, S., et al.: Proximal algorithms. Found. Trends® Optim. **1**(3), 127–239 (2014)
15. Nah, S., Kim, T.H., Lee, K.M.: Deep multi-scale convolutional neural network for dynamic scene deblurring. In: CVPR, vol. 1, no. 2, p. 3 (2017)

16. Kim, J., Lee, J.K., Lee, K.M.: Accurate image super-resolution using very deep convolutional networks. In: Proceedings of the IEEE Conference on Computer Vision and Pattern Recognition, pp. 1646–1654 (2016)

17. Zhang, K., Zuo, W., Chen, Y., Meng, D., Zhang, L.: Beyond a Gaussian denoiser: residual learning of deep CNN for image denoising. IEEE Trans. Image Process. **26**(7), 3142–3155 (2017)

18. Meinhardt, T., Möller, M., Hazirbas, C., Cremers, D.: Learning proximal operators: using denoising networks for regularizing inverse imaging problems. In: IEEE International Conference on Computer Vision, pp. 1781–1790 (2017)

19. Chang, J.R., Li, C.-L., Poczos, B., Kumar, B.V., Sankaranarayanan, A.C.: One network to solve them all-solving linear inverse problems using deep projection models. In: Proceedings of the IEEE Conference on Computer Vision and Pattern Recognition, pp. 5888–5897 (2017)

20. Bigdeli, S.A., Zwicker, M., Favaro, P., Jin, M.: Deep mean-shift priors for image restoration. In: Advances in Neural Information Processing Systems, pp. 763–772 (2017)

21. Schmidt, U., Roth, S.: Shrinkage fields for effective image restoration. In: Proceedings of the IEEE Conference on Computer Vision and Pattern Recognition, pp. 2774–2781 (2014)

22. Jin, M., Roth, S., Favaro, P.: Noise-blind image deblurring. In: 2017 IEEE Conference on Computer Vision and Pattern Recognition (CVPR). IEEE (2017)

23. Chen, Y., Pock, T.: Trainable nonlinear reaction diffusion: a flexible framework for fast and effective image restoration. IEEE Trans. Pattern Anal. Mach. Intell. **39**(6), 1256–1272 (2017)

24. Schmidt, U., Rother, C., Nowozin, S., Jancsary, J., Roth, S.: Discriminative non-blind deblurring. In: 2013 IEEE Conference on Computer Vision and Pattern Recognition (CVPR), pp. 604–611. IEEE (2013)

25. Perona, P., Malik, J.: Scale-space and edge detection using anisotropic diffusion. IEEE Trans. Pattern Anal. Mach. Intell. **12**(7), 629–639 (1990)

26. Hunter, D.R., Lange, K.: A tutorial on MM algorithms. Am. Stat. **58**(1), 30–37 (2004)

27. Zoran, D., Weiss, Y.: From learning models of natural image patches to whole image restoration. In: 2011 IEEE International Conference on Computer Vision (ICCV), pp. 479–486. IEEE (2011)

28. Ioffe, S., Szegedy, C.: Batch normalization: accelerating deep network training by reducing internal covariate shift. arXiv preprint arXiv:1502.03167 (2015)

29. Heide, F., et al.: FlexISP: a flexible camera image processing framework. ACM Trans. Graph. (TOG) **33**(6), 231 (2014)

30. Paris, S., Hasinoff, S.W., Kautz, J.: Local laplacian filters: edge-aware image processing with a laplacian pyramid. ACM Trans. Graph. **30**(4), 68–71 (2011)

31. Burt, P.J., Adelson, E.H.: The Laplacian pyramid as a compact image code. In: Readings in Computer Vision, pp. 671–679. Elsevier (1987)

32. Ghiasi, G., Fowlkes, C.C.: Laplacian pyramid reconstruction and refinement for semantic segmentation. In: Leibe, B., Matas, J., Sebe, N., Welling, M. (eds.) ECCV 2016. LNCS, vol. 9907, pp. 519–534. Springer, Cham (2016). https://doi.org/10.1007/978-3-319-46487-9_32

33. Lai, W.-S., Huang, J.-B., Ahuja, N., Yang, M.-H.: Deep Laplacian pyramid networks for fast and accurate super-resolution. In: Proceedings of the IEEE Conference on Computer Vision and Pattern Recognition, pp. 624–632 (2017)

34. Noh, H., Hong, S., Han, B.: Learning deconvolution network for semantic segmentation. In: Proceedings of the IEEE International Conference on Computer Vision, pp. 1520–1528 (2015)
35. Gu, S., Zhang, L., Zuo, W., Feng, X.: Weighted nuclear norm minimization with application to image denoising. In: Proceedings of the IEEE Conference on Computer Vision and Pattern Recognition, pp. 2862–2869 (2014)
36. Burger, H.C., Schuler, C.J., Harmeling, S.: Image denoising: can plain neural networks compete with BM3D? In: 2012 IEEE Conference on Computer Vision and Pattern Recognition (CVPR), pp. 2392–2399. IEEE (2012)
37. Kingma, D.P., Ba, J.: Adam: a method for stochastic optimization. arXiv preprint arXiv:1412.6980 (2014)
38. Arbelaez, P., Fowlkes, C., Martin, D.: The Berkeley segmentation dataset and benchmark (2007). http://ww.eecs.berkeley.edu/Research/Projects/CS/vision/bsds
39. Roth, S., Black, M.J.: Fields of experts. Int. J. Comput. Vis. **82**(2), 205 (2009)
40. Bevilacqua, M., Roumy, A., Guillemot, C., Alberi-Morel, M.L.: Low-complexity single-image super-resolution based on nonnegative neighbor embedding (2012)
41. Zeyde, R., Elad, M., Protter, M.: On single image scale-up using sparse-representations. In: Boissonnat, J.-D., et al. (eds.) Curves and Surfaces 2010. LNCS, vol. 6920, pp. 711–730. Springer, Heidelberg (2012). https://doi.org/10.1007/978-3-642-27413-8_47
42. Arbelaez, P., Maire, M., Fowlkes, C., Malik, J.: Contour detection and hierarchical image segmentation. IEEE Trans. Pattern Anal. Mach. Intell. **33**(5), 898–916 (2011)
43. Huang, J.-B., Singh, A., Ahuja, N.: Single image super-resolution from transformed self-exemplars. In: Proceedings of the IEEE Conference on Computer Vision and Pattern Recognition, pp. 5197–5206 (2015)
44. Timofte, R., De Smet, V., Van Gool, L.: A+: adjusted anchored neighborhood regression for fast super-resolution. In: Cremers, D., Reid, I., Saito, H., Yang, M.-H. (eds.) ACCV 2014. LNCS, vol. 9006, pp. 111–126. Springer, Cham (2015). https://doi.org/10.1007/978-3-319-16817-3_8
45. Schulter, S., Leistner, C., Bischof, H.: Fast and accurate image upscaling with super-resolution forests. In: Proceedings of the IEEE Conference on Computer Vision and Pattern Recognition, pp. 3791–3799 (2015)
46. Dong, C., Loy, C.C., He, K., Tang, X.: Image super-resolution using deep convolutional networks. IEEE Trans. Pattern Anal. Mach. Intell. **38**(2), 295–307 (2016)
47. Dong, C., Loy, C.C., Tang, X.: Accelerating the super-resolution convolutional neural network. In: Leibe, B., Matas, J., Sebe, N., Welling, M. (eds.) ECCV 2016. LNCS, vol. 9906, pp. 391–407. Springer, Cham (2016). https://doi.org/10.1007/978-3-319-46475-6_25
48. Wang, Z, Liu, D., Yang, J., Han, W., Huang, T.: Deep networks for image super-resolution with sparse prior. In: Proceedings of the IEEE International Conference on Computer Vision, pp. 370–378 (2015)
49. Kim, J., Lee, J.K., Lee, K.M.: Deeply-recursive convolutional network for image super-resolution. In: Proceedings of the IEEE Conference on Computer Vision and Pattern Recognition, pp. 1637–1645 (2016)
50. Tai, Y., Yang, J., Liu, X.: Image super-resolution via deep recursive residual network. In: The IEEE Conference on Computer Vision and Pattern Recognition (CVPR), vol. 1, no. 4 (2017)

# A Deep Learning Approach for Real-Time 3D Human Action Recognition from Skeletal Data

Huy Hieu Pham[1,2]([✉]) [iD], Houssam Salmane[1] [iD], Louahdi Khoudour[1] [iD],
Alain Crouzil[2] [iD], Pablo Zegers[3] [iD], and Sergio A. Velastin[4,5]

[1] Cerema, Equipe-projet STI, 1 Avenue du Colonel Roche, 31400 Toulouse, France
{huy-hieu.pham,houssam.salmane,louahdi.khoudour}@cerema.fr
[2] Université Toulouse III - Paul Sabatier, Institut de Recherche en Informatique de Toulouse, 31062 Cedex 9, Toulouse, France
alain.crouzil@irit.fr
[3] Aparnix, La Gioconda 4355, Santiago, Chile
pablozegers@gmail.com
[4] Cortexica Vision Systems Ltd., London, UK
sergio.velastin@ieee.org
[5] Queen Mary University of London and Department of Computer Science, University Carlos III of Madrid, Madrid, Spain

**Abstract.** We present a new deep learning approach for real-time 3D human action recognition from skeletal data and apply it to develop a vision-based intelligent surveillance system. Given a skeleton sequence, we propose to encode skeleton poses and their motions into a single RGB image. An Adaptive Histogram Equalization (AHE) algorithm is then applied on the color images to enhance their local patterns and generate more discriminative features. For learning and classification tasks, we design Deep Neural Networks based on the Densely Connected Convolutional Architecture (DenseNet) to extract features from enhanced-color images and classify them into classes. Experimental results on two challenging datasets show that the proposed method reaches state-of-the-art accuracy, whilst requiring low computational time for training and inference. This paper also introduces CEMEST, a new RGB-D dataset depicting passenger behaviors in public transport. It consists of 203 untrimmed real-world surveillance videos of realistic normal and anomalous events. We achieve promising results on real conditions of this dataset with the support of data augmentation and transfer learning techniques. This enables the construction of real-world applications based on deep learning for enhancing monitoring and security in public transport.

**Keywords:** Action recognition · Skeletal data · Enhanced-SPMF · DenseNet

**Electronic supplementary material** The online version of this chapter (https://doi.org/10.1007/978-3-030-27202-9_2) contains supplementary material, which is available to authorized users.

F. Karray et al. (Eds.): ICIAR 2019, LNCS 11662, pp. 18–32, 2019.
https://doi.org/10.1007/978-3-030-27202-9_2

# 1    Introduction

Human Action Recognition or HAR for short, plays a crucial role in many computer vision applications such as intelligent surveillance, human-computer interaction or robotics. Although significant progress has been achieved, detecting accurately what humans do in unknown videos is still a challenging task due to numerous challenges, e.g. viewpoint changes, intra-class variation, or surrounding distractions [31]. At present, depth sensor-based HAR is considered as one of the best available methods for overcoming the above obstacles. Cost-effective depth sensors are able to provide 3D structural information of the human body, which is suitable for HAR task. In particular, most of these devices have integrated the real-time skeleton estimation algorithms [34] that are robust to surrounding distractions as well as invariant to camera viewpoints. Therefore, exploiting skeletal data for HAR opens up opportunities for addressing the limitations of RGB and depth modalities. In the literature of skeleton-based action recognition, there are two main issues that need to be solved. The first challenge is how to transform the raw skeleton sequences into an effective representation, which is able to capture the spatio-temporal dynamics of human motions. The second is to model and recognize actions using the motion representation obtained from skeletons. Previous works on this topic can be divided into two main groups: HAR based on hand-crafted features and HAR using deep learning models. The first group of methods extracts hand-crafted local features from skeleton joints and uses probabilistic graphical models such as Hidden Markov Model (HMM) [26], Conditional Random Field (CRF) [8], and Fourier Temporal Pyramid (FTP) [39] to model and classify actions. For instance, since the first work on 3D HAR from depth data was introduced [20], many methods for skeleton-based action recognition have been proposed [8,25,39,41–43,46,47]. The common characteristic of these approaches is that, they extract the geometric features from the 3D coordinates of the skeleton joints and model their temporal information by a generative model. Although promising results have been achieved, most of these approaches are shallow, data-dependent and require a lot of feature engineering. E.g., they require pre-processing input data in which the skeleton sequences need to be segmented or aligned. In contrast, we propose a skeleton-based representation and a learning framework for 3D HAR that learns to recognize actions from the raw skeletons in an end-to-end manner, without dependence on the length of actions.

The second group considers skeleton-based action recognition as a time-series problem and proposes to use Recurrent Neural Networks with Long Short-Term Memory units (RNN-LSTMs) [12] to analyze the temporal evolutions of skeletons. They are considered as the most popular deep learning based approach for the HAR task from skeletons and have achieved high-level performance [6,21,23,33,35,38,51]. The temporal evolutions of skeletons are in fact spatio-temporal patterns. Thus, they can be modeled by memory cells in the structure of RNN-LSTMs. However, RNN-LSTM based methods tend to overemphasize the temporal information and lose spatial information of skeletons [6] – an important characteristic for 3D HAR. Another limitation of RNN-LSTM networks is that they just model the overall temporal dynamics of actions without considering the detailed temporal dynamics of them [19]. Additionally, this approach considers skeletons as a kind of low-level feature by feeding raw skeletal data directly into the network. The huge number of input features makes RNN-LSTMs complex, time-consuming and easily lead to overfitting. Furthermore in many cases, RNN-LSTMs act as a classifier, which cannot extract high-level features for the HAR problem [32]. In this paper, we propose a CNN-based method to extract rich geometric motion features from skeleton sequences and model various temporal dynamics, including both short-term and long-term actions.

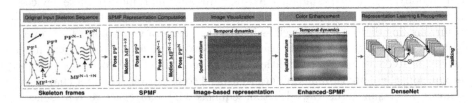

**Fig. 1.** Overview of the proposed approach for real-time 3D action recognition from skeletal data. Each skeleton sequence is encoded as a single RGB image via a skeleton-based representation called SPMF [27]. The SPMF is built from *Pose Feature* vectors (PFs) and *Motion Feature* vectors (MFs), which are estimated from the 3D coordinates of skeletons. A color enhancement technique [30] is adopted to enhance the local textures of SPMF to form the enhanced motion maps, namely Enhanced-SPMF. Finally, they are fed to a deep network for learning image features and performing action classification.

In contrast to the existing approaches, we aim to build an end-to-end deep learning framework for real-time action recognition from skeleton sequences. We believe that an effective motion representation is the key factor influencing recognition performance. Therefore, we propose to encode human poses and motions extracted from the 3D coordinates of skeleton joints into color images. These color-coded images are then enhanced in their local textures by an Adaptive Histogram Equalization (AHE) algorithm [30] before feeding into Deep Convolutional Neural Networks (D-CNNs), which are built based on the DenseNet architecture [14]. Before that, a smoothing filter is applied to reduce the effects of noise on the input skeletal data. The overview of the proposed method is illustrated in Fig. 1. Generally speaking, four hypotheses that motivate us to build a skeleton-based representation and design DenseNets for 3D HAR include: (**1**) human actions can be correctly represented via movements of the skeleton [16]; (**2**) spatio-temporal evolutions of skeletons can be transformed into color images – a kind of 3D tensor that can be effectively learned by D-CNNs [1,3,5]. This hypothesis was proved in our previous studies [27–29]; (**3**) compared to RGB and depth modalities, skeletal data has high-level information with much less complexity. This makes the learning model much simpler and requiring less computation, allowing us to build real-time deep learning framework for HAR task; (4) DenseNet is currently one of the most effective CNN architecture for image recognition. It has a densely connected structure allowing maximal information flow and facilitates features reuse as each layer in its architecture has direct access to the features from previous layers. This helps DenseNet to improve its learning performance. Therefore, we explore and optimise this architecture for learning and recognizing human actions on the proposed image-based representation.

The main contributions of this work are three-fold. **First**, we introduce Enhanced-SPMF (Enhanced Skeleton Pose-Motion Feature) – a 3D motion representation for HAR tasks (Sect. 2). This is an extended representation of SPMF, which was presented in our previous work [27]. The new representation aims to improve the efficiency of the SPMF by using a smoothing filter on input skeleton sequences and a color enhancement technique that could make the proposed Enhanced-SPMF more robust and discriminative. An ablation study on the Enhanced-SPMF demonstrates that the new representation leads to better overall action recognition performance than the SPMF. **Second**, we introduce an end-to-end deep framework based on D-CNNs[1] for learning and recognizing actions from the Enhanced-SPMFs (Sect. 3). This approach is general in the sense that it can be applied to other data modalities, e.g. mocap data or the output of 3D pose estimation algorithms. The proposed method is evaluated on two highly competitive benchmark datasets and achieved state-of-the-art performance on both these two benchmark tasks with high computational efficiency (Sect. 4). **Finally**, we collect and introduce a new RGB-D dataset consisting of real-world surveillance videos for analyzing anomalous and normal events in public transport. Experimental results show that the proposed method achieves promising performance in realistic conditions (Sect. 4).

The rest of this paper is organized as follows: Sect. 2 presents the proposed skeleton-based representation. The proposed deep learning framework is presented in Sect. 3. Datasets and experiments are provided in Sect. 4, including a description of our dataset and the obtained results. Section 5 concludes the paper.

## 2    Enhanced Skeleton Pose-Motion Feature

One of the major challenges in exploiting D-CNNs for skeleton-based action recognition is how a skeleton sequence could be effectively represented and fed to the deep networks. As D-CNNs work well on still images [18], our idea therefore is to encode the spatial and temporal dynamics of skeletons into 2D images [28,29]. Two essential elements for describing an action are static poses and their temporal dynamics. As shown by Zhang et al. in [50], the combination of too many geometric features will lead to lower performance than using only a single feature or several main features. Moreover, joint features such as joint distance and joint motion are stronger features than others [49]. Hence, we decide to transform these two important elements into the static spatial structure of

---

[1] Codes and models are available on our GitHub project at https://bit.ly/2EC9vj9.

a color image. The details of this idea are explained in our previous work [27], in which the spatio-temporal patterns of a skeleton sequence can be encoded into a single color image as a global representation, namely SPMF, via pose and motion feature vectors. Due to the limited space available, detailed description of the SPMF is not included. Instead, we refer the interested readers to [27] for further technical details. Figure 2 shows some SPMF representations in form of an image-based representation obtained from MSR Action3D dataset [20].

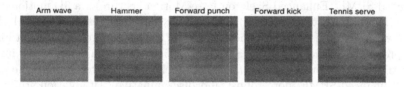

**Fig. 2.** Some SPMF representations obtained from the MSR Action3D dataset [20]. The change in color reflects the change of distance and orientation between the joints.

The color images obtained after the process of encoding mainly reflect the spatio-temporal distribution of skeleton joints. We observe that these images are represented by close contrast values, as can be seen in as Fig. 2. In this case, a color enhancement method can be useful for increasing the contrast of these representations and highlighting the texture and edges of motion maps. This helps to better distinguish similar actions. Therefore, it is necessary to enhance the local features on the generated color images. The Adaptive Histogram Equalization (AHE) [30] is a common approach for this task. This technique is capable of enhancing the local features of an image. Mathematically, let $I$ be a given image, represented as a $r$-by-$c$ matrix of integer pixels with intensity levels in the range $[0, L - 1]$. The histogram of image $I$ will be defined by $H_k = \mathbf{n}_k$, where $\mathbf{n}_k$ is the number of pixels with intensity $k$ in $I$. Hence, the probability of occurrence of intensity level $k$ in $I$ is

$$p_k = \frac{\mathbf{n}_k}{r \times c}, \quad (k = 0, 1, 2, ..., L - 1). \tag{1}$$

The histogram equalized image will be formed by transforming the pixel intensities, $n$, of $I$ by the function

$$T(n) = \texttt{floor}((L - 1) \sum_{k=0}^{n} p_k), \quad (n = 0, 1, 2, ..., L - 1), \tag{2}$$

The Histogram Equalization (HE) method is used for increasing the global contrast of the image. However, it cannot solve the problem of increasing the local contrast. To do this, the image needs to be divided into $\mathcal{R}$ regions and the HE is then applied in each region. This technique is called the Adaptive Histogram Equalization (AHE). Figure 3 shows samples of the enhanced motion maps with $\mathcal{R} = 8$, which we refer to it as Enhanced-SPMF for some actions from the MSR Action 3D dataset [20].

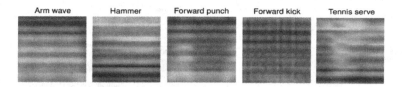

**Fig. 3.** The corresponding Enhanced-SPMF representations after applying the AHE algorithm [30]. This color enhancement step could make the proposed Enhanced-SPMF more robust and discriminative for the representation learning phase with D-CNNs later.

## 3  Deep Learning Model

This section reviews the key ideas behind the DenseNet architecture and presents the proposed deep networks for recognizing actions from the Enhanced-SPMFs.

### 3.1  DenseNet Review

DenseNet [14], a recently proposed CNN model, has some interesting properties. Each layer is connected to all the others within a dense block and all layers can access feature maps from their preceding layers. Besides, each layer receives direct information flow from the loss function through shortcut connections. These properties make DenseNet less prone to overfitting for supervised learning problems. Traditional CNN architectures use the output feature maps $\mathbf{x}_{l-1}$ of the $(l-1)^{\text{th}}$ layer as input to the $l^{\text{th}}$ layer and learn a mapping function $\mathbf{x}_l = \mathcal{H}_l(\mathbf{x}_{l-1})$. Here, $\mathcal{H}_l(\cdot)$ is a non-linear transformation that is usually implemented by a series of operations such as Convolution (**Conv.**), Rectified Linear Unit (**ReLU**) [7], Pooling, and Batch Normalization (**BN**) [15]. When increasing the depth of the network, the problem of optimization becomes complex due to the vanishing-gradient problem and the degradation phenomenon [9]. To solve these problems, [11] introduced ResNet. The key idea behind the ResNet architecture is to add shortcut connections that bypass the non-linear transformations $\mathcal{H}_l(\cdot)$ with an identity function $id(\mathbf{x}) = \mathbf{x}$. Inspired by the philosophy of ResNet, to maximize information flow through layers, Huang et al. [14] proposed DenseNet in which the $l^{\text{th}}$ layer in a dense block receives the feature maps of all preceding layers as inputs. That means

$$\mathbf{x}_l = \mathcal{H}_l(\text{concat}[\mathbf{x}_0, \mathbf{x}_1, \mathbf{x}_2, ..., \mathbf{x}_{l-1}]), \tag{3}$$

where $\text{concat}[\mathbf{x}_0, \mathbf{x}_1, \mathbf{x}_2, ..., \mathbf{x}_{l-1}]$ is a single tensor constructed by concatenation of the previous layer output feature maps. All layers receive direct supervision signal from the loss function through the shortcut connections. Therefore, DenseNets are easy to optimize and resistant to overfitting. In DenseNet, multiple dense blocks are connected via transition layers. Each block with its transition layer produces $k$ feature maps and the parameter $k$ is called as the "*growth rate*" of the network. The function $\mathcal{H}_l(\cdot)$ in the original work [14] is a composite function of three consecutive layers: **BN-ReLU-Conv**.

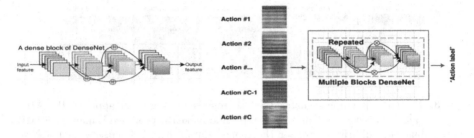

**Fig. 4.** A DenseNet block (**left**). The symbols ⊕ denotes the concatenation operator. We explore and optimize this architecture for learning and recognizing human actions on the proposed image-based representation (**right**).

## 3.2   Network Design

We design D-CNNs based on the DenseNet architecture [14] to learn and classify actions on the Enhanced-SPMF. To study how performance varies with architecture size, we test three different configurations of DenseNet: {DenseNet-16, $k = 12$}; {DenseNet-28, $k = 12$}; and {DenseNet-40, $k = 12$}. Here, the numbers 16, 28, 40 refer to the depth of the network and $k$ is the network growth rate. For computational efficiency, we use three dense blocks on $32 \times 32$ input images. The $\mathcal{H}_l(\cdot)$ function is implemented by a sequence of layers: Batch Normalization (**BN**), advanced activation layer named Exponential Linear Units (**ELU**) [4] and $3 \times 3$ Convolution (**Conv**). Dropout [4] with a rate of 0.2 is used after each **Conv.** to prevent overfitting. The proposed networks can be trained in an end-to-end manner by gradient descent using Adam update rule [17]. During training, we minimize a cross-entropy loss function between the true action label **y** and the predicted action $\hat{\mathbf{y}}$ over the training samples $\mathcal{X}$, by solving the following optimization problem

$$\text{Arg} \min_{\mathcal{W}}(\mathcal{L}_{\mathcal{X}}(\mathbf{y}, \hat{\mathbf{y}})) = \text{Arg} \min_{\mathcal{W}} \left( -\frac{1}{M} \sum_{i=1}^{M} \sum_{j=1}^{C} \mathbf{y}_{ij} \log \hat{\mathbf{y}}_{ij} \right), \tag{4}$$

where $\mathcal{W}$ is the set of weights that will be learned by the model, $M$ denotes the number of samples in training set $\mathcal{X}$ and $C$ is the number of action classes.

## 4   Experiments

The proposed method is first evaluated on two challenging datasets: the MSR Action3D and NTU RGB+D (Sect. 4.1). We then introduce the CEMEST dataset[2] and report experimental results on this dataset. The implementation details of the proposed D-CNNs are also provided in this section (Sect. 4.2).

---

[2] Created by Cerema and Tisséo public transport in France and available for research purposes from https://bit.ly/2SNbrdE.

## 4.1   Datasets and Settings

**MSR Action3D Dataset** [20]: This dataset contains 20 actions performed by 10 subjects. Each skeleton is composed of 20 key joints. Experiments were conducted on 557 action sequences. We follow the protocol proposed by [20]. Specifically, the whole dataset is divided into three subsets: AS1, AS2 and AS3. For each subset, five subjects are selected for training and the rest are used for testing (see Supplemental Material). Data augmentation techniques including random cropping, vertically flipping, and Gaussian filtering have been applied on this dataset.

**NTU RGB+D Dataset** [33]: This Kinect 2 captured dataset is a very large-scale RGB+D dataset. It is currently the largest and state-of-the-art dataset that provides skeletal data for 3D HAR. The NTU RGB+D has more than 56 thousand video samples, 4 millions frames, collected from 40 distinct subjects for 60 different action classes. Each skeleton contains the 3D coordinates of 25 body joints. The authors of this dataset suggested two different evaluation criteria, including Cross-Subject and Cross-View evaluations. For the Cross-Subject setting, the sequences performed by 20 subjects are used for training and the rest sequences are used for testing. In Cross-View setting, the sequences provided by cameras 2 and 3 are used for training while sequences from camera 1 are used for testing (see Supplemental Material). Due to the very large-scale nature of the NTU RGB+D dataset, we do not apply any data augmentation technique on this dataset.

**CEMEST Dataset:** We have collected a new RGB-D dataset, called CEMEST (CErema MEtro STation dataset) using Kinect v2 sensor and carried out experiments on this dataset to verify the effectiveness of the proposed method on a

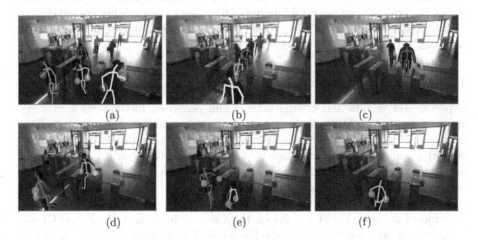

**Fig. 5.** Some samples from the CEMEST dataset: (a), (b) *crossing over the barriers*, (c), (d) *jumping over the ticket barriers* and (e), (f) *sneaking under ticket barriers*.

real-world dataset. The CEMEST was made at a metro station in France without any control of the passenger behavior as well as illumination. It contains three actions including both normal and abnormal behaviors: *crossing normally over the barriers, jumping over the barriers,* and *sneaking under the barriers.* These three behaviors are taken into account for acquisition because they have a significant impact on monitoring and management in public transport. As an example, the French National Railway Company (SNCF) reported that they lost €500 million every year through people trying to cheat the ticket system [37]. In summary, this dataset provides RGB, depth and skeletal data. The skeleton sequences are extracted by Kinect SDK with 25 key joints for each subject, at a frame rate of 30 FPS. All recorded sequences are manually segmented and labeled. Figure 5 shows some samples from the CEMEST. We carried out two experimental evaluations on this dataset. In the first setting, we randomly chose 67% of the data as training set and the remaining 33% is used for testing. In the second setting, the proposed networks are trained on a combination dataset, which is created from a portion of the MSR Action3D [20] and NTU RGB+D [33] datasets (see Supplementary Material for more details). To ensure the number of samples in each action class is balanced, we augmented samples in the MSR Action3D to match the size of the larger dataset. The pre-trained model is then deployed on the CEMEST dataset in the hope that transfer learning will help to solve overfitting problem when training on small dataset. In both experiments, data augmentation (i.e. cropping, flipping, Gaussian filtering) has been used.

## 4.2 Implementation Details

The Enhanced-SPMFs are computed directly from skeletons without using a fixed number of frames. The proposed DenseNets were implemented in Python using Keras. For training, we use mini-batches of 64 images. The weights are initialized as [10]. Adam optimizer [17] is used with an initial learning rate $\eta = 3e-4$. All networks are trained for 250 epochs from scratch.

## 4.3 Experimental Results and Evaluation

Experimental results and comparison of the proposed method with existing approaches on the MSR Action3D dataset are summarized in Table 1. The DenseNet-40 achieves an average accuracy of 99.10% over three subsets, which outperformed previous approaches by [2,6,20,39,42,44,48] and surpassed our previous work on SPMF [27]. Figure 6 (*left*) shows an example of the learning curves of the network during training on this dataset.

For the NTU RGB+D dataset, as shown in Table 2, the proposed DenseNet-40 achieves an accuracy of 79.95% on the Cross-Subject and 87.52% on Cross-View evaluations, respectively. These results demonstrate the effectiveness of the proposed representation and deep learning framework since they surpassed previous state-of-the-art approaches reported in [6,13,21,22,24,33,39,40,50] as well as a higher level of performance than SPMF [27]. Figure 6 (*right*) shows the training loss and test accuracy of the proposed DenseNet-40 on the NTU RGB+D

**Table 1.** Experimental results and comparison with the state-the-art approaches on the MSR Action3D dataset [20]. The best accuracies are in *italics*. Results that surpass previous works are in **bold**.

| Method (protocol of [20]) | AS1 | AS2 | AS3 | Aver. |
|---|---|---|---|---|
| Bag of 3D Points [20] | 72.90% | 71.90% | 71.90% | 74.70% |
| Depth Motion Maps [2] | 96.20% | 83.20% | 92.00% | 90.47% |
| Bi-LSTM [36] | 92.72% | 84.93% | 97.89% | 91.84% |
| Lie Group [39] | 95.29% | 83.87% | 98.22% | 92.46% |
| Hierarchical RNN [6] | 99.33% | 94.64% | 95.50% | 94.49% |
| Graph-Based Motion [42] | 93.60% | 95.50% | 95.10% | 94.80% |
| ST-NBNN [44] | 91.50% | 95.60% | 97.30% | 94.80% |
| ST-NBMIM [45] | 92.50% | 95.60% | 98.20% | 95.30% |
| S-T Pyramid [48] | *99.10%* | 92.90% | 96.40% | 96.10% |
| SPMF [27] | 97.54% | 98.73% | 99.41% | 98.56% |
| Enhanced-SPMF DenseNet-16 (**ours**) | 98.05% | 98.38% | 98.80% | 98.41% |
| Enhanced-SPMF DenseNet-28 (**ours**) | 98.44% | 98.47% | 99.18% | **98.70**% |
| Enhanced-SPMF DenseNet-40 (**ours**) | 98.88% | *99.05%* | 99.24% | *99.10%* |

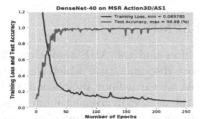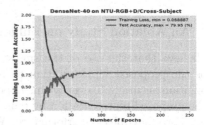

**Fig. 6.** Learning curves of the proposed DenseNet-40 network on the Enhanced-SPMFs obtained from the MSR Action3D and NTU RGB+D

dataset. On the CEMEST dataset, an accuracy of 91.18% has been made by the DenseNet-40 in the first setting. In the second setting, transfer learning is used. The experimental results show that the proposed method reached an accuracy of 95.70%, increasing the performance by nearly 5% compared to the first experiment. This could be explained by the fact that since the CEMEST dataset is quite small, it benefits from the knowledge transfer coming from larger datasets such as the MSR Action3D and NTU RGB+D datasets. This result indicates that the use of data augmentation and transfer learning is crucial to address the small amount of samples in real-world datasets. Figure 7 shows learning curves of the proposed deep learning networks on the CEMEST dataset from scratch (Fig. 7a–c), pre-training on the combined dataset (Fig. 7d–f) and fine-tuning on CEMEST dataset (Fig. 7g–i).

**Table 2.** Experimental results and comparison with the state-the-art approaches on the NTU RGB+D dataset [33]. The best accuracies are in *italics*. Results that surpass previous works are in **bold**.

| Method (protocol of [33]) | Cross-Subject | Cross-View |
|---|---|---|
| Lie Group [39] | 50.10% | 52.80% |
| Hierarchical RNN [6] | 59.07% | 63.97% |
| Dynamic Skeletons [13] | 60.20% | 65.20% |
| Two-Layer P-LSTM [33] | 62.93% | 70.27% |
| ST-LSTM Trust Gates [21] | 69.20% | 77.70% |
| Geometric Features [50] | 70.26% | 82.39% |
| Two-Stream RNN [40] | 71.30% | 79.50% |
| Enhanced Skeleton [24] | 75.97% | 82.56% |
| GCA-LSTM [22] | 76.10% | 84.00% |
| SPMF [27] | 78.89% | 86.15% |
| Enhanced-SPMF DenseNet-16 (**ours**) | 77.89% | **86.55%** |
| Enhanced-SPMF DenseNet-28 (**ours**) | **79.07%** | **86.82%** |
| Enhanced-SPMF DenseNet-40 (**ours**) | *79.95%* | *87.52%* |

### 4.4    An Ablation Study on Enhanced-SPMF

We believe that the use of the smoothing filter and the AHE algorithm [30] helps the proposed representation to be more discriminative, which improves recognition accuracy. To verify this hypothesis, we carried out an ablation study on the proposed representation by removing the color enhancement module and seeing how that affects performance. We observed that this kind of transformation is needed for improving learning performance of deep neural networks. Specifically, we trained the proposed DenseNet-40 on both the SPMFs and Enhanced-SPMFs provided by MSR Action3D dataset [20]. During training, the same hyper-parameters and training methodology were applied. The experimental results indicate that the proposed deep network achieves better recognition accuracy when trained on the Enhanced-SPMF (+1.42%). This result validates our hypothesis above.

### 4.5    Computational Efficiency Evaluation

The proposed learning framework comprises three main stages: (**1**) the computation of Enhanced-SPMF; (**2**) the training stage; and (**3**) the inference stage. To evaluate the computational efficiency of this method, we measure the execution time of each stage on the AS1 subset/MSR Action3D dataset with the proposed DenseNet-40 network, which only has 1.0M parameters. With the implementation in Python using Keras and training on a single GTX Ti 1080 GPU, the training process takes less than one hour to reach convergence. While the inference stage, including the stage (**1**) that is executed on a CPU and the stage (**3**), takes an average of 0.175 s per sequence without parallel processing. This result verifies the appropriateness of our method in terms of computational cost. Additionally, the computation of the Enhanced-SPMF can be implemented on a GPU for real-time applications.

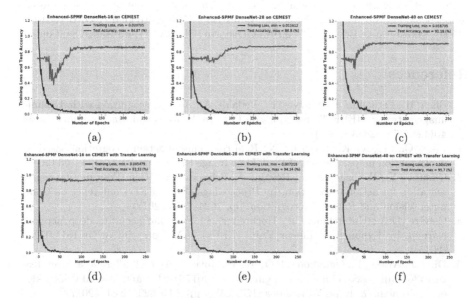

**Fig. 7.** Learning curves of the three proposed deep networks (DenseNet-16, DenseNet-28, DenseNet-40) on CEMEST dataset when trained from scratch (a)-(b)-(c) and fine-tuned on CEMEST dataset (d)-(e)-(f). Our best configuration (DenseNet-40) achieved an accuracy of 91.18% when trained on the CEMEST dataset from scratch. With the support of transfer learning, the proposed method reached an accuracy of 95.70%, increasing the recognition accuracy by nearly 5%.

# 5   Conclusions

We introduced a deep learning framework for 3D action recognition from skeletal data. A new motion representation that captures the spatio-temporal patterns of skeleton movements and encodes them into color images has been proposed. Densely connected networks have been designed to learn and recognize actions from the proposed representation in an end-to-end manner. Experiments on two public datasets have demonstrated the effectiveness of our method, both in terms of accuracy as well as computational time. We also introduced CEMEST, a new real-wold surveillance dataset containing both normal and anomalous events for studying human behaviors in public transport. Experimental results on this dataset show that the proposed deep learning based approach achieved promising results. We are currently expanding this study by adding more visual evidence to the network in order to further gains in performance. A new approach for 3D pose estimation will also be studying to replace depth sensors. The preliminary results are encouraging.

**Acknowledgements.** This research was supported by the Cerema, France. Sergio A. Velastin is grateful for funding from the Universidad Carlos III de Madrid, the EU's 7th Framework Programme for Research, Technological Development and demonstration (grant 600371), Ministerio de Economia, Industria y Competitividad (COFUND2013-51509), Ministerio de Educación, cultura y Deporte (CEI-15-17) and Banco Santander.

# References

1. Bilen, H., Fernando, B., Gavves, E., Vedaldi, A.: Action recognition with dynamic image networks. IEEE Transactions on Pattern Analysis and Machine Intelligence **40**(12), 2799–2813 (2018)
2. Chen, C., Liu, K., Kehtarnavaz, N.: Real-time human action recognition based on depth motion maps. Journal of Real-Time Image Processing **12**(1), 155–163 (2016)
3. Choutas, V., Weinzaepfel, P., Revaud, J., Schmid, C.: Potion: Pose motion representation for action recognition. In: Proceedings of the IEEE Conference on Computer Vision and Pattern Recognition. pp. 7024–7033 (2018)
4. Clevert, D.A., Unterthiner, T., Hochreiter, S.: Fast and accurate deep network learning by Exponential Linear Units (ELUs). arXiv preprint arXiv:1511.07289 (2015)
5. Ding, Z., Wang, P., Ogunbona, P.O., Li, W.: Investigation of different skeleton features for cnn-based 3d action recognition. In: 2017 IEEE International Conference on Multimedia & Expo Workshops (ICMEW). pp. 617–622. IEEE (2017)
6. Du, Y., Wang, W., Wang, L.: Hierarchical recurrent neural network for skeleton based action recognition. In: IEEE CVPR. pp. 1110–1118 (2015)
7. Glorot, X., Bordes, A., Bengio, Y.: Deep sparse rectifier neural networks. In: International Conference on Artificial Intelligence and Statistics (AISTATS). pp. 315–323 (2011)
8. Han, L., Wu, X., Liang, W., Hou, G., Jia, Y.: Discriminative human action recognition in the learned hierarchical manifold space. Image and Vision Computing **28**(5), 836–849 (2010)
9. He, K., Sun, J.: Convolutional neural networks at constrained time cost. In: IEEE CVPR. pp. 5353–5360 (2015)
10. He, K., Zhang, X., Ren, S., Sun, J.: Delving deep into rectifiers: Surpassing human-level performance on ImageNet classification. In: IEEE ICCV. pp. 1026–1034 (2015)
11. He, K., Zhang, X., Ren, S., Sun, J.: Deep residual learning for image recognition. In: IEEE CVPR. pp. 770–778 (2016)
12. Hochreiter, S., Schmidhuber, J.: Long Short-Term Memory. Neural Computation **9**(8), 1735–1780 (1997)
13. Hu, J., Zheng, W.S., Lai, J.H., Jianguo, Z.: Jointly learning heterogeneous features for RGB-D activity recognition. IEEE Transactions on Pattern Analysis and Machine Intelligence **39**, 2186–2200 (2015)
14. Huang, G., Liu, Z., Weinberger, K.Q., van der Maaten, L.: Densely connected convolutional networks. In: IEEE CVPR. p. 3 (2017)

15. Ioffe, S., Szegedy, C.: Batch normalization: Accelerating deep network training by reducing internal covariate shift. In: ICML. pp. 448–456 (2015)
16. Johansson, G.: Visual perception of biological motion and a model for its analysis. Perception & Psychophysics **14**(2), 201–211 (1973)
17. Kingma, D.P., Ba, J.: Adam: A method for stochastic optimization. arXiv preprint arXiv:1412.6980 (2014)
18. LeCun, Y., Bengio, Y., Hinton, G.: Deep learning. nature **521**(7553), 436 (2015)
19. Lee, I., Kim, D., Kang, S., Lee, S.: Ensemble deep learning for skeleton-based action recognition using temporal sliding lstm networks. In: Proceedings of the IEEE International Conference on Computer Vision. pp. 1012–1020 (2017)
20. Li, W., Zhang, Z., Liu, Z.: Action recognition based on a bag of 3D points. In: IEEE CVPR. pp. 9–14 (2010)
21. Liu, J., Shahroudy, A., Xu, D., Wang, G.: Spatio-temporal LSTM with trust gates for 3D human action recognition. In: ECCV. pp. 816–833 (2016)
22. Liu, J., Wang, G., Duan, L.Y., Abdiyeva, K., Kot, A.C.: Skeleton-based human action recognition with global context-aware attention LSTM networks. IEEE Transactions on Image Processing **27**(4), 1586–1599 (2018)
23. Liu, J., Wang, G., Hu, P., Duan, L.Y., Kot, A.C.: Global context-aware attention LSTM networks for 3D action recognition. In: IEEE CVPR. pp. 3671–3680 (2017)
24. Liu, M., Liu, H., Chen, C.: Enhanced skeleton visualization for view invariant human action recognition. Pattern Recognition **68**, 346–362 (2017)
25. Luo, J., Wang, W., Qi, H.: Group sparsity and geometry constrained dictionary learning for action recognition from depth maps. In: IEEE ICCV. pp. 1809–1816 (2013)
26. Lv, F., Nevatia, R.: Recognition and segmentation of 3D human action using HMM and multi-class Adaboost. In: ECCV. pp. 359–372 (2006)
27. Pham, H., Khoudour, L., Crouzil, A., Zegers, P., Velastin, S.A.: Skeletal movement to color map: A novel representation for 3D action recognition with Inception Residual networks. In: IEEE International Conference on Image Processing (ICIP). pp. 3483–3487 (2018)
28. Pham, H.H., Khoudour, L., Crouzil, A., Zegers, P., Velastin, S.: Learning to Recognize 3D Human Action from A New Skeleton-based Representation Using Deep Convolutional Neural Networks. IET Computer Vision (2018)
29. Pham, H.H., Khoudour, L., Crouzil, A., Zegers, P., Velastin, S.A.: Exploiting deep residual networks for human action recognition from skeletal data. Computer Vision and Image Understanding **170**, 51–66 (2018)
30. Pizer, S.M., Amburn, E.P., Austin, J.D., Cromartie, R., Geselowitz, A., Greer, T., ter Haar Romeny, B., Zimmerman, J.B., Zuiderveld, K.: Adaptive histogram equalization and its variations. Computer Vision, Graphics, and Image Processing **39**(3), 355–368 (1987)
31. Poppe, R.: A survey on vision-based human action recognition. Image and Vision Computing **28**(6), 976–990 (2010)
32. Sainath, T.N., Vinyals, O., Senior, A., Sak, H.: Convolutional, Long Short-Term Memory, Fully Connected Deep Neural Networks. In: IEEE ICASSP. pp. 4580–4584 (2015)
33. Shahroudy, A., Liu, J., Ng, T.T., Wang, G.: NTU RGB+D: A large scale dataset for 3D human activity analysis. In: IEEE CVPR. pp. 1010–1019 (2016)
34. Shotton, J., Sharp, T., Kipman, A., Fitzgibbon, A., Finocchio, M., Blake, A., Cook, M., Moore, R.: Real-time human pose recognition in parts from single depth images. Communications of the ACM **56**(1), 116–124 (2013)

35. Si, C., Jing, Y., Wang, W., Wang, L., Tan, T.: Skeleton-based action recognition with spatial reasoning and temporal stack learning. In: Proceedings of the European Conference on Computer Vision (ECCV). pp. 103–118 (2018)

36. Tanfous, A.B., Drira, H., Amor, B.B.: Coding Kendall's shape trajectories for 3D action recognition. In: IEEE CVPR. pp. 2840–2849 (2018)

37. The Local: SNCF increases fines for ticket dodgers. https://bit.ly/2mYaJwW (2015), published 20 February 2015. Accessed 10 July 2018

38. Veeriah, V., Zhuang, N., Qi, G.J.: Differential recurrent neural networks for action recognition. In: IEEE ICCV. pp. 4041–4049 (2015)

39. Vemulapalli, R., Arrate, F., Chellappa, R.: Human action recognition by representing 3D skeletons as points in a lie group. In: IEEE CVPR. pp. 588–595 (2014)

40. Wang, H., Wang, L.: Modeling temporal dynamics and spatial configurations of actions using two-stream recurrent neural networks. In: IEEE CVPR. pp. 3633–3642 (2017)

41. Wang, J., Liu, Z., Wu, Y., Yuan, J.: Mining actionlet ensemble for action recognition with depth cameras. In: IEEE CVPR. pp. 1290–1297 (2012)

42. Wang, P., Yuan, C., Hu, W., Li, B., Zhang, Y.: Graph based skeleton motion representation and similarity measurement for action recognition. In: ECCV. pp. 370–385 (2016)

43. Wang, P., Li, W., Ogunbona, P., Gao, Z., Zhang, H.: Mining mid-level features for action recognition based on effective skeleton representation. In: International Conference on Digital Image Computing: Techniques and Applications (DICTA). pp. 1–8 (2014)

44. Weng, J., Weng, C., Yuan, J.: Spatio-temporal Naive-Bayes Nearest-Neighbor (ST-NBNN) for skeleton-based action recognition. In: IEEE CVPR. pp. 4171–4180 (2017)

45. Weng, J., Weng, C., Yuan, J., Liu, Z.: Discriminative spatio-temporal pattern discovery for 3D action recognition. IEEE Transactions on Circuits and Systems for Video Technology pp. 1–1 (2018)

46. Wu, D., Shao, L.: Leveraging hierarchical parametric networks for skeletal joints based action segmentation and recognition. In: IEEE CVPR. pp. 724–731 (2014)

47. Xia, L., Chen, C.C., Aggarwal, J.: View invariant human action recognition using histograms of 3D joints. In: IEEE CVPR. pp. 20–27 (2012)

48. Xu, H., Chen, E., Liang, C., Qi, L., Guan, L.: Spatio-temporal pyramid model based on depth maps for action recognition. In: IEEE International Workshop on Multimedia Signal Processing (MMSP). pp. 1–6 (2015)

49. Yun, K., Honorio, J., Chattopadhyay, D., Berg, T.L., Samaras, D.: Two-person interaction detection using body-pose features and multiple instance learning. In: IEEE CVPR. pp. 28–35 (2012)

50. Zhang, S., Liu, X., Xiao, J.: On geometric features for skeleton-based action recognition using multilayer LSTM networks. In: IEEE Winter Conference on Applications of Computer Vision (WACV). pp. 148–157 (2017)

51. Zhu, W., et al.: Co-occurrence feature learning for skeleton based action recognition using regularized deep LSTM networks. In: AAAI. p. 8 (2016)

# Image Structure Subspace Learning
# Using Structural Similarity Index

Benyamin Ghojogh$^{(\boxtimes)}$ ⓘ, Fakhri Karray ⓘ, and Mark Crowley ⓘ

Department of Electrical and Computer Engineering, University of Waterloo,
Waterloo, ON, Canada
{bghojogh,karray,mcrowley}@uwaterloo.ca

**Abstract.** Literature has shown that Mean Squared Error is not a promising measure for image fidelity and similarity assessment, and Structural Similarity Index (SSIM) can properly handle this aspect. The existing subspace learning methods in machine learning are based on Euclidean distance or MSE and thus cannot properly capture the structural features of images. In this paper, we define image structure subspace which captures the intrinsic structural features of an image and discriminates the different types of image distortions. Therefore, this paper provides a bridge between image processing and manifold learning opening future research opportunities. In order to learn this subspace, we propose SSIM kernel as a new kernel which can be used in kernel-based machine learning methods.

**Keywords:** Image structure subspace · Subspace learning ·
SSIM kernel · SSIM index · Structural similarity

## 1 Introduction

Although Mean Squared Error (MSE) has many nice mathematical properties, such as convexity, it is not a proper measure for image quality, fidelity, or similarity [1]. MSE, or $\ell_2$ norm, sees the distortions applied on the image with the same eye; however, the image distortions can be categorized into structural and non-structural distortions [2]. The structural distortions, including blurring, Gaussian noise, and JPEG blocking distortion, are noticeable by Human Visual System (HVS). On the other hand, non-structural distortions, including luminance enhancement and contrast change, are not as annoying to HVS as the structural distortions.

One of the most well-known measures suitable for image fidelity assessment is the structural similarity index (SSIM) [2,3] which considers luminance and contrast change as non-structural distortions and other distortions as structural ones. Recently, using SSIM in optimization problems has been noticed in the literature [4]. The distance based on SSIM is quasi-convex under some conditions [5] and satisfies the triangular property as a metric [6]. The SSIM has been used

© Springer Nature Switzerland AG 2019
F. Karray et al. (Eds.): ICIAR 2019, LNCS 11662, pp. 33–44, 2019.
https://doi.org/10.1007/978-3-030-27202-9_3

in many tasks such as image denoising, image restoration, contrast enhancement, image quantization, compression, etc (e.g., see the references in [5]).

Most of the manifold learning and machine learning algorithms have focused on $\ell_2$ norm or MSE [7]. Different subspace learning methods such as Principal Component Analysis (PCA), Kernel PCA, Multi-Dimensional Scaling (MDS) [8], Isomap [9], and Laplacian Eigenmap (LE) [10] have been developed based on MSE. A good question arises here: Why don't we use SSIM in manifold and machine learning? Because SSIM is much more effective than MSE in terms of image structure measurement [1,3]. In this paper, we introduce and define the new concept of *image structure subspace* which is a subspace capturing the intrinsic features of an image in terms of structural similarity and distortions, and can discriminate the various types of image distortions. The image structure subspace can open a broad new area for future research by connecting the fields of manifold learning and image quality assessment. One of the many possible applications of this subspace is selecting among the denoising methods or tuning their parameters [11] which we consider as a future work. In order to learn the image structure subspace, we propose *SSIM kernel* as a new kernel which can be used in kernel-based learning methods [12].

In the remainder of paper, we briefly review SSIM and then we introduce the SSIM kernel. Using SSIM kernel in several subspace learning methods are explained afterwards. Finally, experiments on comparison of kernels and out-of-sample projection are reported.

## 2   Structural Similarity Index

The SSIM between two reshaped image patches $\breve{\boldsymbol{x}}_1 = [x_1^{(1)}, \ldots, x_1^{(q)}]^\top \in \mathbb{R}^q$ and $\breve{\boldsymbol{x}}_2 = [x_2^{(1)}, \ldots, x_2^{(q)}]^\top \in \mathbb{R}^q$, in color intensity range $[0, 255]$, is [2,3]:

$$\mathbb{R} \ni \mathrm{SSIM}(\breve{\boldsymbol{x}}_1, \breve{\boldsymbol{x}}_2) := \left( \frac{2\mu_{x_1}\mu_{x_2} + c_1}{\mu_{x_1}^2 + \mu_{x_2}^2 + c_1} \right) \left( \frac{2\sigma_{x_1}\sigma_{x_2} + c_2}{\sigma_{x_1}^2 + \sigma_{x_2}^2 + c_2} \right) \left( \frac{\sigma_{x_1,x_2} + c_3}{\sigma_{x_1}\sigma_{x_2} + c_3} \right), \quad (1)$$

where $\mu_{x_1} = (1/q)\sum_{i=1}^{q} x_1^{(i)}$, $\sigma_{x_1} = \left[ (1/(q-1))\sum_{i=1}^{q}(x_1^{(i)} - \mu_{x_1})^2 \right]^{0.5}$, $\sigma_{x_1,x_2} = (1/(q-1))\sum_{i=1}^{q}(x_1^{(i)} - \mu_{x_1})(x_2^{(i)} - \mu_{x_2})$, $c_1 = (0.01 \times 255)^2$, $c_2 = 2c_3 = (0.03 \times 255)^2$, and $\mu_{x_2}$ and $\sigma_{x_2}$ are defined similarly for $\breve{\boldsymbol{x}}_2$. The $c_1$, $c_2$, and $c_3$ are for avoidance of singularity [3] and $q$ is the dimensionality of the reshaped image patch.

Because of $c_2 = 2c_3$, the SSIM is simplified to $\mathrm{SSIM}(\breve{\boldsymbol{x}}_1, \breve{\boldsymbol{x}}_2) = s_1(\breve{\boldsymbol{x}}_1, \breve{\boldsymbol{x}}_2) \times s_2(\breve{\boldsymbol{x}}_1, \breve{\boldsymbol{x}}_2)$, where $s_1(\breve{\boldsymbol{x}}_1, \breve{\boldsymbol{x}}_2) := (2\mu_{x_1}\mu_{x_2} + c_1)/(\mu_{x_1}^2 + \mu_{x_2}^2 + c_1)$ and $s_2(\breve{\boldsymbol{x}}_1, \breve{\boldsymbol{x}}_2) := (2\sigma_{x_1,x_2} + c_2)/(\sigma_{x_1}^2 + \sigma_{x_2}^2 + c_2)$. Because of spatial variety of image statistics, the SSIM is usually computed for patches of an image. A sliding window moves pixel by pixel on the two images and calculates the $\mathrm{SSIM}(\breve{\boldsymbol{x}}_1, \breve{\boldsymbol{x}}_2)$ for every patch. We denote the reshaped vectors of the two images by $\boldsymbol{x}_1 \in \mathbb{R}^d$ and $\boldsymbol{x}_2 \in \mathbb{R}^d$, and a reshaped patch in the two images by $\breve{\boldsymbol{x}}_1 \in \mathbb{R}^q$ and $\breve{\boldsymbol{x}}_2 \in \mathbb{R}^q$. Therefore, an SSIM vector denoted by $\boldsymbol{s}(\boldsymbol{x}_1, \boldsymbol{x}_2) \in \mathbb{R}^d$ is obtained whose $i$-th element is SSIM for the patch around the $i$-th pixel.

## 3   SSIM Kernel

We can map the $n$ data points $\{\boldsymbol{x}_i\}_{i=1}^n$, where $\boldsymbol{x}_i \in \mathbb{R}^d$, to a higher-dimensional feature space hoping to have the data fall close to a simpler-to-analyze manifold in the feature space. Suppose $\phi : \boldsymbol{x} \to \mathcal{H}$ is a function which maps the data $\boldsymbol{x}$ to the feature space. In other words, $\boldsymbol{x} \mapsto \phi(\boldsymbol{x})$. Let $t$ denote the dimensionality of the feature space, i.e., $\phi(\boldsymbol{x}) \in \mathbb{R}^t$. We usually have $t \gg d$. If $\boldsymbol{x}$ belongs to the set $\mathcal{X}$, i.e., $\boldsymbol{x} \in \mathcal{X}$, the kernel of two vectors $\boldsymbol{x}_1$ and $\boldsymbol{x}_2$ is $k : \mathcal{X} \times \mathcal{X} \to \mathbb{R}$ and is defined as [12]: $k(\boldsymbol{x}_1, \boldsymbol{x}_2) := \phi(\boldsymbol{x}_1)^\top \phi(\boldsymbol{x}_2)$. The kernel matrix for two datasets $\boldsymbol{X}_1 = [\boldsymbol{x}_{1,1}, \ldots, \boldsymbol{x}_{1,n_1}] \in \mathbb{R}^{d \times n_1}$ and $\boldsymbol{X}_2 = [\boldsymbol{x}_{2,1}, \ldots, \boldsymbol{x}_{2,n_2}] \in \mathbb{R}^{d \times n_2}$ is:

$$\mathbb{R}^{n_1 \times n_2} \ni \boldsymbol{K}(\boldsymbol{X}_1, \boldsymbol{X}_2) := \boldsymbol{\Phi}(\boldsymbol{X}_1)^\top \boldsymbol{\Phi}(\boldsymbol{X}_2), \tag{2}$$

where $\boldsymbol{\Phi}(\boldsymbol{X}_1) := [\phi(\boldsymbol{x}_{1,1}), \ldots, \phi(\boldsymbol{x}_{1,n_1})] \in \mathbb{R}^{t \times n_1}$ and $\boldsymbol{\Phi}(\boldsymbol{X}_2)$ is similarly defined. The kernel between a matrix $\boldsymbol{X} \in \mathbb{R}^{d \times n}$ and a vector $\boldsymbol{x} \in \mathbb{R}^d$ is $\mathbb{R}^n \ni k(\boldsymbol{X}, \boldsymbol{x}) := \boldsymbol{\Phi}(\boldsymbol{X})^\top \phi(\boldsymbol{x})$. We denote the kernel over dataset $\boldsymbol{X}$ by $\boldsymbol{K}_x := \boldsymbol{K}(\boldsymbol{X}, \boldsymbol{X}) \in \mathbb{R}^{n \times n}$. The kernel can be written as [8,13]:

$$\boldsymbol{K}_x = -(1/2)\,\boldsymbol{H}\boldsymbol{D}\boldsymbol{H}, \tag{3}$$

where $\mathbb{R}^{n \times n} \ni \boldsymbol{H} = \boldsymbol{I} - (1/n)\boldsymbol{1}\boldsymbol{1}^\top$ is the centering matrix, $\boldsymbol{I}$ and $\boldsymbol{1}$ are the identity matrix and $[1, \ldots, 1]^\top$, respectively, and $\boldsymbol{D} \in \mathbb{R}^{n \times n}$ is the distance matrix whose $(i, j)$-th element is a distance measure between $\boldsymbol{x}_i$ and $\boldsymbol{x}_j$. For example, if the distance measure for $\boldsymbol{D}$ is $\|\boldsymbol{x}_i - \boldsymbol{x}_j\|_2^2$, we will have $\boldsymbol{K}_x = \boldsymbol{H}\boldsymbol{X}^\top \boldsymbol{X}\boldsymbol{H}$. The elements of $\boldsymbol{D}$ can be measured by a valid distance metric (see [13] and Chapter 2 in [7]). Two examples of distance metrics are Euclidean distance (resulting in metric MDS [8] or PCA) and geodesic distance (resulting in Isomap [9]).

A valid distance metric based on SSIM is [5,6]:

$$\mathbb{R} \ni d(\breve{\boldsymbol{x}}_1, \breve{\boldsymbol{x}}_2) = \sqrt{2 - s_1(\breve{\boldsymbol{x}}_1, \breve{\boldsymbol{x}}_2) - s_2(\breve{\boldsymbol{x}}_1, \breve{\boldsymbol{x}}_2)}. \tag{4}$$

Calculating this metric for every patch, we will have a distance vector $\boldsymbol{d}(\boldsymbol{x}_1, \boldsymbol{x}_2) \in \mathbb{R}^d$ between the two images $\boldsymbol{x}_1$ and $\boldsymbol{x}_2$. We want to have a scalar distance between two images so we use this theorem: The $\ell_2$ norm of a vector of metrics is also a metric (see [5] for proof). Therefore, we define the distance between two images $\boldsymbol{x}_1 \in \mathbb{R}^d$ and $\boldsymbol{x}_2 \in \mathbb{R}^d$ as:

$$\mathbb{R} \ni d(\boldsymbol{x}_1, \boldsymbol{x}_2) := \|\boldsymbol{d}(\boldsymbol{x}_1, \boldsymbol{x}_2)\|_2 = \left[ \sum_{i=1}^d \left( d_i(\breve{\boldsymbol{x}}_1, \breve{\boldsymbol{x}}_2) \right)^2 \right]^{(1/2)}, \tag{5}$$

where $d_i(\breve{\boldsymbol{x}}_1, \breve{\boldsymbol{x}}_2)$ is the distance of Eq. (4) for the $i$-th patch. Note that Eq. (5) is equivalent to the Frobenius norm of the distance map between the two images if we have not reshaped the map to a vector. Calculating Eq. (5) between every two images of the dataset $\boldsymbol{X} = [\boldsymbol{x}_1, \ldots, \boldsymbol{x}_n] \in \mathbb{R}^{d \times n}$ gives us the symmetric distance matrix $\boldsymbol{D} \in \mathbb{R}^{n \times n}$. Finally, according to Eq. (3), we define the *SSIM kernel*:

$$\mathbb{R}^{n \times n} \ni \boldsymbol{S}_x = \boldsymbol{S}(\boldsymbol{X}, \boldsymbol{X}) := -(1/2)\,\boldsymbol{H}\boldsymbol{D}\boldsymbol{H}, \tag{6}$$

where $D$ is calculated using Eq. (5). Similarly, as in Eq. (2), we can have the SSIM kernel between two different datasets: $S(X_1, X_2) = -(1/2) H_1 D H_2$ where $D \in \mathbb{R}^{n_1 \times n_2}$ is similarly calculated between the images, one from $X_1$ and one from $X_2$. Note that $H_1 \in \mathbb{R}^{n_1 \times n_1}$ and $H_2 \in \mathbb{R}^{n_2 \times n_2}$. The SSIM kernel between a matrix $X \in \mathbb{R}^{d \times n}$ and a vector $x \in \mathbb{R}^d$ is:

$$\mathbb{R}^n \ni s(X, x) := -(1/2) H d, \tag{7}$$

where $d \in \mathbb{R}^n$ is the distance vector between $X$ and $x$ where every element is calculated using Eq. (5). The SSIM kernel measures the similarity of data points which are images. Notice that the kernel here should not be confused with the filter kernel in signal processing.

## 4    Image Structure Subspace Learning

The proposed SSIM kernel can be used with various subspace learning methods in machine learning. Here, we briefly review PCA, kernel PCA, metric MDS, Isomap, and LE, and we also explain how we can use this kernel in these methods in order to obtain the image structure subspace.

### 4.1    Kernel Principal Component Analysis

Kernel PCA is based on dual PCA which provides the inner products of the vectors, suitable for use with kernels. In dual PCA, Singular Value Decomposition (SVD) is applied on the centered data $XH = U \Sigma V^\top$ where the columns of $U \in \mathbb{R}^{d \times p}$ and $V \in \mathbb{R}^{n \times p}$ are the $p$ leading left and right singular vectors of $XH$, respectively, and $\Sigma \in \mathbb{R}^{p \times p}$ is a diagonal matrix with the $p$ leading singular values (usually $p \ll d$). In dual PCA, the projection of data is $\mathbb{R}^{p \times n} \ni \widetilde{X} = U^\top XH = \Sigma V^\top$ where $\widetilde{X}$ denotes the projected data. On the other hand, from $XH = U \Sigma V^\top$, we have $U = XHV \Sigma^{-1}$. Therefore, projection of out-of-sample data point, denoted by $x_t \in \mathbb{R}^d$, is $\widetilde{x}_t = \Sigma^{-1} V^\top H X^\top (x_t - \mu)$ where $\mu$ is the mean of training points $X$.

In kernel PCA, data are mapped to the feature space using a kernel. Applying SVD on the centered mapped data $\Phi(X)H$ gives us $\Phi(X)H = U \Sigma V^\top$ where $U \in \mathbb{R}^{t \times p}$, $V \in \mathbb{R}^{n \times p}$, and $\Sigma \in \mathbb{R}^{p \times p}$ include the left singular vectors, right singular vectors, and singular values of $\Phi(X)H$, respectively. In practice, the $V$ and $\Sigma$ are found by solving the eigenvalue problem for $H\Phi(X)^\top \Phi(X)H = HK_x H$. Therefore, the kernel should be double-centered. The eigenvalue problem is $HK_x HV = V \Sigma^2$ where $V$ and $\Sigma$ contain the eigenvectors and square root of eigenvalues of $HK_x H$. After picking the $p$ leading eigenvectors to have $V \in \mathbb{R}^{n \times p}$ and $\Sigma \in \mathbb{R}^{p \times p}$, the projection of data in kernel PCA is:

$$\mathbb{R}^{p \times n} \ni \widetilde{X} = U^\top \Phi(X)H = \Sigma V^\top. \tag{8}$$

Moreover, from $\Phi(X)H = U \Sigma V^\top$ we have $U^\top = \Sigma^{-1} V^\top H \Phi(X)^\top$; therefore, projection of out-of-sample point $x_t$ is:

$$\mathbb{R}^p \ni \widetilde{x}_t = U^\top \phi(x_t) = \Sigma^{-1} V^\top H k(X, x_t). \tag{9}$$

In order to learn the image structure subspace, the kernel $K_x$ can be the SSIM kernel $S_x$. Therefore, $V$ and $\Sigma$ are obtained from $S_x V = V \Sigma^2$. Note that the $S_x$ is already double centered according to Eq. (6). Moreover, for out-of-sample projection, $s(X, x_t)$ is used in place of $k(X, x_t)$ in Eq. (9).

## 4.2 Metric Multi-dimensional Scaling

In metric MDS, the difference of distances in the original and embedded space, i.e., $||D_x - D_{\widetilde{x}}||_F^2$ is minimized, where $||.||_F$ denotes Frobenius norm. The $D_x$ is the distance matrix whose $(i,j)$-th element is $||x_i - x_j||_2^2$ and $D_{\widetilde{x}}$ is defined similarly in the embedded space. This optimization problem is equivalent to minimizing the similarities of data points in the original and the embedded space, i.e., $||X^\top X - \widetilde{X}^\top \widetilde{X}||_F^2$. Solving this optimization problem results in [8]:

$$\mathbb{R}^{p \times n} \ni \widetilde{X} = \Sigma^{(1/2)} V^\top, \tag{10}$$

where $V \in \mathbb{R}^{n \times p}$ and $\Sigma \in \mathbb{R}^{p \times p}$ contain the $p$ leading eigenvectors and square root of eigenvalues of $X^\top X$. Assuming that the kernel over data is linear, i.e., $K_x = \Phi(X)^\top \Phi(X) = X^\top X$, the complete $V \in \mathbb{R}^{n \times n}$ and $\Sigma \in \mathbb{R}^{n \times n}$ are obtained by applying SVD on the kernel:

$$\mathbb{R}^{n \times n} \ni K_x = \Phi(X)^\top \Phi(X) = V \Sigma V^\top. \tag{11}$$

Note that if the kernel in Eq. (11) is obtained from Eq. (3) where $D$ is the geodesic distance matrix, we will have Isomap [9].

In image structure subspace learning, we use SSIM kernel for MDS. Therefore, Eq. (11) becomes: $\mathbb{R}^{n \times n} \ni S_x = V \Sigma V^\top$. The kernel is required to be double centered [8] and the $S_x$ is already double centered according to Eq. (6).

## 4.3 Laplacian Eigenmap

The LE [10] addresses the minimization of $\widetilde{X}^\top L \widetilde{X}$ subject to orthogonality of the embedded data points, i.e., $\widetilde{X}^\top \widetilde{X} = I$, where $L$ is the Laplacian matrix, $L = M - W$. The $W \in \mathbb{R}^{n \times n}$ is the similarity matrix whose $(i,j)$-th element, denoted by $W_{i,j}$, is $\exp(-||\widetilde{x}_i - \widetilde{x}_j||_2^2)$ if the points $x_i$ and $x_j$ are connected in the k-nearest neighbor graph, and zero otherwise. Therefore, the LE uses the Radial Basis Function (RBF) kernel for constructing $W$, where the $k$ largest values of every row of the kernel are utilized. The $M$ is a diagonal matrix whose $(i,i)$-th element is the summation of the $i$-th row of $W$. Note that $\widetilde{X}^\top L \widetilde{X} = (1/2) \sum_{ij} W_{i,j} ||\widetilde{x}_i - \widetilde{x}_j||_2^2$. Therefore, this optimization problem tries to make $\widetilde{x}_i$ and $\widetilde{x}_j$ close to one another when $x_i$ and $x_j$ are similar. Solving this optimization problem results in this eigenvalue problem:

$$L \widetilde{X} = \widetilde{X} \Sigma. \tag{12}$$

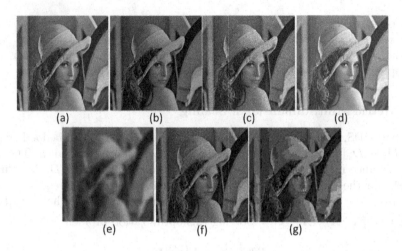

**Fig. 1.** Examples from the training dataset: (a) original image, (b) contrast stretched, (c) Gaussian noise, (d) luminance enhanced, (e) Gaussian blurring, (f) salt & pepper impulse noise, and (g) JPEG distortion.

Therefore, the embedded data points $\widetilde{X}$ are the $p$ trailing eigenvectors (with smallest eigenvalues) of $L$, except the first smallest eigenvector with eigenvalue zero. Note that finally $\widetilde{X}$ should be transposed to have $\widetilde{X} \in \mathbb{R}^{p \times n}$. In image structure subspace learning, we can use the SSIM kernel for constructing $W$. The $k$ largest values in every row of this kernel are used and the other elements will be zero.

## 5    Experiments

### 5.1    Dataset

We made a dataset out of the standard *Lena* image. Six different types of distortions were applied on the original *Lena* image (see Fig. 1), each of which has 20 images in the dataset with different MSE values. Therefore, the size of training set is 121 including the original image. The six used distortions are stretching contrast, Gaussian noise, enhancing luminance, Gaussian blurring, salt & pepper impulse noise, and JPEG distortion. For every type of distortion, 20 different levels of MSE, i.e., from MSE = 45 to MSE = 900 with step 45, were generated in order to have images on the equal-MSE or *iso-error* hypersphere [3].

### 5.2    Comparison of Kernels

We experimented with the basic subspace learning methods using different kernels including our proposed SSIM kernel. The baseline kernels are Radial Basis Function (RBF) $\exp(-\gamma \|x_1 - x_2\|_2^2)$, linear kernel $x_1^\top x_2$, polynomial $(\gamma \, x_1^\top x_2 + 1)^3$, sigmoid $\tanh(\gamma \, x_1^\top x_2 + 1)$, cosine $x_1^\top x_2 / (\|x_1\|_2 \|x_2\|_2)$, and geodesic kernel (Eq. (3) with geodesic distance matrix), where $\gamma := 1/d$. Figures 2 and 3 show the subspaces obtained from experiments using different kernels.

As can be seen in Fig. 2, the image structure subspace propagates the different types of distortions out from the non-distorted original image while the distortions mostly exist on separate trajectories. The more distorted an image is, the further from the original image it is projected or embedded. The subspace obtained using the SSIM kernel discriminates the different distortions much more properly compared to other kernels. In kernel PCA using SSIM, the first dimension puts the luminance enhancement and contrast stretching (non-structural distortions) apart from the structural distortions. Moreover, the third dimension separates the Gaussian blurring as a structural distortion. The fourth dimension shows that the distortions have tilted around this direction in the image distortion subspace. In linear and polynomial kernels, Gaussian noise is not separated from the original image. Also, contrast stretching and impulse noise are treated similarly in a linear kernel. In a polynomial kernel, contrast stretching, impulse noise, and JPEG distortion are not properly separated. The fourth dimension in both linear and polynomial kernels are not promising discriminators.

According to Fig. 2, the results of the SSIM kernel and RBF kernel look very similar, but not identical, especially in the first dimensions. We provide the reason here: Let $d := ||\boldsymbol{x}_1 - \boldsymbol{x}_2||_2$ and $r = d^2$. The Taylor series expansion of RBF kernel is:

$$\exp(-\gamma r) \approx 1 - \gamma r + \frac{\gamma^2}{2}r^2 - \frac{\gamma^3}{6}r^3 + \cdots \tag{13}$$

On the other hand, the SSIM kernel is $\boldsymbol{S}_x \propto -\boldsymbol{D}$ (Eq. (6)). Every element of $\boldsymbol{D}$ is based on $d(\boldsymbol{x}_1, \boldsymbol{x}_2)$ in Eq. (5). We have $d(\boldsymbol{x}_1, \boldsymbol{x}_2) \propto d_i(\breve{\boldsymbol{x}}_1, \breve{\boldsymbol{x}}_2)$. Therefore, $\boldsymbol{S}_x \propto -d_i(\breve{\boldsymbol{x}}_1, \breve{\boldsymbol{x}}_2) = -\sqrt{r}$ where $r = (d_i(\breve{\boldsymbol{x}}_1, \breve{\boldsymbol{x}}_2))^2$. By Taylor series expansion, we have:

$$\boldsymbol{S}_x \propto -\sqrt{r} \approx -\frac{5}{16} - \frac{15}{16}r + \frac{5}{16}r^2 - \frac{1}{16}r^3 + \cdots \tag{14}$$

Comparing Eqs. (13) and (14) gives us the hint for why SSIM and RBF kernels had similar results. Note that the $r$ in the RBF kernel is based on Euclidean distance while the $r$ in SSIM kernel is based on SSIM distance.

In Fig. 3, we can see that the sigmoid kernel does not properly discriminate stretching contrast and impulse noise. Moreover, the Gaussian noise is not well separated from the original image. The cosine kernel separates these two but does not preserve the almost uniform distance of different intensities of a distortion, as we had for SSIM kernel. In the first two dimensions of Isomap, on the other hand, the image with Guassian noise and the original image are not separated, and contrast stretching, impulse noise, and JPEG distortion are not discriminated. In the second, third, and fourth dimensions of Isomap, we see that very high amount of JPEG distortion is noticed while low value of JPEG distortion is not respected.

Figure 3 also includes the subspaces of LE using SSIM kernel and RBF kernel [10]. The LE using SSIM kernel strongly outperforms the LE using RBF kernel

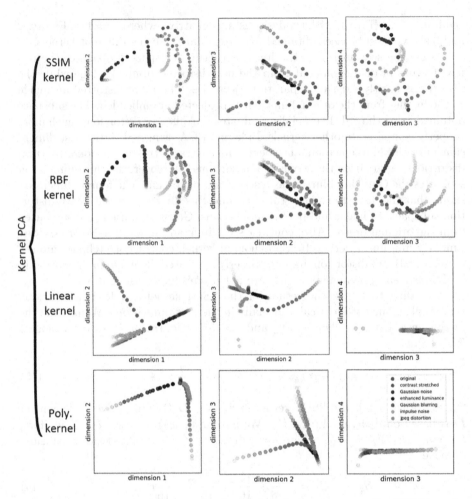

**Fig. 2.** Image structure subspaces: The first to fourth rows correspond to SSIM kernel, RBF kernel, linear kernel (or dual PCA or MDS [7,8]), and polynomial kernel in kernel PCA, respectively. More transparent points correspond to more distorted images.

because its second and third dimensions discriminate contrast stretching (non-structural distortion) from Gaussian blurring (structural distortion). The first and second dimensions of LE using SSIM kernel also show much better scatter of data points in the subspace. That is while LE fails to discriminate the distortions properly. Finally, for the sake of better visualization of what the scatter plots in Figs. 2 and 3 mean, please see Fig. 4.

## 5.3   Out-of-Sample Projection

For out-of-sample projection using the SSIM kernel, we created 12 test images with MSE = 500 having different distortions. Figure 5 shows the test images

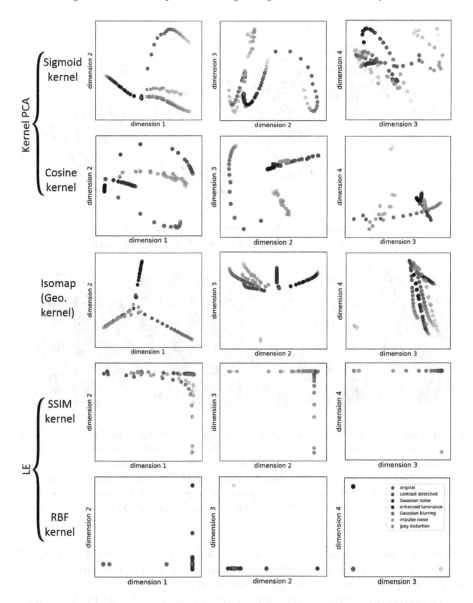

**Fig. 3.** Image structure subspaces: The first and second rows correspond to sigmoid kernel and cosine kernel in kernel PCA, respectively. The third row is for geodesic kernel (Isomap) [9]. The fourth and fifth rows correspond to LE using SSIM kernel and RBF kernel [10], respectively. More transparent points correspond to more distorted images.

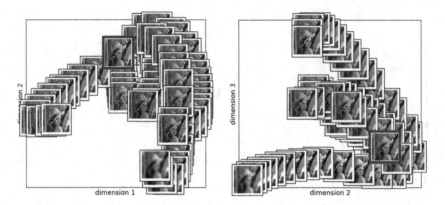

**Fig. 4.** The projected images onto the subspace of kernel PCA using SSIM kernel. The image with a thick red frame is the original image. (Color figure online)

**Fig. 5.** Out-of-sample images with different types of distortions having MSE = 500: (1) stretching contrast, (2) Gaussian noise, (3) luminance enhancement, (4) Gaussian blurring, (5) impulse noise, (6) JPEG distortion, (7) Gaussian blurring + Gaussian noise, (8) Gaussian blurring + luminance enhancement, (9) impulse noise + luminance enhancement, (10) JPEG distortion + Gaussian noise, (11) JPEG distortion + luminance enhancement, and (12) JPEG distortion + stretching contrast.

where the distortions are reported in the caption of figure. Some of the test images have a combination of different distortions in order to evaluate the image structure subspace with harder out-of-sample images.

The projection of these out-of-sample images onto the kernel PCA subspace obtained using SSIM kernel is shown in Fig. 6. As expected, the images 1 to 6 which have solely one type of distortion fall close enough to the projected training samples of their distortion. Note that in dimensions 3 and 4 of projection, some points might be thought to fall onto each other but a 3D imagination shows that they are apart in the other dimension. Image 7 falls between the projection of Gaussian blurring and Gaussian noise. Likewise, Image 8 falls between projection of Gaussian blurring and luminance enhancement, image 9 falls between impulse noise and luminance enhancement, image 10 falls between JPEG distortion and Gaussian noise, image 11 falls between JPEG and luminance, and image 12 falls

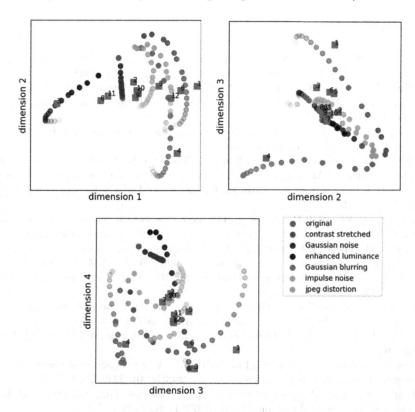

**Fig. 6.** Projection of out-of-sample images onto the image structure subspace. The pink square points are the out-of-sample images. (Color figure online)

between JPEG and stretching contrast. Note that for example, image 12 falls closer to JPEG distortion than to contrast stretching because JPEG distortion is a structural distortion and carries more amount of image quality distortion. In conclusion, the image structure subspace also supports distortion of out-of-sample images even if they have a combination of different distortions.

## 6    Conclusion and Future Direction

This paper introduced image structure subspace which captures the intrinsic features of an image in terms of structural similarity and distortions. This paper opens a new research field for a combination of image processing and manifold learning investigations. The SSIM kernel was also proposed which can be used in kernel-based machine learning algorithms. Experiments showed that the image structure subspace can demonstrate interesting discrimination useful to understand the relative effects of different types of distortions. As a future direction, we seek to develop new manifold learning algorithms based on SSIM in order to learn the defined image structure subspace in other ways.

# References

1. Wang, Z., Bovik, A.C.: Mean squared error: love it or leave it? a new look at signal fidelity measures. IEEE Signal Process. Mag. **26**(1), 98–117 (2009)
2. Wang, Z., Bovik, A.C., Sheikh, H.R., Simoncelli, E.P.: Image quality assessment: from error visibility to structural similarity. IEEE Trans. Image Process. **13**(4), 600–612 (2004)
3. Wang, Z., Bovik, A.C.: Modern image quality assessment. Synth. Lect. Image Video Multimed. Process. **2**(1), 1–156 (2006)
4. Brunet, D., Channappayya, S.S., Wang, Z., Vrscay, E.R., Bovik, A.C.: Optimizing image quality. In: Monga, V. (ed.) Handbook of Convex Optimization Methods in Imaging Science, pp. 15–41. Springer, Cham (2018). https://doi.org/10.1007/978-3-319-61609-4_2
5. Brunet, D., Vrscay, E.R., Wang, Z.: On the mathematical properties of the structural similarity index. IEEE Trans. Image Process. **21**(4), 1488–1499 (2012)
6. Brunet, D., Vrscay, E.R., Wang, Z.: A class of image metrics based on the structural similarity quality index. In: Kamel, M., Campilho, A. (eds.) ICIAR 2011. LNCS, vol. 6753, pp. 100–110. Springer, Heidelberg (2011). https://doi.org/10.1007/978-3-642-21593-3_11
7. Strange, H., Zwiggelaar, R.: Open Problems in Spectral Dimensionality Reduction. SCS. Springer, Cham (2014). https://doi.org/10.1007/978-3-319-03943-5
8. Cox, T.F., Cox, M.A.: Multidimensional Scaling. Chapman and hall/CRC, Boca Raton (2000)
9. Tenenbaum, J.B., De Silva, V., Langford, J.C.: A global geometric framework for nonlinear dimensionality reduction. Science **290**(5500), 2319–2323 (2000)
10. Belkin, M., Niyogi, P.: Laplacian eigenmaps for dimensionality reduction and data representation. Neural Comput. **15**(6), 1373–1396 (2003)
11. McCrackin, L., Shirani, S.: Strategic image denoising using a support vector machine with seam energy and saliency features. In: 2014 IEEE International Conference on Image Processing (ICIP), pp. 2684–2688. IEEE (2014)
12. Hofmann, T., Schölkopf, B., Smola, A.J.: Kernel methods in machine learning. Annal. Stat. **36**, 1171–1220 (2008)
13. Ham, J.H., Lee, D.D., Mika, S., Schölkopf, B.: A kernel view of the dimensionality reduction of manifolds. In: International Conference on Machine Learning (2004)

# Motion-Augmented Inference and Joint Kernels in Structured Learning for Object Tracking

Kumara Ratnayake and Maria A. Amer[✉]

ECE Department, Concordia University, Montreal, Quebec, Canada
amer@ece.concordia.ca

**Abstract.** This paper proposes an object tracking method, where we first predict target dynamics by harmonic means and particle filter in which we exploit kernel machines to derive a new entropy-based observation likelihood distribution. We then employ online Structured SVMs (Structured SVMs) to model object appearance, where we analyze responses of several kernel functions for various feature descriptors and study how such kernels can be optimally combined to formulate a single joint kernel function. We gain efficiency improvements by *(1)* exploiting particle filter for sampling the search space instead of commonly adopted dense sampling strategies, and *(2)* introducing a motion-augmented regularization term during inference to constrain the output search space. We objectively demonstrate that our method strongly competes against state-of-the-art structured object tracking methods.

**Keywords:** Object tracking · Structured learning · SVMs ·
Particle filter · Motion-augmented inference · Joint kernels

## 1 Introduction

Object tracking has widespread video applications, such as traffic, security, and AR. It is challenging due to occlusion, illumination variations, fast motion, deformation, background clutter, low resolution, scale variation, rotation, out-of-view, motion blur, and speed requirements [4,12]. The online-learning based object tracking approach is the most effective among all tracking approaches. In [7], Hare et al. presented Structured output object tracking framework (*Struck*) that integrates the learning and tracking without incorporating ad-hoc update strategies. The appearance is modeled by Haar features and intensity histograms. The target location is computed by obtaining the highest discriminant score of the classifier. To gain efficiency improvements in *Struck*, the authors incorporate a budgeting mechanism which constrains the number of support vectors (SVs). Some of the limitations of *Struck* are lack of dynamic motion modeling, occlusion handling, tracking articulated and deformable objects that undergo scale variations. In [11], Kalal et al. presented discriminative classifier learning method decomposed into tracking, learning and detection (*TLD*). The method incorporates object detector with an optical flow tracker for appearance modeling, which

© Springer Nature Switzerland AG 2019
F. Karray et al. (Eds.): ICIAR 2019, LNCS 11662, pp. 45–54, 2019.
https://doi.org/10.1007/978-3-030-27202-9_4

is subsequently used for correcting any tracking drifts. Because *TLD* is based on interesting points, its performance is particularly suboptimal for articulated objects and when the object undergoes rotation. A graph based discriminative tracker is proposed in [9], which uses tensors to model appearance of the target. In [9], geometric structure of object and its background are differentiated by dedicating multiple graphs. The method reduces the tensor dimensions by exploiting graph embedding. [9] is semi-supervised therefore restricting its use in limited applications.

In this paper, we extend related online-learning based object tracking approaches by (*1*) effective target dynamic modeling, (*2*) formulating joint kernel functions for effective object tracking, (*3*) constraining output search space during inference, and (*4*) exploiting kernel machines to evaluate posterior likelihood.

## 2 The Proposed Tracker

The proposed Motion Inferred Structured Tracker (MIST) consists of two main steps: dynamic modeling and tracking by learning.

### 2.1 Target Dynamic Modeling

Modeling target dynamics is important especially when the motion is large or abrupt. We model target dynamics using Kernelized Harmonic Means (KHM), particle filter, and entropy-based likelihood.

**Kernelized Harmonic Means Propagation:** We represent our dynamic model by a state vector $\mathbf{s} = [s_1 \ s_2]$ to describe the moving target by its position. Typically, the dynamics of $\mathbf{s}$ is represented by a constant velocity model [15]

$$\hat{\mathbf{s}}_{t+1} = \mathbf{s}_t + (\mathbf{s}_t - \mathbf{s}_{t-1}) + \mathbf{n}_t^{\text{HM}}, \tag{1}$$

where $\hat{\mathbf{s}}_{t+1}$ is the predicted state at time $t + 1$ (in frame $F_{t+1}$) and $\mathbf{s}_t$ and $\mathbf{s}_{t-1}$ are the current and previous states at time $t$ and $t - 1$, respectively, and $\mathbf{n}_t^{\text{HM}}$ is system noise modeled by a Gaussian distribution with zero mean and a standard deviation of 0.25. In (1), $(\mathbf{s}_t - \mathbf{s}_{t-1})$ represents constant velocity component computed using two most recent states. We use $N^{\text{HM}}$ prior state vectors and apply KHM to estimate $\Delta\mathbf{s}_t = \mathbf{s}_t - \mathbf{s}_{t-1}$ as $\Delta\mathbf{s}_t = \left( \sum_{l=1}^{N^{\text{HM}}} \frac{k^{\text{HM}}(t-1,t-l)}{\Delta\mathbf{s}_{t-l}} \right)^{-1}$, where

$l \in [1, N^{\text{HM}}]$ is the prior state number and $k^{\text{HM}}(t, t') = \exp\left(-C^{\text{HM}} \cdot (t - t')^2\right)$ is a Gaussian Radial Basis Function (GRBF) kernel with parameter $C^{\text{HM}}$. Since $k^{\text{HM}}(t, t')$ is higher for the most recent state vectors and lower for past state vectors, the later state dynamics are aggregated more into the KHM predicted state vector. Substituting $\Delta\mathbf{s}_t$ in (1), we predict the state dynamics of the target

$$\hat{\mathbf{s}}_{t+1} = \mathbf{s}_t + \frac{1}{\sum_{l=1}^{N^{\text{HM}}} \frac{k^{\text{HM}}(t-1,t-l)}{\Delta\mathbf{s}_{t-l}}} + \mathbf{n}_t^{\text{HM}}. \tag{2}$$

**Particle Filter:** On frame $F_1$, we draw $N_1^P$ particles around the initial Bounding Box (BB) according to a Gaussian distribution. We denote the state of particle $r$ at time $t$ by $\mathbf{u}_t^{(r)}$ and propagate each particles with independent KHM propagation model, i.e., $\mathbf{u}_t^{(r)} \rightarrow \hat{\mathbf{s}}_t^{(r)}$, where $r \in [1, N_t^P]$. The measurement to the particle filter is $\mathbf{z}_t$, which we obtain from the optimal BB estimated by the proposed Support-Vector-Machines (SVMs) inference model (see Sect. 2.2). We consider state dynamic prediction as an estimation problem of the system state $\mathbf{u}_t$ using a sequence of noisy measurement $\mathbf{z}_t$ made on the system. In particle filtering, state $\mathbf{u}_t$ is modeled as a Markovian random process and observation $\mathbf{z}_t$ are assumed to be conditionally independent given the state sequence. We then define, as in [1], $\mathbf{u}_t = f^{\text{ST}}(\mathbf{u}_{t-1}, \bar{\mathbf{n}}_t^{\text{s}})$, $\mathbf{z}_t = f^{\text{OB}}(\mathbf{u}_t, \bar{\mathbf{n}}_t^{\text{o}})$. Both $f^{\text{ST}}(\cdot)$ and $f^{\text{OB}}(\cdot)$ are nonlinear functions and $\bar{\mathbf{n}}_t^{\text{s}}$ and $\bar{\mathbf{n}}_t^{\text{o}}$ are independent non-Gaussian noise processes. We make an inference about $\mathbf{u}_t$ given all the observations up to time $t$, $\mathbf{z}_{1:t} = \{\mathbf{z}_1, ..., \mathbf{z}_t\}$. This is given by the posterior distribution for $\mathbf{u}_t$, $p(\mathbf{u}_t|\mathbf{z}_{1:t})$ [1], which by Bayes' rule is

$$p(\mathbf{u}_t|\mathbf{z}_{1:t}) = \frac{p(\mathbf{z}_t|\mathbf{u}_t)p(\mathbf{u}_t|\mathbf{z}_{1:t-1})}{p(\mathbf{z}_t|\mathbf{z}_{1:t-1})}. \tag{3}$$

Here, $p(\mathbf{z}_t|\mathbf{u}_t)$ is the observation likelihood distribution describing how the observation $\mathbf{z}_t$ depends on state $\mathbf{u}_t$. We assume that system dynamics are governed by a first order Markov process; thus the prior distribution $p(\mathbf{u}_t|\mathbf{z}_{1:t-1})$ can be described by the Chapman-Kolmogorov Equation [1]

$$p(\mathbf{u}_t|\mathbf{z}_{1:t-1}) = \int p(\mathbf{u}_t|\mathbf{u}_{t-1})p(\mathbf{u}_{t-1}|\mathbf{z}_{1:t-1})d\mathbf{u}_{t-1}. \tag{4}$$

$p(\mathbf{u}_t|\mathbf{u}_{t-1})$ is the state transition distribution. Substituting (4) in (3),

$$p(\mathbf{u}_t|\mathbf{z}_{1:t}) = \frac{p(\mathbf{z}_t|\mathbf{u}_t) \int p(\mathbf{u}_t|\mathbf{u}_{t-1})p(\mathbf{u}_{t-1}|\mathbf{z}_{1:t-1})d\mathbf{u}_{t-1}}{p(\mathbf{z}_t|\mathbf{z}_{1:t-1})}. \tag{5}$$

(5) forms the optimal Bayesian solution for inferring the state. However, (5) cannot be analytically solved [1]. Particle filter provides a numerical approximation for the posterior distribution $p(\mathbf{u}_t|\mathbf{z}_{1:t})$ using a discrete set of weighted particles $\mathbf{u}_t^{(r)}$. With such particles, the posterior density in (5) is approximated [1]

$$p(\mathbf{u}_t|\mathbf{z}_{1:t}) \approx \sum_{r=1}^{N_t^P} \tilde{m}_t^{(r)} \cdot \delta(\mathbf{u}_t - \mathbf{u}_t^{(r)}); \quad \tilde{m}_t^{(r)} = \frac{m_t^{(r)}}{\sum_{\bar{r}=1}^{N_t^P} m_t^{(\bar{r})}}, \tag{6}$$

where $\delta(\cdot)$ is the Dirac delta function, $\tilde{m}_t^{(r)}$ is the normalized importance weight of particle $r$ at $F_t$, and $m_t^{(r)}$ [1] is

$$m_t^{(r)} \propto \frac{p(\mathbf{z}_t|\mathbf{u}_t^{(r)})p(\mathbf{u}_t^{(r)}|\mathbf{u}_{t-1}^{(r)})}{q(\mathbf{u}_t^{(r)}|\mathbf{u}_{t-1}^{(r)}, \mathbf{z}_{1:t})} m_{t-1}^{(r)}, \tag{7}$$

where $q(\mathbf{u}_t^{(r)}|\mathbf{u}_{t-1}^{(r)}, \mathbf{z}_{1:t})$ is the importance distribution from which particles are drawn at $F_t$. As with widely adopted Sequential Importance Resampling (SIR) particle filters [6], we choose $q(\mathbf{u}_t^{(r)}|\mathbf{u}_{t-1}^{(r)}, \mathbf{z}_{1:t}) = p(\mathbf{u}_t|\mathbf{u}_{t-1}^{(r)})$ as the state transition distribution, and (7) becomes

$$m_t^{(r)} \propto p(\mathbf{z}_t|\mathbf{u}_t^{(r)}) \cdot m_{t-1}^{(r)}. \tag{8}$$

For improving the efficiency (speed) of the proposed tracker, we use the mean $\mu^{\mathbf{u}}$ and the standard deviation $\sigma^{\mathbf{u}}$ of the motion vectors of the previously estimated $N^{\mathrm{PP}}$ optimal particles to adaptively derive $N_t^{\mathrm{P}}$. To that end, we set the number of particles to the number of locations covered by a circular region with a radius of $\mu^{\mathbf{u}} + 3\sigma^{\mathbf{u}}$; more specifically, $N_t^{\mathrm{P}} = \lceil \pi(\mu^{\mathbf{u}} + 3\sigma^{\mathbf{u}})^2 \rceil$, where $\lceil \cdot \rceil$ rounds up to the nearest integer. The weights $m_t^{(r)}$ are sorted in ascending order and resampled so that the particles with higher weights are multiplied if $N_t^{\mathrm{P}} > N_{t-1}^{\mathrm{P}}$ and those with lower weights are eliminated otherwise.

**Entropy-Based Likelihood:** The observation likelihood model $p(\mathbf{z}_t|\mathbf{u}_t^{(r)})$ in (8) plays an important role in estimating the state $\mathbf{u}_t$. Entropy can be used to measure certainty of distribution; a lower entropy means less uncertainty in the underline distribution. We formulate the observation likelihood using entropy of the similarity-distribution between each particle and the target by exploiting *kernel machines* described in Sect. 2.2. Let $\mathbf{k}^{\mathrm{OL}}$ be a vector of similarity between previous target $\hat{\mathbf{u}}_{t-1}$ and each particle

$$\mathbf{k}^{\mathrm{OL}} = \begin{bmatrix} k(\mathbf{u}_1, \hat{\mathbf{u}}_{t-1}) & k(\mathbf{u}_2, \hat{\mathbf{u}}_{t-1}) & \cdots & k(\mathbf{u}_{N_t^{\mathrm{P}}}, \hat{\mathbf{u}}_{t-1}) \end{bmatrix}, \tag{9}$$

where Joint Kernel Function (JKF) $k(\mathbf{u}, \hat{\mathbf{u}}) = g \cdot k^{\star}(\mathbf{u}^{\star}, \hat{\mathbf{u}}^{\star}) + (1-g) \cdot k^{\diamond}(\mathbf{u}^{\diamond}, \hat{\mathbf{u}}^{\diamond})$. Here, $k^{\star}$ and $k^{\diamond}$ are color and shape kernel functions, and $g$ is a weight. To compute entropy of the similarity scores, we normalize (9) to $\tilde{\mathbf{k}}_r^{\mathrm{OL}} = \frac{\mathbf{k}_r^{\mathrm{OL}} - \min(\mathbf{k}^{\mathrm{OL}})}{\max(\mathbf{k}^{\mathrm{OL}}) - \min(\mathbf{k}^{\mathrm{OL}})}$, and deduce their similarity distribution $p(\mathbf{k}_r^{\mathrm{OL}}|\hat{\mathbf{u}}_{t-1})p(\mathbf{k}_r^{\mathrm{OL}}|\hat{\mathbf{u}}_{t-1}) = \frac{\tilde{\mathbf{k}}_r^{\mathrm{OL}}}{\sum_{r=1}^{N_t^{\mathrm{P}}} \tilde{\mathbf{k}}_r^{\mathrm{OL}}}$. Then, we compute the corresponding entropy score $H$ for $p(\mathbf{k}_r^{\mathrm{OL}}|\hat{\mathbf{u}}_{t-1})$ by

$$H = -\sum_{r=1}^{N_t^{\mathrm{P}}} p(\mathbf{k}_r^{\mathrm{OL}}|\hat{\mathbf{u}}_{t-1}) \log \left( p(\mathbf{k}_r^{\mathrm{OL}}|\hat{\mathbf{u}}_{t-1}) \right), \tag{10}$$

and subsequently we define our observation likelihood

$$p(\mathbf{z}_t|\mathbf{u}_t^{(r)}) = \frac{\exp(-\tilde{\mathbf{k}}_r^{\mathrm{OL}} \cdot H)}{\sum_{\acute{r}=1}^{N_t^{\mathrm{P}}} \exp(-\tilde{\mathbf{k}}_{\acute{r}}^{\mathrm{OL}} \cdot H)}. \tag{11}$$

By substituting (11) in the weight computation in (8), and using Maximum A Posteriori (MAP) rule [5], we obtain the estimated state $\hat{\mathbf{u}}_t \approx \arg\max_{\mathbf{u}_t^{(r)}} \tilde{m}_t^{(r)}$.

## 2.2  Tracking by Learning

The proposed tracking-by-learning is composed of Structured SVMs, conditional model-update, joint kernels, and motion-inferred inference.

**Structured Support-Vector-Machines:** Object tracking is considered as learning a *prediction* function $f : \mathcal{X} \rightarrow \mathcal{Y}$ that maps the space of input features $\mathcal{X}$ to the space of output BBs $\mathcal{Y}$ based on $N^{\text{EX}}$ input-output example pairs $\mathcal{S} = \{(\mathbf{x}_1, \mathbf{y}_1), ..., (\mathbf{x}_{N^{\text{EX}}}, \mathbf{y}_{N^{\text{EX}}})\} \in (\mathcal{X} \times \mathcal{Y})^{N^{\text{EX}}}$. With Structured SVMs in tracking, we discriminatively learn a *scoring* function $\phi : \mathcal{X} \times \mathcal{Y} \in \mathbb{R}$ over input-output example set $\mathcal{S}$. Alternatively, the scoring function $\phi$ maps both output BB $\mathbf{y}$ and its corresponding feature $\mathbf{x}$ to a scalar label. Hence, $\phi$ can be seen as measuring the compatibility of an input-output pairs. (Notice that each BB $\mathbf{y}$ is extracted from the corresponding particle $\mathbf{u}$.) Once the scoring function is learned, the prediction of the output $\hat{\mathbf{y}}$, that constitutes the highest compatibility with the input $\mathbf{x}$, can be obtained by maximizing $\phi$ over all $\mathbf{y} \in \mathcal{Y}$

$$\hat{\mathbf{y}} = f(\mathbf{x}) = \arg \max_{\mathbf{y} \in \mathcal{Y}} \phi(\mathbf{x}, \mathbf{y}). \tag{12}$$

The scoring function is defined [14] in the form of

$$\phi(\mathbf{x}, \mathbf{y}) = \langle \mathbf{w}, \boldsymbol{\Phi}(\mathbf{x}, \mathbf{y}) \rangle, \tag{13}$$

where the weight vector $\mathbf{w}$ is learned with sequentially obtained example pairs in set $\mathcal{S}$, and $\boldsymbol{\Phi}(\mathbf{x}, \mathbf{y})$ is a joint feature map that maps joint input feature and output BBs to a transform space. The specific form of $\boldsymbol{\Phi}(\mathbf{x}, \mathbf{y})$ depends on the nature of the problem. In general, $\boldsymbol{\Phi}(\mathbf{x}, \mathbf{y})$ is not explicitly modeled allowing us to exploit the advantages of kernel machines. Following the standard SVMs derivation, $\phi$ can be learned by minimizing the constrained convex function

$$\min_{\mathbf{w}} \left\{ \tfrac{1}{2} \| \mathbf{w} \|^2 + C^{\text{SVM}} \textstyle\sum_{i=1}^{N^{\text{EX}}} \xi_i \right\}, \quad \text{s.t.} \quad \forall i : \xi_i \geq 0, \forall i \, \forall \mathbf{y} \neq \mathbf{y}_i : \langle \mathbf{w}, \delta \boldsymbol{\Phi}_i(\mathbf{y}) \rangle \geq \Delta(\mathbf{y}_i, \mathbf{y}) - \xi_i, \tag{14}$$

where $i \in [1, N^{\text{EX}}]$, the slack variables $\xi_i$ allow the examples to violate the constraint of being outside of the margin, $\delta \boldsymbol{\Phi}_i(\mathbf{y}) = \boldsymbol{\Phi}(\mathbf{x}_i, \mathbf{y}_i) - \boldsymbol{\Phi}(\mathbf{x}_i, \mathbf{y})$, and $C^{\text{SVM}}$ controls how strongly margin violations are penalized. The loss function $\Delta$ is 1 when the BBs $\bar{\mathbf{y}}$ and $\mathbf{y}$ are disjoint, and is 0 when the BBs are identical. Instead of solving the *primal* optimization problem in (14) directly, its *dual* formulation using the Lagrangian function [14] is obtained

$$\max_{\boldsymbol{\alpha}} -\frac{1}{2} \sum_{\substack{i \\ \mathbf{y} \neq \mathbf{y}_i}} \sum_{\substack{j \\ \bar{\mathbf{y}} \neq \mathbf{y}_j}} \alpha_{i\mathbf{y}} \alpha_{j\bar{\mathbf{y}}} \langle \delta \boldsymbol{\Phi}_i(\mathbf{y}), \delta \boldsymbol{\Phi}_j(\bar{\mathbf{y}}) \rangle + \sum_{i\mathbf{y} \neq \mathbf{y}_i} \Delta(\mathbf{y}_i, \mathbf{y}) \alpha_{i\mathbf{y}},$$

$$\text{s.t.} \quad \forall i : \sum_{\mathbf{y} \neq \mathbf{y}_i} \alpha_{i\mathbf{y}} \leq C^{\text{SVM}}, \forall i \, \forall \mathbf{y} \neq \mathbf{y}_i : \alpha_{i\mathbf{y}} \geq 0, \tag{15}$$

where $j \in [1, N^{\text{EX}}]$ is an index, the Lagrangian multiplier $\alpha$ corresponds to the margin constraint in (14). By solving this dual optimization problem, the weight vector $\mathbf{w} = \sum_{i, \mathbf{y} \neq \mathbf{y}_i} \alpha_{i\mathbf{y}} \delta \boldsymbol{\Phi}_i(\mathbf{y})$ and (13) becomes

$$\phi(\mathbf{x}, \mathbf{y}) = \sum_{i, \bar{\mathbf{y}} \neq \mathbf{y}_i} \alpha_{i\bar{\mathbf{y}}} \langle \delta \boldsymbol{\Phi}_i(\bar{\mathbf{y}}), \boldsymbol{\Phi}(\mathbf{x}, \mathbf{y}) \rangle. \tag{16}$$

Following [3], we define $\beta$

$$\beta_{i\mathbf{y}} = \begin{cases} -\alpha_{i\mathbf{y}}, & \text{if } \mathbf{y} \neq \mathbf{y}_i \\ \sum_{\bar{\mathbf{y}} \neq \mathbf{y}_i} \alpha_{i\bar{\mathbf{y}}}, & \text{otherwise,} \end{cases} \tag{17}$$

and substitute $\beta$ in (15) to form a simplified dual problem

$$\max_{\beta} -\frac{1}{2} \sum_{i, \mathbf{y}} \sum_{j, \bar{\mathbf{y}}} \beta_{i\mathbf{y}} \beta_{j\bar{\mathbf{y}}} k_{ij} - \sum_{i\mathbf{y}} \Delta(\mathbf{y}_i, \mathbf{y}) \beta_{i\mathbf{y}},$$

$$\text{s.t.} \quad \forall i: \sum_{\mathbf{y}} \beta_{i\mathbf{y}} = 0, \forall i \; \forall \mathbf{y}: \beta_{i\mathbf{y}} \leq C^{\text{SVM}} \Delta'(\mathbf{y}_i, \mathbf{y}), \tag{18}$$

where $\Delta'(\mathbf{y}_i, \mathbf{y}) = 1$, if $\mathbf{y} = \mathbf{y}_i$, and $\Delta'(\mathbf{y}_i, \mathbf{y}) = 0$ otherwise. $\Delta(\mathbf{y}_i, \mathbf{y}) = 1 - \frac{\mathbb{A}(\mathbf{y}_i \cap \mathbf{y})}{\mathbb{A}(\mathbf{y}_i \cup \mathbf{y})}$, $\mathbb{A}(\mathbf{y}_i \cap \mathbf{y})$ and $\mathbb{A}(\mathbf{y}_i \cup \mathbf{y})$ are the areas of the intersection and union of $\mathbf{y}_i$ and $\mathbf{y}$. The JKF $k : \mathcal{X} \times \mathcal{X} \in \mathbb{R}$ is the inner product of input-output pairs $(\mathbf{x}_i, \mathbf{y})$ and $(\mathbf{x}_j, \bar{\mathbf{y}})$ mapped in Reproducing Kernel Hilbert Space (RKHS) $\mathcal{H}$ space, i.e.,

$$k\big((\mathbf{x}_i, \mathbf{y}), (\mathbf{x}_j, \bar{\mathbf{y}})\big) = \langle \boldsymbol{\Phi}(\mathbf{x}_i, \mathbf{y}), \boldsymbol{\Phi}(\mathbf{x}_j, \bar{\mathbf{y}}) \rangle. \tag{19}$$

We extract the feature (color and shape) inputs $\mathbf{x}$ from their corresponding BBs $\mathbf{y}$. Hence, without loss of generality, we denote the JKF as $k(\mathbf{x}_i, \mathbf{x}_j)$ omitting $\mathbf{y}$. Substituting $\alpha$ in (16) with $\beta$ in (17), $\phi$ becomes $\phi(\mathbf{x}, \mathbf{y}) = \sum_{i, \bar{\mathbf{y}}} \beta_{i\bar{\mathbf{y}}} k(\mathbf{x}_i, \mathbf{x})$. Often, $\beta$ is sparse. We denote the pairs $(\mathbf{x}_i, \mathbf{y})$ for which $\beta_{i\mathbf{y}} \neq 0$ as SVs. SVs with $\beta_{i\mathbf{y}} > 0$ and $\beta_{i\bar{\mathbf{y}}} < 0$ are referred as positive and negative SVs, respectively.

We adopt Sequential Minimal Optimization (SMO)-style [13] for maximization of (18) because of its efficiency [3]. We select a pair of positive and negative BBs by searching for the maximum and minimum of the gradient of (18), respectively. For example, $\mathbf{y}^+$ is chosen by finding the most important positive sample

$$\mathbf{y}^+ = \arg \max_{\mathbf{y}} -\phi(\mathbf{x}_i, \mathbf{y}) - \Delta(\mathbf{y}_i, \mathbf{y}). \tag{20}$$

For this pair of $\mathbf{y}^+$ and $\mathbf{y}^-$, we optimize their corresponding coefficients $\beta_{i\mathbf{y}}^+$ and $\beta_{i\mathbf{y}}^-$ using SMO-step. If these coefficients are non-zero, we retain $\beta_{i\mathbf{y}}$, the corresponding gradients and SV $(\mathbf{x}_i, \mathbf{y})$. During tracking, both gradient and $\beta_{i\mathbf{y}}$ are updated, and we remove any SV if its $\beta_{i\mathbf{y}}$ becomes zero. In practice, however, the target may not be present in the scene, for example, due to occlusion. Therefore, updating the model every frame results in tracking drift. We thus construct a probability model to determine the target state and update our learning model.

**Conditional Model Update:** During SMO-step, we search for the maximum and minimum of the gradient to select a pair of positive and negative BBs. If their corresponding coefficients ($\beta_{i\mathbf{y}}^+$ and $\beta_{i\mathbf{y}}^-$) are non-zero, we retain the sample as a SV in each frame. Let $\mathbf{x}^{\text{OPT}}$ be the feature vector of the optimally inferred BB $\mathbf{y}^{\text{OPT}}$ and $\mathcal{D}^+$ be the set of positive SVs. We define $p(\mathcal{D}^+|\mathbf{y}^{\text{OPT}}) = \frac{\mu^+}{\mu^+|\mu^-|}$, where $\mu^+ = \sum_{i\in\mathcal{D}^+} \beta_{i\mathbf{y}}^+ k(\mathbf{x}_i, \mathbf{x}^{\text{OPT}})$ and $\mu^- = \sum_{i\in\mathcal{D}^-} \beta_{i\mathbf{y}}^- k(\mathbf{x}_i, \mathbf{x}^{\text{OPT}})$. We retain the current BB as a positive SV only when $\min(p(\mathcal{D}^+, |\mathbf{y}^{\text{OPT}}), \phi(\mathbf{x}^{\text{OPT}}, \mathbf{y})) > C^{\text{CMU}}$. When the target is absent from the scene, $\min(p(\mathcal{D}^+, |\mathbf{y}^{\text{OPT}}), \phi(\mathbf{x}^{\text{OPT}}, \mathbf{y}))$ is lower than $C^{\text{CMU}}$, and we avoid updating the learning model and rely on the proposed motion model for trajectory estimation.

**Adaptive Weighted Joint Kernel:** For the joint kernel formulation in (19), we extract the input feature vector $\mathbf{x}$ from the image regions defined by the BB $\mathbf{y}$. We define $\mathbf{x} = [\mathbf{x}^\star\ \mathbf{x}^\circ]$ by two feature descriptors to characterize the target using color $\mathbf{x}^\star$, and local shape $\mathbf{x}^\circ$. For color features, we use joint Bhattacharyya (Hellinger) kernel $k^\star(\mathbf{x}^\star, \bar{\mathbf{x}}^\star) = \sqrt{\langle\mathbf{x}^\star, \bar{\mathbf{x}}^\star\rangle}$. By incorporating the shape kernel within the JKF, we ensure that input-output pairs with good *geometric*-similarity are assigned with higher similarity score. We construct the local shape kernel $k^\circ$ as GRBF kernel function with $\gamma^\circ = 0.22$, $k^\circ(\mathbf{x}^\circ, \bar{\mathbf{x}}^\circ) = \exp\left(-\gamma^\circ \| \mathbf{x}^\circ - \bar{\mathbf{x}}^\circ \|^2\right)$. Our JKF ensures that the input-output pairs are similar *if and only if* both their inputs and outputs are similar. To this end, we define our joint kernel as the weighted sum of color and global shape kernels. The final JKF yields a smaller output if any one of the two kernels' response is small. This also implies that JKF is stronger than classical kernels defined over single kernel. Formally, given two input-output pairs $(\mathbf{x}, \mathbf{y})$ and $(\bar{\mathbf{x}}, \bar{\mathbf{y}})$, we define adaptive weighted JKF

$$k(\mathbf{x}, \bar{\mathbf{x}}) = \langle\boldsymbol{\Phi}(\mathbf{x}), \boldsymbol{\Phi}(\bar{\mathbf{x}})\rangle = g \cdot k^\star(\mathbf{x}^\star, \bar{\mathbf{x}}^\star) + (1 - g) \cdot k^\circ(\mathbf{x}^\circ, \bar{\mathbf{x}}^\circ) \qquad (21)$$

where $k^\star$ and $k^\circ$ are color and global-shape (Histogram of Oriented Gradients (HoG)) kernels measuring similarity between two feature vectors. The weight $g$ is computed using the color similarity between the target and its background: $g = g_n$; $L_n < k^\star(\mathbf{x}^\star, \bar{\mathbf{x}}^\star) \leq L_{n+1}$, where $\{L_n\}_{n=0}^\infty$ is a monotonically increasing sequence. Experimentally, we obtain $L = \{0, 0.10, 0.25, 0.50, 0.75, 1\}$ and $g = \{0.0, 0.15, 0.25, 0.35, 0.45\}$. Note that a kernel derived by weighted sum of valid kernels holds Mercer's condition. Therefore, (21) is still a valid kernel.

**Motion-Augmented Inference:** JKF based on multiple features is computationally expensive. To gain performance improvements, we introduce a motion-augmented regularization term during inference to constrain the output search space. In the maximization problem (12), we infer the prediction of the output $\hat{\mathbf{y}}$ by maximizing $\phi$ over all possible output $\mathbf{y} \in \mathcal{Y}$, which is intractable. Instead, we leverage proposed dynamic model and restrict the search space to a smaller subspace $\mathcal{Y}^\star \subset \mathcal{Y}$. To this end, we amend our original maximization problem in (12) with a regularization term $\varphi(\mathbf{u}, \mathbf{y})$

$$\hat{\mathbf{y}} = \arg\max_{\mathbf{y} \in \mathcal{Y}^*} \phi(\mathbf{x}, \mathbf{y}) \cdot \varphi(\mathbf{u}, \mathbf{y}), \tag{22}$$

where $\varphi(\mathbf{u}, \mathbf{y})$ is higher (smaller) if a BB $\mathbf{u}$ is closer to (far from) the output $\mathbf{y}$. To reflect this, we compute the relative distance of the dynamic models between the BBs $\mathbf{u}$ and $\mathbf{y}$. We use a distance measure based on $l_2$-norm mapped in the RKHS space, which is subsequently induced by the JKF $k^{\mathrm{MI}}$

$$\begin{aligned}\varphi(\mathbf{u}, \mathbf{y}) &= \exp\left(- \parallel \boldsymbol{\Phi}(\mathbf{u}, \mathbf{y}) - \boldsymbol{\Phi}(\hat{\mathbf{u}}, \hat{\mathbf{y}}) \parallel^2\right) \\ &= \exp\left(2k^{\mathrm{MI}}(\mathbf{u}, \hat{\mathbf{u}}) - k^{\mathrm{MI}}(\mathbf{u}, \mathbf{u}) - k^{\mathrm{MI}}(\hat{\mathbf{u}}, \hat{\mathbf{u}})\right). \end{aligned} \tag{23}$$

The regularization term $\varphi(\mathbf{u}, \mathbf{y})$ incorporated in (22) is not an explicit component of the learning model in (12). Therefore, it simplifies the overall learning task to a greater deal since it allows focusing on a restricted, smaller subspace $\mathcal{Y}^*$. For efficiency and simplicity, we formulate our JKF for motion states $k^{\mathrm{MI}}$ using GRBF kernel with parameter $\gamma^{\mathrm{MI}} = 0.2$, as $k^{\mathrm{MI}}(\mathbf{u}, \hat{\mathbf{u}}) = \exp\left(-\gamma^{\mathrm{MI}} \parallel \mathbf{u} - \hat{\mathbf{u}} \parallel^2\right)$.

## 3  Experimental Results

Algorithm 1 summarizes the proposed method.

The parameters of our algorithm are $N^{\mathrm{HM}} = 8, N^{\mathrm{P}} = 1000, N^{\mathrm{PP}} = 16, C^{\mathrm{SVM}} = 25, C^{\mathrm{CMU}} = 0.02, \gamma^{\mathrm{MI}} = 0.20$, and $\gamma^{\circ} = 0.22$. We used the dataset [15], which includes 11 challenging categories, to compare our method against *Struck* [7], *ASLA* [10], *SCM* [16], *TLD* [11], *CSK* [8], and *L1APG* [2]. We apply the objective measures [15]: center location error (CLE) and average overlap ratio (AOR). Table 1 lists the averaged objective measures for all sequences as well as the average frame rates obtained for all videos. As can be observed from Table 1, our method well outperforms the compared trackers in the overall objective measures. Compared to the 3 most accurate methods (*Struck*, *ASLA*, and *SCM*), the proposed method is the fast with 11.23 Frames Per Seconds (FPS). The sample subjective results show the effectiveness of MIST

**Table 1.** Average measures over the test video sequences. %BestS is the percentage of the sequences that a tracker performs best and second best.

| Tracker | Overlap score | | Center error | | Frame rate | Code |
|---------|------|--------|------|--------|------------|------|
|         | Mean | %BestS | Mean | %BestS | (FPS)      |      |
| *MIST* [Ours] | **0.551** | **0.52** | **26.84** | **0.48** | 11.23 | *C/C++* |
| *Struck* [7] | *0.481* | 0,28 | *50.81* | 0,22 | 9.46 | *C/C++* |
| *ASLA* [10] | 0.457 | *0,38* | 62.17 | 0,22 | 4.88 | *Matlab/C/C++* |
| *TLD* [11] | 0.432 | 0,16 | 52.27 | 0,22 | 24.12 | *Matlab/C/C++* |
| *SCM* [16] | 0.437 | 0,18 | 64.35 | 0,22 | 0.36 | *Matlab/C/C++* |
| *CSK* [8] | 0.400 | 0,14 | 88.88 | 0,16 | **230.72** | *Matlab* |
| *L1APG* [2] | 0.360 | 0,08 | 73.39 | 0,10 | 1.23 | *Matlab/C/C++* |

---

**Algorithm 1:** Proposed online object tracking algorithm MIST.

---

**Input** : Initial BB of the target in $F_1$.
**Output:** Prediction of the output BB $\hat{\mathbf{y}}$ in $F_t$.

1  **repeat**
2     **if** $F_1$ **then**
3        Draw $N_1^{\mathrm{P}}$ particles around the initial BB.
4        **go to** line 12.

5     **for** each particle $r$ **do**
6        Propagate particles according to (2).
7        Evaluate likelihood $p(\mathbf{z}_t|\mathbf{u}_t^{(r)})$ by (10).
8        Update the importance weights $m_t^{(r)}$ using (7).

9     Estimated optimal particle state $\hat{\mathbf{u}}_t$ with $\hat{\mathbf{u}}_t \approx \arg\max_{\mathbf{u}_t^{(r)}} \tilde{m}_t^{(r)}$.
10    Compute number of particles: $N_t^{\mathrm{P}} = \mu^{\mathbf{u}} + 3\sigma^{\mathbf{u}}$.
11    Sort $\{\mathbf{u}_t^{(r)}, m_t^{(r)}\}$ according to $m_t^{(r)}$, and resample.
12    **for** each particle $r$ **do**
13       Extract color $\mathbf{x}^*$ and local shape $\mathbf{x}^\circ$ features.
14       Compute scoring function $\phi(\mathbf{x}, \mathbf{y})$ by $\phi(\mathbf{x}, \mathbf{y}) = \sum_{i,\bar{\mathbf{y}}} \beta_{i\bar{\mathbf{y}}} k(\mathbf{x}_i, \mathbf{x})$.
15       **if** $\min(p(\mathcal{D}^+, |\mathbf{y}^{\mathrm{OPT}}), \phi(\mathbf{x}^{\mathrm{OPT}}, \mathbf{y})) > C^{\mathrm{CMU}}$ **then**
16          Evaluate $g = g_n$; $L_n < k^*(\mathbf{x}^*, \bar{\mathbf{x}}^*) \le L_{n+1}$, and then compute JKF:
17             $k(\mathbf{x}, \bar{\mathbf{x}}) = g \cdot k^*(\mathbf{x}^*, \bar{\mathbf{x}}^*) + (1 - g) \cdot k^\circ(\mathbf{x}^\circ, \bar{\mathbf{x}}^\circ)$.
18          Compute regularization term $\varphi(\mathbf{u}, \mathbf{y})$ by (22).
19          Evaluate $\hat{\mathbf{y}} = \arg\max_{\mathbf{y} \in \mathcal{Y}^*} \phi(\mathbf{x}, \mathbf{y})\varphi(\mathbf{u}, \mathbf{y})$.
20          Select $\{\mathbf{y}^+, \mathbf{y}^-\}$ according to (19).
21          Maximize the dual (17) with SMO-style [13].
22       **else**
23          Derive output BB $\hat{\mathbf{y}}$ using (2)

24 **until** end of video sequence.

---

## 4  Conclusion

In our object tracking method, *first*, we modeled the target dynamics as a random stochastic process, and adopted harmonic means and particle filter to predict dynamics. In our dynamic model, we introduced a new observation likelihood model using kernel machines. We used entropy to evaluate certainty of our observation likelihood distribution. *Second*, we used online structured SVMs to the tracking problem. For modeling the target appearance, we developed an adaptive weighted joint kernel function using color and histogram of gradients.

For learning, we built a probability model to avoid model updates when the target is absent. To gain computational efficiency, we used particle filter for sampling, and introduced a motion-augmented regularization term during inference to constrain the search space. We demonstrated that the proposed method is more effective than related methods against many challenges often encountered in real-world applications, while being computationally efficient.

# References

1. Arulampalam, M.S., Maskell, S., Gordon, N., Clapp, T.: A tutorial on particle filters for online nonlinear/non-Gaussian Bayesian tracking. IEEE Trans. Signal Process. **50**, 174–188 (2002)
2. Bao, C., Wu, Y., Ling, H., Ji, H.: Real time robust $l_1$ tracker using accelerated proximal gradient approach. In: IEEE Conference on Computer Vision and Pattern Recognition, pp. 1830–1837 (2012)
3. Bordes, A., Bottou, L., Gallinari, P., Weston, J.: Solving multiclass support vector machines with LaRank. In: International Conference on Machine Learning, pp. 89–96 (2007)
4. Cai, Y., Wang, H., Chen, X., Chen, L.: Multilevel framework to handle object occlusions for real-time tracking. IET Image Process. **10**(11), 885–892 (2016)
5. Doucet, A., Godsill, S., Andrieu, C.: On sequential monte carlo sampling methods for Bayesian filtering. Stat. Comput. **10**(3), 197–208 (2000)
6. Gordon, N., Salmond, D., Smith, A.: Novel approach to nonlinear/non-Gaussian Bayesian state estimation. IET Radar Signal Proc. **140**(2), 107–113 (1993)
7. Hare, S., et al.: Struck: structured output tracking with kernels. IEEE Trans. PAMI **38**(10), 2096–2109 (2016)
8. Henriques, J.F., Caseiro, R., Martins, P., Batista, J.: Exploiting the circulant structure of tracking-by-detection with kernels. In: Fitzgibbon, A., Lazebnik, S., Perona, P., Sato, Y., Schmid, C. (eds.) ECCV 2012. LNCS, vol. 7575, pp. 702–715. Springer, Heidelberg (2012). https://doi.org/10.1007/978-3-642-33765-9_50
9. Hu, W., Gao, J., Xing, J., Zhang, C., Maybank, S.: Semi-supervised tensor-based graph embedding learning and its application to visual discriminant tracking. IEEE Trans. Pattern Anal. Mach. Intell. **PP**(99), 1 (2016)
10. Jia, X., Lu, H., Yang, M.H.: Visual tracking via adaptive structural local sparse appearance model. In: IEEE Conference on CVPR, pp. 1822–1829 (2012)
11. Kalal, Z., Mikolajczyk, K., Matas, J.: Tracking-learning-detection. IEEE Trans. Pattern Anal. Mach. Intell. **34**(7), 1409–1422 (2012)
12. Kang, B., Zhu, W., Liang, D.: Robust multi-feature visual tracking via multi-task kernel-based sparse learning. IET Image Process. **11**(12), 1172–1178 (2017)
13. Platt, J.: Fast training of support vector machines using sequential minimal optimization. In: Advances in Kernel Methods-Support Vector Learning, vol. 3 (1999)
14. Tsochantaridis, I., Joachims, T., Hofmann, T., Altun, Y.: Large margin methods for structured and interdependent output variables. J. Mach. Learn. Res. **6**, 1453–1484 (2005)
15. Wu, Y., Lim, J., Yang, M.H.: Online object tracking: a benchmark. In: IEEE Conference on Computer Vision and Pattern Recognition, pp. 2411–2418 (2013)
16. Zhong, W., Lu, H., Yang, M.H.: Robust object tracking via sparsity-based collaborative model. In: IEEE Conference on Computer Vision and Pattern Recognition, pp. 1838–1845 (2012)

# An Efficient Algorithm for Computing the Derivative of Mean Structural Similarity Index Measure

Isabel Molina Orihuela[1,2] and Mehran Ebrahimi[2(✉)]

[1] Universidad de Málaga, 31 Bulevar Louis Pasteur, 29010 Málaga, Spain
[2] University of Ontario Institute of Technology, 2000 Simcoe Street North, Oshawa, ON L1H 7K4, Canada
{isabel.orihuela,mehran.ebrahimi}@uoit.ca

**Abstract.** Many inverse problems in imaging can be addressed using energy minimization. The Euclidean distance is traditionally used in data fidelity term of energy functionals, even though it is not an optimal measure of visual quality. Recently the use of Mean Structural Similarity Index Measure (MSSIM) in data fidelity expressions has been examined. Solving such problems requires derivative of MSSIM. We propose an efficient algorithm for computing this derivative using convolutions. We indicate how the computational cost will be reduced to $\mathcal{O}(N \log N)$ from the cost of traditional scheme $\mathcal{O}(m \ N \log N)$ where $N$ is the size of an input image and $m$ is the window size. The proposed algorithm can be used for any inverse problem that traditionally applies L2 norm as a data fidelity measure. We apply the proposed numerical scheme to the inverse problem of image denoising.

**Keywords:** Structural Similarity Index Measure (SSIM) · Mean-SSIM · Inverse problems · SSIM derivative

## 1 Introduction

The analysis of image quality plays a central role in many image processing applications. Over the past decade, new objective image quality assessment measures have been developed that can better estimate image quality perceived by the human specialist [6]. Traditional measures such as the Peak Signal-Noise Ratio (PSNR) or Mean Square Error (MSE) are very simple to calculate, yet they do not necessarily relate to the image quality perceived by a human observer [6]. An original image can be altered with different distortions that are perceived differently, but all of them have the same MSE, see [6]. The proposed similarity measure in [6] known as Structural Similarity Index Measure (SSIM) is based on the hypothesis that the human visual system is adapted to extract structural information of images in such a way that a measure of the structural information can provide a good approximation of the perceived image quality.

© Springer Nature Switzerland AG 2019
F. Karray et al. (Eds.): ICIAR 2019, LNCS 11662, pp. 55–66, 2019.
https://doi.org/10.1007/978-3-030-27202-9_5

In the next Section, we first review the definitions of SSIM, MSSIM and the general formulation of inverse problems using MSSIM as a data fidelity term. This will be followed by a developing a novel technique for efficient derivative estimation of the MSSIM and proving in terms of computational complexity. Finally, preliminary experiments for total variation (TV)-based image denoising will be presented in which MSSIM is employed as a data fidelity term instead of the typical Euclidean distance.

## 2   Background Material

### 2.1   SSIM

The function SSIM measures the similarity between an 'ideal' discrete image $x$ and a distorted version of it $y$ based on three components, luminance, contrast and structure [2,6]. Let $\mu_x$, $\mu_y$ be the mean intensity of images $x$ and $y$ each of size $N$ as

$$\mu_x = \frac{1}{N} \sum_{i=1}^{N} x_i \quad , \quad \mu_y = \frac{1}{N} \sum_{i=1}^{N} y_i.$$

Let $\sigma_x$, $\sigma_y$ and $\sigma_{xy}$ be the standard deviation of $x$, standard deviation of $y$, and covariance between $x$ and $y$ respectively given by $\sigma_x = \left( \frac{1}{N-1} \sum_{i=1}^{N} (x_i - \mu_x)^2 \right)^{\frac{1}{2}}$, $\sigma_y = \left( \frac{1}{N-1} \sum_{i=1}^{N} (y_i - \mu_y)^2 \right)^{\frac{1}{2}}$ and $\sigma_{xy} = \frac{1}{N-1} \sum_{i=1}^{N} (x_i - \mu_x)(y_i - \mu_y)$. The luminance comparison is defined as

$$l(x,y) = \frac{2\mu_x\mu_y + C_1}{\mu_x^2 + \mu_y^2 + C_1},$$

the contrast comparison is calculated as

$$c(x,y) = \frac{2\sigma_x\sigma_y + C_2}{\sigma_x^2 + \sigma_y^2 + C_2},$$

and the structure comparison is defined as

$$s(x,y) = \frac{\sigma_{xy} + C_3}{\sigma_x\sigma_y + C_3},$$

where the constants $C1 = (0.01)^2$ and $C2 = (0.03)^2$ are included to avoid instability when factors $(\mu_x^2 + \mu_y^2)$, $(\sigma_x^2 + \sigma_y^2)$ or $\sigma_x\sigma_y$ are close to zero. Combining the three comparison components, we obtain the SSIM index between images $x$ and $y$ in a scale of 0 to 1 as

$$SSIM(x,y) = [l(x,y)]^\alpha \cdot [c(x,y)]^\beta \cdot [s(x,y)]^\gamma$$

where $\alpha, \beta, \gamma > 0$ are parameters used to assign a weight to each of the three comparison terms. Setting $\alpha = \beta = \gamma = 1$ and $C_3 = \frac{C2}{2}$, we obtain the expression of the SSIM that will be used in this manuscript

$$SSIM(x,y) = \left( \frac{2\mu_x\mu_y + C_1}{\mu_x^2 + \mu_y^2 + C_1} \right) \left( \frac{2\sigma_{xy} + C_2}{\sigma_x^2 + \sigma_y^2 + C_2} \right).$$

## 2.2  MMSIM

The SSIM is applied locally rather than globally, obtaining a local SSIM for each point of an image using a sliding Gaussian window of fixed size. This provides a map which provides information about how the image quality varies spatially. A global SSIM can be obtained by calculating its average. In this case, mean SSIM (MSSIM) is introduced [1,6] as

$$MSSIM(x,y) = \frac{1}{N} \sum_{j=1}^{N} SSIM(x_j, y_j), \tag{1}$$

where $N$ is the number of local windows in the image and $x_j$ and $y_j$ are the $j$-th sample sliding square windows, also referred to as patches, in images $x$ and $y$.

## 2.3  MSSIM as Data Fidelity in Imaging Inverse Problems

As discussed in [5], we typically infer a measurement image $y = H(x) + n$ that is related to an ideal image $x$, through a degradation operator $H$ and some additive noise term $n$. In general we assume that the operator $H$ is known or can be approximated.

To obtain an approximation of the ideal image $x$, given $y$ we can solve a minimization problem

$$\underset{x}{\operatorname{argmin}} \left[1 - MSSIM(H(x), y)\right] + \alpha[R(x)], \tag{2}$$

where $H$ is the degradation operator, $R(x)$ is a regularization term, and $\alpha$ is its corresponding regularization parameter. Notice that the new data fidelity term $[1 - MSSIM(H(x), y)]$ replaces the typical Sum of Squared Differences of $H(x)$ and $y$ in inverse problems as motivated by [5]. In this manuscript, for simplicity we consider the particular case where $H = I$, that is, denoising a given measurement image $y$ and reconstructing the ideal image $x$, where $y = x + n$. In this case, our minimization problem becomes

$$\underset{x}{\operatorname{argmin}} \left[1 - MSSIM(x, y)\right] + \alpha[R(x)]. \tag{3}$$

The same technique that we will develop in this manuscript for computing derivative of MSSIM can be applied to any inverse problem addressed via the minimization in Eq. (2).

## 3  Computing the MSSIM Derivative

The SSIM derivative was computed in the original SSIM papers [6,7] although full details were not given. It was also computed as an essential step in the Maximum Differentiation (MAD) competition [8]. It was later extended in solving optimization problems, e.g. see [3].

In order to apply gradient-based techniques to solve the minimization problem in Eq. (3), we need to find the MSSIM derivative. In this section, we express this derivative efficiently using convolutions. Recall that convolution operator $*$ of two functions $f$ and $w$ is defined as

$$g(x) = (f * w)(x) = \sum_n f(n)w(x - n).$$

**Theorem 1.** *The partial derivative of MSSIM between two images $x$ and $y$ with respect to $x(q)$, i.e, the intensity of image $x$ as location $q$ can be expressed using convolutions as*

$$\frac{\partial MSSIM(x,y)}{\partial x(q)} = \frac{2}{N}\Big((h * G_\sigma)(q) + y(q)(f * G_\sigma)(q) - (g * G_\sigma)(q) - x(q)(j * G_\sigma)(q) + (k * G_\sigma)(q)\Big) \quad (4)$$

*where $N$ is the total number of pixels (also corresponding to the number of patches) in the image, and for every pixel location $p$*

$$h(p) = cs(p)\Big(\frac{\mu_y - \mu_x l(p)}{\mu_x^2 + \mu_y^2 + C_1}\Big),$$

$$f(p) = \frac{l(p)}{\sigma_x^2 + \sigma_y^2 + C_2},$$

$$g(p) = \frac{l(p)\mu_y(p)}{\sigma_x^2 + \sigma_y^2 + C_2},$$

$$j(p) = \frac{l(p)cs(p)}{\sigma_x^2 + \sigma_y^2 + C_2},$$

$$k(p) = \frac{l(p)cs(p)\mu_x(p)}{\sigma_x^2 + \sigma_y^2 + C_2}.$$

*Proof.* First, we find the SSIM derivatives as given in [9]. We can express the SSIM between images $x$ and $y$ at a local patch centered at pixel $p$ as

$$SSIM\,(x(p), y(p)) = \Big(\frac{2\mu_x\mu_y + C_1}{\mu_x^2 + \mu_y^2 + C_1}\Big) \cdot \Big(\frac{2\sigma_{xy} + C_2}{\sigma_x^2 + \sigma_y^2 + C_2}\Big) = l(p)cs(p). \quad (5)$$

where means and standard deviations are computed using $G_\sigma$ which is a Gaussian filter of standard deviation $\sigma$,

$$\mu_x(p) = G_\sigma * P_x, \quad (6)$$
$$\sigma_x^2(p) = G_\sigma * P_x^2 - \mu_x^2(p), \quad (7)$$
$$\sigma_{xy}(p) = G_\sigma * (P_x \cdot P_y) - \mu_x(p)\mu_y(p), \quad (8)$$

where $P_x$ and $P_y$ are patches in $x$ and $y$ centered at pixel $p$ respectively, '$*$' denotes the convolution operator and '$\cdot$' is point-wise multiplication. The values of $\mu_y(p)$ and $\sigma_y^2(p)$ can be computed similar to Eqs. (6) and (7) replacing $x$ with $y$. We need to compute the derivative at pixel $p$ with respect to every pixel location $q$ in every patch. As shown in [9],

$$\frac{\partial SSIM(x(p), y(p))}{\partial x(q)} = \frac{\partial l(p)}{\partial x(q)} cs(p) + l(p) \frac{\partial cs(p)}{\partial x(q)},$$

where

$$\frac{\partial l(p)}{\partial x(q)} = \frac{\partial l(p)}{\partial \mu_x} \cdot \frac{\partial \mu_x}{\partial x(q)} = 2G_\sigma(p - q) \cdot \left( \frac{\mu_y - \mu_x \cdot l(p)}{\mu_x^2 + \mu_y^2 + C_1} \right), \tag{9}$$

and

$$\frac{\partial cs(p)}{\partial x(q)} = \frac{2G_\sigma(p - q)}{\sigma_x^2 + \sigma_y^2 + C_2} \Big( (y(q) - \mu_y) - cs(p)(x(q) - \mu_x) \Big). \tag{10}$$

We apply these derivative approximations to compute the derivative of MSSIM. The partial derivatives of MSSIM are computed as

$$\frac{\partial MSSIM(x, y)}{\partial x(q)} = \frac{1}{N} \sum_p \frac{\partial l(p)}{\partial x(q)} cs(p) + l(p) \frac{\partial cs(p)}{\partial x(q)}, \tag{11}$$

where $N$ is the total number of pixels, also patches, in the image.

Now we expand both parts of the derivatives and show that it can be expressed as a product of convolutions. The first expression on the right hand side of Eq. (11) can be written as

$$\frac{1}{N} \sum_p \frac{\partial l(p)}{\partial x(q)} cs(p)$$

$$= \frac{1}{N} \sum_p 2G_\sigma(p - q) \left( \frac{\mu_y - \mu_x l(p)}{\mu_x^2 + \mu_y^2 + C_1} \right) cs(p)$$

$$= \frac{2}{N} \sum_p cs(p) \left( \frac{\mu_y - \mu_x l(p)}{\mu_x^2 + \mu_y^2 + C_1} \right) G_\sigma(p - q)$$

$$= \frac{2}{N} \sum_p h(p) G_\sigma(p - q)$$

$$= \frac{2}{N} (h * G_\sigma)(q),$$

where $h(p) = cs(p) \left( \frac{\mu_y - \mu_x l(p)}{\mu_x^2 + \mu_y^2 + C_1} \right)$. The second expression can be written as

$$\frac{1}{N} \sum_p l(p) \frac{\partial cs(p)}{\partial x(q)}$$

$$= \frac{1}{N} \sum_p \frac{2l(p) G_\sigma(p - q)}{\sigma_x^2 + \sigma_y^2 + C_2} \Big( (y(q) - \mu_y) - cs(p)(x(q) - \mu_x) \Big)$$

$$= \frac{2}{N} (A + B + C + D),$$

where

$$A = \sum_p \frac{l(p)}{\sigma_x^2 + \sigma_y^2 + C_2} G_\sigma(p - q) y(q)$$

$$= y(q) \sum_p \frac{l(p)}{\sigma_x^2 + \sigma_y^2 + C_2} G_\sigma(p - q)$$

$$= y(q)(f * G_\sigma)(q),$$

with $f(p) = \frac{l(p)}{\sigma_x^2 + \sigma_y^2 + C_2}$,

$$B = -\sum_p \frac{l(p)}{\sigma_x^2 + \sigma_y^2 + C_2} G_\sigma(p - q) \mu_y(p)$$

$$= -\sum_p \frac{l(p)\mu_y(p)}{\sigma_x^2 + \sigma_y^2 + C_2} G_\sigma(p - q)$$

$$= -(g * G_\sigma)(q),$$

with $g(p) = \frac{l(p)\mu_y(p)}{\sigma_x^2 + \sigma_y^2 + C_2}$,

$$C = -\sum_p \frac{l(p)}{\sigma_x^2 + \sigma_y^2 + C_2} G_\sigma(p - q) cs(p) x(q)$$

$$= -x(q) \sum_p \frac{l(p)cs(p)}{\sigma_x^2 + \sigma_y^2 + C_2} G_\sigma(p - q)$$

$$= -x(q)(j * G_\sigma)(q),$$

with $j(p) = \frac{l(p)cs(p)}{\sigma_x^2 + \sigma_y^2 + C_2}$, and

$$D = \sum_p \frac{l(p)}{\sigma_x^2 + \sigma_y^2 + C_2} G_\sigma(p - q) cs(p) \mu_x(p)$$

$$= \sum_p \frac{l(p)cs(p)\mu_x(p)}{\sigma_x^2 + \sigma_y^2 + C_2} G_\sigma(p - q)$$

$$= (k * G_\sigma)(q),$$

with $k(p) = \frac{l(p)cs(p)\mu_x(p)}{\sigma_x^2 + \sigma_y^2 + C_2}$.                              □

The above Theorem can essentially be used to compute the derivative of the MSSIM using convolutions that will be referred to as our proposed algorithm.

## 4  Efficiency

In order to show the efficiency of our proposed algorithm, we analyze its computational complexity. We compare two different paths to compute the MSSIM derivative.

First path evaluating the derivative directly by computing each expression of the sum in Eq. (11) and adding all of these terms, and second path using convolutions as shown in Eq. (4). Suppose the size of the image is $N$ and the size of each patch is $m$. Hence we have $N$ patches of size $m$.

In the first path, we analyze the expression in Eq. (11). For every patch, the calculation consists of two multiplications and an addition of terms depending on $\mu_x$, $\mu_y$, $\sigma_x$, $\sigma_y$ and $\sigma_{x,y}$, which are calculated with convolutions as shown in Eqs. (6, 7 and 8). We know that the computational cost of the convolution using Fast Fourier Transform (FFT) is $\mathcal{O}(N \log N)$, and both terms (Eqs. 9 and 10) are calculated with respect to every pixel $q$ in the patch centered at $p$. Therefore the cost of the calculation is $\mathcal{O}(m \, N \log N)$.

Now using the second path, we analyze the expression in Eq. (4). The calculation consists of two additions, 2 subtractions and 3 multiplications of convolutions and terms depending again on $\mu_x$, $\mu_y$, $\sigma_x$, $\sigma_y$ and $\sigma_{x,y}$. Hence the cost of calculating the derivative using convolutions is $\mathcal{O}(N \log N)$.

We can conclude that the larger the patch-size $m$, the larger is the difference between the two computational complexities. As $m \to N$, the cost of the calculation of the MSSIM derivative gets closer to $\mathcal{O}(N^2 \log N)$, and in general using convolutions via our proposed Theorem provides a more efficient way to calculate the derivatives.

## 5   Experiments and Results

In this Section, we consider the total variation (TV) denoising in which we use the MSSIM as the data fidelity term. Variational calculus tells us that the minimum of the (convex) function

$$E = \int_\Omega \mathbf{g}(x, y, u, u_x, u_y) \, d\boldsymbol{x}$$

can be found by setting the variational derivative equal to zero

$$\nabla E = \frac{d\mathbf{g}}{du} - \frac{d}{dx}\frac{d\mathbf{g}}{du_x} - \frac{d}{dy}\frac{d\mathbf{g}}{du_y} = 0.$$

To solve this equation numerically, we evolve $u$ to the state minimizing $E$

$$\frac{du}{dt} = -\nabla E.$$

Discretizing this equation yields the steepest descent method

$$u^{n+1} = u^n + \Delta t \left[-\nabla E(u^n)\right]. \tag{12}$$

The total variation of an image $u(x, y)$ is

$$\int_\Omega \|\nabla u\| \, d\boldsymbol{x}.$$

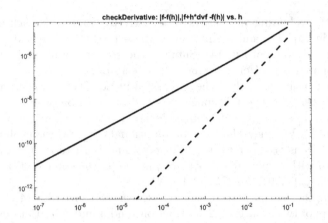

**Fig. 1.** The result of checkDerivative for the implementation of MSSIM derivative: linear decay (solid line) for $|\mathbf{f} - \mathbf{f(h)}|$ and quadratic decay (dashed line) for $|\mathbf{f} + \mathbf{h} * dv\mathbf{f} - \mathbf{f(h)}|$ up to machine precision is shown on a logarithmic scale.

To minimize total variation, we could pick $\mathbf{g} = \|\nabla u\|$, but evolving such a system would eventually lead to a flat image $u = const$. An additional term is needed to determine the balance minimizing the variation with keeping the evolved $u$ similar to the noisy measurement $w$. Traditionally we can add a data fidelity term $\int_\Omega \lambda (u - w)^2 \, d\boldsymbol{x}$, so that $E$ is given by

$$E = \int_\Omega \|\nabla u\| \, d\boldsymbol{x} + \lambda \int_\Omega (u - w)^2 \, d\boldsymbol{x}. \tag{13}$$

Alternatively, we use the new data fidelity term $\int_\Omega MSSIM(u, w) \, d\boldsymbol{x}$, and let $\mathbf{g} = \|\nabla u\| + \lambda MSSIM(u, w)$ as motivated in [5]

$$E = \int_\Omega \|\nabla u\| \, d\boldsymbol{x} + \lambda \int_\Omega MSSIM(u, w) \, d\boldsymbol{x}. \tag{14}$$

To minimize Eq. (14), we first obtain $\nabla E$

$$
\begin{aligned}
\nabla E &= \frac{d\mathbf{g}}{du} - \frac{d}{dx}\frac{d\mathbf{g}}{du_x} - \frac{d}{dy}\frac{d\mathbf{g}}{du_y} \\
&= \lambda \frac{\partial MSSIM(u, w)}{\partial u} - \frac{u_{xx}u_y^2 - 2u_x u_y u_{xy} - u_{yy}u_x^2}{(u_x^2 + u_y^2)^{3/2}},
\end{aligned}
\tag{15}
$$

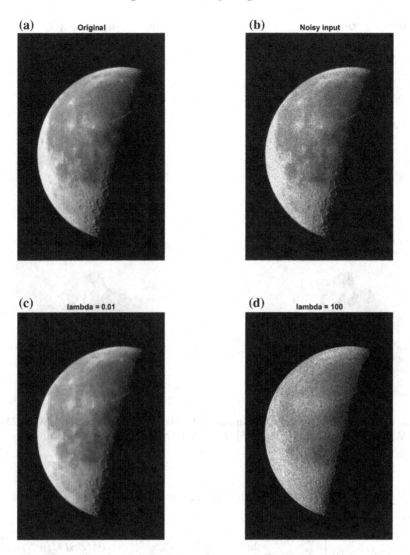

**Fig. 2.** (a) The original moon image. (b) Noisy input, SSIM: 0.29, PSNR: 24.77 (c) TV denoising with $\lambda = 0.01$, SSIM: 0.83, PSNR: 34:84. (d) TV denoising with $\lambda = 100$, SSIM: 0.39, PSNR: 23.92

where we used $u_{xy} = u_{yx}$. Then we evolve the PDE with a small nonzero $\epsilon$ added to the denominator of the fraction term so that the term does not become singular

$$\frac{du}{dt} = -\nabla E$$

$$= \frac{u_{xx}u_y^2 - 2u_x u_y u_{xy} - u_{yy}u_x^2}{\epsilon + (u_x^2 + u_y^2)^{3/2}} - \lambda \frac{\partial MSSIM(u, w)}{\partial u}.$$

**Fig. 3.** (a) The original cameraman image. (b) Noisy input, SSIM: 0.44, PSNR: 23.32. (c) TV denoising with $\lambda = 0.01$, SSIM: 0.82, PSNR: 28.02. (d) TV denoising with $\lambda = 100$, SSIM: 0.08, PSNR: 18.45.

The discretized version is (from Eqs. (12) and (15))

$$
\begin{aligned}
u^{(n+1)} &= u^{(n)} + \Delta t \left[ -\nabla E \right] \\
&= u^{(n)} + \Delta t \left[ \frac{u_{xx}^{(n)} u_y^{(n)2} - 2u_x^{(n)} u_y^{(n)} u_{xy}^{(n)} - u_{yy}^{(n)} u_x^{(n)2}}{\epsilon + (u_x^{(n)2} + u_y^{(n)2})^{3/2}} - \lambda \frac{\partial MSSIM(u^{(n)}, w)}{\partial u^{(n)}} \right].
\end{aligned}
\tag{16}
$$

One of the many traps in optimization is working with an erroneous derivative. The following test provides a simple way of checking the implementation of a derivative. To this end, let $\mathbf{f}$ be a multivariate function $\mathbf{f} : \mathbb{R}^n \longmapsto \mathbb{R}$ and let $\mathbf{v} \in \mathbb{R}^n$ be an arbitrary vector in the Taylor expansion $\mathbf{f}(\mathbf{x} + h\mathbf{v}) = \mathbf{f}(\mathbf{x}) + h d\mathbf{f}(\mathbf{x})\mathbf{v} + \mathcal{O}(h^2)$. A matrix $\mathbf{A}$ is the derivative of $\mathbf{f}$ if and only if the difference $\|\mathbf{f}(\mathbf{x} + h\mathbf{v}) - \mathbf{f}(\mathbf{x}) - h\mathbf{A}\mathbf{v}\|$ is essentially quadratic in $h$. The function checkDerivative (See, e.g., [4]) computes this difference. Here we apply the check-Derivative function to our computed MSSIM derivative and show the result in Fig. 1. The result is consistent as the difference is quadratic with respect to $\mathbf{h}$.

To observe how the TV denoising algorithm with MSSIM data fidelity works (see Eq. (16)), we added zero-mean additive white Gaussian noise to the images 'Moon' (Fig. 2) and 'Cameraman' (Fig. 3) for various parameters $\lambda$ and calculated the SSIM and PSNR values of the results.

As expected, we can perform denoising using the new MSSIM data fidelity term for a proper value of the regularization parameter $\lambda$, e.g., $\lambda = 0.01$ for these images. For a complete list of parameters used along with the checkDerivative results, please refer to our source code which is publicly available on GitHub at https://github.com/ImagingLab/MSSIM.

## 6   Conclusion

In this paper, we introduced a computationally efficient algorithm to calculate the MSSIM derivative used in imaging inverse problems, e.g, image denoising.

The derivative calculation was rigorously obtained based on convolutions in Theorem 1. We also presented preliminary computational experiments to validate the calculation of the MSSIM derivative and applied it to Total Variation denoising method as a data fidelity term. As mentioned, we focused on computing the derivative aimed at denoising (2) problem. To extend the technique for solving (3), chain rule can be used to compute the derivative in a similar way. This will generalize to address a variety of inverse problems including deblurring and super-resolution with a new data fidelity term.

**Acknowledgments.** I.M. is a visiting student from the Universidad de Málaga, Spain. This research was supported in part by an NSERC Discovery Grant for M.E.

## References

1. Brunet, D., Vrscay, E.R., Wang, Z.: On the mathematical properties of the structural similarity index. IEEE Trans. Image Process. **21**(4), 1488–1499 (2012)
2. Hore, A., Ziou, D.: Image quality metrics: PSNR vs. SSIM. In: 2010 20th International Conference on Pattern Recognition (ICPR), pp. 2366–2369. IEEE (2010)
3. Ma, K., Duanmu, Z., Yeganeh, H., Wang, Z.: Multi-exposure image fusion by optimizing a structural similarity index. IEEE Trans. Comput. Imaging **4**(1), 60–72 (2017)
4. Modersitzki, J.: FAIR: Flexible Algorithms for Image Registration, vol. 6. SIAM, New Delhi (2009)
5. Otero, D., Vrscay, E.R.: Solving optimization problems that employ structural similarity as the fidelity measure. In: Proceedings of the International Conference on Image Processing, Computer Vision, and Pattern Recognition (IPCV), page 1. The Steering Committee of the World Congress in Computer Science, Computer (2014)
6. Wang, Z., Bovik, A.C., Sheikh, H.R., Simoncelli, E.P.: Image quality assessment: from error visibility to structural similarity. IEEE Trans. Image Process. **13**(4), 600–612 (2004)
7. Wang, Z., Simoncelli, E.P.: Stimulus synthesis for efficient evaluation and refinement of perceptual image quality metrics. In: Human Vision and Electronic Imaging IX, vol. 5292, pp. 99–109. International Society for Optics and Photonics (2004)

8. Wang, Z., Simoncelli, E.P.: Maximum differentiation (MAD) competition: a methodology for comparing computational models of perceptual quantities. J. Vis. **8**(12), 8–8 (2008)
9. Zhao, H., Gallo, O., Frosio, I., Kautz, J.: Loss functions for image restoration with neural networks. IEEE Trans. Comput. Imaging **3**(1), 47–57 (2017)

# Drift Detection Using SVM in Structured Object Tracking

Kumara Ratnayake and Maria A. Amer[(⊠)]

ECE Department, Concordia University, Montreal, QC, Canada
amer@ece.concordia.ca

**Abstract.** This paper extends structured learning to detect object tracking failures or inaccuracies and reinitialize itself when needed using object segmentation. First, we use binary support vector machines to develop a technique to detect tracking failures (drifts or inaccuracies) by monitoring internal variables of our baseline tracker. We leverage learned examples from our baseline tracker to train the employed binary support vector machines. Second, we propose an automated method to re-initialize the tracker to recover from tracking failures by integrating an active contour based object segmentation and using particle filter to sample bounding boxes for segmentation. We subjectively and objectively show that our extended method outperform classical structured learning approach under various tracking challenges.

**Keywords:** Object tracking · Structured learning · SVMs · Drift detection · Reinitialization · Particle filter · Segmentation

## 1 Introduction

Object tracking has diverse video applications and is an active research field. Challenges in object tracking arise from occlusion, deformation, background clutter, illumination variation, fast motion, etc. To address such challenges, powerful tracking approaches learn object appearance changes online [4–8]. Still, tracking failures (inaccuracies or drift) are inevitable. Recovering from tracking failures requires effective detection of failures and then tracker reinitialization. Integrating segmentation into tracking can alleviate this problem, but segmentation may become erroneous under challenging video scenes. Therefore, relying on segmentation frequently (i.e., each frame) is undesirable.

Approaches integrating segmentation into tracking can be classified based on the employed segmentation method. The paper [6] presents a tracker with a rough segmentation based on graph cut; it aims to track deformable target with a discriminative classifier. The paper [15] presents a tracking method by active contour segmentation, which uses a level set to represent the object and utilizes the Bhattacharyya distance to locate the region that optimally describes the target. Random-walk [11] segmentation is integrated in a patch- and appearance-model

© Springer Nature Switzerland AG 2019
F. Karray et al. (Eds.): ICIAR 2019, LNCS 11662, pp. 67–76, 2019.
https://doi.org/10.1007/978-3-030-27202-9_6

based tracker in [12] that uses a deterministic local optimizer. The JOTS algorithm [13] integrates multi-part tracking and segmentation into a unified energy optimization framework. It uses SLIC superpixels for multi-part segmentation which is used to initialize the tracking at each incoming frame.

Few learning-based trackers explicitly employ failure detection and recovery; *TLD* [9] incorporates object detector with an optical flow tracker, which is subsequently used for correcting drifts. In this paper, we propose to explicitly detect tracking failures using binary Support-Vector-Machines (SVMs) and reinitializes tracking using segmentation and particle filters on-demand, i.e., in the event of failures. Compared to related work, our method (1) explicitly monitors internal variables of a baseline tracker to detect failures, (2) is fully automated, (3) applies segmentation not each frame but only when tracking failures is detected. Running segmentation at each frame has two main drawbacks: intensive computations and segmentation may become inaccurate and mislead the tracking.

In this paper, Sect. 2 presents our method, Sect. 3 discusses its results, and Sect. 4 draws a conclusion.

## 2    Drift-Aware Structured Tracking

This section first summarizes baseline structured tracking (for more details see, e.g., [8,17,18]) and then proposes our drift detection and correction method.

### 2.1    Baseline Structured Tracker

We represent the dynamic model by a state vector $\mathbf{s} = [s_1 \ s_2]$ and predict $\hat{\mathbf{s}}_{t+1}$ its state at time $t + 1$ (in frame $F_{t+1}$) using

$$\hat{\mathbf{s}}_{t+1} = \mathbf{s}_t + \left( \sum_{l=1}^{N^{\mathrm{HM}}} \frac{k^{\mathrm{HM}}(t-1, t-l)}{\Delta \mathbf{s}_{t-l}} \right)^{-1} + \mathbf{n}_t^{\mathrm{HM}}, \tag{1}$$

where $\mathbf{s}_t$ is the current states at time $t$ and $\mathbf{n}_t^{\mathrm{HM}}$ is system Gaussian noise. In (1), we use $N^{\mathrm{HM}}$ (e.g., 8) prior state vectors and apply Kernelized Harmonic Means (KHM) to estimate $\Delta \mathbf{s}_t$ with $k^{\mathrm{HM}}(t, t') = \exp\left(-C^{\mathrm{HM}} \cdot (t - t')^2\right)$ a Gaussian Radial Basis Function (GRBF) kernel with parameter $C^{\mathrm{HM}}$ (e.g., 1.0).

The baseline structured tracker, with joint kernels (4) and motion inference (5), can be summarized as follows. We use Sequential Minimal Optimization (SMO) for maximization problem in structured SVMs for learning, which outputs a scoring function and retains a pool of positive and negative samples to describe variations of object and background, respectively. For the optimization problem, we use a color and global-shape feature joint kernel. Finally, we predict an optimal output of target Bounding Box (BB) by maximizing the scoring function regularized with a motion-augmented term.

A structured tracker typically extracts and compares object features from an image patch within the estimated BB and its example pairs which are learned online. The tracking is learning a *prediction* function $f : \mathcal{X} \to \mathcal{Y}$ that maps the space of input features $\mathcal{X}$ to the space of output BBs $\mathcal{Y}$ based on $N^{\text{EX}}$ input-output example pairs $\mathcal{S} = \{(\mathbf{x}_1, \mathbf{y}_1), \ldots, (\mathbf{x}_{N^{\text{EX}}}, \mathbf{y}_{N^{\text{EX}}})\} \in (\mathcal{X} \times \mathcal{Y})^{N^{\text{EX}}}$. Using structured SVMs, we can discriminatively learn a *scoring* function $\phi : \mathcal{X} \times \mathcal{Y} \in \mathbb{R}$ over $\mathcal{S}$. Alternatively, $\phi$ maps both output BB $\mathbf{y}$ and its feature $\mathbf{x}$ to a scalar label. Hence, $\phi$ can be seen as measuring the compatibility of an input-output pair. Once $\phi$ is learned, the prediction of $\hat{\mathbf{y}}$ highest compatible with $\mathbf{x}$, can be obtained by maximizing $\phi$

$$\hat{\mathbf{y}} = f(\mathbf{x}) = \arg\max_{\mathbf{y} \in \mathcal{Y}} \phi(\mathbf{x}, \mathbf{y}), \tag{2}$$

$\phi(\mathbf{x}, \mathbf{y}) = \langle \mathbf{w}, \boldsymbol{\Phi}(\mathbf{x}, \mathbf{y}) \rangle$ [20], where $\mathbf{w}$ the weight vector, $\boldsymbol{\Phi}(\mathbf{x}, \mathbf{y})$ a joint feature map that maps joint input feature and output BBs to a transform space, and $\langle \cdot, \cdot \rangle$ the inner product in the Reproducing Kernel Hilbert Space (RKHS) [19].

The scoring function $\phi$ can be learned by a *dual* formulation using the Lagrangian function with a multiplier corresponding to the margin constraint [20]. We solve and simplify such dual optimization problem to

$$\max_{\beta} -\frac{1}{2} \sum_{i,\mathbf{y}} \sum_{j,\bar{\mathbf{y}}} \beta_{i\mathbf{y}} \beta_{j\bar{\mathbf{y}}} k_{ij} - \sum_{i\mathbf{y}} \Delta(\mathbf{y}_i, \mathbf{y})\beta_{i\mathbf{y}}, \quad \text{s.t.} \quad \forall i : \sum_{\mathbf{y}} \beta_{i\mathbf{y}} = 0, \forall i \, \forall \mathbf{y} : \beta_{i\mathbf{y}} \leq C^{\text{SVM}} \Delta'(\mathbf{y}_i, \mathbf{y}), \tag{3}$$

where $j \in [1, N^{\text{EX}}]$; $\beta$ the Lagrangian multiplier [2]; $C^{\text{EX}}$ (e.g., 25) controls how strongly margin violations are penalized; $\Delta'(\mathbf{y}_i, \mathbf{y})$ the loss function; and $k\big((\mathbf{x}_i, \mathbf{y}), (\mathbf{x}_j, \bar{\mathbf{y}})\big) = \langle \boldsymbol{\Phi}(\mathbf{x}_i, \mathbf{y}), \boldsymbol{\Phi}(\mathbf{x}_j, \bar{\mathbf{y}}) \rangle$ the Joint Kernel Function (JKF) we define as weighted sum of color $k^{\star}$ and global-shape $k^{\circ}$ kernels

$$k(\mathbf{x}, \bar{\mathbf{x}}) = g \cdot k^{\star}(\mathbf{x}^{\star}, \bar{\mathbf{x}}^{\star}) + (1 - g) \cdot k^{\circ}(\mathbf{x}^{\circ}, \bar{\mathbf{x}}^{\circ}), \tag{4}$$

with $0 \leq g \leq 1$, $k^{\circ}(\mathbf{x}^{\circ}, \bar{\mathbf{x}}^{\circ}) = \exp\left(-\gamma^{\circ} \| \mathbf{x}^{\circ} - \bar{\mathbf{x}}^{\circ} \|^2\right)$, $\gamma^{\circ} = 0.22$, $k^{\star}(\mathbf{x}^{\star}, \bar{\mathbf{x}}^{\star}) = \sqrt{\langle \mathbf{x}^{\star}, \bar{\mathbf{x}}^{\star} \rangle}$. Instead of maximizing $\phi$ over all possible $\mathbf{y} \in \mathcal{Y}$ as in (2), we restrict the search space to $\mathcal{Y}^{\star} \subset \mathcal{Y}$ with a regularization

$$\hat{\mathbf{y}} = \arg\max_{\mathbf{y} \in \mathcal{Y}^{\star}} \phi(\mathbf{x}, \mathbf{y}) \cdot \varphi(\mathbf{u}, \mathbf{y}), \tag{5}$$

where $\mathbf{u}(\mathbf{u}, \mathbf{y})$ is higher if a BB $\mathbf{u}$ is closer to $\mathbf{y}$ as in

$$\varphi(\mathbf{u}, \mathbf{y}) = \exp\left(2k^{\text{MI}}(\mathbf{u}, \hat{\mathbf{u}}) - k^{\text{MI}}(\mathbf{u}, \mathbf{u}) - k^{\text{MI}}(\hat{\mathbf{u}}, \hat{\mathbf{u}})\right), \tag{6}$$

with $k^{\text{MI}}(\mathbf{u}, \hat{\mathbf{u}}) = \exp\left(-\gamma^{\text{MI}} \| \mathbf{u} - \hat{\mathbf{u}} \|^2\right)$ the JKF of motion states with $\gamma^{\text{MI}} = 0.2$. $\hat{\mathbf{u}}$ is the optimal estimate of $\mathbf{u}$.

## 2.2   Failure Detection Using SVM

To detect tracking failure, we form a failure-detection feature vector $\mathbf{x}^{\bullet}$ of internal variables, e.g., scoring function $\phi(\mathbf{x}, \hat{\mathbf{y}})$, global-shape kernel $k^{\circ}(\mathbf{x}^{\circ}, \bar{\mathbf{x}}^{\circ})$, color kernel $k^{\star}(\mathbf{x}^{\star}, \bar{\mathbf{x}}^{\star})$, responses from $k(\mathbf{x}, \bar{\mathbf{x}})$, and motion kernel $k^{\text{MI}}(\mathbf{u}, \hat{\mathbf{u}})$,

$$\mathbf{x}^{\bullet} = \begin{bmatrix} \phi(\mathbf{x}, \hat{\mathbf{y}}) & k(\mathbf{x}, \bar{\mathbf{x}}) & k^{\star}(\mathbf{x}^{\star}, \bar{\mathbf{x}}^{\star}) & k^{\circ}(\mathbf{x}^{\circ}, \bar{\mathbf{x}}^{\circ}) & k^{\text{MI}}(\mathbf{u}, \hat{\mathbf{u}}) \end{bmatrix}. \tag{7}$$

We then formulate failure detection as an SVM classification problem: Given a set of $\bar{N}^{\mathrm{EX}}$ example pairs $\{\mathbf{x}_{\bar{i}}^{\bullet}, y_{\bar{i}}^{\bullet}\}_{\bar{i}=1}^{\bar{N}^{\mathrm{EX}}}$, where $\bar{i} \in [1, \bar{N}^{\mathrm{EX}}]$, $y_{\bar{i}}^{\mathrm{S}} \in \{-1, +1\}$ is the class label of the feature vector $\mathbf{x}_{\bar{i}}^{\bullet}$. We employ binary SVMs as a classifier to detect the tracking failure as follows

$$\min_{\bar{\mathbf{w}}} \left\{ \frac{1}{2} \| \bar{\mathbf{w}} \|^2 + \bar{C}^{\mathrm{SVM}} \sum_{\bar{i}=1}^{\bar{N}^{\mathrm{EX}}} \xi_{\bar{i}}^{\bullet} \right\}, \quad \text{s.t.} \quad \forall \bar{i} : y_{\bar{i}}^{\bullet}(\langle \bar{\mathbf{w}}, \bar{\boldsymbol{\Phi}}(\mathbf{x}_{\bar{i}}^{\bullet}) \rangle + b^{\bullet}) \geq 1 - \xi_{\bar{i}}^{\bullet}, \forall \bar{i} : \xi_{\bar{i}}^{\bullet} \geq 0, \quad b^{\bullet} \in \mathbb{R}, \tag{8}$$

where the weight vector $\bar{\mathbf{w}}$ is learned with sequentially obtained $\bar{N}^{\mathrm{EX}}$ example pairs $\{\mathbf{x}_{\bar{i}}^{\bullet}, y_{\bar{i}}^{\bullet}\}$, $\bar{\boldsymbol{\Phi}}(\mathbf{x}_{\bar{i}}^{\bullet})$ is a nonlinear function that maps $\mathbf{x}_{\bar{i}}^{\bullet}$ to a high-dimensional feature space, the slack variables $\xi_{\bar{i}}^{\bullet}$ allow the examples to violate the constraint of being outside of the margin, $b^{\bullet}$ is the bias term of the separating hyperplane, and $\bar{C}^{\mathrm{SVM}}$ is a parameter which controls how strongly margin violations are penalized.

Using the Lagrangian function [20], the corresponding dual expression of the optimization problem in (8) is obtained

$$\max_{\boldsymbol{\alpha}^{\bullet}} -\frac{1}{2} \sum_{\bar{i}}^{\bar{N}^{\mathrm{EX}}} \sum_{\bar{j}}^{\bar{N}^{\mathrm{EX}}} \alpha_{\bar{i}}^{\bullet} \alpha_{\bar{j}}^{\bullet} y_{\bar{i}}^{\bullet} y_{\bar{j}}^{\bullet} k^{\bullet}(\mathbf{x}_{\bar{i}}^{\bullet}, \mathbf{x}_{\bar{j}}^{\bullet}) + \sum_{\bar{i}}^{\bar{N}^{\mathrm{EX}}} \alpha_{\bar{i}}^{\bullet}, \quad \text{s.t.} \quad \forall \bar{i} : \sum_{\bar{i}}^{\bar{N}^{\mathrm{EX}}} \alpha_{\bar{i}}^{\bullet} y_{\bar{i}}^{\bullet} = 0, \forall \bar{i} : \bar{C}^{\mathrm{SVM}} \geq \alpha_{\bar{i}}^{\bullet} \geq 0, \tag{9}$$

where $\bar{j} \in [1, \bar{N}^{\mathrm{EX}}]$, the Lagrangian multiplier $\boldsymbol{\alpha}^{\bullet}$ corresponds to the margin constraint in (8), and $k^{\bullet}(\mathbf{x}_{\bar{i}}^{\bullet}, \mathbf{x}_{\bar{j}}^{\bullet})$ is

$$k^{\bullet}(\mathbf{x}_{\bar{i}}^{\bullet}, \mathbf{x}_{\bar{j}}^{\bullet}) = \langle \bar{\boldsymbol{\Phi}}(\mathbf{x}_{\bar{i}}^{\bullet}), \bar{\boldsymbol{\Phi}}(\mathbf{x}_{\bar{j}}^{\bullet}) \rangle. \tag{10}$$

By solving (9) using SMO-step [16], we obtain

$$\bar{\mathbf{w}} = \sum_{\bar{i}}^{\bar{N}^{\mathrm{EX}}} \alpha_{\bar{i}}^{\bullet} y_{\bar{i}}^{\bullet} \bar{\boldsymbol{\Phi}}(\mathbf{x}_{\bar{i}}^{\bullet}). \tag{11}$$

We then predict a tracking failures, i.e., $y^{\bullet}(\mathbf{x}^{\bullet}) = -1$,

$$y^{\bullet}(\mathbf{x}^{\bullet}) = \begin{cases} +1, \text{ if } \sum_{\bar{i}}^{\bar{N}^{\mathrm{EX}}} \alpha_{\bar{i}}^{\bullet} y_{\bar{i}}^{\bullet} k^{\bullet}(\mathbf{x}_{\bar{i}}^{\bullet}, \mathbf{x}^{\bullet}) + b^{\bullet} \geq 0 \\ -1, \text{ otherwise.} \end{cases} \tag{12}$$

We construct the kernel $k^{\bullet}(\mathbf{x}_{\bar{i}}^{\bullet}, \mathbf{x}_{\bar{j}}^{\bullet})$ in (10) as a GRBF kernel function with parameter $\gamma^{\bullet} = 1$ as in

$$k^{\bullet}(\mathbf{x}_{\bar{i}}^{\bullet}, \mathbf{x}_{\bar{j}}^{\bullet}) = \exp\left(-\gamma^{\bullet} \| \mathbf{x}_{\bar{i}}^{\bullet} - \mathbf{x}_{\bar{j}}^{\bullet} \|^2\right). \tag{13}$$

For online tracking, the proposed failure detection must be trained online. We assume the target can be correctly tracked for the first $\bar{N}^{\mathrm{EX}}$ frames. This is not a strong assumption since state-of-the-art structured trackers are effective during the first few frames. In each $\bar{N}^{\text{EX}}$ frames, we leverage the structured tracker to select a pair of positive and negative BBs by searching for the maximum and minimum of the gradient of (3), respectively. We extract the failure-detection feature vector $\mathbf{x}^{\bullet}$ corresponding to the positive and negative BBs, and use them to train the binary SVMs classifier online. Once the training is complete, i.e., after the first $\bar{N}^{\text{EX}}$ frames, we predict the tracking failures using (12).

## 2.3  Tracker' Reinitialization Using Segmentation

Effective segmentation methods [3–17, 19–22] require human input (e.g., seeds or initial BB). To automate such input, we leverage object trajectory within the most recent $N^{\bullet}$ frames and we use particle filter to sample and estimate the location of the optimal BB. Once tracking failure is detected, restricting the sampling to the vicinity of the most recent object trajectory is important to prevent outliers caused by background clutter. In what follows, we first discuss our method of BB selection for segmentation with particle filter, and then present how we use segmentation to evaluate the observation likelihood model of particle filter.

Let the state vector $\mathbf{s}^{\bullet} = [s_1^{\bullet} \ s_2^{\bullet} \ s_3^{\bullet} \ s_4^{\bullet}]$ describe the origin $[s_1^{\bullet} \ s_2^{\bullet}]$ and the width and height $[s_3^{\bullet} \ s_4^{\bullet}]$ of the BBs. We can regard making inference about $\mathbf{s}^{\bullet}$ as the estimation of the system state given a series of $\bar{t}$ observations $\mathbf{z}^{\bullet}{}_{1:\bar{t}} = \{\mathbf{z}^{\bullet}{}_1, ..., \mathbf{z}^{\bullet}{}_{\bar{t}}\}$. Our goal is to recursively find the posterior distribution $p(\mathbf{s}^{\bullet}{}_{\bar{t}}|\mathbf{z}^{\bullet}{}_{1:\bar{t}})$ for $\mathbf{s}^{\bullet}{}_{\bar{t}}$. Using Bayes' rule [1]

$$p(\mathbf{s}^{\bullet}{}_{\bar{t}}|\mathbf{z}^{\bullet}{}_{1:\bar{t}}) \propto p(\mathbf{z}^{\bullet}{}_{\bar{t}}|\mathbf{s}^{\bullet}{}_{\bar{t}})p(\mathbf{s}^{\bullet}{}_{\bar{t}}|\mathbf{z}^{\bullet}{}_{1:\bar{t}-1}), \tag{14}$$

where the observation likelihood distribution $p(\mathbf{z}^{\bullet}{}_{\bar{t}}|\mathbf{s}^{\bullet}{}_{\bar{t}})$ describes how the observation $\mathbf{z}^{\bullet}{}_{\bar{t}}$ depends on $\mathbf{s}^{\bullet}{}_{\bar{t}}$, i.e., the origin and size of the BB. We assume the system dynamics can be modeled by a first order Markov process. Using Chapman-Kolmogorov Eq. [1], $p(\mathbf{s}^{\bullet}{}_{\bar{t}}|\mathbf{z}^{\bullet}{}_{1:\bar{t}})$ is calculated

$$p(\mathbf{s}^{\bullet}{}_{\bar{t}}|\mathbf{z}^{\bullet}{}_{1:\bar{t}}) \quad \propto \quad p(\mathbf{z}^{\bullet}{}_{\bar{t}}|\mathbf{s}^{\bullet}{}_{\bar{t}}) \int p(\mathbf{s}^{\bullet}{}_{\bar{t}}|\mathbf{s}^{\bullet}{}_{\bar{t}-1})p(\mathbf{s}^{\bullet}{}_{\bar{t}-1}|\mathbf{z}^{\bullet}{}_{1:\bar{t}-1})d\mathbf{s}^{\bullet}{}_{\bar{t}-1}, \tag{15}$$

where $p(\mathbf{s}^{\bullet}{}_{\bar{t}}|\mathbf{s}^{\bullet}{}_{\bar{t}-1})$ is the state transition distribution. We leverage (1) to propagate the state $\mathbf{s}^{\bullet}$. $p(\mathbf{s}^{\bullet}{}_{\bar{t}}|\mathbf{z}^{\bullet}{}_{1:\bar{t}})$ is approximated by particle filtering using a set of $N^{\text{SP}}$ weights $\omega_{\bar{t},\ell}$ corresponding to the state $\mathbf{s}^{\bullet}{}_{\bar{t},\ell}$.

Using Sequential Importance Resampling (SIR) particle filters [7], $\omega_{\bar{t},\ell}$ is estimated by

$$\omega_{\bar{t},\ell} \propto p(\mathbf{z}^{\bullet}{}_{\bar{t}}|\mathbf{s}^{\bullet}{}_{\bar{t},\ell}) \cdot \omega_{\bar{t}-1,\ell}. \tag{16}$$

Using Maximum A Posteriori (MAP) rule [5], the estimated location and the size of the BB $\hat{\mathbf{s}}^{\bullet}_{\hat{t}}$ is obtained from

$$\hat{\mathbf{s}}^{\bullet}_{\hat{t}} \approx \underset{\mathbf{s}^{\bullet}{}_{\bar{t},\ell}}{\arg\max} \ \tilde{\omega}_{\bar{t},\ell}, \tag{17}$$

where $\tilde{\omega}_{\bar{t},\ell}$ is the normalized weight. $p(\mathbf{z}^{\bullet}{}_{\bar{t}}|\mathbf{s}^{\bullet}{}_{\bar{t},\ell})$ is implicitly required to estimate $\hat{\mathbf{s}}^{\bullet}_{\hat{t}}$ in (17).

To estimate the observation likelihood model $\omega_{\bar{t},\ell}$, we use object segmentation, e.g., the active contour-based method [22], which localizes region-based active contour energies to discriminate non-homogeneous foregrounds from background. For each particle $\mathbf{s}^{\bullet}{}_{\bar{t},\ell}$, we execute [22] $C^{\mathrm{SITR}}$ iterations. We draw $N^{\mathrm{SP}}$ particles equally around each of the object positions in the most recent $N^{\bullet}$ frames. Let $\mathcal{M}$ be the foreground mask returned by [22]. For each particle $\mathbf{s}^{\bullet}{}_{\bar{t},\ell}$, we extract color histogram $\Theta_{\bar{t},\ell}$ only within the area of $\mathcal{M}$. Then, we use $\chi^2$ kernel for defining our observation likelihood

$$p(\mathbf{z}^{\bullet}{}_{\bar{t}}|\mathbf{s}^{\bullet}{}_{\bar{t},\ell}) = \exp\left(-\frac{\|\Theta_{\bar{t},\ell} - \bar{\Theta}\|^2}{|\Theta_{\bar{t},\ell} - \bar{\Theta}|^1}\right), \tag{18}$$

where $\|\cdot\|^2$ and $\|\cdot\|^1$ are $l_2$ and $l_1$ norms, respectively, and $\bar{\Theta}$ is the color histogram of the target reference $\bar{\mathbf{s}}^{\bullet}$ which we obtain by searching for the BB with the minimal gradient within the positive SVMs pool retained in our baseline tracker. We can now estimate the optimal location and size of BB $\hat{\mathbf{s}}^{\bullet}_{\bar{t}}$ using (17) and use it to reinitialize the baseline tracker to recover from failure in $F_t$. Our drift-aware structured tracker MIST-SEG is summarized in Algorithm 1.

---

**Algorithm 1.** Proposed method MIST-SEG

---

    **Input**   : State of internal variables: $\phi(\mathbf{x}, \hat{\mathbf{y}})$, $k(\mathbf{x}, \bar{\mathbf{x}})$, $k^{\star}(\mathbf{x}^{\star}, \bar{\mathbf{x}}^{\star})$, $k^{\circ}(\mathbf{x}^{\circ}, \bar{\mathbf{x}}^{\circ})$,
              $k^{\mathrm{MI}}(\mathbf{u}, \hat{\mathbf{u}})$ in $F_t$.
    **Output:** Prediction of the segmented BB $\hat{\mathbf{s}}^{\bullet}_{\bar{t}}$ in $F_t$.

1  **repeat**
2      Construct the feature vector $\mathbf{x}^{\bullet}$ using (7).
3      Learn the binary SVMs online using the first $\bar{N}^{\mathrm{EX}}$ frames.
4      Predict failure, i.e., $y^{\bullet}(\mathbf{x}^{\bullet}) = -1$, using (12).
5      **if** $y^{\bullet}(\mathbf{x}^{\bullet}) = -1$ **then**
6          Draw $N^{\mathrm{SP}}$ particles around each of the object positions in the most recent $N^{\bullet}$ frames.
7          **for** each particle $\ell$ **do**
8             Propagate particles according to (1).
9             Evaluate the foreground mask $\mathcal{M}$ by [21].
10         Evaluate observation likelihood $p(\mathbf{z}^{\bullet}{}_{\bar{t}}|\mathbf{s}^{\bullet}{}_{\bar{t},\ell})$ by (18).
11         Update the importance weights $\omega_{\bar{t},\ell}$ using (16).
12        Estimate optimal particle state $\hat{\mathbf{s}}^{\bullet}_{\bar{t}}$ with (17).
13        Reinitialize the baseline tracker with $\hat{\mathbf{s}}^{\bullet}_{\bar{t}}$.

14 **until** end of video sequence.

---

# 3   Simulation Results

For testing the proposed MIST Integrated with Segmentation (MIST-SEG), we use video sequences from [23], representing all 11 challenging categories. We compare our method to the segmentation-based tracker JOTS [13], to *TLD* [9] that explicitly employs failure detection and recovery, and to the classical structured tracker Struck [8]. We used a PC with Intel i5 1.8 GHz CPU and 4 GB of RAM and report the mean result of 5 executions on each video sequence. We apply the objective measures [23] center location error (CLE), overlap score (AOR), precision, and success. The parameters of MIST-SEG are $\bar{C}^{\mathrm{SVM}} = 25$, $N^{\bullet} = 16$, $N^{\mathrm{SP}} = 100$, $\bar{N}^{\mathrm{EX}} = 32$, $C^{\mathrm{SITR}} = 10$. We empirically obtained these values by testing MIST-SEG on the same test sequences, i.e., *carDark, david3, trellis, soccer, matrix, car4, sylvester, suv, jumping,* and *fleetface,* each representing a different tracking challenge. Varying these parameters up to 20% does not noticeably affect the effectiveness of the proposed MIST-SEG. Experimentally, we observed that our MIST-SEG is only sensitive to the number of iterations $C^{\mathrm{SITR}}$ that the segmentation is executed. With higher $C^{\mathrm{SITR}}$, the employed method [22] removes more smooth areas of the object through its energy minimization, and with smaller $C^{\mathrm{SITR}}$, it retains more background regions; in both cases, the method [22] is suboptimal in segmenting relevant foreground object from the background.

We have tested MIST-SEG with three segmentation methods: active contour-based (AC) [22], Lazy snapping (LS) [14], and K-means (KM) [10]. Although recent object detection methods such as YOLO, maybe more accurate than the classical object segmentation methods we tested, they do fail when the object class is unknown as the case is in general object tracking. Table 1 lists the averaged AORs, CLEs, %Best score, and frame rates (FPS). As can be seen, using AC clearly outperforms LS and KM.

Table 2 presents average CLE, AOR, %Best, and FPS of MIST-SEGA with automated seeds for [22], of MIST-SEGM with manual seeds for [22], and MIST

**Table 1.** Use of Segmentation Methods [10–17, 19–22]: AOR, CLE, %Best, and FPS (averaged over 11 test sequences). %Best is the ratio of the number of sequences a tracker performs best and second best to the total

| Tracker | AOR | CLE | %Best AOR | %Best CLE | FPS |
|---|---|---|---|---|---|
| *MIST-SEG-AC* | **0.670** | **10.46** | **0.90** | **0.72** | **11.53** |
| *MIST-SEG-LS* | 0.457 | 34.00 | 0.09 | 0.27 | 10.14 |
| *MIST-SEG-KM* | 0.326 | 63.14 | 0.0 | 0.0 | 10.56 |

**Table 2.** Objective AOR, CLE, %Best, and FPS averaged over 51 test sequences from dataset [23]

| Tracker | AOR | CLE | %Best AOR | %Best CLE | FPS |
|---|---|---|---|---|---|
| *MIST-SEGA* | *0.595* | *23.96* | 0,35 | 0.33 | 10.58 |
| *MIST-SEGM* | **0.619** | **18.29** | **0.44** | **0.42** | 7.44 |
| *MIST* (baseline) | 0.551 | 26.84 | 0.20 | 0.24 | 11.23 |
| *Struck* | 0.481 | 50.8 | 0.28 | 0.11 | 9.46 |
| *TLD* | 0.432 | 52.30 | 0.16 | 0.11 | **24.12** |
| *JOTS* | 0.294 | 54.06 | 0.11 | 0.10 | 0.074 |

our baseline structured tracker. As can be observed, MIST-SEG with or without automated seeds outperforms MIST, and manual MIST-SEGM outperforms automated MIST-SEGA. Table 2 also shows that the proposed MIST-SEG quality is superior to the segmentation-based tracker JOTS [13], to TLD [9] with its explicit failure handling, and to classical Struck [8]. We summarize individual results of the 51 test sequences that include 11 challenges [23] as follows: (1) in only 6% of tested sequences AOR and CLE of MIST-SEG are worse than MIST, e.g., AOR 0.327 versus 0.493 in *skiing* video; (2) precision of MIST-SEG is higher than MIST under all challenges except motion blur and deformation, e.g., 0.689 versus 0.767 under blur; and (3) success of MIST-SEG is higher than MIST under all challenges except motion blur, 0.662 versus 0.717. Figure 1 shows cropped BB from video frames; both MIST-SEGM and MIST-SEGA well correct failures and inaccuracies of the baseline MIST (blue BB). We show output BBs manually cropped for a clear presentation.

**Fig. 1.** Sample output BBs comparing MIST-SEGA (magenta), MIST-SEGM (red), and baseline MIST (blue).

## 4 Conclusion

Tracking failure (or drift) is inevitable due to challenges inherent in video signals. This paper investigated failure detection and subsequent tracker reinitialization in structured learning based tracking. To detect failure, we proposed an online binary SVMs framework. For reinitialization, we used recent history of the object trajectory to relocate the lost target based on object segmentation; for this we used particle filter to sample and estimate the target state and segmentation to model the likelihood. Our simulations have shown such integration of segmentation can significantly reduce tracking failures; the performance of our method is not sensitive to drift detection errors but more on tracker reinitialization, i.e., on the object segmentation used. Object segmentation and detection is an active research field and novel methods such [21] can be easily integrated into our approach. We further plan to apply our drift detection and correction approach to recent correlation filter based trackers such as [24].

# References

1. Arulampalam, M.S., Maskell, S., Gordon, N., Clapp, T.: A tutorial on particle filters for online nonlinear/non-Gaussian Bayesian tracking. IEEE Trans. Sign. Process. **50**, 174–188 (2002)
2. Bordes, A., Bottou, L., Gallinari, P., Weston, J.: Solving multiclass support vector machines with LaRank. In: International Conference on Machine learning, pp. 89–96 (2007)
3. Boykov, Y., Jolly, M.P.: Interactive graph cuts for optimal boundary & region segmentation of objects in ND images. In: IEEE International Conference Computer Vision, pp. 105–112, July 2001
4. Danelljan, M., Robinson, A., Shahbaz Khan, F., Felsberg, M.: Beyond correlation filters: learning continuous convolution operators for visual tracking. In: Leibe, B., Matas, J., Sebe, N., Welling, M. (eds.) ECCV 2016. LNCS, vol. 9909, pp. 472–488. Springer, Cham (2016). https://doi.org/10.1007/978-3-319-46454-1_29
5. Doucet, A., Godsill, S., Andrieu, C.: On sequential Monte Carlo sampling methods for Bayesian filtering. Stat. Comput. **10**(3), 197–208 (2000)
6. Godec, M., Roth, P.M., Bischof, H.: Hough-based tracking of non-rigid objects. Comput. Vis. Image Underst. **117**(10), 1245–1256 (2013)
7. Gordon, N., Salmond, D., Smith, A.: Novel approach to nonlinear/non-Gaussian Bayesian state estimation. IET Radar Sign. Proc. **140**(2), 107–113 (1993)
8. Hare, S., et al.: Struck: structured output tracking with kernels. IEEE Trans. Pattern Anal. Mach. Intell. **38**(10), 2096–2109 (2015)
9. Kalal, Z., Mikolajczyk, K., Matas, J.: Tracking-learning-detection. IEEE Trans. Pattern Anal. Mach. Intell. **34**(7), 1409–1422 (2012)
10. Kanungo, T., Mount, D., Netanyahu, N., Piatko, C., Silverman, R., Wu, A.: An efficient k-means clustering algorithm: analysis and implementation. IEEE Trans. Pattern Anal. Mach. Intell. **24**(7), 881–892 (2002)
11. Kim, T.H., Lee, K.M., Lee, S.U.: Generative image segmentation using random walks with restart. In: Forsyth, D., Torr, P., Zisserman, A. (eds.) ECCV 2008. LNCS, vol. 5304, pp. 264–275. Springer, Heidelberg (2008). https://doi.org/10.1007/978-3-540-88690-7_20
12. Kwon, J., Lee, K.M.: Highly nonrigid object tracking via patch-based dynamic appearance modeling. IEEE TPAMI **35**(10), 2427–2441 (2013)
13. Wen, L., et al.: JOTS: joint online tracking and segmentation. In: IEEE International Conference Computer Vision and Pattern Recognition, pp. 2226–2234 (2015)
14. Li, Y., Sun, J., Tang, C.K., Shum, H.Y.: Lazy snapping. Trans. Graph. **23**(3), 303–308 (2004)
15. Ning, J., Zhang, L., Zhang, D., Yu, W.: Joint registration and active contour segmentation for object tracking. IEEE Trans. Circuits Syst. Video Technol. **23**(9), 1589–1597 (2013)
16. Platt, J.: Fast training of support vector machines using sequential minimal optimization. In: Advances in Kernel Methods-Support Vector Learning, vol. 3 (1999)
17. Ratnayake, K., Amer, A.: Object tracking with adaptive motion modeling of particle filter and support vector machines. In: IEEE International Conference on Image Processing, pp. 1140–1144 (2015)
18. Ratnayake, K., Amer, M.A.: Motion-augmented inference and joint kernels in structured learning for object tracking. In: Karray, F., et al. (eds.) ICIAR 2019. LNCS, vol. 11662, pp. 45–54 (2008). https://doi.org/10.1007/978-3-030-27202-9_4

19. Smola, A.J., Schölkopf, B.: A tutorial on support vector regression. Stat. Comput. **14**(3), 199–222 (2004)
20. Tsochantaridis, I., Joachims, T., Hofmann, T., Altun, Y.: Large Margin methods for structured and interdependent output variables. J. Mach. Learn. Res. **6**, 1453–1484 (2005)
21. Wang, J., Chen, K., Yang, S., Loy, C., Lin, D.: Region proposal by guided anchoring. In: IEEE Conference on CVPR, Long Beach, CA, June 2019
22. Wang, X.F., Huang, D.S., Xu, H.: An efficient local Chan-Vese model for image segmentation. Pattern Recogn. **43**(3), 603–618 (2010)
23. Wu, Y., Lim, J., Yang, M.H.: Online object tracking: a benchmark. In: IEEE Conference on Computer Vision and Pattern Recognition, pp. 2411–2418 (2013)
24. Xu, T., Feng, Z.H., Wu, X.J., Kittler, J.: Learning adaptive discriminative correlation filters via temporal consistency preserving spatial feature selection for robust visual tracking. arXiv preprint. arXiv:1807.11348 (2018)

# Principal Component Analysis Using Structural Similarity Index for Images

Benyamin Ghojogh$^{(\boxtimes)}$ ⓘ, Fakhri Karray ⓘ, and Mark Crowley ⓘ

Department of Electrical and Computer Engineering, University of Waterloo,
Waterloo, ON, Canada
{bghojogh,karray,mcrowley}@uwaterloo.ca

**Abstract.** Despite the advances of deep learning in specific tasks using images, the principled assessment of image fidelity and similarity is still a critical ability to develop. As it has been shown that Mean Squared Error (MSE) is insufficient for this task, other measures have been developed with one of the most effective being Structural Similarity Index (SSIM). Such measures can be used for subspace learning but existing methods in machine learning, such as Principal Component Analysis (PCA), are based on Euclidean distance or MSE and thus cannot properly capture the structural features of images. In this paper, we define an image structure subspace which discriminates different types of image distortions. We propose Image Structural Component Analysis (ISCA) and also kernel ISCA by using SSIM, rather than Euclidean distance, in the formulation of PCA. This paper provides a bridge between image quality assessment and manifold learning opening a broad new area for future research.

**Keywords:** Principal Component Analysis · Structural similarity ·
SSIM · Image Structural Component Analysis ·
Image structure subspace

## 1 Introduction

It has been shown that Mean Squared Error (MSE) is not a promising measure for image quality, fidelity, or similarity [1]. The distortions of an image or similarities of two images can be divided into two main categories, i.e., structural and non-structural distortions [2]. The structural distortions, such as JPEG blocking distortion, Gaussian noise, and blurring, are the ones which are easily noticeable by Human Visual System (HVS), whereas the non-structural distortions, such as luminance enhancement and contrast change, do not have large impact on the visual quality of image.

Structural similarity index (SSIM) [2,3] has been shown to be an effective measure for image quality assessment. It encounters luminance and contrast change as non-structural distortions and other distortions as structural ones. Due to its performance, it has recently been noticed and used in optimization problems [4] for tasks such as image denoising, image restoration, contrast

© Springer Nature Switzerland AG 2019
F. Karray et al. (Eds.): ICIAR 2019, LNCS 11662, pp. 77–88, 2019.
https://doi.org/10.1007/978-3-030-27202-9_7

enhancement, image quantization, compression, etc, noticing that the distance based on SSIM is quasi-convex under certain conditions [5].

So far, the fields of manifold learning and machine learning have largely used MSE and Euclidean distance in order to develop algorithms for subspace learning. Principal Component Analysis (PCA) is an example based on Euclidean distance or $\ell_2$ norm. However, MSE is not as promising as SSIM for image structure measurement [1,3] making these algorithms not effective enough in terms of capturing the structural features of image. In this paper, we introduce the new concept of *image structure subspace* which is a subspace capturing the intrinsic features of an image in terms of structural similarity and distortions, and can discriminate the various types of image distortions. This subspace can also be useful for parameter estimation for (or selection between) different denoising methods, but that topic will be dealt with in future work.

The outline and contributions of the paper are as follows: We begin by defining the background methods of SSIM and PCA. We then introduce ISCA using orthonormal bases and kernals by analogy to PCA, where ISCA can be seen as PCA which uses SSIM instead of the $\ell_2$ norm. We then describe an extensive set of experiments demonstrating the performance of ISCA on projection, reconstruction and out-of-sample analysis tasks compared to various kernel PCA methods. The derivations of expressions in this paper are detailed more in the supplementary-material paper which will be released in https://arXiv.org.

## 2   Structural Similarity Index

The SSIM between two reshaped image blocks $\breve{x}_1 = [x_1^{(1)}, \ldots, x_1^{(q)}]^\top \in \mathbb{R}^q$ and $\breve{x}_2 = [x_2^{(1)}, \ldots, x_2^{(q)}]^\top \in \mathbb{R}^q$, in color intensity range $[0, l]$, is [2,3]:

$$\mathbb{R} \ni \mathrm{SSIM}(\breve{x}_1, \breve{x}_2) := \left( \frac{2\mu_{x_1}\mu_{x_2} + c_1}{\mu_{x_1}^2 + \mu_{x_2}^2 + c_1} \right) \left( \frac{2\sigma_{x_1}\sigma_{x_2} + c_2}{\sigma_{x_1}^2 + \sigma_{x_2}^2 + c_2} \right) \left( \frac{\sigma_{x_1,x_2} + c_3}{\sigma_{x_1}\sigma_{x_2} + c_3} \right), \quad (1)$$

where $\mu_{x_1} = (1/q) \sum_{i=1}^q x_1^{(i)}$, $\sigma_{x_1} = \left[ (1/(q-1)) \sum_{i=1}^q (x_1^{(i)} - \mu_{x_1})^2 \right]^{0.5}$, $\sigma_{x_1,x_2} = (1/(q-1)) \sum_{i=1}^q (x_1^{(i)} - \mu_{x_1})(x_2^{(i)} - \mu_{x_2})$, $c_1 = (0.01 \times l)^2$, $c_2 = 2c_3 = (0.03 \times l)^2$, and $\mu_{x_2}$ and $\sigma_{x_2}$ are defined similarly for $\breve{x}_2$. In this work, $l = 1$. The $c_1$, $c_2$, and $c_3$ are for avoidance of singularity [3] and $q$ is the dimensionality of the reshaped image patch. Note that since $c_2 = 2c_3$, we can simplify SSIM to $\mathrm{SSIM}(\breve{x}_1, \breve{x}_2) = s_1(\breve{x}_1, \breve{x}_2) \times s_2(\breve{x}_1, \breve{x}_2)$, where $s_1(\breve{x}_1, \breve{x}_2) := (2\mu_{x_1}\mu_{x_2} + c_1)/(\mu_{x_1}^2 + \mu_{x_2}^2 + c_1)$ and $s_2(\breve{x}_1, \breve{x}_2) := (2\sigma_{x_1,x_2} + c_2)/(\sigma_{x_1}^2 + \sigma_{x_2}^2 + c_2)$. If the vectors $\breve{x}_1$ and $\breve{x}_2$ have zero mean, i.e., $\mu_{x_1} = \mu_{x_2} = 0$, the SSIM becomes $\mathbb{R} \ni \mathrm{SSIM}(\breve{x}_1, \breve{x}_2) = (2\breve{x}_1^\top \breve{x}_2 + c)/(||\breve{x}_1||_2^2 + ||\breve{x}_2||_2^2 + c)$, where $c = (q-1)c_2$ [6]. We denote the reshaped vectors of the two images by $x_1 \in \mathbb{R}^d$ and $x_2 \in \mathbb{R}^d$, and a reshaped block in the two images by $\breve{x}_1 \in \mathbb{R}^q$ and $\breve{x}_2 \in \mathbb{R}^q$. The (squared) distance based on SSIM, which we denote by $||.||_S$, is [5–7]:

$$\mathbb{R} \ni ||\breve{x}_1 - \breve{x}_2||_S := 1 - \mathrm{SSIM}(\breve{x}_1, \breve{x}_2) = \frac{||\breve{x}_1 - \breve{x}_2||_2^2}{||\breve{x}_1||_2^2 + ||\breve{x}_2||_2^2 + c}, \quad (2)$$

where $\mu_{x_1} = \mu_{x_2} = 0$. In ISCA and PCA which inspires ISCA, the data should be centered; therefore, the fact that $\breve{x}_1$ and $\breve{x}_2$ should be centered is useful.

## 3    Principal Component Analysis

Since ISCA is inspired by PCA [8] we briefly review it here. Assume that the orthonormal columns of matrix $U \in \mathbb{R}^{d \times p}$ are the vectors which span the PCA subspace. Then, the projected data $\widetilde{X} \in \mathbb{R}^{p \times n}$ onto PCA subspace and the reconstructed data $\hat{X} \in \mathbb{R}^{d \times n}$ are $\widetilde{X} = U^\top X$ and $\hat{X} = U\widetilde{X} = UU^\top X$, respectively. The squared length of the projected data is $||\hat{X}||_F^2 = ||UU^\top X||_F^2 = \text{tr}(U^\top XX^\top U)$ where $\text{tr}(.)$ and $||.||_F$ denote the trace and Frobenius norm of matrix, respectively. Presuming that the data $X$ are already centered, the $S = XX^\top$ is the covariance matrix; therefore: $||\hat{X}||_F^2 = \text{tr}(U^\top SU)$. Maximizing the squared length of projection where the projection matrix is orthogonal is:

$$\underset{U}{\text{maximize}} \quad \text{tr}(U^\top SU), \quad\quad (3)$$
$$\text{subject to} \quad U^\top U = I,$$

The Lagrangian [9] is: $\mathcal{L} = \text{tr}(U^\top SU) - \text{tr}(\Lambda^\top(U^\top U - I))$, where $\Lambda \in \mathbb{R}^{p \times p}$ is a diagonal matrix including Lagrange multipliers. Equating derivative of $\mathcal{L}$ to zero gives us: $\mathbb{R}^{d \times p} \ni \partial\mathcal{L}/\partial U = 2SU - 2U\Lambda \overset{\text{set}}{=} 0 \implies SU = U\Lambda$. Therefore, columns of $U$ are the eigenvectors of the covariance matrix $S$.

PCA can be looked at with another point of view. The reconstruction error is $R := X - \hat{X} = X - UU^\top X$ where $\mathbb{R}^{d \times n} \ni R = [r_1, \dots, r_n]$ is the matrix of residuals. We want to minimize the reconstruction error:

$$\underset{U}{\text{minimize}} \quad ||X - UU^\top X||_F^2, \quad\quad (4)$$
$$\text{subject to} \quad U^\top U = I.$$

The objective function is $||X - UU^\top X||_F^2 = \text{tr}(X^\top X - XX^\top UU^\top)$. The Lagrangian [9] is: $\mathcal{L} = \text{tr}(X^\top X) - \text{tr}(XX^\top UU^\top) - \text{tr}(\Lambda^\top(U^\top U - I))$, where $\Lambda \in \mathbb{R}^{p \times p}$ is a diagonal matrix including Lagrange multipliers. Equating the derivative of $\mathcal{L}$ to zero gives: $\partial\mathcal{L}/\partial U = 2XX^\top U - 2U\Lambda \overset{\text{set}}{=} 0 \implies XX^\top U = U\Lambda \implies SU = U\Lambda$, which is again the eigenvalue problem for the covariance matrix $S$. Therefore, PCA subspace is the best linear projection in terms of reconstruction error.

As shown above, PCA [8] is based on $\ell_2$ (or Frobenius) norm which is not a promising measure for image quality assessment [1]. In order to have both the minimization of reconstruction error as in PCA and using a proper measure for image fidelity, we propose ISCA.

## 4    Image Structural Component Analysis (ISCA)

### 4.1    Orthonormal Bases for One Image

Our goal is to find a subspace spanned by $p$ directions for some desired $p$. Consider an image block $\breve{x} \in \mathbb{R}^q$ which is centered (its mean is removed). We want to project it onto a $p$-dimensional subspace and then reconstruct it back, where $p \leq q$. Assume $\mathbb{R}^{q \times p} \ni \boldsymbol{U} := [\boldsymbol{u}_1, \ldots, \boldsymbol{u}_p]$ is a matrix whose columns are the projection directions spanning the subspace. The projection and reconstruction of $\breve{\boldsymbol{x}}$ are $\boldsymbol{U}^\top \breve{\boldsymbol{x}}$ and $\boldsymbol{U} \boldsymbol{U}^\top \breve{\boldsymbol{x}}$, respectively. We want to minimize the reconstruction error with orthonormal bases of the subspace; therefore:

$$
\begin{array}{cc}
\underset{\boldsymbol{U} \in \mathbb{R}^{q \times p}}{\text{minimize}} & ||\breve{\boldsymbol{x}} - \boldsymbol{U} \boldsymbol{U}^\top \breve{\boldsymbol{x}}||_S, \\
\text{subject to} & \boldsymbol{U}^\top \boldsymbol{U} = \boldsymbol{I}.
\end{array} \tag{5}
$$

According to Eq. (2) and noticing the orthonormality of projection directions, $\boldsymbol{U}^\top \boldsymbol{U} = \boldsymbol{I}$, we have:

$$
\mathbb{R} \ni f(\boldsymbol{U}) := ||\breve{\boldsymbol{x}} - \boldsymbol{U} \boldsymbol{U}^\top \breve{\boldsymbol{x}}||_S = \frac{\breve{\boldsymbol{x}}^\top (\boldsymbol{I} - \boldsymbol{U} \boldsymbol{U}^\top) \breve{\boldsymbol{x}}}{\breve{\boldsymbol{x}}^\top (\boldsymbol{I} + \boldsymbol{U} \boldsymbol{U}^\top) \breve{\boldsymbol{x}} + c}. \tag{6}
$$

The gradient of the $f(\boldsymbol{U})$ is:

$$
\mathbb{R}^{q \times p} \ni \boldsymbol{G}(\boldsymbol{U}) := \frac{\partial f(\boldsymbol{U})}{\partial \boldsymbol{U}} = \frac{-2 \, (1 + f(\boldsymbol{U}))}{||\breve{\boldsymbol{x}}||_2^2 + ||\boldsymbol{U} \boldsymbol{U}^\top \breve{\boldsymbol{x}}||_2^2 + c} \, \breve{\boldsymbol{x}} \breve{\boldsymbol{x}}^\top \boldsymbol{U}. \tag{7}
$$

We partition a $d$-dimensional image into $b = \lceil d/q \rceil$ non-overlapping blocks each of which is a reshaped vector $\breve{\boldsymbol{x}} \in \mathbb{R}^q$. The parameter $q$ is an upper bound on the desired dimensionality of the subspace of block ($p \leq q$). This parameter should not be a very large number due to the spatial variety of image statistics, yet also not very small so as to be able to capture the image structure. Also note that $p$ is an upper bound on the rank of $\boldsymbol{U} \boldsymbol{U}^\top \in \mathbb{R}^{q \times q}$.

We have $b$ instances of $p$-dimensional subspaces, one for each of the blocks. For projecting an image into the subspace and reconstructing it back, one can project and reconstruct every block of an image separately using the $p$ bases of the block subspace. The overall bases of an image can be visualized in image-form by putting the bases of blocks next to each other (see the experiments in Sect. 6).

Considering all the $b$ blocks in an image, the problem in Eq. (5) becomes:

$$
\begin{array}{cc}
\underset{\boldsymbol{U}_i \in \mathbb{R}^{q \times p}}{\text{minimize}} & \sum_{i=1}^{b} ||\breve{\boldsymbol{x}}_i - \boldsymbol{U}_i \boldsymbol{U}_i^\top \breve{\boldsymbol{x}}_i||_S, \\
\text{subject to} & \boldsymbol{U}_i^\top \boldsymbol{U}_i = \boldsymbol{I}, \quad \forall i \in \{1, \ldots, b\},
\end{array} \tag{8}
$$

where $\boldsymbol{x}_i \in \mathbb{R}^q$ and $\boldsymbol{U}_i \in \mathbb{R}^{q \times p}$ are the $i$-th block and the bases of its subspace, respectively. We can embed the constraint as an indicator function in the objective function [10]:

$$
\begin{array}{cc}
\underset{\boldsymbol{U}_i, \boldsymbol{V}_i \in \mathbb{R}^{q \times p}}{\text{minimize}} & \sum_{i=1}^{b} \big( f(\boldsymbol{U}_i) + h(\boldsymbol{V}_i) \big), \\
\text{subject to} & \boldsymbol{U} - \boldsymbol{V} = \boldsymbol{0},
\end{array} \tag{9}
$$

where $f(\boldsymbol{U}_i) := ||\breve{\boldsymbol{x}}_i - \boldsymbol{U}_i \boldsymbol{U}_i^\top \breve{\boldsymbol{x}}_i||_S$ and $h(\boldsymbol{V}_i) := \mathbb{I}(\boldsymbol{V}_i^\top \boldsymbol{V}_i = \boldsymbol{I})$. The $\mathbb{I}(.)$ denotes the indicator function which is zero if its condition is satisfied and is infinite otherwise. The $U$ and $V$ are defined as union of partitions to form an image-form array, i.e., $U := \cup_{i=1}^{b} U_i$ and $V := \cup_{i=1}^{b} V_i$ [11].

The Eq. (9) can be solved using Alternating Direction Method of Multipliers (ADMM) [10,11]. The augmented Lagrangian for Eq. (9) is: $\mathcal{L}_\rho = \sum_{i=1}^{b} (f(U_i) + h(V_i)) + \mathbf{tr}(\Lambda^\top (U - V)) + (\rho/2)\|U - V\|_F^2 = \sum_{i=1}^{b} (f(U_i) + h(V_i)) + (\rho/2)\|U - V + J\|_F^2 - (\rho/2)\|\Lambda\|_F^2$, where $\Lambda := \cup_{i=1}^{b} \Lambda_i$ is the Lagrange multiplier, $\rho > 0$ is a parameter, and $J := (1/\rho)\Lambda = (1/\rho) \cup_{i=1}^{b} \Lambda_i = \cup_{i=1}^{b} J_i$. Note that the term $(\rho/2)\|\Lambda\|_F^2$ is a constant with respect to $U$ and $V$ and can be dropped. The updates of $U$, $V$, and $J$ are done as [10,11]:

$$U_i^{(k+1)} := \arg\min_{U_i} \left( f(U_i) + (\rho/2)\|U_i - V_i^{(k)} + J_i^{(k)}\|_F^2 \right), \tag{10}$$

$$V_i^{(k+1)} := \arg\min_{V_i} \left( h(V_i) + (\rho/2)\|U_i^{(k+1)} - V_i + J_i^{(k)}\|_F^2 \right), \tag{11}$$

$$J^{(k+1)} := J^{(k)} + U^{(k+1)} - V^{(k+1)}. \tag{12}$$

Considering $\|A\|_F^2 = \mathbf{tr}(A^\top A)$ for a matrix $A$, the gradient of the objective function in Eq. (10) with respect to $U_i$ is $G(U_i) + \rho(U_i - V_i^{(k)} + J_i^{(k)})$ where $G(U_i)$ is defined in Eq. (7). We can use the gradient decent method [9] for solving the Eq. (10). Our experiments showed that even one iteration of gradient decent suffices for Eq. (10) because the ADMM itself is iterative. Hence, we can replace this equation with one iteration of gradient decent.

The proximal operator is defined as [12]:

$$\mathbf{prox}_{\lambda,h}(v) := \arg\min_{u} \left( h(u) + (\lambda/2)\|u - v\|_2^2 \right), \tag{13}$$

where $\lambda$ is the proximal parameter and $h$ is the function that the proximal algorithm wants to minimize. According to Eq. (13), the Eq. (11) is equivalent to $\mathbf{prox}_{\rho,h}(U_i^{(k+1)} + J_i^{(k)})$. As $h(.)$ is indicator function, its proximal operator is projection [12]. Therefore, Eq. (11) is equivalent to $\Pi(U_i^{(k+1)} + J_i^{(k)})$ where $\Pi(.)$ denotes projection onto a set. Here, the variable of proximal operator is a matrix and not a vector. According to [12], if $F$ is a convex and orthogonally invariant function, and it works on the singular values of a matrix variable $A \in \mathbb{R}^{q \times p}$, i.e., $F = f \circ \sigma$ where the function $\sigma(A)$ gives the vector of singular values of $A$, then the proximal operator is:

$$\mathbf{prox}_{\lambda,F}(A) := Q \, \mathbf{diag}\left( \mathbf{prox}_{\lambda,f}(\sigma(A)) \right) \Omega^\top. \tag{14}$$

The $Q \in \mathbb{R}^{q \times p}$ and $\Omega \in \mathbb{R}^{p \times p}$ are the matrices of left and right singular vectors of $A$, respectively. In our constraint $V^\top V = I$, the function $F$ deals with the singular values of $V$. The reason is that we want: $V \overset{\text{SVD}}{=} Q\Sigma\Omega^\top \implies V^\top V = \Omega\Sigma Q^\top Q\Sigma\Omega^\top \overset{(a)}{=} \Omega\Sigma^2\Omega^\top \overset{\text{set}}{=} I \implies \Omega\Sigma^2\Omega^\top\Omega = \Omega \overset{(b)}{\implies} \Omega\Sigma^2 = \Omega \implies \Sigma = I$, where $(a)$ and $(b)$ are because $Q$ and $\Omega$ are orthogonal matrices. Therefore, we can use Eq. (14) for Eq. (11) where $\mathbf{prox}_{\rho,h}(U_i^{(k+1)} + J_i^{(k)})$ sets the singular values of $(U_i^{(k+1)} + J_i^{(k)})$ to one. In summary, Eqs. (10), (11), and (12) can be restated as:

$$U_i^{(k+1)} := U_i^{(k)} - \eta\, G(U_i^{(k)}) - \eta\, \rho\, (U_i^{(k)} - V_i^{(k)} + J_i^{(k)}),$$

$$V_i^{(k+1)} := Q_i \, \mathrm{diag}\Big(\mathbf{prox}_{\rho,h}\big(\sigma(U_i^{(k+1)} + J_i^{(k)})\big)\Big)\, \Omega_i^\top, \qquad (15)$$

$$J^{(k+1)} := J^{(k)} + U^{(k+1)} - V^{(k+1)},$$

where columns of $Q_i \in \mathbb{R}^{q \times p}$ and $\Omega_i \in \mathbb{R}^{p \times p}$ are the left and right singular vectors of $(U_i^{(k+1)} + J_i^{(k)})$ and $\eta > 0$ is the learning rate. Iteratively solving Eq. (15) until convergence gives us the $U_i$ for the image blocks indexed by $i$. The $p$ columns of $U_i$ are the bases for the *ISCA subspace* of the $i$-th block. Unlike in PCA, the ISCA bases do not have an order of importance but as in PCA, they are orthogonal capturing different features of image structure. The $i$-th projected block is $U_i^\top \breve{x}_i \in \mathbb{R}^p$ where its dimensions are *image structural components*. Note that $\breve{x}_i$, whether it is a block in a training image or an out-of-sample image, is centered. It is noteworthy that if we consider only one block in the images, the subscript $i$ is dropped from Eq. (15).

## 4.2   Orthonormal Bases for a Set of Images

So far, if we have a set of $n$ images, we can find the subspace bases $U_i$ for the $i$-th block in each of them using Eq. (15). Now, we want to find the subspace bases $U_i$ for the $i$-th block in *all training images of the dataset*. In other words, we want to find the subspace for the best reconstruction of the $i$-th block in all training images. For this goal, we can look at the optimization problem in Eq. (8) or (9) as an undercomplete auto-encoder neural network [13] with one hidden layer where the input layer, hidden layer, and output layer have $q$, $p$, and $q$ neurons, respectively. The $U_i^\top \breve{x}$ and $U_i U_i^\top \breve{x}$ fill the role of applying the first and second weight matrices to the input, respectively. The weights are $U_i \in \mathbb{R}^{q \times p}$. Therefore, we will have $b$ auto-encoders, each with one hidden layer.

For training the auto-encoder, we introduce the blocks in an image as the input to this network and update the weights $U_i, \forall i$ based on Eq. (15). Note that we do this update of weights with only 'one' iteration of ADMM. Then, we move to the blocks in the next image and update the weights $U_i, \forall i$ again by an iteration of Eq. (15). We do this for all images one by one until an epoch is completed where an epoch is defined as introducing the block in all training images of dataset to the network. After termination of an epoch, we start another epoch to tune the weights $U_i, \forall i$ again. The epochs are repeated until the convergence. The termination criterion can be average reconstruction error $(1/(nb)) \sum_{i=1}^{b} \sum_{j=1}^{n} \|\breve{x}_{j,i} - U_i U_i^\top \breve{x}_{j,i}\|_S < \varepsilon$, where $\varepsilon$ is a small number and $\breve{x}_{j,i}$ is the $i$-th block in the $j$-th image. After training the network, we have one $p$-dimensional subspace for every block in all training images where the columns of the weight matrix $U_i$ span the subspace. Note that because of ADMM, the auto-encoders are trained simultaneously and in parallel. Again, the $p$ columns of $U_i$ are the bases for the *ISCA subspace* of the $i$-th block.

## 5 Kernel Image Structural Component Analysis

We can map the block $\breve{x} \in \mathbb{R}^q$ to higher-dimensional feature space hoping to have the data fall close to a simpler-to-analyze manifold in the feature space. Suppose $\phi : \breve{x} \to \mathcal{H}$ is a function which maps the data $\breve{x}$ to the feature space. In other words, $\breve{x} \mapsto \phi(\breve{x})$. Let $t$ denote the dimensionality of the feature space, i.e., $\phi(\breve{x}) \in \mathbb{R}^t$. We usually have $t \gg q$. The kernel of the $i$-th block in images 1 and 2, which are $\breve{x}_{1,i}$ and $\breve{x}_{2,i}$, is $\phi(\breve{x}_{1,i})^\top \phi(\breve{x}_{2,i}) \in \mathbb{R}$ [14]. The kernel matrix for the $i$-th block among the $n$ images is $\mathbb{R}^{n \times n} \ni \boldsymbol{K}_i := \boldsymbol{\Phi}(\breve{\boldsymbol{X}}_i)^\top \boldsymbol{\Phi}(\breve{\boldsymbol{X}}_i)$ where $\boldsymbol{\Phi}(\breve{\boldsymbol{X}}_i) := [\phi(\breve{x}_{1,i}), \dots, \phi(\breve{x}_{n,i})] \in \mathbb{R}^{t \times n}$. After calculating the kernel matrix, we normalize it [15] as $\boldsymbol{K}_i(a, b) := \boldsymbol{K}_i(a, b)/\sqrt{\boldsymbol{K}_i(a, a)\boldsymbol{K}_i(b, b)}$ where $\boldsymbol{K}_i(a, b)$ denotes the $(a, b)$-th element of the kernel matrix. Afterwards, the kernel is double-centered as $\boldsymbol{K}_i := \boldsymbol{H} \boldsymbol{K}_i \boldsymbol{H}$ where $\mathbb{R}^{n \times n} \ni \boldsymbol{H} := \boldsymbol{I} - (1/n)\boldsymbol{1}\boldsymbol{1}^\top$. The reason for double-centering is that Eq. (2) requires $\phi(\breve{x}_i)$ and thus the $\boldsymbol{\Phi}(\breve{\boldsymbol{X}}_i)$ to be centered (see Eq. (16)). Therefore, in kernel ISCA, we center the kernel rather than centering $\breve{x}$.

According to representation theory [16], the projection matrix can be expressed as a linear combination of the projected data points. Therefore, we have $\mathbb{R}^{t \times p} \ni \boldsymbol{\Phi}(\boldsymbol{U}_i) = \boldsymbol{\Phi}(\breve{\boldsymbol{X}}_i) \boldsymbol{\Theta}_i$ where every column of $\boldsymbol{\Theta}_i := [\boldsymbol{\theta}_1, \dots, \boldsymbol{\theta}_p] \in \mathbb{R}^{n \times p}$ is the vector of coefficients for expressing a projection direction as a linear combination of projected image blocks.

As we did for ISCA, first we consider learning the $b$ subspaces for 'one' image, here. Considering $\boldsymbol{\Phi}(\boldsymbol{U}_i) = \boldsymbol{\Phi}(\breve{\boldsymbol{X}}_i) \boldsymbol{\Theta}_i$ for the $i$-th block in the image, the objective function of Eq. (8) in feature space is $\sum_{i=1}^b \|\phi(\breve{x}_i) - \boldsymbol{\Phi}(\breve{\boldsymbol{X}}_i) \boldsymbol{\Theta}_i \boldsymbol{\Theta}_i^\top \boldsymbol{k}_i\|_S$ where $\mathbb{R}^n \ni \boldsymbol{k}_i := \boldsymbol{\Phi}(\breve{\boldsymbol{X}}_i)^\top \phi(\breve{x}_i)$. Note that $\boldsymbol{\Phi}(\breve{\boldsymbol{X}}_i)$ includes the mapping of the $i$-th block in all the $n$ images while $\phi(\breve{x}_i)$ is the mapping of the $i$-th block in the image we are considering. The constraint of Eq. (8) in the feature space is $\boldsymbol{\Phi}(\boldsymbol{U}_i)^\top \boldsymbol{\Phi}(\boldsymbol{U}_i) = \boldsymbol{\Theta}_i^\top \boldsymbol{K}_i \boldsymbol{\Theta}_i = \boldsymbol{I}$. Therefore, the Eq. (8) in the feature space is:

$$\begin{aligned} \underset{\boldsymbol{\Theta}_i \in \mathbb{R}^{n \times p}}{\text{minimize}} \quad & \sum_{i=1}^b \|\phi(\breve{x}_i) - \boldsymbol{\Phi}(\breve{\boldsymbol{X}}_i) \boldsymbol{\Theta}_i \boldsymbol{\Theta}_i^\top \boldsymbol{k}_i\|_S, \\ \text{subject to} \quad & \boldsymbol{\Theta}_i^\top \boldsymbol{K}_i \boldsymbol{\Theta}_i = \boldsymbol{I}, \quad \forall i \in \{1, \dots, b\}. \end{aligned} \tag{16}$$

Noticing the constraint $\boldsymbol{\Theta}_i^\top \boldsymbol{K}_i \boldsymbol{\Theta}_i = \boldsymbol{I}$ and using Eq. (2), we have:

$$\mathbb{R} \ni f(\boldsymbol{\Theta}_i) := \|\phi(\breve{x}_i) - \boldsymbol{\Phi}(\breve{\boldsymbol{X}}_i) \boldsymbol{\Theta}_i \boldsymbol{\Theta}_i^\top \boldsymbol{k}_i\|_S = \frac{k_i - \boldsymbol{k}_i^\top \boldsymbol{\Theta}_i \boldsymbol{\Theta}_i^\top \boldsymbol{k}_i}{k_i + \boldsymbol{k}_i^\top \boldsymbol{\Theta}_i \boldsymbol{\Theta}_i^\top \boldsymbol{k}_i + c}, \tag{17}$$

where $\mathbb{R} \ni k_i := \phi(\breve{x}_i)^\top \phi(\breve{x}_i)$. The gradient of the $f(\boldsymbol{\Theta}_i)$ is:

$$\mathbb{R}^{n \times p} \ni \boldsymbol{G}(\boldsymbol{\Theta}_i) := \frac{\partial f(\boldsymbol{\Theta}_i)}{\partial \boldsymbol{\Theta}_i} = \frac{-2\left(1 + f(\boldsymbol{\Theta}_i)\right)}{k_i + \boldsymbol{k}_i^\top \boldsymbol{\Theta}_i \boldsymbol{\Theta}_i^\top \boldsymbol{k}_i + c} \boldsymbol{k}_i \boldsymbol{k}_i^\top \boldsymbol{\Theta}_i. \tag{18}$$

We can simplify the constraint $\boldsymbol{\Theta}_i^\top \boldsymbol{K}_i \boldsymbol{\Theta}_i = \boldsymbol{I}$. As the kernel $\boldsymbol{K}_i$ is positive semi-definite, we can decompose it as:

$$\mathbb{R}^{n \times n} \ni \boldsymbol{K}_i \overset{\text{SVD}}{=} \boldsymbol{\Psi} \boldsymbol{\Upsilon} \boldsymbol{\Psi}^\top = \boldsymbol{\Psi} \boldsymbol{\Upsilon}^{(1/2)} \boldsymbol{\Upsilon}^{(1/2)} \boldsymbol{\Psi}^\top = \boldsymbol{\Delta}^\top \boldsymbol{\Delta},$$

where $\mathbb{R}^{n \times n} \ni \mathbf{\Delta} := \mathbf{\Upsilon}^{(1/2)} \mathbf{\Psi}^{\top}$. Therefore, the constraint can be written as: $\mathbf{\Theta}_i^{\top} \mathbf{K}_i \mathbf{\Theta}_i = \mathbf{\Theta}_i^{\top} \mathbf{\Delta}^{\top} \mathbf{\Delta} \mathbf{\Theta}_i = (\mathbf{\Delta} \mathbf{\Theta}_i)^{\top} (\mathbf{\Delta} \mathbf{\Theta}_i) = \mathbf{I}$. In Eq. (16), if we embed the constraint in the objective function [10], we have:

$$\begin{array}{cc} \underset{\mathbf{\Theta}_i, \mathbf{V}_i \in \mathbb{R}^{n \times p}}{\text{minimize}} & \sum_{i=1}^{b} \left( f(\mathbf{\Theta}_i) + h(\mathbf{\Delta} \mathbf{V}_i) \right), \\ \text{subject to} & \mathbf{\Theta} - \mathbf{V} = \mathbf{0}, \end{array} \qquad (19)$$

where $h(\mathbf{\Delta} \mathbf{V}_i) = \mathbb{I}((\mathbf{\Delta} \mathbf{V}_i)^{\top} (\mathbf{\Delta} \mathbf{V}_i) = \mathbf{I})$ and $\mathbf{\Theta} := \cup_{i=1}^{b} \mathbf{\Theta}_i$ and $\mathbf{V} := \cup_{i=1}^{b} \mathbf{V}_i$. Taking $\mathbb{R}^{n \times p} \ni \mathbf{W}_i := \mathbf{\Delta} \mathbf{V}_i$, we can restate Eq. (19) as: $\underset{\mathbf{\Theta}_i, \mathbf{W}_i}{\text{minimize}} \sum_{i=1}^{b} \left( f(\mathbf{\Theta}_i) + h(\mathbf{W}_i) \right)$, subject to $\mathbf{\Delta} \mathbf{\Theta} - \mathbf{W} = \mathbf{0}$, where $\mathbf{W} := \cup_{i=1}^{b} \mathbf{W}_i$. The ADMM solution to this optimization problem is [10,11]:

$$\mathbf{\Theta}_i^{(k+1)} := \arg \min_{\mathbf{\Theta}_i} \left( f(\mathbf{\Theta}_i) + (\rho/2) \| \mathbf{\Delta} \mathbf{\Theta}_i - \mathbf{W}_i^{(k)} + \mathbf{J}_i^{(k)} \|_F^2 \right), \qquad (20)$$

$$\mathbf{W}_i^{(k+1)} := \arg \min_{\mathbf{W}_i} \left( h(\mathbf{W}_i) + (\rho/2) \| \mathbf{\Delta} \mathbf{\Theta}_i^{(k+1)} - \mathbf{W}_i + \mathbf{J}_i^{(k)} \|_F^2 \right), \qquad (21)$$

$$\mathbf{J}^{(k+1)} := \mathbf{J}^{(k)} + \mathbf{\Delta} \mathbf{\Theta}^{(k+1)} - \mathbf{W}^{(k+1)}. \qquad (22)$$

With the similar explanations which we had for Eq. (15), we have:

$$\begin{array}{c} \mathbf{\Theta}_i^{(k+1)} := \mathbf{\Theta}_i^{(k)} - \eta \, \mathbf{G}(\mathbf{\Theta}_i^{(k)}) - \eta \, \rho \, \mathbf{\Delta}^{\top} (\mathbf{\Delta} \mathbf{\Theta}_i^{(k)} - \mathbf{W}_i^{(k)} + \mathbf{J}_i^{(k)}), \\ \mathbf{W}_i^{(k+1)} := \mathbf{Q}_i \, \text{diag} \left( \text{prox}_{\rho,h} (\sigma(\mathbf{\Delta} \mathbf{\Theta}_i^{(k+1)} + \mathbf{J}_i^{(k)})) \right) \mathbf{\Omega}_i^{\top}, \\ \mathbf{J}^{(k+1)} := \mathbf{J}^{(k)} + \mathbf{\Delta} \mathbf{\Theta}^{(k+1)} - \mathbf{W}^{(k+1)}, \end{array} \qquad (23)$$

where columns of $\mathbf{Q}_i \in \mathbb{R}^{q \times p}$ and $\mathbf{\Omega}_i \in \mathbb{R}^{p \times p}$ are the left and right singular vectors of $(\mathbf{\Delta} \mathbf{\Theta}_i^{(k+1)} + \mathbf{J}_i^{(k)})$. Iteratively solving Eq. (23) until convergence gives us the $\mathbf{\Theta}_i$ for the image blocks indexed by $i$. The $p$ columns of $\mathbf{\Theta}_i$ are the bases for the *kernel ISCA subspace* of the $i$-th block. The $i$-th projected block is $\mathbf{\Theta}_i^{\top} \mathbf{k}_i \in \mathbb{R}^p$ and its dimensions are the *kernel image structural components*. Note that $\mathbf{k}_i$, whether it is the kernel over a block in a training image or an out-of-sample image, is normalized and centered. Also, note that we had considered the blocks of only one image for Eq. (23). Again, with the auto-encoder approach, we can solve these equations in successive epochs in order to find the $b$ subspaces for all the $n$ training images.

## 6    Experiments

**Training Dataset:** We formed a dataset out of the standard *Lena* image. Six different types of distortions were applied on the original *Lena* image (see Fig. 1), each of which has 20 images in the dataset with different MSE values. Therefore, the size of the training set is 121 including the original image. For every type of distortion, 20 different levels of MSE, i.e., from MSE = 45 to MSE = 900 with step 45, were generated to have images on the equal-MSE or *iso-error* hypersphere [3].

**Fig. 1.** Examples from the training dataset: (a) original image, (b) contrast stretched, (c) Gaussian noise, (d) luminance enhanced, (e) Gaussian blurring, (f) salt & pepper impulse noise, and (g) JPEG distortion.

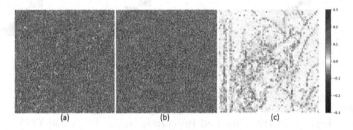

**Fig. 2.** The first dimension of the trained (a) $U$, (b) $V$, and (c) $J$ for ISCA.

**Training:** In our experiments for ISCA, the parameters used were $\rho = 1$ and $\eta = 0.1$, and for kernel ISCA, we used $\rho = 0.1$ and $\eta = 0.1$. We took $q = 64$ ($8 \times 8$ blocks inspired by [6,11]), $p = 4$, and $d = 512 \times 512 = 262144$. One of the dimensions of the trained $U = \cup_{i=1}^{b} U_i$, $V = \cup_{i=1}^{b} V_i$, and $J = \cup_{i=1}^{b} J_i$ for ISCA are shown in Fig. 2. The dual variable $J$ has captured the edges because edges carry much of the structure information. As expected, $U$ and $V$ are close (*Lena* can be seen in them by noticing scrupulously). Note that the variables in kernel ISCA are not $q$-dimensional and thus cannot be displayed in image form.

**Projections and Comparisons:** In order to evaluate the trained ISCA and kernel ISCA subspaces, we projected the training images onto these subspaces. For projecting an image, each of its blocks is projected onto the subspace of that block. After projecting all the images, we used the 1-Nearest Neighbor (1NN) classifier to recognize the distortion type of every block. The 1NN is useful to evaluate the subspace by closeness of the projected distortions. The distortion type of an image comes from a majority vote among the blocks. The linear, Radial Basis function (RBF), and sigmoid kernels were tested for kernel ISCA. The confusion matrices for distortion recognition are shown in Fig. 3. Mostly kernel ISCA performed better than ISCA because it works in feature space; although, ISCA performed better for some distortions like contrast stretching and blurring. Moreover, we compared with PCA and kernel PCA. PCA showed weakness in contrast stretching. RBF and sigmoid kernels in kernel PCA do not perform well for JPEG distortion and contrast stretching, respectively.

**Out-of-sample Projections:** For out-of-sample projection, we created 12 test images with MSE = 500 having different distortions and some having a combi-

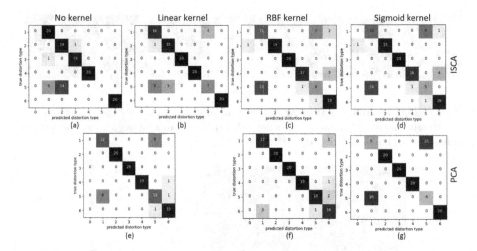

**Fig. 3.** Confusion matrices for recognition of distortion types with a 1NN classifier used in the subspace. Matrices (a) and (e) correspond to ISCA and PCA (or linear-kernel PCA), respectively. Matrices (b) to (d) are for kernel ISCA with linear, RBF, and sigmoid kernels. Matrices (f) and (g) are for kernel PCA with RBF and sigmoid kernels. The 0 label in matrices correspond to the original image and the labels 1 to 6 are the distortion types with the same order as in Fig. 1.

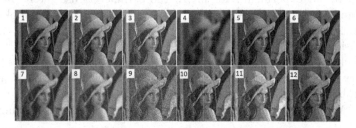

**Fig. 4.** Out-of-sample images with different types of distortions having MSE = 500: (1) stretching contrast, (2) Gaussian noise, (3) luminance enhancement, (4) Gaussian blurring, (5) impulse noise, (6) JPEG distortion, (7) Gaussian blurring + Gaussian noise, (8) Gaussian blurring + luminance enhancement, (9) impulse noise + luminance enhancement, (10) JPEG distortion + Gaussian noise, (11) JPEG distortion + luminance enhancement, and (12) JPEG distortion + stretching contrast.

nation of different distortions (see Fig. 4). We did the same 1NN classification for these images. Table 1 reports the top two votes of blocks for every image with the percentage of blocks voting for those distortions. ISCA did not recognize luminance enhancement well enough because, for Eq. (2), the block is centered while in kernel ISCA, the block is centered in feature space. Overall, both ISCA and kernel ISCA performed very compelling even in recognizing the combination of distortions.

**Table 1.** Recognition of distortions for out-of-sample images. Letters O, C, G, L, B, I, and J correspond to original image, contrast stretch, Gaussian noise, luminance enhanced, blurring, impulse noise, and JPEG distortion, respectively.

| Image | 1 | 2 | 3 | 4 | 5 | 6 | 7 | 8 | 9 | 10 | 11 | 12 |
|---|---|---|---|---|---|---|---|---|---|---|---|---|
| Distortion | C | G | L | B | I | J | B + G | B + L | I + L | J + G | J + L | J + C |
| ISCA | 69.3% O | 49.1% G | 69.7% O | 99.8% B | 30.3% G | 96.4% J | 55.2% B | 98.7% B | 48.9% G | 39.4% J | 96.4% J | 97.9% J |
|  | 30.2% C | 27.2% I | 29.6% C | 0.2% J | 23.8% I | 3.6% B | 19.9% G | 1.3% J | 33.3% I | 32.9% B | 3.6% B | 2.1% B |
| kernel ISCA (linear) | 88.1% C | 59.2% G | 99.8% L | 95.9% B | 37.4% G | 80.4% J | 40.8% G | 93.4% B | 45.6% I | 38.7% G | 70.2% L | 74.1% J |
|  | 11.2% I | 25.2% I | 0.1% O | 3.4% J | 32.3% I | 17.6% B | 33.4% B | 5.8% J | 39.4% G | 21.7% J | 27.0% B | 25.0% B |
| kernel ISCA (RBF) | 72.0% C | 79.1% G | 99.2% L | 70.6% B | 39.6% I | 74.3% J | 44.8% G | 88.1% L | 48.2% L | 33.1% G | 82.8% L | 43.1% J |
|  | 10.9% I | 5.0% B | 0.5% G | 13.1% C | 36.4% C | 13.5% C | 28.5% B | 6.6% B | 37.7% G | 21.6% L | 8.9% G | 30.0% B |
| kernel ISCA (sigmoid) | 80.3% C | 76.3% G | 99.6% L | 76.2% B | 38.5% I | 79.3% J | 47.9% G | 81.7% L | 52.1% L | 37.9% G | 80.7% L | 43.9% J |
|  | 7.6% I | 6.8% I | 0.2% G,B | 10.6% J | 36.5% C | 10.6% C | 24.6% B | 9.8% B | 26.6% G | 19.8% L | 11.3% G | 31.0% B |

**Reconstruction:** The images can be reconstructed after the projection onto the ISCA subspace. For reconstruction, every block is reconstructed as $U_i U_i^\top \breve{x}_i \in \mathbb{R}^q$ where the mean of block should be added to the reconstruction. Similar to kernel PCA, reconstruction cannot be done in kernel ISCA because $\Theta_i \Theta_i^\top k_i \in \mathbb{R}^n \neq \mathbb{R}^q$. Figure 5 shows reconstruction of some of training and out-of-sample images. As expected, the reconstructed images, for both training and out-of-sample images, are very similar to the original images.

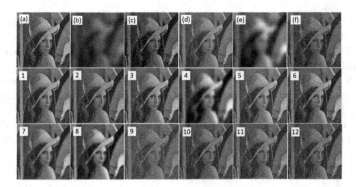

**Fig. 5.** Reconstruction of images in ISCA. Reconstruction of the training images (a), (b), and (c) are shown in (d), (e), and (f), respectively. The reconstruction of out-of-sample images shown in Fig. 4 are shown in the second and third rows.

# 7 Conclusion and Future Direction

This paper introduces the concept of an image structure subspace which captures the structure of an image and discriminates the distortion types. We hope this will open a broad new field for research in this area and build a greatly needed bridge between the worlds of image quality assessment and manifold learning.

For image structure subspace learning, ISCA and kernel ISCA were proposed, taking inspiration from PCA. As future work, we can consider designing deeper auto-encoder [13] with non-linear activation functions for image structure subspace learning.

# References

1. Wang, Z., Bovik, A.C.: Mean squared error: love it or leave it? A new look at signal fidelity measures. IEEE Sign. Proc. Mag. **26**(1), 98–117 (2009)
2. Wang, Z., Bovik, A.C., Sheikh, H.R., Simoncelli, E.P.: Image quality assessment: from error visibility to structural similarity. IEEE Trans. Image Process. **13**(4), 600–612 (2004)
3. Wang, Z., Bovik, A.C.: Modern image quality assessment. Synth. Lect. Image Video Multimedia Process. **2**(1), 1–156 (2006)
4. Brunet, D., Channappayya, S.S., Wang, Z., Vrscay, E.R., Bovik, A.C.: Optimizing image quality. In: Monga, V. (ed.) Handbook of Convex Optimization Methods in Imaging Science, pp. 15–41. Springer, Cham (2017). https://doi.org/10.1007/978-3-319-61609-4_2
5. Brunet, D., Vrscay, E.R., Wang, Z.: On the mathematical properties of the structural similarity index. IEEE Trans. Image Process. **21**(4), 1488–1499 (2012)
6. Otero, D., Vrscay, E.R.: Unconstrained structural similarity-based optimization. In: Campilho, A., Kamel, M. (eds.) ICIAR 2014. LNCS, vol. 8814, pp. 167–176. Springer, Cham (2014). https://doi.org/10.1007/978-3-319-11758-4_19
7. Brunet, D., Vrscay, E.R., Wang, Z.: A class of image metrics based on the structural similarity quality index. In: Kamel, M., Campilho, A. (eds.) ICIAR 2011. LNCS, vol. 6753, pp. 100–110. Springer, Heidelberg (2011). https://doi.org/10.1007/978-3-642-21593-3_11
8. Jolliffe, I.: Principal Component Analysis. Springer, New York (2002). https://doi.org/10.1007/b98835
9. Boyd, S., Vandenberghe, L.: Convex Optimization. Cambridge University Press, Cambridge (2004)
10. Boyd, S., Parikh, N., Chu, E., Peleato, B., Eckstein, J., et al.: Distributed optimization and statistical learning via the alternating direction method of multipliers. Found. Trends® Mach. Learn. **3**(1), 1–122 (2011)
11. Otero, D., Torre, D.L., Michailovich, O.V., Vrscay, E.R.: Alternate direction method of multipliers for unconstrained structural similarity-based optimization. In: Campilho, A., Karray, F., ter Haar Romeny, B. (eds.) ICIAR 2018. LNCS, vol. 10882, pp. 20–29. Springer, Cham (2018). https://doi.org/10.1007/978-3-319-93000-8_3
12. Parikh, N., Boyd, S.: Proximal algorithms. Found. Trends® Optim. **1**(3), 127–239 (2014)
13. Goodfellow, I., Bengio, Y., Courville, A.: Deep Learning, vol. 1. MIT Press, Cambridge (2016)
14. Hofmann, T., Schölkopf, B., Smola, A.J.: Kernel methods in machine learning. Ann. Stat. **36**(3), 1171–1220 (2008)
15. Ah-Pine, J.: Normalized Kernels as similarity indices. In: Zaki, M.J., Yu, J.X., Ravindran, B., Pudi, V. (eds.) PAKDD 2010. LNCS (LNAI), vol. 6119, pp. 362–373. Springer, Heidelberg (2010). https://doi.org/10.1007/978-3-642-13672-6_36
16. Alperin, J.L.: Local Representation Theory: Modular Representations as an Introduction to the Local Representation Theory of Finite Groups, vol. 11. Cambridge University Press, Cambridge (1993)

# Blind Quality Assessment of Multiply Distorted Images Using Deep Neural Networks

Zhongling Wang⬤, Shahrukh Athar$^{(\boxtimes)}$⬤, and Zhou Wang

Department of Electrical and Computer Engineering, University of Waterloo,
Waterloo, ON N2L 3G1, Canada
{zhongling.wang,shahrukh.athar,zhou.wang}@uwaterloo.ca

**Abstract.** In real-world visual content acquisition and distribution systems, a vast majority of visual content undergoes multiple distortions between the source and the end user. However, traditional image quality assessment (IQA) algorithms are usually validated and at times trained on image databases with a single distortion stage. Existing IQA methods for multiply distorted images remain limited in their scope and performance. In this work we design a first-of-its-kind blind IQA model for multiply distorted visual content based on a deep end-to-end convolutional neural network. The network is trained on a newly developed dataset which is composed of millions of multiply distorted images annotated with synthetic quality scores. Our tests on three publicly available subject-rated multiply distorted image databases show that the proposed model outperforms state-of-the-art blind IQA methods in terms of both accuracy and speed.

**Keywords:** Blind image quality assessment ·
Multiply distorted images · Convolutional Neural Networks (CNN) ·
Deep learning · Generalized Divisive Normalization (GDN) ·
Performance evaluation

## 1 Introduction

The goal of objective Image Quality Assessment (IQA) is to predict the visual quality of images as perceived by humans. While simple error-based methods such as the Peak Signal-to-Noise-Ratio (PSNR) were the methods of choice in the past, it has been comprehensively shown to be poorly aligned with human perception of visual quality [1]. Significant strides have been made in the last two decades in designing perceptual quality methods and three major frameworks are now well-established in IQA research [2]: (1) Full-Reference (FR) IQA, (2) Reduced Reference (RR) IQA, and (3) No Reference (NR) or Blind IQA. To evaluate the quality of a distorted image, FR IQA methods require the complete

This work is supported in part by the Natural Sciences and Engineering Research Council of Canada

F. Karray et al. (Eds.): ICIAR 2019, LNCS 11662, pp. 89–101, 2019.
https://doi.org/10.1007/978-3-030-27202-9_8

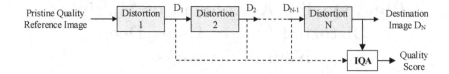

Fig. 1. The framework of a practical media distribution system.

availability of a pristine quality reference image, while RR IQA methods require access to certain features that have been extracted from the reference image. On the other hand, NR IQA methods evaluate the quality of the distorted image in the absence of the reference image. The performance of IQA methods is usually tested on subject rated image databases such as LIVE Release 2 [3,4], TID2008 [5], TID2013 [6], CSIQ [7], VCLFER [8], and CIDIQ [9]. Training for machine learning based IQA methods is also typically done on these databases.

Notwithstanding the significant progress made thus far in perceptual IQA research, the following challenges need to be addressed: (1) Although IQA methods are designed to handle different types of distortions, they are typically designed for images that have undergone a single stage of distortion, that is, they can handle one distortion at a time. This is in contrast to real world media delivery chains where the same visual content can undergo a number of distortions before reaching the end user, as depicted in Fig. 1. Designing IQA methods to deal with simultaneous distortions is quite challenging since the interactions of different distortions need to be accounted for. Thus, IQA for images with multiple simultaneous distortions has been a major challenge that future IQA research needs to address [10]. (2) In practical media delivery systems, access to pristine reference images is either extremely rare or altogether nonexistent, especially at the end user level. This, coupled with the multiple distortion nature of such systems, makes the use of FR and RR IQA infeasible. (3) One way to address the first two challenges is to use NR IQA. However, most NR methods are trained and tested on subject rated databases mentioned earlier, which have images with a single stage of distortion. Although there have been recent advances in the design of NR IQA methods to handle multiply distorted images using some new databases (as will be described later), such progress remains limited in scope. (4) The design of machine learning based IQA methods requires large-scale annotated image databases. However, subject-rated IQA databases, particularly for multiply distorted images remain quite limited, making it difficult to avoid model overfitting or to analyze interactions across distortions. These challenges motivate us to develop an end-to-end deep neural network (DNN) based NR or blind IQA model trained from synthetic scores.

## 2   Related Work

The first IQA database specifically designed for images with multiple simultaneous distortions (multiply distorted images), is the LIVE Multiply Distorted (MD) database [11]. Starting with 15 reference images, LIVE MD has 450 images divided into two parts, one each for the multiple distortion combinations of

(1) Gaussian blur followed by JPEG compression and (2) Gaussian blur followed by Gaussian noise. The MDID2013 database [12] has 12 reference images and one distortion combination of Gaussian blur followed by JPEG compression followed by white noise contamination. Overall, MDID2013 has 324 distorted images. The MDID database [13] has 20 reference images and 1600 multiply distorted images, where distortions are introduced first by adding Gaussian blur and contrast change, then JPEG or JPEG2000 compression, and finally Gaussian noise. The intensity of each distortion type is randomly selected and thus, MDID images may be distorted from 1 to 4 distortions. The MDIVL database [14] is composed of 10 reference images and 750 distorted images which are divided into two parts of (1) Gaussian blur followed by JPEG compression and (2) Gaussian noise followed by JPEG compression. Two databases composed of authentically distorted images, where distortions are not artificially added but captured in real-world environments, have recently been published. The CID2013 database [15] is composed of 480 photographs captured by 79 different cameras of varying quality. The LIVE in the Wild Image Quality Challenge (WC) database [16] is composed of 1162 photographs taken by a diverse set of mobile device cameras.

Recently some blind IQA methods for multiply distorted images have been proposed. SISBLIM [12] is a training-free metric designed for singly and multiply distorted images through the fusion of estimates of noise, blur, JPEG compression, and joint effects. BoWSF [17] selects features sensitive to different distortion types, which are encoded through a Bag-of-Words model and mapped to a quality score. LQAF [18] uses Support Vector Regression (SVR) to map features such as phase congruency, gradient magnitude, gray level gradient co-occurrence matrix and the contrast sensitivity function to quality scores. An enhanced and multi-scale version of LQAF, called MS-LQAF is proposed in [19]. The training-based GWHGLBP [20] uses the gradient-weighted histogram of the local binary pattern (LBP) generated on the gradient map of the distorted image to capture the effects of multiple distortions. Jet-LBP [21] uses color Gaussian jets to generate feature maps from a distorted image. The LBP is applied to these feature maps to ascertain the effect of multiple distortions, leading to a weighted histogram which is mapped to quality scores through SVR. MUSIQUE [22] handles multiply distorted images and operates by performing distortion identification followed by distortion parameter estimation and score generation.

A major challenge in building Convolutional Neural Networks (CNN) for blind IQA is the lack of large-scale subject-rated data for training. Data augmentation by simple geometric transformations is widely used [23–25], though the content variation is still limited by the original training samples and the perceptual quality degradation due to these transformations is ignored. Cropping fixed size small patches from the original image is another popular way to increase training samples, but assigning the subjective quality score of the entire image to all individual patches may introduce significant label noise. The CNN employed in [26] contains 10 convolutional layers and 2 fully connected layers to estimate the quality of $32 \times 32$ image patches. Patch weight estimation was incorporated before score pooling in order to reduce label noise. In [27] the weights of patches were predicted based on Prewitt magnitude of segmentation of an image. In BIECON [24], an FR IQA model was used to derive local scores of $32 \times 32$ patches and then a CNN was pre-trained using these patches with corresponding FR scores. The model was then fine-tuned on a subject-rated dataset. Several models [23, 25, 28–30] alleviate the label noise problem by utilizing larger patches. As a consequence the number of training patches is reduced.

An early CNN-based blind IQA model IQA-CNN [31] was composed of a single convolutional layer with two fully connected layers. Quality scores of $32 \times 32$ image patches were predicted and then averaged to obtain the final result. This model was further extended to IQA-CNN++ [32] which has deeper networks and trained a multi-task CNN by predicting quality and distortion type simultaneously. Fu et al. [33] developed a CNN-based blind IQA model using a different pooling strategy along with a higher number of features compared to [31]. Distortion type information was incorporated in MEON [23], where the distortion classification sub-network was pre-trained without access to subject-rated data, for which a large amount of data is available for training. The quality prediction sub-network of MEON incorporated the distortion type information derived from the first sub-network. The two sub-networks were finally joint optimized on subject-rated datasets. Apart from end-to-end learning methods, some models [29, 30, 34] utilized SVR to predict the quality score based on CNN features. Instead of predicting a single quality score, some models [25, 28] predict the quality distribution of a given image using CNNs. Talebi et al. [25] approximated the score distribution through maximum entropy optimization. Zeng et al. [28] handle this problem by mapping the score to a series of vectorized probability quality representations defined by quality anchors.

A critical problem of the aforementioned learning-based methods including CNN-based models is that they are trained on datasets like LIVE Release 2 [3, 4], LIVE MD [11], LIVE WC [16], CSIQ [7], TID2008 [5] and TID2013 [6], which only have a limited number of subject-rated images. Multi-task learning (such as MEON [23]) and data augmentation only partially mitigate the problem. The lack of training data often leads to overfitting of these models and makes them hard to generalize to new data on which they are not trained. The ultimate goal of a *blind* IQA metric is to be robust to unseen data.

## 3 Proposed Model

We propose a CNN based approach to build a blind IQA model for multiply distorted images, namely End-to-end Optimized deep neural Network using Synthetic Scores (EONSS). EONSS addresses the following design issues: (1) The complex interactions between multiple distortions are learned through the deep CNN of perceptually motivated activation function; (2) a large-scale database of diverse content type and distortion variation is created. Such a database, together with a dedicated synthetic score generation approach, is employed to train the CNN, as opposed to earlier machine learning based methods that used very limited data for training; (3) the trained model operates in a fast manner, suited for practical time-critical applications.

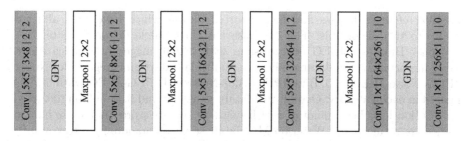

**Fig. 2.** The architecture of the proposed EONSS network. The format of the notation of the convolution layer is (*Conv | kernel width × kernel height | input channel × output channel | stride | padding*).

The network takes a 235 × 235 RGB image patch as input and predicts its quality. 235 × 235 patches contain more visually meaningful content than small patches and can represent the whole image better, therefore alleviating the issue of label noise. However, due to the limited training images in the classic IQA datasets (mentioned earlier), the number of training patches for many models decrease dramatically when larger patch size is utilized. Our model does not suffer from this issue since the number of training images in our dataset is sufficiently large (described later). We illustrate the architecture of the network in Fig. 2. The network consists of 6 stages of processing. Each of the first 4 stages contains a convolutional, generalized divisive normalization (GDN) [35] and max-pooling layer. These 4 stages aim at mapping the 235 × 235 × 3 raw pixels from the image space to a lower-dimensional feature space where perceptually aware image distortions can be quantified more easily. The network reduces the spatial dimension through the use of convolution with stride 2 × 2 in the first 4 stages. 2 × 2 max-pooling is also used after each GDN layers in the first 4 stages to select the neurons that have the highest local response. Finally, the last 2 stages, which consist of 2 fully connected layers and a GDN transform layer in between, map the extracted features to a single quality score. The spatial size of features is reduced to 1 × 1 before they are sent into the last 2 fully connected layers so that the number of weights in the fully connected layers are dramatically reduced. We apply GDN [35] instead of ReLU [36] after the convolution layers in the first 5 stages as the activation function to add non-linearity to the model. Although ReLU [36] is widely used as the activation function in CNNs, it suffers from strong higher-order dependencies, which is often compromised with a much larger network. Here we utilized a bio-inspired normalization transform, GDN, as the activation function. It helps decorrelate the high-dimensional features by using a joint nonlinear gain control mechanism. As a result a much smaller network is needed in order to achieve competitive performance.

The new Waterloo Multiply Distorted (Waterloo MD) IQA database has been used to learn the EONSS model. The construction of this database is beyond the focus of this work and will be covered in detail in our other publications. Suffice it to say that the Waterloo MD database is composed of 3570 pristine reference images and has distorted images which have been afflicted by up to two distortions. The database has three single distortion categories of Noise, Blur and JPEG compression, with 39270 images in each category. More importantly, the database has five multiple distortion categories of Noise-JPEG, Noise-JPEG2000, Blur-JPEG, Blur-Noise and JPEG-JPEG, with 667590 images in each category. Overall the database has around 3.45 million distorted images that have been annotated with synthetic quality scores in place of human subjective ratings. The Waterloo MD database is split randomly into training, validation and testing sets without overlapping image content of size 60%, 20% and 20%, respectively. Since the input dimension of the network is fixed to $235 \times 235 \times 3$, in the training phase, for the sake of time efficiency, we randomly sample one $235 \times 235$ patch from each image if its dimensions are larger. Since our dataset is large, this does not hinder us from creating a sufficiently large training set. In addition, by doing this, we obtain a batch of image patches of greater diversity and therefore significantly increase the time efficiency and prevent overfitting. The image quality of the sampled patch is considered to be the same as the original image during training since the $235 \times 235$ patch size can cover a relatively large area of the original image and therefore is able to contain perceptually meaningful content. In the validation and testing phases, for images with larger dimensions, we sample $235 \times 235$ patches from the original image with a stride of $128 \times 128$ in an overlapping manner. The average of the predicted quality scores of these patches is computed as the predicted quality of the original image.

We follow the approach in [37] to initialize the weights of the convolution layers. Adam [38] is used for optimization. The training batch size is chosen to be 50 and the image patches in each batch are randomly sampled from the training set only. The initial learning rate is set to 0.001 and is decreased by a factor of 10 after every 2 epochs. Other parameters of Adam are set as default. We test the model performance (PLCC and SRCC) on the validation set after each epoch and stop training after 10 epochs when the performance on the validation set reaches a plateau. Finally, the model after 10 epochs of training is applied to the testing set.

## 4 Experimental Results

In addition to evaluating the performance of EONSS on the test set of the new Waterloo MD database, we tested its performance on three publicly available multiply distorted image databases: MDID [13], LIVE MD [11] and MDIVL [14]. It is pertinent to mention here that these three databases were not used in the training and validation process of EONSS, and their ground truths are the mean opinion scores (MOSs) obtained from subjective testing rather than synthetic scores. To compare how EONSS performs against other IQA methods, we also tested the performance of 15 publicly available blind IQA methods. These include two methods designed for multiply distorted images, GWHGLBP [20] and SISBLIM [12], and two methods designed by using CNNs, DeepIQA [26] and

**Table 1.** Performance comparison of IQA algorithms. FR methods are in bold.

| Metric | Part 1: SRCC | | | | Part 2: PLCC | | | |
|---|---|---|---|---|---|---|---|---|
| | MDID | LIVE MD | MDIVL | Weighted Average | MDID | LIVE MD | MDIVL | Weighted Average |
| **IWSSIM** | 0.8911 | 0.8836 | 0.8588 | 0.8812 | 0.8983 | 0.9109 | 0.9056 | 0.9023 |
| EONSS | 0.8297 | 0.7260 | 0.8833 | 0.8274 | 0.8179 | 0.8437 | 0.8744 | 0.8372 |
| CORNIA | 0.7918 | 0.8340 | 0.8336 | 0.8098 | 0.7907 | 0.8679 | 0.8277 | 0.8130 |
| GWHGLBP | 0.7032 | 0.9698 | 0.5841 | 0.7141 | 0.7035 | 0.9663 | 0.5737 | 0.7110 |
| ILNIQE | 0.6900 | 0.8778 | 0.6238 | 0.7025 | 0.7053 | 0.8923 | 0.6303 | 0.7153 |
| dipIQ | 0.6612 | 0.6678 | 0.7131 | 0.6762 | 0.6738 | 0.7669 | 0.7627 | 0.7126 |
| HOSA | 0.6412 | 0.6393 | 0.7399 | 0.6673 | 0.6521 | 0.6768 | 0.7167 | 0.6734 |
| SISBLIM | 0.6554 | 0.8770 | 0.5375 | 0.6594 | 0.6700 | 0.8948 | 0.5724 | 0.6800 |
| NIQE | 0.6523 | 0.7738 | 0.5713 | 0.6501 | 0.6728 | 0.8387 | 0.5688 | 0.6716 |
| **PSNR** | 0.5784 | 0.6771 | 0.6136 | 0.6037 | 0.6091 | 0.7398 | 0.6806 | 0.6493 |
| BIQI | 0.6276 | 0.5556 | 0.5711 | 0.6009 | 0.6372 | 0.7389 | 0.6215 | 0.6493 |
| NRSL | 0.6458 | 0.4145 | 0.6047 | 0.5976 | 0.6502 | 0.4829 | 0.6794 | 0.6311 |
| BRISQUE | 0.4035 | 0.5018 | 0.6647 | 0.4893 | 0.4558 | 0.6045 | 0.6516 | 0.5321 |
| MEON | 0.4861 | 0.1917 | 0.5466 | 0.4550 | 0.5168 | 0.2339 | 0.5722 | 0.4862 |
| DeepIQA[a] | 0.4040 | 0.2379 | 0.5614 | 0.4195 | 0.4215 | 0.2897 | 0.5213 | 0.4271 |
| QAC | 0.3239 | 0.3579 | 0.5524 | 0.3906 | 0.6043 | 0.4145 | 0.5713 | 0.5650 |
| LPSI | 0.0306 | 0.2717 | 0.5736 | 0.2148 | 0.4336 | 0.5464 | 0.5715 | 0.4887 |
| GMLOG | 0.0546 | 0.1841 | 0.2656 | 0.1319 | 0.2626 | 0.3087 | 0.3830 | 0.3023 |

[a] Of the four NR models provided by the authors, the weighted model trained on LIVE Release 2 was used.

MEON [23]. The following state-of-the-art blind IQA methods were also tested for comparison: BIQI [39], BRISQUE [40], CORNIA [41], dipIQ [42], GMLOG [43], HOSA [44], ILNIQE [45], LPSI [46], NIQE [47], NRSL [48], and QAC [49]. The performance of two FR IQA methods, PSNR and the state-of-the-art IWS-SIM [50] was also evaluated to provide a FR reference point. Two performance evaluation criteria were used: Spearman Rank Correlation Coefficient (SRCC) to assess prediction monotonicity and Pearson Linear Correlation Coefficient (PLCC) to assess prediction accuracy [51]. A five-parameter logistic function [4] was used to perform non-linear mapping of objective scores to MOS/DMOS of respective databases before the computation of PLCC. A better objective method should have higher SRCC and PLCC values, ideally close to 1. Parts 1 and 2 of Table 1 respectively show the SRCC and PLCC of all tested methods for all three databases. To provide an overall comparison, weighted average SRCC and PLCC have been provided in Table 1 based on the number of images in the databases and methods in the table have been listed in descending order with respect to the weighted average SRCC numbers.

**Table 2.** Statistical Significance Testing results for competing IQA models [Database Order: MDID, LIVE MD, MDIVL]. Legend: IWSSIM (m1), EONSS (m2), CORNIA (m3), ILNIQE (m4), dipIQ (m5), GWHGLBP (m6), SISBLIM (m7), HOSA (m8), NIQE (m9), PSNR (m10), BIQI (m11), NRSL (m12), QAC (m13), BRISQUE (m14), LPSI (m15), MEON (m16), DeepIQA (m17), GMLOG (m18).

|     | m1 | m2 | m3 | m4 | m5 | m6 | m7 | m8 | m9 | m10 | m11 | m12 | m13 | m14 | m15 | m16 | m17 | m18 |
|-----|----|----|----|----|----|----|----|----|----|-----|-----|-----|-----|-----|-----|-----|-----|-----|
| m1  | ___ | 111 | 111 | 111 | 111 | 101 | 111 | 111 | 111 | 111 | 111 | 111 | 111 | 111 | 111 | 111 | 111 | 111 |
| m2  | 000 | ___ | 101 | 101 | 111 | 101 | 101 | 111 | 1_1 | 111 | 111 | 111 | 111 | 111 | 111 | 111 | 111 | 111 |
| m3  | 000 | 010 | ___ | 101 | 111 | 101 | 101 | 111 | 111 | 111 | 111 | 111 | 111 | 111 | 111 | 111 | 111 | 111 |
| m4  | 000 | 010 | 010 | ___ | 110 | _0_ | 1__ | 110 | 11_ | 11_ | 11_ | 11_ | 11_ | 11_ | 11_ | 11_ | 111 | 111 |
| m5  | 000 | 000 | 000 | 001 | ___ | _01 | _01 | _11 | _01 | 1_1 | 1_1 | _11 | 111 | 111 | 111 | 111 | 111 | 111 |
| m6  | 010 | 010 | 010 | _1_ | _10 | ___ | 11_ | 110 | _1_ | 110 | 11_ | 110 | 11_ | 110 | 11_ | 11_ | 11_ | 111 |
| m7  | 000 | 010 | 010 | 0__ | _10 | 00_ | ___ | _10 | _1_ | 110 | _1_ | _10 | 11_ | 110 | 11_ | 11_ | 11_ | 111 |
| m8  | 000 | 000 | 000 | 001 | _00 | 001 | _01 | ___ | _01 | 10_ | _01 | _1_ | 111 | 111 | 111 | 111 | 111 | 111 |
| m9  | 000 | 0_0 | 000 | 00_ | _10 | _0_ | _0_ | _10 | ___ | 110 | _1_ | _10 | 11_ | 110 | 11_ | 11_ | 11_ | 111 |
| m10 | 000 | 000 | 000 | 00_ | 0_0 | 001 | 001 | 01_ | 001 | ___ | __1 | 01_ | _11 | 11_ | 111 | 111 | 111 | 111 |
| m11 | 000 | 000 | 000 | 00_ | 0_0 | 00_ | _0_ | _10 | _0_ | __0 | ___ | _10 | _1_ | 11_ | 11_ | 11_ | 111 | 111 |
| m12 | 000 | 000 | 000 | 00_ | _00 | 001 | _01 | _0_ | _01 | 10_ | _01 | ___ | 1_1 | 10_ | 1_1 | 111 | 111 | 111 |
| m13 | 000 | 000 | 000 | 00_ | 000 | 00_ | 00_ | 000 | 00_ | _00 | _0_ | 0_0 | ___ | 100 | 10_ | 1__ | 1__ | 1_1 |
| m14 | 000 | 000 | 000 | 00_ | 000 | 001 | 001 | 000 | 001 | 00_ | 00_ | 01_ | 011 | ___ | __1 | _11 | _11 | 111 |
| m15 | 000 | 000 | 000 | 00_ | 000 | 00_ | 00_ | 000 | 00_ | 000 | 00_ | 0_0 | 01_ | __0 | ___ | 01_ | _1_ | 111 |
| m16 | 000 | 000 | 000 | 00_ | 000 | 00_ | 00_ | 000 | 00_ | 000 | 00_ | 000 | 0__ | _00 | 10_ | ___ | 1__ | 1_1 |
| m17 | 000 | 000 | 000 | 000 | 000 | 00_ | 00_ | 000 | 00_ | 000 | 000 | 000 | 0__ | _00 | _0_ | 0__ | ___ | 1_1 |
| m18 | 000 | 000 | 000 | 000 | 000 | 000 | 000 | 000 | 000 | 000 | 000 | 000 | 0_0 | 000 | 000 | 0-0 | 0-0 | ___ |

To draw statistically sound inferences about the performance of IQA methods, we carried out hypothesis testing on model prediction residuals (after nonlinear mapping). First, a simple Kurtosis-based criterion was used to check for Gaussianity of residuals as in [4]. All model prediction residuals had a Kurtosis between 2 and 4, with the exception of GMLOG residuals on MDID database, and were assumed to be Gaussian. This allowed us to compare the model residuals through statistical significance testing by using the $F$-test [52]. The results are shown in Table 2, where "1", "_", or "0" mean that the method in the row is statistically better, indistinguishable, or worse, than the method in the column respectively, with 95% confidence. Each table entry has three digits, which represent testing on the MDID, LIVE MD and MDIVL databases, respectively.

From Tables 1 and 2 the following observations can be made: (1) EONSS performs better than all other blind IQA methods and the FR PSNR on the MDID and MDIVL databases. On LIVE MD, EONSS is statistically outperformed only by CORNIA, GWHGLBP, ILNIQE and SISBLIM, though it needs to be mentioned that GWHGLBP was trained on this very database. (2) Of all the blind

**Table 3.** IQA method execution time.

| Metric | Processing Unit | Execution Time (Seconds) | Execution Time Relative to PSNR |
|---|---|---|---|
| PSNR | CPU | 0.0013 | 1.00 |
| LPSI | CPU | 0.0397 | 30.54 |
| EONSS | GPU | 0.0604 | 46.46 |
| EONSS | CPU | 0.0817 | 62.85 |
| MEON | CPU | 0.0819 | 63.00 |
| MEON | GPU | 0.0876 | 67.38 |
| GMLOG | CPU | 0.1044 | 80.31 |
| HOSA | CPU | 0.1309 | 100.69 |
| QAC | CPU | 0.1357 | 104.38 |
| NRSL[a] | CPU | 0.1421 | 109.31 |
| GWHGLBP[a] | CPU | 0.1469 | 113.00 |
| DeepIQA | GPU | 0.1549 | 119.15 |
| BRISQUE | CPU | 0.1823 | 140.23 |
| NIQE | CPU | 0.2941 | 226.23 |
| BIQI | CPU | 0.4634 | 356.46 |
| IWSSIM | CPU | 0.6067 | 466.69 |
| dipIQ | CPU | 1.6592 | 1276.31 |
| CORNIA | CPU | 2.0304 | 1561.85 |
| SISBLIM | CPU | 2.2005 | 1692.69 |
| ILNIQE | CPU | 2.5227 | 1940.54 |
| DeepIQA | CPU | 6.2818 | 4832.15 |

[a]Feature extraction time only.

IQA methods under test, EONSS and CORNIA are the only robust metrics since they perform consistently well on all three databases (PLCC greater than or close to 0.8). While methods such as SISBLIM, ILNIQE, NIQE, and dipIQ perform well on one database, their performance drops on other databases. (3) Although CORNIA was originally designed by using images with a single distortion, its performance extends well for multiply distorted images. (4) The performance of all blind IQA methods is still a distance away from state-of-the-art FR IQA method IWSSIM, suggesting space for improvement. (5) The computational complexity of all IQA methods under test was evaluated in terms of their execution time to determine the quality of a 1024 × 1024 color image on a desktop computer with a 3.5 GHz Intel Core i7-7800X processor, 16 GB of RAM, NVIDIA GeForce GTX 1050Ti GPU, and Ubuntu 18.04 operating system. The execution time relative to PSNR is given in Table 3, where metrics have been sorted in ascending order with respect to execution time. It appears that EONSS is around twenty or more times faster than competitive methods such as dipIQ, CORNIA, SISBLIM and ILNIQE, making it an excellent choice for practical applications.

## 5  Conclusion

We propose a new deep learning based blind IQA model called EONSS. Compared to other CNN-based models, such as DeepIQA [26] and MEON [23], EONSS uses a much simpler network architecture, but delivers superior performance with fairly low computational cost. The success of EONSS is partially due to its architecture design and its adoption of the perceptually motivated GDN as the activation function, and is also attributed to the Waterloo MD training database, which consists of millions of multiply distorted images whose quality has been synthetically annotated. The enormity and content-diversity of this database has provided sufficient data to the DNN to learn an adequate end-to-end blind IQA model. Since EONSS has been tested on publicly available subject-rated databases which were not part of the training and validation process, its superior performance has also validated the novel methodology of using large-scale synthetically annotated databases for learning new IQA models, providing a new perspective on how to resolve the longstanding problem of the lack of large-scale datasets in IQA research. Detailed account about the construction of the Waterloo MD database will be made available to the IQA community. The trained version of the EONSS model will also be made publicly available to facilitate reproducible research.

## References

1. Wang, Z., Bovik, A.C.: Mean squared error: love it or leave it? A new look at signal fidelity measures. IEEE Signal Process. Mag. **26**(1), 98–117 (2009)
2. Wang, Z., Bovik, A.C.: Modern image quality assessment. Synth. Lect. Image Video Multimedia Process. **2**(1), 1–156 (2006)
3. Sheikh, H.R., Wang, Z., Cormack, L., Bovik, A.C.: LIVE Image Quality Assessment Database Release 2. http://live.ece.utexas.edu/research/Quality/subjective.htm
4. Sheikh, H.R., Sabir, M.F., Bovik, A.C.: A statistical evaluation of recent full reference image quality assessment algorithms. IEEE Trans. Image Process. **15**(11), 3440–3451 (2006)
5. Ponomarenko, N., et al.: TID2008-a database for evaluation of full-reference visual quality assessment metrics. Adv. Modern Radioelectron. **10**(4), 30–45 (2009)
6. Ponomarenko, N., et al.: Image database TID2013: peculiarities, results and perspectives. Signal Process Image Commun. **30**, 57–77 (2015)
7. Larson, E.C., Chandler, D.M.: Most apparent distortion: full-reference image quality assessment and the role of strategy. J. Electron. Imag. **19**(1), 011 006:1–011 006:21 (2010)
8. Zarić, A., et al.: VCL@FER image quality assessment database. AUTOMATIKA **53**(4), 344–354 (2012)
9. Liu, X., Pedersen, M., Hardeberg, J.Y.: CID:IQ – a new image quality database. In: Elmoataz, A., Lezoray, O., Nouboud, F., Mammass, D. (eds.) ICISP 2014. LNCS, vol. 8509, pp. 193–202. Springer, Cham (2014). https://doi.org/10.1007/978-3-319-07998-1_22

10. Chandler, D.M.: Seven challenges in image quality assessment: past, present, and future research. ISRN Signal Process. **2013**, 1–53 (2013). Article ID 905685

11. Jayaraman, D., Mittal, A., Moorthy, A.K., Bovik, A.C.: Objective quality assessment of multiply distorted images. In: Conference Record Asilomar Conference Signals, Systems, and Computers (ASILOMAR), Pacific Grove, CA, USA, pp. 1693–1697, November 2012

12. Gu, K., Zhai, G., Yang, X., Zhang, W.: Hybrid no-reference quality metric for singly and multiply distorted images. IEEE Trans. Broadcast. **60**(3), 555–567 (2014)

13. Sun, W., Zhou, F., Liao, Q.: MDID: a multiply distorted image database for image quality assessment. Pattern Recognit. **61**, 153–168 (2017)

14. Corchs, S., Gasparini, F.: A multidistortion database for image quality. In: Bianco, S., Schettini, R., Trémeau, A., Tominaga, S. (eds.) CCIW 2017. LNCS, vol. 10213, pp. 95–104. Springer, Cham (2017). https://doi.org/10.1007/978-3-319-56010-6_8

15. Virtanen, T., Nuutinen, M., Vaahteranoksa, M., Oittinen, P., Häkkinen, J.: CID2013: a database for evaluating no-reference image quality assessment algorithms. IEEE Trans. Image Process. **24**(1), 390–402 (2015)

16. Ghadiyaram, D., Bovik, A.C.: Massive online crowdsourced study of subjective and objective picture quality. IEEE Trans. Image Process. **25**(1), 372–387 (2016)

17. Lu, Y., Xie, F., Liu, T., Jiang, Z., Tao, D.: No reference quality assessment for multiply-distorted images based on an improved bag-of-words model. IEEE Signal Process. Lett. **22**(10), 1811–1815 (2015)

18. Li, C., Zhang, Y., Wu, X., Fang, W., Mao, L.: Blind multiply distorted image quality assessment using relevant perceptual features. In: Proceedings of IEEE International Conference on Image Processing (ICIP), Quebec City, QC, Canada, pp. 4883–4886, September 2015

19. Li, C., Zhang, Y., Wu, X., Zheng, Y.: A multi-scale learning local phase and amplitude blind image quality assessment for multiply distorted images. IEEE Access **6**, 64 577–64 586 (2018)

20. Li, Q., Lin, W., Fang, Y.: No-reference quality assessment for multiply-distorted images in gradient domain. IEEE Signal Process. Lett. **23**(4), 541–545 (2016)

21. Hadizadeh, H., Bajić, I.V.: Color Gaussian jet features for no-reference quality assessment of multiply-distorted images. IEEE Signal Process. Lett. **23**(12), 1717–1721 (2016)

22. Zhang, Y., Chandler, D.M.: Opinion-unaware blind quality assessment of multiply and singly distorted images via distortion parameter estimation. IEEE Trans. Image Process. **27**(11), 5433–5448 (2018)

23. Ma, K., Liu, W., Zhang, K., Duanmu, Z., Wang, Z., Zuo, W.: End-to-end blind image quality assessment using deep neural networks. IEEE Trans. Image Process. **27**(3), 1202–1213 (2018)

24. Kim, J., Lee, S.: Fully deep blind image quality predictor. IEEE J. Sel. Topics Signal Process. **11**(1), 206–220 (2017)

25. Talebi, H., Milanfar, P.: NIMA: neural image assessment. IEEE Trans. Image Process. **27**(8), 3998–4011 (2018)

26. Bosse, S., Maniry, D., Müller, K., Wiegand, T., Samek, W.: Deep neural networks for no-reference and full-reference image quality assessment. IEEE Trans. Image Process. **27**(1), 206–219 (2018)

27. Li, J., Zou, L., Yan, J., Deng, D., Qu, T., Xie, G.: No-reference image quality assessment using Prewitt magnitude based on convolutional neural networks. Signal Image Video Process. (SIViP) **10**(4), 609–616 (2016)

28. Zeng, H., Zhang, L., Bovik, A.C.: Blind image quality assessment with a proba-
    bilistic quality representation. In: Proceedings of IEEE International Conference
    on Image Processing (ICIP), Athens, Greece, pp. 609–613, October 2018
29. Gao, F., Yu, J., Zhu, S., Huang, Q., Tian, Q.: Blind image quality prediction by
    exploiting multi-level deep representations. Pattern Recognit. **81**, 432–442 (2018)
30. Bianco, S., Celona, L., Napoletano, P., Schettini, R.: On the use of deep learning
    for blind image quality assessment. Signal Image Video Process. (SIViP) **12**(2),
    355–362 (2018)
31. Kang, L., Ye, P., Li, Y., Doermann, D.: Convolutional neural networks for no-
    reference image quality assessment. In: Proceedings of IEEE Conference on Com-
    puter Vision and Pattern Recognition (CVPR), Columbus, OH, USA, pp. 1733–
    1740, June 2014
32. Kang, L., Ye, P., Li, Y., Doermann, D.: Simultaneous estimation of image quality
    and distortion via multi-task convolutional neural networks. In: Proceedings of
    IEEE International Conference on Image Processing (ICIP), Quebec City, QC,
    Canada, pp. 2791–2795, September 2015
33. Fu, J., Wang, H., Zuo, L.: Blind image quality assessment for multiply distorted
    images via convolutional neural networks. In: Proceedings of IEEE International
    Conference on Acoustics, Speech, Signal Processing (ICASSP), Shanghai, China,
    pp. 1075–1079, March 2016
34. Li, J., Yan, J., Deng, D., Shi, W., Deng, S.: No-reference image quality assessment
    based on hybrid model. Signal Image Video Process. (SIViP) **11**(6), 985–992 (2017)
35. Li, Q., Wang, Z.: Reduced-reference image quality assessment using divisive
    normalization-based image representation. IEEE J. Sel. Topics Signal Process.
    **3**(2), 202–211 (2009)
36. Nair, V., Hinton, G.E.: Rectified linear units improve restricted Boltzmann
    machines. In: Proceedings of International Conference on Machine Learning
    (ICML), Haifa, Israel, pp. 807–814, June 2010
37. He, K., Zhang, X., Ren, S., Sun, J.: Delving deep into rectifiers: surpassing human-
    level performance on ImageNet classification. In: IEEE International Conference
    on Computer Vision (ICCV), Santiago, Chile, pp. 1026–1034, December 2015
38. Kingma, D.P., Ba, J.L.: Adam: a method for stochastic optimization. In: Proceed-
    ings of International Conference on Learning Representations (ICLR), San Diego,
    CA, USA, May 2015
39. Moorthy, A.K., Bovik, A.C.: A two-step framework for constructing blind image
    quality indices. IEEE Signal Process. Lett. **17**(5), 513–516 (2010)
40. Mittal, A., Moorthy, A.K., Bovik, A.C.: No-reference image quality assessment in
    the spatial domain. IEEE Trans. Image Process. **21**(12), 4695–4708 (2012)
41. Ye, P., Kumar, J., Kang, L., Doermann, D.: Unsupervised feature learning frame-
    work for no-reference image quality assessment. In: Proceedings of IEEE Confer-
    ence on Computer Vision and Pattern Recognition (CVPR), Providence, RI, USA,
    pp. 1098–1105, June 2012
42. Ma, K., Liu, W., Liu, T., Wang, Z., Tao, D.: dipIQ: blind image quality assessment
    by learning-to-rank discriminable image pairs. IEEE Trans. Image Process. **26**(8),
    3951–3964 (2017)
43. Xue, W., Mou, X., Zhang, L., Bovik, A.C., Feng, X.: Blind image quality assessment
    using joint statistics of gradient magnitude and laplacian features. IEEE Trans.
    Image Process. **23**(11), 4850–4862 (2014)
44. Xu, J., Ye, P., Li, Q., Du, H., Liu, Y., Doermann, D.: Blind image quality assess-
    ment based on high order statistics aggregation. IEEE Trans. Image Process. **25**(9),
    4444–4457 (2016)

45. Zhang, L., Zhang, L., Bovik, A.C.: A feature-enriched completely blind image quality evaluator. IEEE Trans. Image Process. **24**(8), 2579–2591 (2015)
46. Wu, Q., Wang, Z., Li, H.: A highly efficient method for blind image quality assessment. In: Proceedings of IEEE International Conference on Image Processing (ICIP), Quebec City, QC, Canada, pp. 339–343, September 2015
47. Mittal, A., Soundararajan, R., Bovik, A.C.: Making a "Completely Blind" image quality analyzer. IEEE Signal Process. Lett. **20**(3), 209–212 (2013)
48. Li, Q., Lin, W., Xu, J., Fang, Y.: Blind image quality assessment using statistical structural and luminance features. IEEE Trans. Multimedia **18**(12), 2457–2469 (2016)
49. Xue, W., Zhang, L., Mou, X.: Learning without human scores for blind image quality assessment. In: Proceedings of IEEE Conference on Computer Vision and Pattern Recognition (CVPR), Portland, OR, USA, pp. 995–1002, June 2013
50. Wang, Z., Li, Q.: Information content weighting for perceptual image quality assessment. IEEE Trans. Image Process. **20**(5), 1185–1198 (2011)
51. Video Quality Experts Group and others, Final report from the Video Quality Experts Group on the validation of objective models of video quality assessment, Phase II (2003)
52. Sheskin, D.J.: Handbook of Parametric and Nonparametric Statistical Procedures. Chapman & Hall/CRC, Boca Raton (2011)

# Layered Embeddings for Amodal Instance Segmentation

Yanfeng Liu$^{(\boxtimes)}$ ⓘ, Eric T. Psota ⓘ, and Lance C. Pérez ⓘ

University of Nebraska-Lincoln, Lincoln, NE, USA
{yanfeng.liu,epsota,lperez}@unl.edu

**Abstract.** The proposed method extends upon the representational output of semantic instance segmentation by explicitly including both visible and occluded parts. A fully convolutional network is trained to produce consistent pixel-level embedding across two layers such that, when clustered, the results convey the full spatial extent and depth ordering of each instance. Results demonstrate that the network can accurately estimate complete masks in the presence of occlusion and outperform leading top-down bounding-box approaches. Source code available at https://github.com/yanfengliu/layered_embeddings.

**Keywords:** Semantic instance segmentation · Amodal segmentation · Pixel embedding · Occlusion recovery

## 1 Introduction

Instance segmentation extends semantic segmentation by distinguishing between objects of the same class. Instance segmentation methods assign a single instance label to visible pixels, thus each object's full spatial occupancy and depth ordering—two properties that humans instinctively estimate—are not represented in the output. In contrast, when occluded regions are taken into consideration, this is referred to as *amodal segmentation* [8].

To successfully segment occluded regions, the method not only needs to know where occlusions happen, but also the shape of unseen object parts relative to what is observed. If the objects are non-rigid, there can be multiple plausible solutions. On top of the inherent difficulty of the task, the lack of amodal ground truth makes it difficult to develop and evaluate new methods. Li and Malik [8] composited training data from PASCAL VOC 2012 [5] by overlaying foreground masks. However, the resulting images are unnatural, with unrealistic lighting and object scales. Ehsani et al. [4] introduced a synthetic dataset "DYCE" consisting of images rendered from various indoor graphics models at different angles. Zhu et al. [15] introduced the COCO Amodal dataset, consisting of thousands of amodal masks approximated by human annotators. They also provide baseline methods along with suggested performance metrics. Unfortunately, fundamental

© Springer Nature Switzerland AG 2019
F. Karray et al. (Eds.): ICIAR 2019, LNCS 11662, pp. 102–111, 2019.
https://doi.org/10.1007/978-3-030-27202-9_9

flaws in the data generation process (e.g., unrealistic renderings and inconsistent object labels and depth ordering), human errors (e.g., shadows inconsistently being labelled as instances of objects and synonyms/typos for classification labels), and an insufficient number of training images make it difficult to develop and analyze amodal segmentation methods.

We propose a fully-convolutional, end-to-end trainable approach that jointly estimates the presence of occlusion and provides consistent instance labeling across foreground and occluded regions. The method is evaluated on an easily configurable synthetic dataset consisting of various types of shapes with occlusions with precisely known amodal masks. Results demonstrate that the method is capable of accurately estimating layered spatial occupancy and outperforming a state-of-the-art top-down alternative.

## 2  Related Work

Because ground truth instance labels are permutation invariant, the common approach of training deep fully-convolutional networks (FCNs) to detect and segment objects faces the dilemma of an ambiguous target [10]. There are generally two categories of approaches used to achieve instance segmentation. Top-down methods begin by finding the regions (often bounding boxes) that contain each instance, and then performing pixel-wise segmentation of the dominant instance within that region. For example, Mask R-CNN [7] extends Faster R-CNN [11] by adding a branch for segmentation mask prediction in parallel with the other branches (bounding boxes and classification). Li et al. [9] proposed an alternative that uses location-sensitive fully convolutional networks to partition bounding boxes into $3 \times 3$ grids, and then evaluates the likelihood that each partition contains the correct part relative to the other partitions.

The second category, bottom-up methods, begin by assigning attributes to pixels and then clustering them into instances. Examples include those that use pixel embedding to move the high-level detection stage to the end of the process [3,6]. Fathi et al. [6] adopt this principle by training a network to evaluate pairwise pixel similarity. They train a separate model to generate seed points that represent the typicality of a pixel compared to other pixels in the area. Brabandere et al. [3] proposes a discriminative loss function to train pixel embeddings such that they are close within the same instance but far apart for different instances.

The above methods propose a surjective mapping from pixels to instances. However, it is worth considering if this is an optimal representation of semantic instance segmentation. Computer vision often aims to reverse-engineer scenes from images/video, and an assignment of all visible parts to a single membership is an incomplete descriptor. In contrast, the full segmentation masks and relative depth ordering prior to image projection provides a more complete descriptor.

To this end, Yang et al. [13,14] estimate layer ordering as part of instance segmentation and introduce a learned predictor based on relative detection scores, position on the ground plane, and size. They acknowledge the benefits of full spatial segmentations of visible and occluded parts, but their method focuses on the benefits of depth ordering for instance grouping. Chen et al. [2] attempt to fill occluded regions by selecting similar non-occluded exemplar templates from a library; this improves instance segmentation of visible pixels. Uhrig et al. [12] propose to consider explicit depth ordering estimation for instance segmentation. Their method exploits ground truth depth information, but it does not attempt to recover occluded segments. While each of these methods uses the concept of occlusions to improve instance segmentation, none of them explicitly targets the full spatial extents and depth ordering of instances.

Li and Malik [8] use an iterative approach to gradually predict the amodal masks based on the bounding box and classification produced by an object detector. They compute the visible mask and iteratively expand upon it to produce the amodal mask and bounding box. Ehsani et al. [4] propose a GAN-based model to produce both the segmentation and the appearance of the occluded regions, assuming that foreground segmentation is already pre-calculated by other methods. However, their method focuses on crops with one salient object.

Amodal segmentation remains as a challenging task and very few studies and datasets exist. Current methods either focus on a special case of the general problem or extend upon top-down approaches. This paper proposes an alternative bottom-up approach and examines some challenges associated with amodal segmentation.

## 3   Method

The goal of the proposed method is to produce full instance masks for each segmented object as long as part of the object is visible in the image. To circumvent the limitations of DYCE and COCO Amodal datasets, a synthetically generated dataset of shapes is used. The advantages of this set include (1) full control of scene complexity; (2) access to precise ground truth; and (3) rigid shapes where the ground truth is often unique given partial observations.

The dataset has three classes of shapes: triangles, rectangles, and circles. All shapes have a fixed size, but their locations, orientations, and depth orderings are randomized. Shapes have the same color as the background, only distinguished by their black outlines, so that the network cannot cheat by simply detecting color or intensity. This representation forces the network to rely on outlines and be aware of large regions for context.

For training and evaluation, the ground truth masks are arranged in the following manner: foreground semantic classification, occlusion semantic classification, foreground instance labels, and occlusion instance labels. See Fig. 1 for a sample of training data. The proposed method generates the following four outputs: (1) *foreground multi-class semantic segmentation*, that labels pixels as background, foreground, or occluded; (2) *occlusion multi-class semantic segmentation*, that labels occluded pixels as one of the classes; (3) *foreground embedding*, used to cluster foreground pixels into instances; (4) *occlusion embeddings*, that are consistent with visible instances. It is worth noting that occluded pixels are defined as those where one instance occludes another instance. While the method does not consider occlusions caused by background objects, this could trivially be added as another class to the output.

**Fig. 1.** Sample training data. From left to right: input image, foreground class mask, occlusion class mask, foreground instance mask, occlusion instance mask

To train instance embedding across both the foreground and occluded regions, the method uses a variation of the discriminative loss function introduced in [3]. Consider an input image $\mathcal{I}$ and a pair of embedding outputs $\mathcal{E}_f$ and $\mathcal{E}_o$ that contain embedding vectors for the foreground region and occluded region, respectively. The embedding outputs are matrices with the same spatial dimensions (rows and columns) as the input image, where the number of channels $C$ represents the dimensionality of each pixel's embedding. The goal of the network is to map each foreground pixel $p \in \mathcal{I}$ to a $C$-dimensional embedding vector $\mathcal{E}_f(p)$ and each occluded pixel $p \in \mathcal{I}$ to a $C$-dimensional embedding vector $\mathcal{E}_o(p)$ such that embedding vectors for pixels belonging to the same instance are close together in the $C$-dimensional space and embedding vectors for different instances are far apart.

The overall loss consists of three terms: variance $l_{var}$, distance $l_{dst}$, and regularization $l_{reg}$. Let $K$ be the total number of classes, $N_k$ be the number of instances of class $k$, $N$ be the number of ground truth instances and let $\mathcal{R}_f^n \subseteq \mathcal{I}$ and $\mathcal{R}_o^n \subseteq \mathcal{I}$ denote the set of foreground and occluded pixels for instance $n \in \{1, \ldots, N\}$, respectively. Also, let $\mu_n$ be the average embedding vector of all pixels in both the foreground and occlusion embeddings for instance $n$. The variance term and distance term are defined as

$$l_{var} = \frac{1}{N} \sum_{n=1}^{N} \frac{1}{|\mathcal{R}_f^n| + |\mathcal{R}_o^n|} \left( \sum_{p \in \mathcal{R}_f^n} \left[ ||\mu_n - \mathcal{E}_f(p)|| - d_{var} \right]_+^2 \right.$$
$$\left. + \sum_{p \in \mathcal{R}_o(n)} \left[ ||\mu_n - \mathcal{E}_o(p)|| - d_{var} \right]_+^2 \right) \tag{1}$$

and

$$l_{dst} = \sum_{k=1}^{K} \frac{1}{N_k(N_k - 1)} \sum_{n=1}^{N_k} \sum_{\substack{m=1 \\ m \neq n}}^{N_k} \left[ 2d_{dst} - ||\mu_n - \mu_m|| \right]_+^2, \tag{2}$$

where $[a]_+ = max(a, 0)$ is the hinge loss, and $|| \cdot ||$ is L1 distance. Constants $d_{var}$ and $d_{dst}$ are the margins for the variance and distance term. Effectively, $l_{var}$ penalizes pixels that belong to the same instance but are farther than $d_{var}$

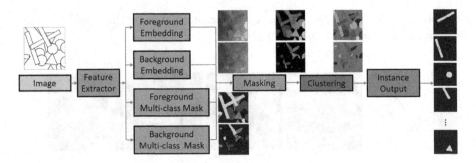

**Fig. 2.** Proposed segmentation architecture.

apart in the embedding space, and $l_{dst}$ penalizes cluster centers that represent different instances but are closer than $d_{dst}$. The regularization term

$$l_{reg} = \frac{1}{N} \sum_{n=1}^{N} ||\mu_n|| \tag{3}$$

prevents the network from minimizing $l_{dst}$ by simple embedding amplification. Finally, the network is trained to minimize $L_{total} = \alpha \cdot l_{var} + \beta \cdot l_{dst} + \gamma \cdot l_{reg}$. Figure 2 presents an example of the method applied to shapes.

The network uses a pre-trained feature extractor and produces a depth-concatenation of four outputs. The four modules share the output from the feature extractor. The method clusters the network's pixel embeddings into instances using the algorithm presented in [3]. A random unlabeled pixel is selected and the embeddings around it within $v_{var}$ are grouped together. The mean embedding of this group is used for the next round of grouping until convergence.

## 4    Implementation Details

The proposed method uses DeeplabV3+ [1] with an Xception backbone as the feature extractor. Its final upsampling and logit layers are removed and the 256-dimensional output is used as features. Input size is set to $256 \times 256$ and the output size is $64 \times 64$. For the loss function, $\alpha = \beta = \gamma = 1, d_{var} = 0.5, d_{dst} = 1.5$. Embedding dimension $C = 6$ and the mean shift threshold for clustering is 1.5, which is consistent with $d_{dst}$. The embedding module consists of 256, 256, 128, and $C$ convolution filters, with RELU activations.

For comparison, Mask R-CNN is selected as a representative model of top-down approaches for baseline due to the success and popularity of the R-CNN family among object detection and segmentation architectures. It is an architecture originally designed only for foreground instance segmentation, but it can be easily modified to perform amodal instance segmentation by fine-tuning on amodal ground truth. Its weights are pre-trained on MS COCO. Its output is

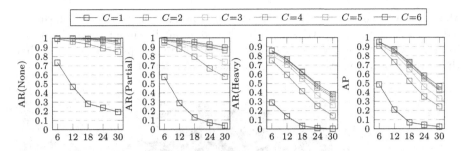

**Fig. 3.** Performance for different number of instances per class and different embedding dimensions $C$. x-axis is number of instances, y-axis is different metrics, and colored lines represent models with different $C$.

upsampled from the original $m \times m$ mask to the corresponding bounding box size and put in the context of the whole image. The final output is resized to $64 \times 64$ to be directly comparable with our method.

All models are trained for 100 epochs in Tensorflow with Adam optimization (learning rate = 0.0001 and batch size = 2). Training examples are generated at runtime with the same initial random seed. Each epoch has 1000 images.

## 5    Results

The embedding model and Mask R-CNN are both evaluated on 1000 shapes images randomly generated with 6 instances per class. Results in Table 1 show that our model outperforms Mask R-CNN on AP, $AP_{50}$, $AR_{None}$, and $AR_{Partial}$.

**Table 1.** Performance of models on 6 instances per class with different NMS threshold $t$ and different number of instances per class $N$

| $N$ | Model | AP | $AP_{50}$ | $AP_{75}$ | $AR_{100}$ | $AP_{None}$ | $AR_{Partial}$ | $AP_{Heavy}$ |
|---|---|---|---|---|---|---|---|---|
| 6 | Ours | **0.7673** | **0.9091** | 0.7800 | 0.7933 | **0.9983** | **0.9637** | 0.6190 |
| | $MRCNN_{t=0.1}$ | 0.5553 | 0.6526 | 0.6249 | 0.5823 | 0.7916 | 0.6986 | 0.4373 |
| | $MRCNN_{t=0.3}$ | 0.6781 | 0.8010 | 0.7706 | 0.7132 | 0.8765 | 0.8417 | 0.5898 |
| | $MRCNN_{t=0.5}$ | 0.7238 | 0.8701 | 0.8187 | 0.7620 | 0.9017 | 0.8768 | 0.6562 |
| | $MRCNN_{t=0.7}$ | 0.7332 | 0.8860 | **0.8323** | 0.7766 | 0.9112 | 0.8822 | 0.6748 |
| | $MRCNN_{t=0.9}$ | 0.6109 | 0.7334 | 0.6800 | **0.8010** | 0.9240 | 0.8978 | **0.6998** |
| 12 | Ours | **0.5262** | **0.7099** | 0.5192 | 0.5697 | **0.9958** | **0.9499** | 0.4049 |
| | $MRCNN_{t=0.1}$ | 0.3564 | 0.4350 | 0.4068 | 0.3730 | 0.7247 | 0.6220 | 0.2562 |
| | $MRCNN_{t=0.3}$ | 0.4641 | 0.5827 | 0.5312 | 0.4887 | 0.8226 | 0.7678 | 0.3715 |
| | $MRCNN_{t=0.5}$ | 0.5127 | 0.6416 | 0.5874 | 0.5399 | 0.8618 | 0.8019 | 0.4290 |
| | $MRCNN_{t=0.7}$ | 0.5203 | 0.6570 | **0.5926** | 0.5533 | 0.8722 | 0.8110 | 0.4424 |
| | $MRCNN_{t=0.9}$ | 0.4022 | 0.5253 | 0.4450 | **0.5856** | 0.8913 | 0.8326 | **0.4702** |

Mask R-CNN achieves better results on $AP_{75}$ when non-max suppression threshold $t = 0.7$, and $AR_{100}$, $AR_{Heavy}$ when $t = 0.9$, but it cannot retain high performance with a single value of $t$. The same performance pattern repeats when the number of instances per class is increased from 6 to 12.

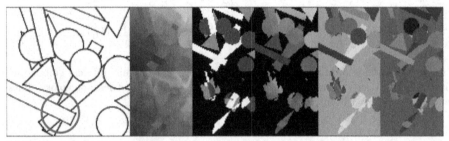

(a) left to right: image, embedding, semantic segmentation mask, masked embedding, labels, ground truth. Top is foreground, and bottom is occlusion

(b) individual instance masks

**Fig. 4.** Failure cases for embedding model. Red circle indicates a triple stack. (Color figure online)

As part of an ablation study, the semantic segmentation prediction for the model is replaced with ground truth. With 6 instances per class, AP increases from 0.7673 to 0.7959 and $AR_{100}$ increases from 0.7933 to 0.8300 when using ground truth; with 12 instances per class, AP increases from 0.5262 to 0.5419 and $AR_{100}$ increases from 0.5697 to 0.6013. These marginal improvements suggest that semantic segmentation is not the primary bottleneck of performance.

In the second part of the ablation study, the instance clustering result is replaced by ground truth. This way, the only source of error is insufficient layers of masks to accommodate the full complexity of occlusions. As Table 2 shows, the performance gains diminishing improvement as the model allows more layers to represent occlusion. Data suggests that three or more layers of mask output in the embedding model instead of just "foreground and occlusion" could improve performance, depending on the complexity of the application.

The embedding model is also trained and evaluated on shapes datasets with different number of instances per class in order to study its embedding capacity. Since embeddings for shapes of different classes are allowed to be similar, the class limited to rectangles in this study. Figure 3 shows that the performance drops when there are more instances of the same class. This happens for two reasons: first, more instances introduce more occlusions, which increases the chance of more than two objects stacking together; second, distinguishing

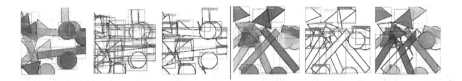

**Fig. 5.** Two failure cases for Mask R-CNN. From left to right, first case: ground truth, unfiltered proposals, filtered proposals; second case: ground truth, filtered proposals, final results

**Table 2.** Performance of instance masks constructed from different number of layers of ground truth. $N$ is the number of instances per class.

| $N$ | Layers | AP | $AP_{50}$ | $AP_{75}$ | $AR_{100}$ | $AP_{None}$ | $AR_{Partial}$ | $AP_{Heavy}$ |
|---|---|---|---|---|---|---|---|---|
| 6 | 2 | 0.8584 | 0.9604 | 0.8614 | 0.8627 | 1.0000 | 0.9927 | 0.7408 |
|  | 3 | 0.9703 | 0.9901 | 0.9802 | 0.9744 | 1.0000 | 0.9997 | 0.9509 |
| 12 | 2 | 0.6594 | 0.8317 | 0.6436 | 0.6611 | 1.0000 | 0.9910 | 0.5251 |
|  | 3 | 0.8703 | 0.9703 | 0.8812 | 0.8729 | 1.0000 | 0.9993 | 0.8206 |
|  | 4 | 0.9584 | 0.9901 | 0.9703 | 0.9629 | 1.0000 | 0.9999 | 0.9475 |

between more instances within the same class requires the model to have higher embedding capacity. Figure 3 also shows that increasing the dimension results in diminishing but consistent improvement on performance. This is because the loss function encourages embeddings of the same instance to be close to one another, and embeddings of different instances to be far away. The penalty on the magnitude of embeddings makes this goal hard to achieve in low dimensions. In higher dimensions it is much easier to find another embedding that is both close to the origin and far enough from other embeddings.

The structure of the embedding model allows easier expansion into three or more layers of masks. Two layers shows its limits when objects are heavily occluded. For example, it is impossible to get correct results in Fig. 4 because there are three objects stacked within the red circle. The model can recover two of them at best. This is the most typical failure case for the proposed embedding model. By evaluating masks constructed from different number of layers of ground truth, Table 1 shows that more layers of masks will lead to better results and that when the number of layers is held constant, performance on heavily occluded regions gets worse because more instances are stacked.

Mask R-CNN has two typical failure cases, as shown in Fig. 5. In the first case, the region proposal network generates the correct bounding boxes for the indicated circles, but some get filtered out during the non-maximum suppression stage. In the second case, both indicated rectangles fit within one bounding box and the mask generator is confused about which one is the salient object.

This points to a fundamental difference between the two types of approaches. Top-down, bounding-box-based approaches have the ability to look at a region multiple times and potentially generate a complete mask each time. However, this also acts as a double-edged sword when multiple objects could appear in the same bounding box and compete for the mask if they are the same class. The embedding model, on the other hand, is a bottom-up, bounding-box-free approach. Each pixel can only have one final embedding per layer, which will then be clustered into an instance label or ignored as background. The trade-off is that, situations like Fig. 5 can be avoided, but, when number of layers of ground truth mask in the training data is insufficient, the best possible performance will have a relatively low upper bound.

## 6    Conclusion

The method presented in this paper pushes the boundaries of a deep network's understanding of images by training it to estimate segmentation masks for unseen parts, and to associate them with visible instances. Experiments show that this bottom-up approach outperforms Mask R-CNN, a typical architecture for instance segmentation, by addressing the fundamental flaw in top-down approaches: the inability of bounding boxes to precisely capture the spatial relationship between cluttered objects. While the method only considers two-layer occlusion scenarios, the network structure can be easily modified to handle an arbitrary number of object types arranged in three or more layers.

Because it is difficult to obtain accurate annotations of occluded parts, the proposed method instead uses a synthetic dataset for training. We hope this and other recent works will motivate the creation of large datasets with ground truth masks representing the full spatial occupancy of occluded instances.

## References

1. Chen, L.-C., Zhu, Y., Papandreou, G., Schroff, F., Adam, H.: Encoder-decoder with atrous separable convolution for semantic image segmentation. In: Ferrari, V., Hebert, M., Sminchisescu, C., Weiss, Y. (eds.) ECCV 2018. LNCS, vol. 11211, pp. 833–851. Springer, Cham (2018). https://doi.org/10.1007/978-3-030-01234-2_49
2. Chen, Y.T., Liu, X., Yang, M.H.: Multi-instance object segmentation with occlusion handling. In: 2015 IEEE Conference on Computer Vision and Pattern Recognition (CVPR), pp. 3470–3478, June 2015
3. De Brabandere, B., Neven, D., Van Gool, L.: Semantic instance segmentation with a discriminative loss function. In: Deep Learning for Robotic Vision, Workshop at CVPR 2017, pp. 1–2. CVPR (2017)
4. Ehsani, K., Mottaghi, R., Farhadi, A.: SeGAN: segmenting and generating the invisible. In: Proceedings of the IEEE Conference on Computer Vision and Pattern Recognition, pp. 6144–6153 (2018)
5. Everingham, M., Van Gool, L., Williams, C.K.I., Winn, J., Zisserman, A.: The pascal visual object classes (VOC) challenge. Int. J. Comput. Vision **88**(2), 303–338 (2010)

6. Fathi, A., et al.: Semantic instance segmentation via deep metric learning. arXiv preprint arXiv:1703.10277 (2017)
7. He, K., Gkioxari, G., Dollár, P., Girshick, R.: Mask R-CNN. In: 2017 IEEE International Conference on Computer Vision (ICCV), pp. 2980–2988. IEEE (2017)
8. Li, K., Malik, J.: Amodal instance segmentation. In: Leibe, B., Matas, J., Sebe, N., Welling, M. (eds.) ECCV 2016. LNCS, vol. 9906, pp. 677–693. Springer, Cham (2016). https://doi.org/10.1007/978-3-319-46475-6_42
9. Li, Y., Qi, H., Dai, J., Ji, X., Wei, Y.: Fully convolutional instance-aware semantic segmentation. In: IEEE Conference on Computer Vision and Pattern Recognition (CVPR), pp. 2359–2367 (2017)
10. Long, J., Shelhamer, E., Darrell, T.: Fully convolutional networks for semantic segmentation. In: Proceedings of the IEEE Conference on Computer Vision and Pattern Recognition, pp. 3431–3440 (2015)
11. Ren, S., He, K., Girshick, R., Sun, J.: Faster R-CNN: towards real-time object detection with region proposal networks. In: Advances in Neural Information Processing Systems, pp. 91–99 (2015)
12. Uhrig, J., Cordts, M., Franke, U., Brox, T.: Pixel-level encoding and depth layering for instance-level semantic labeling. In: Rosenhahn, B., Andres, B. (eds.) GCPR 2016. LNCS, vol. 9796, pp. 14–25. Springer, Cham (2016). https://doi.org/10.1007/978-3-319-45886-1_2
13. Yang, Y., Hallman, S., Ramanan, D., Fowlkes, C.: Layered object detection for multi-class segmentation. In: 2010 IEEE Computer Society Conference on Computer Vision and Pattern Recognition, pp. 3113–3120, June 2010
14. Yang, Y., Hallman, S., Ramanan, D., Fowlkes, C.: Layered object models for image segmentation. IEEE Trans. Pattern Anal. Mach. Intell. **34**(9), 1731–1743 (2012)
15. Zhu, Y., Tian, Y., Metaxas, D., Dollár, P.: Semantic amodal segmentation. In: Proceedings of the IEEE Conference on Computer Vision and Pattern Recognition, pp. 1464–1472 (2017)

# CNN-Based Real-Time Parameter Tuning for Optimizing Denoising Filter Performance

Subhayan Mukherjee$^{(\boxtimes)}$, Navaneeth Kamballur Kottayil, Xinyao Sun, and Irene Cheng

University of Alberta, Edmonton, AB T6G2R3, Canada
{mukherje,kamballu,xinyao1,locheng}@ualberta.ca

**Abstract.** We propose a novel direction to improve the denoising quality of filtering-based denoising algorithms in real time by predicting the best filter parameter value using a Convolutional Neural Network (CNN). We take the use case of BM3D, the state-of-the-art filtering-based denoising algorithm, to demonstrate and validate our approach. We propose and train a simple, shallow CNN to predict in real time, the optimum filter parameter value, given the input noisy image. Each training example consists of a noisy input image (training data) and the filter parameter value that produces the best output (training label). Both qualitative and quantitative results using the widely used PSNR and SSIM metrics on the popular BSD68 dataset show that the CNN-guided BM3D outperforms the original, unguided BM3D across different noise levels. Thus, our proposed method is a CNN-based improvement on the original BM3D which uses a fixed, default parameter value for all images.

**Keywords:** Filter parameter tuning · CNN · Denoising · BM3D · GPU

## 1 Introduction

Image denoising refers to the process of removing noise from a distorted image to recover the clean image. During acquisition, compression or transmission, images and videos often get corrupted by noise. Thus, when the corruption occurs at a particular stage of the processing pipeline, there is a degradation in quality of output of subsequent steps, ultimately affecting the final visualization. This necessitates the image denoising [21] step for signal processing and transmission applications.

In the real world, accurately predicting the result of noise contamination of a clean signal is difficult, as theoretically, there are innumerable possible noise patterns that can contaminate a clean signal. However, most real-world noise patterns can be approximated by Additive White Gaussian Noise (AWGN),

Supported by NSERC Discovery Grant and DND Supplement.

© Springer Nature Switzerland AG 2019
F. Karray et al. (Eds.): ICIAR 2019, LNCS 11662, pp. 112–125, 2019.
https://doi.org/10.1007/978-3-030-27202-9_10

and thus it is commonly discussed in the literature. Consequently, traditional denoising approaches try to model image priors and solve optimization problems, e.g., nonlocal self-similarity (NSS) models [4,9], sparse representation models [13,20] and gradient-based models [26,31]. However, these traditional approaches to denoising are slow due to the optimization process, and thus often unfit for real-time applications. Also, complex and diverse scene content often cannot be denoised effectively using such hand-crafted image priors.

The recent breakthroughs in image denoising come from deep neural networks (DNNs), and especially deep Convolutional Neural Networks (CNNs), which use a discriminative denoising model, e.g., MLP [5], RED-Net [21] and DnCNN [34]. Their superior performance in many instances is mainly due to the modeling capability of CNNs and the computational capacity of modern GPUs for training progressively deeper and deeper networks. These discriminative models based on deep learning often demonstrate better performance that the traditional model-based methods. However, their performance on unseen data (during inference) often varies depending on the type of data they were trained on. If training data for a particular type of application is not representative enough and the model cannot generalize well enough, the denoising performance will suffer, which is an inherent issue with all learning-based approaches. For natural images, if the test image has been significantly distorted with high noise level, causing most structures and fine details in the original image to get visually obfuscated, the discriminative learning approaches often prove insufficient.

This paper proposes and validates a "middle ground" between the above two approaches. It uses the GPU-based implementation of a state-of-the-art model-based approach (namely, the Block Matching 3D filter, BM3D [9]) whose parameter is tuned by our proposed CNN in real time, depending on the characteristics of the noisy input image. This approach is "best-of-both-worlds" in the sense that its denoising workflow has a well-understood theoretical basis and is thus, fully explainable (BM3D algorithm) unlike end-to-end trained CNNs. At the same time, it optimizes denoising quality by tuning the model parameter using a CNN, which can capture more complex characteristics of the input image than what is possible using traditional hand-crafted methods.

In this paper, we consider a "non-blind" denoising scenario like section 5.2.1 of [35], where the noise is assumed to be AWGN with known standard deviation.

## 1.1 Motivation

As discussed earlier, over the last few decades, the various challenges posed by the denoising problem has been analyzed thoroughly by many researchers and a lot of interesting solutions have been proposed. In the non-learning-based category, one of the greatest and recent breakthroughs was achieved by BM3D. Very recently, researchers have found that BM3D out-performs even deep learning-based methods for real-world, non-AWGN noise, e.g. in photographs captured by consumer cameras [24]. Moreover, efficient GPU implementation of BM3D has significantly improved its time performance [17]. BM3D has a lot of input parameters which need to be tuned, though most published denoising methods (learning and non-learning based) compare their performance with BM3D using its default parameter values, as mentioned in the original BM3D paper [9].

In recent years, researchers have experimentally proved that BM3D performance is, in fact, sensitive to its parameter settings and further, that changing some parameter values influence its denoising performance significantly more than changing values of other parameters [2,19]. We repeated those experiments and came to the same conclusion as the researchers that the $\lambda_{3D}$ is one of the few parameters which cause *significant* difference in BM3D's denoising performance.

In BM3D, after grouping of similar (correlated) image blocks (patches), a 3D decorrelating unitary transform is applied to each 3D stack of grouped similar blocks. Enhanced denoising and image detail preservation can only be ensured by choosing a suitable threshold value ($\lambda_{3D}$) for applying a hard thresholding operator on the transform coefficients. This explains why the $\lambda_{3D}$ parameter has significant influence on BM3D denoising quality.

Recently, researchers have tried to adapt the BM3D parameter $\lambda_{3D}$ to the statistical characteristics of the input image and noise [14] using the Noise Invalidation Denoising (NIDe) technique [3]. However, the parameter $\lambda$ used in NIDe for noise confidence interval estimation has been fixed to the constant value 3, and the suitability of the method [14] for real-time performance has not been discussed. Researchers have also attempted to adaptively set the distance threshold for grouping similar image blocks, based on the ratio of the mean and standard deviation and the estimated noise intensity [11]. Motivated by the observation that the Human Vision System is locally adaptive, in another work [12] researchers have tried to vary BM3D parameters according to local perceptual image characteristics in a manner determined by extensive subjective experiments. In yet another work, researchers have tried to incorporate locally-adaptive patch shapes and Principal Component Analysis (PCA) in the 3D transform to improve denoising quality, but at the cost of increasing time complexity many-fold, as well as rendering their algorithm unsuitable for real-time GPU implementation (due to adaptive-shape patches) [10]. Other researchers [2] have used traditional learning algorithms like Naive Bayes, Support Vector Machine (SVM), K Nearest Neighbors (kNN) and Random Forest to train numerous classifiers to set the $\lambda_{3D}$ value for each block based on the block's texture. However, block-wise prediction of $\lambda_{3D}$ is expected to increase the BM3D time complexity significantly. Yet, the authors did not report the time performance of their proposed method. Also, they used $7 \times 7$ sized blocks for classification, but did not report or discuss the possible effects of choosing other block sizes. Lastly, even a very recent attempt at replacing parts of the BM3D pipeline with a CNN did *not* show potential for real-time performance, even using the fastest GPUs available in the market [32].

In this work, we design a Convolutional Neural Network (CNN) that can predict the $\lambda_{3D}$ parameter value which best denoises a noisy image. We compare the performance of our method by comparing the denoising performance of BM3D (using our CNN-estimated parameter value) against the denoising performance of BM3D using the default value for the $\lambda_{3D}$ parameter, as recommended in the original BM3D paper [9].

## 1.2   Our Contribution

To the best of our knowledge, we are the first to propose a simple, shallow CNN-based real-time solution to predict optimum parameter values for a filtering based denoising algorithm. In this paper, we consider such a state-of-the-art algorithm, BM3D as a use case to demonstrate and validate this proposal. We propose a method that is readily implementable on GPUs and (for our use case) enhances the denoising capability of the recent GPU-based BM3D implementation without significantly increasing the overall time complexity.

The rest of this paper is organized as follows: Related work is given in Sect. 2. We present our proposed method in Sect. 3. Experimental results and analysis are in Sect. 4. In Sect. 5, we give the conclusion and future work.

## 2   Related Work

Image denoising is a well studied problem in image processing. Like mentioned earlier, most approaches in the denoising literature rely on modeling image priors [6,9,13,26]. However, this often leads to over-smoothening of the denoised images (loss of image details) due to incorrect assumptions about the prior.

The use of non-linear filters is a popular approach in solving image denoising problems. Non-local means based filters are popular examples. Non-local means are a generalization of bilateral filtering which uses photometric distance as a similarity measure [4]. BM3D is a further improvement on this scheme where a joint filtering is performed after grouping similar patches from the image. The methods that follow this idea are generally slow but produce good quality results.

Another class of methods to denoise images rely on end-to-end deep learning. These methods rely on training convolutional auto-encoders to convert noisy images to clean images. The neural network learns a set of filters which, when convolved with noisy images, would generate a clean version of the image [29,33]. These methods however, often generate images with blurred edges. End-to-end connected networks were limited in their complexity because of the attenuation of gradients in very deep end-to-end frameworks. Neural networks with skip connection were used to solve this issue in Residual network (ResNet) [16]. The skip connections help propagate gradients to train deeper layers. This addition led to further improvements to image sharpness after denoising by end-to-end methods. Variations of the residual network formulation have been proposed in [21] and [34]. The former uses an encoder-decoder skip-layer connection for faster training and better denoising performance, while the latter adopts the residual learning formulation, but uses identity shortcuts instead of multiple residual units.

An alternative approach that is used to solve image denoising problems was pioneered by Trainable nonlinear reaction diffusion (TNRD) [7] and Rapid and accurate image super resolution (RAISR) [25], which rely on learning a set of structure tensor features to select a filter at each pixel. The filtering and aggregation of the results lead to denoised images with a shallow neural network.

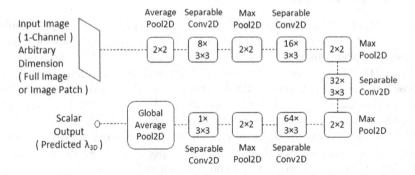

**Fig. 1.** Architecture of proposed CNN. Input: Noisy Image; Output: Predicted $\lambda_{3D}$ value. The GlobalAveragePooling2D layer computes the mean of its input and outputs a single scalar value. During training, the cost function is the mean squared error between this value and the optimum $\lambda_{3D}$ value for the input noisy image. The optimum value is determined while preparing the training data.

## 3   Proposed Method

Our literature survey shows that end-to-end learning based denoising performance may be sensitive to training data for particular application domains, whereas most recent improvements to BM3D involve block-based or region-based locally adaptive parameter tuning, which makes them unsuitable for real-time GPU implementation. In our proposed denoising methodology, we train a shallow, fast CNN to predict the optimum value of the BM3D parameter $\lambda_{3D}$ based only on the whole input noisy image. Subsequently, the BM3D algorithm is used to denoise the noisy input image with its $\lambda_{3D}$ parameter set to the value predicted by the CNN. The CNN is trained with pairs of noisy images and the corresponding optimum $\lambda_{3D}$ values. In its current form, our proposed method requires the CNN be re-trained for different AWGN noise $\sigma$ values (we refer to them as noise *levels*). To clarify, the architecture of the CNN remains the same, but the training data and hence, the weights and biases of the trained model are different for different noise levels. However, BM3D itself requires the noise level as an input parameter ("non-blind"), so this is not an extra requirement imposed by our proposed method. As such, the noise level can be estimated following an approach similar to [2], in which case we can automatically choose the CNN model best suited to that noise level, although this direction has been left as future work. The architecture of the CNN is shown in Fig. 1.

In Fig. 1, each convolutional layer is represented by a box with rounded corners. Output feature map count is indicated by the integer at the top (1, 8,

16, 32, 64) and filter dimension is indicated at the bottom ($3 \times 3$). The same representation holds for the non-global pooling layers, except that the number of feature maps remains unchanged in pooling layers, and are thus not explicitly mentioned (pooling window size is mentioned). From the dimensions of the Input layer, one can observe that we do not put constraints on the width or height of the input image or the batch size. In our experiments, we only constrain the input image to be single channel (gray-scale). Thus, we used the CNN to predict $\lambda_{3D}$ values for input images of arbitrary widths and heights. The AveragePooling2D layer right after the Input layer reduces the image dimension and thus the number of convolutions, leading to faster training and inference. We use $3 \times 3$ separable convolutions [27] to reduce the number of weights to be trained (for faster convergence). For each of the convolution layers shown in Fig. 1, we use the Rectified Linear Unit (ReLU) activation function followed by a MaxPooling2D layer to progressively subsample the feature maps as we move towards the output layer. The pooling window size for all non-global pooling layers in the network is $(2, 2)$. In the GlobalAveragePooling2D (output) layer, we compute the mean of the output of the final convolution layer. The mean is essentially a single scalar value representing the predicted $\lambda_{3D}$ value for the input noisy image. During training, we minimize the Mean Squared Error (MSE) between this mean and the target optimum $\lambda_{3D}$ value for the input image, so that the network can learn to predict the $\lambda_{3D}$ value based on a noisy input image.

### 3.1 Design Motivation

Since the default value for the $\lambda_{3D}$ parameter is 2.7, we chose different ranges of $\lambda_{3D}$ values for different noise levels, always including the value 2.7. We observed that when we select the range $(1.0, 3.0)$, we have a minima with respect to MSE between the denoised image and the clean image, across all noise levels. We show few representative results of this experiment on images of the Sun-Hays dataset [28] in Fig. 2. The $\lambda_{3D}$ values are plotted along the horizontal axis and the MSE values along the vertical axis. To increase legibility, the part of the plot corresponding to $\lambda_{3D}$ values less than 1.5 has been truncated. In the truncated parts, the MSE value was found to display an increasing trend. From all the plots, it can be seen that there is an easily identifiable MSE minima. However, depending on the input image and/or AWGN noise $\sigma$ value, the position of the minima changes. This motivated us to design and train a CNN that could take the noisy image as input and predict the $\lambda_{3D}$ value in order to produce the minimum MSE.

## 4 Results and Discussion

### 4.1 Training Data Generation

For training the CNN shown in Fig. 1, we have to generate the training data. For this purpose, we first combine two publicly available datasets to create our training dataset:

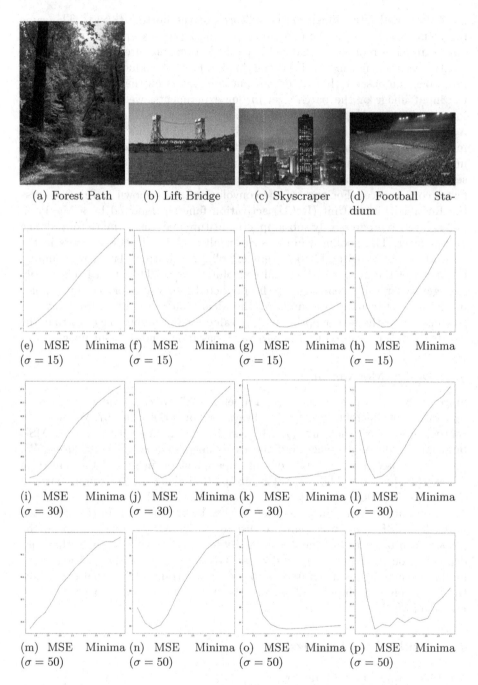

**Fig. 2.** Mean Squared Error (vertical axis) between clean and denoised images of Sun-Hays dataset [28] for different AWGN $\sigma$ values, by varying the $\lambda_{3D}$ parameter (horizontal axis). A distinct minima exists in all cases.

1. McGill Calibrated Colour Image Dataset [23] which contains different categories of natural scenes and thus covers a wide range of textures.
2. The "2017 Unlabeled images [123 K/19 GB]" category of the Microsoft Common Objects in Context (COCO) dataset[1].

We next converted all the above images to grey-scale (single channel, intensity range: 0–255). We then added AWGN noise with three different levels ($15 = $ 'low', $30 = $ 'medium', $50 = $ 'high') to each image. For each noisy version of each image, we denoised (reconstructed) it using the BM3D GPU implementation [17], by varying the value of the $\lambda_{3D}$ parameter as follows: $[1.0, 1.125, 1.250, ..., 2.875, 3.0]$. Thus, for each image corrupted by each of the three noise levels, we have 17 reconstructions using different values of the BM3D $\lambda_{3D}$ parameter. Using each of the three noise levels (15, 30, 50), we compute the MSE of the individual reconstructions with its corresponding clean image, and determine which reconstruction has the minimum MSE (similar to the plots shown in Fig. 2). At each noise level, the $\lambda_{3D}$ parameter value which created the reconstruction having the minimum MSE is assigned as the training label for that noisy image. Thus, the training dataset consists of: 1. *Data*: three versions of an image, each of which is corrupted by a different noise level (low, medium, high), and 2. *Label*: for each version of noisy image, the corresponding $\lambda_{3D}$ parameter value that best denoises it. Thus, from each clean image, we generate three {noisy image, $\lambda_{3D}$ value} pairs for inclusion in our training dataset.

## 4.2   CNN Training Implementation

We implement the CNN shown in Fig. 1 using Keras [8] with TensorFlow-GPU [1] back-end. Given a noisy input image (training data), the CNN is trained to minimize the MSE between its predicted output and the "best" $\lambda_{3D}$ value (training label) for that noisy input image. Thus, we train the CNN three times (separately), once for each noise level. The computer used for training has Ubuntu 16.04 LTS (64-bit) operating system, Intel Core i7-7700K CPU running at 4.20 GHz ($\times 8$ cores), 32 GB system RAM and NVIDIA 1070 GPU with 8 GB GPU RAM. The BM3D GPU implementation took approximately 40–50 ms to generate each training image (for a particular noise level and a particular $\lambda_{3D}$ parameter value). In total, for each noise level, the training data generation took approximately 3 days, but this also includes the time taken to compute the MSEs and determine the minimum MSE for each image. The weights and biases of all CNN layers are initialized by Xavier method [15]. The optimization algorithm used is Adam [18] with $\beta_1 = 0.9$, $\beta_2 = 0.999$, $\epsilon = 10^{-8}$. Learning rate was set to $10^{-3}$ with no decay. The network was trained for 50 epochs for each noise level and took approximately 8 hours for each training session. The images were of varying size ($640 \times 480$ on average) and orientation (portrait/landscape), but the CNN can take images of any size and orientation, so this was not an issue for us. The batch size was set to 1 (one image per batch).

---

[1] http://cocodataset.org/#download.

### 4.3  CNN Performance Evaluation

**Denoising Parameter Prediction and Quantitative Analysis.** Following the most recent denoising literature, we tested the three trained CNN models (one for each noise level) separately on the Berkeley Segmentation Dataset, containing 68 images (BSD68) [22]. As mentioned, for each clean image in the dataset, we converted it to grey-scale and added low, medium and high level AWGN. Then, we used the corresponding trained CNN model to predict the $\lambda_{3D}$ parameter value that would best denoise the given noisy input image. We calculated the PSNR and SSIM [30] for each reconstruction at each noise level for each image. The parameters used to calculate SSIM were the same as those reported in the original paper [30], which have been commonly used in the literature. We averaged the PSNR and SSIM for all 68 images of BSD68 dataset for each of the three noise levels. We also applied BM3D with the default value of the $\lambda_{3D}$ parameter for each test image and each noise level. The results from using our predicted vs. default $\lambda_{3D}$ value in BM3D are summarized in Table 1. The results show superior performance using our CNN-predicted $\lambda_{3D}$, as compared to default $\lambda_{3D}$ for all metrics across all noise levels.

**Table 1.** Performance comparison of proposed CNN-based BM3D parameter prediction

| Average | MSE (Predicted) | MSE (Default) | PSNR (Predicted) | PSNR (Default) | SSIM (Predicted) | SSIM (Default) |
|---------|-----------------|---------------|------------------|----------------|------------------|----------------|
| Noise $\sigma = 15$ | 59.06 | 61.42 | 30.93 | 30.78 | 0.8783 | 0.8708 |
| Noise $\sigma = 30$ | 135.99 | 142.29 | 27.38 | 27.24 | 0.7772 | 0.7669 |
| Noise $\sigma = 50$ | 255.90 | 267.00 | 24.60 | 24.47 | 0.6650 | 0.6547 |

**Qualitative Comparison.** Figure 3 shows two representative clean images and the effect of progressively adding more and more noise (increasing AWGN $\sigma$ value) in order to give the reader a qualitative idea of the three different noise levels used to test our proposed method. We compare a cropped part of a representative denoised image using the default $\lambda_{3D}$ parameter value vs. our CNN-predicted $\lambda_{3D}$ parameter value (Fig. 5). We perform similar comparisons for full images in Fig. 4. From the visual comparison, we can infer that for the most part, the advantage of the parameter prediction lies in greater detail recovery compared to using the fixed, default $\lambda_{3D}$ parameter value (2.7). This also explains the higher SSIM score of the proposed method compared to traditional BM3D which uses a fixed $\lambda_{3D}$ parameter value.

### 4.4    Analysis and Discussion

As can be seen from Table 1, the proposed method of predicting the $\lambda_{3D}$ parameter value based on the input noisy image (instead of using the default value: 2.7) produces better scores with respect to all three metrics (lower MSE, higher PSNR, higher SSIM). It is important to emphasize that, BM3D scores using default parameter values reported in denoising literature are obtained using the traditional CPU-based implementation of BM3D, which is much slower than the GPU-based real-time implementation we use [17]. From Table 1, the most significant improvement is seen in terms of SSIM score for all noise levels. Since SSIM is a score normalized between 0 and 1, even slight increments in SSIM score should be interpreted as noticeable improvements in perceptual image quality.

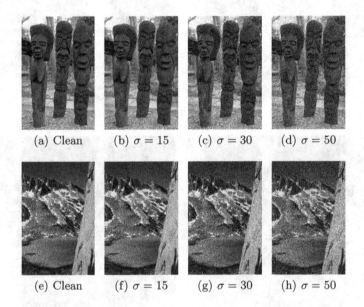

(a) Clean        (b) $\sigma = 15$        (c) $\sigma = 30$        (d) $\sigma = 50$

(e) Clean        (f) $\sigma = 15$        (g) $\sigma = 30$        (h) $\sigma = 50$

**Fig. 3.** Representative images from the BSD68 dataset and all noisy versions thereof.

We found very similar trends as Fig. 2 for the BSD68 dataset as well, but we do not reproduce them here for the sake of brevity. Based on our findings, even if the CNN-predicted $\lambda_{3D}$ value is close to the optimal value, the denoising performance using our method is not affected. On the other hand, fixing the parameter value to 2.7 without taking into consideration the input image characteristics will often produce inferior results, as evident from Fig. 2. It is also worth mentioning that, none of our three trained CNN models ever predicted any $\lambda_{3D}$ parameter value lesser than 1.0 or greater than 3.0. That means, the trained networks are quite stable. In fact, even when preparing the training data, we never came across any image for any noise level whose optimum $\lambda_{3D}$ parameter value lies outside the $(1.0, 3.0)$ range.

(a) Statues (default $\lambda_{3D}$)    (b) Statues (predicted $\lambda_{3D}$)

(c) Mountains (default $\lambda_{3D}$)    (d) Mountains (predicted $\lambda_{3D}$)

**Fig. 4.** Representative denoised images from the BSD68 dataset. Left: using the fixed, default $\lambda_{3D}$ parameter value (2.7); Right: using the CNN-predicted $\lambda_{3D}$ parameter value. Result shown above is for AWGN Noise level $\sigma = 15$. Our method better preserves the details in the statues and mountain walls.

Lastly, the objective of our work is not to prove the superiority of the proposed method to state-of-the-art learning-based denoising methods which often perform end-to-end learning and are thus subject to the limitations of purely learning-based approaches discussed earlier. Rather, we wish to highlight that even the non-learning based state-of-the-art method BM3D which already has a real-time implementation [17] can enhance its denoising quality using our proposed real-time, input image based prediction of its $\lambda_{3D}$ parameter value.

**Time Performance.** Our CNN predicts optimum $\lambda_{3D}$ values for all 68 images of the BSD68 dataset ($481 \times 321$ resolution) in a total of 0.51 s. This translates to an average per-image run time of only 7.5 ms. Our proposed CNN is shallow, uses pooling and separable convolutions. Thus, it runs inference extremely fast, and is ideal for real-time applications when used in conjunction with the real-time BM3D implementation [17] used in this paper.

(a) Train (default $\lambda_{3D}$)          (b) Train (predicted $\lambda_{3D}$)

**Fig. 5.** Cropped and zoomed section of a representative denoised image from the BSD68 dataset. Left: using the fixed, default $\lambda_{3D}$ parameter value (2.7); Right: using the CNN-predicted $\lambda_{3D}$ parameter value. The denoising result shown above is for AWGN Noise level $\sigma = 15$. Our method better preserves the details in the train body's texture.

# 5    Conclusion and Future Work

We proposed a novel approach to use CNNs for real-time image-based parameter prediction to enhance the performance of the state-of-the-art denoising algorithm in the non-learning based category, viz. BM3D. Our proposed CNN accepts images of arbitrary size. Experimental results on the popular BSD68 dataset using multiple widely adopted image denoising quality metrics clearly shows that the proposed approach consistently achieves better results than running BM3D with its default, fixed parameter value across different noise levels.

Future work can target predicting other parameters of BM3D or even those of other denoising algorithms using the proposed approach, as well as automatically choosing the most suitable CNN model based on image noise level estimation.

# References

1. Abadi, M., et al.: TensorFlow: large-scale machine learning on heterogeneous systems (2015). https://www.tensorflow.org/
2. Bashar, F., El-Sakka, M.R.: BM3D image denoising using learning-based adaptive hard thresholding. In: Proceedings of the 11th Joint Conference on Computer Vision, Imaging and Computer Graphics Theory and Applications. SCITEPRESS - Science and and Technology Publications (2016). https://doi.org/10.5220/0005787202040214
3. Beheshti, S., Hashemi, M., Zhang, X.P., Nikvand, N.: Noise invalidation denoising. IEEE Trans. Signal Process. 58(12), 6007–6016 (2010). https://doi.org/10.1109/TSP.2010.2074199
4. Buades, A., Coll, B., Morel, J.M.: A non-local algorithm for image denoising. In: IEEE Computer Society Conference on Computer Vision and Pattern Recognition, CVPR 2005, vol. 2, pp. 60–65. IEEE (2005)
5. Burger, H.C., Schuler, C.J., Harmeling, S.: Image denoising: can plain neural networks compete with BM3D? In: 2012 IEEE Conference on Computer Vision and Pattern Recognition (CVPR), pp. 2392–2399. IEEE (2012)
6. Chatterjee, P., Milanfar, P.: Clustering-based denoising with locally learned dictionaries. IEEE Trans. Image Process. 18(7), 1438–1451 (2009)
7. Chen, Y., Pock, T.: Trainable nonlinear reaction diffusion: a flexible framework for fast and effective image restoration. IEEE Trans. Pattern Anal. Mach. Intell. 39(6), 1256–1272 (2017). https://doi.org/10.1109/TPAMI.2016.2596743
8. Chollet, F., et al.: Keras (2015). https://keras.io
9. Dabov, K., Foi, A., Katkovnik, V., Egiazarian, K.: Image denoising by sparse 3-D transform-domain collaborative filtering. IEEE Trans. Image Process. 16(8), 2080–2095 (2007). https://doi.org/10.1109/TIP.2007.901238
10. Dabov, K., Foi, A., Katkovnik, V., Egiazarian, K.: BM3D image denoising with shape-adaptive principal component analysis. In: Workshop on Signal Processing with Adaptive Sparse Structured Representations (SPARS 2009), April 2009
11. Dai, L., Zhang, Y., Li, Y.: BM3D image denoising algorithm with adaptive distance hard-threshold. Int. J. Signal Process. Image Process. Pattern Recognit. 6(6), 41–50 (2013). https://doi.org/10.14257/ijsip.2013.6.6.04
12. Egiazarian, K., Danielyan, A., Ponomarenko, N., Foi, A., Ieremeiev, O., Lukin, V.: BM3D-HVS: content-adaptive denoising for improved visual quality. Electron. Imaging 2017(13), 48–55 (2017). https://doi.org/10.2352/issn.2470-1173.2017.13.dpmi-083
13. Elad, M., Aharon, M.: Image denoising via sparse and redundant representations over learned dictionaries. IEEE Trans. Image Process. 15(12), 3736–3745 (2006)
14. Elahi, P., Beheshti, S., Hashemi, M.: BM3D mridenoising equipped with noise invalidation technique. In: 2014 IEEE International Conference on Acoustics, Speech and Signal Processing (ICASSP), pp. 6612–6616, May 2014
15. Glorot, X., Bengio, Y.: Understanding the difficulty of training deep feedforward neural networks. In: Proceedings of the Thirteenth International Conference on Artificial Intelligence and Statistics, pp. 249–256 (2010)
16. He, K., Zhang, X., Ren, S., Sun, J.: Deep residual learning for image recognition. In: Proceedings of the IEEE Conference on Computer Vision and Pattern Recognition, pp. 770–778 (2016)
17. Honzátko, D., Kruliš, M.: Accelerating block-matching and 3D filtering method for image denoising on GPUs. J. Real-Time Image Process. (2017). https://doi.org/10.1007/s11554-017-0737-9

18. Kingma, D.P., Ba, J.: Adam: a method for stochastic optimization. arXiv preprint arXiv:1412.6980 (2014)
19. Lebrun, M.: An analysis and implementation of the BM3D image denoising method. Image Process. Line **2**, 175–213 (2012). https://doi.org/10.5201/ipol.2012.l-bm3d
20. Mairal, J., Bach, F., Ponce, J., Sapiro, G.: Online dictionary learning for sparse coding. In: Proceedings of the 26th Annual International Conference on Machine Learning, pp. 689–696. ACM (2009)
21. Mao, X., Shen, C., Yang, Y.B.: Image restoration using very deep convolutional encoder-decoder networks with symmetric skip connections. In: Advances in Neural Information Processing Systems, pp. 2802–2810 (2016)
22. Martin, D., Fowlkes, C., Tal, D., Malik, J.: A database of human segmented natural images and its application to evaluating segmentation algorithms and measuring ecological statistics. In: Proceedings of the 8th International Conference on Computer Vision, vol. 2, pp. 416–423, July 2001
23. Olmos, A., Kingdom, F.A.A.: A biologically inspired algorithm for the recovery of shading and reflectance images. Perception **33**(12), 1463–1473 (2004). https://doi.org/10.1068/p5321
24. Pltz, T., Roth, S.: Benchmarking denoising algorithms with real photographs. In: 2017 IEEE Conference on Computer Vision and Pattern Recognition (CVPR), pp. 2750–2759, July 2017. https://doi.org/10.1109/CVPR.2017.294
25. Romano, Y., Isidoro, J., Milanfar, P.: RAISR: rapid and accurate image super resolution. IEEE Trans. Comput. Imaging **3**(1), 110–125 (2017)
26. Rudin, L.I., Osher, S., Fatemi, E.: Nonlinear total variation based noise removal algorithms. Physica D Nonlinear Phenom. **60**(1–4), 259–268 (1992)
27. Sifre, L.: Rigid-motion scattering for image classification. Ph.D. thesis, Ecole Polytechnique, October 2014
28. Sun, L., Hays, J.: Super-resolution from internet-scale scene matching. In: 2012 IEEE International Conference on Computational Photography (ICCP), pp. 1–12, April 2012. https://doi.org/10.1109/ICCPhot.2012.6215221
29. Vincent, P., Larochelle, H., Lajoie, I., Bengio, Y., Manzagol, P.A.: Stacked denoising autoencoders: learning useful representations in a deep network with a local denoising criterion. J. Mach. Learn. Res. **11**, 3371–3408 (2010)
30. Wang, Z., Bovik, A.C., Sheikh, H.R., Simoncelli, E.P.: Image quality assessment: from error visibility to structural similarity. IEEE Trans. Image Process. **13**(4), 600–612 (2004). https://doi.org/10.1109/TIP.2003.819861
31. Weiss, Y., Freeman, W.T.: What makes a good model of natural images? In: IEEE Conference on Computer Vision and Pattern Recognition, CVPR 2007, pp. 1–8. IEEE (2007)
32. Yang, D., Sun, J.: BM3D-Net: a convolutional neural network for transform-domain collaborative filtering. IEEE Signal Process. Lett. **25**(1), 55–59 (2018). https://doi.org/10.1109/LSP.2017.2768660
33. Ye, X., Wang, L., Xing, H., Huang, L.: Denoising hybrid noises in image with stacked autoencoder. In: 2015 IEEE International Conference on Information and Automation, pp. 2720–2724, August 2015. https://doi.org/10.1109/ICInfA.2015.7279746
34. Zhang, K., Zuo, W., Chen, Y., Meng, D., Zhang, L.: Beyond a Gaussian denoiser: residual learning of deep CNN for image denoising. IEEE Trans. Image Process. **26**(7), 3142–3155 (2017)
35. Zhu, F., Chen, G., Heng, P.A.: From noise modeling to blind image denoising. In: 2016 IEEE Conference on Computer Vision and Pattern Recognition (CVPR), pp. 420–429, June 2016. https://doi.org/10.1109/CVPR.2016.52

# Locally Linear Image Structural Embedding for Image Structure Manifold Learning

Benyamin Ghojogh$^{(\boxtimes)}$ (ID), Fakhri Karray (ID), and Mark Crowley (ID)

Department of Electrical and Computer Engineering, University of Waterloo,
Waterloo, ON, Canada
{bghojogh,karray,mcrowley}@uwaterloo.ca

**Abstract.** Most of existing manifold learning methods rely on Mean Squared Error (MSE) or $\ell_2$ norm. However, for the problem of image quality assessment, these are not promising measure. In this paper, we introduce the concept of an image structure manifold which captures image structure features and discriminates image distortions. We propose a new manifold learning method, Locally Linear Image Structural Embedding (LLISE), and kernel LLISE for learning this manifold. The LLISE is inspired by Locally Linear Embedding (LLE) but uses SSIM rather than MSE. This paper builds a bridge between manifold learning and image fidelity assessment and it can open a new area for future investigations.

**Keywords:** Locally Linear Embedding ·
Locally Linear Image Structural Embedding · Structural similarity ·
SSIM · Image structure manifold

## 1 Introduction

Mean Squared Error (MSE) is not a good measure for image quality assessment [1]. Two different categories of distortions exist, i.e., structural and non-structural distortions [2]. The structural similarity index (SSIM) [2,3] is found to be a very promising measure for image fidelity assessment. It encounters luminance and contrast change as non-structural distortions and other distortions as structural ones. Recently, it has been used in optimization problems for different tasks although it is not convex but quasi-convex under certain conditions [4].

The manifold learning methods are designed mostly based on MSE or the $\ell_2$ norm. Therefore, they do not perform satisfactorily for image quality discrimination. Locally Linear Embedding (LLE) [5] is an example. In this paper, we introduce the new concept of *image structure manifold* which captures the features of image structure and is useful for discriminating the image distortions. We propose Locally Linear Image Structural Embedding (LLISE), in both original and feature space, which uses SSIM distance rather than $\ell_2$ norm. We also

© Springer Nature Switzerland AG 2019
F. Karray et al. (Eds.): ICIAR 2019, LNCS 11662, pp. 126–138, 2019.
https://doi.org/10.1007/978-3-030-27202-9_11

propose the out-of-sample extension of LLISE. The derivations of expressions in this paper are detailed more in the supplementary-material paper which will be released in https://arXiv.org.

## 1.1 Structural Similarity Index

The SSIM between two reshaped image blocks $\breve{x}_1 = [x_1^{[1]}, \ldots, x_1^{[q]}]^\top \in \mathbb{R}^q$ and $\breve{x}_2 = [x_2^{[1]}, \ldots, x_2^{[q]}]^\top \in \mathbb{R}^q$, in color intensity range $[0, l]$, is [2,3]:

$$\mathbb{R} \ni \mathrm{SSIM}(\breve{x}_1, \breve{x}_2) := \left( \frac{2\mu_{x_1}\mu_{x_2} + c_1}{\mu_{x_1}^2 + \mu_{x_2}^2 + c_1} \right) \left( \frac{2\sigma_{x_1}\sigma_{x_2} + c_2}{\sigma_{x_1}^2 + \sigma_{x_2}^2 + c_2} \right) \left( \frac{\sigma_{x_1,x_2} + c_3}{\sigma_{x_1}\sigma_{x_2} + c_3} \right), \quad (1)$$

where $\mu_{x_1} = (1/q) \sum_{i=1}^q x_1^{[i]}$, $\sigma_{x_1} = \left[ (1/(q-1)) \sum_{i=1}^q (x_1^{[i]} - \mu_{x_1})^2 \right]^{0.5}$, $\sigma_{x_1,x_2} = (1/(q-1)) \sum_{i=1}^q (x_1^{[i]} - \mu_{x_1})(x_2^{[i]} - \mu_{x_2})$, $c_1 = (0.01 \times l)^2$, $c_2 = 2c_3 = (0.03 \times l)^2$, and $\mu_{x_2}$ and $\sigma_{x_2}$ are defined similarly for $\breve{x}_2$. In this work, $l = 1$.

Because of $c_2 = 2c_3$, the SSIM is simplified to $\mathrm{SSIM}(\breve{x}_1, \breve{x}_2) = s_1(\breve{x}_1, \breve{x}_2) \times s_2(\breve{x}_1, \breve{x}_2)$, where $s_1(\breve{x}_1, \breve{x}_2) := (2\mu_{x_1}\mu_{x_2} + c_1)/(\mu_{x_1}^2 + \mu_{x_2}^2 + c_1)$ and $s_2(\breve{x}_1, \breve{x}_2) := (2\sigma_{x_1,x_2} + c_2)/(\sigma_{x_1}^2 + \sigma_{x_2}^2 + c_2)$. If the vectors $\breve{x}_1$ and $\breve{x}_2$ have zero mean, i.e., $\mu_{x_1} = \mu_{x_2} = 0$, the SSIM becomes $\mathbb{R} \ni \mathrm{SSIM}(\breve{x}_1, \breve{x}_2) = (2\breve{x}_1^\top \breve{x}_2 + c)/(\|\breve{x}_1\|_2^2 + \|\breve{x}_2\|_2^2 + c)$, where $c = (q-1)c_2$ [6]. We denote the reshaped vectors of the two images by $x_1 \in \mathbb{R}^d$ and $x_2 \in \mathbb{R}^d$, and a reshaped block in the two images by $\breve{x}_1 \in \mathbb{R}^q$ and $\breve{x}_2 \in \mathbb{R}^q$. If $\mu_{x_1} = \mu_{x_2} = 0$, the (squared) distance based on SSIM, which we denote by $\|.\|_S$, is [4,6]:

$$\mathbb{R} \ni \|\breve{x}_1 - \breve{x}_2\|_S := 1 - \mathrm{SSIM}(\breve{x}_1, \breve{x}_2) = \frac{\|\breve{x}_1 - \breve{x}_2\|_2^2}{\|\breve{x}_1\|_2^2 + \|\breve{x}_2\|_2^2 + c}. \quad (2)$$

## 1.2 Locally Linear Embedding

In LLE [5], first a $k$-Nearest Neighbor ($k$-NN) graph is found using pairwise Euclidean distances. Every data point $x_j \in \mathbb{R}^d$ is reconstructed by its $k$ neighbors $\mathbb{R}^{d \times k} \ni X_j := [_1x_j, \ldots, _kx_j]$ where $_rx_j$ denotes the $r$-th neighbor of $x_j$. If $\mathbb{R}^k \ni \widetilde{w}_j := [_1\widetilde{w}_j, \ldots, _k\widetilde{w}_j]^\top$ denotes the reconstruction weights for the $x_j$, the reconstruction problem with the weights adding to one is: minimize $\sum_{j=1}^n \|x_j - \sum_{r=1}^k {_r\widetilde{w}_j} \, {_rx_j}\|_2^2$, subject to $\sum_{r=1}^k {_r\widetilde{w}_j} = 1, \forall j \in \{1, \ldots, n\}$. Then, the data points are embedded using the obtained weights. Take $\mathbb{R}^n \ni w_j := [_1w_j, \ldots, _nw_j]^\top$ where $_rw_j$ is the weight obtained from linear reconstruction if $x_r$ is a neighbor of $x_j$ and is zero otherwise. If $y_j \in \mathbb{R}^p$ denotes the embedded $j$-th data point, the embedding problem with unit covariance is: minimize $\sum_{j=1}^n \|y_j - \sum_{r=1}^n {_rw_j} \, y_r\|_2^2$, subject to $(1/n) \sum_{j=1}^n y_j y_j^\top = I$ and $\sum_{j=1}^n y_j = 0, \forall j \in \{1, \ldots, n\}$. Kernel LLE [7] finds the $k$-NN graph and performs linear reconstruction from the neighbors in the feature space.

# 2   Locally Linear Image Structural Embedding

We partition a $d$-dimensional image $\boldsymbol{x}$ into $b = \lceil d/q \rceil$ non-overlapping blocks each of which is a reshaped vector $\breve{\boldsymbol{x}} \in \mathbb{R}^q$. In LLISE, we find a $p$-dimensional image structure manifold for every block. The $q$ is a parameter and is an upper bound on the desired dimensionality of the manifold of a block ($p \leq q$). This parameter is better not to be a very large number because of spatial variety of image statistics, and not very small to be able to capture the image structure. We denote the $i$-th block in the $j$-th image by $\breve{\boldsymbol{x}}_{j,i} \in \mathbb{R}^q$. In LLISE, we first center every image block by removing its mean.

## 2.1   Embedding the Training Data

**$k$-Nearest Neighbors.** For every block $\breve{\boldsymbol{x}}_i$ ($i \in \{1, \dots, b\}$), amongst the $n$ images, a $k$-NN graph is formed using pairwise Euclidean distances between that $i$-th block in the $n$ images. Therefore, every block in every image has $k$ neighbors. Let $_r\breve{\boldsymbol{x}}_{j,i} \in \mathbb{R}^q$ denote the $r$-th neighbor of $\breve{\boldsymbol{x}}_{j,i}$ and let the matrix $\mathbb{R}^{q \times k} \ni \breve{\boldsymbol{X}}_{j,i} := [_1\breve{\boldsymbol{x}}_{j,i}, \dots, _k\breve{\boldsymbol{x}}_{j,i}]$ include the neighbors of $\breve{\boldsymbol{x}}_{j,i}$.

**Linear Reconstruction by the Neighbors.** For every block $\breve{\boldsymbol{x}}_i$, we want the $j$-th image to be linearly reconstructed by its $k$ neighbors. We minimize the reconstruction error while the vector of reconstruction weights for every image block is a unit vector:

$$
\underset{\widetilde{\boldsymbol{W}}_i}{\text{minimize}} \quad \sum_{i=1}^{b} \varepsilon(\widetilde{\boldsymbol{W}}_i) := \sum_{i=1}^{b} \sum_{j=1}^{n} \left\| \breve{\boldsymbol{x}}_{j,i} - \sum_{r=1}^{k} {_r\widetilde{w}_{j,i}} \, {_r\breve{\boldsymbol{x}}_{j,i}} \right\|_S,
$$

$$
\text{subject to} \quad \sum_{r=1}^{k} {_r\widetilde{w}_{j,i}^2} = 1, \quad \forall i \in \{1, \dots, b\}, \quad \forall j \in \{1, \dots, n\},
$$

(3)

where $\mathbb{R}^{n \times k} \ni \widetilde{\boldsymbol{W}}_i := [\widetilde{\boldsymbol{w}}_{1,i}, \dots, \widetilde{\boldsymbol{w}}_{n,i}]^\top$ includes the weights for the $i$-th block in the images and $\mathbb{R}^k \ni \widetilde{\boldsymbol{w}}_{j,i} := [_1\widetilde{w}_{j,i}, \dots, _k\widetilde{w}_{j,i}]^\top$ includes the weights of linear reconstruction of the $i$-th block in the $j$-th image using its $k$ neighbors. The constraint ensures $\widetilde{\boldsymbol{w}}_{j,i}^\top \widetilde{\boldsymbol{w}}_{j,i} = \|\widetilde{\boldsymbol{w}}_{j,i}\|_2^2 = 1$. Note that we can formulate the problem with the constraint $\sum_{r=1}^{k} {_r\widetilde{w}_{j,i}} = 1$ as in LLE; however, with that constraint, the weights start to explode gradually after some optimization iterations. This problem does not happen in LLE because LLE is solved in closed form and not iteratively.

Take $f(\widetilde{\boldsymbol{w}}_{j,i}) := \left\| \breve{\boldsymbol{x}}_{j,i} - \sum_{r=1}^{k} {_r\widetilde{w}_{j,i}} \, {_r\breve{\boldsymbol{x}}_{j,i}} \right\|_S$ which is restated as $f(\widetilde{\boldsymbol{w}}_{j,i}) = \|\breve{\boldsymbol{x}}_{j,i} - \breve{\boldsymbol{X}}_{j,i} \widetilde{\boldsymbol{w}}_{j,i}\|_S$. According to Eq. (2), the $f(\widetilde{\boldsymbol{w}}_{j,i})$ is simplified to:

$$
\mathbb{R} \ni f(\widetilde{\boldsymbol{w}}_{j,i}) = \frac{\breve{\boldsymbol{x}}_{j,i}^\top \breve{\boldsymbol{x}}_{j,i} + \widetilde{\boldsymbol{w}}_{j,i}^\top \breve{\boldsymbol{X}}_{j,i}^\top \breve{\boldsymbol{X}}_{j,i} \widetilde{\boldsymbol{w}}_{j,i} - 2\widetilde{\boldsymbol{w}}_{j,i}^\top \breve{\boldsymbol{X}}_{j,i}^\top \breve{\boldsymbol{x}}_{j,i}}{\breve{\boldsymbol{x}}_{j,i}^\top \breve{\boldsymbol{x}}_{j,i} + \widetilde{\boldsymbol{w}}_{j,i}^\top \breve{\boldsymbol{X}}_{j,i}^\top \breve{\boldsymbol{X}}_{j,i} \widetilde{\boldsymbol{w}}_{j,i} + c}.
$$

(4)

The gradient of $f(\widetilde{\boldsymbol{w}}_{j,i})$ with respect to $\widetilde{\boldsymbol{w}}_{j,i}$ is:

$$\mathbb{R}^k \ni \nabla f(\widetilde{\boldsymbol{w}}_{j,i}) = \frac{2\,\breve{\boldsymbol{X}}_{j,i}^{\top}\left(\left(1 - f(\widetilde{\boldsymbol{w}}_{j,i})\right)\breve{\boldsymbol{X}}_{j,i}\widetilde{\boldsymbol{w}}_{j,i} - \breve{\boldsymbol{x}}_{j,i}\right)}{\breve{\boldsymbol{x}}_{j,i}^{\top}\breve{\boldsymbol{x}}_{j,i} + \widetilde{\boldsymbol{w}}_{j,i}^{\top}\breve{\boldsymbol{X}}_{j,i}^{\top}\breve{\boldsymbol{X}}_{j,i}\widetilde{\boldsymbol{w}}_{j,i} + c}. \tag{5}$$

The Eq. (3) can be rewritten as:

$$\underset{\widetilde{\boldsymbol{w}}_{j,i},\,\widetilde{\boldsymbol{\xi}}_{j,i}}{\text{minimize}} \quad \sum_{i=1}^{b}\sum_{j=1}^{n}\left(f(\widetilde{\boldsymbol{w}}_{j,i}) + h_1(\widetilde{\boldsymbol{\xi}}_{j,i})\right), \tag{6}$$

$$\text{subject to} \quad \widetilde{\boldsymbol{w}}_{j,i} - \widetilde{\boldsymbol{\xi}}_{j,i} = 0 \;\; \forall i \in \{1,\dots,b\}, \;\; \forall j \in \{1,\dots,n\},$$

where $\mathbb{R}^k \ni \widetilde{\boldsymbol{\xi}}_{j,i} := [_1\widetilde{\xi}_{j,i},\dots,\,_k\widetilde{\xi}_{j,i}]^{\top}$ and $h_1(\widetilde{\boldsymbol{\xi}}_{j,i}) := \mathbb{I}(\widetilde{\boldsymbol{\xi}}_{j,i}^{\top}\widetilde{\boldsymbol{\xi}}_{j,i} = 1)$. The $\mathbb{I}(.)$ denotes the indicator function which is zero if its condition is satisfied and is infinite otherwise. The Eq. (6) can be solved using Alternating Direction Method of Multipliers (ADMM) [8,9]. The augmented Lagrangian is: $\mathcal{L}_\rho = \sum_{i=1}^{b}\sum_{j=1}^{n}\left(f(\widetilde{\boldsymbol{w}}_{j,i}) + h_1(\widetilde{\boldsymbol{\xi}}_{j,i})\right) + (\rho/2)\,||\widetilde{\boldsymbol{w}}_{j,i} - \widetilde{\boldsymbol{\xi}}_{j,i} + \boldsymbol{j}_{j,i}||_2^2 - (\rho/2)\,||\boldsymbol{\lambda}_{j,i}||_2^2$, where $\boldsymbol{\lambda}_{j,i} \in \mathbb{R}^k$ is the Lagrange multiplier, $\rho > 0$ is a parameter, and $\mathbb{R}^k \ni \boldsymbol{j}_{j,i} := (1/\rho)\boldsymbol{\lambda}_{j,i}$. The term $(\rho/2)\,||\boldsymbol{\lambda}_{j,i}||_2^2$ is a constant with respect to $\widetilde{\boldsymbol{w}}_{j,i}$ and $\widetilde{\boldsymbol{\xi}}_{j,i}$ and can be dropped. The updates of $\widetilde{\boldsymbol{w}}_{j,i}$, $\widetilde{\boldsymbol{\xi}}_{j,i}$, and $\boldsymbol{j}_{j,i}$ are performed as [8,9]:

$$\widetilde{\boldsymbol{w}}_{j,i}^{(\nu+1)} := \arg\min_{\widetilde{\boldsymbol{w}}_{j,i}}\left(f(\widetilde{\boldsymbol{w}}_{j,i}) + (\rho/2)\,||\widetilde{\boldsymbol{w}}_{j,i} - \widetilde{\boldsymbol{\xi}}_{j,i}^{(\nu)} + \boldsymbol{j}_{j,i}^{(\nu)}||_2^2\right), \tag{7}$$

$$\widetilde{\boldsymbol{\xi}}_{j,i}^{(\nu+1)} := \arg\min_{\widetilde{\boldsymbol{\xi}}_{j,i}}\left(h_1(\widetilde{\boldsymbol{\xi}}_{j,i}) + (\rho/2)\,||\widetilde{\boldsymbol{w}}_{j,i}^{(\nu+1)} - \widetilde{\boldsymbol{\xi}}_{j,i} + \boldsymbol{j}_{j,i}^{(\nu)}||_2^2\right), \tag{8}$$

$$\boldsymbol{j}_{j,i}^{(\nu+1)} := \boldsymbol{j}_{j,i}^{(\nu)} + \widetilde{\boldsymbol{w}}_{j,i}^{(\nu+1)} - \widetilde{\boldsymbol{\xi}}_{j,i}^{(\nu+1)}, \tag{9}$$

where $\nu$ denotes the iteration. The gradient of the objective function in Eq. (7) is $\nabla f(\widetilde{\boldsymbol{w}}_{j,i}) + \rho\,(\widetilde{\boldsymbol{w}}_{j,i} - \widetilde{\boldsymbol{\xi}}_{j,i}^{(\nu)} + \boldsymbol{j}_{j,i}^{(\nu)})$. We can use the gradient decent method [10] for solving the Eq. (7). Our experiments showed that even one iteration of gradient decent suffices for Eq. (7) because the ADMM itself is iterative. Hence, we can replace this equation with one iteration of gradient decent.

The proximal operator is defined as [11]:

$$\text{prox}_{\lambda,h}(\boldsymbol{v}) := \arg\min_{\boldsymbol{u}}\left(h(\boldsymbol{u}) + (\lambda/2)||\boldsymbol{u} - \boldsymbol{v}||_2^2\right), \tag{10}$$

where $\lambda$ is the proximal parameter and $h$ is the function that the proximal algorithm wants to minimize. According to Eq. (10), the Eq. (8) is equivalent to $\text{prox}_{\rho,h_1}(\widetilde{\boldsymbol{w}}_{j,i}^{(\nu+1)} + \boldsymbol{j}_{j,i}^{(\nu)})$. As $h_1(.)$ is indicator function, its proximal operator is projection [11]. Therefore, Eq. (8) is equivalent to $\Pi(\widetilde{\boldsymbol{w}}_{j,i}^{(\nu+1)} + \boldsymbol{j}_{j,i}^{(\nu)})$ where $\Pi(.)$ denotes projection onto a set. The condition in $h_1(.)$ is $\widetilde{\boldsymbol{\xi}}_{j,i}^{\top}\widetilde{\boldsymbol{\xi}}_{j,i} = 1$; therefore, this projection normalizes the vector by dividing to its $\ell_2$ norm.

In summary, the Eqs. (7), (8), and (9) can be restated as:

$$\widetilde{\boldsymbol{w}}_{j,i}^{(\nu+1)} := \widetilde{\boldsymbol{w}}_{j,i}^{(\nu)} - \eta \, \nabla f(\widetilde{\boldsymbol{w}}_{j,i}^{(\nu)}) - \eta \, \rho \, (\widetilde{\boldsymbol{w}}_{j,i}^{(\nu)} - \widetilde{\boldsymbol{\xi}}_{j,i}^{(\nu)} + \boldsymbol{j}_{j,i}^{(\nu)}),$$

$$\widetilde{\boldsymbol{\xi}}_{j,i}^{(\nu+1)} := (\widetilde{\boldsymbol{w}}_{j,i}^{(\nu+1)} + \boldsymbol{j}_{j,i}^{(\nu)})/\|\widetilde{\boldsymbol{w}}_{j,i}^{(\nu+1)} + \boldsymbol{j}_{j,i}^{(\nu)}\|_2, \tag{11}$$

$$\boldsymbol{j}_{j,i}^{(\nu+1)} := \boldsymbol{j}_{j,i}^{(\nu)} + \widetilde{\boldsymbol{w}}_{j,i}^{(\nu+1)} - \widetilde{\boldsymbol{\xi}}_{j,i}^{(\nu+1)},$$

where $\eta > 0$ is the learning rate. Iteratively solving Eq. (11) until convergence gives us the $\widetilde{\boldsymbol{w}}_{j,i}$ for the $i$-th block in the $j$-th image. Note that Eq. (11) can be solved in parallel for the blocks of images.

**Linear Embedding.** In the previous section, we found the weights of linear reconstruction of the $i$-th block in every image from the $i$-th block in its $k$-NN. We can now find the embedding of the $i$-th block in every image using the obtained weights of reconstruction:

$$\underset{\boldsymbol{Y}_i}{\text{minimize}} \quad \sum_{i=1}^{b} \sum_{j=1}^{n} \Big\| \boldsymbol{y}_{j,i} - \sum_{r=1}^{n} {}_r w_{j,i} \, \boldsymbol{y}_{r,i} \Big\|_S,$$

$$\text{subject to} \quad \frac{1}{n} \sum_{j=1}^{n} \boldsymbol{y}_{j,i} \boldsymbol{y}_{j,i}^\top = \boldsymbol{I}, \quad \sum_{j=1}^{n} \boldsymbol{y}_{j,i} = \boldsymbol{0}, \quad \forall i \in \{1, \ldots, b\}, \tag{12}$$

where $\boldsymbol{I}$ is the identity matrix, the rows of $\mathbb{R}^{n \times p} \ni \boldsymbol{Y}_i := [\boldsymbol{y}_{1,i}, \ldots, \boldsymbol{y}_{n,i}]^\top$ are the embedded $i$-th block in the images, $\boldsymbol{y}_{r,i} \in \mathbb{R}^p$ is the $i$-th embedded block in the $r$-th image, and ${}_r w_{j,i}$ is the weight obtained from the linear reconstruction (previous section) if $\boldsymbol{x}_{r,i}$ is a neighbor of $\boldsymbol{x}_{j,i}$ and zero otherwise. The second constraint ensures the zero mean of embedded blocks. The first and second constraints together satisfy having unit covariance for the embedded image blocks.

Suppose $\mathbb{R}^n \ni \boldsymbol{w}_{j,i} := [{}_1 w_{j,i}, \ldots, {}_n w_{j,i}]^\top$ and let $\mathbb{R}^n \ni \boldsymbol{1}_j := [0, \ldots, 1, \ldots, 0]^\top$ be the vector whose $j$-th element is one and other elements are zero. The Eq. (12) can be restated as:

$$\underset{\boldsymbol{Y}_i}{\text{minimize}} \quad \sum_{i=1}^{b} \sum_{j=1}^{n} \|\boldsymbol{Y}_i^\top \boldsymbol{1}_j - \boldsymbol{Y}_i^\top \boldsymbol{w}_{j,i}\|_S,$$

$$\text{subject to} \quad \frac{1}{n} \boldsymbol{Y}_i^\top \boldsymbol{Y}_i = \boldsymbol{I}, \quad \boldsymbol{Y}_i^\top \boldsymbol{1} = \boldsymbol{0}, \quad \forall i \in \{1, \ldots, b\}. \tag{13}$$

Let $\theta_j(\boldsymbol{Y}_i) := \|\boldsymbol{Y}_i^\top \boldsymbol{1}_j - \boldsymbol{Y}_i^\top \boldsymbol{w}_{j,i}\|_S$. According to Eq. (2), it is simplified to:

$$\mathbb{R} \ni \theta_j(\boldsymbol{Y}_i) = \frac{\text{tr}(\boldsymbol{Y}_i^\top \boldsymbol{M}_{j,i} \boldsymbol{Y}_i)}{\text{tr}(\boldsymbol{Y}_i^\top \boldsymbol{\Psi}_{j,i} \boldsymbol{Y}_i) + c}, \tag{14}$$

where $\text{tr}(.)$ is the trace of matrix, $\mathbb{R}^{n \times n} \ni \boldsymbol{M}_{j,i} := \boldsymbol{1}_j \boldsymbol{1}_j^\top + \boldsymbol{w}_{j,i} \boldsymbol{w}_{j,i}^\top - 2 \, \boldsymbol{1}_j \boldsymbol{w}_{j,i}^\top$, and $\mathbb{R}^{n \times n} \ni \boldsymbol{\Psi}_{j,i} := \boldsymbol{1}_j \boldsymbol{1}_j^\top + \boldsymbol{w}_{j,i} \boldsymbol{w}_{j,i}^\top = \boldsymbol{M}_{j,i} + 2 \, \boldsymbol{1}_j \boldsymbol{w}_{j,i}^\top$. The gradient of $\theta_j(\boldsymbol{Y}_i)$ with respect to $\boldsymbol{Y}_i$ is:

$$\mathbb{R}^{n \times p} \ni \nabla \theta_j(\boldsymbol{Y}_i) = \frac{2}{\text{tr}(\boldsymbol{Y}_i^\top \boldsymbol{\Psi}_{j,i} \boldsymbol{Y}_i) + c} \Big( \boldsymbol{M}_{j,i} - \theta_j(\boldsymbol{Y}_i) \boldsymbol{\Psi}_{j,i} \Big) \boldsymbol{Y}_i. \tag{15}$$

In Eq. (13), we can embed the constraint as an indicator function in the objective function [8]:

$$\underset{Y_i, V_i \in \mathbb{R}^{n \times p}}{\text{minimize}} \sum_{i=1}^{b} \left( \sum_{j=1}^{n} \left( \theta_j(Y_i) \right) + h_2(V_i) \right), \tag{16}$$
$$\text{subject to} \quad Y - V = 0,$$

where $h_2(V_i) := \mathbb{I}(V_i^\top 1 = 0 \wedge (1/n) V_i^\top V_i = I)$. The $U$ and $V$ are union of partitions, i.e., $Y := \cup_{i=1}^{b} Y_i$ and $V := \cup_{i=1}^{b} V_i$ [9].

We can solve the Eq. (16) using Alternating Direction Method of Multipliers (ADMM) [8,9]. The augmented Lagrangian is: $\mathcal{L}_\rho = \sum_{i=1}^{b} \left( \sum_{j=1}^{n} \left( \theta_j(Y_i) \right) + h(V_i) \right) + \text{tr}\left( \Lambda^\top (Y - V) \right) + (\rho/2) \|Y - V\|_F^2 = \sum_{i=1}^{b} \left( \sum_{j=1}^{n} \left( \theta_j(Y_i) \right) + h(V_i) \right) + (\rho/2) \|Y - V + J\|_F^2 - (\rho/2) \|\Lambda\|_F^2$, where $\Lambda := \cup_{i=1}^{b} \Lambda_i$ is the Lagrange multiplier, $\rho > 0$, and $J := (1/\rho)\Lambda = (1/\rho) \cup_{i=1}^{b} \Lambda_i = \cup_{i=1}^{b} J_i$. The term $(\rho/2) \|\Lambda\|_F^2$ is a constant with respect to $Y$ and $V$ and can be dropped. The updates of $Y$, $V$, and $J$ are done as [8,9]:

$$Y_i^{(\nu+1)} := \arg\min_{Y_i} \left( \sum_{j=1}^{n} \left( \theta_j(Y_i) \right) + (\rho/2) \|Y_i - V_i^{(\nu)} + J_i^{(\nu)}\|_F^2 \right), \tag{17}$$

$$V_i^{(\nu+1)} := \arg\min_{V_i} \left( h_2(V_i) + (\rho/2) \|Y_i^{(\nu+1)} - V_i + J_i^{(\nu)}\|_F^2 \right), \tag{18}$$

$$J^{(\nu+1)} := J^{(\nu)} + Y^{(\nu+1)} - V^{(\nu+1)}. \tag{19}$$

The gradient of the objective function in Eq. (17) is $\sum_{j=1}^{n} \left( \nabla \theta_j(Y_i) \right) + \rho \left( Y_i - V_i^{(\nu)} + J_i^{(\nu)} \right)$. Similar to Eq. (7), we replace Eq. (17) with one iteration of gradient descent.

With the same explanation for Eq. (8), Eq. (18) is equivalent to the projection $\Pi(Y_i^{(\nu+1)} + J_i^{(\nu)})$. One of the constraints in Eq. (13) is $Y_i^\top 1 = 0$. Therefore, the row mean of the matrix should removed, i.e., $Y_i := H Y_i$, where $\mathbb{R}^{n \times n} \ni H := I - (1/n)11^\top$ is the centering matrix and $1$ is the vector of ones. The other constraint in Eq. (13) is $(1/n)Y_i^\top Y_i = I$. The variable of proximal operator, which is a projection here, is a matrix and not a vector. According to [11], if $F$ is a convex and orthogonally invariant function and it works on the singular values of a matrix variable $A \in \mathbb{R}^{n \times p}$, i.e., $F = f \circ \sigma$ where the function $\sigma(A)$ gives the vector of singular values of $A$, then the proximal operator is $\mathbf{prox}_{\lambda, F}(A) := Q \, \text{diag}\left( \mathbf{prox}_{\lambda, f}(\sigma(A)) \right) \Omega^\top$. The $Q \in \mathbb{R}^{n \times p}$ and $\Omega \in \mathbb{R}^{p \times p}$ are the matrices of left and right singular vectors of $A$, respectively. In our constraint $(1/n)Y_i^\top Y_i = I$, the function $F$ deals with the singular values of $Y_i$. The reason is that we want: $Y_i \overset{\text{SVD}}{=} Q\Sigma\Omega^\top \implies (1/n)Y_i^\top Y_i = (1/n)\Omega\Sigma Q^\top Q\Sigma\Omega^\top \overset{(a)}{=} (1/n)\Omega\Sigma^2\Omega^\top \overset{\text{set}}{=} I \implies (1/n)\Omega\Sigma^2\Omega^\top\Omega = \Omega \overset{(b)}{\implies} (1/n)\Omega\Sigma^2 = \Omega \implies \Sigma = nI$, where $(a)$ and $(b)$ are because $Q$ and $\Omega$ are orthogonal matrices. Thus, projection onto the second constraint is equivalent to decomposing the matrix with Singular

Value Decomposition (SVD) and setting all the singular values to $n$. To sum up, $\Pi(\boldsymbol{Y}_i^{(\nu+1)} + \boldsymbol{J}_i^{(\nu)})$ first removes the row mean of $(\boldsymbol{Y}_i^{(\nu+1)} + \boldsymbol{J}_i^{(\nu)})$ and then sets the singular values of $(\boldsymbol{Y}_i^{(\nu+1)} + \boldsymbol{J}_i^{(\nu)})$ to $n$. In summary, the Eqs. (17), (18), and (19) can be restated as:

$$
\begin{aligned}
\boldsymbol{Y}_i^{(\nu+1)} &:= \boldsymbol{Y}_i^{(\nu)} - \eta \sum_{j=1}^{n} \left(\nabla\theta_j(\boldsymbol{Y}_i)\right) - \eta\,\rho\left(\boldsymbol{Y}_i - \boldsymbol{V}_i^{(\nu)} + \boldsymbol{J}_i^{(\nu)}\right), \\
\boldsymbol{V}_i^{(\nu+1)} &:= \Pi(\boldsymbol{Y}_i^{(\nu+1)} + \boldsymbol{J}_i^{(\nu)}), \\
\boldsymbol{J}^{(\nu+1)} &:= \boldsymbol{J}^{(\nu)} + \boldsymbol{Y}^{(\nu+1)} - \boldsymbol{V}^{(\nu+1)}.
\end{aligned}
\tag{20}
$$

Iteratively solving Eq. (20) until convergence gives us the $\boldsymbol{Y}_i$ for the image blocks indexed by $i$. The rows of $\boldsymbol{Y}_i$ are the $p$-dimensional embedded image blocks in the *LLISE manifold*. Unlike LLE, the first column of $\boldsymbol{Y}_i$ is not ignored in LLISE because it is not based on $\ell_2$ norm and thus eigenvalue problem.

## 2.2   Embedding the Out-of-Sample Data

There exist two methods in the literature for extension of LLE for out-of-sample embedding. The first method is based on the concept of eigenfunctions [12] and the second method uses linear reconstruction of the out-of-sample data [13]. The first method cannot be used for LLISE because it does not result in closed-form eigenvalue problem as in LLE. We use the second approach.

Suppose we have $n_t$ out-of-sample images and $\check{\boldsymbol{x}}_{j,i}^{(t)}$ denotes the $i$-th block in the $j$-th out-of-sample image. For the $i$-th block in every out-of-sample image, we first find the $k$-NN among the $i$-th block in training images. Let $_r\check{\boldsymbol{x}}_{j,i}^{(t)}$ and $\mathbb{R}^{q\times k} \ni \check{\boldsymbol{X}}_{j,i}^{(t)} := [_1\check{\boldsymbol{x}}_{j,i}^{(t)}, \ldots, _k\check{\boldsymbol{x}}_{j,i}^{(t)}]$ denote the $r$-th training neighbor of $\check{\boldsymbol{x}}_{j,i}^{(t)}$ and the matrix including the training neighbors of $\check{\boldsymbol{x}}_{j,i}^{(t)}$, respectively. We want to reconstruct every out-of-sample image block by its training neighbors:

$$
\begin{aligned}
&\underset{\widetilde{\boldsymbol{W}}_i^{(t)}}{\text{minimize}} \quad \sum_{i=1}^{b} \varepsilon(\widetilde{\boldsymbol{W}}_i^{(t)}) := \sum_{i=1}^{b}\sum_{j=1}^{n_t} \left\| \check{\boldsymbol{x}}_{j,i}^{(t)} - \sum_{r=1}^{k} {_r\widetilde{w}_{j,i}^{(t)}} \; {_r\check{\boldsymbol{x}}_{j,i}^{(t)}} \right\|_S, \\
&\text{subject to} \quad \sum_{r=1}^{k} ({_r\widetilde{w}_{j,i}^{(t)}})^2 = 1, \quad \forall i \in \{1,\ldots,b\}, \;\; \forall j \in \{1,\ldots,n_t\},
\end{aligned}
\tag{21}
$$

where $\mathbb{R}^{n_t \times k} \ni \widetilde{\boldsymbol{W}}_i^{(t)} := [\widetilde{w}_{1,i}^{(t)}, \ldots, \widetilde{w}_{n_t,i}^{(t)}]^\top$ includes the weights, $\mathbb{R}^k \ni \widetilde{w}_{j,i}^{(t)} := [_1\widetilde{w}_{j,i}^{(t)}, \ldots, _k\widetilde{w}_{j,i}^{(t)}]^\top$ includes the weights of linear reconstruction of the $i$-th block in the $j$-th out-of-sample image using the $i$-th block in its $k$ training neighbors. Note that Eq. (21) is similar to Eq. (3) and is solved using Eq. (11) where $\widetilde{w}_{j,i}^{(t)}$, $\check{\boldsymbol{x}}_{j,i}^{(t)}$, and $\check{\boldsymbol{X}}_{j,i}^{(t)}$ are used in the expressions.

The embedding $\boldsymbol{y}_{j,i}^{(t)}$ of the $i$-th block in the $j$-th out-of-sample image, i.e., $\boldsymbol{x}_{j,i}^{(t)}$, is obtained by the linear reconstruction of the embedding of the $i$-th block in its $k$ training neighbors:

$$\mathbb{R}^p \ni \boldsymbol{y}_{j,i}^{(t)} = \sum_{r=1}^{k} {}_r\widetilde{w}_{j,i}^{(t)} \, {}_r\boldsymbol{y}_{j,i}^{(t)}, \tag{22}$$

where ${}_r\boldsymbol{y}_{j,i}^{(t)} \in \mathbb{R}^p$ is the embedding of ${}_r\check{\boldsymbol{x}}_{j,i}^{(t)}$ which was found by the linear embedding of the training data, $\boldsymbol{Y}_i$.

## 3    Kernel Locally Linear Image Structural Embedding

We can map the block $\check{\boldsymbol{x}}_i \in \mathbb{R}^d$ to higher-dimensional feature space hoping to have the data fall close to a simpler-to-analyze manifold in the feature space. Suppose $\boldsymbol{\phi} : \check{\boldsymbol{x}} \to \mathcal{H}$ is a function which maps the data $\check{\boldsymbol{x}}$ to the feature space. In other words, $\check{\boldsymbol{x}} \mapsto \boldsymbol{\phi}(\check{\boldsymbol{x}})$. Let $t$ denote the dimensionality of the feature space, i.e., $\boldsymbol{\phi}(\check{\boldsymbol{x}}) \in \mathbb{R}^t$. We usually have $t \gg d$. The kernel of the $i$-th block in images 1 and 2, which are $\check{\boldsymbol{x}}_{1,i}$ and $\check{\boldsymbol{x}}_{2,i}$, is $k(\check{\boldsymbol{x}}_{1,i}, \check{\boldsymbol{x}}_{2,i}) := \boldsymbol{\phi}(\check{\boldsymbol{x}}_{1,i})^\top \boldsymbol{\phi}(\check{\boldsymbol{x}}_{2,i}) \in \mathbb{R}$.

Let $\boldsymbol{K} = \boldsymbol{\Phi}(\check{\boldsymbol{X}}_i)^\top \boldsymbol{\Phi}(\check{\boldsymbol{X}}_i) \in \mathbb{R}^{n \times n}$ be the kernel between the $i$-th block in the $n$ images. We can normalize it as $\boldsymbol{K}(a,b) := \boldsymbol{K}(a,b)/\sqrt{\boldsymbol{K}(a,a)\boldsymbol{K}(b,b)}$ where $\boldsymbol{K}(a,b)$ denotes the $(a,b)$-th element of the kernel matrix [14]. Then, the kernel is double-centered as $\boldsymbol{K} := \boldsymbol{H}\boldsymbol{K}\boldsymbol{H}$. The reason for double-centering is that Eq. (2) requires $\boldsymbol{\phi}(\check{\boldsymbol{x}}_i)$ and thus the $\boldsymbol{\Phi}(\check{\boldsymbol{X}}_i)$ to be centered. Therefore, in kernel LLISE, we center the kernel rather than centering $\check{\boldsymbol{x}}_i$. Kernel LLISE maps the data to the feature space and performs the steps of $k$-NN and linear reconstruction in the feature space.

### 3.1    Embedding the Training Data

**$k$-Nearest Neighbors.** The Euclidean distance in the feature space is [15]:

$$||\boldsymbol{\phi}(\check{\boldsymbol{x}}_{a,i}) - \boldsymbol{\phi}(\check{\boldsymbol{x}}_{b,i})||_2 = \sqrt{k(\check{\boldsymbol{x}}_{a,i}, \check{\boldsymbol{x}}_{a,i}) - 2k(\check{\boldsymbol{x}}_{a,i}, \check{\boldsymbol{x}}_{b,i}) + k(\check{\boldsymbol{x}}_{b,i}, \check{\boldsymbol{x}}_{b,i})}. \tag{23}$$

For every block $i$ amongst the images, we construct the $k$-NN graph using the distances of the blocks in the feature space. Therefore, every block has $k$ neighbors in the feature space. Let the matrix $\mathbb{R}^{t \times k} \ni \boldsymbol{\Phi}(\check{\boldsymbol{X}}_{j,i}) := [\boldsymbol{\phi}({}_1\check{\boldsymbol{x}}_{j,i}), \dots, \boldsymbol{\phi}({}_k\check{\boldsymbol{x}}_{j,i})]$ include the neighbors of $\check{\boldsymbol{x}}_{j,i}$ in the feature space.

**Linear Reconstruction by the Neighbors.** For finding the reconstruction weights $\mathbb{R}^k \ni \widetilde{\boldsymbol{w}}_{j,i} = [{}_1\widetilde{w}_{j,i}, \dots, {}_k\widetilde{w}_{j,i}]^\top$, the Eq. (3) is used in the feature space:

$$\underset{\widetilde{\boldsymbol{W}}_i}{\text{minimize}} \quad \varepsilon(\widetilde{\boldsymbol{W}}_i) := \sum_{i=1}^{b}\sum_{j=1}^{n} \left|\left| \boldsymbol{\phi}(\check{\boldsymbol{x}}_{j,i}) - \sum_{r=1}^{k} {}_r\widetilde{w}_{j,i} \, \boldsymbol{\phi}({}_r\check{\boldsymbol{x}}_{j,i}) \right|\right|_S,$$

$$\text{subject to} \quad \sum_{r=1}^{k} {}_r\widetilde{w}_{j,i}^2 = 1, \quad \forall i \in \{1, \dots, b\}, \quad \forall j \in \{1, \dots, n\}. \tag{24}$$

Let $f^\phi(\widetilde{\boldsymbol{w}}_{j,i}) := \big\| \boldsymbol{\phi}(\breve{\boldsymbol{x}}_{j,i}) - \sum_{r=1}^{k} {}_r\widetilde{w}_{ij}\, \boldsymbol{\phi}({}_r\breve{\boldsymbol{x}}_{j,i}) \big\|_S$. According to Eq. (2), we have:

$$\mathbb{R} \ni f^\phi(\widetilde{\boldsymbol{w}}_{j,i}) = \frac{k_{j,i} + \widetilde{\boldsymbol{w}}_{j,i}^\top \boldsymbol{K}_{j,i}\, \widetilde{\boldsymbol{w}}_{j,i} - 2\,\widetilde{\boldsymbol{w}}_{j,i}^\top \boldsymbol{k}_{j,i}}{k_{j,i} + \widetilde{\boldsymbol{w}}_{j,i}^\top \boldsymbol{K}_{j,i}\, \widetilde{\boldsymbol{w}}_{j,i} + c}, \tag{25}$$

where $\mathbb{R} \ni k_{j,i} := \boldsymbol{\phi}(\breve{\boldsymbol{x}}_{j,i})^\top \boldsymbol{\phi}(\breve{\boldsymbol{x}}_{j,i})$, $\mathbb{R}^k \ni \boldsymbol{k}_{j,i} := \boldsymbol{\Phi}(\breve{\boldsymbol{X}}_{j,i})^\top \boldsymbol{\phi}(\breve{\boldsymbol{x}}_{j,i})$, and $\mathbb{R}^{k\times k} \ni \boldsymbol{K}_{j,i} := \boldsymbol{\Phi}(\breve{\boldsymbol{X}}_{j,i})^\top \boldsymbol{\Phi}(\breve{\boldsymbol{X}}_{j,i})$. The gradient of $f^\phi(\widetilde{\boldsymbol{w}}_{j,i})$ with respect to $\widetilde{\boldsymbol{w}}_{j,i}$ is:

$$\mathbb{R}^k \ni \nabla f^\phi(\widetilde{\boldsymbol{w}}_{j,i}) = \frac{2\left( (1 - f^\phi(\widetilde{\boldsymbol{w}}_{j,i}))\, \boldsymbol{K}_{j,i}\, \widetilde{\boldsymbol{w}}_{j,i} - \boldsymbol{k}_{j,i} \right)}{k_{j,i} + \widetilde{\boldsymbol{w}}_{j,i}^\top \boldsymbol{K}_{j,i}\, \widetilde{\boldsymbol{w}}_{j,i} + c}. \tag{26}$$

We can use Eq. (11) for solving Eq. (24) where $\nabla f^\phi(\widetilde{\boldsymbol{w}}_{j,i})$ is used in place of $\nabla f(\widetilde{\boldsymbol{w}}_{j,i})$. The linear embedding in kernel LLISE is the same as the linear embedding in LLISE. The rows of obtained $\boldsymbol{Y}_i$ are the $i$-th embedded block of the images in *kernel LLISE manifold*.

## 3.2   Embedding the Out-of-Sample Data

For embedding every out-of-sample image, we reconstruct it by its training neighbors in the feature space. The Eq. (21) in the feature space is:

$$\underset{\widetilde{\boldsymbol{W}}_i^{(t)}}{\text{minimize}} \quad \sum_{i=1}^{b} \varepsilon(\widetilde{\boldsymbol{W}}_i^{(t)}) := \sum_{i=1}^{b} \sum_{j=1}^{n_t} \Big\| \boldsymbol{\phi}(\breve{\boldsymbol{x}}_{j,i}^{(t)}) - \sum_{r=1}^{k} {}_r\widetilde{w}_{j,i}^{(t)}\, \boldsymbol{\phi}({}_r\breve{\boldsymbol{x}}_{j,i}^{(t)}) \Big\|_S,$$

$$\text{subject to} \quad \sum_{r=1}^{k} ({}_r\widetilde{w}_{j,i}^{(t)})^2 = 1, \quad \forall i \in \{1, \ldots, b\}, \quad \forall j \in \{1, \ldots, n_t\}, \tag{27}$$

which is similar to Eq. (24) and is solved similarly. Here, the used kernels are $\mathbb{R} \ni k_{j,i} = \boldsymbol{\phi}(\breve{\boldsymbol{x}}_{j,i}^{(t)})^\top \boldsymbol{\phi}(\breve{\boldsymbol{x}}_{j,i}^{(t)})$, $\mathbb{R}^k \ni \boldsymbol{k}_{j,i} = \boldsymbol{\Phi}(\breve{\boldsymbol{X}}_{j,i}^{(t)})^\top \boldsymbol{\phi}(\breve{\boldsymbol{x}}_{j,i}^{(t)})$, and $\mathbb{R}^{k\times k} \ni \boldsymbol{K}_{j,i} = \boldsymbol{\Phi}(\breve{\boldsymbol{X}}_{j,i}^{(t)})^\top \boldsymbol{\Phi}(\breve{\boldsymbol{X}}_{j,i}^{(t)})$. After finding the weights $\widetilde{\boldsymbol{w}}_{j,i}^{(t)} = [{}_1\widetilde{w}_{j,i}^{(t)}, \ldots, {}_k\widetilde{w}_{j,i}^{(t)}]$ from Eq. (27), the embedding of the out-of-sample $\boldsymbol{x}_{j,i}^{(t)}$ is found using Eq. (22) where ${}_r\boldsymbol{y}_{j,i}^{(t)} \in \mathbb{R}^p$ is the embedding of ${}_r\breve{\boldsymbol{x}}_{j,i}^{(t)}$ in kernel LLISE.

## 4   Experiments

**Training Dataset:** We made a dataset out of the standard *Lena* image. Six different types of distortions were applied on the original *Lena* image (see Fig. 1), each of which has 20 images in the dataset with different MSE values. Therefore, the size of the training set is 121 including the original image. For every type of distortion, 20 different levels of MSE, i.e., from MSE = 45 to MSE = 900 with step 45, were generated to have images on the equal-MSE or *iso-error* hypersphere [3].

**Fig. 1.** Samples from the training dataset: (a) original image, (b) contrast stretched, (c) Gaussian noise, (d) luminance enhanced, (e) Gaussian blurring, (f) salt & pepper impulse noise, and (g) JPEG distortion.

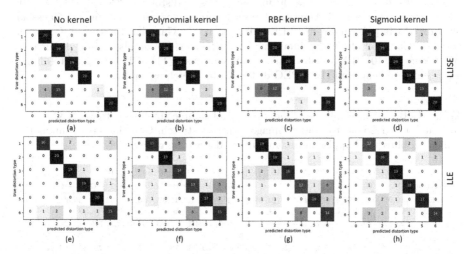

**Fig. 2.** Confusion matrices for recognition of distortion types with a 1NN classifier used in the embedded space. Matrices (a) and (e) correspond to LLISE and LLE, respectively. Matrices (b) to (d) are for kernel LLISE and (f) and (g) are for kernel LLE with polynomial, RBF, and sigmoid kernels, respectively. The 0 label corresponds to the original image and the labels 1 to 6 are the distortion types with the same order as in Fig. 1.

**Embedding the Training Images:** We embedded the blocks in the training images. In $k$-NN, we used $k = 10$. For linear reconstruction, we used $\rho = \eta = 0.1$ in LLISE and $10\rho = \eta = 0.1$ in kernel LLISE. For linear embedding, we used $\rho = \eta = 0.01$. We took $q = 64$ ($8 \times 8$ blocks inspired by [6,9]), $p = 4$, and $d = 512 \times 512 = 262144$. In order to evaluate the obtained embedded manifold, we used the 1-Nearest Neighbor (1NN) classifier to recognize the distortion type of every block. The 1NN is useful to show how to evaluate the manifold by closeness of the embedded distortions. The distortion type of an image comes from a majority vote among the blocks. The polynomial $(\gamma \breve{x}_1^\top \breve{x}_2 + 1)^3$, Radial Basis function (RBF) $\exp(-\gamma \|\breve{x}_1 - \breve{x}_2\|_2^2)$, and sigmoid $\tanh(\gamma \breve{x}_1^\top \breve{x}_2 + 1)$ kernels were tested for kernel LLISE, where $\gamma := 1/q$. The confusion matrices for distortion recognition are shown in Fig. 2. Also, the LLISE and kernel LLISE are compared with LLE and kernel LLE in this figure. Except for impulse noise, LLISE and

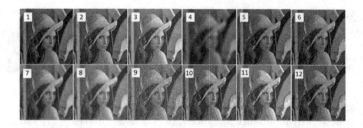

**Fig. 3.** Out-of-sample images with different types of distortions having MSE = 500: (1) stretching contrast, (2) Gaussian noise, (3) luminance enhancement, (4) Gaussian blurring, (5) impulse noise, (6) JPEG distortion, (7) Gaussian blurring + Gaussian noise, (8) Gaussian blurring + luminance enhancement, (9) impulse noise + luminance enhancement, (10) JPEG distortion + Gaussian noise, (11) JPEG distortion + luminance enhancement, and (12) JPEG distortion + stretching contrast.

**Table 1.** Recognition of distortions for out-of-sample images. Letters O, C, G, L, B, I, and J correspond to original image, contrast stretch, Gaussian noise, luminance enhanced, blurring, impulse noise, and JPEG distortion, respectively.

| Image | 1 | 2 | 3 | 4 | 5 | 6 | 7 | 8 | 9 | 10 | 11 | 12 |
|---|---|---|---|---|---|---|---|---|---|---|---|---|
| Distortion | C | G | L | B | I | J | B + G | B + L | I + L | J + G | J + L | J + C |
| LLISE | 42.9% C | 42.2% G | 35.6% L | 44.5% B | 31.2% G | 43.2% J | 46.8% G | 41.3% B | 55.9% G | 33.5% G | 39.6% J | 40.7% J |
|  | 22.8% L | 29.3% I | 29.6% C | 15.7% J | 28.4% I | 16.8% B | 34.4% I | 14.7% J | 39.6% I | 26.5% I | 16.3% B | 16.3% L |
| Kernel LLISE (polynomial) | 69.7% C | 23.7% L | 97.5% L | 74.3% B | 45.4% C | 76.6% J | 20.7% G | 78.1% L | 35.1% G | 27.7% L | 76.9% L | 45.1% J |
|  | 14.7% I | 21.3% G | 0.8% C | 14.5% J | 19.5% I | 13.9% B | 17.9% B | 5.7% I | 23.5% L | 16.6% G | 7.0% B | 28.6% B |
| Kernel LLISE (RBF) | 62.1% C | 25.6% L | 72.6% L | 58.1% B | 42.3% C | 59.6% J | 23.7% B | 58.1% L | 33.3% L | 26.5% L | 57.8% L | 40.0% J |
|  | 12.0% I | 16.1% B | 9.5% C | 16.3% J | 17.0% I | 16.4% B | 18.5% J | 11.9% B | 24.7% G | 19.6% J | 13.0% B | 24.8% B |
| Kernel LLISE (sigmoid) | 63.0% C | 28.5% L | 92.4% L | 68.5% B | 51.9% C | 55.6% J | 39.2% B | 77.8% L | 57.0% L | 31.1% L | 76.1% L | 42.8% J |
|  | 14.5% I | 24.5% C | 3.5% B | 15.5% J | 14.0% I | 19.7% B | 19.5% L | 10.7% B | 12.6% C | 24.6% B | 10.8% B | 29.4% B |
| LLE | C | L | L | B | C | J | B | C | C | L | L | B |
| Kernel LLE (polynomial) | L | C | L | B | C | J | B | L | L | B | L | J |
| Kernel LLE (RBF) | L | C | C | J | C | J | B | L | L | B | L | J |
| Kernel LLE (sigmoid) | C | L | L | B | C | J | J | C | L | C | C | C |

kernel LLISE had better performance compared to LLE and kernel LLE. In other distortions, especially in JPEG distortion and contrast stretch, the performances of LLE and kernel LLE are not acceptable because LLE uses $\ell_2$ norm rather than SSIM distance.

**Out-of-sample Embedding:** For out-of-sample embedding, we made 12 test images with MSE = 500 having different distortions and some having a combination of different distortions (see Fig. 3). Again, for linear reconstruction, we used $\rho = \eta = 0.1$ in LLISE and $10\rho = \eta = 0.1$ in kernel LLISE. The same 1NN classification was done for the test images. Table 1 reports the top two votes of blocks for every image with the percentage of blocks voting for those distortions. This table also shows the recognition of distortions using LLE and kernel LLE. Note that LLE does not perform block-wise and thus it has only one recognition label for the whole image. As expected for LLISE and kernel LLISE, in most cases, at least one of the two top votes recognized the type of distortion(s) the out-of-sample images had. However, LLE and kernel LLE performed poorly on the out-of-sample images.

## 5 Conclusion and Future Work

This paper introduced the concept of an image structure manifold which discriminates the types of distortions applied on the images and captures the structure of an image. A new method, named LLISE, was proposed for learning this manifold in both original and feature spaces. The LLISE is inspired by LLE which uses $\ell_2$ norm. As a possible future work, we seek to design other new methods for learning the image structure manifold.

## References

1. Wang, Z., Bovik, A.C.: Mean squared error: love it or leave it? A new look at signal fidelity measures. IEEE Signal Process. Magaz. **26**(1), 98–117 (2009)
2. Wang, Z., Bovik, A.C., Sheikh, H.R., Simoncelli, E.P.: Image quality assessment: from error visibility to structural similarity. IEEE Trans. Image Process. **13**(4), 600–612 (2004)
3. Wang, Z., Bovik, A.C.: Modern image quality assessment. Synthesis Lect. Image Video Multimedia Process. **2**(1), 1–156 (2006)
4. Brunet, D., Vrscay, E.R., Wang, Z.: On the mathematical properties of the structural similarity index. IEEE Trans. Image Process. **21**(4), 1488–1499 (2012)
5. Roweis, S.T., Saul, L.K.: Nonlinear dimensionality reduction by locally linear embedding. Science **290**(5500), 2323–2326 (2000)
6. Otero, D., Vrscay, E.R.: Unconstrained structural similarity-based optimization. In: Campilho, A., Kamel, M. (eds.) ICIAR 2014. LNCS, vol. 8814, pp. 167–176. Springer, Cham (2014). https://doi.org/10.1007/978-3-319-11758-4_19
7. Zhao, X., Zhang, S.: Facial expression recognition using local binary patterns and discriminant kernel locally linear embedding. EURASIP J. Adv. Signal Process. **2012**, 20 (2012)

8. Boyd, S., Parikh, N., Chu, E., Peleato, B., Eckstein, J., et al.: Distributed optimization and statistical learning via the alternating direction method of multipliers. Found. Trends® Mach. Learn. **3**(1), 1–122 (2011)

9. Otero, D., Torre, D.L., Michailovich, O.V., Vrscay, E.R.: Alternate direction method of multipliers for unconstrained structural similarity-based optimization. In: Campilho, A., Karray, F., ter Haar Romeny, B. (eds.) Image Analysis and Recognition. ICIAR 2018. LNCS, vol. 10882, pp. 20–29. Springer, Cham (2018). https://doi.org/10.1007/978-3-319-93000-8_3

10. Boyd, S., Vandenberghe, L.: Convex Optimization. Cambridge University Press, New York (2004)

11. Parikh, N., Boyd, S.: Proximal algorithms. Found. Trends® Optim. **1**(3), 127–239 (2014)

12. Bengio, Y., Paiement, J.F., Vincent, P., Delalleau, O., Roux, N.L., Ouimet, M.: Out-of-sample extensions for LLE, Isomap, MDS, eigenmaps, and spectral clustering. In: Advances in Neural Information Processing Systems, pp. 177–184 (2004)

13. Saul, L.K., Roweis, S.T.: Think globally, fit locally: unsupervised learning of low dimensional manifolds. J. Mach. Learn. Res. **4**, 119–155 (2003)

14. Ah-Pine, J.: Normalized kernels as similarity indices. In: Zaki, M.J., Yu, J.X., Ravindran, B., Pudi, V. (eds.) PAKDD 2010. LNCS (LNAI), vol. 6119, pp. 362–373. Springer, Heidelberg (2010). https://doi.org/10.1007/978-3-642-13672-6_36

15. Schölkopf, B.: The kernel trick for distances. In: Advances in Neural Information Processing Systems, pp. 301–307 (2001)

# Fitting Smooth Manifolds to Point Clouds in a Level Set Formulation

Hossein Soleimani$^{(\boxtimes)}$, George Poothicottu Jacob, and Oleg V. Michailovich

University of Waterloo, Waterloo, Canada
{h3soleim,gpoothic,olegm}@uwaterloo.ca

**Abstract.** Since its inception, curves and surfaces have been the principal means of representation of observed geometry in computer vision. In many practical applications, one's knowledge of the shapes of real-life objects is obtained through discrete measurements, which are subsequently converted into their continuous counterparts through the process of either curve or surface fitting, depending on the object dimensionality. Unfortunately, the measurement noise due to environmental effects, operator errors and/or hardware limitations makes the fitting problem a challenging one, requiring its solutions to possess a substantial degree of robustness. Moreover, in the case of surface fitting, the use of relatively complex fitting mechanisms might be disadvantageous due to their typically higher computational requirements, which could, in turn, create an implementation bottleneck due to the high dimensionality of the data. Accordingly, in this work, we propose a unified approach to fitting of smooth geometric manifolds, such as curves and surfaces, to point clouds. The proposed method is based on a level-set formulation, which leads to a simple and computationally efficient algorithm, the practical value of which is demonstrated through a series of examples.

**Keywords:** Surface fitting · Point clouds · Level-set functions · Total-variation

## 1 Introduction

The problem of fitting of smooth geometric manifolds, such as spatial curves and surfaces, to finite sets of Euclidean points is unarguably one of the classical problems of image processing and computer vision. Such sets of points, commonly referred to as *point clouds*, are typically acquired by means of range/depth sensors to provide a raw description of the shape and geometry of scanned objects. Due to their irregular and noisy nature, however, point clouds are rarely used by higher level algorithms and visualization software. Instead, the latter "prefer" to process continuous representations of observed geometries, which are derived from point clouds through the process of curve/surface fitting. Virtual and augmented reality, reverse engineering, and medical imaging are only a few examples of application areas, where such fitting problems routinely arise [1].

© Springer Nature Switzerland AG 2019
F. Karray et al. (Eds.): ICIAR 2019, LNCS 11662, pp. 139–149, 2019.
https://doi.org/10.1007/978-3-030-27202-9_12

Moreover, the recent advance in digital scanning technologies has resulted in a widespread proliferation of a variety of new depth/range scanning devices, which often present unexplored challenges from the viewpoint of curve/surface fitting. To cope with these challenges, a broad spectrum of fitting methodologies has been so far proposed [2], which generally differ in their ability to withstand the effects of noise and scarce sampling as well as to effectively deal with non-trivial topologies [3].

The current arsenal of methods for curve/surface fitting is vast, suggesting a variety of possible taxonomies. A particular way to classify such methods could be based on their property of being either *explicit* or *implicit* [4]. In the explicit formulation, it is standard to represent surfaces by means of triangulated meshes obtained based on Voronoi diagrams [5] or Delaunay triangulation [6]. In their core, such methods are based on systematically connecting the points of a cloud until a predefined completeness criterion is met. Under weak noise conditions and in the absence of considerable gaps between data points, explicit representations are known to provide satisfactory and useful results. Unfortunately, their quality degrades quickly when the aforementioned assumptions start to fail.

In implicit representation, curves and surfaces are typically defined by means of either the indicator functions of closed subsets of $\mathbb{R}^d$ or the level sets of Lipschitz-continuous functions [3,7]. Thus, for instance, the fitting procedure in [8] utilized the zero level-set of a distance function, in which case it was also possible to determine the topological types of reconstructed surfaces. While promising in many respects, however, the method lacked in geometric accuracy. In [9], the same group of authors introduced an accurate surface model for unorganized point data. Unfortunately, this work provided little evidence on the performance of the proposed method in the case of incomplete and irregularly sampled data [10]. A method called Poisson Surface Reconstruction was introduced in [11] based on the observation that the normal field of the boundary of a solid can be interpreted as the gradient of the indicator function of a surface, which can, in turn, be used to model this surface in an implicit manner. Further modifications of this method were described in [12], including its adjustments to the case of sparse point clouds and improvements of computational efficiency. An interesting method exploiting the underlying geometric structure of point clouds in combination with a convex formulation of image segmentation was described in [3]. The method has been shown to perform reliably under a variety of conditions, including scenarios with incomplete/scarce data and complex topologies. Yet, to achieve such performance, one requires to possess prior information in the form of point normals, which might not always be available. Finally, a surface fitting formulation based on the concept of function approximation by means of Radial Basis Functions (RBF) was reported in [13]. In addition to its other merits, the method was also shown to be computationally efficient, which makes it particularly valuable when dealing with large data sets [14].

The level-set framework, in which curves and surfaces are defined in terms of the level-set of Lipschitz-continuous functions, offers a number of critical advantages, among which are the simplicity of parameterization and the ability to deal with relatively complex topologies in an easy and straightforward manner. The practical implementation of such methods in the context of curve/surface fitting, however, may be rather challenging, thereby risking to put these methods in disadvantage with respect to other techniques. Accordingly, the main purpose of this work is to introduce a level-set based formulation of the problem of curve/surface fitting which offers two important advantages. First, the formulation is independent of the problem dimensionality, and it can be applied in the cases of curve and surface fitting with virtually no adjustments. Second, the formulation leads to a particularly simple and computationally efficient solution, which allows its application in both time-critical and data-extensive scenarios.

The rest of this paper is organized as follows. Sections 2 and 3 provide a formal description of the fitting problem and its solution, respectively. Experimental results with 2D and 3D point clouds are presented in Sect. 4, followed by a discussion and conclusions in Sect. 5.

## 2   Problem Formulation

Let $\phi : \mathbb{R}^d \to \mathbb{R}$ be a Lipschitz-continuous function (with $d = 2$ and $d = 3$ corresponding to the cases of curve and surface fitting, respectively), whose zero level set

$$\Gamma = \left\{ \mathbf{r} \in \mathbb{R}^d \mid \phi(\mathbf{r}) = 0 \right\}$$

will be used to model the geometric manifold of interest (i.e., either a curve or a surface). In particular, in what follows, the *level-set* function $\phi(\mathbf{r})$ will be defined to be the *signed distance function* (SDF) of the zero level-set $\Gamma$ of $\phi$. Such SDF is given by the unique solution of Eikonal equation

$$\begin{cases} |\nabla\phi(\mathbf{r})| = 1, & \forall \mathbf{r} \in \mathbb{R}^d \\ \phi(\mathbf{r}) = 0, & \forall \mathbf{r} \in \Gamma \end{cases},$$

with $\nabla\phi$ standing for the gradient of $\phi$ and $|\nabla\phi(\mathbf{r})|$ being its magnitude at $\mathbf{r}$.

By the nature of its definition, the value $\phi(\mathbf{r})$ of an SDF $\phi$ returns the distance between $\mathbf{r}$ and the zero-level set $\Gamma$. Thus, given a set of $N$ points $\{\mathbf{r}_i\}_{i=1}^N$, the average cumulative distance between the point cloud and $\Gamma$ can be computed as

$$D(\phi) = \frac{1}{N} \sum_{i=1}^N |\phi(\mathbf{r}_i)|, \tag{1}$$

where the absolute value is used to cancel out the effect of the sign of $\phi$ (which we assume to have negative values inside $\Gamma$). Clearly, the closer the points $\mathbf{r}_i$ to $\Gamma$, the lower the value of $D(\phi)$. Consequently, the fitting problem at hand can be formulated as a minimization problem in $\phi$, whose optimal solution returns the minimum possible value of $D(\phi)$.

An obvious flaw of the above approach consist in its proneness to the "curse of dimensionality". Indeed, in an attempt to minimize $D(\phi)$, the optimization is likely to result in a solution with an excessively variable, fluctuating $\Gamma$ which might contradict the physical nature of the object represented by the point cloud. Such situations are particularly frequent in the case of noisy and/or incomplete (scarce) measurements, which necessitates the use of regularization. To this end, it has been proven effective to penalize the area of $\Gamma$, which (owing to the co-area formula), amounts to requiring the SDF $\phi$ to be a function of bounded variation (BV) [19]. Such functions are known to have relatively small values of their *total-variation* (TV) semi-norms defined as

$$\|\phi\|_{TV} = \int_{\mathbf{r} \in \mathbb{R}^d} |\nabla \phi(\mathbf{r})| \, d\mathbf{r}. \tag{2}$$

Subsequently, to guarantee the zero level-set $\Gamma$ (and, hence, the resulting manifold) has a plausible configuration, the minimization of $D(\phi)$ should be restricted to the functions with relatively small values of TV semi-norms, which leads to an optimization problem of the form

$$\min_{\phi} \{D(\phi) + \lambda \|\phi\|_{TV}\}, \tag{3}$$

where $\lambda > 0$ is a user-defined regularization constant. Denoting the cost functional in (3) by $E(\phi)$, namely $E(\phi) := D(\phi) + \lambda \|\phi\|_{TV}$, its (local) minimizers $\phi^*$ are characterized by the Euler-Lagrange condition

$$\frac{\delta E(\phi^*)}{\delta \phi} = 0, \tag{4}$$

with $\delta E / \delta \phi$ being the first variational derivative of $E(\phi)$. A particularly simple and computationally efficient solution to the above equation is detailed in the following section.

## 3   Proposed Solution

A solution to the Euler-Lagrange equation (4) can be found as a stationary point of the *gradient flow* given by [15]

$$\frac{\partial \phi}{\partial t} = -\frac{\delta E(\phi)}{\delta \phi}, \tag{5}$$

where $t > 0$ is an artificial time that can be thought of as a continuous equivalent of an iteration index. Thus, to implement the gradient flow, the first variational derivative $\delta E / \delta \phi$ needs to be computed first. To this end, one can first redefine $D(\phi)$ as

$$D(\phi) = \frac{1}{N} \sum_{i=1}^{N} |\phi(\mathbf{r}_i)| = \frac{1}{N} \sum_{i=1}^{N} \int |\phi(\mathbf{r})| \, \delta(\mathbf{r} - \mathbf{r}_i) \, d\mathbf{r} = \int |\phi(\mathbf{r})| \, g_N(\mathbf{r}) \, d\mathbf{r}$$

with

$$g_N(\mathbf{r}) = \frac{1}{N} \sum_{i=1}^{N} \delta(\mathbf{r} - \mathbf{r}_i)$$

and $\delta(\mathbf{r})$ be the standard Dirac delta function. In this case, the first variational derivative of $D(\phi)$ can be shown to have the form of

$$\frac{\delta D(\phi)}{\delta \phi} = \text{sign}(\phi) \cdot g_N,$$

where we have adopted the sign function, $\text{sign}(x)$, as a practical approximation of the first-order derivative of $|x|$. On the other hand, the first variational derivative of $\|\phi\|_{\text{TV}}$ is well known to be equal to $-\text{div}(\nabla\phi/|\nabla\phi|)$, with div standing for the operator of divergence. Therefore, combining the two results leads to

$$\frac{\delta E(\phi)}{\delta \phi} = \text{sign}(\phi) \cdot g_N - \lambda \, \text{div}(\nabla\phi/|\nabla\phi|), \tag{6}$$

and, subsequently, to the gradient flow of the form

$$\frac{\partial \phi}{\partial t} = \lambda \, \text{div}(\nabla\phi/|\nabla\phi|) - \text{sign}(\phi) \cdot g_N. \tag{7}$$

The next step is to discretize (7), to which end we take advantage of a *semi-implicit* approach to produce

$$\frac{\phi_{t+\Delta t} - \phi_t}{\Delta t} = \lambda \, \text{div}(\nabla\phi_{t+\Delta t}/|\nabla\phi_{t+\Delta t}|) - \text{sign}(\phi_t) \cdot g_N,$$

where $\phi_t$ and $\phi_{t+\Delta t}$ denote the values of $\phi$ at times $t$ and $t + \Delta t$, respectively. Thus, rearranging the terms in the above numerical approximation, one obtains

$$\phi_{t+\Delta t} - (\lambda \Delta t) \, \text{div}(\nabla\phi_{t+\Delta t}/|\nabla\phi_{t+\Delta t}|) = \phi_t - \Delta t \, \text{sign}(\phi_t) \cdot g_N. \tag{8}$$

To conclude the derivations, we recall that any real subdifferentiable functional $F : \mathcal{X} \to \mathbb{R}$ with a monotone subdifferential (where $\mathcal{X}$ is the Banach space to which $\phi$ is supposed to belong, such as the space of BV functions in our case) can be associated with its *proximal map* $\text{prox}_F : \mathcal{X} \to \mathcal{X}$ defined as [16]

$$\text{prox}_F(\psi) = \arg \inf_{\phi \in \mathcal{X}} \left\{ \frac{1}{2}\|\phi - \psi\|_2^2 + F(\phi) \right\}. \tag{9}$$

In the special case when $F(\phi) = \tau\|\phi\|_{\text{TV}}$, with some $\tau > 0$, one has

$$\text{prox}_{\tau\|\cdot\|_{\text{TV}}}(\psi) = \arg \inf_{\phi \in \mathcal{X}} \left\{ \frac{1}{2}\|\phi - \psi\|_2^2 + \tau\|\phi\|_{\text{TV}} \right\}, \tag{10}$$

which is always well-defined due to the strict convexity of its associated cost functional. Although this operator does not admit a closed-form definition, there are a number of numerical procedures that can be used to compute $\text{prox}_{\tau\|\cdot\|_{\text{TV}}}$ in a computationally efficient manner [17, 18]. It is worthwhile noting that, in the context of image processing, finding efficient numerical methods for computation of $\text{prox}_{\tau\|\cdot\|_{TV}}$ dates back to the seminal work in [19] that pioneered the field of *TV-denoising*.

Now, having the proximal map (10) defined, it can be shown that the update equation in (8) can be alternatively defined as

$$\phi_{t+\Delta t} = \text{prox}_{(\lambda\Delta t)\|\cdot\|_{TV}} \{\phi_t - \Delta t\,\text{sign}(\phi_t) \cdot g_N\}. \tag{11}$$

Consequently, starting from some initial curve/surface $\Gamma$ associated with $\phi_0 = \phi_{t=0}$, an optimal solution to the problem of curve/surface fitting *in the sense of minimum cumulative distance* can be computed as a stationary point of the sequence of fixed-point iterations (i.e., recursive re-substitutions) produced by

$$\phi \mapsto T_{\lambda,\Delta t}\{\phi\}, \tag{12}$$

where $T_{\lambda,\Delta t} : \mathcal{X} \rightarrow \mathcal{X}$ stands for the composition of the proximal map $\text{prox}_{(\lambda\Delta t)\|\cdot\|_{TV}}$ with the simple non-linear map defined by $I - \Delta t\,\text{sign}(\cdot) \cdot g_N$. In practice, we replace $g_N$ with its smooth approximation $g_{N,\sigma}$ obtained via spatial convolution with a normalized, isotropic Gaussian kernel $G_\sigma$ of standard deviation $\sigma$, viz.

$$g_{N,\sigma}(\mathbf{r}) = (g_N * G_\sigma)(\mathbf{r}) = \frac{1}{N}\sum_{i=1}^{N} G_\sigma(\mathbf{r} - \mathbf{r}_i), \quad \forall \mathbf{r} \in \mathbb{R}^d.$$

In practice, such sums can be computed efficiently, e.g., by first uniformly quantizing the values of $\mathbf{r}_i$ to the vertices of a (sufficiently dense) rectangular lattice, and then performing the summation in the domain of a discrete Fourier transform (DFT), followed by an inverse Fourier transformation.

It is interesting to notice that the map $x \mapsto x - \Delta t\,\text{sign}(x)a$, with $0 \leq a \leq 1$, is neither linear nor monotone, and, what is more important, it does not preserve the sign of $x$. Thus, applying this map to an SDF $\phi$ may, in general, forfeit the fundamental property of such $\phi$ to have values of opposite signs on both sides of its zero-level set. To avoid this undesirable effect, it has proven useful to replace the above map by *soft thresholding* $S_{\Delta t g_{N,\sigma}}(x) := \max(|x| - \Delta t\,g_{N,\sigma}, 0) \cdot \text{sign}(x)$ which, similarly to the former, reduces the positive values of $\phi$, while increasing the negative values of $\phi$ by $\Delta t\,g_{N,\sigma}$. (In some sense, both maps try to "shorten the distance" to points $\mathbf{r}_i$, which are represented by the "peaks" of $g_{N,\sigma}$.) However, $S_{\Delta t g_{N,\sigma}}$ provides the additional advantage of continuity, while keeping the sign of its argument intact.

In practical computations, we used $\Delta t \in (0, 1]$, while adapting $\sigma$ recursively according to $\sigma \mapsto \beta\sigma$, starting with some initial $\sigma > 0$ and a predefined $0.9 < \beta < 1$. In this case, the proposed numerical scheme acquires the flavor of a multi-grid method. Particularly, in the beginning of iterations (when $\sigma$ is still relatively large) the intermediate solutions are predominantly effected by a rough collective configuration of the data points as a cloud, while becoming more and more responsive to the individual forces of each point $\mathbf{r}_i$ towards convergence.

To summarize, the final algorithm can be described by the pseudo-code shown below.

**Data:** $\{\mathbf{r}_i\}_{i=1}^N, \phi_0, \lambda, \Delta t, \sigma, \beta,$ #iterations
$i = 1;$
$\phi = \phi_0;$
**while** $i \leq$ #iterations **do**
$\quad\quad g_{N,\sigma}(\mathbf{r}) \leftarrow (1/N) \sum_{i=1}^N G_\sigma(\mathbf{r} - \mathbf{r}_i);$
$\quad\quad \phi \leftarrow T_{\lambda,\Delta t}\{\phi\};$
$\quad\quad \phi \leftarrow \mathrm{ReDist}(\phi);$
$\quad\quad \sigma \leftarrow \beta\,\sigma;$
$\quad\quad i \leftarrow i + 1$
**end**
**Result:** $\phi^* = \phi;$

Note that, for any value of $\Delta t$, $S_{\Delta t g_{N,\sigma}}$ is guaranteed to be a contraction, which, in conjunction with the contractiveness of the proximal map, suggests that the sequence of solutions produced by $\phi \mapsto T_{\lambda,\Delta t}\{\phi\}$ always converges to a stationary point. However, for any given $\phi$, its corresponding $T_{\lambda,\Delta t}\{\phi\}$ does not yield an SDF, in general. For this reason, the above pseudo-code has been augmented with the procedure of *redistancing* ReDist, which effectively replaces a given $\phi \in \mathcal{X}$ with an SDF that has a zero-level set $\Gamma$ identical to that of $\phi^1$. Even thought such mapping may not always be contractive, from the practical point of view, the proposed algorithm has never failed to converge in a relatively small number of iterators (see below), under broad experimental conditions.

## 4    Experimental Results

The proposed method has been tested on a dataset of both 2D and 3D artificial point clouds. In the course of evaluations, the algorithm's performance was tested under a variety of different experimental conditions, as defined by various levels of measurement noise, the presence of skewness in the distribution of $\{\mathbf{r}_i\}_{i=1}^N$ and various fractions of data points assumed to be missing.

In our experiments, the original geometric manifolds (i.e., curves and surfaces) were used as the mean values around which the cloud points $\mathbf{r}_i$ had then been randomly distributed. To this end, we used a centered uniform distribution in conjunction with an offset to emulate the effect of asymmetric sampling. In all the experiments, $\phi_0$ was computed by fast matching initiated at the boundary of the convex hull of its associated data cloud. The values of $\lambda, \Delta t, \sigma$, and $\beta$ were set to be equal to $100, 0.95, 0.03$, and $0.99$, respectively. All coding and simulations were performed in MATLAB (Mathworks Inc, version R2018b).

In the case of symmetric sampling in 2D (i.e., when the number of planar data points is approximately equal on both sides of the original curve), some representative results obtained using the proposed method are shown in Fig. 1,

---

[1] As mentioned earlier, in numerical computations, redistancing is usually performed by means of fast marching [20].

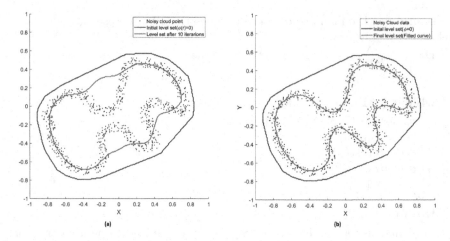

**Fig. 1.** Results applying the proposed algorithm to 2D "noisy" point clouds. (a) optimal solution after 10 iterations, (b) optimal solution after 30 iterations. The blue and red colors correspond to the initial and final solutions, respectively. (Color figure online)

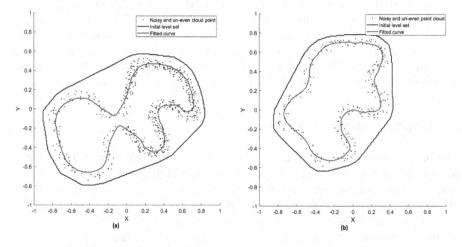

**Fig. 2.** Results analogous to Fig. 1 obtained in the case of asymmetric data sampling.

with Fig. 2 showing analogous results for the case of asymmetric sampling. One can see that, in all the cases, the proposed algorithm has managed to converge to the expected shapes just in a few tens of iterations.

To quantitatively evaluate the proposed algorithm, a distance between the original and fitted manifolds has been computed. In each case, the distance was defined to be the average distance between the points on the fitted manifold and its continuous counterpart. To facilitate the computation of the distances, the original manifolds were chosen to be

- a circle (radius 50), an oval (max radius 50, axis ratio 1:0.5), and a square (side length 100), in the case of $d = 2$,
- a sphere (radius 50) and an ellipsoid (max radius 50, axis ratio 1:1:0.5), in the case of $d = 3$.

The conditions of asymmetric sampling were emulated by sub-sampling the data points on one size of a given manifold by a factor of 2. Moreover, the data points were further subjected to random removals of their localized subsets to imitate the effects of "holes". Finally, all data points were contaminated by additive Gaussian noise with different values of its standard deviation $\sigma_n$.

**Table 1.** Empirical mean cumulative errors (average $\pm$ 1 standard deviation)

|  | Circle | Oval | Square | Sphere | Ellipsoid |
|---|---|---|---|---|---|
| Number of points $N$ | 50 | 50 | 50 | 1200 | 1200 |
| $\sigma_n = 0.03\,R/L$ | $1.93 \pm 0.81$ | $1.85 \pm 1.04$ | $3.41 \pm 2.81$ | $3.68 \pm 0.86$ | $2.61 \pm 0.92$ |
| $\sigma_N = 0.10\,R/L$ | $3.48 \pm 1.65$ | $3.19 \pm 1.75$ | $5.69 \pm 4.24$ | $4.55 \pm 0.96$ | $3.21 \pm 1.05$ |

Table 1 summarizes the results of present quantitative analysis, showing the values of mean cumulative distance for different types of manifolds as well as the values of $N$ and $\sigma_n$. Each entry in Table 1 has been computed as an average of 10 independent trials. As expected, the noisy scenarios with higher extents of skewness and incompletion in measurements results in higher values of the errors. A relative increase of the error can also be observed in the case of square, due to the non-smoothness of its shape. Overall, however, the proposed method demonstrated a stable and reasonably accurate performance. A sample results of surface and curve fitting is shown in Fig. 3.

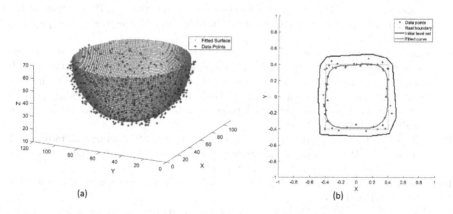

(a)                                                              (b)

**Fig. 3.** Results of fitting the sphere surface and the square curves.

## 5    Conclusion

In this paper, a simple numerical method for fitting closed curves and surfaces of various topologies to points clouds has been presented. The proposed numerical solution was based on implicit discretization, which allows using substantially larger time steps $\Delta t$ (as opposed to explicit schemes), thus improving the rate of convergence. Moreover, the proposed formulation is parameter-free, offering the same unified algorithmic structure in both 2D and 3D settings.

## References

1. Mencl, R., Muller, H.: Interpolation and approximation of surfaces from three-dimensional scattered data points. In: Scientific Visualization, pp. 223–232. IEEE Computer Society (1997)
2. Berger, M., et al.: A survey of surface reconstruction from point clouds. Comput. Graph. Forum **36**(1), 301–329 (2017)
3. Liang, J., Park, F., Zhao, H.: Robust and efficient implicit surface reconstruction for point clouds based on convexified image segmentation. J. Sci. Comput. **54**(3), 577–602 (2013)
4. Poothicottu Jacob, G.: HoloLens framework for augmented reality applications in breast cancer surgery. Master's thesis, University of Waterloo (2018)
5. Franz, A.: Voronoi diagramsa survey of a fundamental geometric data structure. ACM Comput. Surv. (CSUR) **23**(3), 345–405 (1991)
6. De Loera, J.A., Rambau, J., Santos, F.: Triangulations: Structures for Algorithms and Applications. Algorithms and Computation in Mathematics, vol. 25, 1st edn. Springer, Heidelberg (2010). https://doi.org/10.1007/978-3-642-12971-1
7. Carr, J.C., Fright, W.R., Beatson, R.K.: Surface interpolation with radial basis functions for medical imaging. IEEE Trans. Med. Imaging **16**(1), 96–107 (1997)
8. Hoppe, H., DeRose, T., Duchamp, T., McDonald, J., Stuetzle, W.: Surface reconstruction from unorganized points. ACM SIGGRAPH Comput. Graph. **26**(2), 71–78 (1992)
9. Hoppe, H., et al.: Piecewise smooth surface reconstruction. In: Proceedings of the 21st Annual Conference on Computer Graphics and Interactive Techniques, pp. 295–302 (1994)
10. Tang, R., Halim, S., Zulkepli, M.: Surface reconstruction algorithms: review and comparisons. In: The 8th International Symposium on Digital Earth (ISDE) (2013)
11. Kazhdan, M.: Reconstruction of solid models from oriented point sets. In: Proceedings of the Third Eurographics Symposium on Geometry Processing (2005)
12. Kazhdan, M., Hoppe, H.: Screened poisson surface reconstruction. ACM Trans. Graph. (ToG) **32**(3), 29 (2013)
13. Carr, J.C., et al.: Reconstruction and representation of 3D objects with radial basis functions. In: Proceedings of the 28th Annual Conference on Computer Graphics and Interactive Techniques, pp. 67–76 (2001)
14. Khatamian, A., Arabnia, H.R.: Survey on 3D surface reconstruction. J. Inf. Process. Syst. **12**(3), 338 (2016)
15. Caselles, V., Catté, F., Coll, T., Dibos, F.: A geometric model for active contours in image processing. Numerische mathematik **66**(1), 1–31 (1993)
16. Parikh, N., Boyd, S.: Proximal algorithms. Found. Trends® Optim. **1**(3), 127–239 (2014)

17. Chambolle, A.: An algorithm for total variation minimization and applications. J. Math. Imag. Vis. **20**(1–2), 89–97 (2004)
18. https://pythonhosted.org/prox-tv/
19. Rudin, L.I., Osher, S., Fatemi, E.: Nonlinear total variation based noise removal algorithms. Physica D Nonlinear Phenom. **60**(1–4), 259–268 (1992)
20. Sethian, J.: Level Set Methods. Cambridge University Press, Cambridge (1996)

# KFBin: Kalman Filter-Based Approach for Document Image Binarization

Abderrahmane Rahiche$^{(\boxtimes)}$ and Mohamed Cheriet

Synchromedia Lab, École de Technologie Supérieure (ETS), University of Quebec,
Montreal, Canada
`abderrahmane.rahiche.1@ens.etsmtl.ca, mohamed.cheriet@etsmtl.ca`

**Abstract.** In this paper, we propose a novel two-step approach, called KFBin, for the binarization of document images based on the Kalman filtering (KF) technique. In the first step, a state space model is developed as a new document image representation, and then the Kalman filter is applied to track the positions of the foreground and background information and generate two corresponding outputs, which allows the enhancement of the foreground content leading to better legibility of text. Standard thresholding algorithms were used in the second step to generate binary images from the enhanced foreground components. The performance of the proposed approach is validated on a well-known dataset and evaluated using common image binarization quality metrics. Outstanding improvement of the binarization performances of several state-of-the-art binarization methods has been achieved by using the proposed approach. Experimental results point that the poor binarization results of egraded document images can be greatly improved by enhancing their quality.

**Keywords:** Document image binarization · Kalman filter ·
Historical document · Thresholding ·
Foreground/background separation

## 1 Introduction

The binarization of document images is a fundamental step in the pipeline of their analysis. The quality of such operation influences the accuracy of the rest of the document image analysis processes fed by the obtained binary image. Document image binarization is a well-known research problem, and researchers have investigated a variety of document binarization approaches over the past two decades [7]. However, this processing step is not trivial, due to the high variability of degradation types existing on documents, especially historical ones. Therefore, this issue is still a challenging research problem and is still of great interest to the document analysis community.

Binarization (also known as thresholding or foreground-background separation) techniques can be broadly grouped into two groups [13]: thresholding-based strategies and classification-based techniques. Thresholding methods perform the

© Springer Nature Switzerland AG 2019
F. Karray et al. (Eds.): ICIAR 2019, LNCS 11662, pp. 150–161, 2019.
https://doi.org/10.1007/978-3-030-27202-9_13

separation of the pixels of document images into two classes, i.e., foreground and background classes, based on an intensity value called a threshold. Depending on how this thresholding value is set, these techniques can be divided into two main categories, global and local. Global document image binarization methods, such as Otsu's method [18], seek a single optimal threshold for the whole image. These algorithms work well with bimodal intensity histograms, but they fail against non-uniform and degraded images. To overcome these drawbacks, local thresholding techniques have been introduced, such as Sauvola [22], Niblack [16], and Adaptive Otsu (AdOtsu) [14]. Unlike global methods, these methods seek the optimal threshold value for each pixel based on local statistical information obtained from a local area around the pixel. However, both methods might produce poor binarization results when evaluated on low quality document images.

Classification techniques aim to classify each pixel into either a background or a foreground, based on a set of features extracted from the image. In recent years, Deep Learning (DL) [7] and Convolutional Neural Networks (CNN) [2], [26] techniques have also gained a lot of attention from the community of document image analysis. These techniques are known to be able to achieve good performances in various applications. They demonstrate high competitiveness and outperform existing binarization strategies in some cases, as in the recent DIBCO contest [20]. However, these supervised strategies rely heavily on a training step that generally requires a large and representative training set, which can not always be available and may lead to a high computational cost.

In addition, instead of designing a new document binarization method, several hybrid techniques have been proposed to improve the performance of existing binarization techniques, as in [25], [4]. The idea of these hybrid techniques is to combine the advantages and benefits of existing techniques to produce better performance for document image binarization. Other works in the literature [15] introduced additional pre-processing and post-processing steps to the initial binarization schemes to increase their thresholding performances.

In this paper, in order to boost the performance of standard binarization techniques, we propose a novel binarization scheme by combining the Kalman filtering technique with standard binarization approaches. Two main reasons that motivate the proposed approach. First, several prior research [15] highlighted that the low quality of input document images affects considerably the binarization results, and they emphasizes the importance of providing clean and uniform input images to allow binarization algorithms to perform better. Therefore, introducing a pre-processing step for cleaning and enhancing input images will certainly increase the performance of the existing algorithms. Second, the Kalman filter is probably the most widely used technique in statistical signal processing, that processes data samples recursively in a very effective manner [3]. The KF has been used in the literature for image denoising [19], image reconstruction [1], video denoising [11], and object tracking [5]. Contrarily to these works, here we use the KF to map any multi-channel input images (color) to two outputs images, whereby one output contains the enhanced foreground component and the other contains the background component. Thus, using KF as a pre-processing operator will allow us to enhance degraded images and generate clean images that can be efficiently binarized with any standard algorithm.

The remaining of this paper is organized as follows. Section 2 describes the proposed approach. In Sect. 3 we present the obtained results and discuss the performance of our framework. Section 4 is devoted to conclusion and perspectives.

## 2   The Proposed Approach

The proposed method consists of two main steps: (i) A state-space representation and Kalman filtering to generate enhanced and clean images, and then (ii) an image binarization step to obtain the binary image. The details of each step are given in the following subsections.

### 2.1   Step 1: State Space Representation and Kalman Filtering

The KF is designed for linear dynamical systems. Thus, a reformulation of our problem is needed to derive the required linear system. Such a system can be obtained through a state space modeling of a linear mixture model, which is explained in this section.

Let $p$ denotes the number of pixels of a given image. In this step, each component from $n$ multi-channel images (e.g. Red, Green, and Blue channels or from other color space representation) is assembled into one data vector of size $(1 \times p)$. To this end, we used a horizontal scanning scheme to exploit the information embedded in the pixel neighborhood. The $n$ vectors obtained previously are then stacked together to form one data matrix $Y \in \mathbb{R}_+^{n \times p}$ ($n = 3$ in the case of an RGB image).

Then, we can consider the following linear mixture model that considers each observation as a linear mixture of two components, i.e., the foreground ($x_{fg}$) and the background ($x_{bg}$):

$$\begin{bmatrix} y_1(k) \\ y_2(k) \\ .. \\ y_n(k) \end{bmatrix} = \begin{bmatrix} h_{fg1} & h_{bg1} \\ h_{fg2} & h_{bg2} \\ ... \\ h_{fgn} & h_{bgn} \end{bmatrix} \begin{bmatrix} x_{fg}(k) \\ x_{bg}(k) \end{bmatrix}, \quad k = 1, \cdots, p, \tag{1}$$

which can be written in the following compact matrix form:

$$y(k) = \mathbf{H}x(k), \quad k = 1, \cdots, p, \tag{2}$$

where $y$ is a vector of one observation from the matrix $Y$, $x \in \mathbb{R}^{r \times 1}$ is the two mixed components, $r$ is the number of states (components), and $\mathbf{H} \in \mathbb{R}^{n \times r}$ is a signature mixture matrix.

**State Space Representation:** The linear mixing model described by Eq. 2 can be expressed in terms of a state-space model which consists of two main equations, a state equation, and an observation equation.

$$\begin{cases} x_k = \mathbf{A}x_{k-1} + u_k \\ y_k = \phantom{x}\mathbf{C}x_k \phantom{xx} + v_k \end{cases} \tag{3}$$

where the first equation represents the state equation, in which $x_k$ denotes the state vector of the system, $\mathbf{A} \in \mathbb{R}^{r \times r}$ is a known and invariant state mixing process matrix and $u_k$ represents the white additive noise with zero mean and covariance matrix $\mathbf{R}$, i.e, $u_k \sim \mathcal{N}(0, R)$, where $\mathbf{R} = \sigma_u^r I_r$ and $I_r$ is the identity matrix of size $r \times r$. The second equation is the observation (measurement) equation, in which $y_k$ is its observation vector, $\mathbf{C} \in \mathbb{R}^{n \times r}$ is a known and invariant mixing matrix, and $v_k$ is the measurement noise of the mixing system, which is assumed to be a zero mean, white process with covariance matrix $\mathbf{Q}$, i.e, $v_k \sim \mathcal{N}(0, Q)$, where $\mathbf{Q} = \sigma_v^r I_n$ and $I_n$ is the $n \times n$ identity matrix.

**Kalman Filtering:** KF [10] is used to recursively estimate the state variable $x_k$ given by the Eq. 4 while minimizing the mean-squared error between the observed output $y_k$ and the predicted output $\hat{y}_k$. The Kalman filter dynamics are given as follow [30]:

$$\hat{x}_k = x_k + \mathbf{G}_k \Delta y_k, \tag{4}$$

where $G_k$ denotes the Kalman gain matrix, and $\Delta y_k = y_k - \hat{y}_k$ is the residual or the error between the predicted output and the measured value.

The updating rule used for updating the Kalman gain matrix $\mathbf{G}_k$ and the state vector $x_k$ are given as follow:

– *(1) Compute the Kalman gain at the current step $k$:*

$$\mathbf{G}_k = \frac{\mathbf{A}\mathbf{P}_{k|k-1}\mathbf{C}^T}{\mathbf{C}\mathbf{P}_{k|k-1}\mathbf{C}^T + \mathbf{R}} \tag{5}$$

– *(2) Update the estimate of the current state vector:*

$$x_{k|k} = x_k + \mathbf{G}_k \Delta y_k \tag{6}$$

– *(3) Calculate the current error covariance matrix:*

$$\mathbf{P}_{k|k} = \mathbf{P}_{k|k-1} - \mathbf{G}_k \mathbf{C}\mathbf{P}_{k|k-1} \tag{7}$$

– *(4) Predict the next state vector:*

$$x_{k+1|k} = \mathbf{A}x_{k|k} \tag{8}$$

– *(5) Update the error covariance matrix:*

$$\mathbf{P}_{k+1|k} = \mathbf{A}\mathbf{P}_{k|k}\mathbf{A}^T + \mathbf{Q} \tag{9}$$

The new representation obtained by Kalman filter enhance the quality of document images and clean out the degradations which offers a better visualization of documents. As we can see in Fig. 1, the outputs obtained by KF are more representative compared to the gray-level space and any other color space known to be more suitable for the study of historical document images. In Fig. 1, the textual information is enhanced and is more legible, while the degradation and the unwanted background are cleaned up.

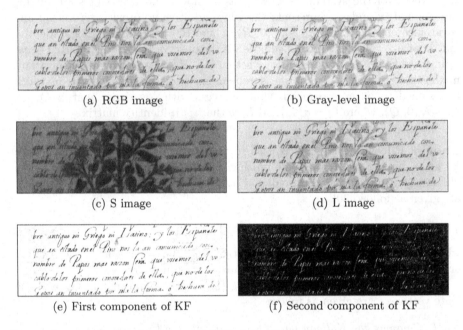

(a) RGB image                    (b) Gray-level image

(c) S image                      (d) L image

(e) First component of KF        (f) Second component of KF

**Fig. 1.** An example showing the use of the Kalman filter as a pre-processing operator for enhancing degraded document image. (a) original RGB image and (b) its corresponding gray-level image. (c) saturation component and (d) luminance component from the HSL color space. (e) and (f) outputs of the Kalman filter.

## 2.2   Step 2: Binarization

The outcomes of the last step are not binary and therefore can not be used directly in high-level document understanding techniques such as text recognition and word spotting. This is clearly observable in Fig. 1-e. Hence, a binarization step is performed to allow the obtention of the desired outcome. For this step, any state-of-the-art binarization method can be applied. In our experiments, we used the adaptive thresholding Sauvola's method [22], a popular approach for the binarization of gray-level images. For the sake of comparison and completeness, we used also Howe's method [8], which is one of the best binarization methods.

# 3   Results and Discussion

For the evaluation of our approach, we consider a dataset from the international Document Image Binarization Contest (DIBCO) collection (2014). This dataset consists of color images of ancient documents.

## 3.1   Evaluation Metrics

To evaluate the performances of the proposed approach, we considered the same metrics adopted by the international Document Image Binarization Contest series [6]. These measures consist of (a) F-Measure (FM) [23]; (b) Pseudo F-measure [21]; (c) Distance Reciprocal Distortion (DRD) [12]; (d) Negative Rate Metric (NRM) [29] and (e) the Accuracy (ACC) metric.

For the sake of reproducibility, we recall the different definitions of these metrics in the following:

- *F-Measure (Fm)*: is a weighted mean of the precision and recall that measures the accuracy of the prediction.

$$Fm = \frac{2 \times Recall \times Precision}{Recall + Precision}, \tag{10}$$

where $Recall = \frac{TP}{TP+FN}$, $Precision = \frac{TP}{TP+FP}$, and $TP$, $FP$, $FN$ denote respectively the True Positive, False Positive, False Negative values extracted from the confusion matrix.

- *Pseudo F-Measure ($F_{ps}$)*: is a modified F-Measure, in which the recall value is calculated from skeletonized ground truth (GT) image:

$$Fm = \frac{2 \times Recall_{Skeleton} \times Precision}{Recall_{Skeleton} + Precision} \tag{11}$$

- *Negative Rate Metric (NRM)*: measures the mismatches between the GT and prediction on the pixel level.

$$NRM = \frac{NR_{FN} + NR_{FP}}{2}, \tag{12}$$

with

$$NR_{FN} = \frac{FN}{FN+TP}, \quad \text{and} \quad NR_{FP} = \frac{FP}{FP+TN}$$

- *Distance Reciprocal Distortion (DRD)*: measures the distortion between two binary images. It is defined as follows [12]:

$$DRD = \frac{\sum_{k=1}^{N} DRD_k}{NUBN}, \tag{13}$$

where $DRD_k$ is the distortion of the $k^{th}$ flipped pixel and is defined as the weighted sum of the pixels in the $5 \times 5$ block of the GT image that differs from the value flipped pixel $B(x,y)_k$ in the predicted image. It is expressed as follows:

$$DRD_k = \sum_{i=-2}^{2} \sum_{j=-2}^{2} [|GT(i,j)_k - B(x,y)_k| \times W_{Nm}(i,j)] \qquad (14)$$

The normalized wight matrix is defined as:

$$W_{Nm}(i,j) = \frac{W_m(i,j)}{\sum_{i=1}^{m} \sum_{j=1}^{m} W_m(i,j)}, \qquad (15)$$

where $NUBN$ is defined as the number of non-uniform (not all black or white pixels) $8 \times 8$ blocks in the GT image [12].

– Peak Signal-to-Noise Ratio (PSNR):

$$PSNR = 10log(\frac{C^2}{MSE}), \qquad (16)$$

were C is the difference between the text and background, and $MSE$ denotes the mean square error between two images.

We should note that the highest is the value of $F_m$, $F_{ps}$, PSNR, or ACC the best is the quality of the binarization. This is indicated by ($\uparrow$) symbol in this paper. In contrast to these metrics, a lower value of NRM and DRD indicates a better quality of the binarization. Similarly, this is indicated by ($\downarrow$) symbol.

## 3.2 Results

In this work, for the first step, we seek to obtain two new images from multi-channel document images, one contains the enhanced foreground and the other corresponds to the background information. Therefore we set the rank model to be $r = 2$. We assume that the two material signatures are independent of each other and formed separately, and we set the state mixing matrix in Eq. 3 to be invariant and given by $\mathbf{A} = I_r$. The process mixing matrix $\mathbf{C}$ that contains the spectral signature of the two materials (i.e., text and paper) is designed by taking the average of the signatures of selected pixels representing the background and the foreground respectively. For initial conditions, $\sigma_u$ and $\sigma_v$ are tuned experimentally to design the two covariance matrices $\mathbf{R}$ and $\mathbf{Q}$ respectively. The initial value of the error covariance matrix $\mathbf{P}_{0|-1}$ is set to be equal to one and the initial value of the state vector $\mathbf{x}_{0|-1}$ is set to be zero.

Our experiments confirmed that other color spaces are more suitable for the study of historical document images as found in the literature [27]. Therefore, in this study, we transformed the original image to the OHTA [17] color space first, and then we used the three channel of the OHTA space as inputs for the Kalman filter. The OHTA transformation given by Eq. 17 is another way to approximate the Principal Component Analysis (PCA) of the RGB components [27].

$$\begin{bmatrix} O \\ H \\ T \end{bmatrix} = \begin{bmatrix} 0.33 & 0.33 & 0.33 \\ 0.5 & 0 & -0.5 \\ -0.25 & 0.5 & -0.25 \end{bmatrix} \begin{bmatrix} R \\ G \\ B \end{bmatrix} \qquad (17)$$

To show the performance of the proposed KBin approach and quantify the improvement obtained using the generated clean images, we conducted two experiments using two state-of-the-art binarization methods, namely, Sauvola's [22] adaptive thresholding method and Howe's method [8], both validated on the H-DIBCO 2014 dataset. For the sake of completeness, we also compare our method with other state-of-the-art methods and recent approaches.

The first series of experiments is conducted using Sauvola's method [8] as a binarization method in the second step. Figure 2 illustrates the results of the two steps. The Kalman filter generates two outcomes (d) and (f). The first image contains the text component and the second one holds the background. The last image of the third row (i) shows the binary image obtained using Sauvola's method to separate the text and background sources. As a reference for comparison, the binary image (h) is generated using the original image (OI) using the same binarization method. As we can see, the resulted binary image compared with the available GT image (g) is of high quality despite the poor intensity of the text information in the original image.

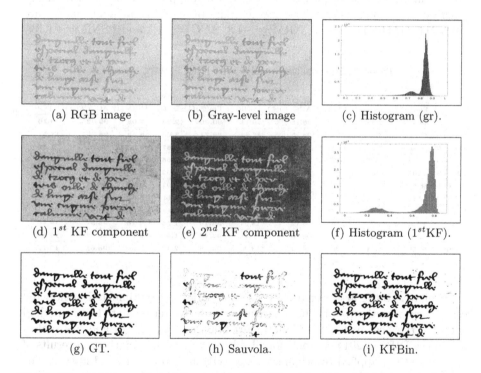

(a) RGB image        (b) Gray-level image        (c) Histogram (gr).

(d) $1^{st}$ KF component    (e) $2^{nd}$ KF component    (f) Histogram ($1^{st}$KF).

(g) GT.            (h) Sauvola.            (i) KFBin.

**Fig. 2.** Binarization results of the proposed KFBin. (a) original RGB image, (b) its corresponding gray-level image, (c) histogram of the gray-level image (b), (d) and (e) are the outputs of the Kalman filter and (f) is the histogram of (d). In the last row, (g) the GT binary image, (h) the binary image obtained from the gray-level image and (i) the binary image obtained by KFBin.

As shown in Figure 2, the histogram of the original gray-level image illustrates the poor intensity of the ink and the low contrast of the original image, whereas the histogram of the first output, i.e, the enhanced image generated by the Kalman filter illustrates a better contrast. The intensity of the ink is corrected and shifted to the darkest side. By applying Sauvola's algorithm directly on the original image, the algorithm was not able to separate correctly between the text and the background information and therefore it produces a poor results. The resulted binary image (h) is not legible. However, using the enhanced image as an input, the same algorithm produced a fairly better result. The quality of the output image (i) is comparable to the GT image (g).

To put particular stress on the usefulness of the proposed pre-processing step using KF operator and the effectiveness of our binarization method, more detailed results are shown in Table 1 that presents the binarization results of Sauvola's method applied on original images (OI) and on clean images generated by the Kalman filter (KF).

It is clearly observable that the results obtained by Sauvola's method are greatly improved with respect to all metrics when applied on the cleaned images generated by Kalman filter. The overall gain obtained for different metrics are Fm = +6.34, DRD = −2.13, NRM = −4.8, ACC = +1.1 and PSNR = +1.13.

**Table 1.** Binarization results in H-DIBCO 2014 dataset.

| Samples | OI + Sauvola | | | | | KFBin(Sauvola) | | | | |
|---|---|---|---|---|---|---|---|---|---|---|
| | Fm(%)($\uparrow$) | DRD($\downarrow$) | NRM($\downarrow$) | ACC(%)($\uparrow$) | PSNR($\uparrow$) | Fm(%)($\uparrow$) | DRD($\downarrow$) | NRM($\downarrow$) | ACC(%)($\uparrow$) | PSNR($\uparrow$) |
| H2014-01 | 88.32 | 2.89 | 9.55 | 98.78 | 19.14 | 90.90 | 2.26 | 7.08 | 99.02 | 20.10 |
| H2014-02 | 87.79 | 3.32 | 9.74 | 98.15 | 17.33 | 88.71 | 3.08 | 8.48 | 98.25 | 17.57 |
| H2014-03 | 96.36 | 2.01 | 3.28 | 99.27 | 21.34 | 96.39 | 1.87 | 2.82 | 99.26 | 21.35 |
| H2014-04 | 92.74 | 2.27 | 6.57 | 97.95 | 16.89 | 94.70 | 1.65 | 4.39 | 98.46 | 18.12 |
| H2014-05 | 90.07 | 3.57 | 8.83 | 97.04 | 15.29 | 92.27 | 2.92 | 5.67 | 97.56 | 16.12 |
| H2014-06 | 38.96 | 21.82 | 37.89 | 88.36 | 9.34 | 92.66 | 2.91 | 4.75 | 97.78 | 16.54 |
| H2014-07 | 92.08 | 2.06 | 5.34 | 98.64 | 18.65 | 91.87 | 2.14 | 5.00 | 98.59 | 18.50 |
| H2014-08 | 94.23 | 1.43 | 4.47 | 99.66 | 24.70 | 94.50 | 1.49 | 3.05 | 99.67 | 24.78 |
| H2014-09 | 93.14 | 1.71 | 5.83 | 98.72 | 18.93 | 94.10 | 1.55 | 4.18 | 98.87 | 19.46 |
| H2014-10 | 92.23 | 1.99 | 6.49 | 98.56 | 18.41 | 93.16 | 1.93 | 4.56 | 98.67 | 18.80 |
| Mean | 86.59 | 4.31 | 9.79 | 97.51 | 18.00 | 92.93 | 2.18 | 4.99 | 98.61 | 19.13 |

Similarly to the first scenario, this second series of experiments is conducted using Howe's method [8] in the binarization step. We recall that Howe's method is one of the best methods for the binarization of text images and has ranked $2^{nd}$ in the DIBCO-2014 competition. Table 2 presents the binarization results of Howe's method applied to original images (OI) and to the cleaned images. The results obtained using the enhanced images show a good improvement compared with the results obtained using original images.

Moreover, Table 3 presents the performance of our approach compared with 7 state-of-the-art binarization methods applied to the H-DIBCO 2014 dataset. We should mention that the results of Sauvola, Howe and the proposed KFBin approach are generated by our validations. The results of Vo [28], DeepOtsu [7],

**Table 2.** Binarization results in H-DIBCO 2014 dataset.

| Samples | OI + Howe | | | | KFBin(Howe) | | | |
|---------|-----------|--|--|--|-------------|--|--|--|
| | Fm(%)(↑) | $F_{ps}$(%)(↑) | DRD(↓) | PSNR(↑) | Fm(%)(↑) | $F_{ps}$(%)(↑) | DRD (↓) | PSNR(↑) |
| H2014-01 | 96.89 | 97.81 | 0.782 | 24.53 | **96.90** | **97.87** | **0.781** | 24.53 |
| H2014-02 | 94.88 | 94.57 | 1.455 | 20.86 | **94.92** | **94.65** | **0.440** | **20.87** |
| H2014-03 | **99.05** | 99.47 | **0.426** | **27.06** | 99.03 | **99.49** | 0.432 | 26.97 |
| H2014-04 | 97.09 | **98.46** | 0.888 | 20.61 | **97.45** | 98.26 | **0.769** | **21.16** |
| H2014-05 | 96.72 | 98.03 | 1.100 | 19.72 | **97.05** | **98.05** | **0.971** | **20.16** |
| H2014-06 | 95.79 | 96.05 | 1.889 | 18.91 | **96.63** | **97.59** | **1.363** | **19.83** |
| H2014-07 | **95.94** | **97.32** | **0.971** | **21.49** | 95.87 | 97.27 | 0.991 | 21.41 |
| H2014-08 | **97.11** | 98.34 | **0.652** | **27.59** | 97.10 | **98.36** | 0.659 | 27.57 |
| H2014-09 | 97.13 | 98.46 | 0.668 | 22.50 | **97.16** | **98.57** | **0.662** | **22.56** |
| H2014-10 | 96.96 | 98.37 | 0.727 | 22.27 | **97.06** | **98.53** | **0.698** | **22.41** |
| **Mean** | 96.76 | 97.69 | 0.956 | 22.55 | **96.92** | **97.86** | **0.877** | **22.75** |

Jia [9], Su [24] and Otsu [18] methods are taken from [7]. As we can see in Table 3, the results show that the performance of our proposed method is comparable to that of Vo's method that is a deep learning based method. The proposed KFBin outperforms the Howe's method of the $2^{nd}$ place in terms of all used metrics.

**Table 3.** Comparison of different algorithms applied to the H-DIBCO2014 dataset.

| Method | Fm | Fps | PSNR | DRD |
|--------|----|----|------|-----|
| Vo [28] | 96.7 | 97.6 | **23.2** | **0.7** |
| KFBin (KF+ Howe) | **96.9** | **97.9** | 22.8 | 0.9 |
| Howe [8] | 96.8 | 97.7 | 22.6 | 1.0 |
| DeepOtsu [7] | 95.9 | 97.2 | 22.1 | 0.9 |
| Jia [9] | 95.0 | 97.2 | 20.6 | 1.2 |
| Su [24] | 94.4 | 95.9 | 20.3 | 1.9 |
| KFBin (KF+ Sauvola) | 92.9 | 94.9 | 19.1 | 2.2 |
| Otsu [18] | 91.7 | 95.7 | 18.7 | 2.7 |
| Sauvola [22] | 86.6 | 87.8 | 18.0 | 4.3 |

## 4  Conclusion

In this paper, a new approach is proposed for the binarization of low quality color document images. The approach makes use of the Kalman filter theory to generate clean outputs from original degraded document images. The enhanced outputs can be efficiently binarized using any state-of-the-art binarization method. Experimental results indicate that the presented approach was able to increase the performance of the binarization algorithms used for validation. The proposed method requires only the determination of the mixing matrix from a few selected pixels, and the estimation of state error covariance matrix, which can be done in an interactive manner. The proposed method is currently applied only on color images. As future work, we are planning to target gray-level images. The selection of initial pixels candidates is also a sensitive and subjective step that we plan to address in the future.

# References

1. Azimi-Sadjadi, M.R., Bannour, S.: Two-dimensional adaptive block Kalman filtering of SAR imagery. IEEE Trans. Geosci. Remote Sens. **29**(5), 742–753 (1991)
2. Calvo-Zaragoza, J., Vigliensoni, G., Fujinaga, I.: Pixel-wise binarization of musical documents with convolutional neural networks. In: 2017 Fifteenth IAPR International Conference on Machine Vision Applications (MVA), pp. 362–365. IEEE (2017)
3. Chang, C.-I.: Discrete-time Kalman filtering for hyperspectral processing. In: Real-Time Recursive Hyperspectral Sample and Band Processing, pp. 49–71. Springer, Cham (2017). https://doi.org/10.1007/978-3-319-45171-8_3
4. Cheriet, M., Moghaddam, R.F., Hedjam, R.: A learning framework for the optimization and automation of document binarization methods. Comput. Vis. Image Underst. **117**(3), 269–280 (2013)
5. Cuevas, E.V., Zaldivar, D., Rojas, R.: Kalman filter for vision tracking (2005)
6. Gatos, B., Ntirogiannis, K., Pratikakis, I.: ICDAR 2009 document image binarization contest (DIBCO 2009). In: 10th International Conference on Document Analysis and Recognition, ICDAR 2009, pp. 1375–1382. IEEE (2009)
7. He, S., Schomaker, L.: DeepOtsu: document enhancement and binarization using iterative deep learning. Pattern Recognit. **91**, 379–390 (2019)
8. Howe, N.R.: Document binarization with automatic parameter tuning. Int. J. Doc. Anal. Recognit. (IJDAR) **16**(3), 247–258 (2013)
9. Jia, F., Shi, C., He, K., Wang, C., Xiao, B.: Degraded document image binarization using structural symmetry of strokes. Pattern Recognit. **74**, 225–240 (2018)
10. Kalman, R.E.: A new approach to linear filtering and prediction problems. J. Basic Eng. **82**(1), 35–45 (1960)
11. Lu, G., Ouyang, W., Xu, D., Zhang, X., Gao, Z., Sun, M.-T.: Deep Kalman filtering network for video compression artifact reduction. In: Ferrari, V., Hebert, M., Sminchisescu, C., Weiss, Y. (eds.) Computer Vision – ECCV 2018. LNCS, vol. 11218, pp. 591–608. Springer, Cham (2018). https://doi.org/10.1007/978-3-030-01264-9_35
12. Lu, H., Kot, A.C., Shi, Y.Q.: Distance-reciprocal distortion measure for binary document images. IEEE Signal Process. Lett. **11**(2), 228–231 (2004)
13. Moghaddam, R.F., Cheriet, M.: A multi-scale framework for adaptive binarization of degraded document images. Pattern Recognit. **43**(6), 2186–2198 (2010)
14. Moghaddam, R.F., Cheriet, M.: Adotsu: An adaptive and parameterless generalization of Otsu's method for document image binarization. Pattern Recognit. **45**(6), 2419–2431 (2012)
15. Nafchi, H.Z., Moghaddam, R.F., Cheriet, M.: Application of phase-based features and denoising in postprocessing and binarization of historical document images. In: 2013 12th International Conference on Document Analysis and Recognition, pp. 220–224. IEEE (2013)

16. Niblack, W.: An introduction to digital image processing (1986)
17. Ohta, Y.I., Kanade, T., Sakai, T.: Color information for region segmentation. Comput. Graph. Image Process. **13**(3), 222–241 (1980)
18. Otsu, N.: A threshold selection method from gray-level histograms. IEEE Trans. Syst. Man Cybern. **9**(1), 62–66 (1979)
19. Pan, J., Yang, X., Cai, H., Mu, B.: Image noise smoothing using a modified Kalman filter. Neurocomputing **173**, 1625–1629 (2016)
20. Pratikakis, I., Zagoris, K., Barlas, G., Gatos, B.: ICDAR 2017 competition on document image binarization (DIBCO 2017). In: 2017 14th IAPR International Conference on Document Analysis and Recognition (ICDAR), vol. 01, pp. 1395–1403, November 2017
21. Pratikakis, I., Gatos, B., Ntirogiannis, K.: ICDAR 2013 document image binarization contest (DIBCO 2013). In: 2013 12th International Conference on Document Analysis and Recognition, pp. 1471–1476. IEEE (2013)
22. Sauvola, J., Pietikäinen, M.: Adaptive document image binarization. Pattern Recognit. **33**(2), 225–236 (2000)
23. Sokolova, M., Lapalme, G.: A systematic analysis of performance measures for classification tasks. Inf. Process. Manage. **45**(4), 427–437 (2009)
24. Su, B., Lu, S., Tan, C.L.: Binarization of historical document images using the local maximum and minimum. In: Proceedings of the 9th IAPR International Workshop on Document Analysis Systems, pp. 159–166. ACM (2010)
25. Su, B., Lu, S., Tan, C.L.: Combination of document image binarization techniques. In: 2011 International Conference on Document Analysis and Recognition, pp. 22–26. IEEE (2011)
26. Tensmeyer, C., Martinez, T.: Document image binarization with fully convolutional neural networks. In: 2017 14th IAPR International Conference on Document Analysis and Recognition (ICDAR), vol. 1, pp. 99–104. IEEE (2017)
27. Tonazzini, A.: Color space transformations for analysis and enhancement of ancient degraded manuscripts. Pattern Recognit. Image Anal. **20**(3), 404–417 (2010)
28. Vo, Q.N., Kim, S.H., Yang, H.J., Lee, G.: Binarization of degraded document images based on hierarchical deep supervised network. Pattern Recognit. **74**, 568–586 (2018)
29. Young, D.P., Ferryman, J.M.: Pets metrics: on-line performance evaluation service. In: 2nd Joint IEEE International Workshop on Visual Surveillance and Performance Evaluation of Tracking and Surveillance, pp. 317–324. IEEE (2005)
30. Zhang, L., Cichocki, A.: Blind deconvolution of dynamical systems: a state space approach. J. Signal Process. **4**(2), 111–130 (2000)

# AVC, HEVC, VP9, AVS2 or AV1? — A Comparative Study of State-of-the-Art Video Encoders on 4K Videos

Zhuoran Li$^{(\boxtimes)}$, Zhengfang Duanmu$^{(\boxtimes)}$, Wentao Liu$^{(\boxtimes)}$, and Zhou Wang$^{(\boxtimes)}$

University of Waterloo, Waterloo, ON N2L 3G1, Canada
{z777li,zduanmu,w238liu,zhou.wang}@uwaterloo.ca

**Abstract.** 4K, ultra high-definition (UHD), and higher resolution video contents have become increasingly popular recently. The largely increased data rate casts great challenges to video compression and communication technologies. Emerging video coding methods are claimed to achieve superior performance for high-resolution video content, but thorough and independent validations are lacking. In this study, we carry out an independent and so far the most comprehensive subjective testing and performance evaluation on videos of diverse resolutions, bit rates and content variations, and compressed by popular and emerging video coding methods including H.264/AVC, H.265/HEVC, VP9, AVS2 and AV1. Our statistical analysis derived from a total of more than 36,000 raw subjective ratings on 1,200 test videos suggests that significant improvement in terms of rate-quality performance against the AVC encoder has been achieved by state-of-the-art encoders, and such improvement is increasingly manifest with the increase of resolution. Furthermore, we evaluate state-of-the-art objective video quality assessment models, and our results show that the SSIM-plus measure performs the best in predicting 4K subjective video quality. The database will be made available online to the public to facilitate future video encoding and video quality research.

**Keywords:** Video compression · Quality-of-experience ·
Subjective quality assessment · Objective quality assessment ·
4K video · Ultra-high-definition (UHD) · Video coding standard

## 1 Introduction

4K, ultra high-definition (UHD), and higher resolution video contents have enjoyed a remarkable growth in recent years. 4K/UHD (4096 × 2160 or 3840 × 2160) video increases the resolution by a factor of four from full-HD (FHD, 1920 × 1080) and offers significantly increased sharpness and fine details.

**Electronic supplementary material** The online version of this chapter (https://doi.org/10.1007/978-3-030-27202-9_14) contains supplementary material, which is available to authorized users.

F. Karray et al. (Eds.): ICIAR 2019, LNCS 11662, pp. 162–173, 2019.
https://doi.org/10.1007/978-3-030-27202-9_14

4K/UHD video displays are believed to deliver better quality-of-experience (QoE) to viewers and are becoming widely available on the consumer market.

While 4K/UHD videos raise the potentials for better user QoE, their higher data rates cast great challenges to video distributions, for which video compression technologies are crucial in controlling the bandwidth of video so as to fit the distribution pipeline. The currently most widely used video coding technologies based on H.264 Advanced Video Coding (AVC) standards hardly meet the requirement. To this end, several modern video encoders including H.265 High Efficiency Video Coding (HEVC) [24], AOMedia Video 1 (AV1) [2], and Audio Video Coding Standard (AVS2) [20] are deliberately optimized for compressing content of 4K and higher resolutions. With many video encoders at hand, it becomes pivotal to compare their performance, so as to choose the best algorithms and find the direction for further advancement. Because the human visual system (HVS) is the ultimate receiver in most applications, subjective evaluation is a straightforward and reliable approach to evaluate the quality of videos. Although expensive and time consuming [26], a comprehensive subjective study has several benefits. First, it provides useful data to study human behaviors in evaluating perceived quality of encoded videos. Second, it supplies a test set to evaluate and compare the relative performance of classical and modern video encoding algorithms. Third, it is useful to validate and compare the performance of existing objective video quality assessment (VQA) models in predicting the perceptual quality of encoded videos. This will in turn provide insights on potential ways to improve them.

Several recent subjective studies have been conducted to evaluate the encoder performance on 4K video compression [3,7,10,23]. It is generally observed that the latest video encoders can deliver 4K contents with better viewer QoE, although the test only covers a small number of contents. In addition, most of the work covers FHD and 4K for HEVC and AVC encoders only. In [27], HEVC encoder is evaluated by using 10 contents under 4K resolution. In [6], the performance of HEVC, AVC, and VP9 [9] at FHD and 4K are compared on 10 contents, from which it is shown that HEVC and VP9 achieve better bitrate reduction than AVC at the same quality level. The performance of the emerging next-generation encoders, AV1 and AVS2, on 4K videos has not been systematically evaluated. In summary, all of the aforementioned studies suffer from the following problems: (1) the test dataset is limited in size; (2) the types of encoders do not fully reflect the state-of-the-art; and (3) the spatial resolutions do not cover commonly used display sizes. Moreover, many tests have been conducted by the developers or participants of the coding standards. Independent datasets and test results commonly available to the public is lacking.

In this work, we conduct subjective evaluation of popular and emerging video encoders on 4K content. Our contributions are threefold. First, we carry out an independent and so far the most comprehensive subjective experiment to evaluate the performance of modern video encoders including AVC [25], VP9 [9], AV1 [1], AVS2 [21] and HEVC [18]. Second, we applied statistical analysis on the subjective data and observe some significant trends. Third, we use the database

**Fig. 1.** Snapshots of source video sequences. (a) Safari. (b) 2D cartoon. (c) News. (d) Teppanyaki. (e) Screen recording. (f) Botanical garden. (g) Tears of steel. (h) Soccer game. (i) Animation. (j) Motor racing. (k) Climbing. (l) Colorfulness. (m) Forest. (n) Lightrail. (o) Dolphins. (p) Dance. (q) Spaceman. (r) Barbecue. (s) Supercar. (t) Traffic.

to evaluate objective VQA models to compare their prediction accuracy and complexity. The database will be made available online for future research.

## 2    Video Database Construction and Subjective Experiment

The video database is created from 20 pristine high-quality videos of UHD resolution (3840×2160, progressive) selected to cover diverse content types, including humans, plants, natural scenes, architectures and computer-synthesized sceneries. All videos have the length of 10 s [8]. The detailed specifications are listed in Table 1 and the screenshots are shown in Fig. 1. Spatial information (SI) and temporal information (TI) [12] that roughly reflect the complexity of the video content are also given in Table 1, which suggests that the video sequences are of diverse spatio-temporal complexity and widely span the SI-TI space. Using the aforementioned video sequences as the source, each video is encoded with AVC, VP9, AV1, AVS2 and HEVC encoders with progressive scan at three spatial resolutions (3840 × 2160, 1920 × 1080, and 960 × 540) and four distortion levels. The detailed encoding configurations are as follows:

- HEVC: We employ x265 [18] with main profile for HEVC encoding. The GOP size is set to 60. Rate control mode is selected to be constant rate factor (CRF). Videos are encoded in "veryslow" speed setting.
- AVC: The x264 [25] with high profile of level 5 is used for AVC encoding. Other settings such as GOP size, rate control mode and speed setting are the same as those of the HEVC configurations.
- VP9: The libvpx software [9] is used for VP9 encoding. The encoding parameters, such as GOP size, rate control mode, etc., are set to be as similar as possible to HEVC. The parameter selection is based on [15].
- AV1: The AV1 reference software aomenc [1] is used for AV1 encoding. The encoding parameters are set to be as similar as possible to HEVC. The parameter selection is based on [15].
- AVS2: The libxavs2 [21] is used for AVS2 encoding. The encoding parameters, such as GOP size and speed setting are set to be as similar as possible to HEVC. The parameter selection is based on the configuration file "encoder_ra.cfg" that comes with AVS2 source code [21].

A small-scale internal subjective test is conducted and the encoding bitrates are adjusted to ensure that the neighboring distortion levels are perceptually distinguishable. Eventually, we obtain 1,200 videos encoded by 5 encoders in 3 resolutions at 4 distortion levels.

Our subjective experiment generally follows the single stimulus methodology as suggested by the ITU-T recommendation P.910 [12]. The experiment setup is normal indoor home settings with ordinary illumination level and no reflecting ceiling walls or floors. All videos are displayed at 3840×2160 resolution on a 28 in. 4K LED monitor with Truecolor (32 bit) at 60 Hz. The monitor is calibrated to meet the ITU-T BT.500 recommendations [11]. Videos are displayed in random order using a customized graphical user interface from which individual subjects' opinion scores are recorded.

A total of 66 naïve subjects, including thirty nine males and twenty seven females aged between 18 and 35, participated in the subjective test. Visual acuity and color vision are confirmed with each subject before the subjective test. To familiarize the subjects with the testing environment, a training session is performed before the formal experiment, in which 3 videos different from those in the formal experiment are rendered. The same methods are used to generate the videos used in the training and testing sessions. Therefore, before the testing session, subjects knew what distortion types would be expected. Subjects were instructed with sample videos to judge the overall video quality based on the

**Table 1.** Spatial Information (SI), Temporal Information (TI), Framerate (FPS), and Description of source videos

| Name | FPS | SI | TI | Description |
|---|---|---|---|---|
| Safari | 24 | 26 | 41 | Animal, smooth motion |
| 2D carton | 25 | 38 | 55 | Animation, camera motion |
| News | 25 | 32 | 45 | Human, static |
| Teppanyaki | 24 | 33 | 32 | Food, average motion |
| Screen recording | 30 | 82 | 12 | Screen content, partial motion |
| Botanical garden | 30 | 112 | 10 | Natural scene, static |
| Tears of steel | 24 | 28 | 61 | Movie, high motion |
| Soccer game | 30 | 54 | 24 | Sports, high motion |
| Animation | 30 | 55 | 32 | Animation, high motion |
| Motor racing | 24 | 57 | 37 | Sports, camera motion |
| Climbing | 30 | 38 | 73 | Game, high motion |
| Colorfulness | 30 | 23 | 65 | Texture, smooth motion |
| Forest | 24 | 46 | 24 | Natural scene, camera motion |
| Lightrail | 30 | 79 | 32 | Architecture, camera motion |
| Dolphins | 25 | 54 | 23 | Animal, smooth motion |
| Dance | 30 | 73 | 32 | Human, high motion |
| Spaceman | 24 | 51 | 2 | Human, static |
| Barbecue | 25 | 100 | 11 | Natural scene, smooth motion |
| Supercar | 25 | 80 | 22 | Sports, average motion |
| Traffic | 30 | 89 | 24 | Architecture, high motion |

distortion level. Due to the limited subjective experiment capacity, we employed the following strategy. Each subject is assigned 10 contents in a circular fashion. Specifically, if subject $i$ is assigned contents 1 to 10, then subject $i+1$ watch contents 2 to 11. Each video is assessed for at least 30 times and more than 36,000 subjective ratings are collected in total. For each subject, the whole study takes about 3 h, which is divided into 6 sessions with five 5-min breaks in-between to minimize the influence of fatigue effect.

We employ 100-point continuous scale as opposed to a discrete 5-point ITU-R Absolute Category Scale (ACR) for three advantages: broader range, finer distinctions between ratings, and demonstrated prior efficacy [16]. After converting the subjective scores to Z-scores per session to account for any differences in the use of the quality scale between sessions, we proceed to an outlier removal process suggested in [11]. No outlier detection is conducted participant-wise. After outlier removal, Z-scores are linearly re-scaled to lie in the range of [0, 100].

The final quality score for each individual video is computed as the average of the re-scaled Z-scores, namely the mean opinion score (MOS), from all valid subjects. Pearson linear correlation coefficient (PLCC) and Spearman rank-order correlation coefficient (SRCC) between the score given by each subject and MOS are calculated. The average PLCC and SRCC across all subjects are 0.79 and 0.78, with standard deviation (STD) of 0.09 and 0.08, respectively, suggesting that there is considerable agreement among different subjects on the perceived quality of the test video sequences.

## 3   Evaluation of Video Encoders

We use the MOS of the test videos described in the previous section to evaluate and compare the performance of the encoders. It is worth noting that the performance comparison is based on the encoder configuration provided earlier, where all encoders are set to configurations equivalent to the 'veryslow' setting of the HEVC encoders.

Sample rate-distortion (RD) curves for individual test videos are given in Fig. 2. From the RD curves of all content, we have several observations. First, AVC under-performs all the other four encoders in most cases, which justifies the performance improvement of the newly developed video encoders in recent years. Second, the performance difference between different encoders, exhibited as the gaps between the RD curves, become increasingly manifest with the increase of resolution from 540p to 1080p, and then to 2160p. This validates the coding gain obtained by the advanced technologies specifically designed for high resolution videos in the newly developed encoders. This observation also justifies the necessity of cross-resolution subjective and objective video quality assessment because the visibility of coding artifacts changes from low to high resolution content. Third, we observe that AV1 achieves the highest bitrate savings for high motion content. This may be explained by the advancement of AV1 motion prediction schemes which utilizes warped motion, global motion tools and more reference frames [17].

In addition to the qualitative analysis, we also compute the average bitrate saving [4,5] of each encoder over another. The result is shown in Table 2, from which we can observe that on average AV1 outperforms the other encoders with a sizable margin. However, it is worth noting that the RD performance gain by AV1 is highly content dependent and that AV1's performance is achieved on the condition of its much higher complexity compared with all other encoders.

The time complexity performance test is done on a Ubuntu 16.04 system with Intel E5-1620 CPU and 32 GB RAM. As shown in Table 3, we can see that AV1 consumes over 500 times of AVC's computational time, which takes the least amount of encoding time. The results suggest that state-of-the-art AVC implementations are still highly competitive choices for time critical tasks, while the encoding speed of AV1 may hinder it from many practical applications.

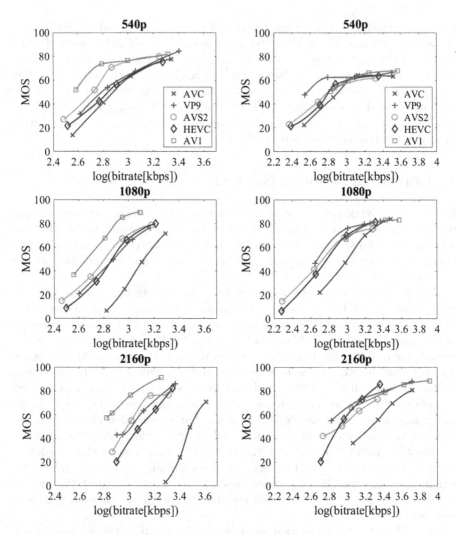

**Fig. 2.** RD curves of AVC, VP9, HEVC, AVS2 and AV1 encoders for 540p, 1080p and 2160p resolutions for Tears of steel (left) and Barbecue (right).

It is worth mentioning that AV1 is still under development and the current version has not been fully optimized for multi-thread encoding. VP9 and HEVC show comparable time complexity, while AVS2 doubles their encoding time. They compromise between compression performance and speed.

**Table 2.** Column BD-rate saving vs. row (negative percentages suggest savings)

| 540p | AVC | HEVC | AVS2 | VP9 | AV1 |
|------|-----|------|------|-----|-----|
| AVC | 0 | - | - | - | - |
| HEVC | −22.7% | 0 | - | - | - |
| AVS2 | −20.3% | −4.7% | 0 | - | - |
| VP9 | −28.9% | −20.5% | −25.7% | 0 | - |
| AV1 | −34.4% | −23.3% | −17.6% | −4.5% | 0 |
| 1080p | AVC | HEVC | AVS2 | VP9 | AV1 |
| AVC | 0 | - | - | - | - |
| HEVC | −42.2% | 0 | - | - | - |
| AVS2 | −45.8% | −9.8% | 0 | - | - |
| VP9 | −47.5% | −18.5% | −18.1% | 0 | - |
| AV1 | −48.7% | −20.1% | −21.4% | −3.5% | 0 |
| 2160p | AVC | HEVC | AVS2 | VP9 | AV1 |
| AVC | 0 | - | - | - | - |
| HEVC | −61.2% | 0 | - | - | - |
| AVS2 | −63.5% | −9.7% | 0 | - | - |
| VP9 | −62.2% | −8.7% | −5.3% | 0 | - |
| AV1 | −63.2% | −9.5% | −15.0% | −16.4% | 0 |

**Table 3.** Encoder relative complexity vs. AVC at 3 resolutions

| | AVC | HEVC | AV1 | VP9 | AVS2 |
|------|-----|------|-----|-----|------|
| 2160p | 1 | 4.2810 | 590.74 | 5.2856 | 9.8568 |
| 1080p | 1 | 4.7314 | 546.19 | 6.6286 | 10.0401 |
| 540p | 1 | 5.2805 | 806.15 | 5.2572 | 11.7716 |

# 4    Performance of Objective Quality Assessment Methods

We use four representative objective VQA models including PSNR, VQM [19], VMAF [13] (version v0.6.1), VMAF-4K [14] (version v0.6.1), and SSIMplus [22] to test their generalizability on novel video encoders. The implementations of the VQA models are obtained from the original authors. Only SSIMplus supports direct cross-resolution video quality evaluation. For the other VQA models, all representations are upsampled to $3840 \times 2160$ using bilinear filter and the VQA is performed on the up-sampled videos. PLCC and SRCC are employed to evaluate the performance of objective VQA models in terms of their effectiveness in predicting MOS.

Table 4 summarizes the overall performance of the VQA models and the breakdown results for three resolutions, where the top VQA models for each evaluation criterion are highlighted in bold. Overall, SSIMplus is the best performing VQA model in most cases. Specifically, the performance gaps between SSIMplus and the other models increases with resolution, and the gap is the largest at 4K/UHD resolution. This justifies the effectiveness of the HVS-based resolution adaptation mechanism underlying the SSIMplus approach [22]. PSNR, the traditional quality model, is the weakest in the current test, which is likely due to its ignorance of any HVS properties. For VQM, we observe major inconsistent scoring across different video content, suggesting that there is space for improvement in VQM in terms of content-adaptation. Our results also show that the VMAF model tends to overestimate the quality scores of AVC videos. This may be because VMAF is a learning-based approach and was originally trained using H.264/AVC compressed videos, but the statistical properties of the artifacts in the newly developed encoding methods are different. For example, HEVC and AV1 encoders produce less blockiness and smoother transition between frames. These features may not be properly captured by VMAF. Somewhat surprisingly, for the VMAF-4K model, which was claimed to be better suited for 4K TV device, the correlation is significantly lower than VMAF even when tested with the 4K dataset. This might be because the VMAF-4K model was trained to cover a very wide range of video resolutions, for which the size of its training dataset may not be sufficient [14]. Using MOS as the ground-truth, we can compare the scores given by any individual subject, and evaluate the performance of the subject in predicting MOS. The average of individual subjects' performance and the standard deviation (STD) between all individual subjects are also given in Table 4. Such "average subject" performance gives us a baseline about the difficulty of the quality assessment task. Using this baseline, we observe that top VQA models such as SSIMplus performs closely to an average subject.

**Table 4.** Performance comparison of VQA models using MOS as ground-truth

| VQA models | | All | | 540p | | 1080p | | 2160p | |
|---|---|---|---|---|---|---|---|---|---|
| | | PLCC | SRCC | PLCC | SRCC | PLCC | SRCC | PLCC | SRCC |
| PSNR | | 0.4197 | 0.4162 | 0.3993 | 0.4143 | 0.4155 | 0.3858 | 0.3259 | 0.3252 |
| VMAF-4K (v0.6.1) | | 0.5505 | 0.5530 | 0.5102 | 0.4726 | 0.5784 | 0.5371 | 0.4601 | 0.4414 |
| VQM | | 0.6154 | 0.6282 | 0.5165 | 0.5357 | 0.6659 | 0.6722 | 0.5831 | 0.6163 |
| VMAF (v0.6.1) | | 0.7371 | 0.7387 | 0.7247 | **0.7018** | 0.7909 | 0.7646 | 0.6335 | 0.6521 |
| SSIMplus | | **0.7930** | **0.7757** | **0.7604** | 0.6874 | **0.8662** | **0.8265** | **0.7469** | **0.7523** |
| Individual subjects | Average | 0.7917 | 0.7819 | 0.7229 | 0.7007 | 0.8287 | 0.8079 | 0.7770 | 0.7584 |
| | STD | ±0.0068 | ±0.0081 | ±0.0108 | ±0.0132 | ±0.0066 | ±0.0077 | ±0.0078 | ±0.0098 |

VQA measurement is often a computationally demanding task but real-world applications such as live QoE monitoring often desire video quality being evaluated in real-time. Figure 3 compares VQA methods' prediction accuracy against speed on videos of 4K resolution, where the speed performance test for VQA methods is done on a Ubuntu 16.04 system with Intel E5-1620 CPU and 32 GB RAM. It appears that the VMAF and VMAF-4K models are much faster than VQM while maintaining a similar level of quality prediction accuracy. Overall, the SSIMplus measure clearly offers the best compromise between speed and accuracy.

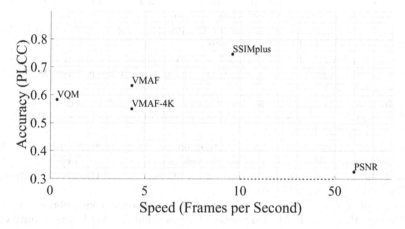

**Fig. 3.** Speed vs. prediction accuracy comparison of VQA models on 4K resolution videos

## 5 Conclusions and Discussion

We conduct an independent and so far the most comprehensive subjective evaluation and performance analysis, specifically on popular and emerging video encoders (AVC, HEVC, VP9, AVS2, and AV1) with video content of diverse resolutions and bitrates. The five video encoders are evaluated across 20 source 4K contents from the view points of content dependency and resolution adaptation. The subjective testing results are also used to test the performance of representative VQA models, among which the SSIMplus measure achieves the best compromise between accuracy and speed. The testing results will be made publicly available to facilitate future video coding and VQA research.

It is important to note that video coding standards define decoders only, and their encoder instantiations and configurations vary significantly from one to another. Due to the limited subjective experiment capacity and the large number of combinations of encoder configurations, absolute "fair" comparison of video decoders or coding standards is extremely difficult. Therefore, conclusions about the performance of video coding standards should be drawn with caution. The current study is valid for the given encoders with the specified encoding configurations only.

# References

1. Alliance for Open Media: AV1 codec source code repository, June 2018. https://aomedia.googlesource.com/aom
2. Alliance for Open Media: The alliance for open media kickstarts video innovation era with "AV1" release, March 2018. https://aomedia.org/the-alliance-for-open-media-kickstarts-video-innovation-era-with-av1-release/
3. Bae, S.H., Kim, J., Kim, M., Cho, S., Choi, J.S.: Assessments of subjective video quality on HEVC-encoded 4K-UHD video for beyond-HDTV broadcasting services. IEEE Trans. Broadcast. **59**(2), 209–222 (2013)
4. Bjontegaard, G.: Calculation of average PSNR differences between RD-curves. In: ITU-T Q. 6/SG16, 33th VCEG Meeting (2001)
5. Bjontegaard, G.: Improvements of the BD-PSNR model, VCEG-AI11. In: ITU-T Q. 6/SG16, 34th VCEG Meeting (2008)
6. Cheon, M., Lee, J.S.: Subjective and objective quality assessment of compressed 4K UHD videos for immersive experience. IEEE Trans. Circuits Syst. **28**(7), 1467–1480 (2018)
7. Deshpande, S.: Subjective and objective visual quality evaluation of 4K video using AVC and HEVC compression. In: SID Symposium Digest of Technical Papers, vol. 43, pp. 481–484 (2012)
8. Fröhlich, P., Egger, S., Schatz, R., Mühlegger, M., Masuch, K., Gardlo, B.: QoE in 10 seconds: are short video clip lengths sufficient for quality of experience assessment? In: Proceedings of IEEE International Conference on Quality of Multimedia Experience, pp. 242–247 (2012)
9. Google: libvpx, July 2018. https://chromium.googlesource.com/webm/libvpx.git
10. Hanhart, P., Rerabek, M., De Simone, F., Ebrahimi, T.: Subjective quality evaluation of the upcoming HEVC video compression standard. In: Applications of Digital Image Processing XXXV, vol. 8499, pp. 1–13 (2012)
11. ITU-R BT.500: Recommendation: methodology for the subjective assessment of the quality of television pictures, January 2012
12. ITU-R BT.910: Recommendation: subjective video quality assessment methods for multimedia applications, April 2008
13. Li, Z., Aaron, A., Katsavounidis, I., Moorthy, A., Manohara, M.: Toward a practical perceptual video quality metric, June 2016. https://medium.com/netflix-techblog/toward-a-practical-perceptual-video-quality-metric-653f208b9652
14. Li, Z., Vigier, T., Callet, P.L.: A VMAF model for 4K, March 2018. ftp://vqeg.its.bldrdoc.gov/Documents/VQEG_Madrid_Mar18/Meeting_Files/VQEG_SAM_2018_025_VMAF_4K.pdf
15. Liu, Y.: AV1 beats x264 and libvpx-vp9 in practical use case, April 2018. https://code.fb.com/video-engineering/av1-beats-x264-and-libvpx-vp9-in-practical-use-case/
16. Ma, K., et al.: Group MAD competition-a new methodology to compare objective image quality models. In: Proceedings of IEEE International Conference on Computer Vision and Pattern Recognition, pp. 1664–1673 (2016)
17. Massimino, P.: AOM - AV1, How does it work? July 2017. https://parisvideotech.com/wp-content/uploads/2017/07/AOM-AV1-Video-Tech-meet-up.pdf
18. MultiCoreWare Inc.: x265, July 2018. https://bitbucket.org/multicoreware/x265
19. Pinson, M.H., Wolf, S.: A new standardized method for objectively measuring video quality. IEEE Trans. Broadcast. **50**(3), 312–322 (2004)
20. PKU-VCL: AVS2 technology (2018). http://www.avs.org.cn/avs2/technology.asp

21. PKU-VCL: AVS2 codec source code repository, January 2018. https://github.com/pkuvcl/xavs2
22. Rehman, A., Zeng, K., Wang, Z.: Display device-adapted video quality-of-experience assessment. In: Human Vision and Electronic Imaging XX, vol. 9394, pp. 1–11 (2015)
23. Řeřábek, M., Ebrahimi, T.: Comparison of compression efficiency between HEVC/H.265 and VP9 based on subjective assessments. In: Applications of Digital Image Processing Xxxvii, vol. 9217, pp. 1–13 (2014)
24. Tan, T., Mrak, M., Baroncini, V., Ramzan, N.: Report on HEVC compression performance verification testing. Joint Collab. Team Video Coding (JCT-VC) (2014)
25. VideoLAN: x264, July 2018. http://git.videolan.org/git/x264
26. Wang, Z., Bovik, A.C.: Mean squared error: love it or leave it? A new look at signal fidelity measures. IEEE Signal Process. Mag. **26**(1), 98–117 (2009)
27. Zhu, Y., Song, L., Xie, R., Zhang, W.: SJTU 4K video subjective quality dataset for content adaptive bit rate estimation without encoding. In: IEEE International Symposium on Broadband Multimedia Systems and Broadcasting, pp. 1–4 (2016)

# An Improved Simulated Annealing Approach for Reconstructing Binary Images with Fixed Number of Strips

Judit Szűcs[✉] and Péter Balázs

Department of Image Processing and Computer Graphics, University of Szeged, Árpád tér 2., Szeged 6720, Hungary
{jszucs,pbalazs}@inf.u-szeged.hu

**Abstract.** We consider the problem of reconstructing binary images from their horizontal and vertical projections and the given number of strips in each row and column. Knowing that the problem is NP-hard, in one of our recent papers (Szűcs, J., Balázs, P.: Variants of simulated annealing for strip constrained binary tomography, LNCS 10986, p. 82–92, 2019) we proposed variants of Simulated Annealing to solve this issue. However, in the same time we revealed different drawbacks of this approach. Here, we enhance the method in two ways: (1) we locally update the number of strips in each iteration, and (2) we apply the Curveball algorithm to avoid getting stuck in local minima. By experimental results we show that the new approach is faster than the former one, and it ensures also better solutions.

**Keywords:** Binary tomography · Image reconstruction · Nonogram · Simulated annealing · Ryser's algorithm · Curveball algorithm

## 1 Introduction

Binary Tomography investigates the reconstruction of binary images from their projections, i.e., sets of line sums taken along parallel lines from different directions [4]. When only the horizontal and vertical projections are given the problem is known to be solvable in polynomial time. However, the solution is usually not uniquely determined. A common way to reduce the number of feasible solutions is to assume that the image to reconstruct satisfies some geometrical, topological, or more complex properties. This, however, can cause the reconstruction problem to be NP-hard. In this case the reconstruction can be formulated as a function minimization problem which is then solved by deterministic or stochastic minimizers.

Motivated by nonogram puzzles, in [1] we introduced a texture-like prior, the number of strips in each row and column. We suggested a deterministic integer programming approach and a stochastic method (Simulated Annealing - SA) to solve the problem, and found that the SA-based method was much faster.

© Springer Nature Switzerland AG 2019
F. Karray et al. (Eds.): ICIAR 2019, LNCS 11662, pp. 174–185, 2019.
https://doi.org/10.1007/978-3-030-27202-9_15

Then, in [8] we proposed different strategies to initialize the SA-based approach. Among the different variants, the so-called RyserSA proved to be the best one. Unfortunately, its running time was rather high and it often got stuck into a local minimum. The aim of this paper is to eliminate these drawbacks of the method by (1) locally updating the number of strips in each iteration, and (2) by applying the Curveball algorithm to avoid getting stuck in local minima.

The structure of the paper is the following. Section 2 is for the problem outline. In Sect. 3 we describe the method based on SA and show how to improve it. In Sect. 4 we present experimental results and provide an explanation of them. Finally, we summarize our work in Sect. 5.

## 2  Problem Outline

We represent the binary images by binary matrices where 1 stands for the object (black) and 0 stands for the background (white) pixels. Then, the horizontal (vertical) projection of the image is the vector of the row (column) sums of the image matrix, respectively. The basic problem of Binary Tomography is the following.

**Problem.** BINARY TOMOGRAPHY (BT)
**Input:** Two non-negative integer vectors $H \in \mathbb{Z}^m$ and $V \in \mathbb{Z}^n$.
**Output:** A binary matrix of size $m \times n$, if it exists, with row sum vector $H$ and column sum vector $V$.

A *switching component* in a binary matrix $A \in \{0,1\}^{m \times n}$ is a set of four positions $(i,j), (i',j), (i,j'), (i',j')$ $(1 \le i, i' \le m,\ 1 \le j, j' \le n)$ such that $a_{ij} = a_{i'j'}$ and $a_{i'j} = a_{ij'} = 1 - a_{ij}$. An *elementary switching* changes the 1s of a switching component to 0s, and the 0s to 1s. Clearly, this operation does not affect the row and column sums. We recall the followings from [6]:

**Proposition 1.** *Problem* BT *can be solved in* $\mathcal{O}(mn)$ *time.*

**Proposition 2.** *The presence of switching components is a sufficient and necessary condition for non-uniqueness of the solution.*

**Proposition 3.** *All the solutions of the same problem can be accessed from an arbitrary initial solution by applying a sequence of elementary switchings.*

The aforementioned problem has a natural connection to the logic puzzles called nonograms. To formally describe this problem, we introduce the notion of *strips* which are non-extendible (i.e., maximal) segments of black pixels of a row or column. Formally, given a binary matrix $A$ of size $m \times n$, a sequence of consecutive positions $(i, j_s), (i, j_{s+1}), \ldots, (i, j_{s+l-1})$ (where $l$ is a positive integer, and $1 \le j_s \le n$) in the $i$-th row $(1 \le i \le m)$ form a *strip* if $a_{i,j_s} = 1, a_{i,j_{s+1}} = 1, \ldots, a_{i,j_{s+l-1}} = 1$, and $a_{i,j_s-1} = 0$ and $a_{i,j_s+l} = 0$ (if the latter two positions exist). The length of the strip is given by $l$. Strips of columns can be defined in an analogous way.

The length of each strip in the rows of the matrix $A$ can be encoded by an integer matrix $LH$ of size $m \times n$, where $lh_{ij}$ is the length of the $j$-th strip from the left, in the $i$-th row. Entries not used to indicate strips are set to 0. Similarly, a matrix $LV$ of size $n \times m$ can describe the length of each strip in the columns of $A$. Now, the problem is given as follows.

**Problem.** NONOGRAM
**Input:** Two non-negative integer matrices $LH$ of size $m \times n$ and $LV$ of size $n \times m$.
**Output:** A binary matrix of size $m \times n$, if it exists, in each row and column having strips of length prescribed by $LH$ and $LV$, respectively.

In contrast to BT, NONOGRAM is in general an NP-complete problem [9]. We define the following intermediate problem.

**Problem.** STRIP CONSTRAINED BINARY TOMOGRAPHY (SCBT)
**Input:** Four non-negative integer vectors $H \in \mathbb{Z}^m$, $V \in \mathbb{Z}^n$, $SH \in \mathbb{Z}^m$, and $SV \in \mathbb{Z}^n$.
**Output:** A binary matrix of size $m \times n$, if it exists, with row sum vector $H$, column sum vector $V$, and in each row and column having the number of strips prescribed by $SH$ and $SV$, respectively.

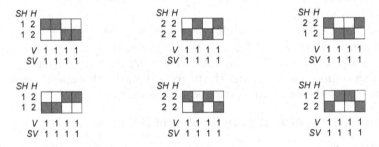

**Fig. 1.** Examples of uniqueness and non-uniqueness of the SCBT problem. The images of the left column cannot be distinguished by their $H$, $V$, $SH$, and $SV$ vectors, thus, the solution in this case is non-unique. The same holds for the images in the middle column. Notice also that an elementary switching cannot transform one solution into the other. Images of the right column are uniquely determined by their vectors, even though they contain switching components.

This problem is also NP-complete in general and its solution is not always uniquely determined (Fig. 1) [8]. Figure 1 also gives an example of the following observation.

**Proposition 4.** *For certain inputs, problem SCBT can have several solutions, such that one cannot be transformed into the other by a sequence of elementary switchings.*

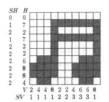 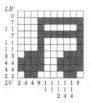

**Fig. 2.** Instances of the BT, SCBT, and Nonogram problems, from left to right, respectively. Padding zero elements of the matrices $LH$ and $LV$ are not indicated.

The three problems and their connections are presented in Fig. 2.

## 3    Simulated Annealing for Solving SCBT

Following [1] we formulate SCBT as an optimization problem, where the aim is to minimize

$$f(\mathbf{x}) = ||H - H'||_2 + ||V - V'||_2 + ||SH - SH'||_2 + ||SV - SV'||_2 , \quad (1)$$

where $H$, $V$, $SH$, $SV$ are the input vectors and $H'$, $V'$, $SH'$, $SV'$ are the corresponding vectors belonging to the current solution image $\mathbf{x}$. We use simulated annealing (SA) [5] to minimize (1) (see Algorithm 1).

---

**Algorithm 1.** Simulated Annealing

---

1: $s \leftarrow$ initial state
2: $T_1 \leftarrow$ initial temperature
3: $k \leftarrow 1$
4: $\alpha \in (0.5, 1)$
5: $\beta \in (0, 1)$
6: **while** $(stoppingCriteria == FALSE)$ **do**
7:     $tempStay := 0$
8:     **while** $(tempStay < \beta \cdot f(s))$ **do**
9:         $actual := neighbor(s)$
10:         **if** $(f(actual) < f(s))$ **then**
11:             $s := actual$
12:         **else if** $(e^{\frac{f(s)-f(actual)}{T_k}} > rand(0,1))$ **then**
13:             $s := actual$
14:         **end if**
15:         $tempStay := tempStay + 1$
16:     **end while**
17:     $T_{k+1} := T_k \cdot \alpha$
18:     $k := k + 1$
19: **end while**

---

Starting from an initial solution, in every iteration the method selects a neighbor solution and accepts it if its objective function value is smaller than the former one. However, the recently selected solution can also be accepted with a given probability (based on the actual temperature and the objective function value), even if its objective function value is worse as before. Parameter $\alpha$ is to control lowering the temperature, while $\beta$ defines a maximum rate of the possibly denied proposals on the current temperature. The method runs until one of the stopping criteria is met.

### 3.1    SA with Ryser's Algorithm

In [8] the authors investigated different strategies to set the initial state of the SA method, and they found that the best variant was to start out from a solution of the BT problem. From, Proposition 1, we know that omitting the $SH$ and $SV$ vectors (thus, relaxing SCBT to BT) the $H$ and $V$ vectors can be satisfied (if a solution exists) in $\mathcal{O}(mn)$ time with Ryser's method [6]. Furthermore, Proposition 3 ensures that by elementary switchings, all the solutions of the BT problem can be reached. However, no efficient method is known to visit all of them, therefore checking all solutions of BT whether they satisfy the vectors $SH$ and $SV$ seems not feasible. Nevertheless, starting from an arbitrary solution of BT, and applying randomly chosen elementary switchings to generate the new suggestions (the neighbor of the current state), we only have to focus on the $\|SH - SH'\|_2 + \|SV - SV'\|_2$ term of the objective function as the remaining part is 0. This method is called RyserSA.

### 3.2    SA with Curveball Algorithm

We can interpret the binary image matrices as presence-absence matrices. There are several methods how to reorganize them without altering row and column totals. One of these approaches is the so-called *Curveball algorithm* published in [2,3,7] (the name comes from the idea based on trading baseball cards). We can use this algorithm as follows. The initialization step is the same as in the RyserSA method. Then, the algorithm randomly chooses two rows from the current image matrix (*Step 1*), and collects the unique items from them (*Step 2*). Thus, we get two lists: the first containing the elements which are 1s in the first row and 0s in the second row, the second containing the elements which are 0s in the first row and 1s in the second row. The length of the smaller list is denoted by $l$. In *Step 3* the algorithm randomly chooses one element from each list. Thus, the upper 1 and the lower 1 values of a switching component is defined. Finally, the items of the switching components are inverted (*Step 4*). *Steps 2–4* are iterated $k$ times (where $k \in \{0, 1, \ldots, l\}$ is randomly chosen in each iteration). We call this method CurveballSA.

### 3.3    Local Update of the Strip Vectors

Both RyserSA and CurveballSA operate with switching components which do not affect the projections but can have an impact on the number of strips. Since the objective function must be evaluated in each iteration it is important to keep its processing time as low as possible. Our key observation is that the vectors $SH$ and $SV$ can be locally updated based on the followings:

- If one object pixel is deleted from the interior of a strip, then one new strip appears (the old one breaks into two pieces), thus the number of strips increases by 1. For example, in Fig. 3a there are two strips, and if we delete the marked object pixel, there will be 3 strips (Fig. 3b).
- If one object pixel is added between two strips (that have only one non-object pixel in between), then the two strips are merging, and thus the number of strips decreases by 1. For example, in Fig. 3c there are two strips, and if we add an object pixel to the marked place, there will be only one strip (Fig. 3d).
- If one object pixel is added to a strip border, there is no change in the number of strips (Fig. 3e and f).
- If one object pixel is deleted from a strip border, there is no change in the number of strips (Fig. 3g and h).
- If a new single object pixel appears (having no neighbor object pixels) then the number of strips increases by 1. If a single object pixel is deleted (having no neighbor object pixels) then the number of strips decreases by 1.

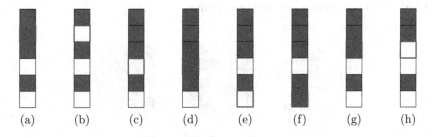

(a)     (b)     (c)     (d)     (e)     (f)     (g)     (h)

**Fig. 3.** Examples for a new strip appearing (a–b), two strips are merging (c–d), and there is no change (e–f and g–h).

## 4   Experimental Results

In order to investigate the effect of the local update and the Curveball strategy we conducted several experiments on different datasets. The parameters of the SA algorithm has been set manually, in an empirical way. The stopping criteria of the algorithm is to reach 1 000 000 iterations or to perform 3 000 iterations without improving the solution. The initial temperature is set to $T_1 = 350$ and the cooling schedule is controlled by $\alpha = 0.99$. The SA algorithm may stay in identical temperature for some iteration, in our case this is defined by $\beta = 0.035$. The tests were performed on a QuadCore Intel Core i7-4770 processor, 3800 MHz with 8 GB RAM. The algorithms were implemented in MATLAB.

For the numerical evaluation, beside calculating the value of the objective function of (1), we also calculated the *pixel error* defined as

$$E(O, R) = \frac{\sum_{ij} |o_{ij} - r_{ij}|}{m \cdot n} ,$$

where $O$ and $R$ is the original and the reconstructed image, respectively, and $m \times n$ is the size of the image.

## 4.1  Random Images

In the first experiment we generated 10-10 binary images of sizes $3 \times 3, 4 \times 4, \ldots, 256 \times 256$, containing $0\%, 10\%, \ldots, 100\%$ randomly chosen object pixels (Fig. 4). Figure 5 shows the average running times of the RyserSA and CurveballSA methods, using local update of the number of strips. As a comparison we report here that without a local update the running time of RyserSA can be as high as 400 s on the hardest instances of this dataset, thus the local update indeed significantly decreased the running time. Clearly, CurveballSA performs much more switchings, thus its execution time is higher (and would be much more higher without the local update). Concerning the value of the objective function, from Fig. 6 we deduce that both methods perform similar and they both can ensure low function values.

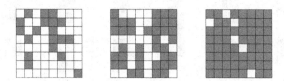

**Fig. 4.** Images with 30%, 60%, and 90% randomly chosen object pixels (from left to right, respectively).

## 4.2  Web Paint-by-Number

The second test was conducted on images of size $20 \times 20$ from real nonogram games (Fig. 7), which were downloaded from [10]. The results are shown in Table 1. The better final objective function values are highlighted in bold. It is clearly seen that in all cases the CurveballSA algorithm performs better, and RyserSA was more often stuck in local minima. It is also seen that CurveballSA needs higher running time. Unfortunately, but not surprisingly, the pixel error is high. This phenomenon is due to the high number of feasible solutions caused by the switching components present in the image, and the issue was already addressed in [8].

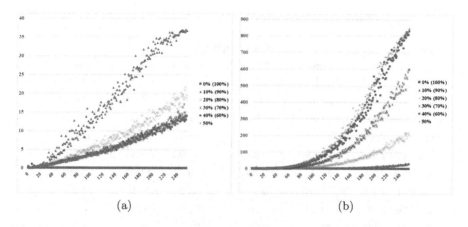

**Fig. 5.** Mean running time in seconds (vertical axis) of the RyserSA and the CurveballSA methods for different sized images (horizontal axis), respectively.

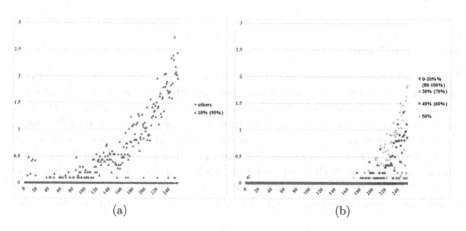

**Fig. 6.** Mean final objective function value (vertical axis) of the RyserSA and the CurveballSA methods for different sized images (horizontal axis), respectively.

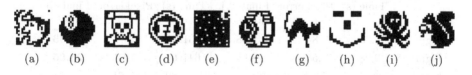

**Fig. 7.** Example images from Web Paint-by-Number.

**Table 1.** Results of Web Paint-by-Number images.

| Figure | RyserSA | | | CurveballSA | | |
|---|---|---|---|---|---|---|
| | Time (s) | Pixel error (%) | Final obj. value | Time (s) | Pixel error (%) | Final obj. value |
| Figure 7a | 3.61 | 39.65 | 0.51 | 1.53 | 39.70 | **0.00** |
| Figure 7b | 1.11 | 18.00 | 6.09 | 147.70 | 10.60 | **1.78** |
| Figure 7c | 2.54 | 27.00 | 2.47 | 6.99 | 23.70 | **0.00** |
| Figure 7d | 2.36 | 37.95 | 1.36 | 2.03 | 35.05 | **0.00** |
| Figure 7e | 1.36 | 12.15 | 0.00 | 0.15 | 11.60 | 0.00 |
| Figure 7f | 2.23 | 31.60 | 3.99 | 63.28 | 26.45 | **0.20** |
| Figure 7g | 0.10 | 20.45 | 7.96 | 152.05 | 20.50 | **1.53** |
| Figure 7h | 1.22 | 32.15 | 6.96 | 138.55 | 30.30 | **2.80** |
| Figure 7i | 3.21 | 36.60 | 0.93 | 1.70 | 37.30 | **0.00** |
| Figure 7j | 1.54 | 24.85 | 4.40 | 50.79 | 26.00 | **0.17** |

### 4.3  TomoPhantom Images

Finally, we conducted tests on 22 different images of size $128 \times 128$, that we called TomoPhantoms, and which were used in other papers to test the efficacy of binary tomographic reconstruction algorithms. Since the images were now more complex, in this experiment we increased the number of possible iterations. The new stopping criteria was to reach 3 000 000 iterations or to perform 6 000 iterations without improving the solution. In Fig. 8 representatives of the dataset are given with the corresponding numerical evaluation in Table 2. The better final objective values are highlighted in bold. The CurveballSA algorithm, again, performed much better, but as before, in needs higher running time than

**Table 2.** Results of TomoPhantom images.

| Figure | RyserSA | | | CurveballSA | | |
|---|---|---|---|---|---|---|
| | Time (s) | Pixel error (%) | Final obj. value | Time (s) | Pixel error (%) | Final obj. value |
| Figure 8a | 0.25 | 12.84 | 148.98 | 1161.94 | 12.61 | **45.33** |
| Figure 8b | 0.28 | 8.55 | 78.61 | 641.15 | 7.69 | **23.65** |
| Figure 8c | 0.23 | 17.61 | 118.90 | 4.89 | 17.61 | 118.90 |
| Figure 8d | 0.27 | 20.00 | 149.69 | 1065.55 | 20.47 | **37.00** |
| Figure 8e | 0.77 | 1.93 | 32.52 | 2427.76 | 1.82 | **2.20** |
| Figure 8f | 24.80 | 36.99 | 11.70 | 861.91 | 37.86 | **4.04** |
| Figure 8g | 0.21 | 16.11 | 98.47 | 3.73 | 16.11 | 98.47 |
| Figure 8h | 0.23 | 13.43 | 138.35 | 1276.23 | 11.51 | **28.68** |

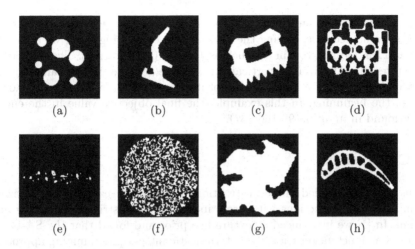

Fig. 8. TomoPhantom images.

RyserSA. There are some instances, where the final objective values are the same for both methods. These correspond to the cases where both methods stuck in the initially guessed local minima causing short running time but high objective function value of the CurveballSA algorithm. These 'hard' instances should be more deeply investigated in the future.

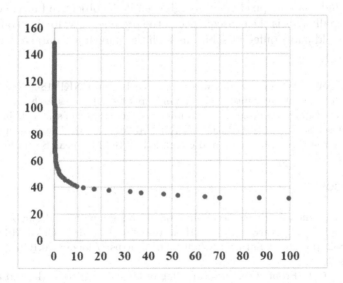

Fig. 9. Objective function values during the iterations for Fig. 8a. The number of million iterations is given on vertical axis and the actual objective values on the horizontal axis. Dots are only drawn when the value decreased in the corresponding iteration.

As a final insight into the problem, in Fig. 9 we show how the objective function value decreases during the iterations in case of Fig. 8a, if we allow the `CurveballSA` method to run as much as 100 000 000 iterations. The number of million iterations is given on vertical axis and the actual objective values on the horizontal axis. After a huge number of iterations the decrease is much slower than in the beginning. In this example, the final objective value in the end is 31.70 (found in iteration 99 166 737).

## 5    Conclusions

In this paper we studied the reconstruction of binary images from their horizontal and vertical projections with prescribed number of strips in each row and column. In [1] we introduced a texture-like prior and found that the SA-based method was much faster than the deterministic integer programming approach. In [8] we suggested different strategies to initialize the SA-based approach and found that the `RyserSA` is the best one. Here, we improved the aforementioned SA-based algorithm from two aspects. First, we described how to locally update the number of strips in each iteration, that highly reduced the running time of the method. Second, we introduced the Curveball algorithm to choose neighbor solutions, in order to prevent the algorithm to stuck in local minima. We found that the `CurveballSA` algorithm performs better for real images than the `RyserSA` algorithm. Unfortunately the former method needs much higher running time. An efficient implementation of this method is among our future plans. We also found that the pixel error is high even if the objective function value is relatively small. This is the consequence of the presence of switching components which can yield many different solutions with the same input data, as we already reported in [8].

**Acknowledgements.** Judit Szűcs was supported by the UNKP-18-3 New National Excellence Program of the Ministry of Human Capacities. This research was supported by the project "Integrated program for training new generation of scientists in the fields of computer science", no. EFOP-3.6.3-VEKOP-16-2017-00002. The project has been supported by the European Union and co-funded by the European Social Fund.

## References

1. Balázs, P., Szűcs, J.: Reconstruction of binary images with fixed number of strips. In: Campilho, A., Karray, F., ter Haar Romeny, B. (eds.) ICIAR 2018. LNCS, vol. 10882, pp. 11–19. Springer, Cham (2018). https://doi.org/10.1007/978-3-319-93000-8_2
2. Carstens, C.J.: Proof of uniform sampling of binary matrices with fixed row sums and column sums for the fast curveball algorithm. Phys. Rev. E **91**(4), 042812 (2015)
3. Carstens, C.J., Berger, A., Strona, G.: A unifying framework for fast randomization of ecological networks with fixed (node) degrees. MethodsX **5**, 773–780 (2018)

4. Herman, G.T., Kuba, A.: Discrete Tomography: Foundations, Algorithms, and Applications. ANHA. Springer, New York (1999). https://doi.org/10.1007/978-1-4612-1568-4

5. Kirkpatrick, S., Gelatt, C.D., Vecchi, M.P., et al.: Optimization by simulated annealing. Science **220**(4598), 671–680 (1983)

6. Ryser, H.J.: Combinatorial properties of matrices of zeros and ones. Can. J. Math. **9**, 371–377 (1957)

7. Strona, G., Nappo, D., Boccacci, F., Fattorini, S., San-Miguel-Ayanz, J.: A fast and unbiased procedure to randomize ecological binary matrices with fixed row and column totals. Nat. Commun. **5**, 4114 (2014)

8. Szűcs, J., Balázs, P.: Variants of simulated annealing for strip constrained binary tomography. In: Barneva, R.P., Brimkov, V.E., Kulczycki, P., Tavares, J.M.R.S. (eds.) CompIMAGE 2018. LNCS, vol. 10986, pp. 82–92. Springer, Cham (2019). https://doi.org/10.1007/978-3-030-20805-9_8

9. Ueda, N., Nagao, T.: NP-completeness results for nonogram via parsimonious reductions. Preprint (1996)

10. Wolter, J.: Web Paint-by-Number. https://webpbn.com/

# WaveM-CNN for Automatic Recognition of Sub-cellular Organelles

Duc Hoa Tran[✉], Michel Meunier, and Farida Cheriet

Polytechnique Montréal, Montréal, Canada
{duc-hoa.tran,michel.meunier,farida.cheriet}@polymtl.ca

**Abstract.** This paper proposes a novel deep learning architecture WaveM-CNN for efficient recognition of sub-cellular organelles in microscopic images. Essentially, multi-resolution analysis based on wavelet decomposition and convolution neural network (CNN) are combined in the architecture. In each wavelet transformed sub-space, discriminative features are extracted by convolution kernels to provide various pattern characteristics of the same organelle. The generated feature maps are concatenated and passed directly to the fully connected layers of the classifier. In order to reduce the computational time and improve performance on limited dataset, transfer learning method is adopted, with the utilization of compact MobileNet model. Experiments on two benchmark datasets **CHO** and **2D HeLa** are conducted to evaluate the performance of the proposed model on fluorescence microscopic images of sub-cellular organelles. The classification accuracies of **98.4**% and **96.1**% are achieved on these two datasets respectively, which are significantly higher than both hand-crafted feature based methods and recent deep learning based models.

**Keywords:** Deep learning · Multi-resolution · Microscopic image · Wavelet transform

## 1 Introduction

One important application of microscopic image analysis is to specify the sub-cellular structures inside a cell where there are proteins of interest. The localization where the proteins are produced by given genes is an essential factor to determine the possible function of such genes. Proteins of similar sequence structures could function differently due to their different compartment localization within the same cell [2].

Microscopic image interpretation is a challenging problem even for experimented pathologists. The output images from typical acquisition systems may have a high resolution but actual objects of interest may only have ten to twenty times smaller resolution [15]. Furthermore, there is usually a strong variability in the organelles shape within the same class, while inter-class variability is relatively small. Thanks to advances in statistical pattern recognition, the acquired

© Springer Nature Switzerland AG 2019
F. Karray et al. (Eds.): ICIAR 2019, LNCS 11662, pp. 186–194, 2019.
https://doi.org/10.1007/978-3-030-27202-9_16

microscope images could be automatically and objectively analyzed based on sets of annotated example data.

Algorithms for automatic object classification in microscopic images are essentially composed of feature extraction and classification stages. In conventional hand-crafted feature extraction methods, the set of local characteristics in images such as points, edges or intensity distribution in neighborhood regions are designed specifically for each target dataset [1,3,6,8,10,11,13]. Then popular efficient classifiers such as Support Vector Machine (SVM) or Artificial Neural Network (ANN) are applied to determine the class of object based on its extracted features. The classification accuracy by these approaches could be relatively high for microscopic images. However, the drawback of hand-crafted based methods is time-consuming and difficult to obtain relevant features for a wide range of datasets: designed parameters could be not optimal for new target images other than the specific images for which they were crafted [14]. Recent efforts tried to develop efficient pattern recognition systems inspired by deep learning algorithms. Unlike methods based on hand-crafted feature extraction, deep learning models automatically learn optimal feature representation from image pixel data to perform classification task directly. Noticeable results are recently produced by using CapsNet network [16] or ensembling multiple Convolution Neural Networks [5,12]. Nevertheless, the reported performance can not overcome the highest result achieved by the previous conventional methods.

This project aims to improve the accuracy compared to recent state of the art deep learning methods and surpass the highest results achieved by conventional hand-crafted feature based methods. Our main contribution in this study are summarized as below:

- Designing a novel multi-resolution architecture, combining 2D wavelet decomposition and the Convolution Neural Network architecture.
- Exploiting compact convolution neural network MobileNet-v1 [7] for automatically extracting features on microscopic image benchmarks.
- Achieving accurate classification of sub-cellular organelles using proposed model without the need for data augmentation.

## 2    Method

This section describes our proposed WaveM-CNN architecture to improve classification accuracy of sub-cellular organelles in microscopic images, as presented in Fig. 1. First, multi-resolution information is obtained by 2D discrete wavelet transformation. Then, a set of pretrained CNNs is used to extract features in each band of transformed image. Finally, an ensemble network is formed by concatenating generated feature maps to pass through fully connected layers for classification.

### 2.1    Image Decomposition

As the first step, each image is decomposed into a set of filtered images by wavelet transform which is commonly used for representation of an image at multiple

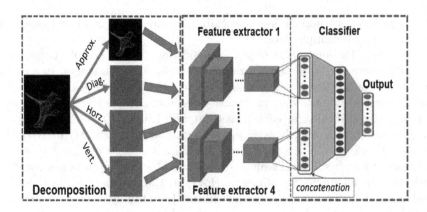

**Fig. 1.** The wavelet based multi-resolution convolution neural network architecture

levels of resolution or scale. One interesting advantage this wavelet-based multi-resolution analysis is that some features which might not be detected at one resolution could be easily uncovered at another. In this work simple Haar function are applied for the transformation to investigate the effectiveness of proposed approach. Experiments with more sophisticated functions would be done in the future work. The discrete Haar filters are applied on both rows and columns of the image to produce four component images: one approximation and three image details in corresponding horizontal, vertical and diagonal orientations. In general, given the image of size $M \times N = 2^m \times 2^n$, the decomposition outputs at $i^{th}$ level are calculated by [9]:

$$y_{hh}^{(i)}(u,v) = \sum_{l=1}^{2^{n-i+1}} \left[ \sum_{k=1}^{2^{m-i+1}} h(k-2u)y_{hh}^{(i-1)}(k,l) \right] h(l-2v) \tag{1}$$

$$y_{hg}^{(i)}(u,v) = \sum_{l=1}^{2^{n-i+1}} \left[ \sum_{k=1}^{2^{m-i+1}} h(k-2u)y_{hh}^{(i-1)}(k,l) \right] g(l-2v) \tag{2}$$

$$y_{hg}^{(i)}(u,v) = \sum_{l=1}^{2^{n-i+1}} \left[ \sum_{k=1}^{2^{m-i+1}} g(k-2u)y_{hh}^{(i-1)}(k,l) \right] h(l-2v) \tag{3}$$

$$y_{gg}^{(i)}(u,v) = \sum_{l=1}^{2^{n-i+1}} \left[ \sum_{k=1}^{2^{m-i+1}} g(k-2u)y_{hh}^{(i-1)}(k,l) \right] g(l-2v) \tag{4}$$

With $u \in \{1, 2, \cdots, 2^{m-i}\}$ and $v \in \{1, 2, \cdots, 2^{n-i}\}$

In the above equations, $y_{hh}^{(i)}$ represents components that contain the approximation coefficients of original image, whereas $y_{hg}^{(i)}$, $y_{gh}^{(i)}$ and $y_{gg}^{(i)}$ are for horizontal details, vertical details and diagonal details coefficients, respectively. $h = \{1/\sqrt{2}, 1/\sqrt{2}\}$ and $g = \{1/\sqrt{2}, -1/\sqrt{2}\}$ represent well known Haar wavelet low-pass filter and high-pass filter. At the initial step: $y_{hh}^{(0)} = Original\ image$ and in this work, only one level of decomposition is performed, thus $i = 1$.

## 2.2 Feature Extraction

After the original images are decomposed into sub-bands, the MobileNet-v1 CNN [7] is used as feature extractor due to its advantage of small number of parameters and hence, less computation cost. It is a dedicated small architecture introduced for implementation on systems having limited hardware resource, for e.g mobile devices, and thus, it could be integrated in a microscope system. Its principal algorithm is based on *depthwise separable convolution* concept, in which the convolution operation is replaced by *depthwise convolution* followed by *pointwise convolution* [7]. As such, the convolution kernels do not need to have corresponding number of channels to operate on all input channels altogether but just have a single channel to operate on each of them. The generated features maps are then merged by using **1 x 1** convolution kernels which number depends on the desired output channels. To gain advantage of reduced training time, computation cost and enhanced accuracy, this work utilizes the MobileNet-v1 CNN model which is pretrained on the popular ImageNet dataset [4] of over one million natural images.

## 2.3 Wavelet Based Multi-resolution CNN Architecture

As illustrated in Fig. 1, a set of four feature extraction modules in the previous section is combined in parallel to carry out the analysis of each decomposed image simultaneously. The feature maps generated independently from all pathways are concatenated to be processed together by the next fully connected layers. This approach of feature combination is found to be more efficient than ensemble methods which use voting scheme with weight averaging or weight learning through training process. Finally, the softmax function is applied at the output to determine the corresponding class of the object. This network model could be trained normally as a single network without dividing the training into multiple steps. Its parameters are initialized following truncated normal distribution with zero mean and standard deviation of 0.001. A learning rate of 0.01 is applied and the optimal number of training epochs is less than 20 epochs with a training batch size of 100 images.

## 2.4 Validation Method

The performance of proposed model is evaluated using two benchmark datasets that are publicly available, CHO and 2D HeLa dataset [1]. CHO is a dataset of fluorescence microscopic images of Chinese Hamster Ovary cells, which consists of more than three hundred images produced by five different fluorescent markers. While 2D HeLa contains fluorescence microscopic images of HeLa cells stained with various dyes for targeting specific organelles. There are totally around nine hundreds cell images, with ten different labels. The two benchmark datasets are not suffering from imbalanced classes as there is no significant difference in number of images in each class.

The model performance is validated through conventional five-fold cross-validation method. In each dataset, the whole images are divided by five subsets, each contains 20% of total number of images, collected from all classes. Each time, one subset is used as testing set to measure the accuracy while the remaining subsets are used as training set. In order to avoid serious bias-variance trade-off or over-fitting problem, we follow the *early stopping retraining* policy. First, within the above training set, 75% of the images are used as training data while other 25% of the images are used as validation data. The accuracy performance on validation data is used to determine the optimal number of training epochs for early stopping before over-fitting. Then, the whole training set, including the validation set, is used as the training data to retrain the model, according to the number of training epochs recorded in previous step. The average accuracy after thirty runs, in which image subsets are reshuffled randomly, is the reported classification accuracy to compare with similar previous works.

## 3    Results and Discussion

We first conduct extensive experiments on the CHO dataset according to the validation method described in previous section. The obtained average confusion matrix is shown in Fig. 2 where the prediction accuracy for any single class is at least 96.0%. In addition, the precision and specificity of the model for each class of CHO dataset are presented in Table 1. The lowest sensitivity and specificity among classes are respectively 96.0% and 99.2%.

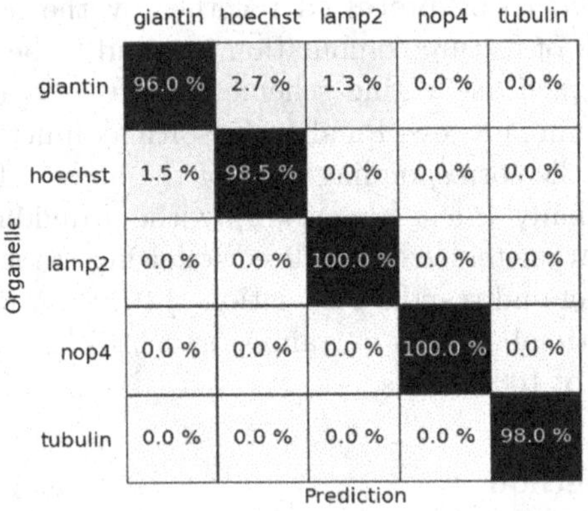

| | giantin | hoechst | lamp2 | nop4 | tubulin |
|---|---|---|---|---|---|
| giantin | 96.0 % | 2.7 % | 1.3 % | 0.0 % | 0.0 % |
| hoechst | 1.5 % | 98.5 % | 0.0 % | 0.0 % | 0.0 % |
| lamp2 | 0.0 % | 0.0 % | 100.0 % | 0.0 % | 0.0 % |
| nop4 | 0.0 % | 0.0 % | 0.0 % | 100.0 % | 0.0 % |
| tubulin | 0.0 % | 0.0 % | 0.0 % | 0.0 % | 98.0 % |

Prediction

**Fig. 2.** Confusion matrix for CHO classes

In comparison with previous work, as can be seen from Table 2, our model classification accuracy is at least 3% higher than the conventional hand-crafted feature extraction based methods. Moreover, its performance outweighs recent deep neural network based models, including ensemble multi-scale CNN network.

**Table 1.** Precision and specificity for each CHO class

| Class | giantin | hoechst | lamp2 | nop4 | tubulin |
|---|---|---|---|---|---|
| Sensitivity | 96.0% | 98.5% | 100.0% | 100.0% | 98.0% |
| Specificity | 99.6% | 99.2% | 99.6% | 99.7% | 100.0% |

**Table 2.** Performance of various classifiers for CHO images

| Type | Methods | Acc. (%) |
|---|---|---|
| Hand-crafted feature extraction based method | Neural network using Zernike moments and Haralick texture features [1] | 88.00 |
| | Weighted Neighbor Distances using a Compound Hierarchy of Algorithms Representing Morphology [13] | 95.00 |
| Deep learning based method | Single network of AlexNet [5] | 29.00 |
| | Single network of GoogleNet [5] | 91.00 |
| | Multi-scale convolution neural network with 22 CONV. + 2 FC. [5] | 94.00 |
| | **Our proposed WaveM-CNN** | **98.4** |

A larger dataset of HeLa cell images is subsequently used to validate our model performance. The average confusion matrix for HeLa dataset is shown in Fig. 3. Obviously, some types of cells are more difficult to distinguish exactly but our model ensures the classification accuracy of more than 90% and most of the time it is over 95%. Table 3 represents the precision and specificity values of the model for each class. Noticeably, the specificity is at least 98.9% for any HeLa organelles.

**Table 3.** Precision and specificity for each HeLa class

| Class | Actin | DNA | Endosome | Golgia | Microtubules |
|---|---|---|---|---|---|
| Sensitivity | 100.0% | 98.8% | 91.1% | 98.8% | 98.9% |
| Specificity | 99.9% | 100.0% | 98.9% | 99.1% | 99.9% |
| | Golgpp | Lysosome | ER | Nucleolus | Mitochondria |
| Sensitivity | 90.6% | 95.0% | 96.5% | 98.8% | 91.4% |
| Specificity | 99.9% | 99.4% | 99.0% | 100.0% | 99.7% |

Early works on classification of HeLa dataset based on hand-crafted feature extraction could achieve relatively good result as indicated in Table 4. However, the large number of specific and dedicated feature sets made it difficult to adapt to new set of images, even similar types of organelles. More recent works try to enhance the transfer-ability but they can not avoid degraded performance. In fact, the deficit is very large with regards to the highest benchmark. Table 4 also shows recent accuracy levels achieved by Deep learning based methods,

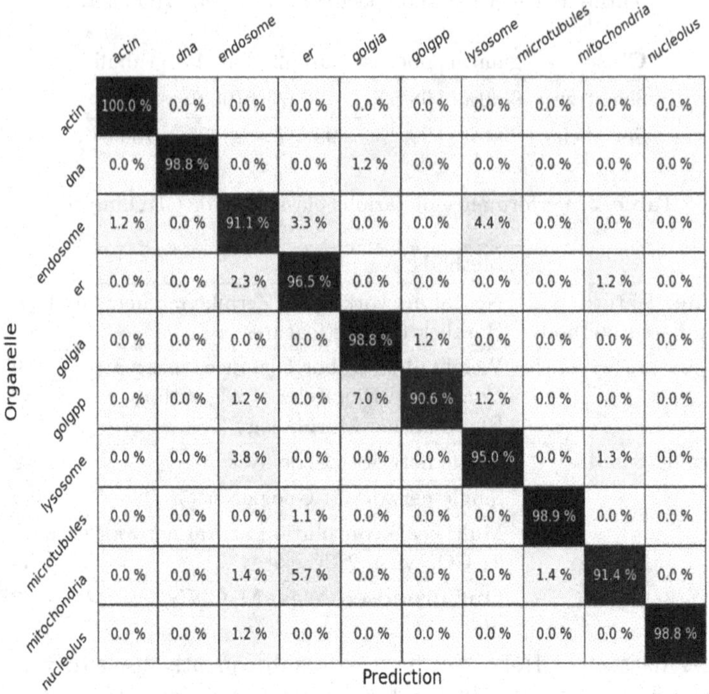

**Fig. 3.** Confusion matrix for HeLa classes

**Table 4.** Performance of various classifiers for HeLa images

| Type | Methods | Acc. (%) |
|---|---|---|
| Hand-crafted feature extraction based method | Neural Network with a set of 174 features(morphological, Haralick texture, Zernike moments) [8] | 91.50 |
| | Neural Network with a set of 26 Haralick texture features [3] | 95.30 |
| | SAHLBP (BoW(VQ) + SPM + SVM) [11] | 84.49 |
| | SIFT+SAHLBP (BoW(VQ) + SPM + SVM) [11] | 86.20 |
| | SIFT(BoW(LLC) + SPM + Softmax) [10] | 89.37 |
| Deep learning based method | Single network of AlexNet [5] | 11.00 |
| | Single network of GoogleNet [5] | 91.00 |
| | Single network of Inception-Resnet-v2 [12] | 92.00 |
| | Single network of CapsNet [16] | 93.08 |
| | Multi-scale convolution neural network with 22 CONV. + 2 FC. [5] | 91.00 |
| | Multiple heterogeneous network of Inception-v3, Resnet152, Inception-Resnet-v2 [12] | 92.57 |
| | **Our proposed WaveM-CNN** | **96.10** |

including single transfer learning convolution neural network and ensemble network models. For single CNN networks, except for AlexNet, both GoogleNet and Inception-Resnet-v2 could equally produce an accuracy as high as 92%. Although recent CapsNet model could achieve the highest accuracy rate of 93.08% but this value is about 3% lower than accuracy rate provided by our WaveM-CNN. Some of recent works also try to apply well known ensemble technique on classification task of 2D HeLa images. Two recent works were identified, one uses seven-scale CNN model which is trained from scratch [5] and the other uses triple heterogeneous pretrained CNNs [12]. Even though these methods provide good results, our model achieves around 3.5% gain compared to the best method providing 92.57%.

## 4   Conclusions

We present a novel deep learning architecture that combines the power of multi-resolution analysis by wavelet transform and feature extraction with convolution neural network. The proposed model outperforms previous published works applied on the same datasets of microscopic fluorescent images. Further experiments on other datasets will be conducted to consolidate the transferring ability and generalization of the classification results. This work applied the compact network MobileNet-v1, which has much less parameters than well known deep neural networks such as ResNet or Inception.

## References

1. Boland, M., Markey, M., Murphy, R.: Automated recognition of patterns characteristic of subcellular structures in fluorescence microscopy images. Cytometry **33**(3), 366–375 (1998)
2. Boland, M., Murphy, R.: A neural network classifier capable of recognizing thepatterns of all major subcellular structures in fluorescence microscope images of HeLa cells. Bioinformatics **17**(12), 1213–1223 (2001)
3. Chebira, A., et al.: A multiresolution approach to automated classification of protein subcellular location images. BMC Bioinform. **8**(1), 210 (2007)
4. Deng, J., Dong, W., Socher, R., Li, L.J., Li, K., Fei-Fei, L.: ImageNet: a large-scale hierarchical image database. In: CVPR 2009, pp. 248–255 (2009)
5. Godinez, W.J., Hossain, I., Lazic, S.E., Davies, J.W., Zhang, X.: A multi-scale convolutional neural network for phenotyping high-content cellular images. Bioinformatics **33**(13), 2010–2019 (2017)
6. Hamilton, N.A., Pantelic, R.S., Hanson, K., Teasdale, R.D.: Fast automated cell phenotype image classification. BMC Bioinform. **8**(1), 110 (2007)
7. Howard, A.G., et al.: MobileNets: efficient convolutional neural networks for mobile vision applications. CoRR (2017). http://arxiv.org/abs/1704.04861
8. Huang, K., Murphy, R.F.: Boosting accuracy of automated classification of fluorescence microscope images for location proteomics. BMC Bioinform. **5**(1), 78 (2004)

9. Wang, H., Vieira, J.: 2-D wavelet transforms in the form of matrices and application in compressed sensing. In: 2010 8th World Congress on Intelligent Control and Automation, pp. 35–39, July 2010

10. Lin, D., Lin, Z., Sun, L., Toh, K., Cao, J.: LLC encoded bow features and softmax regression for microscopic image classification. In: 2017 IEEE International Symposium on Circuits and Systems (ISCAS), pp. 1–4, May 2017

11. Liu, D., Wang, S., Huang, D., Deng, G., Zeng, F., Chen, H.: Medical image classification using spatial adjacent histogram based on adaptive local binary patterns. Comput. Biol. Med. **72**, 185–200 (2016)

12. Nguyen, L.D., Lin, D., Lin, Z., Cao, J.: Deep CNNs for microscopic image classification by exploiting transfer learning and feature concatenation. In: 2018 IEEE International Symposium on Circuits and Systems (ISCAS), pp. 1–5, May 2018

13. Orlov, N.: WND-CHARM: multi-purpose image classification using compound image transforms. Pattern Recogn. Lett. **29**(11), 1684–1693 (2008)

14. Parnamaa, T.: Accurate classification of protein subcellular localization from high-throughput microscopy images using deep learning. G3: Genes, Genomes, Genet. **7**(5), 1385–1392 (2017)

15. Ranzato, M., Taylor, P., House, J., Flagan, R., LeCun, Y., Perona, P.: Automatic recognition of biological particles in microscopic images. Pattern Recogn. Lett. **28**(1), 31–39 (2007)

16. Zhang, X., Zhao, S.G.: Fluorescence microscopy image classification of 2D HeLa cells based on the CapsNet neural network. Med. Biol. Eng. Comput. **57**(6), 1187–1198 (2019)

# Tracking in Urban Traffic Scenes from Background Subtraction and Object Detection

Hui-Lee Ooi$^{(\boxtimes)}$, Guillaume-Alexandre Bilodeau, and Nicolas Saunier

Polytechnique Montréal, Montréal, Canada
{hui-lee.ooi,gabilodeau,nicolas.saunier}@polymtl.ca

**Abstract.** In this paper, we propose to combine detections from background subtraction and from a multiclass object detector for multiple object tracking (MOT) in urban traffic scenes. These objects are associated across frames using spatial, colour and class label information, and trajectory prediction is evaluated to yield the final MOT outputs. The proposed method was tested on the Urban tracker dataset and shows competitive performances compared to state-of-the-art approaches. Results show that the integration of different detection inputs remains a challenging task that greatly affects the MOT performance.

**Keywords:** Multiple object tracking · Urban traffic scene ·
Road user detection

## 1 Introduction

The task of multiple object tracking (MOT) is to produce a set of trajectories that represent the actual real-life movements of the objects of interest across frames. In the context of urban scenes such as traffic intersection, MOT is performed for the road users (vehicles, pedestrians, cyclists, motorcyclists, etc.) as objects of interest for the purpose of traffic control and management to improve traffic while mitigating the adverse impacts. Due to the nature of such settings, interactions among the objects are expected and frequent, thus leading to object occlusions. Compared to conventional traffic scenes where the speeds of the road users are usually more consistent and directions homogeneous, MOT in urban traffic scenes remains a difficult and challenging task as it deals with objects interacting in different directions and speeds. Furthermore, because of the typical camera setups used, object scales varies significantly, which can make them difficult to detect.

The advances and reported good results in recent years of multiclass object detection algorithms with deep learning [4] have prompted us to integrate them into the tracking process. In addition, the class label information can provide a useful description of objects to help with their association across frames in the

© Springer Nature Switzerland AG 2019
F. Karray et al. (Eds.): ICIAR 2019, LNCS 11662, pp. 195–206, 2019.
https://doi.org/10.1007/978-3-030-27202-9_17

tracking steps. However, the recent work of Ooi et al. [10] has shown that tracking with a multiclass object detector (MOD) is very challenging since detections are often incorrect or missing. Since the incorrect or missing detection of an object at that stage can propagate and leave a huge impact on the final tracking results, we seek to improve the detection inputs in order to achieve better MOT results. Therefore, we extend the work of Ooi et al. [10] by using as inputs, detections from both a MOD and a background subtraction algorithm. To handle the problem of occlusion, a Kalman filter is used for prediction when an object of interest is not seen at the detection stage. This helps in keeping track of object of interest that might have been hidden by other objects at certain time steps during the lifespan of the trajectory.

In this paper, we introduce a MOT solution for urban traffic scenes with fused inputs from the integration of background subtraction inputs [2] with detections from a pre-trained MOD. Our two main contributions are: (1) a novel method to fuse detections from two sources that may contradict each other and (2) an object descriptor based on object class labels and their learned detection confidence.

## 2    Related Works

MOT usually comprises several steps: (1) object detection, (2) appearance modeling, and (3) data association. A large part of the past literature on MOT emphasized the challenge of data association [3] and its effect on MOT performance. Researchers proposed sophisticated data association strategies that often extend the Hungarian algorithm. For example, the Joint probabilistic data association filter (JPDAF) tracks objects based on the most likely outcome for each trajectory by considering every detection available, as well as missing or spurious detections [1,12]. Another example is the minimum-cost flow algorithm that formulates the data association problem as finding the shortest path from the apparition of the object to its last appearance in the scene [11].

On the other hand, object detection is necessary before data association, as poor detections will severely deteriorate the tracking performance. Hence, some previous MOT solutions have proposed combining detection methods to allow better object inputs for improved tracking in the end. The main drawback of using inputs from background subtraction is the difficulty of distinguishing the merging, fragmentation and splitting of objects. In cases where multiple road users are in close proximity, partial occlusion will cause the incorrect merging of these road users. IMOT (Improved Multiple Object Tracking) was introduced by Beaupré et al. [2] as an improved version of background subtraction using edge processing and optical flow, converting blobs of objects into compact bounding boxes that outline individual objects if there is evidence based on motion that two or more objects were grouped together.

More generally, the MOT problem in urban scenes was tackled several times in the past. A combination of background subtraction and feature points were proposed in Urban tracker [6]. Based on detections from background subtraction, objects are described by several keypoints which provide robustness to partial occlusion as a subset of keypoints can be matched if they are not all hidden. MKCF [15] was proposed as a solution for MOT, combining the background subtraction with multiple individual KCF (Kernelized Correlation Filters) single object trackers [5]. This method capitalizes on the robustness of newer visual object tracker. It shows good performances even if it uses rudimentary data association. Saunier et al. [13] used optical flow to detect the motion of objects of interest and the classic Kanade-Lucas-Tomasi (KLT) framework [14] to match road users from frame to frame. Recently, Ooi et al. [10] used a MOD for road user tracking. However, the tracking performance was severely impacted by the inadequate and inconsistent detections across frames.

## 3    Methods

Three steps are involved in the proposed MOT strategy: (i) Fusion of objects from detection methods, (ii) Object description, and (iii) The association of objects across frames. Our proposed method is illustrated in Fig. 1. It starts by fusing the input from a multiclass object detector (MOD) and from the improved background subtraction method IMOT. The resulting object detections are then tracked. Objects are described using colour, position and the class labels coming from the MOD. Then, data association is performed.

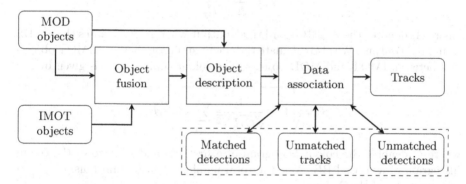

**Fig. 1.** Overview of our tracking framework. Object detections from two methods are first fused. They are described and associated across frames using sets of matched and unmatched tracks and detections. Based on these, the final tracks are outputted.

### 3.1    Object Fusion

In our proposed method, we integrate the bounding boxes from both IMOT and MOD into our tracking framework. The MOD objects are the result of the application of a pre-trained deep learning detection network, in our case RFCN [4], that was fine-tuned on the MIO-TCD dataset [8] containing varied road users such as cars, buses, bicycles, pedestrians, pickup trucks, etc. IMOT objects are the results of a post-processing over a background subtraction method in order to separate erroneously merged road users using edges and optical flow [2].

The objects from the two sources are matched and filtered before starting the tracking process. Due to the nature of IMOT objects, there could be some small bounding boxes that are not relevant as a result of shaking cameras and moving background elements. On the other hand, MOD objects will include long-term stationary road users that are beyond the scope of interest of our applications and there are occasions where objects of interest are missed out [10]. We hypothesize that the merged inputs can be fed into the tracker to give more satisfactory tracking results. However, results are often contradictory, sometimes IMOT gives better results while sometimes, it is MOD. One cannot simply merge the two sets of detections.

The following fusion strategy is proposed. We assume that all IMOT objects are relevant to the tracking framework as stray small IMOT objects that are not representative of objects of interest are filtered out according to size prior to the matching. IMOT objects were shown to be more reliable. They also had better performance in detecting the objects in the scene. MOD objects are used to provide class labels and to merge fragmented IMOT objects.

For matching the input objects of both sources, we compared their similarities in terms of bounding box (BB) overlaps and colour histogram. The BB overlap $S_o$ is given by

$$S_o = \frac{A_i \cap B_j}{A_i \cup B_j},$$  (1)

where $A_i$ denotes the $i^{th}$ BB from IMOT output whereas $B_j$ denotes the $j^{th}$ BB from MOD output. We also calculate the colour similarity between IMOT objects and between IMOT and MOD objects. The colour similarity $S_c$ is given by

$$S_c = \sqrt{1 - \frac{1}{\sqrt{\bar{G}\bar{H}N^2}} \sum_{i=1}^{N} \sqrt{G_i H_i}},$$  (2)

where $G$ denotes the colour histogram of a first BB and $H$ denotes the colour histogram of a second BB. $N$ is the total number of histogram bins. $\bar{G}$ and $\bar{H}$ are the mean of the $N$ bins.

Pairings between IMOT objects and MOD objects are performed based on the overlap of the BBs with Eq. 1 and a threshold $T_o$. IMOT objects that are matched with MOD objects will benefit from the class label information of MOD objects for data association in the tracking phase. On the contrary, IMOT objects that do not matched with MOD objects will be fed into the tracker with a dummy class label. There are cases where the matching is not one-to-one. For instance, several IMOT objects could be matched with the same MOD object and vice versa, though the latter is a rare occurrence since IMOT objects are usually smaller in size and more compact. MOD objects, on the other hand, are larger and often encompassed several objects at the same time. Hence, the merging of input objects is performed only on the IMOT objects and only if the colour of the objects to merge are similar enough based on Eq. 2.

Algorithm 1 describes the process for obtaining the final fused inputs for the MOT task. If multiple IMOT objects are matched to a particular MOD object, the colour histogram similarities of the multiple IMOT objects will be compared among themselves using the Bhattacharyya distance (Eq. 2) and a threshold $T_c$. If the similarity is high, then these objects are thought to be fragmented parts of an object and hence the BB from the MOD object would be taken as the input for the tracker. If the similarity is low, these objects will be considered individually in the subsequent steps. Figure 2 illustrates how fragmented parts of an object are fused together to recover the whole object after taking into consideration the output of the MOD.

**Fig. 2.** Example of the merging of objects. Blue BBs: MOD objects, red BBs: IMOT objects, white BB: resulting fusion of the two inputs into the whole object (pedestrian). (Color figure online)

Colour similarity is used for merging IMOT because there are cases where the BB from the MOD object contains more than one actual object that should not be merged. Hence, care must taken to handle the different cases. To avoid excessive merging of IMOT objects that overlap with often large MOD objects, merging IMOT based on pairings between objects from the two approaches will only be evaluated if there is significant overlap (larger than $T_m$). Finally, when a single IMOT object is matched with multiple MOD objects, the similarity in terms of BB overlap and colour histogram will be used to determine the final label from MOD that will be used with the IMOT object.

### 3.2 Data Association Costs

The cost of assigning pairings among the objects across frames is calculated by using the Hungarian algorithm [7]. The cost of matching a detected object and a tracked object is in the range of 0 and 1. The lower the cost, the more likely the two objects are referring to the same object.

For matching the objects across frames, the spatial cost $C_d$ is measured by the spatial distance between BBs of the compared objects using

$$C_d = 1 - max(0, \frac{T_d - \bar{SD}}{T_d}) \qquad (3)$$

**Algorithm 1.** IMOT and MOD object fusion

---

1: **procedure** IMOT-MOD PAIRING
2:     **for each** IMOT objects **do**
3:         **for each** MOD objects **do**
4:             Compute overlap of BBs with Eq. 1
5:             **if** $S_o >= T_o$ **then**
6:                 Assign as pairs and update pairing matrix
7: **procedure** MERGING MULTIPLE IMOT INTO SINGLE DETECTION OBJECT
8:     **for each** MOD objects **do**
9:         **if** Pair with more than one IMOT **then**
10:            **for each** IMOT objects that are paired **do**
11:                Compute colour similarity with Eq. 2
12:                **if** $S_o >= T_m$ and $S_c <= T_c$ **then**
13:                    Use MOD object as tracker input, discard the IMOT object
14:                **else** Keep IMOT object
15: **procedure** UPDATE IMOT OBJECT WITH LABEL FROM PAIRED MOD OBJECT
16:     **for each** Remaining IMOT objects **do**
17:         **if** No pairing found **then**
18:             Use the IMOT as tracker input with dummy label
19:         **else if** One-to-one pairing found **then**
20:             Use the IMOT as tracker input with label from paired MOD
21:         **else**
22:             **for each** Paired MOD objects **do**
23:                 Compute $S_c$ and $S_o$ of IMOT with each MOD object
24:                 Use IMOT as input with label of MOD object with largest similarity

---

$$\bar{SD} = \frac{1}{4}(|x_{D,min} - x_{T,min}| + |y_{D,min} - y_{T,min}| +$$
$$|x_{D,max} - x_{T,max}| + |y_{D,max} - y_{T,max}|), \quad (4)$$

where $x_{min}$ and $y_{min}$ denotes the minimum x and y coordinates, whereas $x_{max}$ and $y_{max}$ denotes the maximum x and y coordinate of an object. $T$ indicates an object that is currently tracked and $D$ indicates a detected object in a frame. $\bar{SD}$ is the mean spatial distance of the $x$ coordinates and $y$ coordinates of the four corners of the BBs of the compared objects whereas a fixed parameter $T_d$ is used to penalize objects that are too far and to normalize $C_s$.

For describing objects in terms of appearance, colour cost $C_c$ is computed based on the Bhattacharyya distance on colour histogram as in Eq. 2, where $G$ denotes the colour histogram of a detection and $H$ denotes the colour histogram of a currently tracked object. $N$ is the total number of histogram bins (we used 256).

Finally, the class labels are also considered in the matching cost. Detection confidence is used in our formulation. $C_l$ is given by

$$C_l = \begin{cases} 1 - 0.5 \times (W_i + W_j) & \text{if } L_i = L_j \\ 1 & \text{if } L_i \neq L_j, \end{cases} \quad (5)$$

where $L_i$ denotes the class label of object $i$ and $W_i$ its confidence value (between 0 and 1). As we will see in the results, using the confidence value from the MOD, and not just the class label for the cost is a beneficial strategy since confidence values tend to be similar in consecutive frames for a given object.

The final association cost is a combination of $C_d, C_c, C_l$, and is given by

$$C_{final} = \alpha C_d + \beta C_c + \gamma C_l, \tag{6}$$

where $\alpha, \beta, \gamma$ denotes the weights for the corresponding cost.

### 3.3  Overall Tracking Framework

In the tracking phase, each input object that appeared at the start of the video will be included into a set that contains all the active objects, thereafter denoted as the tracked objects. New input objects in the subsequent frames are denoted as detected objects and are matched accordingly to the tracked objects. We enforce one-to-one matching using the Hungarian algorithm [7], since it is expected that there exists only one true object at the next frame that corresponds to a currently tracked object. In addition, because of the non-ideal cases caused by occlusions or objects missing from the inputs that are common in urban scenes, some predictions are used to compensate the shortcomings of the inputs.

Hence, for each processed frame, sets of matched detections, unmatched detections and unmatched tracks are obtained. Matched detections are essentially the successful pairings of detected objects and tracked objects. Unmatched detections refers to detected objects without pairing with the existing set of tracked objects. This can be due to the entrance of a new object into the scene or as a result of spurious detections from the inputs. Unmatched tracks are when there is no corresponding pairing found in the set of detected objects. This is usually due to occlusion or being missed by IMOT, but also by objects that have left the scene.

For each active tracked objects, a Kalman filter is used to get a prediction of its expected location in the subsequent frame based on its history. If the tracked objects are matched with the detected objects, the prediction result will be discarded and the tracked object will be updated with information from the latest matched detected object. In the case where a tracked object is unable to find a matching counterpart in the set of detected objects, the prediction result may be used instead if it is deemed good. For each step of a track, the state or quality of the tracking is defined as "D" (Detection), "GP" (Good Prediction), "BP" (Bad Prediction) or "UP" (Uncertain Prediction). Overlap between the prediction result and the previous position in the trajectory (history) is used to evaluate the quality of a prediction. If the previous time stamp is marked as "D" (indicating it is from a matched pairing) or "GP" (indicating it as a reasonably good prediction), there is a good chance that the trajectory history is reliable. Hence, if the overlap is high (larger than $T_p$) between the prediction at the current step and the previous history step, the prediction result will be used and the state will be marked as "GP". If the overlap is not good, the state will be marked as "BP" and the prediction result will not be used. Instead the previous result in the tracking history will be used. For cases of unmatched tracked objects with a history that is not marked "D" or GP, the state will be marked at "UP" since there is no known reliable history that can be used to verify the current prediction. Algorithm 2 summarizes the inspection of the tracking prediction quality.

---

**Algorithm 2.** Checking prediction quality for unmatched tracks

---
1: **procedure** PREDICTION QUALITY
2:    **for each** Unmatched track **do**
3:        **if** Previous time step is "D" or "GP" **then**
4:            **if** Overlap of prediction with previous time step $< T_p$ **then**
5:                Use BB output from previous time step and mark as "BP"
6:            **else**
7:                Use prediction and mark as "GP"
8:        **else**
9:            Use prediction but mark as "UP"

---

At the end of the tracking process, trajectories with significant amount of "BP" and "UP" will be removed eventually since these final trajectories are likely to contain incorrect prediction that does not reflect the actual movement of the objects of interest.

For active track management, when a tracked object is unable to find a matching detection object for $T_n$ frames, the object is assumed to have left the scene. The track will therefore be terminated along with its last $T_n$ steps of tracking results removed since they are most likely not valid.

## 4   Experiments

The proposed method was tested on the Urban tracker dataset [6] and compared with several state-of-the-art methods. We also performed an ablation study on the data association cost components. The dataset includes four videos: Rouen, Sherbrooke, St-Marc and Rene-Levesque. We chose this dataset because it includes a large variety of object classes and background subtraction is applicable.

The tracking performance is evaluated by using the CLEAR MOT metrics [9] that are comprised of MOTA (Multiple Object Tracking Accuracy) and MOTP (Multiple Object Tracking Precision). MOTA evaluates the tracking performance by taking into consideration the number of objects that are mismatched, the false positives (FP) and false negatives (FN). MOTP evaluates the quality of the localization of the matches by checking the similarity of true positives (TP) with the corresponding targets in ground truths.

We also report the following information. Ground truth (GT) is the number of actual object instants in the whole video. Misses are missing GT object instances in tracks. FP are spurious object detections that are not in the ground truth. Mismatches are the number of tracks that suffer from object identity switches. The identification of correct tracks, misses and FP are based on the overlap of bounding boxes from our tracking output with respect to the ones of the ground truth. We used a threshold of 0.3 for the overlap in tracking performance evaluation as proposed by Beaupré et al. [2]. In our experiments, $T_o = 0.05$, $T_m = 0.5$, $T_c = 0.5$, $T_d = 0.5$ and $T_p = 0.01$.

### 4.1 Ablation Study

We start our evaluation of our method with an ablation study on the data association cost. The individual effects of the cost components are compared in Table 1. Generally it is observed that the spatial cost has the smallest number of mismatches and FP for all the evaluated videos. Since the spatial cost is based on the proximity of BBs, it is an essential component that describes the similarity of objects to determine across frames. In the results for St-Marc and Rene-Levesque, it has the highest number of correct tracks compared to the other association costs.

Colour cost gives slightly inferior tracking performance, having more FP and mismatches with slightly fewer correct tracks compared to the spatial cost. This could be due to presence of multiple objects that share similar colour properties and the fact that proximity is ignored. In addition, since BBs contain a certain portion of background as well (depending how well the object is enclosed in the BB), this might not be the best cost component. However, it can disambiguate the association of nearby objects with different colours.

Lastly, the class label cost gives the lowest performing tracking results due to reasons similar to the colour cost. There could be several objects that share the same class label in the same frame. With only the class label information it is often insufficient to do the right pairings. Also, some IMOT objects are fed into the tracker with dummy class labels since they are not paired with MOD objects in the object fusion stage. Nevertheless, the performance with this feature is better than expected thanks to the similarity of confidence values for the same object between frames. Since, the confidence value is used in Eq. 5, objects are both discriminated by their class and the confidence value.

### 4.2 Comparison with State-of-the-Art Methods

The performance of the proposed method is compared with previous state-of-the-art work, IMOT [2], Urban tracker [6], MKCF [15] and Ooi et al. [10] that were evaluated on the Urban tracker dataset. For the data association cost, the weights of spatial, colour and label costs are 0.6, 0.3 and 0.1 respectively for $\alpha, \beta$ and $\gamma$. As shown in Table 2, the proposed method yields better tracking performance than Urban Tracker, MKCF and Ooi et al. [10]. Overall, IMOT outperformed all evaluated methods, even though our proposed method performs the best in terms of MOTA for the video St-Marc and is second best in terms of MOTA on Sherbrooke. It is noted, however, that the proposed method gives

**Table 1.** Comparison of individual association cost components for the four videos of the Urban tracker dataset. **Bolface** indicates best result.

|  | Cost | GT | Correct tracks | Misses | FP | Mismatches | MOTP | MOTA |
|---|---|---|---|---|---|---|---|---|
| Rouen | Distance | 2627 | 2125 | 502 | **519** | 19 | **0.604** | **0.604** |
|  | Colour |  | 2126 | 501 | 560 | 28 | 0.603 | 0.586 |
|  | Label |  | **2128** | **499** | 804 | 143 | **0.604** | 0.450 |
| Sherbrooke | Distance | 4429 | 3029 | 1400 | **400** | 1 | 0.582 | **0.593** |
|  | Colour |  | **3030** | **1399** | 401 | 6 | 0.582 | 0.592 |
|  | Label |  | 3006 | 1423 | 503 | 45 | **0.584** | 0.555 |
| St-Marc | Distance | 8375 | **6068** | **2307** | **515** | **73** | 0.696 | **0.654** |
|  | Colour |  | 6041 | 2334 | 591 | 93 | 0.696 | 0.640 |
|  | Label |  | 5820 | 2555 | 1161 | 293 | **0.700** | 0.521 |
| Rene-Levesque | Distance | 9418 | **2701** | **6717** | **530** | 0 | 0.740 | **0.231** |
|  | Colour |  | 2694 | 6724 | 538 | 15 | 0.741 | 0.227 |
|  | Label |  | 2596 | 6822 | 687 | 80 | **0.746** | 0.194 |

a low MOTA for Rene-Levesque. Fusion of objects in the proposed method is not working well for this particular video as the objects in the scene are very small, and inevitably they get incorrectly paired with MOD bounding boxes that are usually large and imprecise for small objects. Consequently, this affects the overall MOT performance. In fact, Ooi et al. [10] used only detection inputs, which was not able to track any object in this video. It was already demonstrated that the use of only MOD objects as inputs for the MOT does not work well for this particularly challenging video. The good MOTP values obtained by Ooi et al. [10] show that MOD BBs although not very reliable can give object locations that are sometimes more precise.

**Table 2.** Comparison of the proposed method performance with state-of-the-art approaches. **Boldface** indicates best results, *italic* indicates second best.

|  | Our method | | IMOT | | Urban tracker | | MKCF | | Ooi et al. | |
|---|---|---|---|---|---|---|---|---|---|---|
|  | MOTP | MOTA | MOTP | MOTA | MOTP | MOTA | MOTP | MOTA | MOTP | MOTA |
| Rouen | 0.604 | 0.601 | *0.620* | *0.670* | 0.617 | **0.696** | 0.582 | 0.501 | **0.687** | −0.188 |
| Sherb. | 0.582 | *0.595* | *0.590* | **0.690** | 0.576 | 0.404 | 0.553 | 0.317 | **0.749** | 0.027 |
| St-Marc | *0.696* | **0.654** | 0.682 | *0.653* | 0.691 | 0.638 | 0.652 | 0.463 | **0.723** | −0.366 |
| Rene-L. | **0.741** | 0.230 | *0.705* | **0.613** | 0.582 | *0.565* | 0.531 | 0.334 | NA | NA |

## 4.3   Discussion

The integration of objects from IMOT and a MOD is proposed in order to better capture the objects of interest during the tracking process. It was expected that the combined inputs can complement each other, producing better inputs compared to the inputs produced individually from the different approaches. For instance, with the presence of fragmented objects from background subtraction that are difficult to group together, having a reference BB from the MOD that encompasses the whole object could be a useful indicator to improve the representation of the complete object. However, from the experiments, we have noticed the tendency of the MOD to generate large BBs that often include areas that do not belong to the object of interest. While in certain frames, it is helpful to have such BBs showing objects that are partially occluded, there are many occasions that such BBs include several objects of interest as one detection, especially for objects of small sizes such as pedestrians in urban traffic scene.

This led to a difficulty of tracking them effectively as the input objects to the tracker are already merged as one whole object instead of distinct objects. In addition, there are cases where IMOT objects encompassed more than one object of interest that appeared on the scene as well due its origin of background subtraction. As an effort to mitigate these effects, we have imposed a stricter merging threshold to reduce the amount of incorrect fusion of objects. To distinguish the case between combining BBs of fragmented parts into one whole object, and the case of having multiple objects interacting in close proximity, we take into consideration the colour of IMOT objects to make the merging decision.

The excessive inclusion of areas that are not relevant may impact the tracking process as well. This is because the colour histogram will consider the background portion that was included in the BB for object description in the association cost for matching across frames, leading to possibly less accurate descriptions of the objects of interest. However, despite the effort to differentiate the two cases, some missed objects are still missed in the final tracking outputs because of the imperfect representation of some objects of interest that get fed into the tracker. The missed objects could be the result of MOD objects that are not paired with the available IMOT objects. Indeed, sometimes the MOD can detect object that IMOT cannot.

## 5   Conclusion

In this paper, we presented a novel approach for fusing input objects from a multiclass object detector and an improved object extraction approach based on background subtraction for multiple object tracking. We use the integrated set of objects into a proposed MOT framework that associates objects across frames using spatial, colour and class label information to form trajectories in challenging urban traffic scenes. The prediction quality of unmatched objects in the MOT paradigm is evaluated to further improve the final tracking results. Results show that our method is competitive, but that it is very challenging to combine detections from multiple sources. First, they may not detect the same objects, and secondly, even if the same objects are detected, objects are not bounded in the same way. Our ablation study show that using class labels and their confidence can contribute positively to the data association cost function.

**Acknowledgments.** This research is funded by FRQ-NT (Grant: 2016-PR-189250) and Polytechnique Montréal PhD Fellowship. The Titan X used for this research was donated by the NVIDIA Corporation.

# References

1. Bar-Shalom, Y., Daum, F., Huang, J.: The probabilistic data association filter. IEEE Control Syst. Mag. **29**(6), 82–100 (2009)
2. Beaupré, D.A., Bilodeau, G.A., Saunier, N.: Improving multiple object tracking with optical flow and edge preprocessing (2018). arXiv preprint: arXiv:1801.09646
3. Bewley, A., Ge, Z., Ott, L., Ramos, F., Upcroft, B.: Simple online and realtime tracking. In: 2016 IEEE International Conference on Image Processing (ICIP), pp. 3464–3468. IEEE (2016)
4. Girshick, R., Donahue, J., Darrell, T., Malik, J.: Region-based convolutional networks for accurate object detection and segmentation. IEEE Trans. Pattern Anal. Mach. Intell. **38**(1), 142–158 (2016)
5. Henriques, J.F., Caseiro, R., Martins, P., Batista, J.: High-speed tracking with kernelized correlation filters. IEEE Trans. Pattern Anal. Mach. Intell. **37**(3), 583–596 (2015)
6. Jodoin, J.P., Bilodeau, G.A., Saunier, N.: Tracking all road users at multimodal urban traffic intersections. IEEE Trans. Intell. Transp. Syst. **17**(11), 3241–3251 (2016)
7. Kuhn, H.W.: The Hungarian method for the assignment problem. Naval Res. Logist. Q. **2**(1–2), 83–97 (1955)
8. Luo, Z., et al.: MIO-TCD: a new benchmark dataset for vehicle classification and localization. IEEE Trans. Image Process. **27**(10), 5129–5141 (2018)
9. Milan, A., Leal-Taixé, L., Reid, I., Roth, S., Schindler, K.: MOT16: a benchmark for multi-object tracking (2016). arXiv preprint: arXiv:1603.00831
10. Ooi, H.-L., Bilodeau, G.-A., Saunier, N., Beaupré, D.-A.: Multiple object tracking in urban traffic scenes with a multiclass object detector. In: Bebis, G., et al. (eds.) ISVC 2018. LNCS, vol. 11241, pp. 727–736. Springer, Cham (2018). https://doi.org/10.1007/978-3-030-03801-4_63
11. Pirsiavash, H., Ramanan, D., Fowlkes, C.C.: Globally-optimal greedy algorithms for tracking a variable number of objects. In: CVPR 2011, pp. 1201–1208, June 2011
12. Rezatofighi, S.H., Milan, A., Zhang, Z., Shi, Q., Dick, A., Reid, I.: Joint probabilistic data association revisited. In: 2015 IEEE International Conference on Computer Vision (ICCV), pp. 3047–3055, December 2015
13. Saunier, N., Sayed, T.: A feature-based tracking algorithm for vehicles in intersections. In: The 3rd Canadian Conference on Computer and Robot Vision (CRV 2006), p. 59. IEEE (2006)
14. Shi, J., Tomasi, C.: Good features to track. In: IEEE CVPR, pp. 593–600 (1994)
15. Yang, Y., Bilodeau, G.-A.: Multiple object tracking with kernelized correlation filters in urban mixed traffic. In: 2017 14th Conference on Computer and Robot Vision (CRV), pp. 209–216. IEEE (2017)

# An Improved Weighted Average Reprojection Image Denoising Method

Halimah Alsurayhi and Mahmoud R. El-Sakka[✉]

Western University, 1151 Richmond Street, London, ON N6A 3K7, Canada
halsuray@uwo.ca, elsakka@csd.uwo.ca

**Abstract.** Patch-based denoising algorithms have an effective improvement in the image denoising domain. Weighted Average (WAV) reprojection algorithm is a simple and effective patch-based spatial domain denoising algorithm. In this paper, an improved WAV reprojection algorithm is proposed. It improves the method by adaptively deciding the patch sizes to be used based on the image structure. The image structure is identified using a classification method based on the structure tensor matrix. The classification result is also utilized to improve the identification of similar patches in the image. The experimental results show that the denoising performance of the proposed method is better than that of the original WAV reprojection algorithm.

**Keywords:** Denoising · Patch-based ·
Weighted Average (WAV) reprojection algorithm · Structure tensor ·
Classification

## 1 Introduction

Image denoising is an important process to restore the original image signals from the noisy ones. The main objective in image denoising is to reduce noise while preserving edges and textures.

Recently, patch-based denoising algorithms have become extremely popular in the denoising field. They take the advantage of the similarity within the images, where image signals are restored by performing averaging between the similar patches in the image. Buades et al. [1] have introduced a patch based algorithm called Non-Local Means (NLM) for image denoising.

Variants of NLM algorithm have been proposed to improve its performance by adaptively selecting some of the internal parameters. Some of these variants have assigned the smoothing parameter adaptively based on the image structure [2,10,12], or based on the noise level [14]. Some other variants are based on selecting the patch size adaptively using the image structure [4,7,13]. Beside the adaptive patch size, Deledalle et al. [3] proposed a shape adaptive patches to address the problem of the halo of noise around the edges. Some other variants have improved the NLM algorithm by improving the method of computing the similarity between patches [5,8,11].

© Springer Nature Switzerland AG 2019
F. Karray et al. (Eds.): ICIAR 2019, LNCS 11662, pp. 207–215, 2019.
https://doi.org/10.1007/978-3-030-27202-9_18

One of the significant improvements in the patch-based denoising methods is the WAV reprojection algorithm [9] which has moved the reprojection method from the patch space to pixel space.

In this paper, we propose to improve the WAV reprojection algorithm by adaptively selecting the patch size based on the image structure. We used the structure tensor matrix to classify the image into three regions. In addition, we used the classification results to improve identifying similar patches.

This paper is organized as follow, Sect. 2 presents an explanation of the WAV reprojection algorithm and the proposed method to improve it. Section 3 demonstrates some of the experimental results. The conclusion is drawn in Sect. 4.

## 2    Methodology

In the WAV algorithm, the denoising is performed in three basic steps: (1) groping similar patches, (2) performing the denoising for each patch, and (3) reprojecting the denoised patches to the pixel domain (Fig. 1).

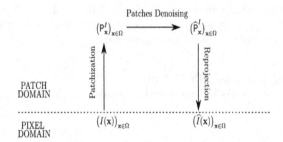

**Fig. 1.** The three basic steps of the WAV algorithm [9]

In the first step, similar patches are identified based on the Euclidean distance between image patches. To estimate a pixel $x$, a weighted average of various estimations of $x$ is calculated as follow:

$$\hat{I}_{Wav}(x) = \sum_{i=1}^{W^2} \beta_i \hat{P}_i (W^2 - i + 1) \tag{1}$$

The weight $\beta_i$ is based on minimizing the variance between patches. Because the WAV reprojection algorithm uses the flat kernel, $\beta_i$ is proportional to the number of patches used to estimate $\hat{P}_i$, and $\sum_{i=1}^{W^2} \beta_i = 1$.

In the last step of the WAV reprojection algorithm, the denoised patches are reprojected to the pixel domain.

Note that, in the original NLM algorithm, only the central pixel in each patch is used to estimate the current processed pixel [1], which degrades the performance of the denoising and creates the halo of noise around the edges.

The WAV reprojection algorithm takes the advantage of the whole patch, i.e., all pixels in the patch are exploited, which enhances the denoising performance.

Edges are preserved better with a small patch size while smooth regions have better denoising performance with large patch size [12,13]. In the WAV reprojection algorithm, the patch size has set to be fixed regardless of the image structure. So, we propose an *adaptive* patch size WAV reprojection algorithm that is based on the image structure.

We used the two eignvalues of the structure tensor matrix [6] to classify the image pixels. The structure tensor matrix is defined as follow:

$$T_\sigma = \begin{bmatrix} j_{11} & j_{12} \\ j_{21} & j_{22} \end{bmatrix} = \begin{bmatrix} G_\sigma * (g_x(i,j))^2 & G_\sigma * g_x(i,j)g_y(i,j) \\ G_\sigma * g_y(i,j)g_x(i,j) & G_\sigma * (g_y(i,j))^2 \end{bmatrix} \tag{2}$$

where $g_x$ and $g_y$ are the gradient information in $x$ and $y$ directions, and $G_\sigma$ is the Gaussian kernel. Then, the two eigenvalues are calculated:

$$\lambda_1 = \frac{1}{2}\left(j_{11} + j_{22} + \sqrt{(j_{11} - j_{22})^2 + 4j_{12}^2}\right) \tag{3}$$

$$\lambda_2 = \frac{1}{2}\left(j_{11} + j_{22} - \sqrt{(j_{11} - j_{22})^2 + 4j_{12}^2}\right) \tag{4}$$

where $j_{11} = G_\sigma * (g_x(i,j))^2$, $j_{22} = G_\sigma * (g_y(i,j))^2$, and $j_{12} = G_\sigma * g_x(i,j)g_y(i,j)$. We follow the classification methods provided by [12,13] to classify the image into three regions. The absolute difference between the two eigenvalues $\lambda_1$ and $\lambda_2$ is then calculated.

$$\lambda = |\lambda_1 - \lambda_2| \tag{5}$$

Then, the following classification scheme is used to classify image pixels:

$$(i,j) \in \begin{cases} c_1 & \lambda(i,j) \leq \lambda_2 \frac{(\lambda_1-\lambda_2)}{n} \\ c_2 & \lambda(i,j) \leq \lambda_2 \frac{2(\lambda_1-\lambda_2)}{n} \\ .. & \\ c_n & \lambda(i,j) \leq \lambda_2 \frac{n(\lambda_1-\lambda_2)}{n} \end{cases} \tag{6}$$

This classification is inaccurate, as some pixels may belong to more than one class. So, we combined it with the discontinuity indicator provided by [12]. The discontinuity indicator classify image pixels into smooth, edge and noise. If $\lambda(i,j)$ is large, the pixel is considered to be on edge. If $\lambda(i,j)$ is small and the two eigenvalues are also small, the pixel is considered to be on smooth region. The pixel is noise if $\lambda(i,j)$ is small but the two eigenvalues are large.

In our method, we classify the image pixels into three classes based on a comparison that made upon the two eigenvalues of the structure tensor matrix. We compare the two eigenvalues of each pixel in each resulted class from Eq. 6 with a specified *threshold* value. If the two eigenvalues are smaller than the *threshold*, the pixel is considered to be in a smooth area. If the maximum eigenvalue $\lambda_1$ is larger than the *threshold* and the minimum eigenvalue $\lambda_2$ is smaller than the *threshold*, the pixel is considered on edge. The pixel is on texture or a noise if the two eigenvalues are larger than the *threshold*.

$$(i,j) \in \begin{cases} Smooth & \lambda_1 < \tau, \ \lambda_2 < \tau \\ Edge & \lambda_1 > \tau, \ \lambda_2 < \tau \\ Texture/Noise & \lambda_1 > \tau, \ \lambda_2 > \tau \end{cases} \tag{7}$$

where $\tau$ is the threshold value, and it has set to be 40.

(a)           (b)           (c)           (d)

**Fig. 2.** The improved classification results on Lena image. (a) noisy image with noise $\sigma = 10$, (b) its classification result, (c) noisy image with noise $\sigma = 60$, (d) its classification result (Color figure online)

(a)           (b)           (c)           (d)

**Fig. 3.** The improved classification results on butterfly image. (a) noisy image with noise $\sigma = 10$, (b) its classification result, (c) noisy image with noise $\sigma = 60$, (d) its classification result (Color figure online)

In addition, we apply a preprocessing step to improve the classification results. The image is denoised first using the original WAV reprojection algorithm. This step has improved the classification result especially at the low noise levels. The texture areas can be classified as a third class when the noise level is less than or equal to 30. However, when the noise level is high, the third class represents the noise. The resulted classifications are shown in Figs. 2 and 3 for Lena and Butterfly images, respectively, with two different noise levels ($\sigma = 10$ and $\sigma = 60$). The blue color presents the smooth areas, the red color presents the edges, and the green color presents the texture or noise areas. When the noise level is low ($\sigma = 10$), the green color shows the texture only. While texture and noise are presented in green color when noise level is high ($\sigma = 60$). The resulted classification is then used as a mask on the noisy image. In the patchization step, patches similar to the reference patch contribute into the averaging process only if their central pixels belong to the same class. That decreases the number of un-similar patches from contributing in the averaging process.

In addition, an adaptive patch size is assigned to each pixel based on the class the pixel is belong to. A large patch size is assigned to pixels on smooth areas, and a small patch size is assigned to pixels on edges. For the texture, a smaller patch size is assigned. Figure 4 shows the block diagram of the proposed scheme. The next section explains the experimental results used to assign the best patch size for each class.

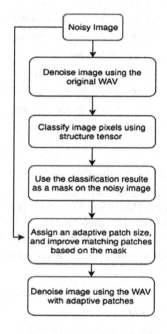

**Fig. 4.** The basic steps of our improved method

## 3   Experimental Results

We compared the performance of our adaptive WAV reprojection method with the original WAV algorithm. The restored images are compared in term of the peak signal-to-noise ratio (PSNR), and the visual quality. The PSNR is defined as:

$$PSNR = 10 \, \log_{10} \left( \frac{(MAX)^2}{MSE} \right) \tag{8}$$

where MSE is *Mean Squared Error* between the original image corrupted image, $MAX$ is the maximum pixel intensity value. In our experiments, we targeted the natural scene images. We used 25 images. The images are contaminated by additive white Gaussian noise with various levels of noise to assess the performance of each class at each noise level and when using different patch sizes.

**Table 1.** The mean PSNR values of smooth areas in 25 different natural scene images using 10 different noise levels

| Noise level | $5 \times 5$ | $7 \times 7$ | $9 \times 9$ | $11 \times 11$ | $13 \times 13$ |
|---|---|---|---|---|---|
| 10 | 37.16 | 37.27 | **37.31** | 37.21 | 37.00 |
| 20 | 33.12 | 33.28 | 33.35 | **33.36** | 33.32 |
| 30 | 30.74 | 30.96 | 31.03 | **31.04** | 31.02 |
| 40 | 29.13 | 29.40 | 29.48 | **29.50** | 29.49 |
| 50 | 27.86 | 28.19 | 28.28 | **28.30** | 28.30 |
| 60 | 26.90 | 27.28 | 27.39 | **27.41** | 27.40 |
| 70 | 26.14 | 26.58 | 26.70 | **26.72** | **26.72** |
| 80 | 25.48 | 25.95 | 26.07 | **26.10** | **26.10** |
| 90 | 24.90 | 25.40 | 25.53 | **25.56** | **25.56** |
| 100 | 24.34 | 24.88 | 25.03 | **25.06** | **25.06** |
| Mean | 28.58 | 28.92 | 29.02 | **29.03** | 29.00 |

Tables 1, 2 and 3 show the resulted mean PSNR values for smooth, edges and texture/noise areas respectively. The patch size $11 \times 11$ have the best mean PSNR value in smooth areas. Pixels on edges have the best results when patch size of $7 \times 7$ is used. For the texture areas, patch size of $5 \times 5$ has the best mean PSNR performance. As the third class (texture) represents noise, when the noise level is more than 30, patch size of $11 \times 11$ is assigned. The patch size, $w \times w$, is selected as shown below:

$$w = \begin{cases} 11, & Smooth, \ (Texture/Noise \ (\sigma > 30)) \\ 7, & Edge \\ 5, & Texture/Noise \ (\sigma \leq 30) \end{cases} \tag{9}$$

The WAV reprojection algorithm has used a fixed patch size of $9 \times 9$ for the entire image. For the searching window size, $9 \times 9$ is used in both methods.

Our adaptive method has improved the denoising performance. It produced better PSNR values than the original WAV reprojection method. Table 4 presents the mean PSNR values for 10 images at 10 different noise levels. In addition, the edges and textures are preserved better in our adaptive method due to applying small patch sizes at the edge and texture areas. Figure 5 shows how our adaptive method has reduced the artefact around Lena's eyes. Figure 6 also shows that the artefact has been reduced with our proposed method. The PSNR performance for those areas are reported.

**Table 2.** The mean PSNR values of edge areas in 25 different natural scene images using 10 different noise levels

| Noise level | $5 \times 5$ | $7 \times 7$ | $9 \times 9$ | $11 \times 11$ | $13 \times 13$ |
|---|---|---|---|---|---|
| 10 | **32.81** | 32.62 | 32.22 | 31.85 | 31.58 |
| 20 | 28.46 | **28.60** | 28.54 | 28.34 | 28.11 |
| 30 | 25.70 | **25.82** | 25.77 | 25.64 | 25.46 |
| 40 | 23.81 | **23.87** | 23.78 | 23.63 | 23.44 |
| 50 | 22.47 | **22.48** | 22.37 | 22.21 | 22.02 |
| 60 | 21.59 | **21.60** | 21.48 | 21.32 | 21.14 |
| 70 | 20.98 | **21.02** | 20.93 | 20.79 | 20.64 |
| 80 | 20.68 | **20.78** | 20.72 | 20.61 | 20.49 |
| 90 | 20.49 | **20.66** | 20.64 | 20.56 | 20.47 |
| 100 | 20.41 | 20.65 | **20.68** | 20.64 | 20.57 |
| Mean | 23.74 | **23.81** | 23.71 | 23.56 | 23.39 |

**Table 3.** The mean PSNR values of texture areas (or noise) in 25 different natural scene images using 10 different noise levels

| Noise level | $5 \times 5$ | $7 \times 7$ | $9 \times 9$ | $11 \times 11$ | $13 \times 13$ |
|---|---|---|---|---|---|
| 10 | **29.47** | 29.05 | 28.78 | 28.63 | 28.56 |
| 20 | **25.25** | 24.89 | 24.61 | 24.43 | 24.34 |
| 30 | **23.29** | 23.18 | 23.03 | 22.94 | 22.88 |
| 40 | 22.37 | 22.44 | **22.45** | 22.42 | 22.39 |
| 50 | 22.33 | 22.53 | 22.61 | **22.63** | 22.58 |
| 60 | 22.67 | 23.00 | 23.13 | **23.17** | 23.13 |
| 70 | 22.92 | 23.32 | 23.49 | **23.54** | 23.53 |
| 80 | 22.94 | 23.39 | 23.56 | **23.62** | 23.61 |
| 90 | 22.79 | 23.29 | 23.47 | **23.53** | 23.52 |
| 100 | 22.47 | 23.02 | 23.22 | **23.29** | **23.29** |
| Mean | 23.65 | 23.81 | **23.84** | 23.82 | 23.78 |

**Table 4.** The PSNR values for 10 different natural images in 10 noise levels

| Noise level | 10 | 20 | 30 | 40 | 50 | 60 | 70 | 80 | 90 | 100 |
|---|---|---|---|---|---|---|---|---|---|---|
| Original WAV | 34.14 | 30.87 | 28.74 | 27.11 | 25.93 | 25.01 | 24.30 | 23.72 | 23.19 | 22.74 |
| Proposed method | **34.37** | **31.01** | **28.96** | **27.31** | **26.20** | **25.29** | **24.58** | **23.94** | **23.34** | **22.81** |

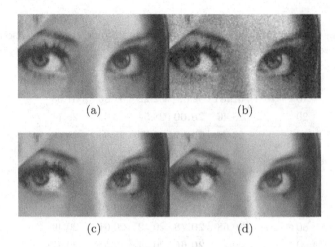

**Fig. 5.** A zoomed portion from Lena image denoised using the original WAV reprojection algorithm and our proposed method. (a) a portion from original Lena image, (b) noisy image with noise $\sigma = 10$ (PSNR = 23.82), (c) denoised image with the original WAV reprojection algorithm (PSNR = 34.22), (d) denoised image using our improved method (PSNR = 34.84).

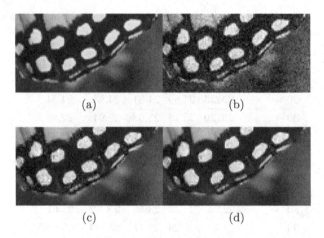

**Fig. 6.** A zoomed portion from butterfly image denoised using the original WAV reprojection algorithm and our proposed method. From left to right and up to bottom: a portion from original Lena image, noisy image with noise $\sigma = 20$ (PSNR = 22.47), image with the original WAV reprojection algorithm (PSNR = 25.96), denoised image using our improved method (PSNR = 26.69).

## 4   Conclusion

In this paper, an improved WAV reprojection algorithm is presented. The image pixels is first classified into three regions: smooth, edges, and texture (or noise). Then, an adaptive patch size is assigned for each class. In addition, grouping similar patches has improved by the resulted classification mask. Experimental results show the improvement of our methods over the original WAV reprojection algorithm, especially around the edges.

# References

1. Buades, A., et al.: A non-local algorithm for image denoising. In: IEEE Computer Society Conference on Computer Vision and Pattern Recognition, vol. 2, pp. 60–65 (2005)
2. Chen, M., Yang, P.: An adaptive non-local means image denoising model. In: 2013 6th International Congress on Image and Signal Processing (CISP), vol. 1, pp. 245–249. IEEE (2013)
3. Deledalle, C.-A., Duval, V., Salmon, J.: Non-local methods with shape-adaptive patches (NLM-SAP). J. Math. Imaging Vis. **43**(2), 103–120 (2012)
4. Hu, J., Luo, Y.-P.: Optik non-local means algorithm with adaptive patch size and bandwidth. Optik Int. J. Light Electron Opt. **124**(22), 5639–5645 (2013)
5. Hu, J., Pu, Y., Wu, X., Zhang, Y., Zhou, J.: Improved DCT-based nonlocal means filter for MR images denoising. Comput. Math. Methods Med. **2012**, 1–14 (2012)
6. Knutsson, H.: Representing local structure using tensors. In: 6th Scandinavian Conference on Image Analysis, Oulu, Finland, pp. 244–251. Linköping University Electronic Press (1989)
7. Lan, X., Shen, H., Zhang, L.: An adaptive non-local means filter based on region homogeneity. In: IEEE Seventh International Conference on Image and Graphics, pp. 50–54 (2013)
8. Peter, J.D., Ramya, R.: A novel adaptive non local means for image de-noising. Procedia Eng. **38**, 3278–3282 (2012)
9. Salmon, J., Strozecki, Y.: Patch reprojections for non-local methods. Signal Process. **92**(2), 477–489 (2012)
10. Verma, R., Pandey, R.: Grey relational analysis based adaptive smoothing parameter for non-local means image denoising. Multimed. Tools Appl. **77**(19), 25919–25940 (2018)
11. Wu, K., Zhang, X., Ding, M.: Curvelet based nonlocal means algorithm for image denoising. AEU Int. J. Electron. Commun. **68**(1), 37–43 (2014)
12. Zeng, W., Du, Y., Hu, C.: Noise suppression by discontinuity indicator controlled non-local means method. Multimed. Tools Appl. **76**(11), 13239–13253 (2017)
13. Zeng, W., Lu, X.: Region-based non-local means algorithm for noise removal. Electron. Lett. **47**(20), 1125–1127 (2011)
14. Zhu, S., Li, Y., Li, Y.: Two-stage non-local means filtering with adaptive smoothing parameter. Optik Int. J. Light Electron Opt. **125**(23), 7040–7044 (2014)

# Hybrid HMM/DNN System for Arabic Handwriting Keyword Spotting

Ahmed Cheikh Rouhou[1,3,4(✉)], Yousri Kessentini[1,2,4], and Slim Kanoun[3,4]

[1] Digital Research Center of Sfax, Sfax, Tunisia
`ahmed.cheikhrouhou@crns.rnrt.tn`
[2] LITIS Laboratory, St Etienne du Rouvray, France
`yousri.kessentini@litislab.eu`
[3] National Engineering School of Sfax, Sfax, Tunisia
`slim.kanoun@gmail.com`
[4] MIRACL Laboratory Sfax, Sfax, Tunisia

**Abstract.** Deep Neural Networks (DNN) have been incorporated in handwriting recognition systems and have proven their effectiveness. This paper presents an efficient hybrid word spotting system for Arabic handwritten documents. We investigate the optimal integration of different discriminative DNN in the standard DNN-HMM hybrid system. Well-trained Bi-Directional Long Short-term Memory (BLSTM), Time Delay Neural Network (TDNN) and LSTM are compared in the discriminative stage. The second stage is based on HMM and integrates a context dependent character modeling. Experiments are made with Arabic handwritten document text lines extracted from the publicly available dataset KHATT. We conclude that the hybrid approach appears to be well suited for Arabic handwriting word spotting compared to the classical GMM-HMM model.

**Keywords:** Arabic handwritten · Word spotting · HMM · Hybrid · BLSTM · LSTM · TDNN

## 1 Introduction

Documents play vital role in our daily life, they are used to store information and to save thoughts and notes. Quite recently, considerable attention has been paid to digitize these documents for storage, transmission and processing. Since valuable information could be found in forms of information, mail, bank statements and pieces of identification (ID cards and passports), researchers are working on solutions for extracting information from these documents.

Several publications have appeared in recent years documenting the KeyWord Spotting (KWS) technique. A KWS system aims to find words in document images [18]. This technique is used to index documents depending on specific information and querying textual handwritten texts. The literature shows two main approaches for the keyword spotting according to the type of the keyword.

F. Karray et al. (Eds.): ICIAR 2019, LNCS 11662, pp. 216–227, 2019.
https://doi.org/10.1007/978-3-030-27202-9_19

The Query By Example (QBE) approach takes a word image as query. Using matching techniques, a system retrieves possible keyword occurrences based on visual similarities [11–13]. However, such solution requires the existence of an input image to process the KWS. Besides, handwritten documents could have a large number of writers with different writing styles and this dissimilarity makes the matching technique more difficult in this context. Meanwhile, the research has focused on the Query By String (QBS) approach. The input query is a text string. Generally, a recognition-based system decodes input images and detects the most suitable position of the keyword during recognition.

Recognition-based keyword spotting systems are more practical. They overtake multi-writers and multi-fonts limitations. Added to that, they can process noisy documents. Nevertheless, KWS decoding process requires a recognition kernel trained with labeled document images. To avoid word segmentation error, KWS systems generally process line images [30,31]. [14–17] have proposed HMM-based systems for keyword spotting. They have demonstrated that the hidden markov model are adequate for keyword modelling and text-alignment. The used technique is based on a line model containing keyword model between two fillers that absorb any non-keyword output. The proposed HMMs are generative approaches and use Gaussian Mixture Model (GMM) to estimate the emission probability of each state. Authors in [32] have proposed a discriminative keyword spotting system based on Bi-directional Long Short-Term Memory Recurrent Neural Network. The main contribution in this work is modifying the algorithm of Connectionist Temporal Classification (CTC) to support keyword spotting. However, the major drawback of this technique is the absence of exact alignment of the output and it cannot provide the exact boundaries of the keyword. Consequently, hybrid techniques have been introduced to surpass these previously-cited problems and propose more efficient systems. Such systems add a discriminative stage to the HMM decoding. This optical classifier performs recognition and provides estimation for the HMM model to retrieve keywords. Deep neural network hybrids have been proven to be the most efficient optical classifier in hybrid approaches as indicated in [19–22]. Authors in [19] present a bench-marking of different neural networks hybrids architectures for KWS and they have demonstrated that the BLSTM-HMM is as efficient as a hybrid system.

To the authors' best knowledge, very few publications can be found in the literature that address Arabic handwriting keyword spotting. Some query by example approaches has been proposed by [23,24,27]. They are all applied to historical Arabic images and use matching technique adapted to the Arabic script. For QBS approaches, [25] and [26] use HMM for keyword spotting in handwritten Arabic documents. These systems readjust the standard HMM KWS application without including the specifics of the Arabic script. In handwritten script, Arabic texts usually contain ligatures and most of the characters are attached.

In this study, we propose different hybrid architectures for keyword spotting dealing with Arabic handwritten documents. Firstly, we created a context-dependent HMM models for Arabic characters (trigraphs) instead of the basic

HMM configuration. Added to that, decision tree based clustering was applied to produce the minimal number of HMM states needed to model Arabic characters. Next, we trained a Time delay Neural Network (TDNN), LSTM-RNN and a BLSTM-RNN to estimate the HMM. Then, we compare all the proposed hybrid HMM/NN architecture, using the KHATT dataset [29], to give the best performance obtained.

The remainder of the paper is organized into 4 sections: Sect. 2 describes the different parts of the proposed system. In Sect. 3, we give more details about how the system was trained. Section 4 shows the performances of our system. And finally, a conclusion of this work is presented and we discuss some perspectives in Sect. 5.

## 2    Proposed System

In this paper, we explore different HMM-DNN (Deep Neural Network) architectures for keyword spotting in Arabic handwritten documents (See Fig. 1). First, we apply image normalization as a pre-process task for the system. Next, we use the HOG descriptor to produce frame sequences for each line image. Then, these sequences are fed to the DNN in order to estimate the suitable HMM state for each frame. Finally, a decoding strategy is implemented to detect keywords in line images. The following section contains a detailed description of different parts of the system.

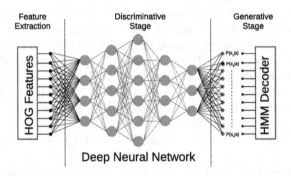

**Fig. 1.** HMM-DNN hybrid

### 2.1    Image Preprocessing Task

In our experiment, we used line images of the publicly available KHATT database. These images are written by different writers then scanned at different resolutions. Hence, the scanning process influences the images and adds some noisy pixels. Added to that, we found some distorted images in the dataset. Therefore, in order to maintain good performances for the system, some pre-processing tasks are required:

- **Normalization:** Fix the rotated and slanted text lines which are highly presented in Arabic handwritten text.
- **Median Filter:** Remove the noisy pixels from images. This filter smoothes the text lines and preserves punctuation and character edges.
- **Padding removal (Cropping):** After normalizing the image, some extra blank spaces could be found and may result in incoherence between images and provided ground truth when we train the system. Consequently, we implement a cropping algorithm that removes these empty regions in images.

### 2.2   Feature Extraction

In our contribution, we implemented the Histogram of Oriented Gradient (HOG) for feature extraction. This descriptor [1] is widely used for object recognition. Shapes and local objects are represented by the distribution of local gradients orientations. Our implementation of this descriptor is based on a sliding window that runs through line images to produce sequences of HOG features. By testing different configuration, best results were obtained using a window of 8 pixels width with 2 pixels step for the sliding factor. Each frame is divided into 8 small regions called cells. Then, HOG features are calculated for each cell to produce a feature vector that includes 64 feature per frame. We added 6 pixel-based features (centroides, upper and lower pixels positions and densities) for additional information.

### 2.3   HMM Stage

We created a keyword-based HMM that forces the decoder to detect the most suitable position for the text query (see Fig. 2). Next, the image was subject to another HMM pass without modeling the keyword (filler decoding).

**Fig. 2.** Decoding HMM model

Using this technique, we compared the results from the two previous decoding steps to calculate the score and the position of a keyword in a line image. The score is calculated by subtracting log-likelihood of the keyword-based decoded scores from filler-based scores, then divided by the number of frame to normalize the score. The equation that describes the obtained final score is as follows:

$$Score_{final} = \frac{\log P(X) - \log P(X|Keyword)}{N_{frames}} \tag{1}$$

At this stage, the system can decide if a keyword has been found in the given image, by checking if the calculated score is above a pre-defined threshold.

The created HMMs model the letters of the Arabic script, numbers, ligatures and punctuation. In this stage, HMMs are called monographs. To enhance this technique, we introduced the context-dependency of the models [9]. Each character is represented with its successor (right context) and predecessor (left context). This modeling called the trigraphs presentation of different characters. Accordingly, the number of models is enormously increased as any character may be surrounded by any other monograph. This amount of models cannot be trained with our available images dataset: most of the trigraphs would have poor number of examples.

The Arabic script contains 28 letters that could have up to 4 different shapes. Adding numbers, ligatures and punctuation, we need to generate HMM states for 153 characters. Based on previous experiments, we model each character (monographs) with 3 states connected from left to right. Thus, the number of these models is too large and need to be reduced. Firstly, we collect the seen trigraphs extracted by executing monographs HMM alignments on the image training set. Then, we use the decision tree clustering to tie the states of HMM models. In fact, this technique gathers similar states to reduce redundancy. Lastly, the final number of states has been reduced to 475 (See Fig. 3).

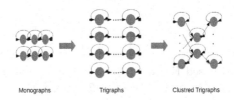

Monographs          Trigraphs          Clustred Trigraphs

**Fig. 3.** HMM modeling

## 2.4 DNN Stage

Deep neural networks are being implemented in many research fields for classification. The main property, that makes these networks suitable for this task, is the flexibility of the network architecture. For document recognition, classifying a data sequence has been improved with introducing time delay neural networks (TDNN) [3] and recurrent neural networks (RNN) [2]. In this paper, three different DNN implementations were used: TDNN, LSTM-RNN and BLSTM-RNN. Each architecture have to estimate the HMM emission probability for decoding keywords. A network configuration contains an input layer, output layer and hidden layers. Since we have 70 features representing each frame of the sequence, we need to assign 70 entries in the input layer. Likewise, the output of the network is 475 values obtained from a soft-max layer that corresponds to the HMM states count.

**Time Delay Neural Network.** Time delay neural network is a simple feed-forward DNN. The main purpose of this network is to process sequential data. The temporal aspect of the sequence is preserved using the layer activation delay in the network. Deep layers activations depend on delayed outputs of the previous layers. Appending the time-delay created between layers, the final output of the DNN are calculated from a wide temporal context called the total delay length.

The time aspect in time delay neural network is inserted starting from the input of the network. Our feed-forward networks have 6 layers. The first layer splices 9 frames initially from the input layer (current frame with 4 right context frames and 4 left context frames). The input dimension is 630 and the output is normalized to 300. The second, fourth and last layers do not splice the inputs but they just propagate the data. Third and fifth layers join 2 outputs with 2 frame delays from the last layer. Its input dimension is 600 and outputs 300 after normalization.

**Recurrent Neural Network.** Another proposed method to process sequential data with DNN is through the addition of a recurrent connection within the layers. This DNN type is called Recurrent Neural Network (RNN). The recurrence in RNNs makes the network aware of the previously calculated outputs. It takes advantage of the order and relations between the elements in a sequence [4].

Since revolutionary results has been published in the data sequence classification problems with RNNs, researchers are focusing on improving networks elements and architectures. They created the Bi-Directional Recurrent Neural Network (B-RNN) [5]. It deals with both left and right contexts in a sequence for decision. However, the main problem observed in these versions of recurrent neural networks is the disappearing of the previous sequence information through time, called gradient vanishing [6].

Long Short-Term Memory cells [7] are invented to control the memory created in recurrent neural networks. Information from the input sequence could overwrite or append the stocked memory. Therefore, an LSTM based neural network increases the performance of recognition-based system fed with time series data. Noticeably, a Bi-Directional LSTM [5] has been announced as a BRNN containing LSTM cells.

The role of hidden layers, in BLSTM-NN, is to transform the input features to the suitable output activation. Further, each layer is composed from 3 sublayers: forward LSTM layer and backward LSTM layer (1024 LSTM cell for each layer) to build the BLSTM context and a projection layer containing 256 neurons to reduce the computational complexity of the RNN structure [8]. Our LSTM implementation has the same configuration of the BLSTM but without backward LSTM. Figure 4 shows the BLSTM neural network architecture with its components.

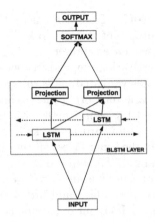

**Fig. 4.** BLSTM-NN architecture

## 3  System Training

The proposed hybrid system relies on two main stages: one is discriminative (deep neural network) and the other is generative (HMM). Training these components was a challenge: the DNN output must be trained using the HMM alignment of the input image, and the HMM itself needs to be trained and optimized to give a great alignment.

After preparing the previously mentioned hidden markov models configuration, line images ground-truth are transformed to HMM states alignments. This is a mandatory step to provide the network with the target class for each frame, during the train phase. The soft-max layer of the deep neural network calculates the posteriors of each class. Thus, Bayes' rule is used to obtain HMM state emission probability:

$$P(X_t|S_{n|t}) = \frac{P(S_{n|t}|X_t)P(X_t)}{P(S_{n|t})} \simeq \frac{P(S_{n|t}|X_t)}{P(S_{n|t})} \qquad (2)$$

where:

- $X_t$: input frame at time t.
- $S_{n|t}$: State n at time t ($1 < n < 475$).
- $P(S_{n|t})$: Prior probability for $S_{n|t}$ calculated from the appearance of each state in the alignments.
- $P(S_{n|t}|X_t)$: Posterior probability for $S_{n|t}$ calculated from DNN softmax layer. Let '$a_t$' denotes the output layer values where $a_t = \{a_{1|t}, .., a_{n|t}, .., a_{475|t}\}$:

$$P(S_{n|t}|X_t) = Softmax(a_{n|t}) = \frac{exp(a_{n|t})}{\sum_{m=1}^{m=475} exp(a_{m|t})} \qquad (3)$$

Since we configured the architecture of our different deep neural networks, we train each network with line images to adjust the weights of the different connections within the network. The back-propagation through time [10] is used to optimize these weights and we use the cross entropy to calculate the error between the feed-forward pass of the network and the suitable target for the frame:

$$Entropy(t) = \sum_{(X,z)} \sum_{k=1}^{475} z_k Ln(P(S_{k|t}|X_t)) \tag{4}$$

where $z_k$ is the target value of the output $k$.

Obviously, the algorithm has to repeat this process to all the line images and for many iterations until the network has nothing to optimize.

## 4 Experiments

### 4.1 Datasets

KHATT database [29] contains up to 9327 line images written by 1000 writers. The hosted-version of the database contains images at 300DPI resolutions and divided into two datasets: set for writer identification and another set for text recognition. We used the second set that contains 5524 line images: 4524 used for training, 500 for validation and 500 for test.

### 4.2 Deep Neural Networks Training Settings

The implementation of our system was carried with KALDI Speech Recognition Toolkit [33]. Deep Neural networks training and system evaluation were achieved using NVIDIA Tesla K80 GPU. Table 1 shows the different configurations of the deep neural networks.

Table 1. Deep neural networks configurations

| Parameter | BLSTM | LSTM | TDNN |
|---|---|---|---|
| Initial learning rate | 0.0006 | 0.0006 | 0.005 |
| Final learning rate | 6e–05 | 6e–05 | 0.0005 |
| Momentum | 0.5 | 0.5 | 0.5 |
| Number of iterations | 390 | 390 | 220 |

### 4.3 KWS Results

The evaluation of the systems is obtained by calculating Recall and Precision measures for 25, 50 and 100 keywords list. Recall is the fraction of the successfully

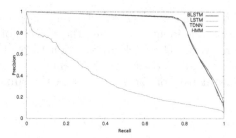

**Fig. 5.** Performances of the different architectures

retrieved keyword positions that are relevant to the query, and the precision denotes the fraction of all the retrieved keyword positions for the query.

Figure 5 presents the different performances of the proposed hybrid systems for 50 input keyword. In fact, we add an implementation of basic GMM-HMM keyword spotting based on [28]. As expected, the results show that the recall-precision variations of the BLSTM-HMM hybrid system has the higher break-even point[1] 83% (Fig. 6). The LSTM-HMM results are too close to the BLSTM and its break point value reaches 81% (Fig. 7), followed by the TDNN with 80% (Fig. 8) and 37% for the HMM (Fig. 9).

Figures 6, 7, 8 and 9 illustrate the efficiency of all the systems with the variation of the number of the keywords used for query. It is predictable that increasing the number of input keyword decreases the system performances. The simple HMM results are very poor compared to the DNN-based systems. The discriminative stage has a huge impact on the recognition rate of the approach. For the DNN implementation, results are slightly changed. The BLSTM-RNN has the best performance among the different DNN, due to the bi-directional context of the network compared with the LSTM-RNN. The TDNN have access to the left and right time context, but recurrence of the BLSTM-RNN and the memory implementation in such network are more efficient.

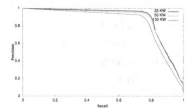

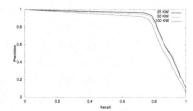

**Fig. 6.** Performances of the BLSTM/ HMM

**Fig. 7.** Performances of the LSTM/ HMM

---

[1] **Break-even Point:** Given a precision-recall curve, the precision/recall break-even point is the value at which the precision is equal to recall.

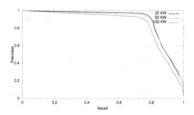

**Fig. 8.** Performances of the TDNN/HMM

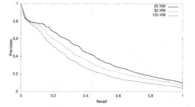

**Fig. 9.** Performances of the HMM

## 5   Conclusion

In this paper, we studied different DNN-hybrid architecture for Arabic handwritten keyword spotting. After that, we adapted the context dependent for Arabic script modeling to cope with the ligatures and overlapping letters. To our knowledge, this is the first study to investigate the performances of such systems applied for Arabic handwriting keyword spotting. It was clearly shown that DNN hybrid systems give very interesting results. The BLSTM-NN has the best overall performances with up to 83% break-even point value for keyword spotting.

Future work will consider new architectures of neural network and explore the use of the convolutional neural network for feature extraction.

## References

1. Rodriguez, J.A., et al.: Local gradient histogram features for word spotting in unconstrained handwritten documents. In: Proceedings of International Conference on Frontiers in Handwriting Recognition (ICFHR 2008), pp. 7–12 (2008)
2. Hammer, B.: On the approximation capability of recurrent neural networks. Neurocomputing **31**(14), 107–123 (2000)
3. Peddinti, V., et al.: A time delay neural network architecture for efficient modeling of long temporal contexts. In: INTERSPEECH (2015)
4. Lipton, Z.C.: A critical review of recurrent neural networks for sequence learning. The Computing Research Repository (2015)
5. Schuster, M., Paliwal, K.K.: Bidirectional recurrent neural networks. IEEE Trans. Signal Process. **45**(11), 2673–2681 (1997)
6. Hochreiter, S., Bengio, Y., Frasconi, P., Schmidhuber, J.: Gradient flow in recurrent nets: the difficulty of learning long-term dependencies. In: Kremer, S.C., Kolen, J.F. (eds.) A Field Guide to Dynamical Recurrent Neural Networks. IEEE Press (2001)
7. Hochreiter, S., Schmidhuber, J.: Long short-term memory. Neural Comput. **9**(8), 1735–1780 (1997)
8. Sak, H., Senior, A., Beaufays, F.: Long short-term memory based recurrent neural network architectures for large vocabulary speech recognition. The Computing Research Repository (2014)
9. Bianne-Bernard, A.-L., Menasri, F., Mohamad, R.A.-H., Mokbel, C., Kermorvant, C., Likforman-Sulem, L.: Dynamic and contextual information in HMM modeling for handwritten word recognition. IEEE Trans. Pattern Anal. Mach. Intell. **33**, 2066–2080 (2011)

10. Mozer, M.C.: A focused backpropagation algorithm for temporal pattern recognition. In: Backpropagation, pp. 137–169 (1995)
11. Rusinol, M., Aldavert, D., Toledo, R., Llads, J.: Efficient segmentation-free keyword spotting in historical document collections. Pattern Recogn. **48**(2), 545–555 (2015)
12. Vidal, E., Toselli, A.H., Puigcerver, J.: High performance Query-by-Example keyword spotting using Query-by-String techniques. In: 2015 13th International Conference on Document Analysis and Recognition (ICDAR), Tunis, pp. 741–745 (2015)
13. Fink, G.A., Rothacker, L., Grzeszick, R.: Grouping historical postcards using query-by-example word spotting. In: 2014 14th International Conference on Frontiers in Handwriting Recognition, Heraklion, pp. 470–475 (2014)
14. Kessentini, Y., Paquet, T.: Keyword spotting in handwritten documents based on a generic text line HMM and a SVM verification. In: 2015 13th International Conference on Document Analysis and Recognition (ICDAR), Tunis, pp. 41–45 (2015)
15. Aldavert, D., Rusinol, M., Toledo, R., Llados, J.: Integrating visual and textual cues for query-by-string word spotting. In: International Conference on Document Analysis and Recognition, pp. 511–515 (2013)
16. Rothacker, L., Fink, G.A.: Segmentation-free query-by-string word spotting with bag-of-features HMMs. In: International Conference on Document Analysis and Recognition, Nancy, France (2015)
17. Puigcerver, J., Toselli, A.H., Vidal, E.: Word-graph and character-lattice combination for KWS in handwritten documents. In: 2014 14th International Conference on Frontiers in Handwriting Recognition, Heraklion, pp. 181–186 (2014)
18. Rath, T.M., Manmatha, R.: Word spotting for historical documents. IJDAR **9**, 139–152 (2007)
19. Bideault, G., Mioulet, L., Chatelain, C., Paquet, T.: Benchmarking discriminative approaches for word spotting in handwritten documents. In: 2015 13th International Conference on Document Analysis and Recognition (ICDAR), Tunis, pp. 201–205 (2015)
20. Frinken, V., Fischer, A., Manmatha, R., Bunke, H.: A novel word spotting method based on recurrent neural networks. IEEE Trans. Pattern Anal. Mach. Intell. **34**(2), 211–224 (2012)
21. Thomas, S., Chatelain, C., Heutte, L., Paquet, T., Kessentini, Y.: A deep HMM model for multiple keywords spotting in handwritten documents. Pattern Anal. Appl. **18**, 1003–1015 (2015)
22. Weillmer, M., Eyben, F., Graves, A., Schuller, B., Rigoll, G.: A Tandem BLSTM-DBN architecture for keyword spotting with enhanced context modeling. In: Proceedings of NOLISP (2009)
23. Brik, Y., Chibani, Y., Hadjadji, B., Zemouri, E.T.: Keyword-guided Arabic word spotting in ancient document images using Curvelet descriptors. In: 2014 International Conference on Multimedia Computing and Systems (ICMCS), Marrakech, pp. 57–61 (2014)
24. Kassis, M., El-Sana, J.: Automatic synthesis of historical Arabic text for word-spotting. In: 2016 12th IAPR Workshop on Document Analysis Systems (DAS), Santorini, pp. 239–244 (2016)
25. Wshah, S., Kumar, G., Govindaraju, V.: Multilingual word spotting in offline handwritten documents. In: Proceedings of the 21st International Conference on Pattern Recognition (ICPR 2012), Tsukuba, pp. 310–313 (2012)

26. Khayyat, M., Lam, L., Suen, C.Y.: Arabic handwritten word spotting using language models. In: 2012 International Conference on Frontiers in Handwriting Recognition, Bari, pp. 43–48 (2012)

27. Zirari, F., Ennaji, A., Nicolas, S., Mammass, D.: A methodology to spot words in historical Arabic documents. In: 2013 ACS International Conference on Computer Systems and Applications (AICCSA), Ifrane, pp. 1–4 (2013)

28. Fischer, A., Keller, A., Frinken, V., Bunke, H.: Lexicon-free hand-written word spotting using character HMMS. Pattern Recogn. Lett. **33**(7), 934–942 (2012)

29. Mahmoud, S.A., et al.: KHATT: an open Arabic offline handwritten text database. Pattern Recogn. **47**(3), 1096–1112 (2014)

30. Kessentini, Y., Paquet, T., Hamadou, A.B.: A multi-lingual recognition system for Arabic and Latin handwriting. In: 2009 10th International Conference on Document Analysis and Recognition (2009)

31. Kessentini, Y., Paquet, T., Hamadou, A.B.: Multi-script handwriting recognition with N-streams low level features. In: 2008 19th International Conference on Pattern Recognition (2008)

32. Frinken, V., Fisher, A., Manmatha, R., Bunke, H.: A novel word spotting method based on recurrent neural networks. IEEE Trans. Pattern Anal. Mach. Learn. **34**, 211–224 (2012)

33. Povey, D., Ghoshal, A., et al.: The Kaldi Speech Recognition Toolkit. ASRU (2011)

# A Reconstruction-Free Projection Selection Procedure for Binary Tomography Using Convolutional Neural Networks

Gergely Pap[1], Gábor Lékó[2(✉)], and Tamás Grósz[1]

[1] Department of Computer Algorithms and Artificial Intelligence,
University of Szeged, Árpád tér 2, Szeged 6720, Hungary
{papg,groszt}@inf.u-szeged.hu
[2] Department of Image Processing and Computer Graphics, University of Szeged,
Árpád tér 2, Szeged 6720, Hungary
leko@inf.u-szeged.hu

**Abstract.** In discrete tomography sometimes it is necessary to reduce the number of projections used for reconstructing the image. Earlier, it was shown that the choice of projection angles can significantly influence the quality of the reconstructions. In this study, we apply convolutional neural networks to select projections in order to reconstruct the original images from their sinograms with the smallest possible error. The training of neural networks is generally a time-consuming process, but after the network has been trained, the prediction for a previously unseen input is fast. We trained convolutional neural networks using sinograms as input and the desired, algorithmically determined k-best projections as labels in a supervised setting. We achieved a significantly faster projection selection and only a slight increase in the Relative Mean Error (RME).

**Keywords:** Projection selection · Binary tomography ·
Convolutional Neural Network · Reconstruction-free

## 1 Introduction

In the field of image processing, the selection of the appropriate projections plays a key role in the reconstruction of binary images. Computed Tomography [4,8] generates the 2D cross-section images of 3D objects using its projections taken from different directions. The object itself may be regarded as a 3D function representing the X-ray attenuation value at each point of the object, while projections are the line integrals of this function measured on the path of the X-ray beams, turned into a vector. Gathering all the projections from the different directions, we get the sinogram of an object. In most cases, hundreds of projections are needed to produce a high quality reconstruction. However, in some

© Springer Nature Switzerland AG 2019
F. Karray et al. (Eds.): ICIAR 2019, LNCS 11662, pp. 228–236, 2019.
https://doi.org/10.1007/978-3-030-27202-9_20

cases, it is not possible to gather a large number of projections, due to physical and/or time limitations.

Discrete tomography [5,6] employs the assumption that the cross-section image to be reconstructed contains only a few different intensities which are known in advance. This allows us to reconstruct the object with a smaller set of projections and still get an acceptable quality. The purpose of binary tomography is to reconstruct objects containing only one single type of material in a non-destructive way, mostly in industrial cases. However it also could be applied in medical fields for structures such as a particular type of tissue in bones or prostheses. The slices of a binary object can be represented by binary matrices (images), where 1 and 0 denote the presence and the absence of the material, respectively. The range of choice in the case of a small number of projections (say, 20 at most) is quite large.

In [14,19] the authors showed that in most of the cases, the correct selection of the projection angles has a big impact on the reconstruction quality. It means that it is important to find the most informative angles for the reconstruction. There are two main types of projection selection, namely offline and online. In the former case, the sampled angles are known and the projections have already been acquired, i.e. we have a so-called blueprint data [13,18]. In the latter case, the number of projections in not known in advance. However, one can define an upper threshold for the projection number. The adaptive projection selection algorithms allow one to perform dense sampling in the information-rich areas and sparse sampling in the information-poor areas [1–3].

The previously mentioned papers provide a good overview of the available approaches for finding the most informative angles. All of these algorithms focus on solving the problem of projection selection using procedural algorithms. Recently, deep learning approaches, especially Convolutional Neural Networks (CNNs) have achieved tremendous success in various fields such as classification [12], segmentation [15], denoising [20], super resolution [10,16] and removing low-dose related CT noise [9]. Although neural networks are widely used in image processing tasks, in the current literature we could not find any studies that concentrate on how to solve the task of projection selection using machine learning algorithms, or any general process in which CNNs could replace a step regarding reconstruction.

The main aim of this paper is to show that neural networks are capable of solving a complex task like projection selection without any reconstruction step (and to significantly decrease the running time of this process for the online scenario).

The structure of the paper is the following. In Sect. 2, we briefly describe artificial and convolutional neural networks, and in Sect. 3 we outline the methods that we used for projection selection using CNNs. In Sect. 4, we provide details about our experimental frameset. In Sect. 5, we describe how the evaluation of our method was performed, while in Sect. 6 we present the experimental results. Finally, in Sect. 7 we draw some conclusions and make some suggestions for future research.

## 2    Artificial and Convolutional Neural Networks

Artificial neural networks have provided an efficient and reliable tool for statistical pattern recognition. Neural networks are capable of learning many tasks in the diverse field of computer science and they are also applied frequently to other related disciplines. CNNs generally make use of convolutional layers (2 dimensional in the case of binary images) in which the convolutional neurons respond to a predefined window of perception. Each neuron has its kernel and these kernels are convolved with the image data. After computation with every possible position with its step size, a pooling layer is applied, which computes the maximum (or in some cases the average) of the convolved features. This is necessary to reduce the parameter space and to make the features translation invariant. After the desired number of convolutional and pooling layers, the collected activation values are flattened and connected to a dense neural network, which attempts to solve a classic machine learning task (e.g. classification or regression).

## 3    Presented Method Using CNN for Projection Selection

Figure 1 summarizes the main steps of our method. The model's architecture consists of 3 convolutional layers with $(5, 5)(3, 3)(3, 3)$ kernel sizes, respectively, followed by two fully connected dense layer with 500 and 180 units. We use ReLU (Rectified Linear Unit) activations as the non-linearities, aside from the last layers' sigmoid function. Between the convolutions we apply maximum pooling with a size of $(3, 3)$. First, the CNN takes a sinogram as input and a dense classifier connected to it outputs 180 activation values optimizing the MSE (Mean Squared Error) using *Adam* (adaptive moment estimation), corresponding to the available directions. Next, these values are thresholded to get the minimum number of projections required for each entity. Since we might end up with more than the required number of projections, a K-means clustering is applied to determine the exact angles to be used in the reconstruction process. We found that the output values of the sigmoid units responsible for angles close to the ground truth are relatively high, which makes clustering them a necessary step. (e.g. often 89-90-91-92 are essential for precise reconstruction, but only one of them should be chosen. Lastly, calculating the RME between the original image and the images reconstructed using the 3 methods explored here (labels, predictions and equiangular projections) gives an estimate of the effectiveness of the selection procedure.

## 4    Test Frameset

Our image database consisted of 8983 phantoms (icons) of varying structural complexity, each with size $64 \times 64$ pixels. To create the train dataset, we performed a modified version of the SFS (Sequential Forward Selection) method [13]. We started the algorithm without initial angles, which resulted in the first

Input: sinogram (180 by 91)    3 x Convolution2D    Dense 500 +
Sigmoid output 180

Thresholding activations and clustering    Reconstruction and RME calculation

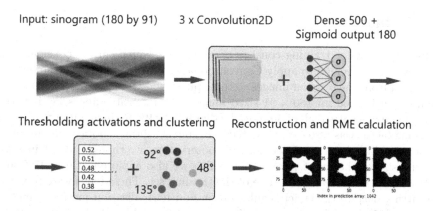

**Fig. 1.** Our proposed pipeline. The input for the CNN is a sinogram, while the output of the network is 180 activation values (one for each direction) upon which we threshold and use K-means clustering. Afterwards, we reconstruct the images and calculate the RME.

two being selected by the algorithm the same way as it would choose in the case of a bigger number of angles. We did not quite follow the method described in the article, because we ran this algorithm just once, instead of their 18 Multistart. The reason for these changes is that the SFS's running time was much too long for 8983 images. Furthermore, with this approach we obtained the sequence of the most informative angles. They turned out to be feasible owing to the fact that many of the experiments needed to be done with a different number of label projections (e.g. 4–8). Therefore only having as many projections as needed for the label data could be done without losing the valuable data contained in the algorithmically selected and ordered labels. The labels stored the information in descending order, with the first containing the angle with the most valuable information for minimising the reconstruction error. This way of selecting projections resulted in having only a local optimum with the most informative angles instead of calculating a global one. However, in our case the former was also as applicable to the given task as the latter.

For the projection selection we used the same setup as the authors in [13], except for the above-mentioned changes in the SFS algorithm. For the validation of our CNN, the reconstructions were performed using the thresholded version of the *skimage* python package's SART [4] algorithm. The output of SART is an image with intensity values around 0 and 1. The quality of the reconstructions using the predictions was measured with the Relative Mean Error (RME) defined as

$$RME(\mathbf{x}^*, \mathbf{y}^S) = \frac{\sum_i |x_i^* - y_i^S|}{\sum_i x_i^*} , \tag{1}$$

where $\mathbf{x}^*$ is the blueprint and $\mathbf{y}^S$ is the reconstructed image from angle set $S$. Our experiments were all performed on 4 NVIDIA Tesla K10 GPUs for equal measurement conditions.

## 5    Evaluation

Since our input for training consists of sinograms, which can be considered as 2D images, we decided to apply Convolutional Neural Networks. The sinograms extracted from the original images were 91 pixels wide for each projection direction, which formed an $180 \times 91$ sized image. The intensity ranges lay between 0–91, so we normalized all of our data by dividing by 91. Reducing input shape by a scaling factor was also experimented with, but we did not notice any improvement regarding accuracy. Based on this observation, we thought about increasing the size of the input parameters, which we also explored using 32760 and 65160 points of data as the source of the training set. These trials were prone to overfitting despite the strict regularisation and normalisation methods applied (dropout [17], batch normalisation [7]). To sum up, 180 by 91 pixels seems to be the optimal size for training the networks, as smaller input features decreased the accuracy of the reconstructions, while larger input spaces led to overfitting (not to mention the increase in training time and memory requirements).

Standard evaluation methods used for scoring neural network predictions might be misleading in the case of a task such as the one presented here. The reason for this is that a label mostly depends on the basic geometrical properties of the input image and it might generate some artifacts resulting from degree-favouritism (selection of common projections such as 0 or 90) or it might find equiangular projections to be the best predictions. The latter might be regarded as the closest one to every possible label projection, but this produces sub-optimal reconstructions. Thus, the images were rotated randomly to eliminate or lessen the effect of the above mentioned problem. Since the main purpose of projection selection procedure is to outperform the Naive equiangular [18] approach by choosing the required angles in order to achieve a lower reconstruction error. To further investigate this issue and to get a better understanding of the selected projections, our method was compared to both the algorithmically selected projection angles, and to the equiangular angle set calculated as $i\frac{180°}{P} \mid i = 0, \ldots, P-1$, where $P$ denotes the number of projections used in each case. We will simply refer to the former projection selection method as Label (as it was the training objective of our neural nets) and the latter as Naive, following the authors of [18].

Here, 10-fold cross-validation [11] was used during the training of our network and we based our RME values and other statistical calculations on these runs.

## 6    Results

In Table 1, we present the RME and Standard Deviation (STD) values of the different methods with 4-6-8 angles, respectively. The •/○ symbols denote when the differences are statistically significant (•) or not (○), using a t-test with a significance level of 0.05. The results are statistically significant only with 8 projections.

The RME values computed from the label projections are naturally the smallest of the three, followed by our CNN approach. The equiangular approach produces the highest RMEs, meaning that the reconstructed images differed from the original ones the most using the Naive angle set. Using our 10-fold cross-validation test evaluations we analyzed the RME values obtained using the 3 methods with 4 projections. We also present our findings in Table 2. In 37 cases our CNN managed to predict a set of projections that was as good as the labels. We note here that these values are from the test set containing examples never encountered during the training of the model. We should add that the more angles we have, the closer we will be to the equiangular approach in terms of minimising the RME. Some of the reconstruction results with the RME values can be seen in Fig. 2 with 8 projections.

**Table 1.** Average of RME and Standard Deviation values calculated from 10 runs for the three different approaches. The significance values were computed pairwise for Naive-Label, Label-CNN and Naive-CNN and the significant statistical differences are presented column-wise with the symbols of ●/○.

| 4 projections | Label | CNN | Naive |
|---|---|---|---|
| RME | 0.3817 ○ | 0.4015 ○ | 0.4912 ○ |
| STD | 0.2078 | 0.2189 | 0.2903 |
| 6 projections | Label | CNN | Naive |
| RME | 0.3196 ○ | 0.3430 ○ | 0.3866 ○ |
| STD | 0.1723 | 0.1723 | 0.2341 |
| 8 projections | Label | CNN | Naive |
| RME | 0.2746 ● | 0.2940 ● | 0.3128 ● |
| STD | 0.1842 | 0.2174 | 0.2312 |

**Table 2.** The number of images on which the 3 distinct methods gave the smallest RME values are shown along the diagonal. The other cells show where two approaches gave the same RME value.

| 4 projections | Label | CNN | Naive |
|---|---|---|---|
| Label | 4676 | 37 | 19 |
| CNN | 37 | 3096 | 14 |
| Naive | 19 | 14 | 1141 |

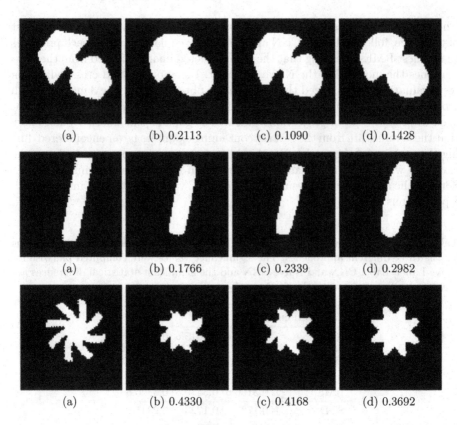

**Fig. 2.** Reconstruction from 180 projections (a), results of the Label (b), the CNN approach (c) and the Naive approach (d). The values under the figures are the RME values compared to (a). The first row shows a case where the CNN selected the most informative projections. Reconstructing from labels produced the smallest RME in the second row. The last row showcases one image when the equiangular set gave the best score.

## 7    Conclusions

In this study, we trained a Convolutional Neural Network to select projections for the accurate reconstruction of binary tomography images. After training, prediction is achieved using K-means clustering to get a smaller set of projection data. After comparing the procedural algorithm and the results obtained using a neural network, we observed only a small increase in the RME values compared to the reconstructions from label projections (but performance-wise we achieved a notable improvement with the former). We found that CNNs can be applied to projection selection tasks by training in a multilabel classification scenario. To the best of our knowledge, this was the first attempt to predict projections of binary images for reconstruction using CNNs and to perform projection selection without any reconstruction step. In the future, we intend to include various projection selection problems and approaches originating from different CT or tomography methods and to evaluate our method using other quality measurements than RME.

**Acknowledgements.** Gábor Lékó was supported by the UNKP-18-3 New National Excellence Program of the Ministry of Human Capacities. Tamás Grósz was supported by the National Research, Development and Innovation Office of Hungary through the Artificial Intelligence National Excellence Program (grant no.: 2018-1.2.1-NKP-2018-00008). This research was supported by the project "Integrated program for training new generation of scientists in the fields of computer science", no EFOP-3.6.3-VEKOP-16-2017-0002. The project was supported by the European Union and co-funded by the European Social Fund. We acknowledge the support of the Ministry of Human Capacities, Hungary, grant 20391-3/2018/FEKUSTRAT. The authors would also like to thank István Megyeri for his valuable advice.

# References

1. Batenburg, K.J., Palenstijn, W.J., Balázs, P., Sijbers, J.: Dynamic angle selection in binary tomography. Comput. Vis. Image Underst. **117**(4), 306–318 (2013)
2. Dabravolski, A., Batenburg, K., Sijbers, J.: Dynamic angle selection in x-ray computed tomography. Nucl. Instrum. Methods Phys. Res., Sect. B **324**, 17–24 (2014)
3. Haque, M.A., Ahmad, M.O., Swamy, M.N.S., Hasan, M.K., Lee, S.Y.: Adaptive projection selection for computed tomography. IEEE Trans. Image Process. **22**(12), 5085–5095 (2013)
4. Herman, G.T.: Fundamentals of Computerized Tomography: Image Reconstruction from Projections. ACVPR, 2nd edn. Springer Publishing Company, London (2009). https://doi.org/10.1007/978-1-84628-723-7
5. Herman, G.T., Kuba, A.: Discrete Tomography: Foundations, Algorithms, and Applications. Birkhäuser, Basel (1999)
6. Herman, G.T., Kuba, A.: Advances in Discrete Tomography and Its Applications. Birkhäuser, Basel (2007)
7. Ioffe, S., Szegedy, C.: Batch normalization: accelerating deep network training by reducing internal covariate shift. CoRR abs/1502.03167 (2015)
8. Kak, A.C., Slaney, M.: Principles of Computerized Tomographic Imaging. IEEE Press, New York (1988)
9. Kang, E., Min, J., Ye, J.C.: A deep convolutional neural network using directional wavelets for low-dose x-ray CT reconstruction. Med. Phys. **44**(10), e360–375 (2017)
10. Kim, J., Kwon Lee, J., Mu Lee, K.: Accurate image super-resolution using very deep convolutional networks. In: The IEEE Conference on Computer Vision and Pattern Recognition (CVPR), June 2016
11. Kohavi, R.: A study of cross-validation and bootstrap for accuracy estimation and model selection. In: International Joint Conference on Artificial Intelligence (IJCAI), vol. 14, March 2001
12. Krizhevsky, A., Sutskever, I., Hinton, G.E.: Imagenet classification with deep convolutional neural networks. In: Neural Information Processing Systems 25, January 2012
13. Lékó, G., Balázs, P.: Sequential projection selection methods for binary tomography. In: Barneva, R.P., Brimkov, V.E., Kulczycki, P., Tavares, J.M.R.S. (eds.) CompIMAGE 2018. LNCS, vol. 10986, pp. 70–81. Springer, Cham (2019). https://doi.org/10.1007/978-3-030-20805-9_7

14. Nagy, A., Kuba, A.: Reconstruction of binary matrices from fan-beam projections. Acta Cybernetica **17**(2), 359–385 (2005)
15. Ronneberger, O., Fischer, P., Brox, T.: U-Net: convolutional networks for biomedical image segmentation. In: Navab, N., Hornegger, J., Wells, W.M., Frangi, A.F. (eds.) MICCAI 2015. LNCS, vol. 9351, pp. 234–241. Springer, Cham (2015). https://doi.org/10.1007/978-3-319-24574-4_28
16. Shi, W., et al.: Real-time single image and video super-resolution using an efficient sub-pixel convolutional neural network. In: Real-Time Single Image and Video Super-Resolution Using an Efficient Sub-Pixel Convolutional Neural Network, June 2016
17. Srivastava, N., Hinton, G., Krizhevsky, A., Sutskever, I., Salakhutdinov, R.: Dropout: a simple way to prevent neural networks from overfitting. J. Mach. Learn. Res. **15**, 1929–1958 (2014)
18. Varga, L., Balázs, P., Nagy, A.: Projection selection algorithms for discrete tomography. In: Blanc-Talon, J., Bone, D., Philips, W., Popescu, D., Scheunders, P. (eds.) ACIVS 2010. LNCS, vol. 6474, pp. 390–401. Springer, Heidelberg (2010). https://doi.org/10.1007/978-3-642-17688-3_37
19. Varga, L., Balázs, P., Nagy, A.: Direction-dependency of binary tomographic reconstruction algorithms. Graph. Models **73**(6), 365–375 (2011). Computational Modeling in Imaging Sciences
20. Zhang, K., Zuo, W., Chen, Y., Meng, D., Zhang, L.: Beyond a Gaussian denoiser: residual learning of deep CNN for image denoising. Trans. Img. Proc. **26**(7), 3142–3155 (2017)

# Augmenting Reality of Tracked Video Objects Using Homography and Keypoints

Julien Valognes, Niloufar Salehi Dastjerdi, and Maria Amer[✉]

Concordia University, Montreal, QC, Canada
`amer@ece.concordia.ca`

**Abstract.** Augmented reality (AR) and object tracking are active research fields and few research exists that combines both. We propose a markerless video AR system that applies video-processing tasks on the input video and virtual-data processing tasks on the virtual data and then adaptively relates both virtual and real data. The proposed system tracks a target and enables the user to select virtual data such as objects, images, or texts, for augmentation but adapted to the current state of the target. For adaptation, the virtual data is segmented to be overlaid on the target. To account for zoom, scaling, translation, and rotation of tracked object, and to make a proper alignment of virtual data, the system applies a homography estimation based on a feature point detector. Augmentation is performed on extracted keyframes of the input video. Experimental results show promising different AR applications of the proposed system, e.g., social media or industrial maintenance. No objective measures are known for video AR systems. We propose to use the image histogram to objectively measure performance by showing the histograms of the segmented virtual object before and after applying estimated homography is preserved.

**Keywords:** Augmented reality · Object tracking ·
Object segmentation · Keyframe extraction · Keypoint detection ·
Ferns · Homography estimation

## 1    Introduction

Augmented reality (AR) adds virtual data over real world content. A typical AR system consists of registration and tracking. Registration is the proper alignment of virtual data to the real world objects [12, 22]. Tracking in AR refers to estimating the camera 3D pose. Video object tracking refers to following the target between consecutive frames. There are two types of AR: marker-based and markerless. Marker-based AR systems [8, 17] use a set of predefined patterns, artificial landmarks, or fiducial markers. Markerless AR combined with camera-tracking [9, 20] relies on visual features (e.g., color) or interest points (e.g., corners).

© Springer Nature Switzerland AG 2019
F. Karray et al. (Eds.): ICIAR 2019, LNCS 11662, pp. 237–245, 2019.
https://doi.org/10.1007/978-3-030-27202-9_21

This paper proposes a markerless AR system in which virtual data (selected by the user) are overlaid on real objects and are on-line adjusted by accounting for scaling, translation and rotation in order to fit the state of the tracked object selected in a given video. Unlike conventional AR systems, the proposed system does not require camera calibration. The core of the proposed system are three main steps: tracking, feature detection, and homography estimation. Key feature detection is based on random Ferns and combined with a stochastic procedure allowing to detect the most stable keypoints in the non-initial frame based on random deformation of the image.

Next, we discuss related work and differences to our system. Although there are many AR applications [5–14], little research [12,14,19,22] has been done for developing AR and object tracking. In [22], the authors proposed a PC-based markerless AR application to render a 3D object on top of the reference image using four steps: detection, description, matching and pose estimation. The difference to our work is that they used fixed reference image to augment another object on top of it; our system can augment any object selected by the user from any image to overlay on the tracked object. The authors of [12] presented an AR application in order to blend two videos. They segmented an object to overlay it on another video sequence. SIFT and HoG descriptors were used to detect the interest points and extract the features from a video image. The difference to [12] is that our system overlays selected object on the tracked object in all frames or only keyframes. Moreover, our study uses Ferns [18] instead of SIFT. The authors in [18] show that Ferns can rely on a low-cost keypoint extraction while SIFT reuses intermediate data from the keypoint extraction to compute canonic scale and orientations and the descriptors. Lehiani et al. [14] presented a technique for mobile AR, based on KAZE descriptors [1] to identify the object of interest. KAZE describes 2D features using nonlinear diffusion filtering. The authors utilized pose estimation for AR tracking to determine a transformation that relates the object reference frame according to camera coordinate system. Different than Lehiani et al. [14], we do not require camera calibration. Park et al. [19] proposed a method to track multiple 3D objects for AR using object detection and tracking. Contrary to our featured-based system, their approach is model-based where each target object has a CAD 3D model. In addition, they used pre-extracted keyframes from the video shot of the object from various viewpoints. Each input frame is matched against the keyframes and features lying on the objects over consecutive frames are tracked. In our work, we track objects in each frame and use keyframes for augmentation.

This paper presents the proposed system in Sect. 2, experimental results in Sect. 3, and a summary and conclusion in Sect. 4.

## 2    Proposed System

We propose a markerless AR system which augments real-world video objects with adaptive virtual data. Adaptation means that the virtual data need to be adjusted so to fit the state of current real objects. The adaptive augmentation may be applied either to each input frame or to a selected frame (e.g., keyframe). Figure 1 shows the block diagram of our system having three main modules: keyframe extraction, video processing and virtual-data processing. Not all frames in a video present significant information. Often, a frame has a slight difference from its previous frame. Approaches for extracting keyframes are based on motion patterns, frame descriptors, or visual features. For faster processing, keyframe extraction can be performed on a set of $N$ previous video frames and in parallel to video processing tasks. We use the method in [4] to extract keyframes.

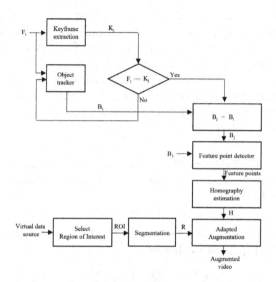

**Fig. 1.** Block diagram of the proposed AR system; $B_1 \in F_1$

## 2.1   Video Processing for AR

Our video processing module consists of three main steps: object tracking, feature detection, and homography estimation. The user creates a bounding box (BB) around the target in the first frame. Any object tracking method can be used to find the BB of the object in subsequent frames. Let $F_i, i = 1, \cdots, n$ be the input video frames, $K_j, j = 1, \cdots, m; m < n$ be the extracted keyframes, $B_1$ be the user-selected BB in $F_1$, $B_i$ be the output of the tracker in $F_i$, and $B_j$ be the output of the tracker in the keyframe $K_j$.

The first frame BB (i.e, $B_1$), called model image, is used to initialize Ferns feature point detector [18] so to detect keypoints in the output BB ($B_j$) in future frames. To detect keypoints, $B_1$ is deformed several times using random affine deformations and Harris corners are detected in the deformed $B_1$. Then, the most stable keypoints are selected in $B_1$, based on how many times they appear in the deformed $B_1$ versions, and a unique class ID is assigned to each of the keypoints using Ferns. This Ferns classification uses patches $I$ in $B_1$ and a number of ferns, each is a set of binary features $f$ as in

$$f = \begin{cases} 1 : I(\mathbf{d_1}) \leq I(\mathbf{d_2}), \\ 0 : \text{otherwise} \end{cases} \tag{1}$$

where $\mathbf{d_1}$ and $\mathbf{d_2}$ are two randomly sampled locations in $I$ centered at a keypoint. In our system, Ferns applies to both $B_1$ and $B_j$ and detects up to 1000 feature key points inside the $B_1$ and $B_j$. The output of Ferns is a list of extracted feature points in $B_1$ and in $B_j$, which are matched to estimate a homography matrix $H$. This homography estimation is required to handle scaling, rotation, and translation of the tracked (augmented) object. To compute the homography matrix, we use Random Sample Consensus (RANSAC) [6] which requires at least four correspondences to achieve a successful homography estimation between $B_1$ and $B_j$. Let $X$ and $x$ be the projective coordinates of the same point in $B_1$ and $B_j$, respectively; the homography transformation is

$$X = Hx. \tag{2}$$

This homography has 8 degrees of freedom and can consequently be computed from four point correspondences. The corresponding homogeneous system of equations is solved by

$$X_l \times H x_l = 0, \tag{3}$$

in which $H$ is computed using the source $(x_l, y_l)$, target $(X_l, Y_l)$, and vector of source points $(\mathbf{x_l})$. Equation (3) becomes

$$\begin{bmatrix} \mathbf{0}^\mathrm{T} & -\mathbf{x_l^T} & Y_l \mathbf{x_l^T} \\ \mathbf{x_l^T} & \mathbf{0}^\mathrm{T} & -X_l \mathbf{x_l^T} \\ -Y_l \mathbf{x_l^T} & X_l \mathbf{x_l^T} & \mathbf{0}^\mathrm{T} \end{bmatrix} h = 0, \tag{4}$$

which results in equations of the form $\mathbf{A_l} h = 0$, with $\mathbf{A_l}$ being the rows of the left matrix and $\mathbf{h}$ being a $9 \times 1$ vector made of the entries of the homography matrix $H$.

## 2.2   Virtual Data Processing

The third module of our system processes virtual data using virtual data selection, segmentation, homography transformation, and augmentation on the real object $B_j$ in keyframe $K_j$. The user can select a virtual data source such as a text or an image, in order to overlay it on $B_j$, as needed. When an image is selected as the virtual data source, the user can select any region of interest (ROI) and indicates (with a click or a BB) where to add it in $K_j$. The system segments the ROI by applying an interactive segmentation method such as [7]. After segmentation, the system applies the homography matrix estimated in (4) on $R$, the segmented ROI, in order to handle scaling, rotation, and translation of real and virtual objects and create an augmented adapted object. Thus, our system allows the augmented ROI to undergo perspective changes similar to the tracked object for a proper augmented video.

# 3  Experimental Results

We have implemented our system on an Intel(R) Xeon(R) 3.60 GHz PC with 16 GB RAM and under MSVC 2015 using C++. For segmenting the virtual ROI, we apply the interactive segmentation graph cuts (G-CUTS) [7], where the user selects certain continuous sets of pixels (strokes) of background and foreground to perform segmentation; the strokes provide clues on what the user intends to segment. We use Struck [11] to track the target; a recent tracking method such as [3] can be used for better performance.

To detect feature points, we use Ferns [18] for its ability to match points in consecutive frames by applying a scoring system which separates the best point matches from its other descriptors. Ferns outputs are compared to SIFT [16] and TILDE [21] in Fig. 2 on "Graffiti" from the HPatches benchmark [2]. Figure 2(a) shows Ferns matched descriptors highlighted in blue. In comparison, SIFT and TILDE outputs in Figs. 2(b) and (c) have no scoring system to isolate best matches from the rest of their descriptors. Obtaining only the best matches is crucial as it better enables homography estimation necessary for augmentation; for this, Ferns is preferred. Indeed, Fig. 2(e) displays "Graffiti" subject to perspective changes of the image in (d), and Fig. 2(f) shows the perspective change Ferns estimates from (d) to (e); the blue rectangle on (f) is a visual representation of the perspective change Ferns estimates from the feature points.

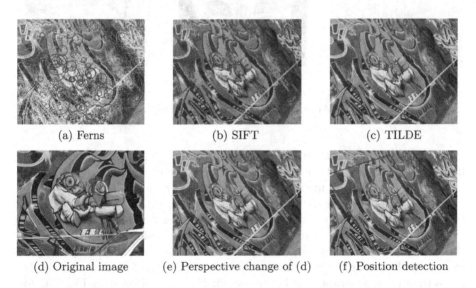

(a) Ferns               (b) SIFT               (c) TILDE

(d) Original image    (e) Perspective change of (d)    (f) Position detection

**Fig. 2.** Feature point detection: comparison over "Graffiti" (Color figure online)

Figure 3 shows the steps of the proposed system using a masking application; in Fig. 3(b), a user selects a ROI and strokes from the image for augmentation and the ROI is segmented as in Fig. 3 (c). Figure 3(d) shows the result of applying Ferns on the target; circles are centered at model keypoints; white circles indicate matched keypoints in $B_1$ and $B_j$, and the radius of each circle depends on the scale of its corresponding keypoint in Ferns. Figure 3(e) shows homography estimation applied on the segmented ROI allowing its transformation, so to fit on the zoom-out target. Figure 3(f) indicates the proper augmentation of the mask.

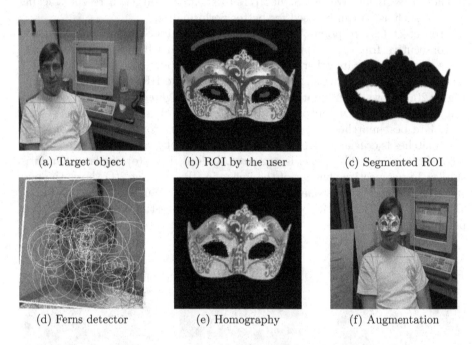

(a) Target object          (b) ROI by the user          (c) Segmented ROI

(d) Ferns detector          (e) Homography          (f) Augmentation

**Fig. 3.** Augmentation for "Dudek": masking face

Figure 4 presents augmentation applied on "Singer1"; the user selects the ROI from the same video and the system has changed the dress of one of the singers in a keyframe to make a uniform appearance for both singers as in Fig. 4(d). In Fig. 5, the virtual data is from the image "Doll" [15]; (c) and (d) show augmentation under left and right rotation; (f) and (e) under zoom-in and zoom-out.

The image histogram is preserved under image transformations [10]; we use the histogram here as an objective performance measure for our system; we expect the histograms of the segmented virtual object before and after applying estimated homography to be preserved; this is confirmed in Fig. 6(a) for all 4 transformations for the mask in Fig. 3 (e). Figure 6(b) shows the effect of augmentation on the histograms of the target in Fig. 5 (d); as seen, correct homography and augmentation output a histogram of the target after augmentation as the addition of the histograms of the target before augmentation and the virtual object after homography.

(a) Target object    (b) ROI by the user    (c) Segmented ROI    (d) Augmentation

**Fig. 4.** Augmentation for "Singer1": unify dresses

(a) Target object            (b) Virtual image      (c) Augment under left rotation

(d) Augment under right rotat. (e) Augment under zoom-in  (f) Augment under zoom-out

**Fig. 5.** Head cover under appearance changes

By definition, video AR systems are developed for specific applications and thus their output differ. Therefore, no one set of objective measures exists to compare our system with existing video AR systems. We propose to use the image histogram as an objective measure for augmentation; however, more research is required. In our system, the virtual object is manually selected by the user using a BB so to segment it out and display it on the tracked object. The object tracking step follows the real object, and the feature detection is applied on the virtual object, not on the background, so to match feature points of the target object at each keyframe. The performance of our system thus heavily depends on the object tracking since major tracking failure may render the homography estimation useless. However, object tracking is a very active field with major recent advances where new methods achieve high stable performance [13]. Ferns feature detector requires a sufficiently large window size; thus the user-selected BB should not be too small. Our AR system serves as a prototype for planar objects but a 3D video AR system would have to capture objects in 3D so to apply that transformation on a 3D virtual object. In this case, 3D keypoints and 3D transformations are required.

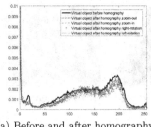

(a) Before and after homography.

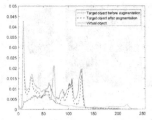

(b) Before and after augmentation.

**Fig. 6.** Histograms before and after processing.

## 4    Conclusion

We proposed a system that combines AR and video processing to augment real objects with virtual data in keyframes. Our video processing tracked a target and estimated both feature points and homography transformation of the target compared to its initial state. Our AR module applied interactive segmentation to segment the user-selected virtual ROI for augmentation. To match tracked and virtual objects, we used a point feature detector (Ferns) to estimate homography which handles scaling, translation, and rotation of both tracked and virtual objects so to achieve proper augmentation. Our results showed that well augmentation can be achieved under challenging video conditions. We verified the performance using the histogram that was preserved under different transformations. Our system requires two user inputs: an object to track in the first frame and virtual data to augment. The rest of the system is automated and can be easily adapted to requirements of the different AR applications, for example, social media or industrial maintenance.

## References

1. Alcantarilla, P.F., Bartoli, A., Davison, A.J.: KAZE features. In: Fitzgibbon, A., Lazebnik, S., Perona, P., Sato, Y., Schmid, C. (eds.) ECCV 2012. LNCS, vol. 7577, pp. 214–227. Springer, Heidelberg (2012). https://doi.org/10.1007/978-3-642-33783-3_16
2. Balntas, V., Lenc, K., Vedaldi, A., Mikolajczyk, K.: HPatches: a benchmark and evaluation of handcrafted and learned local descriptors. In: Proceedings of IEEE Conference on Computer Vision Pattern Recognition (2017)
3. Bertinetto, L., Valmadre, J., Golodetz, S., Miksik, O., Torr, P.H.S.: Staple: complementary learners for real-time tracking. In: The IEEE Conference on Computer Vision and Pattern Recognition (CVPR), June 2016
4. Dastjerdi, N.S., Valognes, J., Amer, M.: Effective keyframe extraction from RGB and RGB-D video sequences. In: International Conference on Image Processing Theory, Tools and Applications, pp. 1–5. IEEE, Montreal, Quebec, November 2017
5. Eisert, P., Fechteler, P., Rurainsky, J.: 3-D tracking of shoes for virtual mirror applications. In: Proceedings of IEEE Conference on Computer Vision Pattern Recognition, Anchorage, AK, pp. 1–6, 23–28 June 2008

6. Fischler, M., Bolles, R.: Random sample consensus: a paradigm for model fitting with applications to image analysis and automated cartography. Commun. ACM **24**, 381–395 (1981)

7. Freedman, D., Turek, M.: Illumination-invariant tracking via graph cuts. In: Proceedings IEEE Conference on CVPR, San Diego, USA, pp. 10–17, 20–25 June 2005

8. Fuji, T., Mitsukura, Y., Moriya, T.: Interactive augmented reality art book to promote Malaysia traditional game. IEEE Computer, Communications, and Control Technology (I4CT), Langkawi, Malaysia, pp. 203–208, September 2014

9. Genc, Y., Riedel, S., Souvannavong, F., Akinlar, C., Navab, N.: Marker-less tracking for AR: a learning-based approach. In: IEEE-C-ISMAR, Darmstadt, Germany, pp. 295–304, October 2002

10. Hadjdemetriou, E., Grossberg, M., Nayar, S.: Histogram preserving image transformations. Int. J. Comput. Vis. **45**, 5–23 (2001)

11. Hare, S., et al.: Struck: structured output tracking with kernels. IEEE Trans. Pattern Anal. Machine Intell. **38**, 2096–2109 (2016)

12. Khandelwal, P., Swarnalatha, P., Bisht, N., Prabu, S.: Detection of features to track objects and segmentation using GrabCut for application in marker-less augmented reality. Elsevier Procedia Comput. Sci. **58**, 698–705 (2015)

13. Kristan, M., et al.: The sixth visual object tracking VOT2018 challenge results. In: IEEE European Conference on Computer Vision Workshops (2018)

14. Lehiani, Y., Maidi, M., Preda, M., Ghorbel, F.: Object identification and tracking for steady registration in mobile augmented reality. In: Proceedings of IEEE International Conference on Signal and Image Processing Applications (ICSIPA), Kuala Lumpur, Malaysia, pp. 54–59, 19–21 October 2015

15. Liu, T., Sun, J., Zheng, N., Tang, X., Shum, H.: Learning to detect a salient object. In: Proceedings of IEEE Conference on CVPR, USA, pp. 353–367, June 2007

16. Lowe, D.: Distinctive image features from scale-invariant keypoints. Int. J. Comput. Vis. **60**, 91–110 (2004)

17. Motokurumada, M., Ohta, M., Yamashita, K.: A video-based augmented reality system. In: IEEE 17th International Symposium on Consumer Electronics (ISCE), Taiwan, pp. 213–214, June 2013

18. Ozuysal, M., Calonder, M., Lepetit, V., Fua, P.: Fast keypoint recognition using random ferns. IEEE Trans. Pattern Anal. Machine Intell. **32**, 448–461 (2010)

19. Park, J., Seo, D., Ku, M., Jung, I., Jeong, C.: Multiple 3D object tracking using ROI and double filtering for augmented reality. In: Proceedings of IEEE International Conference on Multimedia and Ubiquitous Engineering (MUE), Crete, Greece, pp. 317–322, 28–30 June 2011

20. Vacchetti, L., Lepetit, V., Fua, P.: Stable real-time 3D tracking using online and offline information. IEEE Trans. Pattern Anal. Machine Intell. **26**, 1385–1391 (2004)

21. Verdie, Y., Yi, K., Fua, P., Lepetit, V.: Tilde: a temporally invariant learned detector. In: Proceedings of IEEE Conference on Computer Vision Pattern Recognition (2015)

22. Yee, T., Arshad, H., Abdullah, A.: Development of a PC-based markerless augmented reality. In: Proceedings of IEEE International Conference on Electrical Engineering and Informatics, Bali, Indonesia, pp. 49–53, 10–11 August 2015

# Initial Conditions of Reaction-Diffusion Algorithm Designed for Image Edge Detection

Atsushi Nomura[✉]

Faculty of Education, Yamaguchi University,
Yoshida 1677-1, Yamaguchi 753-8513, Japan
anomura@yamaguchi-u.ac.jp

**Abstract.** Image edges refer to steep brightness changes and provide fruitful information on image structures. This paper proposes initial conditions of a reaction-diffusion algorithm designed for image edge detection. The algorithm utilizes a network in which FitzHugh-Nagumo neurons are placed at grid points and connected to their neighboring ones. Each FitzHugh-Nagumo neuron simulates a process of excitation and inhibition observed in biological nerve axon, and is described with a pair of time-evolving ordinary differential equations (ODEs) stated by activator and inhibitor variables. The network is originally derived from discretization of FitzHugh-Nagumo type reaction-diffusion equations described by partial differential equations (PDEs). It is known that the network creates stationary pulses at edge positions of image brightness distribution provided as initial conditions. Steep brightness changes initiate processes of excitation and inhibition, and pulses having excited states at edge positions remain at their original positions, as time proceeds. However, the network is insensitive to relatively weak edges having gradual brightness changes. The novel initial conditions proposed here are composed of absolute gradients of multi-scale images. The algorithm with the initial conditions is applied to test images of BSDS300 dataset, and its performance is quantitatively confirmed by F-measure, in comparison with other edge detection algorithms.

**Keywords:** Edge detection · Reaction-diffusion · FitzHugh-Nagumo · Initial conditions · PDEs approach · Performance evaluation

## 1 Introduction

Reaction-diffusion algorithm refers to a set of computational procedures governed by reaction-diffusion equations or their discretized ones for tasks of image processing and computer vision research. Since the reaction-diffusion equations have a mathematical formulation of diffusion equations coupled with reaction functions, the algorithm is the extension of diffusion equation based algorithm [1]

© Springer Nature Switzerland AG 2019
F. Karray et al. (Eds.): ICIAR 2019, LNCS 11662, pp. 246–251, 2019.
https://doi.org/10.1007/978-3-030-27202-9_22

in the partial differential equations (PDEs) approach [2]. In general, reaction-diffusion algorithm numerically computes the equations from certain initial conditions, and provides results for its task in finite duration.

We have proposed a reaction-diffusion algorithm designed for image edge detection [3,4]. The algorithm utilizes a discretized version of FitzHugh-Nagumo type reaction-diffusion equations, which simulates a pulse propagation phenomenon along biological nerve axon having a process of excitation and inhibition [5]. The equations are discretized with a finite difference method for numerical computation, and the discretization results in a network or lattice of FitzHugh-Nagumo neurons placed at grid positions and coupled with their neighboring ones.

This paper contributes to improve performance of the reaction-diffusion algorithm designed for edge detection by proposing its initial conditions. Although our previous algorithm [4] successfully detected image edges having steep brightness changes, it failed to detect weak edges having relatively gradual changes, which sometimes provide fruitful information on object boundaries. In order to enhance the gradual changes, we propose novel initial conditions composed of multi-scale blurred images. The performance of the algorithm is confirmed with BSDS300 dataset [6,7] in comparison with other algorithms.

## 2   The Algorithm

Let $u(x,t)$ be a distribution of space $x$ at time $t$. A diffusion equation governing $u(x,t)$ with its diffusion coefficient $D$ is

$$\partial u/\partial t = D\nabla^2 u, \tag{1}$$

in which $\partial/\partial t$ is a temporal partial derivative, and $\nabla$ is a gradient operator of a spatial distribution. If an image $I(x)$ is provided for the initial condition of Eq. (1),

$$u(x,0) = I(x), \tag{2}$$

the solution of Eq. (1) in infinite one-dimensional space becomes a Gaussian filtering [8] of

$$u(x,t) = \int_{-\infty}^{\infty} G(x,\xi,t)I(\xi)d\xi = \frac{1}{2\sqrt{D\pi t}} \int_{-\infty}^{\infty} I(\xi)e^{-(x-\xi)^2/(4Dt)}d\xi = G*I, \tag{3}$$

in which $G(x,\xi,t)$ is a Gaussian function and the symbol $*$ is a convolution operator.

A FitzHugh-Nagumo type reaction-diffusion model having activator $u(x,t)$ and inhibitor $v(x,t)$ simulates a pulse propagation phenomenon along nerve axon [5]. The model consists of a pair of equations described by

$$\partial u/\partial t = D_u\nabla^2 u + f(u,v) + S(x,t), \quad \partial v/\partial t = D_v\nabla^2 v + g(u,v), \tag{4}$$

with reaction functions $f(u, v)$ and $g(u, v)$, and an external stimulus $S(x, t)$; $D_u$ and $D_v$ are diffusion coefficients. The reaction functions $f(u, v)$ and $g(u, v)$ of the FitzHugh-Nagumo model are

$$f(u, v) = [u(u - a)(1 - u) - v] / \varepsilon, \quad g(u, v) = u - bv, \tag{5}$$

with the constants $a, b$ and $\varepsilon$ $(0 < \varepsilon \ll 1)$.

We previously proposed a reaction-diffusion algorithm utilizing a discretized system of Eq. (4) in image edge detection [3,4]. Absolute gradient of a blurred image

$$A(x) = |\nabla G * I| \tag{6}$$

is provided for the initial conditions of the algorithm, as follows:

$$u(x, t) = A(x), (-\tau \le t < 0) \quad v(x, -\tau) = \varepsilon f(A(x), 0), \tag{7}$$

and the external stimulus is given by

$$S(x, t) = \mu A(x) \times [1 - U(t)] \tag{8}$$

in which $\mu$ is a constant; $U(t)$ is a step function giving 0 in $t < 0$ and 1 in $t \ge 0$. Note that we define the model of Eq. (4) in $-\tau < t$ (see [4] for more detail).

After finite duration in computing Eq. (4), an edge map $E$ is created by

$$E = \{x | u(x, t) > 1/2\}, \tag{9}$$

in which $u(x, t) > 1/2$ denotes an excited state of the FitzHugh-Nagumo model. In this paper, we propose to replace the initial conditions of Eq. (7) by

$$u(x, t) = \frac{\sum_i A_i(x)}{G * \sum_i A_i(x)}, (-\tau \le t < 0) \quad v(x, -\tau) = \varepsilon f(u(x, -\tau), 0), \tag{10}$$

in which $A_i(x)$ denotes Eq. (6) and is computed with Eq. (1) at time instances $t_i, i = 1, 2, \cdots N$. The key point of Eq. (10) is that the proposed initial conditions take sum of multi-scales of the given image $I$ and is normalized by its blurred one; this enhances weak edges having gradual brightness changes.

## 3    Experimental Results and Discussions

Performance of the proposed algorithm was confirmed with BSDS300 dataset [6, 7], which consists of 200 training images and 100 test ones. After determining the optimal parameter settings of the proposed algorithm with the training images, we applied the algorithm to the test images and evaluated its performance by F-measure. The optimal parameter settings were $D_u = 2, D_v = 3, a = 0.1, b = 4.0, \varepsilon = 1.0 \times 10^{-3}, \tau = 0.03, \mu = -5.0$. The FitzHugh-Nagumo model of Eq. (4) was discretized with a finite difference of time $\delta t = 1.0 \times 10^{-4}$ and that of space $\delta x = 0.5$; the higher order terms were eliminated.

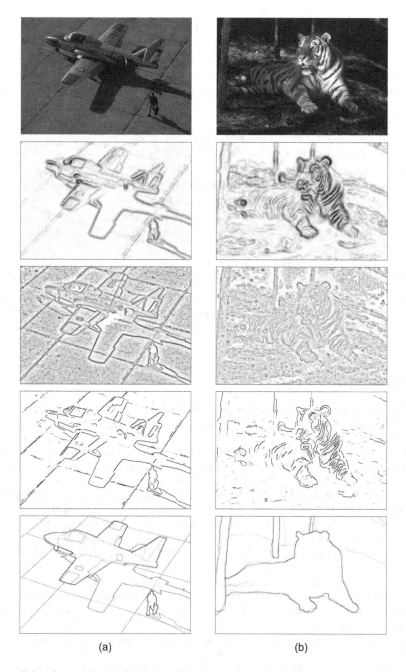

**Fig. 1.** Edge detection results on the two test images of (a) 'airplane' (#37073) and (b) 'tiger' (#108082) contained in BSDS300 dataset [6]. From top to bottom, given images, absolute gradient of the blurred images of Eq. (6), initial conditions $u(x, -\tau)$ of Eq. (10), edge maps created by the proposed algorithm and the ground-truth edge maps are shown. In the created edge maps, small edges having less than 3 pixels long were eliminated. These two results were evaluated as (a) $F = 0.83$ and (b) $F = 0.33$.

The performance evaluation result of the proposed algorithm was $F = 0.60$ for the test images; the larger F-measure shows the better performance. On the same dataset, that of the typical edge detection algorithm: gPb [7] was $F = 0.70$ and that of the classical algorithm Canny [9] was $F = 0.58$; these evaluation results shown in [10] were imported here for comparison. Although the proposed algorithm was evaluated slightly better than Canny, gPb was significantly better than the proposed algorithm.

Let us discuss edge detection results created from the two images 'airplane' and 'tiger' shown in Fig. 1. Figure 1(a) shows that the proposed algorithm successfully detected weak edges in the background; this is the evidence of effectiveness of the proposed initial conditions. On the other hand, Fig. 1(b) shows that the algorithm failed to detect contours of a tiger (the target object of the image). In order to detect the contours, we need to take account of discontinuity of texture patterns. This is the future work remaining in the reaction-diffusion algorithm.

In conclusion, this paper proposed novel initial conditions provided for the reaction-diffusion algorithm designed for image edge detection. The initial conditions are composed of sum of absolute gradient of multi-scale blurred images normalized by its blurred one. By applying the algorithm with the proposed initial condition to BSDS300 dataset, we confirmed its performance in comparison with other existing algorithms.

# References

1. Perona, P., Malik, J.: Scale-space and edge detection using anisotropic diffusion. IEEE Trans. Pattern Anal. Mach. Intell. **12**(7), 629–639 (1990). https://doi.org/10.1109/34.56205
2. Aubert, G., Kornprobst, P.: Mathematical Problems in Image Processing - Partial Differential Equations and the Calculus of Variations, 2nd edn, p. 379. Springer, New York (2006). https://doi.org/10.1007/978-0-387-44588-5
3. Nomura, A., Okada, K., Mizukami, Y.: Preprocessing in a reaction-diffusion algorithm designed for image edge detection. In: Proceedings of 2016 IEEE International Symposium on Signal Processing and Information Technology (ISSPIT), pp. 166–171 (2016). https://doi.org/10.1109/ISSPIT.2016.7886028
4. Nomura, A., Okada, K., Mizukami, Y.: Reaction-diffusion algorithm designed for image edge detection and its performance evaluation. In: Proceedings of the 12th International Conference on Computer Graphics, Visualization, Computer Vision and Image Processing, Part of the IADIS MCCSIS 2018, pp. 269–276 (2018)
5. Murray, J.D.: Mathematical Biology, 2nd edn. Springer, Heidelberg (1993). https://doi.org/10.1007/978-3-662-08542-4
6. The Berkeley Segmentation Dataset and Benchmark. https://www2.eecs.berkeley.edu/Research/Projects/CS/vision/grouping/segbench/. Accessed 24 May 2019
7. Martin, D., Fowlkes, C., Tal, D., Malik, J.: A database of human segmented natural images and its application to evaluating segmentation algorithms and measuring ecological statistics. In: Proceedings of 8th International Conference on Computer Vision, vol. 2, pp. 416–423 (2001)
8. Koenderink, J.J.: The structure of images. Biol. Cybern. **50**(5), 363–370 (1984). https://doi.org/10.1007/BF00336961

9. Canny, J.: A computational approach to edge detection. IEEE Trans. Pattern Anal. Mach. Intell. PAMI **8**(6), 679–698 (1986). https://doi.org/10.1109/TPAMI.1986.4767851

10. Arbelaez, P., Maire, M., Fowlkes, C., Malik, J.: Contour detection and hierarchical image segmentation. IEEE Trans. Pattern Anal. Mach. Intell. **33**(5), 898–916 (2010). https://doi.org/10.1109/TPAMI.2010.161

# Vision-Based Target Objects Recognition and Segmentation for Unmanned Systems Task Allocation

Wenbo Wu[1]($\boxtimes$), Pierre Payeur[1], Omar Al-Buraiki[1],
and Matthew Ross[2]

[1] Faculty of Engineering, University of Ottawa, Ottawa, ON, Canada
{wwu039,ppayeur,oalbu060}@uottawa.ca
[2] School of Psychology, University of Ottawa, Ottawa, ON, Canada
mross094@uottawa.ca

**Abstract.** This paper investigates the potential of deep learning methods to detect and segment objects from vision sensors mounted on autonomous robots to support task allocation in unmanned systems. An object instance segmentation framework, Mask R-CNN, is experimentally evaluated and compared with previous architecture, Faster R-CNN. The former model adds an object mask prediction branch in parallel with the existing branches for target objects location and class recognition, which represents a significant benefit for autonomous robots navigation. A comparison of performance between the two architectures is carried over scenes of varying complexity. While both networks perform well on recognition and bounding box estimation, experimental results show that Mask R-CNN generally outperforms Faster R-CNN, particularly because of the accurate mask prediction generated by this network. These results support well the requirements imposed by an automated task allocation mechanism for a group of unmanned vehicles.

**Keywords:** Object recognition · Deep learning · Classification ·
Segmentation · Unmanned systems · Task allocation ·
Collective robots coordination

## 1 Introduction

Unmanned systems are called to play a prominent role in the transportation industry, search-and-rescue operations, as well as in various military applications. To achieve their goal, autonomous robots still require significant improvement before self-determination of task distribution among the agents can be performed with minimal human intervention. Autonomous robots working in collaboration are investigated from the perspective of specialization, beyond particularities related only to their mechanical and physical construction. Specialization is defined at the capability level, from hardware and software embedded on specific agents, such as sensors, actuators, communication means, or computational resources. Addressing the problem of task allocation for robotic agents to perform specific missions from the point of view of their specialized capabilities leads to effective labor division. Under such a task allocation

F. Karray et al. (Eds.): ICIAR 2019, LNCS 11662, pp. 252–263, 2019.
https://doi.org/10.1007/978-3-030-27202-9_23

framework, individual agents interact with target objects as a cooperative team while dedicating the most qualified agent to perform specific tasks in response to perceived constraints in the environment. For it to be effective, reliable perception of these constraints is critical. This paper reports on an empirical study that investigates the potential of deep learning methods to recognize and segment target objects in unstructured environments from vision sensors mounted on autonomous robots. The objective is to experimentally evaluate the reliability of modern object recognition and segmentation methods to support efficient and responsive automated task allocation for unmanned robotic systems.

With the application of Convolutional Neural Networks (CNNs) to image recognition, unprecedented performance in object detection and segmentation was achieved in the last decade, especially with a family of methods referred to as region-based convolutional neural networks (R-CNNs) [1]. Such models are investigated here in the specific context of object recognition through vision sensors mounted on unmanned vehicles, such as UGVs or UAVS. Under the specialization constraints described above, objects considered of interest in a given environment are those that can be associated with a specific task to be executed by one or some of the robotic agents. The problem of visual target objects recognition and segmentation studied in this paper consists of deciding, for a given image, whether a certain class of objects is present and determining its location in space in order to efficiently and reliably support the allocation of the most competent agent to reach out to that given target object and perform a task on it. For the sake of development, the objects considered are inspired from search-and-rescue (SAR) operations. These include tasks such as finding and rescuing a person, reading signs to find direction in an environment, finding and opening doors, or finding and climbing stairs. The goal of this research is to experimentally identify deep learning structures that offer the best potential for target objects recognition and segmentation to support the coordination of specialized autonomous robotic agents.

## 2 State-of-the-Art

Multi-agent unmanned systems are comprised of multiple robots that interact with each other, while exhibiting collective behavior in their interaction with the environment. Previous work in multi-agent unmanned robotic systems has introduced various task-agent assignment solutions that emphasize the combination of forces contributed by all agents. For instance, techniques such as maximum agent-task matching [2], that match an equal number of robotic agents and tasks, or perfect matching [3], that assigns $n$ robots to $m$ tasks, consider robotic agents as equal contributors. Others leverage space division to allocate robotic agents based on proximity, with the task forming a grid assignment algorithm [4]. More elaborate models privilege a labor division approach, such as [5] that formulates a state transition probabilistic model to allocate changing tasks to agents, or monitor the object-action relevance [6, 7]. Wu et al. [8] take inspiration from the ant colony labor division model and use an environmental stimulus to transfer the individual agents between only two task states for the entire set of targets. However, these approaches do not attempt to match specialized capabilities of the individual autonomous agents with features detected on objects in their environment. Recent work has addressed the problem of task allocation from the perspective of specialized agents, while leveraging recognized characteristics on target objects [9].

Features detection and object class recognition on target objects that robotic agents encounter while exploring a workspace play a critical role for a reliable estimation of the respective agents' qualification and match with their specialization. Moreover, multi-agent navigation is closely related with the problem of target object detection, since the selected agent must be directed toward that target with maximum efficiency. Therefore, target object segmentation, simultaneously with classification, represents a major advantage. For these reasons, state-of-the-art deep learning methods that perform class-level detection simultaneously with segmentation of an object instance in an image are considered in this investigation. The Faster R-CNN, a region-based convolutional neural network [10], and the Mask R-CNN [11], which offers excellent potential for class-level detection combined with pixel-precise mask segmentation of each instance are closely studied and experimentally evaluated. The latter not only detects instances of different classes of objects in an image but also generates an image map that highlights the pixel distribution of each instance.

Faster R-CNN is a two-stage architecture for object detection [10]. The first stage is formed of a Region Proposal Network (RPN), shown in Fig. 1, that identifies potential candidates as regions of interest (RoI) with bounding boxes. It takes an image as input and outputs a set of rectangular object proposals, each with an objectness score. RPN is formed of a classifier and a regressor. The classifier determines the probability of a proposal containing the target object, while the regressor refines the coordinates of the proposals. For each object proposal, a pooling layer extracts a fixed-length feature vector from the feature map. The second stage extracts features from each proposal and performs category classification and bounding box regression. This is achieved by a sequence of fully connected layers that branch into two sibling outputs: one produces softmax probability estimates over K object classes plus a background class, and the other layer outputs real-valued numbers that position the bounding-box for each of the K object classes.

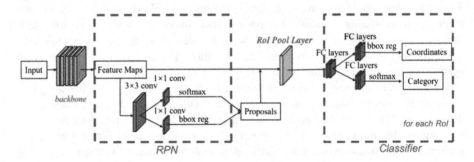

**Fig. 1.** Detailed two-stage structure of Faster R-CNN architecture.

Mask R-CNN architecture also supports a two-stage framework [11], as shown in Fig. 2. The first stage scans the image and generates proposals, while the second stage classifies the proposals and generates bounding boxes and segmentation masks that more accurately define the area occupied by each recognized object instance. The first stage performs similarly to Region Proposal Network in Faster R-CNN. However, in the second stage, the RoIAlign layer replaces the RoIPool layer to address misalignments introduced by the RoIPool operation in Faster R-CNN. A third branch is added as well in the classifier for predicting segmentation masks on each RoI, in parallel with the existing branches for classification and bounding box regression. The supplementary mask branch is a small Fully Convolutional Network (FCN) [12] that is applied to each RoI to predict a segmentation mask in a pixel-to-pixel manner. A mask encodes a specific input object's spatial layout. This data provides a more accurate definition of instances than the class labels or box offsets that are generated as fixed-size outputs by fully connected layers. In the operational context considered here, while the most qualified specialized agent is assigned solely from the recognized object class with highest confidence, or objectness score, the supplementary extraction of the spatial distribution of a recognized target object as a precisely segmented mask provides a more accurate pixel-to-pixel correspondence with each recognized object in the environment. This is of immediate benefit to plan the navigation of the assigned specialized robot toward the target object.

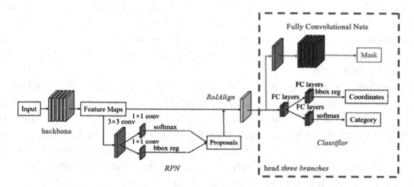

**Fig. 2.** Detailed two-stage structure of Mask R-CNN architecture.

## 3  Methodology

An experimental evaluation of two considered deep learning architectures, Faster R-CNN and Mask R-CNN, is conducted under the constraints imposed by the requirement to automate the task allocation process for specialized autonomous mobile agents. This application of object recognition and segmentation calls for reliable detection and classification of instances of predetermined objects of relevance in various environments. Specific intervention scenarios of relevance in SAR operations using heterogeneous mobile agents are considered, that include: inspecting space with vehicles equipped with multispectral sensors; recognizing doors to trigger the intervention of specialized agents equipped with a robotic arm and hand; recognizing people in various states (lost, unconscious, trapped, injured) to allocate specialized agents equipped with oxygen tank, or evacuation mechanisms; or recognizing posted signage to involve mobile agents equipped with high resolution cameras and natural language processing algorithms to find directions in unmapped environments.

Moreover, to refine the task-agent matching process beyond a simple lookup table allocation procedure, confidence in every target object detected and classified is estimated. It is well recognized that automated object recognition is not entirely reliable. The selected architectures must therefore provide a dynamic estimate of the degree of confidence on every instance of a recognized target object. This metric is directly leveraged in the task allocation framework that identifies the most qualified agent in accordance with the characteristics of the target. Finally, beyond object detection and classification from vision sensors, it is preferable to achieve accurate localization of the corresponding targets in the scene, for planning the trajectory of the allocated robotic agent identified to perform the given task. This section details the investigation process that was conducted to experimentally determine the suitability of deep learning object recognition architectures under these requirements.

### 3.1 Backbone Network

For experimental evaluation of the Mask-R CNN architecture, the implementation uses a Residual Network of depth 50 (ResNet-50) [13] and a Feature Pyramid Network (FPN) [14] architectures as a convolutional backbone for extracting features. ResNet-50 consists of 5 stages, each one involving a series of convolution layers of the same dimension. FPN extracts RoI features from different levels of the feature pyramid according to their scale.

For performing a comparison with Faster R-CNN, and given the similarity in between the topologies, a Faster R-CNN architecture was not trained individually. Instead the Mask R-CNN implementation was trained for the classification and bounding box branches while the mask branch was deactivated. The RoIPool layer was replaced with the RoIAlign layer for these tests. Section 4.1 reports on their comparative performance. Based on these early results, and given the extra benefits provided by the Mask R-CNN topology in extracting a precise segment for each object instance, further investigation concentrated on the latter architecture.

### 3.2 Data Preparation

Given that an image mask detailing the area occupied by every object instance is also generated by the Mask R-CNN architecture, the PASCAL Visual Object Classes (PASCAL VOC 2007) dataset [15] was selected for experimentation. The dataset contains 9963 images with predefined bounding boxes over 20 object categories, of which "person" is of immediate interest. For the sake of validation, other classes available such as "car", "train", "plants", are associated with tasks of interest in the considered scenarios. Besides the category annotation, this dataset provides a bounding box offset and segmentation masks annotation over 632 images. For these experiments, 400 images from the 632 having a mask label were selected as a training set, and another 100 images were used for testing, while comparing with the ground truth provided by the predefined classes and segmentation masks.

### 3.3   Evaluation Metrics

The evaluation metrics used for object detection and segmentation is the mean Average Precision (mAP). The value is calculated by generating predictions for each image in the test set, finding the average precision (AP) for each class independently, and taking the mean across all classes. For each class, every object detected of that class is classified as either a true positive (TP) or a false positive (FP). A true positive detection is defined as an object's bounding box having an intersection-over-union (IoU) ratio of at least 0.5 with the bounding box of the corresponding ground truth. Otherwise it is considered a false positive. For class recognition, precision measures the accuracy of the class prediction. For the segmentation component, AP is evaluated using the segmentation mask regions IoU, that is the IoU of the pixels in the segmented mask and ground truth mask.

### 3.4   Implementation Details

The network was initialized with a pre-trained model on the Microsoft COCO dataset [16] that provides a large number of pre-labelled images suited for object detection, but no mask segmentation. The head branches of the network were further adjusted and trained on the PASCAL VOC 2007 dataset that contains labelled mask areas. The training was performed in 3 stages, as shown in Fig. 3, that consisted of: (*i*) fixing all layers except the head, and train the head part; (*ii*) unfreezing the layers in ResNet-50 stage 4 and up, to train the region proposal part and head part; and (*iii*) unfreezing all layers and fine-tuning the whole model.

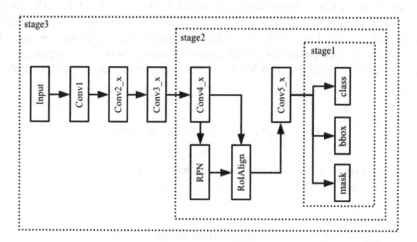

**Fig. 3.**   Three stages training strategy.

During the whole process, a stochastic gradient descent (SGD) optimizer was used, with starting learning rate of 0.001, weight decay of 0.0001, momentum of 0.9 and gradient clip norm of 5.0. Only in the last fine-tuning stage the learning rate is reduced to 0.0001.

The training was performed on an 8G memory NVIDIA Tesla P4 GPU configured in virtual machine supported by Google Compute Engine. The first stage was trained for 15 epochs, the second stage for 15 epochs and the third stage for 10 epochs. This limitation is mainly due to the significant amount of time and memory needed for training. It took about 1.46 h to train all 3 steps. Table 1 reports on the training time for each stage. In the testing phase, object recognition speed reached 3 to 5 frames per second.

**Table 1.** Training time per stage.

|          | Epochs | Steps per epoch | Average training time per epoch per step |
|----------|--------|-----------------|------------------------------------------|
| Stage 1  | 15     | 300             | 333 ms                                   |
| Stage 2  | 15     | 300             | 398 ms                                   |
| Stage 3  | 10     | 300             | 442 ms                                   |

## 4   Experimental Results

### 4.1   Comparative Object Class Recognition and Bounding Box Detection Results

A comparison on object detection performance (considering a bounding box mAP with a threshold at IoU = 0.5 for true positives, denoted by $mAP_{50}^{bb}$) between the Mask R-CNN and Faster R-CNN architectures is shown in Table 2. For Mask R-CNN, the full model was trained but only the category classification and the bounding box outputs were considered. For Faster R-CNN model, the implementation detailed in Sect. 3.1 was used and the corresponding classification and the bounding box outputs considered. The results demonstrate that Mask R-CNN outperforms Faster R-CNN on object detection.

**Table 2.** Object detection results comparison.

|                                    | Backbone network | $mAP_{50}^{bb}$ (%) |
|------------------------------------|------------------|---------------------|
| Faster R-CNN (with RoIAlign)       | ResNet-50-FPN    | 43.85               |
| Mask R-CNN                         | ResNet-50-FPN    | 59.36               |

### 4.2   Target Object Instances Segmentation Results

Images from the testing part of PASCAL VOC 2007 dataset were randomly selected and used for monitoring the performance of the Mask R-CNN model at recognizing instances of objects in the 20 classes and segmenting these objects. The mean average precision (mAP) achieved for instance segmentation is 67.0% over 100 test images. The precision for object recognition is 73.3%. Figure 4 illustrates the class, bounding box and segmentation mask prediction results and compares them with ground truth on various objects.

In Fig. 4a–f the bounding box (dotted lines) predictions closely correspond to the ground truth, while the segmentation mask predictions (colored areas) also match well, tend to be continuous, and form relatively accurate segmentation of the objects

| Ground Truth | Prediction Results | Ground Truth | Prediction Results |
|---|---|---|---|
|  |  | 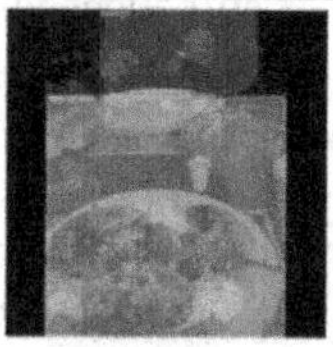 |  |
| a) car (yellow); person1(pink); person2 (blue); person3 (purple); person4 (green); person5 (yellow); person6 (red) | b) car (purple, 97.3%); person1 (yellow, 99.2%); person2 (cyan, 98.3%); person3 (red, 99.8%); person4 (green, 98.9%); person5 (blue, 99.6%); person6 (pink, 97.7%) | c) person (red); dining table (blue) | d) person (red, 98.4%); dining table (blue, 99.1%) |
|  |  |  |  |
| e) person1 (green); train (red); person2 (blue) | f) person1 (blue, 99.6 %); train (red, 99.6%); person2 (green, 91.8%) | g) potted plant (blue); person (yellow); potted plant (purple); potted plant (green); potted plant (red) | h) potted plant (yellow, 99.1 %); person (blue, 99.6%); potted plant (purple, 98.9%); potted plant (red, 98.2%); potted plant (green, 99.4%) |
|  |  |  |  |
| i) horse (red); person (green) | j) horse (red, 97.7%); person (green, 99.6%) | k) chair (blue); tvmonitor (red); chair (green) | l) chair (green, 97.7%); tvmonitor (purple, 99.0%); chair (red, 95.6%); false positive dining table (cyan, 61.4%) |

**Fig. 4.** Prediction results versus ground truth for class recognition with corresponding confidence level, and segmentation results on test samples from the PASCAL VOC 2007 dataset.

detected. Color codes are not associated to specific classes, which explains the change of color in between matched instances in the ground truth and prediction results images. Confidence level in the class prediction, shown in percentage under each prediction result, also offers excellent reliability, reaching over 95% in these examples. No false positive detection takes place, and only one person who is not fully visible on the upper right edge of Fig. 4b is missed.

When it comes to situations where the shape of objects is slender, as shown in Fig. 4g–h, or where an object is partially occluded, as shown in Fig. 4i–j, the trained Mask R-CNN architecture still succeeds to recognize and locate these instances with a high confidence level, but degradation is observed on the precision of the segmentation mask. Besides, in Fig. 4k–l, the desk, which is not a formal class in the PASCAL VOC 2007 dataset, was falsely recognized as a dining table, due to the similarity between the two types of objects. This result actually demonstrates that the Mask R-CNN architecture for target object recognition offers a significant level of robustness and is not restricted to visually explicit appearance of instances. This is a particularly suitable characteristic for application in automated task allocation for unmanned systems, as scenarios in which a group of autonomous vehicles are typically involved are far from being perfectly constrained and predefined. The fact that a lower level of confidence (61.4%) is associated with the recognition of a desk as a dining table serves as an indicator to the task allocation scheme to act with care, perhaps even triggering validation by a human supervisor before dispatching a robotic agent.

Given the limited number of 400 images used for training, with no more than 20 images for each class, and a training over only 40 epochs in 3 stages, as detailed in Table 1, the experimental recognition and segmentation results demonstrate the validity of the Mask R-CNN architecture for the application considered.

Validation was also performed on arbitrary images, not contained in the PASCAL VOC 2007 dataset, but depicting objects from classes the Mask R-CNN has learned to recognize (here a car, bus, person, TV monitor, sheep). A diversified range of complexity for object recognition cases in indoor and outdoor scenes is illustrated in Fig. 5. A single object (car) is successfully detected with 99.6% confidence in Fig. 5a, while the trailer is not detected as a false positive. Multiple instances of various classes are also properly classified and well segmented in Fig. 5b–f with confidence level varying from 65.7% to 99.9%, and with a limited number of false detections on smaller objects.

Given the two convolutional neural networks architectures investigated for object recognition in the context of automated robotic task allocation, the Mask R-CNN demonstrated its ability and reliability to recognize and locate instances of objects from a diversity of classes and with only limited training. The architecture proved its capability to associate accurate confidence level to the recognized classes, which provides an important trade-off between accuracy and flexibility, an important characteristic for the management of unmanned systems operating in less than perfect conditions and uncontrolled environments. Moreover, the architecture reliably generates detailed segmentation mask information to separate instances of objects. This characteristic provides additional benefits over only category classification and determination of a rectangular bounding box surrounding each object, as predicted by the Faster R-CNN architecture. Precise segmentation of an instance of target object leads to

**Fig. 5.** Prediction results for class recognition with confidence level, and segmentation on arbitrary images not from the training dataset but sharing similar classes.

efficient path planning for the most competent agent to navigate toward the identified target, which further reduces critical response time in search-and-rescue operations. The segmented area also determines a very specific search region in an image to detect and recognize features at a higher level of resolution, which opens the door to multi-stage object recognition to allocate specialized agents with more specificity.

## 5   Conclusion

This experimental investigation of modern convolutional neural network architectures to perform target objects detection, recognition and segmentation from vision sensors mounted on-board unmanned vehicles as an entry point to an automated task-agent allocation process demonstrated that the recently introduced Mask R-CNN architecture provides reliable performance for category classification, bounding box estimation and mask extraction of object instances in scenarios of various complexity. This solution supports well the requirements imposed by an automated task allocation mechanism for a heterogeneous group of specialized unmanned vehicles.

Future work will involve further refining the training of the architecture to comprehend more classes of immediate relevance to search-and-rescue operations, involving more substantial number of samples images and larger number of training epochs, which expectedly will lead to even better performance on specific class recognition and accurate segmentation of instances. Multi-stage recognition of specific features embedded in classes defined at a higher-level, as studied here, will be pursued with a stack of specialized CNNs. Further experimental validation will be performed with live image sequences collected from real-robot embedded cameras.

**Acknowledgements.** The authors wish to acknowledge the support from Department of National Defence of Canada toward this research under the Innovation for Defence Excellence and Security (IDEaS) program.

# References

1. Girshick, R., Donahue, J., Darrell, T., Malik, J.: Rich feature hierarchies for accurate object detection and semantic segmentation. In Proceedings of the IEEE Conference on Computer Vision and Pattern Recognition (2014)
2. Korte, B., Vygen, J.: Combinatorial Optimization: Theory and Algorithms. Algorithms and Combinatorics. Springer, Heidelberg (2008). https://doi.org/10.1007/3-540-29297-7
3. Hall, P.: On representatives of subsets. In: Gessel, I., Rota, G.C. (eds.) Classic Papers in Combinatorics. Modern Birkhäuser Classics, pp. 58–62. Birkhäuser, Boston (2009). https://doi.org/10.1007/978-0-8176-4842-8_4
4. Smith, S.L., Bullo, F.: Target assignment for robotic networks: asymptotic performance under limited communication. In: Proceedings American Control Conference, New York, NY, pp. 1155–1160 (2007)
5. Jones, C., Mataric, M.J.: Adaptive division of labor in large-scale minimalist multi-robot systems. In: Proceedings of the IEEE/RSJ International Conference on Intelligent Robots and Systems, Las Vegas, NV, USA, vol. 2, pp. 1969–1974 (2003)
6. Lang, T., Toussaint, M.: Relevance Grounding for Planning in Relational Domains. In: Buntine, W., Grobelnik, M., Mladenić, D., Shawe-Taylor, J. (eds.) ECML PKDD 2009. LNCS (LNAI), vol. 5781, pp. 736–751. Springer, Heidelberg (2009). https://doi.org/10.1007/978-3-642-04180-8_65
7. Toussaint, M., Plath, N., Lang, T., Jetchev, N.: Integrated motor control, planning, grasping and high-level reasoning in a blocks world using probabilistic inference. In: Proceedings of the IEEE International Conference on Robotics and Automation, Anchorage, AK, USA, pp. 385–391 (2010)
8. Wu, H., Li, H., Xiao, R., Liu, J.: Modeling and simulation of dynamic ant colony's labor division for task allocation of UAV swarm. Phys. A **491**, 127–141 (2018)
9. Al-Buraiki, O., Payeur, P.: Agent-Task assignation based on target characteristics for a swarm of specialized agents. In: 13th Annual IEEE International Systems Conference, Orlando, FL, pp. 268–275, April 2019
10. Ren, S., He, K., Girshik, R., Sun, J.: Faster R-CNN: towards real-time object detection with region proposal networks. In: Proceedings of the 28th International Conference on Neural Information Processing Systems, vol. 1, pp. 91–99, December 2015
11. He, K., Gkioxari, G., Dollar, P., Girshick, R.: Mask R-CNN, In: Proceedings of the IEEE International Conference on Computer Vision (2017)
12. Long, J., Shelhamer, E., Darrell, T.: Fully convolutional networks for semantic segmentation. In: Proceedings of the IEEE Conference on Computer Vision and Pattern Recognition, pp. 3431–3440, June 2015
13. He, K., Zhang, X., Ren, S., Sun, J.: Deep residual learning for image recognition. In: Proceedings of the IEEE Conference on Computer Vision and Pattern Recognition, pp. 770–778 (2016)
14. Lin, T.-Y., Dollar, P., Girshick, R., He, K., Hariharan, B., Belongie, S.: Feature pyramid networks for object detection. In: Proceedings of the IEEE Conference on Computer Vision and Pattern Recognition, pp. 936–944 (2017)

15. Everingham, M., Van Gool, L., Williams, C.K.I., Winn, J., Zisserman, A.: The PASCAL Visual Object Classes (VOC) challenge. Int. J. Comput. Vision **88**(2), 303–338 (2010)
16. Lin, T.-Y., et al.: Microsoft COCO: Common Objects in Context. In: Fleet, D., Pajdla, T., Schiele, B., Tuytelaars, T. (eds.) ECCV 2014. LNCS, vol. 8693, pp. 740–755. Springer, Cham (2014). https://doi.org/10.1007/978-3-319-10602-1_48

# Bayesian Learning of Infinite Asymmetric Gaussian Mixture Models for Background Subtraction

Ziyang Song, Samr Ali[(✉)], and Nizar Bouguila

Concordia University, Montreal, Canada
{zi_on,al_samr}@encs.concordia.ca, nizar.bouguila@concordia.ca

**Abstract.** Background subtraction plays an important role in many video-based applications such as video surveillance and object detection. As such, it has drawn much attention in the computer vision research community. Utilizing a Gaussian mixture model (GMM) has especially shown merit in solving this problem. However, a GMM is not ideal for modeling asymmetrical data. Another challenge we face when applying mixture models is the correct identification of the right number of mixture components to model the data at hand. Hence, in this paper, we propose a new infinite mathematical model based on asymmetric Gaussian mixture models. We also present a novel background subtraction approach based on the proposed infinite asymmetric Gaussian mixture (IAGM) model with a non-parametric learning algorithm. We test our proposed model on the challenging Change Detection dataset. Our evaluations show comparable to superior results with other methods in the literature.

**Keywords:** Infinite asymmetric gaussian mixture model ·
Gibbs sampling · MCMC · Metropolis-Hastings ·
Background subtraction

## 1 Introduction

Background subtraction is an active area of research in computer vision [1,2]. It is performed by using a reference image that contains only the background without any moving objects then subtracting the new frame from this image and thresholding to obtain the foreground [3]. Hence, it mainly involves the automatic segmentation of foreground regions in video sequences from the background [4]. This has many consequent applications such as in video surveillance [5], object detection [6], and anomaly detection [7].

Gaussian mixture models (GMM) is a commonly deployed approach that has been proposed for statistical modeling of foreground [8,9]. However, GMMs are not necessarily the ideal model since the background and foreground pixels are not always distributed according to a Gaussian distribution [10]. Hence, we

© Springer Nature Switzerland AG 2019
F. Karray et al. (Eds.): ICIAR 2019, LNCS 11662, pp. 264–274, 2019.
https://doi.org/10.1007/978-3-030-27202-9_24

investigate the employment of the asymmetric Gaussian mixture (AGM) which has two variance parameters for the left and right sides of each of the mixture components [11].

Parameter learning is one of the challenges required for the use of mixture models. A variety of algorithms may be deployed to achieve this purpose. For instance, the expectation maximization algorithm for the maximum likelihood method is one of the famous learning approaches [12]. Nonetheless, this deterministic approach suffers from several drawbacks that include over-fitting and high dependency on initialization [8,9]. This compromises the efficiency of the learning algorithm and negatively impacts the accuracy of the model. The author in [13] recently studied Bayesian learning of AGM. Such sampling-based approaches include the Markov Chain Monte Carlo (MCMC) introduces prior and posterior distributions in order to address the over-fitting issues whereby the dependency between the mixture parameters and mixture components is eradicated [14,15].

In this paper, we propose a novel mathematical model by extending the AGM to the infinity [16]. This addresses another important challenge that arises when applying mixture models; choosing the correct number of mixture components. We use the Dirichlet process [17,18] for precise allocation of the observations in and determining the number of components for the proposed model, the infinite asymmetric Gaussian mixture (IAGM). We apply a hierarchical Bayesian learning approach for the proposed model.

The contributions of this paper are then summarized as: (i) proposal and derivation of the IAGM model; (ii) hierarchical Bayesian learning of the IAGM model; (iii) testing and evaluation of the IAGM model for the background subtraction application. The rest of this paper is organized as follows. In Sect. 2, we outline the IAGM model and present a complete learning algorithm. We evaluate our proposed model for the background subtraction application and compare it to three other models in Sect. 3. Finally, we conclude the paper in Sect. 4.

## 2    Infinite Asymmetric Gaussian Mixture Model

### 2.1    Mathematical Model

A finite AGM model is denoted by:

$$p(\mathcal{X} \mid \Theta) = \prod_{i=1}^{N} \sum_{j=1}^{M} p_j p(X_i \mid \xi_j) \tag{1}$$

where $\mathcal{X} = (X_1, \ldots, X_N)$ is the $N$ observations dataset, each observation $X_i = (X_{i1}, \ldots, X_{iD})$ could be represented as $D$-dimensional random variable. $M \geq 1$ is the number of mixture components, $\Theta = (p_1, \ldots, p_M, \xi_1, \ldots, \xi_M)$ defines the complete set of parameters fully characterizing the mixture model where $\vec{p} = (p_1, \ldots, p_M)$ is the mixing weights which must be positive and sum to one, and $\xi_j$ is the set of parameters of mixture component $j$.

The asymmetric Gaussian density for each component, $p(X_i \mid \xi_j)$, is then given by:

$$p(X_i \mid \xi_j) \propto \prod_{k=1}^{D} \frac{1}{(S_{l_{jk}})^{-\frac{1}{2}} + (S_{r_{jk}})^{-\frac{1}{2}}} \times \begin{cases} \exp\left[-\frac{S_{l_{jk}}(X_{ik}-\mu_{jk})^2}{2}\right] & if\ X_{ik} < \mu_{jk} \\ \exp\left[-\frac{S_{r_{jk}}(X_{ik}-\mu_{jk})^2}{2}\right] & if\ X_{ik} \geq \mu_{jk} \end{cases} \tag{2}$$

where $\xi_j = (\mu_j, S_{l_j}, S_{r_j})$ is the parameter set for the asymmetric Gaussian distribution with $\mu_j = (\mu_{j_1}, \ldots, \mu_{j_d})$, $S_{l_j} = (S_{l_{j_1}}, \ldots, S_{l_{j_d}})$ and $S_{r_j} = (S_{r_{j_1}}, \ldots, S_{r_{j_d}})$. $\mu_{jk}$, $S_{l_{jk}}$ and $S_{r_{jk}}$ are the mean, the left precision and the right precision of the $k$th dimensional distribution. In this paper, we assume independence so that the covariance matrix of $X_i$ is diagonal matrix. This assumption allows us to avoid costly computation during deployment.

We introduce the latent indicator variable $Z = (Z_1, \ldots, Z_N)$, $Z_i$ for each observation $X_i$ to indicate which component it belongs to. $Z_i = (Z_{i1}, \ldots, Z_{iM})$ where hidden label $Z_{ij}$ is assigned as 1 if $X_i$ belongs to component j otherwise will be set to 0. The likelihood function is then defined by:

$$p(\mathcal{X} \mid Z, \Theta) = \prod_{i=1}^{N} p(X_i \mid \xi_j)^{Z_{ij}} \tag{3}$$

Given the mixing weights $\vec{p}$ with $p_j = Z_{ij} = 1$, for $j = 1, \ldots, M$, $Z$ is given a Multinomial prior:

$$p(Z \mid \vec{p}) = Multi(\vec{p}) = \prod_{j=1}^{M} p_j^{n_j} \tag{4}$$

where $n_j$ is the number of observations that are associated with component $j$. The mixing weights are considered to follow a symmetric Dirichlet distribution with a concentration parameter $\alpha/M$:

$$p(\vec{p} \mid \alpha) \sim Dirichlet(\frac{\alpha}{M}, \ldots, \frac{\alpha}{M}) = \frac{\Gamma(\alpha)}{\Gamma(\frac{\alpha}{M})^M} \prod_{j=1}^{M} p_j^{\frac{\alpha}{M}-1} \tag{5}$$

We then integrate out the mixing weights $\vec{p}$ to obtain the prior of $Z$:

$$p(Z \mid \alpha) = \int p(Z \mid \vec{p}) p(\vec{p} \mid \alpha) d\vec{p} = \frac{\Gamma(\alpha)}{\Gamma(N+\alpha)} \prod_{j=1}^{M} \frac{\Gamma(\frac{\alpha}{M} + n_j)}{\Gamma(\frac{\alpha}{M})} \tag{6}$$

The conditional prior for a single indicator is then denoted by:

$$p(Z_{ij} = 1 \mid \alpha, Z_{-i}) = \frac{n_{-i,j} + \frac{\alpha}{M}}{N - 1 + \alpha} \tag{7}$$

Where the subscript $-i$ defines all indexes except $i$, $Z_{-i} = (Z_1, \ldots, Z_{i-1}, Z_{i+1}, \ldots, Z_N)$, $N_{-i,j}$ is the number of observations excluding $X_i$ in component $j$.

Next, we extend the model to infinity by updating the posteriors of indicators in Eq. (7) with $M \to \infty$:

$$p(Z_{ij} = 1 \mid \alpha, Z_{-i}) = \begin{cases} \frac{n_{-i,j}}{N-1+\alpha}, & if \ n_{-i,j} > 0 \\ \frac{\alpha}{N-1+\alpha}, & if \ n_{-i,j} = 0 \end{cases} \tag{8}$$

where $n_{-i,j} > 0$ occurs only when component $j$ is represented. Thus, an observation $X_i$ is associated with an existing component by a certain probability proportional to the number of observations already allocated to this component; while a new (when unrepresented) component is proportional to $\alpha$ and $N$. Given the conditional priors in Eq. (7), the conditional posteriors are obtained by multiplying the priors with Eq. (3) resulting in:

$$p(Z_{ij} = 1 \mid ...) = \begin{cases} \frac{n_{-i,j}}{N-1+\alpha} \prod_{k=1}^{d} p(X_{ik} \mid \xi_{jk}), & if \ n_{-i,j} > 0 \\ \frac{\alpha}{N-1+\alpha} \int p(X_i \mid \xi_j) p(\xi_j \mid \lambda, r, \beta_l, \beta_r, w_l, w_r) d\xi_j, & if \ n_{-i,j} = 0 \end{cases} \tag{9}$$

where the hyperparameter $\alpha$ is defined by an inverse Gamma prior with shape parameter $a$ and mean $b$ chosen as follows:

$$p(\alpha^{-1}) \propto \alpha^{-\frac{3}{2}} \exp(-\frac{1}{2\alpha}) \tag{10}$$

Given the likelihood of $\alpha$ in Eq. (6), the posterior is then:

$$p(\alpha \mid M, N) \propto \frac{\alpha^{\frac{M-3}{2}} \exp(-\frac{1}{2\alpha})\Gamma(\alpha)}{\Gamma(N+\alpha)} \tag{11}$$

The conditional posterior for $\alpha$ depends only on number of observations, $N$, and the number of components, $M$. The logarithmic representation of posteriors is log-concave, so we can sample $\alpha$ by using the Adaptive Rejection Sampling (ARS) method [19].

## 2.2   Bayesian Learning

In this section, we describe an MCMC-based approach for learning the proposed IAGM model as shown in Fig. 1. The means of the component $\mu_{jk}$ are given Gaussian priors with hyperparameters $\lambda$ and $r$ as follows:

$$p(\mu_{jk} \mid \lambda, r) \sim \mathcal{N}(\lambda, r^{-1}). \tag{12}$$

where the mean, $\lambda$, and precision, $r$, hyperparameters are common to all components in a specific dimension. $\lambda$ is given Gaussian priors with mean $e$ and variance $f$, and $r$ is given Gaussian priors and inverse Gamma priors with shape parameter $g$ and mean parameter $h$ respectively:

$$p(\lambda) \sim \mathcal{N}(e, f) \tag{13}$$

$$p(r) \sim \Gamma(g, h) \tag{14}$$

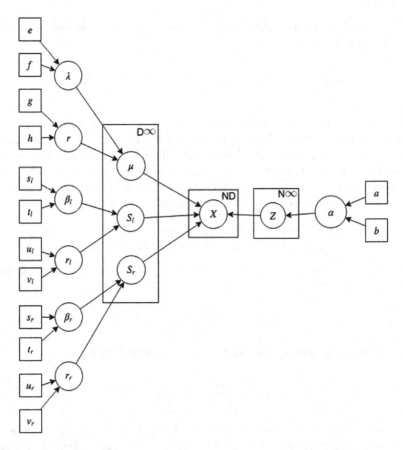

**Fig. 1.** Graphical model representation of the IAGM model. The random variables are in circles, and the model parameters in squares. The number mentioned in the right upper corner of the plates indicates the number of repetition of the contained random variables. The arcs describe the conditional dependencies between variables.

where $e$ and $f$ will be $\mu_y$ and $\sigma_y^2$, the mean and variance of the observations which are used for the parameters of the Gaussian priors. The Gamma priors use constant values 1 as shape $g$ and $\sigma_y^2$ as mean $h$ to represent.

The conditional posterior distribution for the mean $\mu_{jk}$ is then computed by multiplying the likelihood from Eq. (3) by the prior Eq. (12) as follows:

$$p(\mu_{jk} \mid X_k, S_{l_{jk}}, S_{r_{jk}}, \lambda, r) \propto \mathcal{N}(\frac{S_{l_{jk}} \sum_{i:X_{ik}<\mu_{jk}}^n X_{ik} + s_{r_{jk}} \sum_{i:X_{ik}\geq\mu_{jk}}^n X_{ik} + r\lambda}{r + ps_{l_{jk}} + (n_j - p)s_{r_{jk}}},$$

$$\frac{1}{r + ps_{l_{jk}} + (n_j - p)s_{r_{jk}}}) \tag{15}$$

Where $X_k$ is the $k$th dimensional observation allocated to component $j$. $n_j$ is the count of $X_k$ and $p$ is the count of $X_k$ which are less than $\mu_{jk}$. $\sum_{i:X_{ik}<\mu_{jk}} X_{ik}$ and $\sum_{i:X_{ik}\geq\mu_{jk}}^n X_{ik}$ are the sums of the observations which are less than and greater than $\mu_{jk}$ respectively. For the hyperparmeters $\lambda$ and $r$, we use hyperposteriors to update parameters. Equation (12) plays the role of the likelihood function. As such, we combine Eq. (12), Eq. (13) and Eq. (14) to obtain the following posteriors:

$$p(\lambda \mid \mu_{1k}, \ldots, \mu_{Mk}, r) \propto \mathcal{N}(\frac{\mu_y \sigma_y^{-2} + r \sum_{j=1}^{M} \mu_{jk}}{\sigma_y^{-2} + Mr}, \frac{1}{\sigma_y^{-2} + Mr}) \tag{16}$$

$$p(r \mid \mu_{1k}, \ldots, \mu_{Mk}, \lambda) \propto \Gamma(M+1, \frac{M+1}{\sigma_y^2 + \sum_{j=1}^{M}(\mu_{jk} - \lambda)^2}) \tag{17}$$

The component precision $S_{l_{jk}}$ and $S_{r_{jk}}$ are given Gamma priors with common hyperparameters $\beta$ and $w^{-1}$ as follows:

$$p(S_{l_{jk}} \mid \beta, w) \sim \Gamma(\beta, w^{-1}), \quad p(S_{r_{jk}} \mid \beta, w) \sim \Gamma(\beta, w^{-1}) \tag{18}$$

where $\beta$ is given inverse Gamma priors with shape parameter $s$ and mean parameter $t$, and $w$ is given Gamma priors with shape parameters $u$ and $v$:

$$p(\beta^{-1}) \sim \Gamma(s, t) \tag{19}$$

$$p(w) \sim \Gamma(u, v) \tag{20}$$

Where we set both of mean and shape parameters of hyperprior $\beta$ as constant value 1, and mean and shape parameters of hyperprior $w$ are defined as 1 and $\sigma_y^2$ respectively. The conditional posterior distribution for left precision $S_{l_{jk}}$ and right precision $S_{r_{jk}}$ are obtained by multiplying the likelihood from Eq. (3) by the prior Eq. (18) as follows:

$$p(S_{l_{jk}} \mid X_k, \mu_{jk}, S_{r_{jk}}, \beta, w) \propto (S_{l_{jk}}^{-\frac{1}{2}} + S_{l_{jk}}^{-\frac{1}{2}}) S_{l_{jk}}^{\frac{\beta}{2}-1}$$
$$\exp\left[-\frac{S_{l_{jk}} \sum_{i:X_{ik} < \mu_{jk}}^{n}(x_{ik} - \mu_{jk})^2}{2} - \frac{w\beta S_{l_{jk}}}{2}\right] \tag{21}$$

Random samples of posteriors can be drawn by using the MCMC method. In our work, we use Metropolis–Hastings algorithm to sample precision parameters. For the hyperparameters $\beta$ and $w$, the equation Eq. (18) plays the role of the likelihood function. Combining Eq. (12), Eq. (19), and Eq. (20), we obtain the following posteriors:

$$p(\beta_l \mid S_{l_{1k}}, \ldots, S_{l_{Mk}}, w_l) \propto \Gamma(\frac{\beta_l}{2})^{-M} \exp(-\frac{1}{2\beta_l})(\frac{\beta_l}{2})^{\frac{M\beta_l-3}{2}}$$
$$\prod_{j=1}^{M}(w_l S_{l_{jk}})^{\frac{\beta_l}{2}} \exp(-\frac{\beta_l w_l S_{l_{jk}}}{2}) \tag{22}$$

$$p(w_l \mid S_{l_{1k}}, \ldots, S_{l_{Mk}}, \beta_l) \propto \Gamma(M\beta_l + 1, \frac{M\beta_l + 1}{\sigma_y^{-2} + \beta_l \sum_{j=1}^{M} S_{l_{jk}}}) \tag{23}$$

where we only show the left side of $\beta$ and $w$ parameters with similar posteriors for the right side parameters. The posterior distribution of precision $\beta$ is not a standard form, but its logarithmic posterior is log-concave. Therefore, we can sample from the distribution for $\log(\beta)$ using ARS technique and transform the resultant to get values for $\beta$.

The proposed complete algorithm can be summarized by the following:

---

**Algorithm 1.** IAGM algorithm

---

1: **procedure**
2:     initialize assignments and parameters
3: *loop:*
4:     Update mixture parameters $\mu_j$, $S_{l_{jk}}$ and $S_{r_{jk}}$ from posteriors in Eq. (15) and Eq. (21).
5:     Update hyperparameters $\lambda$, $r$, $\beta$, $w$ and Dirichlet process concentration parameter $\alpha$ from posteriors in Eq. (16), (17), (22), (23) and (11).
6:     Update the indicators conditioned on the other indicators and the hyperparameters from Eq. (9).
7:     The convergence criteria is reached when the difference of the current value of joint posteriors and the previous value is less than $10^{-4}$. Otherwise, repeat above procedures until convergence.

---

## 3    Experimental Setup

### 3.1    Background Subtraction Application

In this section, we employ the proposed IAGM model for video background subtraction with a pixel-level evaluation approach as in [8]. The background subtraction methodology starts off by constructing the model using the proposed IAGM model. After applying the learning algorithm for the model, we discriminate between the mixture components for the representation of foreground and background pixels for each of the new input frames.

Assume that each video frame has $P$ number pixels such that $\vec{\mathcal{X}} = (\mathcal{X}_1, \ldots, \mathcal{X}_P)$ then each pixel $\mathcal{X}$ is assigned as a foreground or background pixel according to the trained IAGM model $p(\mathcal{X} \mid \Theta) = \prod_{i=1}^{N} \sum_{j=1}^{M} p_j p(X_i \mid \xi_j)$. Components that occurs frequently, i.e. high $p$ value, and with a low standard deviation $S^{-\frac{1}{2}}$) are modeled as the background.

Accordingly, the value of $p_j / (||S_{l_j}^{-\frac{1}{2}}|| + ||S_{r_j}^{-\frac{1}{2}}||)$ is used to order the mixture components, where $p_j$ is the mixing weight for component $j$, $||S_{l_j}^{-\frac{1}{2}}||$ and $||S_{r_j}^{-\frac{1}{2}}||$ are the respective norms of left and right standard deviations of the $j$ component [8]. The first $B$ number of components are chosen to model the background, with $B$ estimated as:

$$B = \arg\min_b \sum_{j=1}^{b} p_j > T \tag{24}$$

where $T$ is a measure of the minimum proportion of the data that represents the background in the scene, and the rest of the components are defined as foreground components.

## 3.2 Results and Discussion

We apply the proposed algorithm to the Change Detection dataset [20]. The dataset consists of six categories with a total of 31 videos totaling 90,000 frames. Each of the categories (baseline, dynamic background, camera jitter, shadows, intermittent object motion, and thermal) contains around 4 to 6 different videos sequences from low-resolution IP cameras.

In this paper, we have selected five videos from the Change Detection dataset to evaluate our proposed methodology. We initialize the IAGM by incrementally increasing the threshold multiple times and choosing the optimum parameter setting. We adopt the threshold factor $T = 0.9$ in our method. We set the maximum component number for the algorithm as 9 and the standard deviation factor $K = 2$. Evaluations of the proposed IAGM can be observed in the confusion matrices in Fig. 2. Moreover, Fig. 3 show visual results of our proposed method on samples frames in the Library and Street Light video sequences.

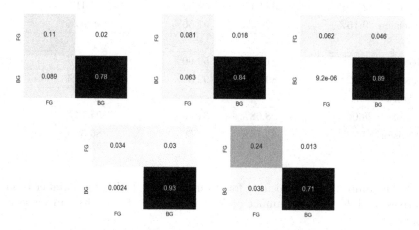

**Fig. 2.** Confusion matrices of the proposed method employed for background subtraction on the boulevard (top left), abandoned box (top center), street light (top right), sofa (bottom left), and library (bottom right) videos where FG denotes the foreground and BG denotes the background.

We also compare our results with three other methods from the literature. These include the Gaussian mixture model-based background subtraction algorithms by Sauffer et al. [8] and Zivkovic [9] as well as the finite asymmetric Gaussian mixture model by Elguebaly et al. [3]. We evaluate the performance of the algorithms in terms of the recall and the precision metrics. These are defined respectively as Recall $= TP/(TP + FN)$ and precision $= TP/(TP + FP)$ where

**Fig. 3.** A sample frame from Street Light (left) and Library (right) video sequences and the detected foreground object respectively.

**Table 1.** Experimental results for the background subtraction application.

|  | Stauffer et al. [8] | Zivkovic [9] | Elguebaly et al. [3] | IAGM (proposed) |
|---|---|---|---|---|
| *Boulevard* | | | | |
| Recall | 83.21% | 79.77% | 79.54% | 84.72% |
| Precision | 40.02% | 43.79% | 61.13% | 55.80% |
| *Abandoned Box* | | | | |
| Recall | 45.74% | 45.64% | 45.18% | 81.53% |
| Precision | 65.52% | 62.14% | 67.41% | 56.23% |
| *Street Light* | | | | |
| Recall | 32.25% | 33.94% | 30.33% | 57.41% |
| Precision | 89.16% | 92.47% | 97.56% | 99.99% |
| *Sofa* | | | | |
| Recall | 51.62% | 51.41% | 59.90% | 53.56% |
| Precision | 85.92% | 89.25% | 92.52% | 93.41% |
| *Library* | | | | |
| Recall | 28.00% | 28.68% | 31.33% | 94.74% |
| Precision | 84.76% | 81.76% | 94.66% | 86.52% |

$TP$ is the number of true positive foreground pixels, $FN$ is the number of false negatives, and $FP$ is the number of false positives. The results can be seen in Table 1.

As can be observed in Table 1, the proposed IAGM model mostly outperforms the other methodologies in terms of the recall metric, while achieving comparable precision results. For instance, IAGM attains better recall results for the Street Light video sequence with a near perfect precision. This clearly demonstrates the effectiveness of our proposed model and approach.

In particular, our approach detects more foreground pixels; most of which are clustered correctly. This ensures comparable precision results compared with the other algorithms. Our method does not remarkably improve the precision metric due to the sensitivity of the proposed method to the change in environments. With higher number of detected foreground pixels, our approach shows significant improvement in the recall metric. This improvement is especially distinct for the Library video.

These improvements are due to the nature of the IAGM model that is capable of accurately capturing the asymmetry of the observations. This higher flexibility of asymmetric Gaussian distribution allows the incorporation of the different shape distributions of objects. Furthermore, the extension to the infinite mixture using the Dirichlet process with a stick-breaking construction increases adaptability of the proposed model. Hence, we addressed both the parameter learning and the mixture component number determination challenges. These advantages provide a more efficient model for background subtraction.

## 4   Conclusion

We propose a new infinite mixture model, IAGM, that is capable of modeling the asymmetry of data in contrast to the traditionally deployed GMM. Moreover, we address the challenges of parameter learning and choosing the right number of components through the employment of Bayesian learning and extension of the AGM model to infinity. Furthermore, we demonstrate the efficiency of our model by utilizing it for the background subtraction application. Our achieved results are comparable to three different methods in terms of precision, and superior in terms of the recall metric. Finally, our future plan considers Variational Inference to improve learning speed.

**Acknowledgments.** The completion of this research was made possible thanks to the Natural Sciences and Engineering Research Council of Canada (NSERC).

## References

1. Sakpal, N.S., Sabnis, M.: Adaptive background subtraction in images. In: 2018 International Conference on Advances in Communication and Computing Technology (ICACCT), pp. 439–444, February 2018
2. Fan, W., Bouguila, N.: Video background subtraction using online infinite dirichlet mixture models. In: 21st European Signal Processing Conference, EUSIPCO 2013, Marrakech, Morocco, 9–13 September, pp. 1–5 (2013)
3. Elguebaly, T., Bouguila, N.: Background subtraction using finite mixtures of asymmetric gaussian distributions and shadow detection. Mach. Vis. Appl. **25**(5), 1145–1162 (2014)
4. Tang, C., Ahmad, M.O., Wang, C.: Foreground segmentation in video sequences with a dynamic background. In: 2018 11th International Congress on Image and Signal Processing, BioMedical Engineering and Informatics (CISP-BMEI), pp. 1–6. IEEE (2018)
5. Hedayati, M., Zaki, W.M.D.W., Hussain, A.: Real-time background subtraction for video surveillance: from research to reality. In: 2010 6th International Colloquium on Signal Processing its Applications, pp. 1–6, May 2010
6. Bouguila, N., Ziou, D.: Using unsupervised learning of a finite dirichlet mixture model to improve pattern recognition applications. Pattern Recogn. Lett. **26**(12), 1916–1925 (2005)

7. Bilge, Y.C., Kaya, F., Cinbis, N.,Çelikcan, U., Sever, H.: Anomaly detection using improved background subtraction. In: 2017 25th Signal Processing and Communications Applications Conference (SIU), pp. 1–4, May 2017

8. Stauffer, C., Grimson, W.E.L.: Adaptive background mixture models for real-time tracking. In: Proceedings 1999 IEEE Computer Society Conference on Computer Vision and Pattern Recognition (Cat. No PR00149), vol. 2, pp. 246–252. IEEE (1999)

9. Zivkovic, Z.: Improved adaptive gaussian mixture model for background subtraction. In: null, pp. 28–31. IEEE (2004)

10. Wang, D., Xie, W., Pei, J., Lu, Z.: Moving area detection based on estimation of static background. J. Inf. Comput. Sci. $2$(1), 129–134 (2005)

11. Fu, S., Bouguila, N.: A bayesian intrusion detection framework. In: 2018 International Conference on Cyber Security and Protection of Digital Services (Cyber Security), pp. 1–8 (2018)

12. Bouguila, N., Ziou, D.: Unsupervised selection of a finite dirichlet mixture model: an mml-based approach. IEEE Trans. Knowl. Data Eng. $18$(8), 993–1009 (2006)

13. Elguebaly, T., Bouguila, N.: Simultaneous high-dimensional clustering and feature selection using asymmetric gaussian mixture models. Image Vision Comput. $34$, 27–41 (2015)

14. Carlin, B.P., Chib, S.: Bayesian model choice via markov chain monte carlo methods. J. Roy. Stat. Soc.: Ser. B (Methodol.) $57$(3), 473–484 (1995)

15. Elguebaly, T., Bouguila, N.: A nonparametric bayesian approach for enhanced pedestrian detection and foreground segmentation. In: IEEE Conference on Computer Vision and Pattern Recognition, CVPR Workshops 2011, Colorado Springs, CO, USA, 20–25 June, pp. 21–26 (2011)

16. Elguebaly, Tarek, Bouguila, Nizar: Infinite generalized gaussian mixture modeling and applications. In: Kamel, Mohamed, Campilho, Aurélio (eds.) ICIAR 2011. LNCS, vol. 6753, pp. 201–210. Springer, Heidelberg (2011). https://doi.org/10.1007/978-3-642-21593-3_21

17. Bouguila, N., Ziou, D.: A countably infinite mixture model for clustering and feature selection. Knowl. Inf. Syst. $33$(2), 351–370 (2012)

18. Bouguila, N.: Infinite liouville mixture models with application to text and texture categorization. Pattern Recogn. Lett. $33$(2), 103–110 (2012)

19. Rasmussen, C.E.: The infinite gaussian mixture model. In: Solla, S.A., Leen, T.K., Müller, K. (eds.) Advances in Neural Information Processing Systems, vol. 12, pp. 554–560. MIT Press, Cambridge (2000)

20. Wang, Y., Jodoin, P.M., Porikli, F., Konrad, J., Benezeth, Y., Ishwar, P.: CDnet 2014: an expanded change detection benchmark dataset. In: Proceedings of the IEEE Conference on Computer Vision and Pattern Recognition Workshops, pp. 387–394 (2014)

# Deep Demosaicing for Edge Implementation

Ramchalam Ramakrishnan[1], Shangling Jui[2], and Vahid Partovi Nia[1(✉)]

[1] Huawei Noah's Ark Lab, Montreal, Canada
vahid.partovinia@huawei.com
[2] Huawei Kirin Solution, Shanghai, China

**Abstract.** Most digital cameras use sensors coated with a Color Filter Array (CFA) to capture channel components at every pixel location, resulting in a mosaic image that does not contain pixel values in all channels. Current research on reconstructing these missing channels, also known as *demosaicing*, introduces many artifacts, such as *zipper effect* and *false color*. Many deep learning demosaicing techniques outperform other classical techniques in reducing the impact of artifacts. However, most of these models tend to be over-parametrized. Consequently, edge implementation of the state-of-the-art deep learning-based demosaicing algorithms on low-end edge devices is a major challenge. We provide an exhaustive search of deep neural network architectures and obtain a Pareto front of Color Peak Signal to Noise Ratio (CPSNR) as the performance criterion versus the number of parameters as the model complexity that outperforms the state-of-the-art. Architectures on the Pareto front can then be used to choose the best architecture for a variety of resource constraints. Simple architecture search methods such as exhaustive search and grid search requires some conditions of the loss function to converge to the optimum. We clarify these conditions in a brief theoretical study.

**Keywords:** Deep learning · Demosaicing · Edge computing · Network architecture search

## 1 Introduction

Deep Learning is changing lives on a day to day basis. Overparametrization of deep models can have an impact in their deployment for variety of applications. For instance, model size could adversely affect the real-time updates in mobile phone implementation. Moreover, the training and inference time increases for a large model. For instance, ResNet152 takes 1.5 weeks to train on the Image-Net dataset using one Nvidia TitanX GPU [4]. In terms of hardware, much of the impact of such models is in the energy consumption. As an example, Dynamic Random Access Memory (DRAM) consumes most of the energy at inference. Therefore, it is imperative to reduce the model size [3].

© Springer Nature Switzerland AG 2019
F. Karray et al. (Eds.): ICIAR 2019, LNCS 11662, pp. 275–286, 2019.
https://doi.org/10.1007/978-3-030-27202-9_25

The success of deep learning models has been proven in many high-level vision tasks such as image classification and object detection. However, deep learning solutions are less explored for low-level vision problems where the edge implementation is an obligation. Previous work shows the effectiveness on other low-level vision problems such as image denoising and image demosaicing [16]. Here we explore various architectures for demosaicing, with the aim of finding suitable models for deployment on the edge. It is imperative to make use of models that can be stored on edge devices.

## 2    Demosaicing

Image demosaicing involves interpolating full-resolution images from incomplete color samples produced by an image sensor. Limitations in camera sensor resolution and sensitivity leads to the problem of mosaicing. For a digital camera to capture or produce a full color image, it uses sensors to detect all 3 colors (RGB) at every pixel location. One way this is done involves using a beam-splitter to project the image onto three separate sensors, see Fig. 1a, one for each color (RGB). Color filters are placed in front of each sensor to filter specific wavelengths such that three full-channel color images are obtained. This is a costly process that is generally used in scientific-grade microscopes. Most digital cameras, on the other hand, make use of just one sensor coated with a Color Filter Array (CFA). In this system, one color component is captured at every pixel location and the missing channels are reconstructed. The resultant image is often called a mosaic image, derived from the CFA's mosaic pattern. This mosaic image is then subjected to software-based interpolation, resulting in a full-resolution image; a process termed as *demosaicing*.

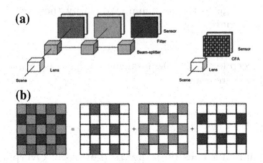

**Fig. 1.** a. Optical path for multi-chip and single-chip digital camera, b. Bayer Pattern in single-chip digital cameras, borrowed from [6]. (Color figure online)

Various existing CFA patterns are currently used, with the Bayer CFA being the most commonly used approach for mosaicing. The Bayer CFA measures the green image on *quincinx* grid, and the red/blue on the rectangular grids (Fig. 1b). The green channel has higher sampling because the human retina has a higher sensitivity toward the green wavelength.

Let $I^{CFA} : \mathbb{Z}^2 \rightarrow \mathbb{Z}^3$ denote an $M \times N$ Bayer CFA image. If we consider the sampling pattern shown in Fig. 1b, then the mosaic image is as follows:

$$I(i,j) = \begin{cases} R_{i,j} & \text{for i odd and j even,} \\ B_{i,j} & \text{for i even and j odd,} \\ G_{i,j} & \text{Otherwise,} \end{cases} \quad (1)$$

where $R_{i,j}$, $G_{i,j}$, $B_{i,j}$ includes values between 0 and 255. To estimate the missing two missing channels for each pixel location using demosaicing,

$$\hat{I}(i,j) = \begin{cases} (R_{i,j}, \hat{B}_{i,j}, \hat{G}_{i,j}) & \text{for i odd and j even,} \\ (\hat{R}_{i,j}, B_{i,j}, \hat{G}_{i,j}) & \text{for i even and j odd,} \\ (\hat{R}_{i,j}, \hat{B}_{i,j}, G_{i,j}) & \text{Otherwise,} \end{cases} \quad (2)$$

where $\hat{R}_{i,j}, \hat{G}_{i,j}, \hat{B}_{i,j}$ are the estimates for the channels at each pixel location.

Demosaicing approaches are divided into various categories: 1. Edge-sensitive methods, 2. Directional interpolation and decision methods, 3. Frequency domain approaches, 4. Wavelet-based methods, 5. Statistical reconstruction techniques, and 6. Deep learning [9]. Early studies in bi-linear/bi-cubic [18] and spline interpolation make use of single-channel interpolation techniques that treat each channel separately, without using the inter-channel information and correlation. For instance, bi-linear interpolation computes the red value of a non-red pixel as the average of the 2/4 adjacent red pixels; this method is then repeated with the blue and green pixels. Many comparatively advanced algorithms use the results of bi-linear interpolation as a baseline. These algorithms make use of a weighted average of the neighboring pixels to fill the missing channel values.

Recently, neural network approaches like convolutional neural networks (CNN) have been effectively used for joint denoising and demosaicing [2]. This method down-samples the mosaiced image using multiple convolutions and computes the residual at lower resolution; this is further concatenated with the input mosaic image. The final output is then calculated using another group of convolutions at full resolution to reconstruct the full resolution image. Studies [14] have also used Deep Residual Learning for image demosaicing for Bayer CFA. This neural network uses a two-stage architecture: (1) the first step recovers an intermediate result of the Green and Red/Blue channel separately as a guiding prior to use as input for the second stage, (2) the final demosaiced image is reconstructed.

The current state-of-the-art model, DMCNN-VD [13] architecture (Fig. 2) consists of a deep network that uses same dimensions for the input and output layers. They use the Bayer CFA mosaic layer and 20 blocks (CNN, BN, SELU), instead of the 3 layers in the DMCNN model.

## 2.1 Artifacts

Although various approaches to the demosaicing problem have been discussed, most techniques have a propensity to introduce unwanted artifacts into the

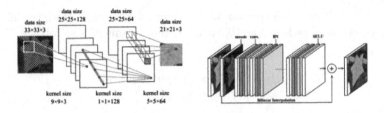

**Fig. 2.** DMCNN (left) and DMCNN-VD (right) architectures introduced in [13].

resulting images. A previous study shows that bi-linear interpolation of mosaic images results in various structural errors [5], such as the two homogeneous areas with 2 gray levels of low and high intensity ($L$ and $H$, $L<H$) represented in Fig. 3.1. Another artifact introduced is the mismatch in the green and blue/red channel intensity.

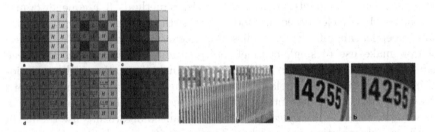

**Fig. 3.** (1) a: Gray image, b: CFA of a, c: Bi-linear interpolation result, d e f: interpolation in color plane, borrowed from [19]. (2) Zipper Effect and False color - Original image and bi-linear interpolated image. (Color figure online)

These 2 artifacts are generalized as *zipper effect* and *false color*. The zipper effect is an abrupt or sudden change in intensity over the neighboring pixels, generally seen along the edges (Fig. 3.2a). False colors (Fig. 3.2b), on the other hand, are pseudo-colors that are not an accurate representation of the original image. This generally occurs due to inconsistencies in color channels of the original mosaic image. Both these effects are categorized as misguidance color artifacts, generated as a result of wrong interpolation direction. Interestingly, these artifacts are observed even when the interpolation direction is appropriate. However, the effects in this case are less evident when compared to misguided color artifacts. Many deep learning demosaicing techniques outperform other classical techniques in reducing the impact of artifacts.

### 2.2 Performance Evaluation

A common demosaicing approach is to capture the ground truth images using a professional 3-sensor camera, convert them into a mosaic format using Bayer

CFA, interpolate using a demosaicing algorithm, and then compare the results with the ground truth image. Widely used performance criteria are mean Squared Error (MSE) or the equivalent Peak Signal to Noise Ratio (PSNR). The Kodak/McMaster [17] dataset is generally used as a baseline because of the realistic scenes and varied complexities. The MSE in each color plane is:

$$\text{MSE}(k) = \frac{1}{MN} \sum_{i=1}^{M} \sum_{j=1}^{N} \{\hat{I}_k(i,j) - I_k(i,j)\}^2, \tag{3}$$

where $\hat{I}_k(i,j)$ is the predicted and $I_k(i,j)$ is the original pixel color component. Another measure is the Color Mean Squared Error (CMSE) ([9]) which averages over the color channel as well,

$$\text{CMSE}(I, \hat{I}) = \frac{1}{3MN} \sum_{k \in \{\text{R,G,B}\}} \sum_{i=1}^{M} \sum_{j=1}^{N} \{\hat{I}_k(i,j) - I_k(i,j)\}^2, \tag{4}$$

The peak signal to noise ratio (PSNR) is defined as,

$$\text{PSNR}(k) = 10 \log_{10} \left( \frac{R^2}{\text{MSE}} \right), \tag{5}$$

where R is 1.0 (for float datatype), R is 255 (for integer datatype).

The Color Peak Signal to Noise Ratio (CPSNR) is computed using CMSE. Higher the PSNR value, better is the quality of the demosaiced image.

## 3 Architecture Search

For the exhaustive search of architectures, we made use of various parameters chosen based on state-of-the-art models to obtain the Pareto front between negative CPSNR as the loss and the number of parameters as the model complexity. To make the comparisons fair, we ran each model for 500 epochs and retrained the state-of-the-art architecture in this new setting. The various hyperparameters for exhaustive search were mostly discrete and are as follows:

1. The use of depthwise separable convolutions [11], similar to MobileNet V2 architecture [10], over the traditional convolutional layers as per the state-of-the-art models.
2. The number of filters used in the models (16, 32, 64, 128 and 256).
3. Number of blocks, each block consisted of sets of (i) depthwise separable (ii) standard convolution, and (iii) activation function, chosen from (3, 5, 7 blocks).
4. We use a constant kernel size of 3 × 3 since much of the hardware has shown to be optimized for this convolution [8].
5. The length of skip connections (1,2).
6. The use of cosine annealing [7] or a fixed learning rate.

Some of the reasoning behind choosing the search space is as follows:

1. Primary reason for choosing this range of filter and block values was to obtain networks that have a smaller number of parameters and FLOPs as the current state-of-the-art networks. The filters and block size dominate the parameter density in a network. We defined an upper bound based on this.
2. Motivated from [8], choosing equal channel width minimizes memory access cost (MAC). Hence, we retained the same channel width across all the layers.
3. Furthermore, [8] computed the relative costs of using group convolution, so we used the depth-wise convolution in all the layers.
4. Moreover, for deployment in edge devices, various restrictions are placed based on the platform for inference. In this problem, the model size, the number of FLOPs and MAC play a key role in inference time. For instance, the largest model we have has around $7 \times 10^5$ parameters and $5.2 \times 10^6$ multiplication FLOPs. Deploying such a model would have severe consequences in the overall usability of the edge device
5. We chose a lower bound on the number of filters, around the region, based on the smallest state-of-the-art model, i.e. DMCNN [13].
6. We used point-wise convolutions to avoid the use of fully-connected layers as the last layer, and therefore reduce the model size.

Our goal in this study was to explore architectures that improve the state of the art models by using fewer number of parameters and maintaining reasonable accuracy for edge implementation.

## 4   Methodology and Theory

Neural architecture search is a discrete optimization problem. Here, we used an exhaustive search over a small space, where the convergence to the optimum in the designed space is trivial and independent of the loss function, because all points are evaluated. However, most of these neural architecture search techniques are motivated by a very large design space. We show that as the designed space gets infinitely large, even simple methods such as exhaustive search and grid search, require some minimal properties of the loss function to converge to the optimum. Exhaustive search and grid search techniques are common optimization methods that rely only on function evaluation. Therefore, it is counterintuitive that finding the optimum point using these techniques may require some mathematical assumptions about the search space, or the objective function. Motivated from the derivative-free optimization theory, we aim at clarifying some minimal conditions that the exhaustive search and grid search converges to the optimum.

Let us set the notation first. We denote a vector using bold $\boldsymbol{\theta}$ and an element of the this vector using unbold $\theta$. The search space can be a mix of continuous or discrete parameters and denoted by $\Theta$. Suppose a neural network is uniquely defined by its hyperparameters embedded in $\boldsymbol{\theta} \in \Theta$. Note that the complexity of each network might differ. Complexity may be defined as the number of parameters of the network, inference delay, training time, etc. Often the objective is to discover the neural network with minimum loss (or maximum accuracy) on a fixed validation set. Let's denote the validation loss of the neural network with $\mathcal{L}(\boldsymbol{\theta})$ and its complexity $\mathcal{C}(\boldsymbol{\theta})$. It is preferable to minimize $\mathcal{L}(\boldsymbol{\theta})$ and $\mathcal{C}(\boldsymbol{\theta})$ at the same time, i.e. between two neural networks with the same validation loss $\mathcal{L}(.)$, the neural network with smaller complexity $\mathcal{C}(.)$ is preferred. To simplify the theoretical analysis we assume that $\mathcal{C}(.)$ is fixed and focus on minimizing the validation loss function $\mathcal{L}(.)$ regardless of $\mathcal{C}(.)$. In the context of demosaicing $\mathcal{L}(.)$ is the negative CPSNR and $\mathcal{C}(.)$ is the number of model parameters.

Assume the minimum exists within the search space $\Theta$

$$\underset{\boldsymbol{\theta}\in\Theta}{\operatorname{argmin}} \, \mathcal{L}(\boldsymbol{\theta}) \neq \emptyset \tag{6}$$

Let's define the exhaustive search algorithm to minimize $\mathcal{L}(.)$ as

1. Enumerate: $\{\boldsymbol{\theta}_0, \boldsymbol{\theta}_1, \ldots, \boldsymbol{\theta}_K\}$.
2. Initialize: $k = 0, \boldsymbol{\theta}^* = \boldsymbol{\theta}_0, \mathcal{L}^* = \mathcal{L}(\boldsymbol{\theta}_0)$.
3. Evaluate $\mathcal{L}(\boldsymbol{\theta}_{k+1})$.
4. If $\mathcal{L}(\boldsymbol{\theta}_{k+1}) < \mathcal{L}^*$, then update $\boldsymbol{\theta}^* = \boldsymbol{\theta}_{k+1}, \mathcal{L}^* = \mathcal{L}(\boldsymbol{\theta}_{k+1})$.
5. If $k < K$ then $k = k + 1$ go to 3, otherwise end.

It is trivial that after iterating the algorithm for $K$ iterations, the global minimum of the objective function is obtained $(\boldsymbol{\theta}^*, \mathcal{L}(\boldsymbol{\theta}^*))$, for simplicity of notation we may denote $(\boldsymbol{\theta}^*, \mathcal{L}^*)$ where

$$\boldsymbol{\theta}^* = \underset{\theta\in\Theta}{\operatorname{argmin}} \, \mathcal{L}(\boldsymbol{\theta}), \mathcal{L}^* = \underset{\theta\in\Theta}{\min} \, \mathcal{L}(\boldsymbol{\theta}).$$

Convergence to the optimum requires no restriction on the loss function $\mathcal{L}(.)$ except the existence of the minimum (6). However, if the algorithm is iterated only $k < K$ iterations there is no guarantee of convergence to the minimum.

Often the cardinality $||\Theta|| = K$ is a large value because in a real scenario a grid search on the hyperparameter vector $\boldsymbol{\theta}$ is implemented, where the search becomes NP-hard, $K = \mathcal{O}\left(e^d\right)$ where $d = \dim(\boldsymbol{\theta})$, and the algorithm is run only $k < K$ iterations depending on computation budget.

In the following sections we explore under what conditions the exhaustive search convergence is assured. Suppose the search space is large but is countable, $K = \infty$. Infinitely many evaluations requires more conditions on $\mathcal{L}(.)$. For simplicity of the notation we may assume $\Theta \subset \mathbb{R}^d$ where $d = \dim(\boldsymbol{\theta})$. Suppose the minimum argument and the objective value at iteration $k$ of exhaustive search is denoted by $(\boldsymbol{\theta}_k^*, \mathcal{L}_k^*)$.

**Theorem 1.** *If $\Theta$ is dense and $\mathcal{L}(.)$ is continuous, the exhaustive search converges to the minimum value*

$$\lim_{k\to\infty} \mathcal{L}_k^* = \mathcal{L}^*.$$

*Proof.* Take the optimal solution $\boldsymbol{\theta}^* \in \Theta$ and because $\mathcal{L}(.)$ is continuous and $\Theta$ is dense

$$\exists \delta > 0, \boldsymbol{\theta}_k \in \Theta_k \text{ where } ||\boldsymbol{\theta}_k - \boldsymbol{\theta}^*|| < \delta, |\mathcal{L}(\boldsymbol{\theta}_k) - \mathcal{L}(\boldsymbol{\theta}^*)| < \epsilon,$$

or equivalently $\mathcal{L}(\theta_k) < \mathcal{L}(\theta^*) + \epsilon$. On the other hand $\forall k, \mathcal{L}(\theta^*) \leq \mathcal{L}(\theta_k^*) \leq \mathcal{L}(\theta_k)$ and by definition $\mathcal{L}^* = \mathcal{L}(\theta^*), \mathcal{L}_k^* = \mathcal{L}(\theta_k^*)$, so

$$\mathcal{L}^* \leq \mathcal{L}_k^* \leq \mathcal{L}(\theta_k) \leq \mathcal{L}^* + \epsilon,$$

$$\implies \lim_{k \to \infty} \mathcal{L}_k^* = \mathcal{L}^*.$$

**Theorem 2.** *If $\Theta$ is compact and $\theta^* = \mathrm{argmin}_{\theta \in \Theta} \mathcal{L}(\theta)$ is unique, the exhaustive algorithm converges to the unique minimum.*

*Proof.* $\forall k, \theta_k \in \Theta$ which is compact, so there is a sub-sequence that converges to $\theta_k^*$, call it $\theta_{ik}^*$

$$\lim_{k \to \infty} \lim_{i \to \infty} \theta_{ik}^* = \tilde{\theta}.$$

By continuity of $\mathcal{L}(.)$

$$\lim_{k \to \infty} \lim_{i \to \infty} \mathcal{L}(\theta_{ik}^*) = \mathcal{L}(\tilde{\theta}),$$

but from Theorem 1 we know $\lim_{k \to \infty} \mathcal{L}(\theta_k^*)$, therefore $\tilde{\theta} \in \Theta$. From the uniqueness of the minimum $\tilde{\theta} = \theta^*$.

The convergence of exhaustive search relies on the continuity of $\mathcal{L}(.)$. It is easy to construct cases where the exhaustive search fails to converge if $\mathcal{L}(.)$ is non-continuous [1]. Although exhaustive search is the first tool to explore the discrete space, in a continuous space exhaustive search is in-feasible. Therefore optimizing over a continuous parameter such as learning rate, annealing rate, regularization constant, etc requires other tools. Bayesian optimization [12] is often used and some open source packages are available [15]. However, grid search is still one of the most used tool to tune a continuous parameter.

Grid search on multiple variables is cumbersome as a large dimension of the search variable $d$ implies the evaluation set being $\mathcal{O}(n^d)$. Multivariate grid search algorithm over the set $\prod_{i=1}^{d}[a_i, b_i] \subset \mathbb{R}^d$ is as follows:

1. Initialize number of grid evaluation $n \in \mathbb{N}$.
2. Set the step size $\delta_i = \frac{b_i - a_i}{n-1}, i = 1, \ldots, d$.
3. Create the grid search space with step iteration $j$

$$\Theta_n = \{\theta \mid \theta = l_i + j\delta_i, j = 0, \ldots, n-1, i = 1, \ldots, d\}$$

4. Evaluate the objective function $\mathcal{L}(.)$ for all $n^d$ grid points $\theta \in \Theta_n$.
5. Find the grid search solution $(\theta_n^*, \mathcal{L}_n^*)$ where

$$\theta_n^* = \mathrm{argmin}_{\theta \in \Theta_n} \mathcal{L}(\theta), \quad \mathcal{L}_n^* = \min_{\theta \in \Theta_n} \mathcal{L}(\theta).$$

Grid search on $d$ variables is NP-hard, so it is commonly implemented only on one element of the vector $\theta$ while keeping the other elements fixed to certain values. Therefore, it makes more sense to explore the convergence of the grid search on a uni-variate variable $\theta$.

Suppose the continuous uni-variate parameter $\theta \in [a, b]$ achieves its minimum at $(\theta^*, \mathcal{L}^*)$. The uni-variate parameter $\theta$ is a continuous element, such as the learning rate, and is also an element of the vector $\boldsymbol{\theta}$, in which the vector $\boldsymbol{\theta}$ fully determines the neural network.

The grid search convergence result relies on creating a nearly dense set $\Theta_n$ by choosing a large number of grid evaluation $n$. The convergence also depends on $\mathcal{L}(\theta)$ being Lipschitz continuous, i.e.

$$\forall \theta, \theta' \in [a, b], |\mathcal{L}(\theta) - \mathcal{L}(\theta')| \leq M|\theta - \theta'|,$$

where $M$ is the Lipschitz constant.

**Theorem 3.** *Suppose $\mathcal{L}(.)$ is Lipschitz continuous on $\theta \in [a, b]$ and a grid search is run over $n$ grids to create $\Theta_n$ with step size $\delta$, then*

$$\mathcal{L}_n^* - \frac{M\delta}{2} \leq \mathcal{L}^*$$

*Proof.* Suppose $\theta^* \in \Theta$, take $\boldsymbol{\theta}_n \in \Theta_n$ as a grid search candidate. For any point in the grid $\Theta_n$, define the closest point to $\theta^*$ in the grid space $\theta_n^* = \text{argmin}_{\theta_n \in \Theta_n} |\theta_n - \theta^*|$. The distance between two consecutive points is $\delta$, so $|\theta_n^* - \theta^*| \leq \frac{\delta}{2}$. By the Lipschitz continuity of $\mathcal{L}(.)$

$$|\mathcal{L}(\theta_n^*) - \mathcal{L}(\theta^*)| \leq M|\theta_n^* - \theta^*| \leq \frac{M\delta}{2}$$

$$\implies \mathcal{L}_n^* - \frac{M\delta}{2} \leq \mathcal{L}^*.$$

Theorem 3 means for a finite $n$, $\mathcal{L}_n^*$ may never reach the true minimum $\mathcal{L}^*$ as $\mathcal{L}^* \leq \mathcal{L}_n^*$, but improves swiftly as $\delta$ gets smaller by evaluating a smaller step size or equivalently by increasing the number of evaluations $n$; the lower-bound improves by $\mathcal{O}(n^{-1})$.

## 5 Application

We first describe the dataset that was used for our experiments and elaborate on the results obtained.

Flickr500 data is used by [13] to generate around 3.5 million patches. The authors choose the images with some criteria such as (i) being colorful enough to obtain the proper color distributions of real world, (ii) high-frequency patterns in the images and (iii) of high-quality. However, there are some key points missing in the description to re-generate the exact results such as:

1. Specifications on exactly how the patches are generated from the original Flickr500 images (related to the stride etc while cropping the patches).
2. Specifications on how to apply the Bayer CFA for creating the mosaic image.

Therefore, some assumptions were made while generating our data.

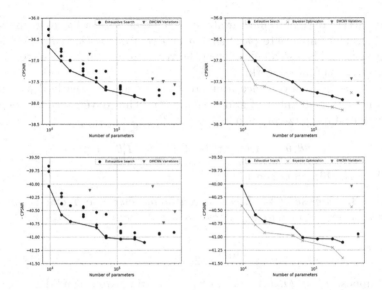

**Fig. 4.** Pareto front of MCM dataset 18 photos with standard error 0.53 (top panels) compared to and Kodak dataset 24 photos standard error 0.66 (bottom panels). Left panels is exhaustive search versus right Bayesian Optimization of learning rate and regularization constant implemented on Pareto architectures.

1. We generated random patches of $32 \times 32 \times 3$ to obtain approximately 1.5 million image patches from the 500 images. Since the method is not specified, we used random points in the image and extracted patches from the random points. 1382400 patches were used for the training set and 153600 patches for the validation set. Note: In the paper, they use patches of size $33 \times 33 \times 3$ but we used $32 \times 32 \times 3$ because the training is much faster on GPU due the dimensions being a power of 2 for tiling.
2. The Bayer CFA generation is also based on the python package. We used the default setting of $RGGB$ and filled the missing channels with zeros to maintain the channel dimensions.
3. All the results in the section were calculated against the McMaster dataset (MCM) containing 18 photos (58000 patches created), and the Kodak images containing 24 photos (78408 patches created).

The Pareto front of our exhaustive search is shown in Fig. 4. The $y$-axis represents the validation loss $\mathcal{L}(.)$ which indicates the negative CPSNR and the $x$-axis represents the model complexity $\mathcal{C}(.)$, which is the total number of parameters in the model. The standard error for each experiment is calculated and as they are comparable, they produce a similar prediction interval.

Most of the architectures in the search space outperform the current state-of-the-art (SOTA) as in Fig. 4 in a similar setting, see also Table 1. The total number of parameters in the current SOTA is approximately $7 \times 10^5$. Architectures on the Pareto front maintain the same accuracy while significantly reducing the number of parameters. In our search the effect of cosine annealing was not obvious and would need further tuning on cycle rate. The ResNet skip connections length of 2 blocks worked better than 1.

Some of the models on the Pareto front are shown in the table below in comparison to the current state-of-the-art models for the MCM dataset. Once the initial search was completed, the models from the Pareto front architectures were fed through a Bayesian optimizer using the ORION package [15], to optimize the learning rate and regularization constant for $L_2$ regularization. Figure 4 indicates further improvement over the initial CPSNR obtained with a fixed learning rate $10^{-4}$ and regularization constant $10^{-8}$, so Bayesian optimization is recommended as an extra step after the architecture search as including it in the first step would further increase the complexity of the search. In our experiments, the PSNR was calculated separately for each image in the test dataset; the final CPSNR value was the mean of all the PSNRs of all images in the dataset.

**Table 1.** The negative CPSNR denoted by $\mathcal{L}(.)$ versus the number of parameters denoted by $\mathcal{C}(.)$ for few architectures of the search space on the MCM dataset. The first line in bold shows the state-of-the-art.

| Model | No of blocks | Skip length | $\mathcal{L}(.)$ | Standard Error | $\mathcal{C}(.)$ |
|---|---|---|---|---|---|
| **64 filter** | **20** | **20** | **−37.58** | **0.66** | **710275** |
| 64 filter | 15 | 15 | −37.51 | 0.62 | 487171 |
| 64 filter | 10 | 10 | −37.45 | 0.64 | 338435 |
| 256 filter | 3 | 2 | −37.77 | 0.68 | 420879 |
| 128 filter | 7 | 2 | −37.94 | 0.67 | 252431 |
| 128 filter | 5 | 2 | −37.82 | 0.69 | 182287 |

## 6   Conclusion

Our designed space with a simple exhaustive search outperforms the state of the art and brings a range of loss versus complexity for edge implementation with varying resource constraints. Although in most of architecture search, the number of evaluations and complex search algorithm implementation is the bottleneck, here we showed using prior vision domain knowledge, we can overcome these drawbacks and a simple exhaustive search becomes an effective search tool. We only focused on demosaicing as an example of a low-vision problem where edge implementation is an obligation. We wonder whether a similar approach is useful in edge implementation of other low vision problems. A simple theoretical study suggests the continuity of the loss function and compactness of the search space for exhaustive and grid search to converge to the optimum.

**Acknowledgement.** We want to acknowledge Jingwei Chen, Yanhui Geng, and Heng Liao for their support. Qiang Tang and Shao Hua Chen from HiSilicon Vancouver IC Lab kindly assisted us in initiating and developing demisaicing research direction. We appreciate the assistance of Huawei media research lab of Japan that provided us details about demosaicing and camera sensors. We declare our deep gratitude to Charles Audet and Sébastien Le Digabel who introduced to us the theory behind derivative-free optimization.

# References

1. Audet, C., Hare, W.: Derivative-Free and Blackbox Optimization. SSORFE. Springer, Cham (2017). https://doi.org/10.1007/978-3-319-68913-5
2. Gharbi, M., Chaurasia, G., Paris, S., Durand, F.: Deep joint demosaicking and denoising. ACM Trans. Graph. **35**(6), 191 (2016)
3. Han, S., et al.: Eie: efficient inference engine on compressed deep neural network. SIGARCH Comput. Archit. News **44**(3), 243–254 (2016)
4. Han, S., Pool, J., Tran, J., Dally, W.J.: Learning both weights and connections for efficient neural networks. CoRR abs/1506.02626 (2015)
5. Chang, L., Tan, Y.P.: Hybrid color filter array demosaicking for effective artifact suppression. J. Electron. Imaging **15**, 15–17 (2006)
6. Li, X., Gunturk, B.K., Zhang, L.: Image demosaicing: a systematic survey (2007)
7. Loshchilov, I., Hutter, F.: SGDR: stochastic gradient descent with restarts. CoRR
8. Ma, N., Zhang, X., Zheng, H., Sun, J.: Shufflenet V2: practical guidelines for efficient CNN architecture design. CoRR abs/1807.11164 (2018)
9. Menon, D., Calvagno, G.: Color image demosaicking: an overview. Image Commun. **26**(8–9), 518–533 (2011)
10. Sandler, M., Howard, A.G., Zhu, M., Zhmoginov, A., Chen, L.: Inverted residuals and linear bottlenecks: mobile networks for classification, detection and segmentation. CoRR abs/1801.04381 (2018)
11. Sifre, L., Mallat, S.: Rigid-motion scattering for texture classification. CoRR abs/1403.1687 (2014)
12. Snoek, J., Larochelle, H., Adams, R.P.: Practical bayesian optimization of machine learning algorithms. In: Advances in Neural Information Processing Systems, vol. 25, pp. 2951–2959. Curran Associates, Inc., New York (2012)
13. Syu, N., Chen, Y., Chuang, Y.: Learning deep convolutional networks for demosaicing. CoRR abs/1802.03769 (2018)
14. Tan, H., Xiao, H., Lai, S., Liu, Y., Zhang, M.: Deep residual learning for image demosaicing and blind denoising, August 2018
15. Tsirigotis, C., Bouthillier, X., Corneau-Tremblay, F., Henderson, P., Askari, et al.: Oríon: experiment version control for efficient hyperparameter optimization (2018)
16. Xie, J., Xu, L., Chen, E.: Image denoising and inpainting with deep neural networks. In: Advances in Neural Information Processing Systems, vol. 25 (2012)
17. Yu, K., Wang, C., Yang, S., et al.: An effective directional residual interpolation algorithm for color image demosaicking. Appl. Sci. **8**, 680 (2018)
18. Yu, W.: Colour demosaicking method using adaptive cubic convolution interpolation with sequential averaging. IEEE Proc. - Vis. Image Sig. Process. **153**(5), 666–676 (2006)
19. Zhen, R., Stevenson, R.L.: Image demosaicing. In: Celebi, M.E., Lecca, M., Smolka, B. (eds.) Color Image and Video Enhancement, pp. 13–54. Springer, Cham (2015). https://doi.org/10.1007/978-3-319-09363-5_2

# A Scene-Based Augmented Reality Framework for Exhibits

Julien Li-Chee-Ming, Zheng Wu, Randy Tan, Ryan Tan,
Naimul Mefraz Khan[(✉)], Andy Ye, and Ling Guan

Ryerson Multimedia Research Laboratory, Ryerson University, Toronto,
ON M5B 2K3, Canada
n77khan@ryerson.ca

**Abstract.** This paper presents a novel augmented reality (AR) framework specifically targeting scene-based exhibits. Unlike traditional AR libraries that rely on specific image targets, the proposed framework utilizes a bag-of-words model for scene recognition, which enables recognition and subsequent launch of AR experiences under challenging environments. Moreover, the proposed framework utilizes relocalization capabilities of the popular ORB-SLAM algorithm to track the user's movement after recognition of a particular exhibit. We demonstrate the efficacy of the proposed framework through a complete mobile app designed for a local museum, where artifacts are enhanced through AR.

**Keywords:** Bag-of-words · SLAM · Object recognition · Scene recognition

## 1 Introduction[1]

Augmented Reality (AR) is a live view of a real-world environment whose elements are augmented by computer-generated content such as text, sound, video, or animation. Recently AR has become a ubiquitous mode of application development due to the adoption of new technologies, such as mobiles devices, computer vision, 3D rendering, image recognition, and cloud computing. The commercial market for AR applications is projected to increase from $5.2 billion in 2016 to more than $162 billion in 2020 [1]. In an exhibit scenario, such as a museum or a gallery, AR has huge potential to increase visitor engagement. Instead of reading static text or visuals that typically accompany such exhibits, an AR solution can present dynamic content in a context aware manner with accurate registration and tracking.

This work presents a novel framework for accurate scene recognition and tracking specifically geared towards creating AR exhibits for museums. The primary contributions of this work can be summarized as follows:

1. *Perform fast and accurate scene recognition on mobile devices*: The initialization of a good AR experience for an object on display greatly depends on accurately recognizing the 3D object so that virtual content can be retrieved and aligned with

---

[1] NSERC's financial support for this research work through a Collaborative Research and Development (CRD) Grant (#507333-16) is much appreciated.

F. Karray et al. (Eds.): ICIAR 2019, LNCS 11662, pp. 287–296, 2019.
https://doi.org/10.1007/978-3-030-27202-9_26

the real-world view through the device's camera. Unlike traditional image target-based approaches for initialization that is prevalent in commercial SDKs such as Vuforia [2], ARCore [3], ARKit [4], we utilize a 2D to 3D matching algorithm that is traditionally used for scene recognition. We show that for challenging AR initialization scenarios, the scene recognition algorithm succeeds while image-based targets fail.

2. *Perform robust real-time tracking on mobile devices*: For a smooth AR experience, real-time tracking is essential once the AR content is retrieved and initially aligned. A state-of-the-art Simultaneous Localization and Mapping (SLAM) algorithm [5] is utilized to work with the recognition module in delivering a seamless AR experience. To further speed up tracking, the mobile devices' Inertial Measurement Units (IMUs) are utilized to interpolate orientation between SLAM-based tracking calls.

Using the algorithms, a prototype application was developed for the newly renovated Canada Science and Technology Museum (CSTM), where various museum artifacts were recognized, and highly immersive educational experiences were initiated based on recognition and tracked in real-time using SLAM.

## 2 Related Work

The usage of AR in exhibits has recently attracted some attention. [6] promoted MRsionCase, a device-free mixed reality (MR) showcase that presents spatially consistent visual and auditory information with physical exhibits. However, the proposed system displays only 2D images at a fixed position, which lacks depth perception and interactivity. [7] built a museum display in the Mawangdui Han Dynasty Tombs and overlaid virtual archaeological relics onto real exhibits. The Vuforia SDK [2] was used to perform object recognition and camera motion tracking. Although the AR experience did not require external infrastructure, it needed a calibration grid in the mapping stage that must be approximately the same size as the object being mapped. This process becomes cumbersome with large artifacts. [8] developed a museum tour guide application which gives users access guiding services and other functions interactively. The proposed navigator relies on pre-installed sensor beacons for localization. [9] is our own previous work, where we developed a large-area augmented reality exhibit for the Fort York National Historic Site, where multiple users can experience the same shared events simultaneously. We utilized specialized hardware that performed radio-frequency-based tracking. The work presented here demonstrates that a similar experience can be achieved using only a mobile device's camera.

## 3 Background

A key challenge in an AR-based exhibit design is localizing the user with respect to the world. Typically, image-based targets are used in commercial libraries such as Vuforia [2], ARCore [3], ARKit [4], where a 2D image is utilized at the recognition stage to localize the user. However, in challenging scenarios such as low light, distance from 2D image, such recognition fails, as we see in the experimental results section. Another alternative is to entirely depend on relocalization with SLAM. However, as we show, the relocalization approach is prone to drift due to accumulated errors and it is difficult to achieve real-time performance with acceptable accuracy on mobile devices. Although ARCore/ARKit has good native implementation of SLAM, none of the libraries have consistent relocalization, and the libraries only support newer devices. Instead, we approach the problem in two stages: (1) 3D scene recognition; where we utilize a bag-of-word models to recognize the current exhibit instead of the traditional 2D image approach for robust recognition; and (2) camera motion tracking; where we enable relocalization within SLAM to track the user's movement.

Decoupling the recognition from tracking ensures consistent launch of AR experiences followed by tracking. Any potential drifts/slowdown arising from SLAM does not affect the initialization of the experience. The bag-of-words model provides instantaneous and robust recognition, which enhances user experience.

### 3.1 Scene Recognition

[10] surveyed methods for scene recognition and argued that appearance-based image-to-image matching techniques perform better than map-to-map and image-to-map methods. Within appearance-based methods, the bag of words methods (BoW) have the highest performance. [11] proposed the bag of binary words obtained from BRIEF descriptors along with the very efficient FAST feature detector, reducing the time needed for feature extraction by more than one order of magnitude. However, BRIEF is not invariant to rotation nor scale, which limited the system to in-plane trajectories and loop closures with similar point of view. [12] extend that work using ORB, which are rotation invariant and can deal with changes in scale. The bag of binary words method DBoW2 [11] is used for image to image matching mainly for the purpose of scene recognition inside SLAM algorithms [12]. Scene recognition within SLAM algorithms are used for relocalization and loop closing. Relocalization uses image to image matching to allow for SLAM algorithms to recover from tracking failure which would render previously mapped data useless in visual odometry algorithms. Loop closing reduces the odometry drift error by detecting paths to revisited areas and then minimizes the error over the path. This work will apply DBoW2 to recognize the artifact being viewed by the camera and trigger its AR experience.

### 3.2 Camera Motion Tracking

From an AR context, tracking based on visual features mostly use some variant of Simultaneous Localization and Mapping (SLAM). The objective of SLAM in an AR context is to anchor the virtual objects to their position in the real world, regardless of the motion of the user. To accomplish this, the system must be able to track the camera pose (i.e., 3D position and orientation) relative to the anchor point. The chosen SLAM system for this work is ORB-SLAM [5], which runs three parallel threads: tracking, mapping, and loop closing. ORB-SLAM uses ORB features in their localization, tracking, mapping, and loop closing. The ORB feature allows the algorithm to have real-time performance without relying on GPUs and provided some robustness to lighting changes and invariance to rotation and scaling. All the functions using the same descriptor also allows ORB-SLAM to be efficient in both memory and execution time by preventing the need to compare different descriptors. ORB-SLAM uses DBoW2 when performing relocalization and loop closure detection. These functions allow ORB-SLAM to have more re-usability and more robustness while maintaining its real-time performance.

The tracking thread maintains camera localization and determines when a new keyframe should be added. The local mapping thread oversees the mapping of the keyframes. The loop closing thread then takes the new keyframe and map points to calculate a similarity score to its closest matches using DBoW2. If the frames pass a threshold then the thread will attempt to minimize the mean square error of the entire loop rather than minimize local error.

# 4    Methodology

This section explains how the scene recognition module and the tracking module are integrated to deliver a novel AR experience for museums. Four modules were developed (Fig. 1): An offline module to perform training for scene recognition; an offline module to generate and save a map for each artifact; an online module to perform scene recognition; and an online module to perform motion tracking.

ORB-SLAM was selected to perform camera motion tracking in Modules 2 and 4, as it has been shown to perform well on mobile devices [13]. DBoW2 was selected to perform object recognition in Modules 1 and 3 because it has also been shown to performance well on mobile devices [14]. Further, DBoW2 is used for ORB-SLAM's relocalization and loop closing, which facilitated the integration of the modules. The software libraries were built for Android and integrated as Unity 3D game engine plugins. Rendering the AR content was also performed by Unity 3D.

## 4.1    Module 1: Training for Scene Recognition

Training for scene recognition is an offline process performed by the museum staff, which involves capturing images of each artifact from various vantage points. These vantage points are predictions of how the user will view the artifact with their mobile device. Images were captured using various image resolutions and aspect ratios, and from various heights, viewing angles, and distances from the artifact. These images were processed using DBoW2. 10 to 20 images were captured per artifact, as this number produced a sufficiently small database size, while maintaining high precision and recall rates for object recognition. A verification step was developed to further increase the precision and recall of DBoW2. Specifically, DBoW2 returns the object and image with the highest match score. An object was accepted if it was returned 7 times among 10 consecutive images, as this ratio provided an acceptable balance between reliability and real-time performance.

The visual vocabulary was created by [12] in an offline step with the dataset Bovisa 2008-09-01 [15]. This dataset is a sequence with outdoors and indoors areas, yielding a

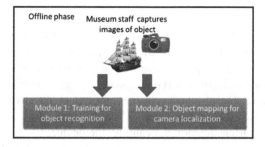

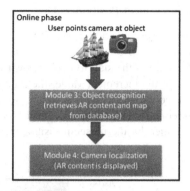

**Fig. 1.** The two phases performed by the museum staff and the user respectively

vocabulary that provides good results in both scenarios. ORB features were extracted from ten thousand images from the dataset and a vocabulary of 6 levels and 10 clusters per level was built, getting one million words. Such a big vocabulary is suggested in [11] to be efficient for recognition in large image databases.

The vocabulary had a file size of 43 MB. The training database generated by DBoW2 had a file size of 14 MB. Both files are stored onboard the mobile device when the application is installed. On a Google Pixel, the average load time for the files were $4.2 \pm 0.4$ s and $5.4 \pm 0.2$ s, respectively.

### 4.2 Module 2: Object Mapping for Camera Localization

Object mapping is an offline phase performed by the museum staff. The purpose of this module is to generate and save a map that will be used for online localization. The map generated by ORB-SLAM is a pose graph connecting 3D map points and keyframes. Where a 3D map point consists of a 3D world position and an ORB descriptor, and a keyframe consists of an image's camera pose and ORB feature points in the image, each with its associated 3D map point. The mapping process involved capturing images of each artifact from various vantage points. As in the object recognition training phase, these vantage points were predictions of where the user will view the artifact. Thus, the map contained keyframes captured from various heights, viewing angles, and distances from the artifact, Tracking must be maintained throughout the mapping process, thus the images were processed in real-time using ORB-SLAM, as opposed to collecting images or video and post-processing the frames. The generated maps are stored onboard the mobile device upon installation of the application, thus the file size of each artifact's map was limited to a maximum of 10 megabytes. On a Google Pixel, a map with this file size had an average load time of $1.83 \pm 0.58$ s and average processing time for the localization module of $1.85 \pm 0.69$ s (Table 1).

### 4.3   Object Positioner Tool

The object positioner tool (Fig. 2) is used by the museum staff to calibrate the AR content's pose with respect to its corresponding map. The tool provides a menu button that allows the staff to load the artifact's AR content and map. The staff is then able to select the increment value, the type of transformation (i.e., translate, rotate, or scale), the coordinate system axis, and the direction of adjustment (i.e., positive or negative direction). The calibrated offsets for each artifact are saved. When the application is installed by the museum visitor, these offsets are stored locally on the device.

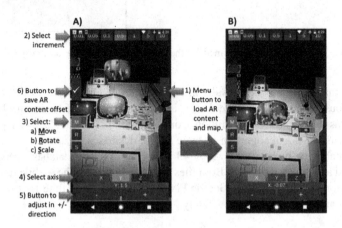

**Fig. 2.** (A) Misalignment between the real TV screen and the AR content (TV screen). (B) The Positioner Tool has been used to align the AR content with the real TV screen. The AR content's pose with respect to the map (green cubes) is stored. (Color figure online)

### 4.4   Module 3: Scene Recognition

Scene recognition is an online phase performed by the museum visitor. The user points the mobile device's camera at an object and DBoW2 recognizes the object, the corresponding map and AR content is then retrieved from the database, and the camera localization module is started. This module requires the vocabulary and the training database files. As previously mentioned, both files are stored locally on the mobile device when the application is installed.

### 4.5   Module 4: Camera Localization

Camera localization is an online phase performed by the museum visitor. The user points the mobile device's camera at an object. Once Module 3 recognizes the object and retrieves the object's map from the database, this module estimates the camera pose with respect to the object (i.e., map of the object). This process allows the AR content to be displayed in the correct pose on the screen of the user's mobile device.

ORB-SLAM is used in Localization Mode, a lightweight localization algorithm used in mapped areas. In this mode the local mapping and loop closing threads are deactivated and the camera continuously localizes using the tracking thread.

## 5  Experiments

The AR application was built for the Android operating system. Figure 3 shows the Cheerful Oak Stove artifact (circa 1920). When the user views the artifact using the mobile device's camera, the object recognition module automatically retrieves the corresponding AR content and map from the database. The AR content allows the user to virtually interact with the artifact by dragging logs of wood into the stove via the mobile device's touch screen. The user then places a lit match in the stove to set the wood on fire. The tracking module applies the camera localization on every frame; this allows the AR content to maintain alignment with the artifact as the user moves the camera to view the artifact from different perspectives.

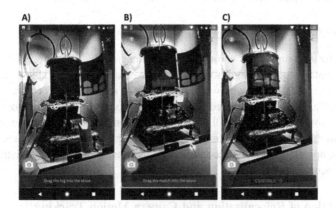

**Fig. 3.**  Stove artifact with AR content.

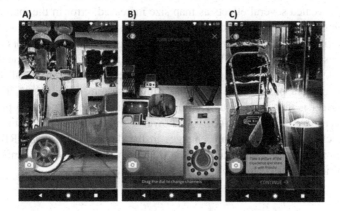

**Fig. 4.**  (A) Gas pump, (B) TV, (C) Snow blower.

Figure 4 shows three other artifacts: (A) A Shell twin visible gasoline pump (circa 1925), (B) A Philco Predicta television (TV) (circa 1959), and C) an Outboard Marine Corporation snow blower (circa 1963). In the AR experience for the gas pump, the glass cylinders fill with fuel. A 1925 Chevrolet drives into camera's field of view. The AR experience for the television is automatically triggered by the object recognition module when the user points the mobile device's camera at the television artifact. The AR experience includes an animated television screen showing a black and white video.

There were 8 AR experiences in total. Table 1 shows results from 10 trials at each experience. Where each trial involved the user opening the application, going through the AR experience, then closing the application. The results include the average time taken for DBoW2 to recognize the object, properties of the ORB-SLAM map, the average time taken for ORB-SLAM to localize with respect to the map, and the average reprojection error upon relocalization. The reprojection error is the image distance between a projected point belonging to the 3D AR content and its corresponding 2D point in the image. 5 check points, evenly spread throughout the object, were measured to calculate each scene's reprojection error with $640 \times 480$ pixels.

## 5.1  Evaluation of Scene Recognition

DBoW2 performed uniformly across all experiences, with 100% precision and recall, and approximately equal recognition times. As we can see from Table 1, the average recognition time of 0.47 s is well within the realm of real-time performance for launch of an AR scene. We also attempted at traditional image target-based recognition with Vuforia [2], however, for almost all the artifacts, the image targets were not recognized even with slight changes in lighting or viewing angle. This demonstrates that for a practical AR application, scene recognition holds more potential for a distraction-free user experience.

## 5.2  Evaluation of Relocalization and Camera Motion Tracking

Larger artifacts (e.g., the TV, the gas pump, and the Union Station lamp) required larger areas to be mapped, resulting in larger map file sizes and map load times. The experiments revealed several effects as map size increased: error in the map increased, the map points were sparser, and less ORB features were extracted from smoother images, resulting in longer localization times and larger reprojection errors (Table 1). The results also indicate that the localization time is too long for real-time AR applications. Thus, instead of invoking relocalization at every frame, it is called once to initialize the camera pose in the map's coordinate system, the device's IMU-based rotational tracker is then used to update the camera orientation. The IMU provides an orientation estimate every frame (20 Hz), however the pose drifts over time and the rotational tracker does not estimate changes in the device's position. ORB-SLAM's relocalization is called in a separate thread at 0.5 Hz, based on the results in Table 1, to provide a periodic drift correction.

**Table 1.** Results from 10 trials at each experience. The results include the average time taken to recognize the object, properties of the ORB-SLAM, the average time taken to localize the camera, and the average reprojection error upon relocalization.

| Scene | Recognition time (s) | # key frames | # map points | File size (Mb) | Map load time (s) | Localization time (s) | Reprojection error (pixels) |
|---|---|---|---|---|---|---|---|
| Ray gun | 0.61 ± 0.26 | 62 | 939 | 2.9 | 1.58 ± 0.52 | 1.83 ± 0.48 | 23.76 ± 13.12 |
| Ship | 0.42 ± 0.66 | 61 | 849 | 3.5 | 1.25 ± 0.48 | 1.55 ± 0.37 | 17.81 ± 10.63 |
| Microphone | 0.60 ± 0.13 | 64 | 778 | 2.9 | 1.45 ± 0.37 | 1.91 ± 0.81 | 45.88 ± 24.47 |
| Snow blower | 0.54 ± 0.30 | 62 | 982 | 4.7 | 1.82 ± 0.72 | 1.47 ± 0.39 | 36.05 ± 11.95 |
| Stove | 0.46 ± 0.25 | 60 | 884 | 3.2 | 1.28 ± 0.58 | 2.12 ± 0.22 | 30.87 ± 20.54 |
| Gas Pump | 0.35 ± 0.63 | 96 | 1095 | 4.1 | 1.91 ± 0.71 | 2.70 ± 0.56 | 52.38 ± 23.27 |
| TV | 0.23 ± 0.12 | 96 | 1338 | 6.5 | 2.54 ± 0.97 | 2.1 ± 0.41 | 69.42 ± 15.81 |
| Lamp | 0.58 ± 0.23 | 124 | 1673 | 8.8 | 2.83 ± 0.25 | 2.49 ± 0.31 | 75.23 ± 24.91 |
| **Mean** | **0.47 ± 0.32** | **89.75 ± 35.16** | **1067.25 ± 299.91** | **4.56 ± 2.09** | **1.83 ± 0.58** | **1.85 ± 0.69** | **41.43 ± 16.84** |

# 6    Conclusion

In this work, we proposed an AR framework that intelligently combines 3D scene recognition with the relocalization capabilities of SLAM to provide a smooth user experience, where AR scenes are instantly launched through scene recognition, and user's movement is tracked through SLAM-based motion tracking. We demonstrate that utilizing scene recognition results in successful AR experience design in a challenging museum environment with low light and multiple viewing angles, where traditional image target-based recognition fails. We provide detailed performance analysis of the framework with an Android application, where timings, file sizes, and error metrics for each module of the framework is presented and analyzed.

Future work involves developing a cloud processing module to offload recognition and tracking computations to a server to improve performance and provide a tool for central managing and distribution of maps for easy application administration.

# References

1. IDC, Worldwide Semiannual Augmented and Virtual Reality Spending Guide (2016)
2. PCT Inc. (2019). https://developer.vuforia.com/
3. Google (2019). https://developers.google.com/ar/discover/
4. Apple (2019). https://developer.apple.com/arkit/
5. Mur-Artal, R., Montiel, J.M., Tardós, J.D.: ORB-SLAM: a versatile and accurate monocular slam system. IEEE Trans. Robot. **31**(5), 1147–1163 (2015)
6. Kim, H., Nagao, S., Maekawa, S., Naemura, T.: MRsionCase a glasses-free mixed reality showcase for surrounding multiple. In: ACM SIGGRAPH Asia (2012)
7. Han, D., Li, X., Zhao, T.: The application of augmented reality technology on museum exhibition—a museum display project in Mawangdui Han Dynasty Tombs. In: International Conference on Virtual, Augmented and Mixed Reality, pp. 394–403 (2017)

8. Tsai, T.-H., Shen, C.-Y., Lin, Z.-S., Liu, H.-R., Chiou, W.-K.: Exploring location-based augmented reality experience in museums. In: Antona, M., Stephanidis, C. (eds.) UAHCI 2017, Part II. LNCS, vol. 10278, pp. 199–209. Springer, Cham (2017). https://doi.org/10. 1007/978-3-319-58703-5_15

9. Khan, N.M., et al.: Towards a shared large-area mixed reality system. In: IEEE ICME Workshop on Mobile Multimedia Computing, pp. 1–6 (2016)

10. Williams, B., et al.: A comparison of loop closing techniques in monocular SLAM. Robot. Auton. Syst. **57**(12), 1188–1197 (2009)

11. Gálvez-López, D., Tardós, J.D.: Bags of binary words for fast place recognition in image sequences. IEEE Trans. Robot. **28**(5), 1188–1197 (2012)

12. Mur-Artal, R., Tardós, J.D.: Fast relocalisation and loop closing in keyframe-based SLAM. In: IEEE International Conference on Robotics and Automation, pp. 846–853 (2014)

13. Shridhar, M., et al.: Monocular slam for real-time applications on mobile platforms (2015)

14. Li, P., Qin, T., Hu, F., Shen, S.: Monocular visual-inertial state estimation for mobile augmented reality. In: IEEE International Symposium on Mixed and Augmented Reality (2017)

15. Bonarini, A., et al.: RAWSEEDS: robotics advancement through web-publishing of sensorial and elaborated extensive data sets. In: Intelligent Robots and Systems Workshop on Benchmarks in Robotics Research (2006)

# Existence, Uniqueness and Asymptotic Behaviour of Intensity-Based Measures Which Conform to a Generalized Weber's Model of Perception

Dongchang Li[1], Davide La Torre[2,3], and Edward R. Vrscay[1(✉)]

[1] Department of Applied Mathematics, Faculty of Mathematics,
University of Waterloo, Waterloo, ON N2L 3G1, Canada
d235li@edu.uwaterloo.ca, ervrscay@uwaterloo.ca
[2] SKEMA Business School, 06902 Sophia Antipolis, France
davide.latorre@skema.edu
[3] Department of Economics, Management and Quantitative Methods,
University of Milan, 20122 Milan, Italy
davide.latorre@unimi.it

**Abstract.** In this paper, we report on further progress on our study of "Weberized" metrics for image functions presented at ICIAR 2018. These metrics allow greater deviations at higher intensity values and lower deviations at lower intensity values in accordance with Weber's model of perception. The purpose of this paper is to address some important mathematical details that were not considered in the ICIAR 2018 paper, e.g., (a) proving the existence and uniqueness of greyscale density functions $\rho_a(y)$ which conform to Weber's model, (b) complete description of the dominant asymptotic behaviour of the density functions $\rho_a(y)$ for $y \to \infty$ and $y \to 0^+$ for the cases (i) $0 < a < 1$ and (ii) $a > 1$, (c) a method of computing the asymptotic expansion of $\rho_a(y)$ for $y \to \infty$ to any number of terms for the case $0 < a < 1$.

## 1 Introduction

In this paper we report on some recent progress on the formulation and analysis of image function metrics designed to perform better than standard $L^2$-based metrics in terms of perceptual image quality. It is a continuation of work presented at ICIAR 2018 [4] and ICIAR 2014 [3], to which the interested reader is referred for more details.

Very briefly, in [3] we used the idea of "Weberizing" distance functions to show that the logarithmic $L^1$ distance between two image functions conforms to Weber's standard model of perception. The method employed in [3] could be viewed as rather *ad hoc*. In [4], we approached the problem from a more mathematical point of view, by employing appropriate nonuniform measures over the greyscale intensity to produce a class of alternate metrics between image functions. (The idea of such measures over greyscale space was introduced in [2].)

© Springer Nature Switzerland AG 2019
F. Karray et al. (Eds.): ICIAR 2019, LNCS 11662, pp. 297–308, 2019.
https://doi.org/10.1007/978-3-030-27202-9_27

These measures were defined by (nonconstant) greyscale density functions which conform (at least asymptotically, in the limit $I \to \infty$) to Weber's generalized model of perception. (The term "conform" will be defined in Sect. 2 below.)

By Weber's generalized model of perception we mean the following: Given a greyscale background intensity $I > 0$, the minimum change in intensity $\Delta I$ perceived by the human visual system (HVS) is related to $I$ as follows,

$$\frac{\Delta I}{I^a} = C, \tag{1}$$

where $a > 0$ and $C$ is constant, or at least roughly constant over a significant range of intensities $I$. The case $a = 1$ corresponds to the standard Weber model which is employed in practically all applications [7]. There are situations, however, in which other values of $a$, in particular, $a = 0.5$, may apply – see, for example, [5]. From Eq. (1), a Weberized distance between two functions $u$ and $v$ should tolerate greater/lesser differences over regions in which they assume higher/lower intensity values. The degree of toleration will be determined by the exponent $a$ in Eq. (1).

As mentioned in [4], the well known structural similarity (SSIM) measure [8,9] is already Weberized, according to the standard model $a = 1$, since it may be rewritten in terms of intensity ratios. This may well be quite sufficient in practice, but it would be interesting to investigate how SSIM could be modified to conform to the more general case, i.e., $a \neq 1$.

In [4], we showed that for $0 \leq a \leq 1$, the density function $\rho_a(I)$ which conforms, at least asymptotically, to Weber's model of perception is $\rho_a(I) = 1/I^a$. (In the case $a = 0$, i.e., zero Weber effect, $\rho_0(y) = 1$ corresponds to uniform Lebesgue measure in $I$-space.) The image function metrics produced by the measures which correspond to these density functions are as follows,

$$0 \leq a < 1: \quad D_a(u,v) = \int_X \left| u(x)^{-a+1} - v(x)^{-a+1} \right| dx$$

$$a = 1: \quad D_1(u,v) = \int_X \left| \ln u(x) - \ln v(x) \right| dx. \tag{2}$$

As mentioned in [4], it is more convenient to work with the $L^2$-based analogues of these metrics.

The primary purpose of this paper is to address some important mathematical details that were not considered in [4], including the following:

1. The results in [4] were obtained under the assumption of the existence of a continuous density function $\rho_a(I)$ for $a > 0$. In Sect. 2, we outline the main steps in a proof of the existence of a unique density function $\rho_a(y)$ which satisfies an invariance result (Eq. (9) below) that guarantees "conformity" to Weber's generalized model of perception. It is very interesting, at least from a mathematical viewpoint, to see how the "equal-area condition" in Eq. (9) is associated with the famous Abel functional equation.
2. In Sect. 3, the dominant asymptotic behaviour of the density functions $\rho_a(y)$ for $y \to \infty$ and $y \to 0^+$ are obtained in the cases (i) $0 < a < 1$ and (ii) $a > 1$.

All of these results are obtained by means of an asymptotic analysis of an "equal-area integral," cf. Eq. (9). (In [4], the result for $y \to \infty$ in the case $0 < a < 1$ was obtained using a differential equation approach.)

3. A method of computing the asymptotic expansion of $\rho_a(y)$ for $y \to \infty$ to any number of terms in the case $0 < a < 1$ is also presented in Sect. 3.

Finally, in Sect. 2, we address and correct a couple of unfortunate typographical errors which appeared in [4], specifically in Theorem 2 of that paper.

The basic mathematical ingredients of our formalism are as follows:

1. The **base (or pixel) space** $X \subset \mathbb{R}^n$ on which our signals/images are supported. Here, without loss of generality since our discussion is purely theoretical, we simply consider the one-dimensional case $X = [a, b]$.
2. The **greyscale range:** For an $A > 0$, $\mathbb{R}_g = [A, B]$, where $B < \infty$.
3. The **signal/image function space** $\mathcal{F} = \{u : X \to \mathbb{R}_g \mid u$ is measurable$\}$. From our definition of the greyscale range $\mathbb{R}_g$, $u \in \mathcal{F}$ is positive and bounded almost everywhere, i.e., $0 < A \leq u(x) \leq B < \infty$ for almost every $x \in X$. A consequence of this boundedness is that $\mathcal{F} \subset L^p(X)$ for all $p \geq 1$, where the $L^p(X)$ function spaces are defined in the usual way. For any $p \geq 1$, define a metric $d_p$ on $\mathcal{F}$ can be defined in the usual way, i.e.,

$$d_p(u, v) = \|u - v\|_p = \left[ \int_X [u(x) - v(x)]^p \, dx \right]^{1/p}, \quad u, v \in L^2(X). \quad (3)$$

## 2 Existence and Uniqueness of Greyscale Density Functions $\rho_a(y)$ for Generalized Weber's Model of Perception

In [4], we defined a class of intensity-dependent distance functions between functions in the space $\mathcal{F}$ as summarized below.

Consider two functions $u, v \in \mathcal{F}$ and define the following subsets of the base space $X = [a, b]$:

$$X_u = \{x \in X \mid u(x) \leq v(x)\} \qquad X_v = \{x \in X \mid v(x) \leq u(x)\}, \quad (4)$$

so that $X = X_u \cup X_v$. The sketch in Fig. 1 below should help with the visualization of our procedure.

The distance $D$ between $u$ and $v$ will be defined as an integration over vertical strips of width $dx$ and centered at $x \in [a, b]$. The contribution of each strip will **not**, in general, be determined by the usual lengths of the strips, i.e., the quantities $|u(x) - v(x)|$, but rather the **sizes** of the intervals $(u(x), v(x)] \subset \mathbb{R}_g$ and $(v(x), u(x)] \subset \mathbb{R}_g$ as assigned by a **measure** $\nu$ that is supported on the greyscale interval $\mathbb{R}_g = [A, B]$. The measures of the two intervals shown in the figure will be denoted as $\nu(u(x), v(x)]$ and $\nu(v(x), u(x)]$, respectively. The distance between $u$ and $v$ associated with the measure $\nu$ is now defined as follows,

$$D(u, v; \nu) = \int_{X_u} \nu(u(x), v(x)] \, dx \; + \; \int_{X_v} \nu(v(x), u(x)] \, dx, \quad (5)$$

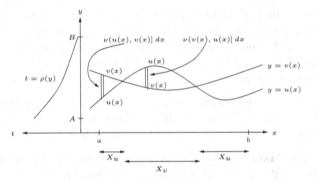

**Fig. 1.** Sketch of two nonnegative greyscale functions $u(x)$ and $v(x)$ with strips of width $dx$ that will contribute to the distance $D(u, v; \nu)$. A density function $\rho(y)$ over the greyscale range $\mathbb{R}_g = [A, B]$ is sketched at the left.

It is convenient to consider measures which are defined by continuous, non-negative density functions $\rho(y)$ for $y > 0$. (Such measures will be absolutely continuous with respect to Lebesgue measure.) Given a measure $\nu$ with density function $\rho$, then for any interval $(y_1, y_2] \subset \mathbb{R}_g$,

$$\nu(y_1, y_2] = \int_{y_1}^{y_2} \rho(y)\, dy = P(y_2) - P(y_1), \qquad (6)$$

where $P'(y) = \rho(y)$. The distance function $D(u, v; \nu)$ in Eq. (5) then becomes

$$D(u, v; \nu) = \int_X |P(u(x)) - P(v(x))|\, dx. \qquad (7)$$

**Special Case:** $\nu = m_g$, uniform Lebesgue measure on $\mathbb{R}_g$, where $\rho(y) = 1$ so that $P(y) = y$ in Eq. (7). This is the measure employed in most function metrics, e.g., the $L^p$ metrics in Eq. (3). The associated metric is

$$D(u, v, m_g) = \int_{X_u} [v(x) - u(x)]\, dx + \int_{X_v} [u(x) - v(x)]\, dx = \int_X |u(x) - v(x)|\, dx, \qquad (8)$$

the well known $L^1$ distance between $u$ and $v$.

As discussed in [4], the constancy of the Lebesgue density function $\rho(y) = 1$ implies that all greyscale intensity values are weighted equally in the computation of distances between image functions. However, Weber's model of perception in Eq. (1) suggests that for $a > 0$, the density function $\rho_a(y)$ should be a *decreasing* function of intensity $y$: As the intensity value increases, the HVS will tolerate greater differences between $u(x)$ and $v(x)$ before being perceived. We shall also require the density function $\rho_a(y)$ to conform to Weber's model in Eq. (1) according to the following criterion.

**Definition:** For a given $a > 0$, suppose that Weber's model of perception in Eq. (1) holds for a particular value of $C > 0$ for all values of $I \geq A$. (See Note 3 below.) We say that a measure $\nu_a(y)$ defined by the density function $\rho_y(y)$ **conforms to** or **accommodates** this Weber model if the following condition holds for all $I \geq A$,

$$\nu_a(I, I + \Delta I) = \int_I^{I+\Delta I} \rho_a(y)\, dy = K,\tag{9}$$

for some constant $K$, where $\Delta I = CI^a$ is the minimum change in perceived intensity at $I$ according to Eq. (1).

Equation (9) may be viewed as an invariance result with respect to perception. Its graphical interpretation in terms of equal areas enclosed by the density curve $\rho_a(y)$ is shown in Fig. 2 below.

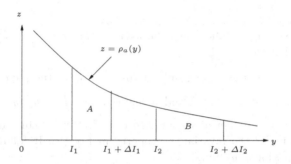

**Fig. 2.** Graphical interpretation of the "equal areas" invariance result in Eq. (9). Area of $A$ = Area of $B$.

## Notes

1. In the special case, $a = 1$, i.e., Weber's standard model, $\rho_1(y) = 1/y$ and $\nu(I, I + \Delta I) = \ln(1 + C)$ [4].
2. We may also include the special case $a = 0$, i.e., an absence of Weber's model, in the above definition. In this case $\rho_0(y) = 1$ so that $\nu = m_g$, Lebesgue measure on $\mathbb{R}_g$.
3. As mentioned earlier, Weber's model in Eq. (1) is valid only over a limited range of intensities. The requirement that Eq. (9) be true for all $I > A$ is imposed in order to establish the asymptotic behaviour of the density functions $\rho_a(y)$ for large $y$.

From Notes 1 and 2 above, it is natural to conjecture that for $a > 0$ in general, $\rho_a(y) = 1/y^a$ or at least approaches $1/y^a$ asymptotically as $y \to \infty$. It is easy to show that equality does not hold for $a \neq 1$. In [4], however, we proved that the asymptotic result holds for $0 < a < 1$. Unfortunately, there are two typographical errors in the presentation of this result, namely Theorem 2 in [4]:

(i) it is valid for $0 < a < 1$ and not $a > 0$ as stated, (ii) the asymptotic result $\rho_a(y) \approx 1/y^a$ is valid for $y \to \infty$ and not $y \to 0^+$ as stated. (These errors do not appear in the proof of the theorem given in the Appendix.)

We now present a significant improvement of the results obtained in [4] in terms of mathematical rigor, as summarized in Sect. 1. The following result, although seemingly trivial, will have some important consequences.

**Theorem 1:** For given values of $a > 0$ and $C > 0$, let $\rho_a(y)$ satisfy the invariance condition in Eq. (9). Then $\int_A^\infty \rho_a(y)\, dy = \infty$.

**Sketch of Proof:** Let $y_0 = A$, and $y_{n+1} = y_n + Cy_n^a$ for $n \geq 0$. It is not difficult to show that $y_n \to \infty$ as $n \to \infty$. Furthermore, from Eq. (9),

$$\int_A^{y_n} \rho_a(y)\, dy = nK \to \infty \quad \text{as} \quad n \to \infty. \tag{10}$$

This result already establishes that the asymptotic property $\rho_a(y) \sim 1/y^a$ as $y \to \infty$ cannot hold for $a > 1$.

In preparation for the main result of this section of the paper, let $g(y)$ be a continuous function on $[A, \infty)$ and define $G(x) = \int_A^x g(y)\, dy$ for all $x \geq A$. Clearly, $G(A) = 0$. Furthermore, suppose that for fixed values of $a > 0$ and $C > 0$, $g(y)$ satisfies the invariance property in Eq. (9). It follows that $G(x)$ satisfies the following equation,

$$G(x + Cx^a) - G(x) = K, \quad x \geq A. \tag{11}$$

For convenience, we define $f(x) = x + Cx^a$ and divide both sides of Eq. (11) by $K$ to obtain the equation,

$$H(f(x)) - H(x) = 1, \tag{12}$$

where $H(x) = K^{-1}G(x)$. Equation (12) is known as **Abel's equation**, a well known **functional equation** [6].

We now state the main result of this section of the paper.

**Theorem 2:** For given values of $a > 0$ and $C > 0$, there exists a unique, continuous function $\rho_a(y)$ defined on $[A, \infty)$ which satisfies Eq. (9).

**Sketch of Proof:** Consider the following linear functional equation for the function $g(x)$ for $x \geq A$,

$$g(x + Cx^a)(1 + aCx^{a-1}) - g(x) = 0. \tag{13}$$

(This equation may be obtained by differentiating both sides of Eq. (9) with respect to $x$ with the assumption that $g(x)$ is continuous.) Equation (13) is a

special case of the following family of linear functional equations studied by
Belitskii and Lyubich in [1],

$$P(x)\psi(F(x)) + Q(x)\psi(x) = \gamma(x), \quad x \in X, \tag{14}$$

where $X$ is the topological space over which the equation is being considered.
Here, $X = [A, \infty)$, $P(x) = 1 + aCx^{a-1}$, $F(x) = 1 + aCx^a$, $Q(x) = -1$ and
$\gamma(x) = 0$. In [1], it is shown that if the Abel equation associated with Eq. (14),
namely,

$$\phi(F(x)) - \phi(x) = 1, \tag{15}$$

has a continuous solution $\phi(x)$, then Eq. (14) is *totally solvable*, i.e., it has a
continuous solution $\psi(x)$ for every continuous function $\gamma(x)$.

The existence of continuous solutions to Eq. (15) depends on the iteration
dynamics of the function $F(x)$ on the space $X$. In this case, $F(x) = x + Cx^a$ is
an increasing function on $X = [A, \infty)$, the dynamics of which is quite straightforward: $F : X \to X$ and for all $x \in X$, $F^n(x) \to \infty$ as $n \to \infty$. As such, the
conditions of Corollary 1.6 of [1] are satisfied, i.e., every compact set $S \in X$ is
wandering under the action of $F$. Therefore, Eq. (15) has a continuous solution
(unique up to a constant, i.e., if $\phi(x)$ satisfies Eq. (15), then so does $\phi(x) + C$
for any $C \in \mathbb{R}$). This, in turn, implies that Eq. (14) has a unique, nonzero,
continuous solution.

Additional analysis of Eqs. (13) and (9) yields the following properties of
$\rho_a(y)$ for $a > 0$ which we state without formal proof because of space limitations:

1. $\rho_a(y) > 0$ for all $x > 0$. (Or at least we choose a positive solution of Eq. (13).
   If $g(x)$ is a solution to Eq. (13), then so is $Cg(x)$ for any $C \in \mathbb{R}$.
2. $\rho_a(y)$ is decreasing on $[0, \infty)$ and $\rho_a(y) \to 0$ as $y \to \infty$. This is to be expected:
   In Eq. (9), the length of the interval $[x, x + Cx^a]$ increases with $x$. The equal-
   area condition would dictate that $\rho_a(y)$ decrease with $y$.
3. As $y \to 0^+$, $\rho_a(y) \to \infty$. This is expected from the equal-area condition since
   the length of the interval $[x, x + Cx^a]$ decreases as $x \to 0^+$.

# 3    Asymptotic Behaviour of Density Functions $\rho_a(y)$

The determination of the asymptotic behaviour of the density functions $\rho_a(y)$ is
centered on the equal-area property of Eq. (9).

**Asymptotic Behaviour of $\rho_a(y)$ as $y \to \infty$ for the Case $0 < a < 1$**

**Theorem 3:** For a given $a \in (0, 1)$ and $C > 0$, the asymptotic expansion of the
Weber density function $\rho_a(y)$ satisfying Eq. (9) has the following form,

$$\rho_a(y) = \sum_{n=0}^{\infty} \frac{A_n}{y^{a+n(1-a)}} \quad \text{as} \quad y \to \infty. \tag{16}$$

The first three terms of this expansion are

$$\rho_a(y) = \frac{1}{y^a} + \frac{1}{2}aC\frac{1}{y} - \frac{1}{12}aC^2(2a-1)\frac{1}{y^{2-a}} + \cdots. \tag{17}$$

Note that the leading term of this expansion is in agreement with the asymptotic result presented in [4].

The expansion in Eq. (16) is obtained by repeated use of the following important result.

**Lemma 1:** For $x > 0$, $0 < a < 1$ and $b > 0$,

$$\int_x^{x+Cx^a} \frac{1}{y^b}\, dy = Cx^{a-b} - \frac{1}{2}bC^2 x^{2a-b-1} + \cdots \quad \text{as} \quad x \to \infty. \tag{18}$$

**Sketch of Proof of Lemma:** Use antiderivative of $1/y^b$ (considering the cases $b \neq 1$ and $b = 1$ separately). For $b \neq 1$, let $(x + Cx^a)^{1-b} = x^{1-b}(1 + Cx^{a-1})^{1-b}$ and expand the term in parenthesis via binomial series. Similar procedure for $b = 1$ involving the ln function and binomial series.

**Sketch of Proof of Theorem 3:** Here are the first few steps involved in the derivation of Eq. (16).

1. Setting $b = a$ in Eq. (18) yields

$$\int_x^{x+Cx^a} \frac{1}{y^a}\, dy = C + O(x^{a-1}) \quad \text{as} \quad x \to \infty, \tag{19}$$

which implies that the equal-area condition in Eq. (9) is satisfied, to leading order, by $\rho_a(y) \sim 1/y^a$, in agreement with the asymptotic result of [4].
2. Set $b = a$ in Eq. (18) and rewrite it as follows,

$$\int_x^{x+Cx^a} \frac{1}{y^a}\, dy - C = -\frac{1}{2}aC^2 x^{a-1} + O(x^{2a-2}) \quad \text{as} \quad x \to \infty. \tag{20}$$

3. Up to a constant, the first term on the right side of Eq. (20) has the same behaviour, $x^{a-1}$, as the first term in Eq. (18) in the case $b = 1$. Now multiply both sides of Eq. (18) in the case $b = 1$ by the factor $-\dfrac{1}{aC}$ and subtract the resulting equation from Eq. (20) to obtain the result,

$$\int_x^{x+Cx^a} \left[ \frac{1}{y^a} + \frac{1}{2}aC\frac{1}{y} \right] dy - C = O(x^{2a-2}) \quad \text{as} \quad x \to \infty. \tag{21}$$

The term in square brackets is an improved approximation of $\rho_a(y)$ as $y \to \infty$ in terms of the equal-area condition of Eq. (9).
4. Higher order terms in Eq. (18) involve powers of the form $x^{n(a-1)}$. Matching these terms with the leading term $x^{a-b}$ in Eq. (18) is accomplished by selecting $b = a + n(1 - a)$ for $n \geq 0$, yielding the expansion in Eq. (16).

**Asymptotic Behaviour of $\rho_a(y)$ as $y \to \infty$ for the Case $a > 1$**
Recall, from Theorem 1, that in the case $a > 1$, we do not expect that $\rho_a(y) \sim 1/y^a$ as $y \to \infty$. This is confirmed by the following result, which can easily be derived with some elementary Calculus:

**Lemma 2:** For a given $a > 0$ and $C > 0$, define the function

$$G_{a,b}(x) = \int_x^{x+Cx^a} \frac{1}{y^b} \, dy, \quad x > 0. \tag{22}$$

1. If $0 < b \leq 1$, then $G_{a,b}(x) \to \infty$ as $x \to \infty$.
2. If $b > 1$, then $G_{a,b}(x) \to 0$ as $x \to \infty$.

This leads us to consider functions which may involve $\ln y$ along with the term $1/y$. The following result, which can also be derived via Calculus, is helpful.

**Lemma 3:** For a given $a > 0$ and $C > 0$ define the function

$$H_{a,p}(x) = \int_x^{x+Cx^a} \frac{1}{y \, (\ln y)^p} \, dy, \quad x > 0. \tag{23}$$

1. If $0 < p < 1$, then $H_{a,p}(x) \to \infty$ as $x \to \infty$.
2. If $p = 1$, then $H_{a,1}(x) \to \ln a$ as $x \to \infty$.
3. If $p > 1$, then $H_{a,p}(x) \to 0$ as $x \to \infty$.

The above result suggests that $\rho_a(y) \sim 1/(y \ln y)$ as $y \to \infty$ for $a > 1$. Using some results from the asymptotic analysis involved in the proof of Lemma 3, we obtain the following two-term approximation,

$$\rho_a(y) \simeq \frac{1}{y \ln y} - \left( \frac{\ln C}{a} \right) \frac{1}{y \, (\ln y)^2} \quad \text{as} \quad y \to \infty. \tag{24}$$

This result is interesting in that the leading-order term is independent of $a$, unlike the situation for $a \leq 1$.

Further asymptotic analysis of this case will be quite complicated due to the possible mixed presence of powers of $y$ and $\ln y$ in the denominators of additional terms in the expansion.

**Asymptotic Behaviour of $\rho_a(y)$ as $y \to 0^+$**

There is a reciprocity with regard to the integrals involved in the previous analysis of $y \to \infty$ and those involved in the case $y \to 0^+$, It is quite straightforward to show, for example, that an analysis of the asymptotic limit $x \to 0^+$ for the case $0 < a < 1$ employs the same equations as those used in the analysis of $x \to \infty$ for the case $a > 1$. For this reason, we simply state the two major results below:

$$0 < a < 1: \quad \rho_a(y) \simeq \frac{1}{y \ln y} - \left( \frac{\ln C}{a} \right) \frac{1}{y \, (\ln y)^2} \quad \text{as} \quad y \to 0^+,$$

$$a > 1: \quad \rho_a(y) = \frac{1}{y^a} + \frac{1}{2} aC \frac{1}{y} - \frac{1}{12} aC^2 (2a - 1) \frac{1}{y^{2-a}} + \cdots \text{as} \quad y \to 0^+,$$

where the second result is the truncation of an asymptotic expansion of the same form, and the same constants $A_n$, as in Eq. (16).

**Some Comments on These Asymptotic Results**
The asymptotic analysis of the density functions $\rho_a(y)$ in the case $y \to 0^+$ is more of a theoretical exercise since we are working with the range space $\mathbb{R}_g = [A, B]$ with lower "cutoff" intensity level $A > 0$. Indeed, the validity of Weber's model for low intensity values is also questionable. We are more interested in the high-intensity region and expect that the behaviour of $\rho_a(y)$ is well described by the asymptotic formulas for $y \to \infty$. In fact, as was done in [4], we consider only the leading-order behaviour of the asymptotic expansions: Although it would be an interesting mathematical exercise, the inclusion of subdominant terms would most probably be "overkill" in practice, especially in light of the fact that Weber's model is, in itself, an approximation.

## 4    Revisiting the Distance Functions Associated with the Density Functions $\rho_a(y)$

**The Case $0 < a < 1$**
The metrics associated with the leading asymptotic behaviour of the density functions, $\rho_a(y) \sim 1/y^a$ for $0 \le a \le 1$, were presented in Eq. (2). As mentioned in [4], it is rather difficult – although not impossible – to work with these $L^1$-based metrics so we consider their $L^2$-based analogues,

$$0 \le a < 1: \quad D_{2,a}(u, v) = \left[ \int_X \left[ u(x)^{-a+1} - v(x)^{-a+1} \right]^2 dx \right]^{1/2}$$

$$a = 1: \quad D_{2,a}(u, v) = \left[ \int_X \left[ \ln u(x) - \ln v(x) \right]^2 dx \right]^{1/2}. \quad (25)$$

It is rather straightforward to show that these metrics are equivalent to the $L^2$ metric on our space $F(X)$, i.e., $p = 2$ in Eq. (3). First let us recall the Mean Value Theorem of elementary Calculus:

**Theorem 4:** Let $g : [A, B] \to \mathbb{R}$ be continuous on $[A, B]$ and differentiable on $(A, B)$. Then for any $y_1, y_2 \in [A, B]$, there exists a $c$ between $y_1$ and $y_2$ such that

$$g(y_2) - g(y_1) = g'(c)(y_2 - y_1). \quad (26)$$

In what follows, we shall also exploit the fact that for $u \in F(X)$, $A \le u(x) \le B$ for a.e. $x \in X = [a, b]$.

1. $0 < a < 1$. For a fixed $a \in (0, 1)$, we apply the Mean Value Theorem to the function $g(y) = y^{-a+1}$ on $[A, B]$ with $A > 0$, as follows. Then for a.e. $x \in [a, b]$,

$$u(x)^{-a+1} - v(x)^{-a+1} = \frac{1 - a}{c^a} (u(x) - v(x)), \quad (27)$$

where $c$ lies between $u(x)$ and $v(x)$. Taking absolute values, and noting that $A < c < B$, we obtain the inequalities for a.e. $x \in [a, b]$,

$$\frac{1 - a}{B^a} |u(x) - v(x)| \le \left| u(x)^{1-a} - v(x)^{1-a} \right| \le \frac{1 - a}{A^a} |u(x) - v(x)|. \quad (28)$$

Now square all terms, integrate over $[a, b]$ and take square roots to obtain the result,

$$\frac{1-a}{B^a} d_2(u, v) \leq D_{2,a}(u, v) \leq \frac{1-a}{A^a} d_2(u, v). \tag{29}$$

2. $a = 1$. The Mean Value Theorem is now applied to the function $g(y) = \ln y$ on $[A, B]$. For a.e. $x \in [a, b]$,

$$\ln u(x) - \ln v(x) = \frac{1}{c}(u(x) - v(x)), \tag{30}$$

where $c$ lies between $u(x)$ and $v(x)$. Noting once again that $A < c < B$, and proceeding as in the previous case, we arrive at the result,

$$\frac{1}{B} d_2(u, v) \leq D_{2,1}(u, v) \leq \frac{1}{A} d_2(u, v). \tag{31}$$

**The Case $a > 1$**

This case was not considered in [4] because of a lack of knowledge of the large-$y$ behaviour of the density function $\rho_a(y)$ for $a > 1$ at the time. The asymptotic result in Eq. (24) suggests that we consider a distance function of the following form for the case $a > 1$,

$$D_a(u, v) = \int_X |\ln(\ln u(x)) - \ln(\ln v(x))| \, dx, \tag{32}$$

with $L^2$ analogue,

$$D_{2,a}(u, v) = \left[ \int_X [\ln(\ln u(x)) - \ln(\ln v(x))]^2 \, dx \right]^{1/2}. \tag{33}$$

In this case, it may be desirable that the lower greyscale limit $A > e$, in which case $\ln(\ln y) > 0$ for $y \in \mathbb{R}_g$.

Mathematically, the problem of approximating functions in this metric is a very interesting one, and worthy of further study. Whether or not this problem has any practical value is related to the question of whether or not Weber's model is useful or even valid in the case $a > 1$. These, of course, are open questions at this time.

## 5   Concluding Remarks

In this paper, we have addressed some important mathematical details involving intensity-based measures that were not considered in our earlier ICIAR 2018 paper [4]. From a practical perspective, the most important details are (a) the proof of existence and uniqueness of greyscale density functions $\rho_a(y)$ which conform, in the "equal area sense," to Weber's generalized model of perception and (b) their dominant asymptotic behaviour in the case $y \to \infty$. Of course, the actual practical value of these results remains to be explored. In our previous works, admittedly, an examination of the applications of this method was limited to a few simple examples. More work could, and should, be done here and perhaps the area of high dynamic range imaging would serve as a good testing ground.

The "equal area condition" of Eq. (9) represents a unique way of looking at Weber's generalized model of perception. Not only is it interesting from a theoretical, i.e., mathematical, perspective but it also yields a concrete result, namely, a measure $\nu_a$ defined by a density function $\rho_a(y)$ which, in turn, defines a metric which "conforms" to Weber's model. It would be most interesting to investigate whether such a condition, or suitable modification thereof, applies to other models, including those outside of perception/image processing.

**Acknowledgements.** We gratefully acknowledge that this research has been supported in part by the Natural Sciences and Engineering Research Council of Canada (ERV) in the form of a Discovery Grant as well as Assistantships from the Department of Applied Mathematics and the Faculty of Mathematics, University of Waterloo (DL).

# References

1. Belitskii, G., Lyubich, Y.: The Abel equation and total solvability of linear functional equations. Studia Mathematica **127**(1), 81–97 (1998)
2. Forte, B., Vrscay, E.R.: Solving the inverse problem for function and image approximation using iterated function systems. Dyn. Contin. Discret. Impuls. Syst. **1**, 177–231 (1995)
3. Kowalik-Urbaniak, I.A., La Torre, D., Vrscay, E.R., Wang, Z.: Some "Weberized" $L^2$-based methods of signal/image approximation. In: Campilho, A., Kamel, M. (eds.) ICIAR 2014. LNCS, vol. 8814, pp. 20–29. Springer, Cham (2014). https://doi.org/10.1007/978-3-319-11758-4_3
4. Li, D., La Torre, D., Vrscay, E.R.: The use of intensity-based measures to produce image function metrics which accommodate Weber's models of perception. In: Campilho, A., Karray, F., ter Haar Romeny, B. (eds.) ICIAR 2018. LNCS, vol. 10882, pp. 326–335. Springer, Cham (2018). https://doi.org/10.1007/978-3-319-93000-8_37
5. Michon, J.A.: Note on the generalized form of Weber's Law. Percept. Psychophys. **1**, 329–330 (1966)
6. Targonski, G.: Topics in Iteration Theory. Vandenhoeck & Ruprecht, Göttingen (1981)
7. Wandell, B.A.: Foundations of Vision. Sinauer, Sunderland (1995)
8. Wang, Z., Bovik, A.C.: Mean squared error: love it or leave it? a new look at signal fidelity measures. IEEE Sig. Proc. Mag. **26**, 98–117 (2009)
9. Wang, Z., Bovik, A.C., Sheikh, H.R., Simoncelli, E.P.: Image quality assessment: from error visibility to structural similarity. IEEE Trans. Image Process. **13**(4), 600–612 (2004)

# HMM Based Keyword Spotting System in Printed/Handwritten Arabic/Latin Documents with Identification Stage

Ahmed Cheikh Rouhou[1,3,4(✉)], Yousri Kessentini[1,2,4], and Slim Kanoun[3,4]

[1] Digital Research Center of Sfax, Sfax, Tunisia
ahmed.cheikhrouhou@crns.rnrt.tn
[2] LITIS Laboratory, St Etienne du Rouvray, France
yousri.kessentini@litislab.eu
[3] National Engineering School of Sfax, Sfax, Tunisia
slim.kanoun@gmail.com
[4] MIRACL Laboratory Sfax, Sfax, Tunisia

**Abstract.** In this paper, we propose a novel script independent approach for word spotting in printed and handwritten multi-script documents. Since each writing type and script needs to be processed using a specific spotting engine, the proposed system proceeds on two stages: First, a one-step identification method of the writing type and the script of the input image document. The identification system is based on HMM and does not need any additional resources (training, preprocessing, feature extraction) besides those used in the spotting step. Second, a specific word spotting method is used to detect any given keyword in document images. The proposed spotting system is lexicon-free, i.e., able to spot arbitrary keywords that are not required to be known at the training stage. The global system has been evaluated on mixed corpus of public databases such as KHATT, KAFD for Arabic script and ALTID, RIMES for Latin script. The experimental results on both document-level writing type and script type identification and keyword spotting confirm the effectiveness of the proposed scheme.

**Keywords:** Word spotting · Script identification · HMM · Handwriting · Machine printed · Multi-script · Arabic · Latin

## 1 Introduction

With the increasing communication between different world communities, a vast amount of documents and forms are sent to companies for processing. These documents have different writing types (printed/handwritten) and various scripts (Latin, Arabic, Indian, Chinese ...). The automatic processing of such digitized corpora is a real challenge since each script and writing type needs to be processed using a specific recognition engine. Consequently, writing type and script need to be identified in order to design a generic spotting system.

Few studies have focused on multi-script word spotting systems. One possible answer to this problem is to propose script independent techniques which should

© Springer Nature Switzerland AG 2019
F. Karray et al. (Eds.): ICIAR 2019, LNCS 11662, pp. 309–320, 2019.
https://doi.org/10.1007/978-3-030-27202-9_28

be invariant to the script type [1,2]. In [3], the authors proposed a spotting system for Arabic, Latin and Sanskrit scripts using Gradient, Structural and Concavity features and Dynamic Time Warping for matching. A similar approach is proposed in [4] using statistical Moment based features and cosine similarity metric. The proposed framework is evaluated on three languages: English, Hindi and Sanskrit. In [5], authors propose a script independent word spotting framework using script independent methods for feature extraction, training and recognition. The system was evaluated on three languages: English, Arabic and Devanagari. The main drawback of this work is that is not able to automatically identify the script.

One other possible strategy is to identify the script type in a first stage and use the suitable spotting system in the second stage. Script identification has been very much studied during the last years. The task consists in predicting the script of the document and its writing type (printed/handwritten). Recent studies are broadly grouped into global, local and hybrid approaches depending on the structure of the input data such as bloc images, line images, word images or connected components. A global identification approach is presented in [6] to discriminate between Arabic and Latin scripts in printed and handwritten documents. Three different feature sets based on gray-level co-occurrence matrices, Gabor filters and wavelets are compared using a K-Nearest Neighbor (KNN) classifier. A line based identification approach is proposed in [7] using structural characteristics to discriminate between printed and handwritten Latin texts. In [8], a word-level system to identify Farsi and Arabic scripts is proposed using structural features, histogram features and profile features. Lately, Saidani et al. [9] have proposed an Arabic/Latin and printed/handwritten word discrimination approach based on HOG descriptors. In [10], the authors propose an identification system working at the connected component level for the discrimination of handwritten and printed Bangla and English scripts.

In this paper, we present a novel approach to spot printed and handwritten multi-script documents. To the best of our knowledge, this is the first work to deal with documents with different writing types and scripts. The proposed system does not use any prior knowledge about the script and proceeds in two stages: First, an identification stage identifies the writing type (printed/handwritten) and the script (Latin/Arabic) of the input image document. Second, a specialized HMM based word spotting system is used to detect any given keyword in the document image.

The remaining of this paper is organized as follows. In Sect. 2, we present the general architecture of the proposed multi-script handwritten/printed keyword spotting system including line segmentation, preprocessing and feature extraction steps. In Sect. 3, we describe our HMM based identification system including the modeling, training and decoding steps. The experimental evaluation is described in Sect. 4. In the last section, our main conclusions are drawn and some future perspectives are suggested.

## 2    Multi-script Handwriting/Printed Word Spotting System

The proposed spotting system proceeds in several steps as presented in Fig. 1. It takes as input a document image. In the first step, documents are segmented into lines. Then, preprocessing is applied to each input line image. In the next step, HOG based features are extracted from a sequence of overlapping sliding windows spanning each document line. Then, a line level identification system is used to identify the script and the writing type of each line. The script and writing type of the document are deduced by combining the identification results obtained at the line level. Finally, a specific word spotting system is used to detect any given keyword in the document image. We describe in the following sections the line segmentation, preprocessing, and feature extraction steps, which are common to the identification and the spotting sub-systems.

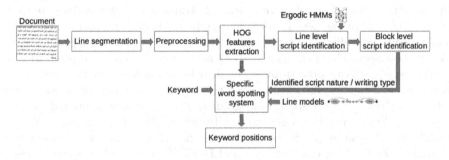

**Fig. 1.** Global system description

### 2.1    Line Segmentation

The line segmentation process is an important and difficult task, mainly due to variable skew angles along the document or even along the text line, and adjacent text lines. We have implemented a line segmentation method based on a connected component analysis (see [11] for details). To improve the line segmentation quality, we propose an algorithm based on connected-components-analysis in order to remove the peripheral noise belonging to other lines. Figure 2 shows the result of this algorithm on a text line image. For every connected-component (CC) with certain size (SCC) in the line image, the proposed algorithm is invoked to label it as a peripheral or non peripheral CC. A connected-component is labeled as peripheral if it touches the peripheral areas of the line image and does not belong to the baseline writing zone.

### 2.2    Preprocessing

Preprocessing is applied to line images in order to eliminate noise and ease the feature extraction procedure. In an ideal handwriting model, the words are

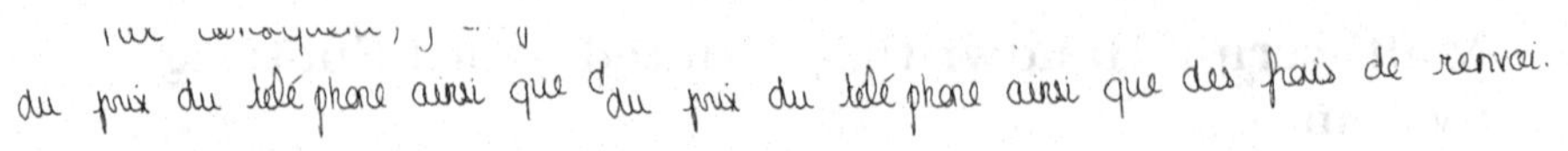

(a) Input Image                    (b) Output Image

**Fig. 2.** Line segmentation cleaning

supposed to be written horizontally and with vertical ascenders and descenders. In real situations, such conditions are rarely met. We use skew and slant correction so as to normalize text line images. A contour smoothing is then applied to eliminate small blobs on the contour.

### 2.3   Feature Extraction

We use Histogram of Oriented Gradient (HOG) [12] as a feature descriptor for the discrimination of handwritten, printed Arabic and Latin scripts. Indeed, in [13], the authors achieved a detailed study of HOG descriptors application and proved their efficiency for the identification of handwritten/printed Arabic/Latin scripts. The main idea of HOG is to represent the local properties of shapes, which are captured through the distribution of local gradients intensity in a particular region. HOG features are computed by dividing the image region into small "cells". One histogram of gradient orientations is computed in each cell. Then, histograms are concatenated, bringing a final high dimensional representation of local properties of the image region. Line images are divided into a sequence of local regions or frames and HOG features are computed for each frame. The dimensionality of the feature vectors used in our experiments is 64.

### 2.4   Script and Writing Type Identification

The proposed identification system aims to discriminate between Arabic and Latin scripts for both handwritten and printed writing types. To this end, we have chosen to use Hidden Markov Models (HMM) given their ability to learn a better representation of the script specificities and to absorb the writing variability. The system takes the line images represented by their corresponding HOG features sequences as input. HOG features sequences are organized left to right and right to left to feed the specific (Arabic/Latin) HMM models in order to describe the natural writing order of the scripts.

We define four basic HMM models associated to each writing type and script namely Handwritten Arabic, Printed Arabic, Handwritten Latin and Printed Latin. The four models are defined by an ergodic structure concatenating all character models of the corresponding script. These HMMs are trained from four script specific training corpus. The Latin characters set of the model consists of 72 models corresponding to the 52 upper and lower case Latin characters, numerical digits and accented letters. The Arabic character set of models is made up of 150 character to account for the various shapes an Arabic character may have depending on its position within the word (beginning, middle, end position within a word). Other models account for additional symbols such as "shadda". For both Latin and Arabic scripts, each character model is composed of four emitting states. The observation probabilities are modeled by Gaussian Mixtures. The embedded training is used where all character models are trained in parallel using Baum-Welch algorithm applied on line examples.

The identification of the script and the writing type is performed by processing each input line image using the Viterbi algorithm and finding the maximum probability path for each of the 4 defined HMMs and then decide among those models for the most likely one. Arabic and Latin models are fed with the same feature stream but choosing a left-right ordering for latin script models and a right-left ordering for the Arabic models. The processing steps of the identification system are summarized in Fig. 3.

Document script and writing type identification is performed by the combination of the line level script identification results, by majority voting.

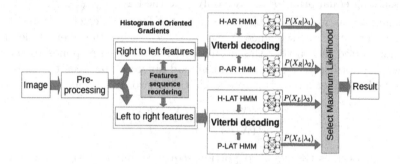

**Fig. 3.** Identification system overview

## 3   Line Based Spotting System

The spotting system takes as input a document image where the script and the writing type have been identified in the previous stage. Its output is the hypothesized keywords in the document and their respective position. The spotting system proceeds at the line level and does not need the line segmentation into words. The main idea is to build one HMM for an entire line which consists of a filler model accounting for irrelevant words for the task and the model of the keyword. These two alternative models are put in parallel in the proposed line model see Fig. 4. The keyword model represents the keyword character sequence that can occur at the beginning, in the middle, or at the end of the text line. The filler model is typically an ergodic graphical model composed of all characters used in the identification system.

Decoding a text line image characterized by an observed feature vector sequence $X = x_1, \ldots, x_N$ using the global line model $\omega$ is performed using

**Fig. 4.** Global line model containing the keyword, and the filler model. The line model is also made of a space model ("SP"), and structural initial and final models.

the Viterbi algorithm which returns the most likely character sequence and its associated likelihood $P(X|\omega)$.

It is well known that likelihood scores are insufficient measures to assess the confidence of a hypothesis. Instead, posterior probabilities are preferred as they account for a normalized score which can be obtained by applying Bayes' rule:

$$P(\omega|X) = \frac{P(X|\omega) \times P(\omega)}{P(X)} \tag{1}$$

Assuming equal priors $P(\omega)$, we only take the terms $\frac{P(X|\omega)}{P(X)}$.

Generally, in word spotting problems, $P(X)$ can be calculated by decoding the feature vector sequence $X = x_1, \ldots, x_N$ using the filler model $F$. It is demonstrated in [14] that this normalized line score corresponds to the normalized keyword score, because the likelihood difference between the global line model and the filler model is zero outside the keyword position.

$$\frac{P(X|\omega)}{P(X|F)} = \frac{P(X_{s,e}|K)}{P(X_{s,e}|F)} \tag{2}$$

where $X_{s,e}$ designs the keyword portion sequence and $K$ designs the keyword model.

The final score $S_K$ is obtained by normalizing the log-likelihood difference with the width of the keyword $L_K = e - s$.

$$S_K = \frac{\log P(X|\omega) - \log P(X|F)}{L_K} \tag{3}$$

### 3.1   Modeling the Inter-PAWs Space for Arabic Script

Arabic script is always cursive even when printed. Words consist of connected components or sub-words, and these are often called Part of Arabic Words (PAWs) in the literature. The presence of PAWs in Arabic words increases the complexity of spotting due to the lack of clear boundaries between words. In fact, in Arabic script, there is no difference between inter-PAWs space and intra-words space (see Fig. 5).

We believe that taking into account the inter-PAWs spaces in the word spotting model could enhance the system accuracy. With a great inter-PAWs space,

**Fig. 5.** An Arabic text line showing differences between inter-PAWs spaces and intra-words spaces

the system may produce random output labels between PAWs. Moreover, if the system detects a large space between PAWs, this will affect the spotting process, and only a portion of the keyword will be detected. Therefore, we define the inter-PAWs space as a HMM model named sp-PAW, trained like the other character models using all inter-PAWs space utterances in the training set. This model is integrated in the global line model as presented in Fig. 6.

**Fig. 6.** Global line model integrating the inter-PAWs spaces: First, the system detects the possible PAWs using the ASCII-presentation of the keyword. Second, the sp-PAW model is inserted between PAWs in the Keyword Model.

## 4    Experiments and Results

### 4.1    Script Identification Results

To evaluate the performance of our identification system, a corpus was collected from different public word datasets. For Arabic script, handwritten samples (HA) are collected from the KHATT dataset [15] which contains 9327 line images written by 1000 people. The printed dataset is collected from the KAFD dataset [16] containing line images with 40 fonts and 10 sizes. 6 fonts (Andalus, Arabic Transparent, DecoType Naskh, Tahoma, Simplified Arabic and M Unicode Sara), and 6 font sizes (6, 8, 10, 12, 14 and 16) are used. Latin handwritten line images are extracted from the RIMES dataset used for the ICDAR 2011 handwriting recognition competitions [17]. Printed line images are collected from the newly published database ALTID [18]. The database is made up of 12000 line images for training, 2000 line images for validation and 4000 line images for test.

Table 1 displays the line level confusion matrix of our identification system. The major diagonal terms indicate the proportion of correctly identified samples while the off-diagonal terms indicate the proportion of misclassified samples.

From this matrix, it can be observed that an average identification rate of 97.1% is achieved. The results analysis shows that the proposed system correctly identifies printed Latin and handwritten Arabic lines in respectively 99.6% and 99.8% of the cases. Figure 7 shows some examples where the system fails to identify the text lines script correctly. We notice that a large number of the confused samples are due to the low quality of the line segmentation (see Fig. 7(a)), or to the presence of crossed-out text in the line image (see Fig. 7(b) or to the use of some fonts which look like handwriting (see Fig. 7(c) (d)).

**Table 1.** The line-level script identification system performances

|        | H-AR    | P-AR    | H-LAT  | P-LAT   |
|--------|---------|---------|--------|---------|
| H-AR   | **99.8%** | 0.1%  | 0%     | 0.1%    |
| P-AR   | 0.1%    | **90.9%** | 9%   | 0%      |
| H-LAT  | 11%     | 0%      | **89%** | 0%     |
| P-LAT  | 0%      | 0.1%    | 0.3%   | **99.6%** |

To evaluate our system at the document level, we used a test document image dataset composed of 182 handwritten Latin documents, 246 handwritten Arabic documents, 115 printed Arabic documents and 234 printed Latin documents. As shown in Table 2, the proposed system provides good results at the document level. An average identification rate of 98% is achieved.

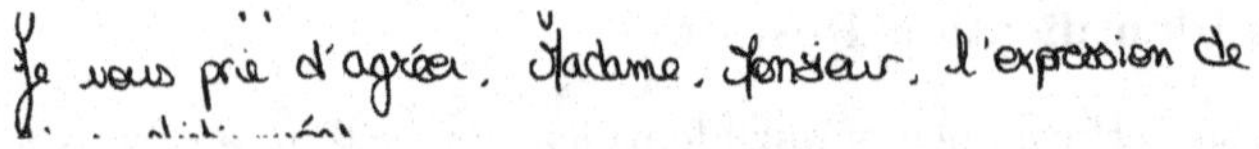

(a) Latin handwriting identified as Arabic handwriting

(b) Arabic handwriting identified as Arabic printed

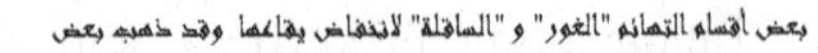

(c) Arabic printed identified as Arabic handwriting

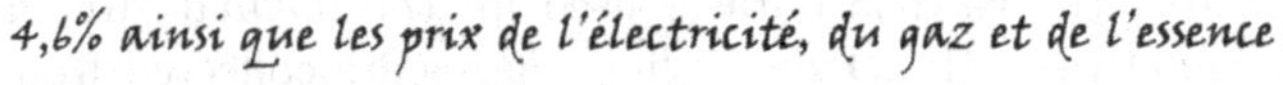

(d) Latin printed identified as Latin handwriting

**Fig. 7.** Examples of incorrectly identified line images

**Table 2.** The document-level script identification system performances

|         | H-AR   | P-AR   | H-LAT  | P-LAT |
|---------|--------|--------|--------|-------|
| H-AR    | **100%** | 0%   | 0%     | 0%    |
| P-AR    | 0%     | **99.2%** | 0.8%  | 0%    |
| H-LAT   | 6.9%   | 0%     | **93.1%** | 0%  |
| P-LAT   | 0%     | 0%     | 0%     | **100%** |

## 4.2   Word Spotting Results

To evaluate the performance of our spotting system, experiments have been conducted on three datasets: RIMES dataset for handwritten Latin script, KHATT dataset for handwritten Arabic script and KAFD dataset for printed Arabic script. In order to evaluate the spotting system, we computed recall (R) and precision measures (P). To this end, the number of true positives (TP), false positives (FP), and false negatives (FN) were evaluated for all possible threshold values. From these values, a recall-precision curve was presented by cumulating these values over all keyword queries.

$$R = \frac{TP}{TP + FN} \quad P = \frac{TP}{TP + FP} \tag{4}$$

The HMM-based spotting results for handwritten Latin script, printed Arabic script and handwritten Arabic script are presented in Figs. 8, 9 and 10, respectively. The recall-precision curves are given using a global threshold, i.e the threshold value is independent of the keyword. Experiments were conducted using 25, 50 and 100 keywords to investigate the effect of different number of keywords on the system performance. The system performance was noticed to be affected by the size of the keyword list because its precision decreases as the size of the list increases. This can be explained by the fact that some keywords are more difficult to retrieve (for instance the short ones) than some others (the longer ones). Figure 11 shows some examples of qualitative results where our system correctly detected the keyword and in Fig. 13 some examples where it failed.

To evaluate the influence of the inter-PAWs space modeling process, we represent in Fig. 13 the performance of our word spotting system with and without inter-PAWs space modeling using precision and recall. It was noted that the inter-PAWs space modeling process gives a better result on Handwritten Arabic documents independently of the number of keywords. For printed Arabic documents, we obtained similar results with and without inter-PAWs space modeling. This is due to the variation in handwriting, especially irregular spaces between sub-words and words (Fig. 12).

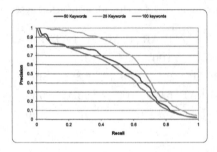

**Fig. 8.** Word spotting performance on handwritten Latin script

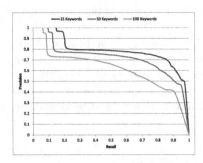

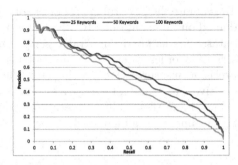

**Fig. 9.** Word spotting performance on printed Arabic script

**Fig. 10.** Word spotting performance on handwritten Arabic script

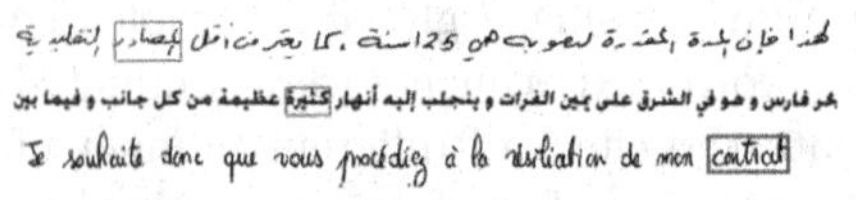

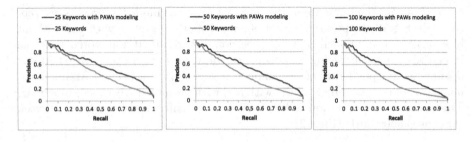

**Fig. 11.** Some examples of qualitative results where our system detected keywords

**Fig. 12.** Some examples of qualitative results where our system fails to detect keywords. A box is drawn around the detected keyword, correct keyword is underlined.

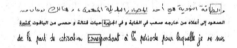

**Fig. 13.** Word spotting performance on KHATT database with and without inter-PAWs space modeling

# 5    Conclusion and Future Works

In this paper, we presented a spotting system in multi-script handwritten and printed documents. The proposed system proceeds in two steps: First, an identification system identifies the writing type (printed/handwritten) and the script (Latin/Arabic) of the input image document. Second, a specific HMM based word spotting system is used to detect any given keyword in document images. The proposed spotting system relies on a global line modeling based on HMMs, without the need for word or character segmentation. Future works consist in generalizing our system to deal with more scripts. Also, we aim to reduce the computational complexity of our identification system by decreasing the number of states in the ergodic HMMs using a state HMM clustering algorithm. Finally, an extension to the search for regular expressions would be interesting.

# References

1. Kessentini, Y., Paquet, T., Benhamadou, A.-M.: Multi-script handwriting recognition with n-streams low level features. In: 19th International Conference on Pattern Recognition ICPR 2008, pp. 1–4, December 2008
2. Kessentini, Y., Paquet, T., Hamadou, A.B.: A multi-lingual recognition system for Arabic and Latin handwriting. In: 2009 10th International Conference on Document Analysis and Recognition, pp. 1196–1200, July 2009
3. Srihari, S.N., Srinivasan, H., Huang, C., Shetty, S.: Spotting words in Latin, Devanagari and Arabic scripts. Vivek: Indian J. Artif. Intell. **16**, 2 (2006)
4. Bhardwaj, A., Jose, D., Govindaraju, V.: Script independent word spotting in multilingual documents, pp. 48–54 (2008)
5. Wshah, S., Kumar, G., Govindaraju, V.: Statistical script independent word spotting in offline handwritten documents. Pattern Recogn. **47**(3), 1039–1050 (2014)
6. Baati, K., Kanoun, S., Benjlaiel, M.: Différenciation d'écritures arabe et latine de natures imprimée et manuscrite par approche globale. In: Colloque International Francophone sur l'Ecrit et le Document (CIFED2010), Sousse, Tunisia, pp. 1–12, March 2010
7. Kavallieratou, E., Stamatatos, S.: Discrimination of machine-printed from handwritten text using simple structural characteristics. In: 2004 Proceedings of the 17th International Conference on Pattern Recognition, ICPR 2004, vol. 1, pp. 437–440, August 2004
8. Mozaffari, S., Bahar, P.: Farsi/Arabic handwritten from machine-printed words discrimination. In: 2012 International Conference on Frontiers in Handwriting Recognition (ICFHR), pp. 698–703, September 2012
9. Saidani, A., Kacem, A., Belaid, A.: Arabic/latin and machine-printed/handwritten word discrimination using hog-based shape descriptor. ELCVIA Electron. Lett. Comput. Vis. Image Anal. **14**(2), 1–23 (2015)
10. Zhou, L., Lu, Y., Tan, C.L.: Bangla/English script identification based on analysis of connected component profiles. In: Bunke, H., Spitz, A.L. (eds.) DAS 2006. LNCS, vol. 3872, pp. 243–254. Springer, Heidelberg (2006). https://doi.org/10.1007/11669487_22
11. Paquet, T., Heutte, L., Koch, G., Chatelain, C.: A categorization system for handwritten documents. Int. J. Doc. Anal. Recogn. **15**(4), 315–330 (2012)

12. Rodríguez, J.A., Perronnin, F.: Local gradient histogram features for word spotting in unconstrained handwritten documents. In: International Conference on Frontiers in Handwriting Recognition (2008)
13. Saidani, A., Kacem Echi, A., Belaid, A.: Arabic/Latin and machine-printed/handwritten word discrimination using HOG-based shape descriptor. ELCVIA: Electron. Lett. Comput. Vis. Image Anal. **14**, 1–23 (2015)
14. Fischer, A., Keller, A., Frinken, V., Bunke, H.: Lexicon-free handwritten word spotting using character HMMs. Pattern Recogn. Lett. **33**(7), 934–942 (2012)
15. Mahmoud, S.A., et al.: KHATT: an open arabic offline handwritten text database. Pattern Recogn. **47**(3), 1096–1112 (2014)
16. Luqman, H., Mahmoud, S.A., Awaida, S.: KAFD arabic font database. Pattern Recogn. **47**(6), 2231–2240 (2014)
17. Grosicki, E., El-Abed, H.: Icdar 2011 - French handwriting recognition competition. In: 2011 International Conference on Document Analysis and Recognition (ICDAR), pp. 1459–1463, September 2011
18. Chtourou, I., Rouhou, A.C., Jaiem, F.K., Kanoun, S.: ALTID: Arabic/Latin text images database for recognition research. In: 2015 13th International Conference on Document Analysis and Recognition (ICDAR), pp. 836–840. IEEE (2015)

# Image Analysis

# Emotion Recognition with Spatial Attention and Temporal Softmax Pooling

Masih Aminbeidokhti, Marco Pedersoli[✉], Patrick Cardinal[✉], and Eric Granger[✉]

Laboratoire d'imagerie, de vision et d'intelligence artificielle (LIVIA), École de technologie supérieure, Montreal, Canada
masih.aminbeidokhti.1@ens.etsmtl.ca,
{marco.pedersoli,patrick.cardinal,eric.granger}@etsmtl.ca

**Abstract.** Video-based emotion recognition is a challenging task because it requires to distinguish the small deformations of the human face that represent emotions, while being invariant to stronger visual differences due to different identities. State-of-the-art methods normally use complex deep learning models such as recurrent neural networks (RNNs, LSTMs, GRUs), convolutional neural networks (CNNs, C3D, residual networks) and their combination. In this paper, we propose a simpler approach that combines a CNN pre-trained on a public dataset of facial images with (1) a spatial attention mechanism, to localize the most important regions of the face for a given emotion, and (2) temporal softmax pooling, to select the most important frames of the given video. Results on the challenging EmotiW dataset show that this approach can achieve higher accuracy than more complex approaches.

**Keywords:** Affective computing · Emotion recognition ·
Attention mechanisms · Convolutional neural networks

## 1 Introduction

Designing a system capable of encoding discriminant features for video-based emotion recognition is challenging because the appearance of faces may vary considerably according to the specific subject, capture conditions (pose, illumination, blur), and sensors. It is difficult to encode common and discriminant spatio-temporal features of emotions while suppressing these context- and subject-specific facial variations.

Recently, emotion recognition has attracted attention from the computer vision community because state-of-the-art methods are finally providing results that are comparable with human performance. Thus, these methods are now becoming more reliable, are beginning to be deployed in real-world applications [2]. However, at this point, it is not yet clear what is the right recipe of success in terms of machine learning architectures. Several state-of-the-art methods [7,9] originating from challenges in which multiple teams provide results on the same

© Springer Nature Switzerland AG 2019
F. Karray et al. (Eds.): ICIAR 2019, LNCS 11662, pp. 323–331, 2019.
https://doi.org/10.1007/978-3-030-27202-9_29

benchmark without having access training-set annotations. Although these challenges measure improvements in the field. One a drawback of challenges is that result focuses mostly on final accuracy of approaches, without taking into account other factors such as their computational cost, architectural complexity, quantity of hyper-parameters to tune, versatility, generality of the approach, etc. As a consequence, there is no clear cost-benefit analysis for component appearing in top-performing methods and often represent complex deep learning architectures.

In this paper, we aim to shed some light on these issues by proposing a simple approach for emotion recognition that (i) is based on the very well-known VGG16 network which is pre-trained on face images; (ii) has a very simple yet performing mechanism to aggregate temporal information; and (iii) uses an attention model to select which part of the face is the most important to recognize a certain emotion. For the selection of the approach to use, we show that a basic convolutional neural network such as VGG can perform as well or even better than more complex models when pre-trained on clean data. For temporal aggregation, we show that softmax pooling is an excellent way to select information from different frames because it is a generalization of max and average pooling. Additionally, in contrast to more complex techniques (e.g. attention), it does not require additional sub-networks and therefore additional parameters to train, which can easily lead to overfitting when dealing with relatively small datasets, a common problem in this field. Finally, we show that for the selection of the most discriminative parts of a face for recognizing an emotion, an attention mechanism is necessary to improve performance. For doing that, we built a small network with multiple attention heads [8] that can simultaneously focus on different parts of a human face.

The rest of the paper is organized as follows. The next section described related work. Then, our methods based on spatial attention and temporal softmax are presented. Finally, in our experimental evaluation, we show the importance of our three system components and compare them with other similar approaches.

## 2   Related Work

Attention models increase the interpretability of deep neural networks internal representations by capturing where the model is focusing its attention when performing a particular task. Sharma et al. [14] proposed a Soft-Attention LSTM model to selectively focus on parts of the video frames and classify videos after taking a few glimpses. As far as we know, unlike similar task such as action recognition, there has been relatively little work that explores spatial-attention for emotion recognition. Zhang et al. [10] proposed attention based on fully convolutional neural network for audio emotion recognition which helped the model to focus on the emotion-relevant regions in speech spectrogram.

For capturing temporal dependencies between video frames in video classification, recurrent neural networks (RNN), particularly long short-term memory

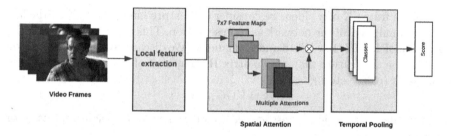

**Fig. 1.** The CNN takes the video frame as its input and produces local features. Using the local features, the multi-head attention network computes the weight importance of each local image feature. The aggregated representation is computed by multiplying multi-head attention output and the local image features. This representation is then propagates through temporal softmax pooling to extract global features over the entire video.

(LSTM) [4] have been applied in numerous papers [1,9,12]. However, the accuracy on video classification with these RNN-based methods were the same or worse, which may indicate that long-term temporal interactions are not crucial for video classification. Karpathy et al. [5] explored multiple approaches based on pooling local spatio-temporal features extracted by CNNs from video frames. However, their models display only a modest improvement compared to single-frame models. In the emotion detection task, Knyazev et al. [7] exploited several aggregation functions (e.g., mean, standard deviation) allowing the incorporation of temporal features. Inspired by the attention mechanism in [8], our proposed method explores the potential use of a self-attentive network in emotion recognition.

## 3 Proposed Model

We now describe our method based on spatial attention and temporal softmax pooling for the task of emotion recognition in videos. We broadly consider three major parts: local feature extraction, local feature aggregation and global feature classification. The overall model architecture is shown in Fig. 1. The local feature extraction uses a pre-trained CNN, the spatial feature aggregation is implemented using an attention network, and the temporal feature classification uses a softmax pooling layer. Given a video sample $S_i$ and its associated emotion $y_i \in \mathbb{R}^E$, we represent the video as a sequence of $F$ frames $[\mathbf{X}_{0,i}, \mathbf{X}_{1,i}, .., \mathbf{X}_{F,i}]$ of size $W \times H \times 3$.

### 3.1 Local Feature Extraction

We use the VGG-16 architecture with the pre-trained VGG-Face Model [13] for extracting an independent description of a face on each frame in the video. For a detailed procedure of face extraction, see the experimental results in Sect. 4.

For a given frame $\mathbf{X}$ of a video, we consider the feature map produced by the last convolutional layer of the network as representation. This feature map has spatial resolution of $L = H/16 \times W/16$ and $D$ channels. We discard the spatial resolution and reshape the feature map as a matrix $\mathbf{R}$ composed of $L$ $D$-dimensional local descriptors (row vectors).

$$\mathbf{R} = VGG_{16}(\mathbf{X}) \tag{1}$$

These descriptors will be associated to a corresponding weight and used for the attention mechanism.

### 3.2 Spatial Attention

For the spatial attention we rely on the self-attention mechanism [15], which aggregates a set of local frame descriptors $\mathbf{R}$ into a single weighted sum $v$ that summarizes the most important regions of a given video frame:

$$v = a\mathbf{R}, \tag{2}$$

where $a$ is a row vector of dimension $L$, which defines the importance of each frame region. The weights $a$ are generated by a two-layers fully connected network that associates each local feature (row of $\mathbf{R}$) to a corresponding weight:

$$a = softmax(w_{s2}tanh(\mathbf{W}_{s1}\mathbf{R}^{\top})). \tag{3}$$

$\mathbf{W}_{s1}$ is then a weight matrix of learned parameters with shape $U \times D$ and $w_{s2}$ is a vector of parameters with size $U$. The softmax function ensures that the computed weights are normalized, i.e. sum up to 1.

This vector representation usually focuses on a specific region in the facial feature, like the mouth. However, it is possible that multiple regions of the face contain different type of information that can be combined to obtain a better idea of the person emotional state. Based on [8], in order to represent the overall emotion of the facial feature, we need multiple attention units that focus on different parts of the image. For doing that, we transform $w_{s2}$ into a matrix $\mathbf{W}_{s2}$ of size $R \times L$, in which every row represents a different attention:

$$\mathbf{A} = softmax(\mathbf{W}_{s2}tanh(\mathbf{W}_{s1}\mathbf{R}^{\top})). \tag{4}$$

Here the softmax is performed along the second dimension of its input. In the case of multiple attention units, the aggregated vector $v$ becomes a matrix $D \times N$ in which each row represents a different attention. This matrix will be then flattened back to a vector $v$ by concatenating the rows in a single vector. Thus, with this approach, a video is now represented as a $F \times (ND)$ matrix $\mathbf{V}$ in which every row is the attention based description of a video frame. To reduce the possible overfitting of the multiple attentions, similarly to [8] we regularize $\mathbf{A}$ by computing Frobenius norm of matrix $(\mathbf{A}\mathbf{A}^{\top} - I)$ and adding it to the final loss. This enforces diversity among the attentions and resulted very important in our experiments for good results.

### 3.3 Temporal Pooling

After extracting the local features and aggregating them using the attention mechanism for each individual frame, we have to take into account frame features over the whole video. As the length of a video can be different for each example, we need an approach that support different input lengths. The most commonly used approaches are average and max pooling; however, these techniques assume that every frame of the video has the same importance in the final decision (average pooling) or that only a single frame is considered as a general representation of the video (max pooling). In order to use the best of both techniques, we use an aggregation based on softmax, which can be considered a generalization of the average and max pooling. In practice, instead of performing the classical softmax on the class scores, to transform them in probabilities to be used with cross-entropy loss, we compute the softmax on the class probabilities and the video frames jointly. Given a video sample $\mathbf{S}$, after feature extraction and spatial attention we obtain a matrix $\mathbf{V}$ in which each row represents the features of a frame. These features are converted into class scores thorough a final fully connected layer $\mathbf{O} = \mathbf{W}_{sm}\mathbf{V}$. In this way $\mathbf{O}$ is a $F \times E$ matrix in which an element $o_{c,f}$ is the score for class $c$ of the frame $f$. We then transform the scores over frames and classes in probabilities with a softmax:

$$p(c, f|\mathbf{S}) = \frac{exp(o_{c,f})}{\sum_{j,k} exp(o_{j,k})}. \tag{5}$$

In this way, we obtain a joint probability on class $c$ and frame $f$. From this, we can marginalize over frames $p(c|\mathbf{S}) = \sum_f p(c, f|S)$ and obtain a classification score that can be used in the training process using cross-entropy loss:

$$\mathcal{L}_{CE} = \sum_i -\log(p(y_i|\mathbf{S}_i)). \tag{6}$$

On the other hand, the same representation can be marginalized over classes $p(f|\mathbf{S}) = \sum_c p(c, f|\mathbf{S})$. In this case, it will give us information about the most important frames of a given video (see Fig. 2). This mechanism looks very similar to attention, but it has the advantage to not require an additional network to compute the attention weights. This can be important in cases for which the training data is limited and adding a sub-network with additional parameters to learn could lead to overfitting. In this case, the weight associated to each frame and each class are computed as a softmax of the score obtained.

## 4    Experiments

### 4.1 Data Preparation

We evaluate our models based on AFEW database, which is used in the audio-video sub-challenge of the EmotiW [3]. AFEW is collected from movies and TV reality shows, which contains 773 video clips for training and 383 for validation. We extract the frame faces using the dlib [6] detector for achieving effective facial images. Then faces are aligned to a frontal position and stored in a resolution of $256 \times 256$ pixels, ready to be passed to VGG16.

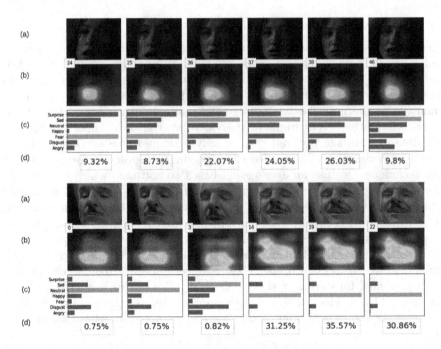

**Fig. 2.** Video frames for a few time-steps for an example of sadness and anger. (a) Original video frames (b) Image regions attended by the spatial attention mechanism. Whiter regions represent the most important parts of the face to recognize a certain emotion for the attention. (c) Emotion probability for each frame. The red bar shows the selected emotion. (d) Temporal importance for selected frames. To make those values more meaningful they have been re-normalized between 0 and 100%. (Color figure online)

## 4.2 Training Details

To overcome overfitting during training we sampled 16 random frames form the video clips. Before feeding the facial image to the network we applied data augmentation: flipping, mirroring and random cropping of the original image. We set weight decay penalty to 0.00005 and use SGD with momentum and warm restart [11] as optimization algorithm. All models are fine-tuned for 30 epochs, but we use a learning rate of 0.00001 for the backbone CNN parameters and 0.1 for the rest of the parameters.

## 4.3 Spatial Attention

Table 1 reports the accuracy based on the AFEW validation dataset. We compare our softmax-based temporal pooling with different configurations of attention by varying the number of attention models and the used regularization. Using just one attention does not helps to improve the overall performance. This is probably due to the fact that a single attention usually focuses on a specific part of the face, like a mouth. However, there can be multiple regions in a face that together forms the overall emotion of the person. Thus, we evaluate our model with 2 and 4 attentions. The best results are obtained with 2 attention models and a strong regularization that enforces the models to focus on different parts of the face. We observe that, adding more than two attentions do not improve the overall performance. This is probably due overfitting. We also compare with our re-implementation of cluster attention with shifting operation (SHIFT) [10], but results are lower than our approach. In Fig. 2(b) we show that the throughout the frames, model not only captures the mouth, which in this case is the most important part for detecting the emotion but also in the first three frames focuses on the eyes as well.

**Table 1.** We evaluate the performance of the proposed spatial attention and compare it with a baseline model without it (first row). TP is our temporal softmax, while SA is the spatial attention. The second column reports the number of attention models used and the third column the amount of regularization as described in Sect. 4.2. Finally the last column reports the accuracy on the validation set.

| Model | # Att. | Reg. | ACC |
|-------|--------|------|-----|
| $VGG_{16} + TP$ | - | - | 46.4% |
| $VGG_{16} + TP + SHIFT$ | 2 | - | 45.0% |
| $VGG_{16} + TP + SA$ | 1 | 0 | 47.6% |
| $VGG_{16} + TP + SA$ | 2 | 0.1 | 48.9% |
| $VGG_{16} + TP + SA$ | 2 | 1 | **49.0%** |
| $VGG_{16} + TP + SA$ | 4 | 0.1 | 48.3% |
| $VGG_{16} + TP + SA$ | 4 | 1 | 48.6% |

## 4.4   Temporal Pooling

In this section we compare the performance of different kind of temporal pooling. The simplest approach is to consider each video sample $i$ frame independent from the others $p(c|\mathbf{S}_i) = \prod_f p(c, f|\mathbf{X}_{f,i})$ and associating the emotion class $c$ of a video to all its frames. In this case the loss becomes:

$$\mathcal{L}_{CE} = \sum_i -\log(p(c|\mathbf{S}_i)) = \sum_i \sum_f -log(p(c, f|\mathbf{X}_{f,i})), \qquad (7)$$

which can be computed independently from each frame. In this way we can avoid to keep in memory at the same time all the frames of a video. However assuming that each frame of the same video is independent from the others, it is a very restrictive assumption and it is in contrast with the common assumption used in learning of identically independently distributed samples. We notice that this approach is equivalent to perform an average pooling (VGG+AVG) on the scoring function before the softmax normalization. This can explain the lower performance of this kind of pooling.

In Table 2 we report results of different pooling approaches. We report results for [9] in which they use VGG16 with an LSTM model to aggregate frames (LSTM). We compare it with a VGG16 model trained with average pooling (AVG) and our softmax temporal pooling (TP). Finally we also consider the model with our temporal pooling and spatial attention (TP+SP). It is interesting to note that our model, even if not explicitly reasoning on the temporal scale, (i.e. every frame is still computed independently, but then the scores are normalized with the softmax) outperforms a model based on LSTM a state-of-the-art recurrent neural network. This suggest that for emotion recognition it is not really important the sequentiality of the facial postures, but the presence of certain key patterns.

**Table 2.** We compare our softmax temporal aggregation (VGG+TP) with the approach of [9] based on recurrent neural networks (VGG+LSTM) and average pooling (VGG+AVG). Our temporal pooling is already slightly better than a more complex approach based on a recurrent network that keep memory of the past frames. Finally, if we add the spatial attention (VGG+TP+SA), we obtain a gain of almost 3 points.

| Model | ACC |
|---|---|
| $VGG_{16} + LSTM$ [9] | 46.2% |
| $VGG_{16} + AVG$ | 46.0% |
| $VGG_{16} + TP$ | 46.4% |
| $VGG_{16} + TP + SA$ | **49.0%** |

## 5   Conclusion

In this paper we have presented two simple strategies to improve the performance of emotion recognition is video sequences. In contrast to previous approaches using recurrent neural networks for the temporal fusion of the data, in this paper we have shown that a simple softmax pooling over the emotion probabilities, that selects the most important frames of a video, can lead to promising results. Also, to obtain more reliable results, instead of fusing multiple sources of information or multiple learning models (e.g. CNN+C3D), we have used a multi-attention mechanism to spatially select the most important regions of an image. For future work we plan to use similar techniques to integrate other sources of information such as audio.

# References

1. Chen, S., Jin, Q.: Multi-modal dimensional emotion recognition using recurrent neural networks. In: Proceedings of the 5th International Workshop on Audio/Visual Emotion Challenge, AVEC 2015, pp. 49–56. ACM, New York, NY, USA (2015). https://doi.org/10.1145/2808196.2811638, http://doi.acm.org/10.1145/2808196.2811638

2. Cowie, R., et al.: Emotion recognition in human-computer interaction. IEEE Signal Process. Mag. **18**(1), 32–80 (2001). https://doi.org/10.1109/79.911197

3. Dhall, A., Goecke, R., Lucey, S., Gedeon, T.: Collecting large, richly annotated facial-expression databases from movies. IEEE Multimed. **19**(3), 34–41 (2012). https://doi.org/10.1109/MMUL.2012.26

4. Hochreiter, S., Schmidhuber, J.: Long short-term memory. Neural Comput. **9**(8), 1735–1780 (1997). https://doi.org/10.1162/neco.1997.9.8.1735

5. Karpathy, A., Toderici, G., Shetty, S., Leung, T., Sukthankar, R., Fei-Fei, L.: Large-scale video classification with convolutional neural networks. In: CVPR (2014)

6. King, D.E.: Dlib-ml: a machine learning toolkit. J. Mach. Learn. Res. **10**, 1755–1758 (2009)

7. Knyazev, B., Shvetsov, R., Efremova, N., Kuharenko, A.: Leveraging large face recognition data for emotion classification. In: 2018 13th IEEE International Conference on Automatic Face & Gesture Recognition (FG 2018), pp. 692–696. IEEE (2018)

8. Lin, Z., et al.: A structured self-attentive sentence embedding. arXiv preprint arXiv:1703.03130 (2017)

9. Liu, C., Tang, T., Lv, K., Wang, M.: Multi-feature based emotion recognition for video clips. In: Proceedings of the 20th ACM International Conference on Multimodal Interaction, ICMI 2018, pp. 630–634. ACM, New York, NY, USA (2018). https://doi.org/10.1145/3242969.3264989, http://doi.acm.org/10.1145/3242969.3264989

10. Long, X., Gan, C., de Melo, G., Wu, J., Liu, X., Wen, S.: Attention clusters: Purely attention based local feature integration for video classification. CoRR abs/1711.09550 (2017). http://arxiv.org/abs/1711.09550

11. Loshchilov, I., Hutter, F.: SGDR: stochastic gradient descent with restarts. CoRR abs/1608.03983 (2016). http://arxiv.org/abs/1608.03983

12. Lu, C., et al.: Multiple spatio-temporal feature learning for video-based emotion recognition in the wild. In: Proceedings of the 20th ACM International Conference on Multimodal Interaction, ICMI 2018, pp. 646–652. ACM, New York, NY, USA (2018). https://doi.org/10.1145/3242969.3264992, http://doi.acm.org/10.1145/3242969.3264992

13. Parkhi, O.M., Vedaldi, A., Zisserman, A.: Deep face recognition. In: British Machine Vision Conference (2015)

14. Sharma, S., Kiros, R., Salakhutdinov, R.: Action recognition using visual attention. CoRR abs/1511.04119 (2015). http://arxiv.org/abs/1511.04119

15. Vaswani, A., et al.: Attention is all you need. In: Advances in Neural Information Processing Systems, pp. 5998–6008 (2017)

# CNN-Based Watershed Marker Extraction for Brick Segmentation in Masonry Walls

Yahya Ibrahim[1]([✉]), Balázs Nagy[1,2], and Csaba Benedek[1,2]

[1] 3in Research Group, Faculty of Information Technology and Bionics,
Pázmány Péter Catholic University, Esztergom, Hungary
ibrahim.yahya@itk.ppke.hu
[2] Institute for Computer Science and Control, Hungarian Academy of Sciences,
Budapest, Hungary
{nagy.balazs,benedek.csaba}@sztaki.mta.hu

**Abstract.** Nowadays there is an increasing need for using artificial intelligence techniques in image-based documentation and survey in archeology, architecture or civil engineering applications. Brick segmentation is an important initial step in the documentation and analysis of masonry wall images. However, due to the heterogeneous material, size, shape and arrangement of the bricks, it is highly challenging to develop a widely adoptable solution for the problem via conventional geometric and radiometry based approaches. In this paper, we propose a new technique which combines the strength of deep learning for brick seed localization, and the Watershed algorithm for accurate instance segmentation. More specifically, we adopt a U-Net-based delineation algorithm for robust marker generation in the Watershed process, which provides as output the accurate contours of the individual bricks, and also separates them from the mortar regions. For training the network and evaluating our results, we created a new test dataset which consist of 162 hand-labeled images of various wall categories. Quantitative evaluation is provided both at instance and at pixel level, and the results are compared to two reference methods proposed for wall delineation, and to a morphology based brick segmentation approach. The experimental results showed the advantages of the proposed U-Net markered Watershed method, providing average F1-scores above 80%.

**Keywords:** Documentation application · Brick segmentation ·
Deep learning · U-Net · Watershed

## 1 Introduction

Image-based analysis of man-built structures is considered as a core step of many applications, such as stability analysis in civil engineering, condition estimation and damage detection of buildings in architecture, digital documentation in archeology or maintenance and restoration in cultural heritage preservation.

© Springer Nature Switzerland AG 2019
F. Karray et al. (Eds.): ICIAR 2019, LNCS 11662, pp. 332–344, 2019.
https://doi.org/10.1007/978-3-030-27202-9_30

The surveyors in these processes need to extract comprehensive information about the studied sites, among others about the current conditions, the possible further actions, types of appropriate treatment, and the expected consequences of any intervention.

By investigating building masonry - either ancient walls or modern buildings - accurate detection and outlining of their structural components is a key initial step of the documentation process. The separation is based the fact that a masonry wall is a heterogeneous material that contains individual units (bricks, blocks, ashlars, irregular stones and others) and joints (mortar, clay, chalk etc.) between the main units, which bind the units together. Note that for simpler discussion, in our paper we use henceforward the term *brick* to describe the main units of any type, and the term *mortar* to describe the joints.

Manual segmentation of a large set of masonry images is time-consuming due the great number of bricks in an image, and such labeling is often inaccurate and unreproducible, as the output also depends on the experience of the operator. Thus, there is an increasing need nowadays for efficient automated processing. Moreover, due to various threats on the buildings (wars, natural disasters, etc.), quick and accurate documentation has become particularly necessary on precious archeology sites in the last decade.

In the paper we present a novel image based automated brick segmentation approach, which combines the strength of deep learning algorithms for robust brick localization under highly varying conditions, and the classical Watershed algorithm for accurate brick outline extraction and removal of mortar regions. We also introduce a new manually labeled dataset of diverse masonry images, which is used to train and test our approach, enabling its quantitative comparison to the state-of-the-art.

The paper is structured as follows. In Sect. 2 we summarize related work and the main contributions of the proposed approach. In Sect. 3 we introduce the proposed algorithm in details, while we present a detailed qualitative and quantitative evaluation in Sect. 4. We conclude our work in Sect. 5, with mentioning remarks for future work.

## 2    Related Work

In an earlier study [4] adopt various pixel-based and object-oriented image processing technologies for detecting and characterizing the structural damage in historical buildings based on multi-spectral measurements. Oses et al. [8] focus on the classification of built heritage masonry for determining the necessary degree of protection in different buildings, using an automatic image-based delineation method. Riveiro et al. [9] present an automatic color-based algorithm for segmenting masonry structures, based on an improved marker-controlled Watershed. However, this later algorithm [9] purely focuses on the morphological analysis of quasi-periodic masonry walls, where the geometry of masonry courses follows horizontal rows, which condition does not hold very often - especially for ancient walls (see Fig. 4). Sithole et al. [12] propose a semi-automatic segmentation algorithm to detect the bricks in masonry walls, working on *3D point cloud data* obtained by laser scanning. Although using such data sources becomes widespread in archeology and architecture nowadays, the 2D image based investigation addressed in this paper still has significance in particular for processing archive measurements, or in situations when long scanning surveys are not feasible. Since the method of [12] is based on the 3D triangulation of the 3D point cloud, reflectance, and RGB triplets, it cannot be suit to 2D data in a straightforward way. Similar issues appear by the work of Bosché et al. [2], who introduce a method that simultaneously considers 3D information both in global and local levels for segmenting the walls into regions corresponding to bricks and mortar joints.

Focusing on the development of a widely applicable and purely 2D image based approach, automatic brick segmentation in masonry images is a notably challenging task due to several reasons [12] like similarity in surface texture between the bricks and the mortar, challenges caused by the lighting conditions, varying dimension and shape of the bricks and the mortar regions. Moreover, walls of different ages, built from various materials, and having different status appear significantly differently in the photos (see Fig. 2, 3(a)).

While deep learning (DL) algorithms have achieved remarkable success in various computer vision applications (segmentation, classification, detections, etc.) in a wide range of fields from medical images [14,15], scene understandings [13] or autonomous driving [1], we only find a few references yet for application of DL methods in architecture or cultural heritage documentation. In addition, existing methods [3,6] use deep learning rather for classification of the available images of the architectural heritage, instead of segmentation and feature extraction for detailed analysis.

The widely used Watershed algorithm [10] is a classical mathematical morphological method for image segmentation, and instance separation of definite object classes. The recently proposed Deep Watershed (DW) technique [1] realizes a possible way of combining deep learning with Watershed, however that method differs from our solution both from a methodological point of view, and in terms of the desired output. DW expects as input besides the raw camera image an accurate region mask obtained by semantic segmentation, which contains several touching or partially occluded instances of a given object class, such as vehicles or pedestrians in a traffic scene. Therefore, DW aims to participate each homogeneous blob of the semantic map into tightly connected individual objects, which is implemented through a cascade usage of a direction network for estimating a vector from each object candidate point to the respective object center, and a second net which aims to approximate the Watershed energy for instance separation. On the other hand, in our case the brick instances are usually *not* tightly connected since they are mostly separated by the mortar regions, thus brick detection within a wall segment includes the separation the individual bricks from the mortar and from the neighboring bricks, which are sometimes slightly contacting (see Fig. 5). Another difference is that instead of training different Convolutional Neural Networks (CNNs) for region level semantic segmentation of the input image, and instance separation within the regions of interest (ROIs) [1], we use a single CNN that simultaneously provides information for ROI filtering, mortar removal and brick separation. Details of the proposed method are presented in the next section.

## 3    Proposed Method

The goal of the proposed method is to automatically extract the individual brick instances from 2D images taken from masonry walls of any types. Our approach is based on the widely used Watershed image segmentation algorithm [10], which considers the image as a topographic surface, where intensities of pixels correspond to altitude values. In the classical form of technique [10], local minima are extracted in the altitude map, then watersheds are defined by the lines that separate adjacent minima basins. As a usual artifact of the approach, the Watershed transform itself yields to oversegment masonry images, since the color values may strongly vary within the individual brick and mortar regions. A straightforward extension is applying markers in the process [10], so that we only enable flooding from specific seed points or internal markers taken inside each individual (brick) object, meantime we also use external markers for the mortar regions, which do not correspond to any brick instances.

The proposed algorithm can be divided into two main steps. The first one is a CNN-based delineation step, which aims to separate the regions of bricks from the mortar and other background regions in the image. The second step implements the Watershed-based segmentation of brick instances using external and internal markers extracted from the delineation output.

For giving a complete overview, Fig. 1 shows the dataflow of our method, with demonstrating the results of the subsequent filtering steps for a selected input image. The algorithms marked with arrows are detailed in Sects. 3.1, 3.2.

### 3.1    Deep Learning Based Delineation for Separation of Brick and Mortar Regions

The first step of our approach is the delineation of the bricks in order to distinguish them from the mortar. Applying conventional edge detectors (such as Sobel or Canny) to tackle the problem is a straightforward solution in the literature, however experiments show that their performance is highly sensitive to image noise and contrast parameters. Riveiro's delineation algorithm [9] relies on the gradient of the pixel intensity attribute for making this distinction step. Oses et al. [8] have proposed a heuristic algorithm that describes the geometric arrangement of blocks in the wall by a set of straight segments, which are extracted from image region boundaries that are created by using histogram based image quantization. However, even by using these complex delineation algorithms, the efficiency is limited to some specific (regular) wall structures [9], or the output is only used for classification of various sorts of masonry walls instead of segmenting the structural elements [8]. (We present later comparative tests between our algorithm and these methods in Sect. 4.3.)

Instead of using noisy hand-crafted features, our key idea is to solve the delineation task by a Convolutional Neural Network (CNN). Our choice was the U-Net network proposed by Ronneberger et al. [11] for biomedical image segmentation, however it has already been applied with a great success in many segmentation tasks, and in addition it is able to reach high accuracy using a relatively small dataset. The U-Net architecture (see Fig. 1(a)) can be decomposed into two main parts: (i) the encoder part consists of several convolution layers with ReLU (Rectified Linear Unit) activation function followed by max pooling layers while the decoder part (ii) consists of up-convolution and convolution layers. (i) encodes the image into a compact feature representation then (ii) decodes the features into a gray scale image which represents the local probabilities of the predicted classes.

To train the network we need input-target pairs. In our case the input is a 3-channel RGB image (raw photo), while the target is a binary mask where white pixels correspond to the brick regions, and black ones to the mortar between the bricks and to the background of the masonry walls (see Fig. 2). The prediction of the U-Net is a grayscale image, where high intensity values indicate the brick regions (Fig. 3(d)).

From a technical point of view, it should be noted that we trained U-Net using the Adam optimizer (Adaptive moment Estimation) with a binary cross entropy cost function and the number of epochs was 100.

### 3.2   Brick Instance Segmentation by a Sketch-Driven Watershed Algorithm

The second step of the proposed algorithm is responsible for extracting the accurate outlines of the brick instances, relying on the previously obtained grayscale delineation map. As the U-Net outputs in Figs. 3(d) and 4(b) demonstrate, the delineation maps are quite reliable, however they might be noisy near to the brick boundaries, and some bricks are contacting, making simple connected component analysis (CCA) based separation prone to errors. To overcome these drawbacks, we apply a marker based Watershed [10] segmentation. (In Sect. 4.3 we also illustrate experimentally the difference between using CCA and Watershed algorithm.)

First, we binarize the delineation map via simple thresholding, and calculate the *inverse distance transform* (IDT) map of the obtained binary mask $(M)$. Our aim is to extract a single compact seed region within each brick instance, which can be used as internal marker for the Watershed algorithm. Since the IDT map may have several false local minima, we apply the H−minima transform [7], which suppresses all minima under a given $H$-value (used $H = 5$ pixels). The H−minima suppression step is illustrated in 1D in Fig. 1(b) and (c).

Finally, we apply flooding from the obtained H−minima regions, so that we consider the inverse of $M$ (i.e. all mortar or non-wall pixels) as an external marker map, whose pixels cannot be assigned to any bricks. Results of the obtained brick contours are displayed over the input images in Fig. 4(c).

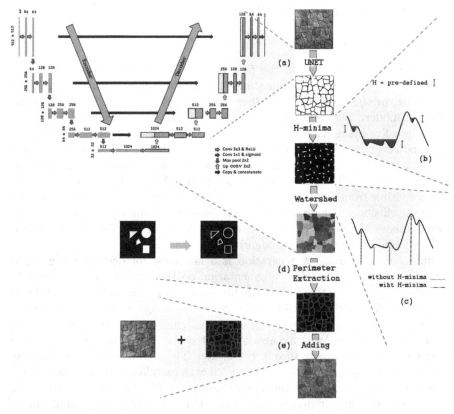

**Fig. 1.** Dataflow of our method. (a) U-Net model (b) H-minima algorithm (c) The Watershed H-minima (d) Perimeter Extraction (e) Adding step.

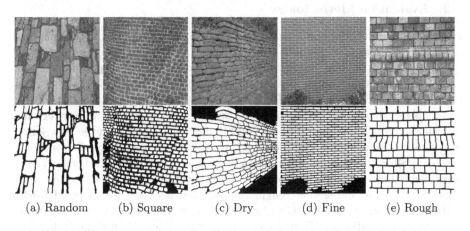

(a) Random     (b) Square     (c) Dry     (d) Fine     (e) Rough

**Fig. 2.** Samples from the dataset and with displaying the ground truth labels, (a) Random rubble masonry, (b) Square rubble masonry, (c) Dry rubble masonry, (d) Ashlar fine, (e) Ashlar rough.

## 4    Experiment and Results

### 4.1    Dataset Generation

For training and evaluation of the proposed U-Net markered Watershed technique, we have created a new annotated dataset containing images of masonry walls from various locations, including both ancient walls and facades of new-fashioned modern buildings. Depending on the wall structures, we divided the images into five main classes: three types of rubble masonry (Random, Square, Dry), and two types of ashlar (Fine, Rough). Note that the samples within each class may still differ in shape and size parameters of the bricks, while the mortar regions can be thin, tick or completely missing. Meantime, in the images the walls are visible from different viewpoints, while different lighting conditions and shadowing effects can be present. The new dataset contains overall 162 manually labeled images of size $512 \times 512$, where we used 117 images for training, 13 for validation and 32 for testing the algorithm.

Since large training set generation is a key issue for deep learning based methods, we also applied data augmentation on the training set by randomly rotating the images up to $+90°$, randomly shifting the images in horizontal and vertical direction with an offset up to 5% of the image width, and optionally applied shearing and horizontal flipping transforms, and zooming up to 5% of the size of the image. We have also augmented the test image set in a similar manner to expand the relevance of evaluation. The annotation follows the way described in Sect. 3.1. The images are labeled with two classes: background (black pixels in the mask) represents the mortar and the non-wall regions in the images, and foreground (white) represents the bricks. For each wall class, a sample image with the corresponding annotated mask is shown in Fig. 2.

### 4.2    Evaluation Methodology

In the experimental phase, we separately analyze the efficiency of the delineation step, and the final brick segmentation results.

To evaluate the delineation, we compare pixel-wise the output map of our U-Net component and other state-of-the-art methods (see Fig. 3(b)–(d)) to the expected Ground Truth masks (Fig. 3(e)). Since the correctness of the structure can be better described by the pixel-level accuracy of the thinner mortar regions, we calculate pixel-level Precision (Pr) and Recall (Rc) values from the viewpoints of the mortar pixels, and take the F1-score as the harmonic mean of Pr and Rc.

For evaluating the final brick segmentation results by the markered Watershed algorithm, we calculate both (i) object level and (ii) pixel level metrics. First of all, an unambiguous assignment is taken between the detected bricks (DB) and the ground truth (GT) bricks (i.e every GT object is matched to at most one DB candidate). To find the optimal assignment we use the Hungarian algorithm [5], where for a given DB and GT object pair the quality of matching is proportional to the intersection of union (IOU) between them, and we only take into account the pairs that have IOU higher then a pre-defined threshold 0.5. Thereafter, object and pixel level matching rates are calculated as follows:

(i) At object (brick) level, we count the number of True Positive (TP), False Positive (FP) and False Negative (FN) hits, and compute the *object level* precision, recall and F1-score values. Here TP corresponds to the number detected bricks (DBs) which are correctly matched to the corresponding GT objects, FP refers to DBs which do not have GT pair, while FN includes GT objects without any matches among the DBs.

(ii) At pixel level, for each correctly matched DB-GT object pair, we consider the pixels of their intersection as True Positive (TP) hits, the pixels that are in the predicted brick but not in the GT as False Positive (FP), and pixels of the GT object missing from the DB as False Negative (FN). Thereafter we compute the *pixel level* evaluation metrics precision, recall and F1-score and the intersection of unions (IOU). Finally the evaluation metric values for the individual objects are averaged over all bricks, by weighting each brick with its total area.

### 4.3 Performance Evaluation

In this section, we analyze the performance of the proposed approach on the test data, based on the different evaluation parameters defined in Sect. 4.2.

We start with the discussion of the delineation step. Demonstrative sample results of using the state-of-the-art delineation methods and our method are shown in Fig. 3, and the corresponding quantitative evaluation values are provided in Table 1. We can confirm, that the proposed U-Net based method can detect the outlines of the bricks with high accuracy (above 80%) for any types of walls, significantly surpassing the reference methods, which suffer both from false detection and misdetection effects. While the reference techniques show better results by processing photos of walls with regularly shaped and aligned bricks, their performance is drastically degraded for the irregularly structured stone walls. In summary, we found neither of the two reference methods [8,9] capable for providing efficient markers for the Watershed process.

Next we evaluate the final output of brick segmentation based on the provided U-Net mask. Figure 4 shows the results of our algorithm step by step for three sample images. The first row represents the input images, the second one the delineation map by U-Net, the third row displays our brick segmentation

**Table 1.** Evaluation of the delineation step. Comparison of state-of-the-art methods and our proposed U-Net-based approach.

| Method | F1-score (%) | Precision (%) | Recall (%) |
|---|---|---|---|
| Riveiro method [9] | 23.65 | 37.04 | 17.71 |
| Oses method [8] | 22.58 | 39.57 | 16.91 |
| Proposed method | **81.57** | **81.16** | **82.14** |

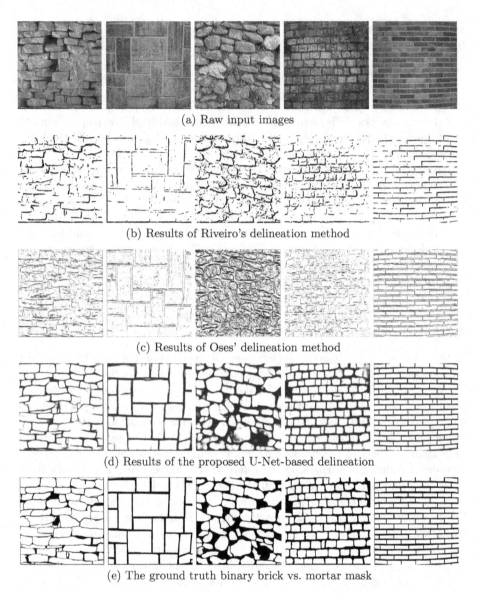

(a) Raw input images

(b) Results of Riveiro's delineation method

(c) Results of Oses' delineation method

(d) Results of the proposed U-Net-based delineation

(e) The ground truth binary brick vs. mortar mask

**Fig. 3.** Comparison between the-state-of-the-art delineation methods and our method; (a) images; (b) Riveiro's method; (c) Oses' method; (d) Our U-Net based delineation output; (e) Ground truth

output (green lines represent the outlines of the bricks), which is followed by the visualization of the ground truth segmentation. Table 2 shows the quantitative object and pixel level results of the complete workflow. We can conclude that our algorithm provides high quality output for the different wall categories of the

(a) Sample images

(b) U-Net prediction results

(c) Result of the proposed brick segmentation algoritm based on (b)

(d) Ground truth

**Fig. 4.** The results by applying our method step by step for many types of walls; (a) input images; (b) U-Net prediction results; (c) Final segmentation results where the green line is to identify each brick; (d) Ground truth

test dataset, as the brick and pixel level F1-scores are measured in almost every cases between 76% and 97%. The best results are naturally observed for the ashlar fine subset, which contains high contrasted photos of modern buildings with simple and regular brick layouts. However, as both qualitative and quantitative examples shows, the proposed method can generally handle very different masonry types, and it shows graceful degradation in cases of more challenging samples, such as random masonry.

The necessity of applying the marker based Watershed process instead of using a simple connected component analysis (CCA) approach becomes evident by checking Fig. 5 and Table 3. Figure 5 displays for a sample region the brick segmentation result by CCA and by the proposed Watershed algorithm in parallel. As shown, if some mortar sections are missing or misdetected, neighboring bricks can be erroneously merged into the same object by CCA, while the Watershed approach efficiently handles these situations. Table 3 confirms that such effects may also cause notable differences in quantitative performance parameters, especially for *rough ashlar* walls.

**Table 2.** Evaluation of brick segmentation. Object (brick) and pixel level precision, recall, F1-score and IOU values for the *augmented* test dataset.

| Wall Categories | Number of (augm) images | Recall (%) | | Precision (%) | | F1-score (%) | | IOU (%) |
|---|---|---|---|---|---|---|---|---|
| | | Brick level | Pixel level | Brick level | Pixel level | Brick level | Pixel level | Pixel level |
| Random rubble masonry | 304 | 83.80 | 82.08 | 77.69 | 83.03 | 79.93 | 81.87 | 71.31 |
| Square rubble masonry | 411 | 85.23 | 78.35 | 69.87 | 86.10 | 75.56 | 78.85 | 69.91 |
| Dry rubble masonry | 375 | 84.97 | 85.04 | 73.54 | 87.47 | 77.74 | 85.36 | 76.66 |
| Ashlar Fine | 268 | **97.53** | **96.43** | **97.67** | **92.18** | **97.58** | **94.19** | **89.12** |
| Ashlar rough | 244 | 81.47 | 84.19 | 79.57 | 78.34 | 79.87 | 81.92 | 69.38 |
| Average | 1602 | 86.38 | 84.53 | 78.34 | 85.67 | 81.23 | 83.98 | 74.88 |

**Table 3.** Object (brick) level F1-scores of connected component analysis (CCA) and the proposed Watershed technique for brick segmentation using in both cases our U-Net based delineation maps as input.

| The method | Random | Square | Dry | Fine | Rough | Average |
|---|---|---|---|---|---|---|
| CCA | 77.46 | **77.44** | 76.23 | 95.76 | 67.02 | 78.63 |
| Prop. Watershed | **79.93** | 75.56 | **77.74** | **97.58** | **79.87** | **81.23** |

  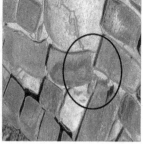

(a) U-Net based mask          (b) CCA labeling result    (c) Prop. Watershed result

**Fig. 5.** Comparison of the brick segmentation results with connected component analysis (CCA) and the proposed Watershed technique based on the same U-Net mask.

## 5   Conclusion

This paper introduced a novel technique for automated brick segmentation in masonry wall images by a joint utilization of the U-Net convolutional neural network and the Watershed segmentation algorithm. The U-Net part provided a high quality delineation map, which enabled efficient marker extraction for the Watershed process. We have shown in a new dataset of diverse masonry photos, that the proposed approach significantly surpasses earlier gradient-driven solutions, and it is largely robust against various noise effects, different illumination conditions, viewpoint and varying masonry types.

Further work will focus on making tests on an extended dataset, and performance comparison of different CNN architectures (like FCN, SegNet, etc.) for the problem. We also plan to expand our studies for 3D point clouds primarily from archaeological sites, with exploiting the advantages of the depth information for brick separation. Another relevant research chapter may deal with wall classification, age or architectural style estimation based on the extracted features.

**Acknowledgement.** This work was supported by the National Research, Development and Innovation Fund (grants NKFIA K-120233 and KH-125681), and by the Szechenyi 2020 Program (grants EFOP-3.6.2-16-2017-00013 and 3.6.3-VEKOP-16-2017-00002). Budapest, Hungary.

## References

1. Bai, M., Urtasun, R.: Deep watershed transform for instance segmentation. In: Proceedings of the IEEE Conference on Computer Vision and Pattern Recognition, Honolulu, Hawaii, pp. 5221–5229 (2017)
2. Bosché, F., Valero, E., Forster, A., Wilson, L., Leslie, A.: Evaluation of historic masonry substrates: towards greater objectivity and efficiency, June 2016. https://doi.org/10.4324/9781315628011-8

3. Llamas, J., Lerones, P.M., Zalama, E., Gómez-García-Bermejo, J.: Applying deep learning techniques to cultural heritage images within the INCEPTION project. In: Ioannides, M., et al. (eds.) EuroMed 2016. LNCS, vol. 10059, pp. 25–32. Springer, Cham (2016). https://doi.org/10.1007/978-3-319-48974-2_4
4. Hemmleb, M., Weritz, A.F., Schiemenz, B.A., Grote, C.A., Maierhofer, C.: Multispectral data acquisition and processing techniques for damage detection on building surfaces. In: ISPRS Commission V Symposium, pp. 1–6, January 2006
5. Kuhn, H.W.: The Hungarian method for the assignment problem. Naval Res. Logistic Q. **2**, 83–97 (1955)
6. Llamas, J.M., Lerones, P., Medina, R., Zalama, E., Gómez-García-Bermejo, J.: Classification of architectural heritage images using deep learning techniques. Appl. Sci. **7**, 992 (2017). https://doi.org/10.3390/app7100992
7. Muñoz, X., Freixenet, J., Cufi, X., Marti, J.: Strategies for image segmentation combining region and boundary information. Pattern Recogn. Lett. **24**, 375–392 (2003). https://doi.org/10.1016/S0167-8655(02)00262-3
8. Oses, N., Dornaika, F., Moujahid, A.: Image-based delineation and classification of built heritage masonry. Remote Sensing **6**(3), 1863–1889 (2014). https://doi.org/10.3390/rs6031863
9. Riveiro, B., Conde, B., Gonzalez, H., Arias, P., Caamaño, J.: Automatic creation of structural models from point cloud data: the case of masonry structures. ISPRS Ann. Photogrammetry Remote Sens. Spat. Inf. Sci. **II–3/W5**, 3–9 (2015). https://doi.org/10.5194/isprsannals-II-3-W5-3-2015
10. Roerdink, J.B., Meijster, A.: The watershed transform: definitions, algorithms and parallelization strategies. Fundam. Inf. **41**(1–2), 187–228 (2000). http://dl.acm.org/citation.cfm?id=2372488.2372495
11. Ronneberger, O., Fischer, P., Brox, T.: U-Net: convolutional networks for biomedical image segmentation. In: Navab, N., Hornegger, J., Wells, W.M., Frangi, A.F. (eds.) MICCAI 2015. LNCS, vol. 9351, pp. 234–241. Springer, Cham (2015). https://doi.org/10.1007/978-3-319-24574-4_28
12. Sithole, G.: Detection of bricks in a masonry wall. Int. Arch. Photogrammetry Remote Sens. Spat. Inf. Sci. **XXXVII**, 567–572 (2008)
13. Tao, Y., Palasek, P., Ling, Z., Patras, I.: Background modelling based on generative Unet. In: IEEE International Conference on Advanced Video and Signal Based Surveillance (AVSS), pp. 1–6, August 2017. https://doi.org/10.1109/AVSS.2017.8078483
14. Zhang, K., et al.: Multi-scale colorectal tumour segmentation using a novel coarse to fine strategy. In: Proceedings of the British Machine Vision Conference (BMVC), pp. 97.1–97.12, September 2016. https://doi.org/10.5244/C.30.97
15. Zyuzin, V., et al.: Identification of the left ventricle endocardial border on two-dimensional ultrasound images using the convolutional neural network Unet. In: 2018 Ural Symposium on Biomedical Engineering, Radioelectronics and Information Technology (USBEREIT), pp. 76–78, May 2018. https://doi.org/10.1109/USBEREIT.2018.8384554

# Improving Person Re-identification by Background Subtraction Using Two-Stream Convolutional Networks

Mahmoud Ghorbel[1(✉)], Sourour Ammar[1,2(✉)], Yousri Kessentini[1,2(✉)], and Mohamed Jmaiel[1,3(✉)]

[1] Digital Research Center of Sfax, 3021 Sfax, Tunisia
mahmoud.ghorbel1991@gmail.com,
{sourour.ammar,yousri.kessentini}@crns.rnrt.tn
[2] MIRACL Laboratory, Sfax University, Sfax, Tunisia
[3] ReDCAD Laboratory, Sfax University, Sfax, Tunisia
mohamed.jmaiel@redcad.org

**Abstract.** The field of person re-identification is facing problems related to the variation of illumination and background scenes. In order to reduce the impact of those variations, we propose in this work a two-stream re-identification system based on a siamese network (S-CNN). The proposed system takes as input a pair of person images: the original image and the image without background. In the background subtraction step, a segmentation network (SEG-CNN) is used to detect the person body part and capture a complementary information. We experimentally prove that the combination of the two streams (images with and without background) improves the recognition rates. In the rank-1, the improvement is respectively of 2% and 4% for Market-1501 and DukeMTMC-reID datasets.

**Keywords:** Person re-identification · Background subtraction · Siamese CNN

## 1  Introduction

Last years have seen the emergence of the field of person re-identification. Thanks to the development of new methods in the domain of machine learning and increasing calculation power of new GPUs, problems related to data recognition became easier to solve and we are getting more and more accurate results. Nowadays, Deep Learning is the most used method to solve problems related to person recognition and identification. Convolutional neuronal networks (CNN) have proved that they can give a great result in image recognition. Thanks to the increase of the computer calculation capability, and the availability of large image datasets, CNN are going deeper and deeper and become one of the most used data analysis techniques. Person re-identification is considered as an image matching problem which aims to match two images of the same person that come

© Springer Nature Switzerland AG 2019
F. Karray et al. (Eds.): ICIAR 2019, LNCS 11662, pp. 345–356, 2019.
https://doi.org/10.1007/978-3-030-27202-9_31

from two different non-overlapping cameras irrespective of the changes that can be related to the complex variations of lighting, pose, point of view or the resolution of images. For a person query image, we aim to return the corresponding identity in the top ranks. In practice, this is a challenging task as generally, many images with a similar background can contain different persons and the same person can be captured under different background. The availability of the large-scale person datasets allowed the use of deep learning for the person re-identification. Several studies have addressed the person re-identification problem by exploiting CNN networks. Since the emergence of solutions based on deep leaning, almost all papers focusing on person re-identification presented an approach using the deep neural network architecture.

Due to the fact that the re-ID problem is an image to image comparison, most of previous works used multi-input architectures which are models based on multi-CNN with shared weights and bias in order to compare two or more images. However, there are some papers that present a one CNN approach with only one input image [18]. For the multi-input networks, the input image number can be two [1, 4, 7, 10, 17, 23], three [6], or four [5].

One of the first works that used deep learning for person re-identification with a pair of images as input is [10] which presented a novel filter pairing neural network (FPNN) to simultaneously manage misalignment, background disorder, photometric and geometric variations.

The paper [1] proposed a method focusing on the dissimilarity of local mid-level features between two images by the use of a layer that computes cross-input neighborhood differences. Given a pair of images as input, the network outputs a similarity value indicating whether the two input images represent the same person or not. The approach of [17] is almost the same approach presented in [1] except for the number of layers and filter's shapes.

Authors in [7] proposed a network that is able to do classification and verification at the same time. They introduced a Loss specific dropout unit where the operation depends on whether the output is fed into the classification subnet subject to the classification loss or the verification subnet with a pairwise verification loss.

Rather than using the Euclidean or cosine distance between a pair of person images as a metric, authors in [4] introduced a CNN network that learns the representation by this images pair and directly returns a similarity score which is used to solve a ranking problem.

Yao et al. [18] introduced Part Loss Network (PL-Net) structure. PL-Net is composed of a basic network and an extension to calculate the partial loss of the person. It is trained to simultaneously minimize part loss and global classification loss.

Zheng et al. [23] proposed a Siamese convolutional network that combines the losses of verification and identification. This network learns both a discriminant integration and a similarity measure, thus fully exploiting the re-ID annotations.

Authors in [6] presented a multi-channel parts-based convolutional neural network model that is able to extract jointly global full-body and local body-parts features of an input person image. The CNN model is trained by an improved triplet loss function in order to pull the instances of the same person closer, and at the same time push the instances belonging to different persons further from each other in the learned feature space. Chen et al [5] proposed a quadruplet loss, allowing the model output to have a larger inter-class variation and a smaller intra-class variation compared to the triplet loss.

Beside the use of multi-input networks, some articles presented solutions based on segmented images [3,9,15,20]. Unlike other works that learn features from the whole image, which contains both body part and background, they introduced some methods to extract information from a specific part of the image which are less exposed to changes caused by position and background variation. Parsing segmentation for person re-identification based on CNN became possible thanks to the large dataset named Look Into Person (LIP) [11] that contains more than 50,000 annotated images with 19 semantic part labels.

In this paper, we propose a two-stream re-identification architecture based on a siamese network (S-CNN) to solve the background bias problem. The proposed approach proceeds in two steps. First, we use a segmentation network (SEG-CNN) to detect the person body part and subsequently remove the background from the image. Then, a two-stream re-identification system based on a siamese network takes as input a pair of person images (with and without background) to extract a complementary information. The results of the two S-CNN are combined to provide the final result. To evaluate our proposed system, we conducted experiments on two large datasets which are Market-1501 [21] and DukeMTMC-reID [22].

This article is organized as follows. We first present our method in Sect. 2 where the implementation details are provided. Then, we present the experimental results in Sect. 3. Finally, we conclude in Sect. 4.

## 2   Overview of the Proposed Method

In this section, we present the proposed method. We can divide our approach into three separated steps (see Fig. 1). The first step is the background subtraction, which consists in detecting the person body part and subsequently removing the background from the image. The second step is the re-identification witch takes as input a pair of person images (with and without background) and gives as output two similarity measures vectors. Finally, the third step is the combination of the two stream outputs.

### 2.1   The Segmentation Step

To reduce the impact of the background variation caused by the person movement and the use of multiple cameras, we propose to remove the background to let the network learning only from the person body part. Figure 2 shows an example of two images of the same person taken by two different cameras. The first one is with a light background while the second is with a dark background, even the texture is not the same. We believe that features extracted from the

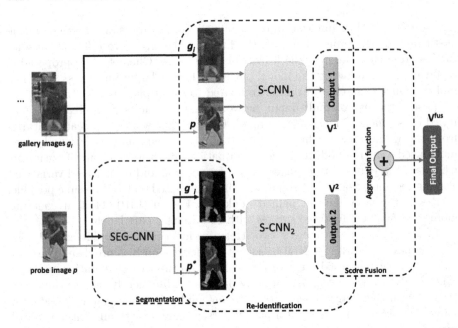

**Fig. 1.** Our framework architecture aims to combine the outputs of the first S-CNN trained on the full images and the second S-CNN trained on the subtracted background images

person body part can capture a complementary information in order to reduce the impact of the background variation and improve the re-identification performances.

The proposed segmentation network (SEG-CNN) is inspired by the work proposed in [11]. Unlike [11] which aims to segment the person body parts and to estimate the pose, we have modified the network architecture to segment the whole body part. Since the body region is detected, we apply a binary mask to remove the background (see Fig. 3).

The SEG-CNN is a deep residual network based on ResNet-101 [8] with atrous spatial pyramid pooling (ASPP) in the output layer in order to make the segmentation more robust. In addition, in order to generate the context used in the refinement phase, two convolutions Res-5 are following. A segmentation loss and a structure-sensitive loss are also used to calculate the similarity between the output image and the ground truth (see Fig. 4).

Since there are no annotated Market-1501 and DukeMTMC-reID datasets for the segmentation field, we use the LIP dataset to train our SEG-CNN.

## 2.2    The Re-identification Step

The re-identification network used in this paper is a convolutional Siamese network (S-CNN) that combines the verification and identification losses [23]. S-CNN is a two-input network formed by two parallel ResNet-50 CNNs pre-trained

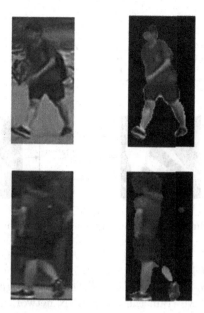

**Fig. 2.** On the left, two images of the same person with two different backgrounds and on the right the same two images without backgrounds

**Fig. 3.** A full image (left), the binary mask (center) and image with only body part of the person (right) from the Market-1501 dataset

on the ImageNet dataset [14] with shared weights and bias. We modified the ResNet-50 network architecture by removing the final fully Connected layer and adding three additional convolutional layers and one square layer are added [8].

The training phase is done on two steps. In the first step, we train the ResNet-50 as a single CNN network with only one image as input. We set the maximum number of training epochs to 20. The learning rate is fixed to 0.001 and the batch size to 16. We choose the categorical-cross-entropy to output a probability over all identities for each image. To update the network parameters, the stochastic gradient descent (SGD) is used to minimize the loss function. Data augmentation is applied to make the training dataset larger by the use of transformations like shear-range, width-shift-range, height-shift-range and horizontal-flip. 90% of the

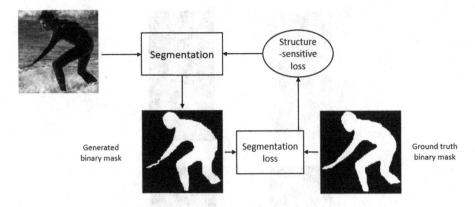

**Fig. 4.** Illustration of the segmentation training process

training images are used for training and 10% are used for validation. The same process is done to train the second network using the segmented images.

In the second step, we train the full S-CNN network using alternated positive and negative pairs. As shown in Fig. 5, the network learns to minimize the distance between two images of the same person and to maximize the distance between two images of two different persons so that maximize inter-class differences, and minimize intra-class differences. For the identification parts, the categorical cross-entropy is used as a loss function combined to a Softmax function that returns a categorical probability distribution. For the binary classification part, the binary cross-entropy is used with a sigmoid function. To compare high-level features extracted from the pair images, Euclidean distance is used.

### 2.3 Scores Fusion

In the literature, many fusion strategies were developed [2]. We can distinguish two types of fusion: early fusion and late fusion. The early fusion is a feature-level-fusion where the output of unimodal analysis is fused before the training. In the late fusion, output of unimodal analysis is used to learn separate scores for each modality. After the fusion, a final score is computed by combining the individual classifier outputs.

In this paper, we adopt a late fusion to combine the output of the first S-CNN trained on the full images dataset and the output of the second S-CNN trained on the images without background.

Given a probe image $p$ and a gallery set $G$ with $N$ images, with $G = \{g_1, g_2, ..., g_N\}$, the output of the first S-CNN is a vector $V^1 = \{S_1^1, S_2^1, ..., S_N^1\}$ of $N$ similarity measures $S_i^1$ computed between the probe image $p$ and each image $g_i$ of the gallery. Similarly, the second S-CNN measures the similarity between the segmented probe image $p^*$ and each segmented image $g_i^*$ in the gallery. It gives as output a vector $V^2 = \{S_1^2, S_2^2, ..., S_N^2\}$.

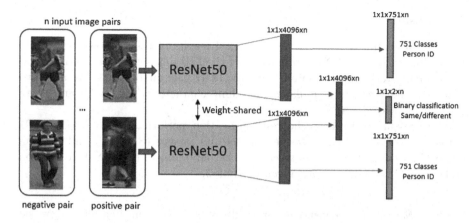

**Fig. 5.** In our S-CNN, two ResNet-50 are used to extract separately two features vectors from a pair of images, which are used to predict respectively the identity of the two input images (751 classes for the Martket-1501 dataset) and to predict the binary classification

The final similarity measure $V^{fus}$ is computed by combining the output of each S-CNN (see Eq. 1). For that, different combination rules are tested in this work like weighted sum, weighted product and vote.

$$V^{fus} = V^1 \oplus V^2 \tag{1}$$

## 3   Experiments

### 3.1   Datasets

To train the segmentation network, we use the LIP dataset [11]. LIP dataset provides a more detailed understanding of image contents by the segmentation of a human image into multiple semantics parts. It is composed of more than 50,000 richly annotated images with 19 semantic body parts indicating the head, the hair, the left arm, the right arm, etc. semantic part labels and 16 body joints, captured from a wide range of viewpoints, occlusions and background complexities.

To evaluate our proposed methods, the experiments are conducted on two publicly available large-scale person re-identification datasets which are Market-1501 [21] and DukeMTMC-reID [22].

The Market-1501 dataset is composed of 32,667 images of 1501 subjects divided into 751 identities for training phase and 750 for testing phase. Images are captured by five high-resolution and one low-resolution cameras.

The DukeMTMC-reID dataset consists of 36,411 bounding boxes of 1812 different persons, 1404 of them appearing in more than two cameras and 408 identities which appear in only one camera. DukeMTMC-ReID is divided into 702 identities for training and 702 identities for testing.

## 3.2   Results

We present in this section the experimental results of the proposed approach. For training the SEG-CNN, we have used the LIP dataset as Market-1501 and DukeMTMC-reID do not contain semantic body part annotations. We used two evaluation metrics, the cumulative matching characteristics (CMC) and mean average precision (mAP).

We present in Table 1 the re-identification performance on Market-1501 dataset of the first S-CNN trained on the full images (S-CNN$_1$) and the second S-CNN trained on the subtracted background images (S-CNN$_2$). Results on DukeMTMC-reID dataset are given in Table 2.

**Table 1.** Market-1501 re-identification results of S-CNN$_1$ trained on full images and S-CNN$_2$ trained on background subtracted images.

| Method | rank-1 | rank-5 | rank-10 | mAP |
|--------|--------|--------|---------|-----|
| S-CNN$_1$ | **79.78** | **91.12** | **94.09** | **63.94** |
| S-CNN$_2$ | 69.85 | 74.17 | 88.53 | 52.80 |

**Table 2.** DukeMTMC-reID re-identification results of S-CNN$_1$ trained on full images and S-CNN$_2$ trained on background subtracted images

| Method | rank-1 | rank-5 | rank-10 | mAP |
|--------|--------|--------|---------|-----|
| S-CNN$_1$ | **69.97** | **83.52** | **87.11** | **53.11** |
| S-CNN$_2$ | 57.63 | 72.39 | 78.23 | 41.29 |

The obtained results on both datasets show that the S-CNN$_1$ trained on the full images gives the best results. The rank-1/mAP scores for S-CNN$_1$ are 79.78%/63.94% for the Market-1501 dataset, and 69.97%/53.11% for the DukeMTMC-reID dataset. Compared to S-CNN$_2$, the improvement in rank-1/mAP accuracy is 9.93%/11.14% for the Market-1501 dataset and 12.34%/11.82% for the DukeMTMC-reID dataset. This can be explained by the bad segmentation quality of some test images. Figure 6 shows an image example from Market-1501 dataset where the SEG-CNN fails to perfectly segment the body part.

We present in Table 3 the combination result of the two stream S-CNN outputs. We have evaluated different combination rules like vote, weighted sum and weighted product. We report in Table 3 the obtained results of the weighted sum combination strategy with different values of $\alpha$ and $\beta$ which gives the best performance. $\alpha$ and $\beta$ are weights of S-CNN$_1$ and S-CNN$_2$.

The best result for the Market-1501 dataset is obtained with $\alpha = 0.7$ and $\beta = 0.3$ (see Table 3). For the DukeMTMC-reID dataset when $\alpha = 0.75$ and $\beta = 0.25$ we get the best value for rank-1 = 73.87 while the best rank-5, rank-10 and mAP are obtained for $\alpha = 0.7$ and $\beta = 0.3$ (see Table 4).

**Fig. 6.** Since the SEG-CNN is only trained on LIP dataset, some images in Market-1501 and DukeMTMC-reID are not well segmented.

**Table 3.** Fusion result with different values of $\alpha$ and $\beta$ on Market-1501 dataset.

| $\alpha$ and $\beta$ values | rank-1 | rank-5 | rank-10 | mAP |
|---|---|---|---|---|
| $\alpha = 0.9, \beta = 0.1$ | 81.20 | 91.76 | 94.62 | 65.63 |
| $\alpha = 0.8, \beta = 0.2$ | 81.73 | 92.13 | 94.77 | 66.64 |
| $\alpha = 0.7, \beta = 0.3$ | **81.79** | **92.31** | **94.83** | **66.78** |
| $\alpha = 0.6, \beta = 0.4$ | 81.47 | 91.89 | 94.74 | 66.44 |

The obtained results on both datasets show that the combination of the two streams S-CNN$_1$ and S-CNN$_2$ significantly improves the re-identification performances. Comparing to S-CNN$_1$ results, the improvement in rank-1/mAP scores is 2.01%/2.84% for the Market-1501 dataset and 3.9%/4.26% for the DukeMTMC-reID dataset. This improvement confirms that the features extracted from only the body part provide complementary information to the full person image features.

Table 5 compares the performance of our approach with other state-of-the-art methods. It can be shown that we achieve competitive results on both datasets.

**Table 4.** Fusion result with different values of $\alpha$ and $\beta$ on DukeMTMC-reID dataset.

| $\alpha$ and $\beta$ values | rank-1 | rank-5 | rank-10 | mAP |
|---|---|---|---|---|
| $\alpha = 0.9, \beta = 0.1$ | 72.63 | 84.56 | 87.83 | 55.32 |
| $\alpha = 0.8, \beta = 0.2$ | 73.51 | 85.18 | 88.33 | 56.75 |
| $\alpha = 0.75, \beta = 0.25$ | **73.87** | 84.96 | 88.64 | **57.37** |
| $\alpha = 0.7, \beta = 0.3$ | 73.60 | **85.27** | **88.95** | **57.37** |
| $\alpha = 0.6, \beta = 0.4$ | 73.60 | 85.05 | 88.64 | 57.20 |

**Table 5.** Comparison with the state-of-the-art results on the Market-1501 and DukeMTMC-reID datasets.

| Method | Market-1501 | | DukeMTMC-reID | |
|---|---|---|---|---|
| | rank-1 | mAP | rank-1 | mAP |
| BoW+kissme [21] | 44.42 | 20.76 | 25.13 | 12.17 |
| LOMO+XQDA [12] | - | - | 30.75 | 17.04 |
| Null Space [19] | 55.43 | 29.87 | - | - |
| Basel(R)+LSRO [22] | 78.06 | 56.23 | 67.68 | 47.13 |
| ReRank [25] | 77.11 | 63.63 | - | - |
| Verif+Identif [23] | 79.51 | 59.87 | 68.9 | 49.3 |
| **Ours** | 81.79 | **66.78** | 73.87 | **57.37** |
| PAN [24] | 82.81 | 63.35 | 71.59 | 51.55 |
| APR [13] | **84.29** | 64.67 | 70.69 | 51.88 |
| SVDNet [16] | 82.3 | 62.1 | **76.7** | 56.8 |

## 4    Conclusions

In this paper, we present a novel two-stream convolutional network for person re-identification. This framework is composed of a segmentation step that aims to subtract the background from images. In the re-identification phase, the outputs of two-stream siamese networks are combined which provides a complementary information for re-identification. We show that the proposed approach brings improvement over the two datasets in re-identification accuracy. We report competitive re-identification accuracy to the state-of-the-art approaches. In the future, more investigations will be made to improve the performance of the segmentation by training the SEG-CNN on the same re-identification datasets. In addition, we will focus in building a multi-task network that combines segmentation and re-identification in the same architecture.

**Acknowledgement.** This project is carried out under the MOBIDOC scheme, funded by the EU through the EMORI program and managed by the ANPR. We gratefully acknowledge the support of NVIDIA Corporation with the donation of the Titan Xp GPU used for this research.

## References

1. Ahmed, E., Jones, M., Marks, T.K.: An improved deep learning architecture for person re-identification. In: Proceedings of the IEEE Conference on Computer Vision and Pattern Recognition, pp. 3908–3916 (2015)
2. Besbes, B., Ammar, S., Kessentini, Y., Rogozan, A., Bensrhair, A.: Evidential combination of SVM road obstacle classifiers in visible and far infrared images. In: 2011 IEEE Intelligent Vehicles Symposium (IV), pp. 1074–1079, June 2011

3. Chen, D., Zhang, S., Ouyang, W., Yang, J., Tai, Y.: Person search via a mask-guided two-stream CNN model. In: Proceedings of the European Conference on Computer Vision (ECCV), pp. 734–750 (2018)
4. Chen, S.Z., Guo, C.C., Lai, J.H.: Deep ranking for person re-identification via joint representation learning. IEEE Trans. Image Process. 25(5), 2353–2367 (2016)
5. Chen, W., Chen, X., Zhang, J., Huang, K.: Beyond triplet loss: a deep quadruplet network for person re-identification. In: Proceedings of the IEEE Conference on Computer Vision and Pattern Recognition, pp. 403–412 (2017)
6. Cheng, D., Gong, Y., Zhou, S., Wang, J., Zheng, N.: Person re-identification by multi-channel parts-based CNN with improved triplet loss function. In: Proceedings of the IEEE Conference on Computer Vision and Pattern Recognition, pp. 1335–1344 (2016)
7. Geng, M., Wang, Y., Xiang, T., Tian, Y.: Deep transfer learning for person re-identification. arXiv preprint arXiv:1611.05244 (2016)
8. He, K., Zhang, X., Ren, S., Sun, J.: Deep residual learning for image recognition. In: Proceedings of the IEEE Conference on Computer Vision and Pattern Recognition, pp. 770–778 (2016)
9. Kalayeh, M.M., Basaran, E., Gökmen, M., Kamasak, M.E., Shah, M.: Human semantic parsing for person re-identification. In: Proceedings of the IEEE Conference on Computer Vision and Pattern Recognition, pp. 1062–1071 (2018)
10. Li, W., Zhao, R., Xiao, T., Wang, X.: Deepreid: deep filter pairing neural network for person re-identification. In: Proceedings of the IEEE Conference on Computer Vision and Pattern Recognition, pp. 152–159 (2014)
11. Liang, X., Gong, K., Shen, X., Lin, L.: Look into person: joint body parsing & pose estimation network and a new benchmark. IEEE transactions on pattern analysis and machine intelligence (2018)
12. Liao, S., Hu, Y., Zhu, X., Li, S.Z.: Person re-identification by local maximal occurrence representation and metric learning. In: Proceedings of the IEEE Conference on Computer Vision and Pattern Recognition, pp. 2197–2206 (2015)
13. Lin, Y., Zheng, L., Zheng, Z., Wu, Y., Yang, Y.: Improving person re-identification by attribute and identity learning. arXiv preprint arXiv:1703.07220 (2017)
14. Russakovsky, O., et al.: Imagenet large scale visual recognition challenge. Int. J. Comput. Vision 115(3), 211–252 (2015)
15. Song, C., Huang, Y., Ouyang, W., Wang, L.: Mask-guided contrastive attention model for person re-identification. In: Proceedings of the IEEE Conference on Computer Vision and Pattern Recognition, pp. 1179–1188 (2018)
16. Sun, Y., Zheng, L., Deng, W., Wang, S.: Svdnet for pedestrian retrieval. In: Proceedings of the IEEE International Conference on Computer Vision, pp. 3800–3808 (2017)
17. Wu, L., Shen, C., Hengel, A.V.D.: Personnet: person re-identification with deep convolutional neural networks. arXiv preprint arXiv:1601.07255 (2016)
18. Yao, H., Zhang, S., Hong, R., Zhang, Y., Xu, C., Tian, Q.: Deep representation learning with part loss for person re-identification. IEEE Trans. Image Process. 28(6), 2860–2871 (2019)
19. Zhang, L., Xiang, T., Gong, S.: Learning a discriminative null space for person re-identification. In: Proceedings of the IEEE Conference on Computer Vision and Pattern Recognition, pp. 1239–1248 (2016)
20. Zhao, G., Jiang, J., Liu, J., Yu, Y., Wen, J.R.: Improving person re-identification by body parts segmentation generated by gan. In: 2018 International Joint Conference on Neural Networks (IJCNN), pp. 1–8. IEEE (2018)

21. Zheng, L., Shen, L., Tian, L., Wang, S., Wang, J., Tian, Q.: Scalable person re-identification: a benchmark. In: Proceedings of the IEEE International Conference on Computer Vision, pp. 1116–1124 (2015)
22. Zheng, Z., Zheng, L., Yang, Y.: Unlabeled samples generated by gan improve the person re-identification baseline in vitro. In: Proceedings of the IEEE International Conference on Computer Vision, pp. 3754–3762 (2017)
23. Zheng, Z., Zheng, L., Yang, Y.: A discriminatively learned CNN embedding for person reidentification. ACM Trans. Multimedia Comput. Commun. Appl. (TOMM) **14**(1), 13 (2018)
24. Zheng, Z., Zheng, L., Yang, Y.: Pedestrian alignment network for large-scale person re-identification. IEEE Transactions on Circuits and Systems for Video Technology (2018)
25. Zhong, Z., Zheng, L., Cao, D., Li, S.: Re-ranking person re-identification with k-reciprocal encoding. In: Proceedings of the IEEE Conference on Computer Vision and Pattern Recognition, pp. 1318–1327 (2017)

# Safely Caching HOG Pyramid Feature Levels, to Speed up Facial Landmark Detection

Gareth Higgins[1](✉), Ling Guan[1](✉), Azhar Quddus[2](✉),
and Ali Shahidi Zandi[2](✉)

[1] Ryerson University, Toronto, ON M5B 2K3, Canada
{gareth.higgins,ling.guan}@ee.ryerson.ca
[2] Alcohol Countermeasure Systems Corp., Toronto, ON M9W 6J2, Canada
{aquddus,aszandi}@acs-corp.com
https://www.ryerson.ca/multimedia-research-laboratory/,
https://acs-corp.com/

**Abstract.** A problem in object detection is finding the scale of interest, which is often solved by multi-scale analysis. One of the drawbacks of multi-scale analysis is that all scales are weighted equally important. We extend [7] to video data, using our method which caches Histogram of Oriented Graidents (HOG) feature levels. Utilizing a Bayesian Network (Bayes Net) to discover a policy for when partial or full pyramid updates are required to prevent loss of tracking. Without sacrificing significant accuracy from the original implementation.

**Keywords:** Face pose detection · HOG pyramid · Bayesian Network

## 1 Introduction

Face detection has always been an area of interest in computer vision. With deeper analysis focusing on problems such as pose/orientation estimation, and face recognition/identification. Recently deep learning techniques have been showing promising results for detection [3,4], and identification. However traditional machine learning algorithms still provide state of the art performance for pose estimation, especially over multiple scales.

Pose estimation, and facial landmark detection, often serve as the first stage in more complex tasks. In the entertainment industry this includes real time facial mapping between live actors, and computer generated models. Previously this has required motion capture markers. While in health monitoring, and security an emerging subject of interest is emotion, and attention recognition, which requires the tracking of individual facial features. In particular HOG continues to be a state of the art approach for facial landmark extraction, and pose estimation [1].

Supported by Alcohol Countermeasure Systems Corp.

F. Karray et al. (Eds.): ICIAR 2019, LNCS 11662, pp. 357–363, 2019.
https://doi.org/10.1007/978-3-030-27202-9_32

## 2    Proposed System

Our work is an extension of [7] which originally targets image data, and is un-optimized for video data. The approach they take is to build a mixture of tree-structured part models, where each part is described by a HOG feature. We recognize that multi-scale HOG Pyramid adds a considerable number of extra calculations which are not always relevant, nor required. This is because all scales at which a subject of interest could occur must have HOG performed each frame. Our goal is to find a balance between accuracy, and processing speed. We achieve this by utilizing slightly stale information, which is still highly correlated to new frames. A similar approach is common in video processing, known as frame skip. We extend that idea to feature levels within a HOG pyramid, however unlike frame skip we utilize cached data from previous frames.

### 2.1    Feature Caching

*Conjecture 1.* Upper levels of the HOG pyramid, which are far from the level of interest will change less between frames and do not need to updated as frequently.

*Conjecture 2.* Lower levels of the HOG pyramid, which are far from the level of interest are unlikely to contribute data distinguishable from noise, and can be ignored.

Under these assumptions, the accuracy penalty from not updating distant feature levels is low. This introduces two issues, deciding frequency of update based on distance, and determining when data has become too outdated to be useful. Recently this concept has also been applied to Residual Networks (ResNets) where a policy network controls which layers will be utilized in a forward pass, dubbed BlockDrop [6]. ResNet successively decreases output feature size, by combining neighbouring cells, which is a similar operation to multi-scale analysis.

For any frame in which the scale of interest is not known, run the original full algorithm. If latency is not acceptable, then under the assumption that the subject has not moved too far, the queued frames can be dropped. After a candidate scale is discovered, prioritize it over other feature scale levels. Feature level updates are then scheduled based on their difference to the scale, or scales of interest. This reduces the workload that must occur in every frame. This works naturally for subjects on the same scale level, and can be extended to subjects at different scales. The degenerate case occurs when a subject exists at each scale. This case is unlikely, as the scale space is often over selected. This method does not completely ignore feature levels, it simply updates them less frequently, which makes it differ from a traditional frame skip approach.

### 2.2    Partial Update

During a partial update, each scale will not be updated every frame. The number of frames between updates $U_p$ is shown in Eq. (1), where $S_i$ are scales which contain a detected subject of interest, and $S_p$ are all the scales to be updated.

$$U_p = \lfloor (\min_{S_i} S_i - S_p)^\gamma \rceil \tag{1}$$

The non-updated HOG features, are still considered when calculating the model of best fit in the subsequent step.

The exponent $\gamma$ is chosen to maintain high update rate on near scales, while lowering update rate of distant scales. Larger values of $\gamma$ are more likely to cause issue with tracking, but provide better performance.

## 2.3  Caching Policy

In order to maintain accuracy, and reduce result latency in fast moving scenes, a Bayes Net provided by the Infer.Net framework [2] is used to discover a policy for deciding when the HOG features need to be recalculated. The action taken can be no update, partial update, or full update. With full update being the most costly with regards to time. Our Bayes Net uses an input feature vector with five items:

1. Summation of frame motion vectors within area of interest
2. Information quality (staleness)
3. Previous frame pose change Occurrence
4. Previous frame scale change Occurrence
5. Previous frame fit model successfully

And outputs a prediction of the optimal action to prevent divergence from the original implementation, and the confidence in the prediction.

The advantage of the Bayes Net is that it is very lightweight, both in inference, and in training. It also accepts unknowns as inputs, which allows us to deal with cases where we have just lost tracking, or have not yet acquired tracking. We train the Bayes Net on a single segment of video, with a good range of motion that sweeps through all the model poses. Since we are looking for a hint, not the exact policy this does not require a large database to train. We show that the Bayes Net provides results than randomly dropping frames.

Recently many consumer grade cameras also include on board video encoders, such as H.264. Instead of recalculating the motion vectors at a software level, we extract them directly from the H.264 encoded video. The quality of the vectors is low, however they have practically zero performance cost since they are generated by the device automatically. We find that they contain sufficient information to suggest when it is safe to avoid recalculating feature levels. Initially the motion vectors of the whole image are considered. Once the algorithm has successfully completed an iteration, candidate bounding boxes are available based on the fit models. In order to detect motion which may occur at the edge of the bounding box, as a subject moves, we use an enlarged copy of the bounding box. Subsequent frames consider only the motion vectors which fall within these bounding boxes.

Additionally since [7] is designed for standalone images there is no previously predicted model data which can be leveraged. However when moving to video data, after a candidate model is found we can restrict the model search to adjacent models, which are more probable.

The information quality is a measure of how old the information contained in the HOG feature pyramid are. This feature was chosen, to help predict how long processing can continue based on stale data. The expectation is that as the data quality drops, the uncertainty in the Bayes Net will rise until eventually it predict that loss of tracking would occur if a more substantial HOG pyramid update is not performed.

The Bayes Net is used to predict which action would be required to prevent loss of accuracy, in object tracking. In addition to the recommended action, we also obtain the probability that the Bayes Net believes in this outcome. For low confidence results, we opt to be cautious, and perform a more comprehensive update than the recommended. With more evidence and testing, a more aggressive stance could be taken to balance accuracy, and performance.

## 3　Results

In order to test our method, we utilize the YouTube Faces DB [5]. We use approximately 400 videos chosen at random from the database to demonstrate that our method does not negatively affect the accuracy of the original algorithm by an appreciable amount. We also show that we can realize a large performance gain. Our modified algorithm at best takes only 37% of the time to process the same video, since we are able to avoid calculating unused HOG features. To compare the execution time difference we use relative difference, Eq. (2) (Table 1).

$$\text{Relative Difference} = \frac{x - x_{ref}}{x_{ref}} \tag{2}$$

**Table 1.** Performance difference between original algorithm being naively applied to each frame, and our method.

| Relative Difference | | |
|---|---|---|
| Best | Mean | Worst |
| −0.6347 | −0.3876 | 0.0969 |

Since mean can often skew the results favourably, by hiding outliers we also show in Fig. 1 the histogram of the performance speed up. Over 60% of the videos processed by the modified algorithm, take less than 50% of the original processing time. The left primary vertical axis denotes the number of videos which achieved a particular speed up. While the right secondary vertical axis denotes the cumulative sum of videos.

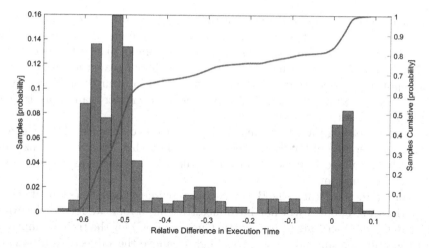

**Fig. 1.** Histogram of time difference, compared to original in YouTube Faces DB using 433 randomly selected videos

In scenes that contain a lot of motion, in which cached information cannot be utilized, we pay a performance penalty for no gain. The ten percent slower worst case is caused by the construction of the feature vector, and performing inference, when such analysis provides no benefit, this is an expected result. In scenes with low motion, we realize the largest gain, using only 36% of the time compared to the original algorithm.

After observing the performance increase, we verify that our algorithm does not negatively impact the accuracy of the original algorithm. First we confirm

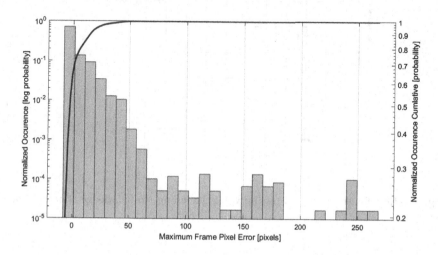

**Fig. 2.** Histogram of maximum pixel error in YouTube Faces DB over 400 randomly selected videos.

that the discovered model is detected at the same scale as the original algorithm. Next we perform nearest neighbour between the keypoints in our results, and that of the base algorithm. We then record the maximum pixel error, and mean pixel error based on the result of the nearest neighbour search for each frame. It is important to note that shows Fig. 2 this result in logarithmic scale. Even though there are some occurrences of very large error, greater than 50 pixels they represent less than 1% of the total occurrences.

When comparing the algorithms our modified version has less than 10 pixels of error for over 84% of the frames. Our results show that it is safe to utilize the previously calculated HOG levels in very diverse environments as generally the pixel error is quite low.

In order to show that the Bayes Net is providing good hints about when not performing updates will not introduce tracking errors, we record the Area under Receiver Operating characteristic Curve (ARoC) for the training input, a thirty second webcam video shot from slightly above the subject. Additionally to show that it generalizes we also test an uncorrelated video, from a Microsoft Kinect, shot looking up at the subject. Shown in Fig. 3 we find that in general the prediction performs better than randomly guessing.

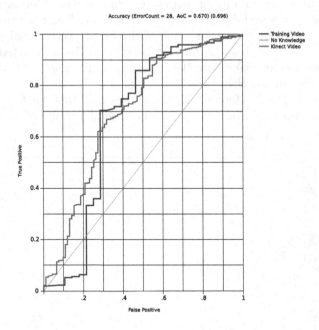

**Fig. 3.** ARoC for training, and testing video, including No knowledge (random selection)

# 4   Conclusion

Combining Bayesian prediction, with multi-scale analysis provides a cheap, and effective way of estimating the value of a frame. With this information we avoid recalculating sections which will not contribute new data. This reduces the work of subsequent stages, which need to utilize facial landmark information; without sacrificing considerable accuracy.

Since the training of the Bayes Net is incredibly light weight, it may be possible to incorporate an online adaptive algorithm, which can further optimize away unnecessary feature level updates. Alternatively it may be possible to use a Reinforcement Learning (RL) technique to discover a more complex policy at the cost of extra additionally training time, and data.

# References

1. Baltrusaitis, T., Zadeh, A., Lim, Y.C., Morency, L.P.: Openface 2.0: facial behavior analysis toolkit. In: 2018 13th IEEE International Conference on Automatic Face & Gesture Recognition (FG 2018), pp. 59–66. IEEE (2018)
2. Minka, T., Winn, J., Guiver, J., Zaykov, Y., Fabian, D., Bronskill, J.: Infer.NET 2.7, microsoft Research Cambridge (2018). http://research.microsoft.com/infernet
3. Redmon, J., Divvala, S., Girshick, R., Farhadi, A.: You only look once: unified, real-time object detection. In: Proceedings of the IEEE Conference on Computer Vision and Pattern Recognition, pp. 779–788 (2016)
4. Redmon, J., Farhadi, A.: YOLO9000: better, faster, stronger. CoRR abs/1612.08242 (2016). http://arxiv.org/abs/1612.08242
5. Wolf, L., Hassner, T., Maoz, I.: Face recognition in unconstrained videos with matched background similarity. IEEE (2011)
6. Wu, Z., et al.: Blockdrop: dynamic inference paths in residual networks. In: Proceedings of the IEEE Conference on Computer Vision and Pattern Recognition, pp. 8817–8826 (2018)
7. Zhu, X., Ramanan, D.: Face detection, pose estimation, and landmark localization in the wild. In: 2012 IEEE Conference on Computer Vision and Pattern Recognition, pp. 2879–2886 June 2012. https://doi.org/10.1109/CVPR.2012.6248014

# Construction and Optimization of Feature Descriptor Based on Dynamic Local Intensity Order Relations of Pixel Group

Wen-Hung Liao[1,2]([✉]), Carolyn Yu[1,2], and Yi-Chieh Wu[1,2]

[1] Department of Computer Science, National Chengchi University, Taipei, Taiwan
whliao@nccu.edu.tw
[2] Pervasive Artificial Intelligence Research (PAIR) Labs, Hsinchu, Taiwan

**Abstract.** With the prevalence of smart embedded systems, the amount of images being captured and processed on mobile devices have grown significantly in recent years. Image feature descriptors which play crucial roles in detection or recognition tasks are expected to exhibit robust matching performance while at the same time maintain reasonable storage requirement. Among the local feature descriptors that have been proposed previously, local intensity order patterns (LIOP) demonstrated superior performance in many benchmark studies. As LIOP encodes the ranking relation in a point set (with $N$ elements), however, its feature dimension increases drastically ($N!$) with the number of a neighboring sampling points around a pixel. To alleviate the dimensionality issue, this paper presents a local feature descriptor by considering pairwise intensity relation in a pixel group, thereby reducing feature dimension to the order of $C_2^N$. In the proposed method, the threshold for assigning order relation is set dynamically according to local intensity distribution. Different weighting schemes, including linear transformation and Euclidean distance, have also been investigated to adjust the contribution of each pairing relation. Ultimately, dynamic local intensity order relations (DLIOR) pattern is devised to effectively encode intensity order relation of each pixel group. Experimental results indicate that DLIOR consumes less storage space than LIOP but achieves comparable or superior feature matching performance using benchmark data set.

**Keywords:** Local feature descriptors ·
Dynamic intensity order relations · Image matching

## 1 Introduction

In recent years, camera has become the standard build-in component for various embedded systems, including smart phones, internet of things (IOT) devices and unmanned aerial vehicles (UAV). As a result, the amount of image/video being captured and processed have grown at a fast pace. Devising effective feature descriptors for robust image recognition has been a lasting endeavor for computer

© Springer Nature Switzerland AG 2019
F. Karray et al. (Eds.): ICIAR 2019, LNCS 11662, pp. 364–375, 2019.
https://doi.org/10.1007/978-3-030-27202-9_33

vision researchers for a long time. With the dominance of deep neural networks, however, recent trend has shifted to the search for feature representation using low-bit storage and simple distance metric to speed up the processing while maintaining satisfactory recognition performance.

Local intensity order pattern (LIOP) was formulated to exploit intensity order relationship in a neighborhood to arrive at a feature encoding scheme that exhibit certain invariance properties. Although the authors have reported encouraging results in [1], a known disadvantage of LIOP is that its feature dimension increases drastically with the number of sampling points in the neighboring group.

To address this issue, local intensity order relation (LIOR) pattern was devised by considering the degree of dissimilarity between pixel intensities, thereby limiting the growth of dimensions [2]. In the comparative analysis provided in [2], LIOR can achieve similar performance using only 1/2 or 1/3 the feature dimension. In this work, we further refine and improve the originally defined LIOR by introducing dynamic threshold for determining order relations as well as different weighting schemes to adjust the contribution of each order relation to the encoding mechanism. The proposed extension known as dynamic local intensity order relation (DLIOR) patterns allow more flexibility in constructing the feature descriptor and provide insight into the effects of different parameter settings in feature matching performance.

The remainder of this paper is organized as follows. In Sect. 2 we review related work, specifically, LIOP and LIOR, and discuss how these local feature descriptors are constructed. Section 3 elucidates our proposed methodology and possible strategies for setting parameters to form a more compact and robust descriptor. In Sect. 4, we compare and discuss experimental results using standard benchmark. Section 5 concludes this paper with a brief summary.

## 2    Related Work

The local intensity order pattern (LIOP) proposed by Wang et al. [1] has been shown to exhibit better performance than SIFT, DAISY and HRI-CSLTP in terms of recall rate. Since both LIOR and DLIOR descriptor are motivated by LIOP, a brief overview of the key stages involved in constructing LIOP will be provided in this section. Details regarding the formulation of LIOR will be presented subsequently.

### 2.1    LIOP

Given an image patch, pixel intensity value is used to divide the patch into $B$ sub-regions called ordinal bins. In each bin, a collection of $N$ samples is first identified within a neighborhood of radius $R$. We then consider the order relations of $N$ points, which has a total of $N!$ combinations, and increment the corresponding index in the histogram of size $N!$. This process will be repeated for selected points in all bins, generating a feature vector of size $B \times N!$. To illustrate, let us set $N = 3$. Then there will be $3! = 6$ different permutations of order relations among these three samples (excluding 'equality' relation). To be exact, the six order relations are: $(1 \prec 2 \prec 3)$, $(1 \prec 3 \prec 2)$, $(2 \prec 1 \prec 3)$, $(2 \prec 3 \prec 1)$, $(3 \prec 1 \prec 2)$, and $(3 \prec 2 \prec 1)$.

As the total bin number is 6, three pixels with intensity values $(10, 20, 30)$ has an order relation $(1 \prec 2 \prec 3)$, generating an index of 1. The triplet $(30, 10, 20)$ will produce an index of 4 $(2 \prec 3 \prec 1)$. The original formulation of LIOP embeds the equality relation by interpreting all the three triplets $(10, 10, 30)$, $(10, 30, 30)$ and $(10, 10, 10)$ as $(1 \prec 2 \prec 3)$. Since the order relations are more stable when the intensity differences between samples are larger, LIOP assigns a weight to the descriptor according to Eq. 1:

$$w(x) = \Sigma_{i,j} sgn(|I(x_i) - I(x_j)| - T_w) + 1 \tag{1}$$

where $sgn()$ is the sign function and $T_w$ is a predefined threshold. This is equivalent to counting the number of dissimilar samples in a group. Therefore, groups containing more disparate samples will exercise more influence.

Feature dimension is obviously a concern when it comes to the choice of $N$. LIOP is claimed to have higher discriminative power as it exploits the local information using the intensity order of all the $N$ sampled neighboring points. It appears that a larger $N$ will encode more local structures and hence yield more accurate representation. However, feature dimension is proportional to $N!$, and grows very quickly as $N$ increases. In practice, only three settings of $N$ (3, 4 and 5) have been tested in [1].

A updated version of LIOP has been disclosed in [3]. The performance of this revised LIOP is shown to be superior than the original LIOP by adopting an enlarged image patch, among other modifications. The proposed descriptor, namely, DLIOR will be evaluated against the modified LIOP in the subsequent sections.

## 2.2 LIOR Series

How do we encode ranking relations while keeping the feature vector at a reasonable size? Instead of comparing all $N$ samples that generates $N!$ permutations, the relationship between two elements at one time can be compared and encoded, reducing the total number of relations to $C_2^N$. The resulting histogram has a dimension of order $O(N^2)$, much lower than the original $O(N!)$. Image descriptor constructed based on the above principle is named local intensity order relations (LIOR) feature.

Two versions of LIOR feature have been defined. LIOR-1 is obtained by encoding concordant/discordant relations of pairs of elements selected from a pixel group. LIOR-2 further exploits the degree of concordance/discordance to arrive at a different encoding scheme. The overall process for constructing LIOR is very similar to that of LIOP. The main difference lies in the way we compare and encode the relations among $N$ pixels in a set.

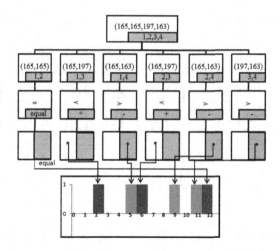

**Fig. 1.** Constructing LIOR-1 using $N = 4$ as an example.

**LIOR-1.** In LIOR-1, the relative magnitude of two elements from the set of $N$ pixels is examined. A total of $N(N-1)/2$ pairwise comparisons are carried out. An array of size $N(N-1)$ is allocated to record the relationship. For two pixels $P_a$ and $P_b$, if $I(P_a) < I(P_b)$, the entry corresponding to $(a, b)$ will be incremented, and vice versa. If there is a tie, this information will be recorded in an extra dimension, resulting in a final dimension of $N(N-1)+1$ for LIOR-1 feature.

Take $N = 4$, for example, with four pixel values 165, 165, 197 and 163. An array of size $4 * (4-1) + 1 = 13$ will first be allocated. Then pairwise comparison of (165, 165), (165, 197), (165, 163), (165, 197), (165, 163) and (197,163), are performed respectively, as illustrated in Fig. 1. For the first pair, since $165 = 165$, dimension #12 will be incremented. For the second pair, since $165 < 197$, dimension #2 will be incremented, and so on. The final descriptor is constructed by accumulating the LIOR-1 of all points in each ordinal bin, then by concatenating them together.

**LIOR-2.** In LIOR-2, the degree of intensity difference between two pixels $P_a$ and $P_b$ is further exploited to define a new encoding mechanism. A fixed threshold $T$ will be specified, and the number of relationship between two pixels increases from 2 ($>$ and $<$) to 4 ($>>$, $>$, $<$ and $<<$, excluding tie), as listed in Eq. (2).

$$\begin{cases} \text{case 1,} & \text{if } I(P_b) - I(P_a) < -T \\ \text{case 2,} & \text{if } -T < I(P_b) - I(P_a) < 0 \\ \text{case 3,} & \text{if } 0 < I(P_b) - I(P_a) < T \\ \text{case 4,} & \text{if } T < I(P_b) - I(P_a) \end{cases} \quad (2)$$

Figure 2 provides examples of constructing LIOR-2 using $N = 4$ and two different thresholds, $T = 20$ and $T = 30$. Indeed, different choices of thresholds

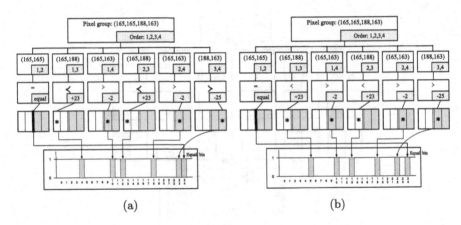

**Fig. 2.** Examples of constructing LIOR-2 [2] using $N = 4$ with different threshold values. (a) $T = 20$ (b) $T = 30$.

for intensity difference will produce distinct feature descriptors. Proper setting of this parameter will be the central topic in the formulation of dynamic LIOR. Table 1 compares the feature dimension of LIOP, LIOR-1, and LIOR-2 with 6 ordinal bins and different $N$s.

**Table 1.** Comparing feature dimension of LIOP, LIOR-1 and LIOR-2

| N | B | LIOP | LIOR-1 | LIOR-2 |
|---|---|---|---|---|
| 4 | 6 | $6 \times 4! = 144$ | $D_1(4) = 6 \times 13 = 78$ | $D_2(4) = 6 \times 25 = 150$ |
| 5 | | $6 \times 5! = 720$ | $D_1(5) = 6 \times 21 = 126$ | $D_2(5) = 6 \times 41 = 246$ |
| 6 | | $6 \times 6! = 4320$ | $D_1(6) = 6 \times 31 = 186$ | $D_2(6) = 6 \times 61 = 366$ |
| 7 | | $6 \times 7! = 30240$ | $D_1(7) = 6 \times 43 = 258$ | $D_2(7) = 6 \times 85 = 510$ |
| 8 | | $6 \times 8! = 214920$ | $D_1(8) = 6 \times 57 = 342$ | $D_2(8) = 6 \times 113 = 678$ |

Experimental results show that both LIOR-1 and LIOR-2 produce comparable matching scores with respect to LIOP, with relatively smaller feature dimension, or equivalently, storage cost in most cases. The performance of LIOR-2 is slightly better than LIOR-1, at the cost of almost twice the feature dimension. However, it shows weakness in coping with illumination change, especially for low brightness images. In general, LIOP-2 produces best results when more pixels in a set are compared.

A few issues come into light when carefully examining the construction of LIOR features. Firstly, the thresholds for asserting 'equality' relation in LIOR-1 and ordering relation in LIOP-2 are fixed regardless of the image intensity distribution (or histogram). Secondly, in the original LIOR, contribution of each pairing relation is weighted by the absolute intensity difference between two pixels.

Therefore, images with different gray level distributions could yield very dissimilar encodings even though the content is nearly identical. Thirdly, the distance between pair of pixels in a neighborhood is different. Consequently, the contribution could also be modified accordingly. The next section will discuss various approaches to address the aforementioned deficiencies in order to build a compact and robust descriptor for feature representation.

## 3   Proposed Methodology

An observation of image intensity distribution motivates the adoption of dynamic thresholds in determining pixel order relations. Given an image along with the detected feature points obtained using the Harris-Affine detector described in [4] in Fig. 3, intensity difference of point pairs in a pixel group is calculated and compared in Fig. 4 (four patches are listed for illustration purpose). Obviously, in patch-4, the total count of the difference of point pairs which is less than the threshold (which is empirically set to 20 in LIOR-2), is significantly larger than that of other patches. We speculate if the difference of intensity distribution will influence the representativeness of LIOR. A variety of adaptive settings are exploited and illustrated as follows.

(a)                                    (b)

**Fig. 3.** Bikes. (a) Original image (b) With detected feature points

### 3.1   Setting Dynamic Threshold

Since the intensity difference of point pairs in a pixel group is fluid, an adaptive threshold $\theta_d$ according to statistics of intensity difference among patches is preferred. The standard deviation of the pixel value difference ($\sigma$) will be computed as the basis for the dynamic threshold. Several different configurations will also be discussed in the subsequent experimental results.

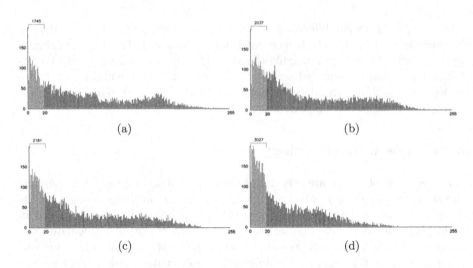

**Fig. 4.** Comparison of intensity difference of point pairs in a pixel group. The marked red area indicates the amount of the difference of point pairs which is less than *Threshold* = 20. (a)–(d) contain results from patch-1 to patch-4.

### 3.2 Weight Assignment Schemes

New weight assignment strategies are designed to decrease the effect of variance of intensity difference among patches. Two methods for weighting bins are considered:

1. *Square root:* In the first step, pixel difference of point pairs is processed according to Eq. 3, where $x$ is the intensity difference, and $\theta$ is a static or dynamic threshold. By applying Eq. 3, the range of w is limited to $0 \leq w \leq \sqrt{255 - \theta} < 16$.

$$w = \begin{cases} \sqrt{x}, & \text{if } x < \theta \\ \sqrt{x - \theta}, & \text{if } x \geq \theta \end{cases} \tag{3}$$

2. *Linear transformation:* Next, the weight is reduced further by applying Eq. 4. Using this method, we can restrict the accumulated bin value effectively.

$$w' = base + \alpha \times w \tag{4}$$

### 3.3 Dynamic Weight Settings Based on Euclidean Distance

When $N$ is greater than 3, the geometric distances of each point pairs differ in a pixel group. Figure 5 provides an illustration of for $N = 4$ and 5. Take Fig. 5(b) for example: $\overline{x_4 x_5} < \overline{x_2 x_5}$. The relation of $(x_4, x_5)$ should be play a more important role than the relation of $(x_2, x_5)$ as the former pair is closer. Setting a weight dynamically based on the Euclidean distance of the point pairs seems justifiable.

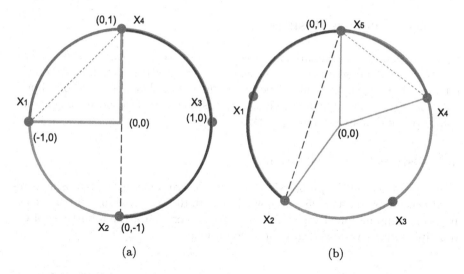

**Fig. 5.** Distance of point pairs with different $N$. (a) $N = 4$ (b) $N = 5$

To speed up the calculation, the parameters of original LIOP can be retrieved. Given an arbitrary point pair $(x_i, x_j)$ belongs to a pixel group, where $i \neq j$, and $N$ is the number of pixel group. The Euclidean distance between $(x_i, x_j)$ can be computed according to Eqs. 5 and 6. A normalized version which ranges from 0 to 1 is shown in Eq. 7.

$$d(i,j) = min(|i - j|, |i + N - j|) \tag{5}$$

$$L_2(x_i, x_j) = 2 \times cos((\frac{1}{2} - \frac{d}{N}) \times \pi) \tag{6}$$

$$NL_2(x_i, x_j) = cos((\frac{1}{2} - \frac{d}{N}) \times \pi) \tag{7}$$

Finally, the base weight function is listed in Eq. 8. Two other variations are given in Eqs. 9 and 10, respectively.

$$Weight_{pair}(x_i, x_j) = \frac{1}{cos((\frac{1}{2} - \frac{d}{N}) \times \pi)} \tag{8}$$

$$Weight_{pair_+}(x_i, x_j) = (\frac{1}{cos(\frac{1}{2} - \frac{d}{N}) \times \pi)})^2 \tag{9}$$

$$Weight_{pair_-}(x_i, x_j) = \sqrt{\frac{1}{cos((\frac{1}{2} - \frac{d}{N}) \times \pi)}} \tag{10}$$

## 4     Experimental Results

In this section, the benchmark employed for performance evaluation is first introduced. Next, the base weight adjustment experiment is conducted. Based on the settings of the optimal result, experiments including dynamic threshold, linear transformation, and dynamic weight settings based on Euclidean distance are conducted and analyzed subsequently.

### 4.1     Data Set and Evaluation

The performance of the proposed local image descriptors is evaluated using standard benchmark data set [5], as shown in Fig. 6. Rotation, scaling blurring, compression, illumination change and noise are present to test the robustness of the descriptor under various degradation conditions.

**Fig. 6.** The dataset of Affine Covariant Feature [5].

Nearest neighbor distance ratio is employed to determine the degree of matching between two features. In this method, if the nearest distance divided by the second nearest distance is smaller than a predefined threshold (as 0.5), it is classified as a correct match. The matching score (abbreviated as M.S.) between two images is computed according to Eq. 11:

$$M.S. = 100 \times \frac{Number\ of\ correct\ matches}{Min.\ number\ of\ features\ in\ two\ images} \qquad (11)$$

## 4.2   Dynamic Threshold

In all the experiments, we adopted an enlarged image patch as was done in the revised LIOP. Based on the standard deviation of the pixel value difference ($\sigma$), several parameter settings of dynamic threshold ($\theta_d$) are tested and listed in Table 2. Other parameters are fixed in this experiment: $B = 6$, $R = 6$, and the weight function is computed using Eq. 3. The result shows that accuracy is improved after incorporating dynamic thresholds. The optimal combination for is $\theta_d = \sigma \times 2$, and equal $= 8$. ('equal' denotes the range within which the intensity of two pixels is considered the same.)

**Table 2.** DLIOR: results of dynamic threshold

| N | 8 | 7 | 6 | 5 | 4 | 8 | 7 | 6 | 5 | 4 |
|---|---|---|---|---|---|---|---|---|---|---|
| $\theta_d$ | $\sigma \times 2$ | | | | | $\sigma \times 1.5$ | | | | |
| equal | 5 | | | | | 5 | | | | |
| Avg | 39.78 | 39.75 | 39.55 | 38.9 | 37.94 | 39.49 | 39.34 | 39.2 | 38.71 | 37.55 |
| $\theta_d$ | $\sigma \times 2$ | | | | | $\sigma \times 1.5$ | | | | |
| equal | 8 | | | | | 8 | | | | |
| Avg | 39.84 | 39.8 | 39.63 | 39.07 | 38.03 | 39.41 | 39.19 | 39.22 | 38.68 | 37.6 |

**Table 3.** DLIOR: results of weight adjustment - square root ($B = 6, R = 6, equal = 2$)

| N | 8 | 7 | 6 | 5 | 4 | 8 | 7 | 6 | 5 | 4 | 8 | 7 | 6 | 5 | 4 |
|---|---|---|---|---|---|---|---|---|---|---|---|---|---|---|---|
| $\theta_s$ | 50 | | | | | 55 | | | | | 60 | | | | |
| Avg | 38.99 | 38.82 | 38.62 | 38.16 | 37.22 | 39.14 | 38.95 | 38.77 | 38.25 | 37.27 | 39.31 | 39.05 | 38.83 | 38.44 | 37.24 |

## 4.3   Weight Adjustment

**Square Root.** In this version of weight adjustment, square root for weight is applied according to Eq. 3. The parameters derived from LIOP and LIOR-2 are configured as follows: $B = 6$, $R = 6$, $equal = 2$. The results are shown in Table 3. For this experiment, static threshold $\theta_s = 60$ produces the best outcome. This value of $\theta_s$ will be employed in all following experiments.

**Linear Transformation.** Equation 4 is applied and several configurations are also tested, as shown in Table 4. The following parameters are fixed in this experiment: $\theta_d = \sigma \times 2$, and $equal = 5$. The best performance is observed when $base = \sigma/2$ and $\alpha = 0.5$.

**Table 4.** DLIOR: results of weight adjustment - linear transformation

| N | 8 | 7 | 6 | 5 | 4 | 8 | 7 | 6 | 5 | 4 | 8 | 7 | 6 | 5 | 4 |
|---|---|---|---|---|---|---|---|---|---|---|---|---|---|---|---|
| base | 5 | | | | | 7 | | | | | 3 | | | | |
| $\alpha$ | 0.5 | | | | | 0.3 | | | | | 0.7 | | | | |
| Avg. | 40.06 | 39.84 | 39.74 | 38.97 | 38.02 | 40.06 | 39.94 | 39.73 | 39.02 | 38.13 | 39.88 | 39.88 | 39.72 | 38.94 | 38.07 |
| base | 8 | | | | | 15 | | | | | 20 | | | | |
| $\alpha$ | 0.5 | | | | | 0.5 | | | | | 0.5 | | | | |
| Avg. | 40.12 | 39.96 | 39.79 | 39.03 | 38.08 | 40.14 | 39.97 | 39.75 | 39.05 | 38.1 | 40.13 | 39.96 | 39.74 | 39.03 | 38.09 |
| base | $\sigma/2$ | | | | | | | | | | | | | | |
| $\alpha$ | 0.5 | | | | | | | | | | | | | | |
| Avg. | *40.18* | 40.02 | 39.78 | 39.12 | 38.08 | | | | | | | | | | |

## 4.4  Dynamic Weight Settings Based on Euclidean Distance

Weight adjustment based on Euclidean distance is implemented here. Using different weight functions, from Eqs. 8 to 10, the results are summarized in Table 5. The best performance can be observed when applying Eq. 10.

**Table 5.** DLIOR: results of dynamic weight settings based on Euclidean distance

| N | 8 | 7 | 6 | 5 | 4 | 8 | 7 | 6 | 5 | 4 | 8 | 7 | 6 | 5 | 4 |
|---|---|---|---|---|---|---|---|---|---|---|---|---|---|---|---|
| $\theta_d$ | $\sigma \times 2$ | | | | | | | | | | | | | | |
| equal | 5 | | | | | | | | | | | | | | |
| Weight function | Eq. 8 | | | | | Eq. 9 | | | | | Eq. 10 | | | | |
| Avg. | 40.08 | 39.93 | 39.73 | 38.92 | 37.99 | 39.27 | 39.13 | 39.06 | 38.45 | 37.74 | *40.27* | 40.13 | 39.86 | 39.1 | 38.07 |

## 4.5  Comparison with Revised LIOR

Based on the above experiments, the best performance of DLIOR can be obtained using the following parameter settings: $N = 8$, $B = 6$, $R = 6$, $base = \sigma/2$, $\alpha = 0.5$, $\theta_d = \sigma \times 2$, $equal = 8$. Table 6 compares each image category as well as average matching scores for LIOP and DLIOR. The results show that DLIOR can achieve better performance than LIOP in most image categories. In addition, if minor degradation (less than 1%) in the accuracy is allowed, DLIOR patterns with $N = 5, 6$ or $7$ that use only 1/3 to 1/2 of the original dimensionality can become alternative solutions with lower storage requirements.

**Table 6.** Comparing performance of LIOP and DLIOR

| N | Method | Dimension | Bark | Bikes | Boat | Graf | Leuven | UBC | Wall | Trees | Average |
|---|--------|-----------|------|-------|------|------|--------|-----|------|-------|---------|
| 4 | LIOP | 144 | 18.52 | 58.6 | 30.78 | 24.8 | 54 | 74.04 | 29.32 | 16.84 | 38.36 |
| 5 | LIOP | 720 | 18.76 | 58.98 | 33.8 | 25.94 | 55.36 | 75.02 | 31.44 | 19.8 | **39.89** |
| 6 | **LIOP** | 4320 | 18.8 | 59.24 | 34.44 | 26.28 | 54.84 | 75.72 | 32.32 | 20.96 | *40.33* |
| 7 | LIOP | 30240 | 18.6 | 58.06 | 33.28 | 25.7 | 54.54 | 74.9 | 31.48 | 19.08 | 39.46 |
| 4 | DLIOR | 150 | 18.12 | 58.54 | 31.86 | 24.82 | 49.1 | 75.26 | 30.26 | 17.14 | 38.14 |
| 5 | DLIOR | 246 | 18.72 | 59.34 | 32.78 | 26.22 | 52.2 | 75.52 | 31.18 | 18.72 | 39.34 |
| 6 | DLIOR | 366 | 18.64 | 59.58 | 33.58 | 26.52 | 52.4 | 76.04 | 32.34 | 20.64 | 39.97 |
| 7 | DLIOR | 510 | 18.8 | 60.04 | 33.96 | 26.96 | 52.82 | 75.96 | 32.5 | 20.98 | 40.25 |
| 8 | **DLIOR** | 678 | 18.78 | 59.84 | 34.34 | 26.82 | 53.32 | 76.26 | 32.7 | 21.96 | *40.5* |

# 5   Conclusion

In this paper, we have extended the LIOR pattern defined in [2] by considering dynamic settings of key parameters based on image statistics. Extensive experimental analysis has been carried out to assess the effectiveness of different assignment strategies. Performance comparison is made against the updated version of LIOP. In most image categories, the proposed DLIOR achieve better accuracy than LIOP using comparable feature dimension. Additionally, when minor reduction in matching accuracy is permitted, DLIOR grants flexibility in the selection of feature size, enabling a sensible trade-off between available computational resources and required performance.

**Acknowledgments.** This work is supported by the Ministry of Science and Technology, Taiwan under Grants no. MOST-108-2634-F-004-001 through Pervasive Artificial Intelligence Research (PAIR) Labs.

# References

1. Wang, Z., Fan, B., Wu, F.: Local intensity order pattern for feature description. In: 2011 IEEE International Conference on Computer Vision (ICCV), pp. 603–610. IEEE (2011)
2. Liao, W.-H., Wu, C.-C., Lin, M.-C.: Feature descriptor based on local intensity order relations of pixel group. In: 2016 23rd International Conference on Pattern Recognition (ICPR). IEEE (2016)
3. Wang, Z., Fan, B., Wang, G., Wu, F.: Exploring local and overall ordinal information for robust feature description. IEEE Trans. Pattern Anal. Mach. Intell. **38**(11), 2198–2211 (2016)
4. Mikolajczyk, K., Schmid, C.: Scale & affine invariant interest point detectors. Int. J. Comput. Vis. **60**(1), 63–86 (2004)
5. Miksik, O., Mikolajczyk, K.: Evaluation of local detectors and descriptors for fast feature matching, In: 21st International Conference on Pattern Recognition (ICPR), pp. 2681–2684 (2012)

# Segmentation of Breast MRI Scans in the Presence of Bias Fields

Hossein Soleimani$^{(\boxtimes)}$, Jose Rincon, and Oleg V. Michailovich

University of Waterloo, Waterloo, Canada
{h3soleim,jrincon,olegm}@uwaterloo.ca

**Abstract.** Magnetic Resonance Imaging (MRI) is currently considered to be the most sensitive tool for imaging-based diagnostic and presurgical assessment of breast cancer. In addition to their valuable diagnostic contrasts, MRI scans also provide a superb delineation of breast anatomy, which facilitates a number of related clinical applications, among which are breast density estimation and bio-mechanical modeling of breast tissue. Such applications, however, require one to know the disposition of various types of the tissue, thus warranting the procedure of image segmentation. In the case of breast MRI, the latter is known to be a challenging problem due to the relatively complicate nature of measurement noises, which is particularly problematic to deal with in the presence of bias fields. Accordingly, in this work, we introduce a simple method that can be used to "gaussianize" the noise statistic, which allows the problem of image segmentation to be formulated in the form of a simple optimization problem. In this formulation, segmentation of breast MRI scans can be completed in only a few iterations as demonstrated by our experiments involving both *in silico* and *in vivo* MRI data.

**Keywords:** Breast MRI · Image segmentation · Bias fields · Numerical optimization

## 1 Introduction

Breast cancer is the most common malignancy diagnosed in women worldwide. Although the introduction of screening mammography has resulted in a massive reduction in the mortality rates of breast cancer, the efficacy of mammography remains limited due to its relatively low sensitivity. For this reason, for women at increased risk breast cancer, it is often necessary to use alternative screening technologies, among which is Magnetic Resonance Imaging (MRI). Particularly, MRI is currently recommended for screening asymptomatic women at high risk for breast cancer related to inherited genetic mutations, family history of breast carcinoma and some other risk factors [1]. Moreover, in addition to screening, breast MRI is routinely used in other clinical scenarios, such as preoperative assessment in women with newly diagnosed breast carcinoma [2].

The relatively high sensitivity of MRI to pathological changes in the breast is favorably complemented by its ability to accurately depict the breast anatomy.

© Springer Nature Switzerland AG 2019
F. Karray et al. (Eds.): ICIAR 2019, LNCS 11662, pp. 376–387, 2019.
https://doi.org/10.1007/978-3-030-27202-9_34

For this reason, breast MRI scans have been successfully used to facilitate a number of related clinical applications, including breast density estimation, prone-to-supine breast MRI registration and mammography-MRI image fusion. Whilst different in terms of their aims and outcomes, these applications share a common need for classification of image values according to various types of breast tissue the latter are supposed to depict. This classification is usually formulated as a problem of *image segmentation* [3,4], which is in the focus of this work.

The problem of segmentation of breast MRI scans have been addressed in several studies using a range of different approaches, such as thresholding-based and gradient-based image segmentation, active contours, machine learning and others [5]. Thus, for example, an adaptation of the fuzzy c-means method with a specially designed kernel was proposed in [6], while a solution to the problem of segmentation of dermal and fibroglandular tissue by means of k-means clustering was described in [7]. An alternative use of the fuzzy c-means method, resulting in an adaptive and semi-automatic algorithm for segmentation of fibroglandular and adipose tissue, was introduced in [9]. In [8], a similar idea of semi-automatic segmentation was realized based on the method of region growing. Unfortunately, the manual selection of seed points as well as the relatively high computational complexity of this method somewhat weaken its otherwise excellent performance.

The recent advent and proliferation of the theory and tools of deep learning has substantially expanded the possibilities of image segmentation as well. Thus, for example, a particular architecture of deep neural networks (DNN), known as U-net, was used to segment fibroglandular and adipose tissues in [10]. It has been shown that the use of DNN allowed a substantial increase in the accuracy of image segmentation, notably outperforming many alternative approaches. It should be noted, however, that the performance of DNNs usually improves *pro rata* with the size of training sets (e.g., manually segmented MRI scans, in the case at hand). Thus, generalizing the method of [10] to a wide range of different densities and geometries of the breast could be potentially problematic.

When searching for relatively simple yet robust methods of segmentation of breast MRI scans, statistical methods based on use of *mixture models* deserve special noting. In particular, the assumption on image values to obey a Gaussian Mixture Model (GMM) was exploited in [11,12]. In this case, the GMM model is typically fitted by means of the Expectation Maximization (EM) algorithm [13], properly modified to account for spatial dependencies between same-class labels (using, e.g., the Markov Random Field model [12]).

For relatively high values of signal-to-noise ratio (SNR), the GMM is known to provide an adequate approximation of the probability distribution of breast MRI scans. At low SNR, however, the quality of this statistical model is known to plummet, causing notable segmentation artifacts. To resolve this problem, in the present work, we consider the use of *Rician* Mixture Modeling (RMM) [14], which is known to be a more natural and accurate statistical description in the case of MRI. To avoid dealing with the generally complex nature of RMM fitting, we introduce a simple "gaussianization" procedure which effectively reduces the Rician case to a Gaussian one. Moreover, the proposed method can explicitly account for the effect of bias fields [17], ultimately leading to a straightforward optimization problem. The latter is shown to admit a computationally efficient solution, which can be found in just a few iterations. What is more important is that the proposed algorithm has been observed to outperform GMM-based segmentation at low SNR (as expected). This result is confirmed using experiments with both phantom (*in silico*) and real-life (*in vivo*) data.

The remainder of the paper is organized as follows. The proposed method and its numerical implementation are summarized in Sect. 2, while Sect. 3 presents the results of our numerical experiments. Finally, Sect. 4 concludes the paper with a discussion of its principal findings.

## 2   Proposed Method

### 2.1   Image Preprocessing

To set the notations, let $\Omega \in \mathbb{R}^3$ be a volumetric image domain over with an MRI scan $F : \Omega \to \mathbb{R}$ is assumed to be defined. The scan $F$ is also assumed to be contaminated by a bias field $B : \Omega \to \mathbb{R}$, the effect of which is usually considered to be multiplicative. Consequently, in the absence of other artifacts and noises, the corresponding observed image $G$ could be modeled as

$$G(\mathbf{r}) = F(\mathbf{r})B(\mathbf{r}), \quad \mathbf{r} \in \Omega. \tag{1}$$

In practical settings, $G$ is always contaminated by Rician noise, which leads to a relatively complex analysis in the presence of $B$. To simplify the model, one can redefine (1) in the logarithmic domain as

$$g(\mathbf{r}) = \mathcal{R}_{\mathcal{L}}\left\{f(\mathbf{r}) + b(\mathbf{r})\right\}, \quad \mathbf{r} \in \Omega, \tag{2}$$

with $g$, $f$ and $b$ standing for $\log G$, $\log F$ and $\log B$, respectively, and with $\mathcal{R}_{\mathcal{L}}\{\cdot\}$ being a symbolic representation of the effect of the log-transformed Rician noise. The latter can be shown to behave similarly to a Gaussian noise, except for the presence of occasional "spikes", which can be attributed to the relatively large mass of the left-side tail of a log-Rician distribution. In its Subplot A, Fig. 1 depicts some examples of Rician probability densities $\mathcal{R}(x \,|\, \sigma, \nu)$ for $\sigma = 1$ and $\nu = 1, 2, 3$. Note how the shapes of the densities transform from asymmetric to Gaussian-like as $\nu$ increases. Subplot B of the same figure, on the other hand, shows the corresponding log-Rician probability densities $\mathcal{R}_{\mathcal{L}}(y \,|\, \sigma, \nu)$ (with $y = \log x$). Note that, for all $\nu$, the densities have a Gaussian-like appearance, with the exception of their heavy left tail.

Clearly, dealing with the log-Rician noise offers few advantages over the Rician case, unless the former is properly "gaussianized" so that $\mathcal{R}_{\mathcal{L}}\{f(\mathbf{r}) + b(\mathbf{r})\}$ can be approximately replaced with $f(\mathbf{r}) + b(\mathbf{r}) + u(\mathbf{r})$, where $u(\mathbf{r})$ obeys a Gaussian distribution. Note that such "gaussianization" should, in fact, be able to suppress the impulsive component of the log-Rician noise. Such a result can be achieved by means of the procedure of *outlier shrinkage* as given by

$$g(\mathbf{r}) \mapsto g(\mathbf{r}) - \mathcal{S}_\lambda\left\{g(\mathbf{r}) - \bar{g}(\mathbf{r})\right\}, \quad \forall \mathbf{r} \in \Omega, \tag{3}$$

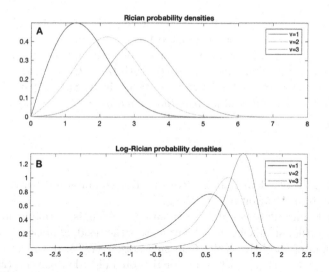

**Fig. 1.** (Subplot A) Rician probability densities $\mathcal{R}(x \mid \sigma, \nu)$ for $\sigma = 1$ and $\nu = 1, 2, 3$; (Subplot B) Corresponding log-Rician densities $\mathcal{R}_{\mathcal{L}}(y \mid \sigma, \nu)$, with $y = \log x$.

where $\bar{g}$ stands for a median-filtered version of $g^1$, while $\mathcal{S}_\lambda$ denotes the operator of soft thresholding given by

$$\mathcal{S}_\lambda(z) = \min(z + \lambda, 0) + \max(z - \lambda, 0),$$

where $\lambda > 0$ is a predefined threshold value.

The action of outlier shrinkage is straightforward. With the original image $f$ being a piece-wise smooth function and $b$ being a smooth field, the residuals $g - \bar{g}$ can be reasonably assumed to be dominated by noise. When subjected to soft thresholding, the noise retains its largest values which are likely to be associated with its impulsive ("spiky") component. Subsequently, the latter is subtracted from $g$, thus making the residual noise to behave in a nearly Gaussian manner.

Despite its conceptual and computational simplicity, the procedure of outlier shrinkage has demonstrated considerable efficacy for properly set values of $\lambda$. In this work, the latter has been set to be equal two times the median absolute deviation (MAD) of the residual $g - \bar{g}$ [15].

## 2.2   Two-Class Segmentation Model

The anatomy of breast is fairly complex. However, when it comes to the T1/T2 contrasts, which are typically used in breast MRI, there are two main tissue classes that are usually targeted by image segmentation algorithms. These classes correspond to fibroglandular and adipose tissue, which we will refer below to as

---

[1] In practical computations, a $3 \times 3$ median filter has proven to be an adequate choice.

the dense and fat tissues, respectively[2]. Accordingly, in what follows, the problem of image segmentation will be formulated for a two-class scenario. In this case, the objective of image segmentation becomes to partition the domain $\Omega$ into two mutually exclusive subdomains $\Omega_d$ and $\Omega_f$ (with $\Omega = \Omega_d \cup \Omega_f$ and $\Omega_d \cap \Omega_f = \emptyset$) associated with the dense and fat tissues, respectively. Such a partition can, in turn, be described in terms of an *partition function* $\xi : \Omega \to \{0, 1\}$ given by

$$\xi(\mathbf{r}) = \begin{cases} 1, & \mathbf{r} \in \Omega_d \\ 0, & \mathbf{r} \in \Omega_f. \end{cases}$$

Consequently, the problem of image segmentation can be equivalently formulated as a problem of estimation of function $\xi$.

One way to formulate the above estimation problem is by taking advantage of the effect of outlier shrinkage, which guarantees the residual noise contaminating $g$ is approximately additive white Gaussian noise (AWG). In this case, it seems reasonable to assume the class-conditional probability densities $p(g(\mathbf{r}) \,|\, \mathbf{r} \in \Omega_d)$ and $p(g(\mathbf{r}) \,|\, \mathbf{r} \in \Omega_f)$ to be Gaussian with their means equal to $\mu_d + b(\mathbf{r})$ and $\mu_f + b(\mathbf{r})$, respectively. Under this assumption, the problem of estimation of $\xi$ can be expressed as an optimization problem of the form

$$\min_{\xi,\mu_d,\mu_f,b} \left\{ \lambda_d \sum_{\mathbf{r}\in\Omega} \xi(\mathbf{r})|g(\mathbf{r}) - \mu_d - b(\mathbf{r})|^2 + \lambda_f \sum_{\mathbf{r}\in\Omega} (1 - \xi(\mathbf{r}))|g(\mathbf{r}) - \mu_f - b(\mathbf{r})|^2 \right\}$$

$$\text{s.t. } \xi(\mathbf{r}) \in \{0, 1\}, \; \forall \mathbf{r} \in \Omega, \tag{4}$$

for some regularization parameters $\lambda_d, \lambda_f > 0$. It is important to emphasize that, in (4), both $\mu_d$ and $\mu_f$ as well as the bias field $b$ are treated as optimization variables, similarly to $\xi$.

The problem defined by (4) is a non-convex integer optimization problem, a solution to which would have been quite difficult to find in general. To overcome this difficulty, one can try to "relax" the problem by letting the values of $\xi(\mathbf{r})$ be anywhere within the interval $[0, 1]$ (instead of being trapped at either 0 or 1), while restricting the optimal $\xi^*$ to the class of piece-wise smooth functions. This can be accomplished by minimizing the value of the *total variation* (TV) semi-norm of $\xi$ that is given by

$$\|\xi\|_{\mathrm{TV}} = \sum_{\mathbf{r}\in\Omega} |\nabla\xi(\mathbf{r})|,$$

where $\nabla\xi$ denotes the (discrete) gradient of $\xi$ and $|\nabla\xi(\mathbf{r})|$ stands for its magnitude at position $\mathbf{r}$. Consequently, the resulting minimization problem acquires the following form [18]

---

[2] In the absence of contrast enhancement, dermal and tumorous tissues have a visual appearance similar to that of dense tissue. For this reason, tumors are often included in the "dense" class.

$$\min_{\xi,\mu_d,\mu_f,b} \left\{ \lambda_d \sum_{r\in\Omega} \xi(\mathbf{r})|g(\mathbf{r}) - \mu_d - b(\mathbf{r})|^2 + \lambda_f \sum_{r\in\Omega}(1 - \xi(\mathbf{r}))|g(\mathbf{r}) - \mu_f - b(\mathbf{r})|^2 + \right.$$

$$\left. + \|\xi\|_{\mathrm{TV}} + I_{[0,1]}(\xi) \right\}, \tag{5}$$

where $I_{[0,1]}$ stands for the indicator function of the closed interval $[0,1]$ that is given by

$$I_{[0,1]}(z) = \begin{cases} 0, & 0 \le z \le 1, \\ \infty, & \text{otherwise} \end{cases}.$$

Additionally, one can also take advantage of the fact that, in practice, the bias field $b$ is a smooth slowly varying function, which can approximated by a polynomial of a relatively low order. Specifically, let $\{\varphi_k\}_{k=0}^{K}$ be a set of polynomials of orders $0, 1, \ldots, K$. Then, with $\Phi_{i,j,k}(\mathbf{r}) = \Phi_{i,j,k}(\mathbf{r}_1, \mathbf{r}_2, \mathbf{r}_3) = \varphi_i(\mathbf{r}_1)\varphi_j(\mathbf{r}_2)\varphi_k(\mathbf{r}_3)$, the bias field $b$ can then be approximated as

$$b(\mathbf{r}) = \sum_{i=0}^{K}\sum_{j=0}^{K}\sum_{k=0}^{K} c_{i,j,k}\Phi_{i,j,k}(\mathbf{r})$$

or, more concisely, as $b(\mathbf{r}) = \Phi(\mathbf{r})c$. Consequently, the problem of estimation of the bias field $b$ can be reduced to the equivalent problem of estimation of its polynomial coefficients $c \in \mathbb{R}^{(K+1)^3}$. In this case, the optimization problem (5) becomes

$$\min_{\xi,\mu_d,\mu_f,c} \left\{ \lambda_d \sum_{r\in\Omega} \xi(\mathbf{r})|g(\mathbf{r}) - \mu_d - \Phi(\mathbf{r})c|^2 + \lambda_f \sum_{r\in\Omega}(1 - \xi(\mathbf{r}))|g(\mathbf{r}) - \mu_f - \Phi(\mathbf{r})c|^2 + \right.$$

$$\left. + \|\xi\|_{\mathrm{TV}} + I_{[0,1]}(\xi) \right\}. \tag{6}$$

In this work, to define $\Phi(\mathbf{r})$, Bernstein polynomials have been used [19]. This choice is by no means exclusive, and alternative definitions of polynomial bases could have been used instead.

## 2.3    Numerical Solution

While much more tractable compared with its original version, the optimization problem (6) can still benefit further simplifications. To this end, one can first split the (optimization) variables to yield an equivalent problem of the form

$$\min_{\xi,\mu_d,\mu_f,c} \left\{ \lambda_d \sum_{r\in\Omega} \xi(\mathbf{r})|g(\mathbf{r}) - \mu_d - \Phi(\mathbf{r})c|^2 + \lambda_f \sum_{r\in\Omega}(1 - \xi(\mathbf{r}))|g(\mathbf{r}) - \mu_f - \Phi(\mathbf{r})c|^2 + \right.$$

$$\left. + \|\eta\|_{\mathrm{TV}} + I_{[0,1]}(\xi) \right\}, \quad \text{s.t. } \xi = \eta. \tag{7}$$

In this case, the augmented Lagrangian of the new problem can be defined as

$$\mathcal{L}(\xi, \eta, \mu_d, \mu_f, c, y) =$$
$$= \lambda_d \sum_{\mathbf{r} \in \Omega} \xi(\mathbf{r}) |g(\mathbf{r}) - \mu_d - \Phi(\mathbf{r})c|^2 + \lambda_f \sum_{\mathbf{r} \in \Omega} (1 - \xi(\mathbf{r})) |g(\mathbf{r}) - \mu_f - \Phi(\mathbf{r})c|^2 +$$
$$+ \|\eta\|_{\mathrm{TV}} + I_{[0,1]}(\xi) + \frac{\delta}{2} \sum_{\mathbf{r} \in \Omega} |\xi(\mathbf{r}) - \eta(\mathbf{r}) + y(\mathbf{r})|^2, \qquad (8)$$

where $y$ denotes a scaled version of the vector of Lagrange multipliers and $\delta > 0$ is a smoothing parameter (e.g., $\delta = 0.5$).

At this point, one can use the Alternating Directions Method of Multipliers (ADMM) [16] to minimize $\mathcal{L}(\xi, \eta, \mu_d, \mu_f, c, y)$ with respect to the primal variables (i.e., w.r.t. $\xi, \eta, \mu_d, \mu_f$, and $c$) *iteratively* using the following steps.

- Step 1:     $\xi^{t+1} = \arg \min_{\xi} \mathcal{L}(\xi, \eta^t, \mu_d^t, \mu_f^t, c^t, y^t)$
- Step 2:     $\eta^{t+1} = \arg \min_{\eta} \mathcal{L}(\xi^{t+1}, \eta, \mu_d^t, \mu_f^t, c^t, y^t)$
- Step 3:     $(\mu_d^{t+1}, \mu_f^{t+1}, c^{t+1}) = \arg \min_{\mu_d, \mu_f, c} \mathcal{L}(\xi^{t+1}, \eta^{t+1}, \mu_d, \mu_f, c, y^t)$

Once the primary variables have been updated, the dual variable $y$ is updated according to

$$y^{t+1}(\mathbf{r}) = y^t(\mathbf{r}) + \xi^{t+1}(\mathbf{r}) - \eta^{t+1}(\mathbf{r}), \quad \forall \mathbf{r} \in \Omega.$$

Although the number of update steps above could look prohibitively large at the first glance, they all admit either closed-form or efficiently solutions, which considerably reduces the cost of each ADMM iteration. Specifically, the updates can be performed as follows.

**Solution to Step 1.** The update in $\xi$ requires solving a simple quadratic minimization problem, followed by orthogonally projecting its solution onto the interval $[0, 1]$. Moreover, the update can be performed separately at each $\mathbf{r}$ according to

$$\xi(\mathbf{r})^{t+1} = \Pi_{[0,1]} \left\{ \eta^t(\mathbf{r}) - y^t(\mathbf{r}) + \frac{\lambda_f - \lambda_d}{\delta} \left( g(\mathbf{r}) - (\mu_f^t - \mu_d^t) - \Phi(\mathbf{r})c^t \right) \right\},$$

where $\Pi_{[0,1]}(z) = \max\{\min\{z, 1\}, 0\}$ denotes the operator of orthogonal projection onto $[0, 1]$.

**Solution to Step 2.** The update in $\eta$ requires solving a norm minimization problem of the form

$$\eta^{t+1} = \arg \min_{\eta} \left\{ \frac{1}{2} \sum_{\mathbf{r} \in \Omega} |\eta(\mathbf{r}) - (\xi^{t+1}(\mathbf{r}) + y^t(\mathbf{r}))|^2 + \frac{1}{\delta} \|\eta\|_{\mathrm{TV}} \right\}.$$

This problem has the format of well-known *TV de-noising* [20], which can be efficiently solved by a number of numerical methods. In this work, to solve this problem, the fixed-point algorithm of [21] has been used.

**Solution to Steps 3.** To derive an equation for the update of $\mu_d$, $\mu_f$ and $c$, it is convenient to think of $\Phi(\mathbf{r})$ as an $N \times M$ matrix, with $N$ equal to the number of voxels in $\Omega$ and $M = (K+1)^3$ being the total number of polynomial coefficients used for representation of $b$. In an analogous manner, both $g$ and $\xi^{t+1}$ can be also thought of as column vectors of length $N$, with a similar interpretation of $c$ as a length $M$ (column) vector.

Using the notational simplifications above, let $\theta \in \mathbb{R}^{M+2}$ be a new vector obtained via concatenation of $\mu_d$, $\mu_f$ and $c$, namely $\theta = [\mu_d, \mu_f, c^T]^T$. Also, let $A_d$ and $A_f$ be two $N \times (M+2)$ matrices obtained by augmenting $\Phi$ with a zero $\mathbf{0}$ and a unit $\mathbf{1}$ column as $A_d = [\mathbf{1}\,\mathbf{0}\,\Phi]$ and $A_f = [\mathbf{0}\,\mathbf{1}\,\Phi]$, respectively. Finally, let $W_d$ and $W_f$ be two diagonal matrices defined by vectors $\lambda_d\,\xi^{t+1}$ and $\lambda_d\,(1-\xi^{t+1})$, correspondingly, as well. Then, with

$$B = A_d^T W_d A_d + A_f^T W_f A_f \quad \text{and} \quad \beta = (A_d^T W_d + A_f^T W_f)g,$$

the optimal value of $\theta$ can be shown to be a solution to the linearly constrained quadratic program given by

$$\arg\min_\theta \ \theta^T B\theta - 2\beta^T\theta, \quad \text{s.t.} \ e^T\theta = 0, \tag{9}$$

with $e \in \mathbb{R}^{M+2}$ of the form $e = [1, 1, 0, 0, \ldots, 0]^T$. Note that the constraint $\nu^T\theta = 0$ is added to guarantee the attainment of a solution with $\mu_d \neq \mu_f$, thus enforcing the photometric discrepancy between the dense and fat tissues.

When applied to the constrained problem in (9), the Karush-Kuhn-Tucker optimality conditions result in a system of linear equations in the primal optimal $\theta^*$ and the dual optimal $\nu^*$ variables that is given by [22]

$$\begin{bmatrix} B & e \\ e^T & 0 \end{bmatrix} \begin{bmatrix} \theta^* \\ \nu^* \end{bmatrix} = \begin{bmatrix} \beta \\ 0 \end{bmatrix}. \tag{10}$$

The above system of equation is straightforward to solve to find $\theta^*$, from which the values of $\mu_d^{t+1}$, $\mu_f^{t+1}$, and $c^{t+1}$ can be extracted.

### 2.4 Algorithm Convergence

In a series of both computer simulations and experiments with real-life breast MRI data, the proposed algorithm has demonstrated stable and consistent convergence in less than 20 iterations, using $\lambda_d = \lambda_f = 0.1$ and $\delta = 0.5$. Once the optimal $\xi^*$ was computed, its corresponding domain partition/segmentation was defined as

$$\Omega_d = \{\mathbf{r} \in \Omega \mid \xi^*(\mathbf{r}) \geq 0.5\} \quad \text{and} \quad \Omega_f = \{\mathbf{r} \in \Omega \mid \xi^*(\mathbf{r}) < 0.5\}.$$

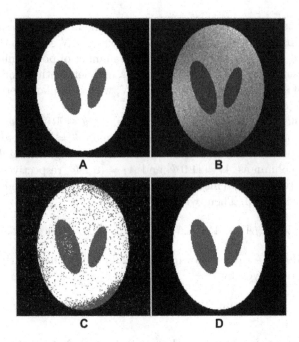

**Fig. 2.** (Subplot A) Cross-sectional slice of a 3-D phantom; (Subplot B) Same slice contaminated by a bias field and Rician noise; (Subplot C) Segmentation obtained using the GMM-based method of [18]; (Subplot D) Segmentation obtained using the proposed method.

## 3   Experimental Results

The performance of the proposed method for segmentation of breast MRI scans has been tested using both phantom and real-life data. In the former case, a 3-D version of the Shepp-Logan phantom has been used as a model of the breast, while in the latter case we used the breast MRI scans acquired with a 3T Signa™ Premier MRI scanner (GE Healthcare, Inc.) at the Princess Margaret Cancer Center (Toronto, Canada). As a reference method, the GMM-based algorithm of [18] has been used.

Some representative results produced by the reference and proposed methods are shown in Figs. 2 and 3 corresponding to the case of *in silico* and *in vivo* experiments, respectively. One can see that the Gaussian model is incapable of adequately capturing the nature of Rician noise, resulting in erroneous segmentation. The proposed method, on the other hand, has been able to produce valuable results at low SNR and in the presence of sizable bias.

Moreover, using the phantom data allowed us to compare the performance of the reference and proposed methods in a quantitative way. As a figure of merit,

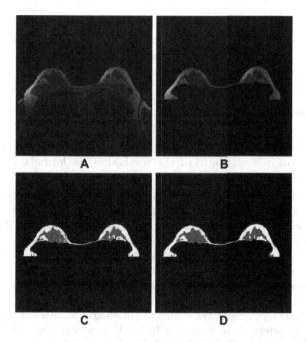

**Fig. 3.** (Subplot A) Axial slice of a 3-D breast MRI volume; (Subplot B) Same slice contaminated by a bias field and Rician noise; (Subplot C) Segmentation obtained using the GMM-based method of [18]; (Subplot D) Segmentation obtained using the proposed method.

we used the Dice Similarity Coefficient (DCS) which is defined as

$$\mathrm{DSC} = \frac{2|X \cap Y|}{|X| + |Y|},$$

where $X$ and $Y$ denote two non-empty sets of size $|X|$ and $|Y|$, respectively. Note that, with $X$ being the true $\Omega_d$ (or, alternatively, $\Omega_f$) and $Y$ being its estimate, the values of DCS are distributed between 0 and 1, with the latter corresponding to the case of perfect segmentation.

**Table 1.** Quantitative comparison of the reference and proposed methods.

| SNR(in dB) | DSC (reference method) | DSC (proposed method) |
|---|---|---|
| 6.6 | 0.86 | 0.97 |
| 7.0 | 0.65 | 0.94 |
| 7.4 | 0.65 | 0.91 |
| 7.8 | 0.69 | 0.95 |
| 12.0 | 0.86 | 0.97 |
| 12.3 | 0.79 | 0.97 |

The quantitative comparisons have been performed at different levels of SNR and bias field contamination. Table 1 demonstrates the obtained results for a representative set of SNR values. One can see that, in all these cases, the proposed method outperforms the reference segmentation by a substantial margin.

## 4    Conclusion

In this work, a new method of segmentation of breast MRI scans has been described. A principle attribute of the method is its formulation in the logarithmic domain in conjunctions with proper "gaussianization". It has been shown that such preprocessing allows on to substantially simplify the problem of image segmentation, leading to a computationally efficient numerical solution that remains accurate and stable for a wide range of values of SNR as well as in the presence of sizable bias fields.

## References

1. Monticciolo, D.L., Newell, M.S., Moy, L., Niell, B., Monsees, B., Sickles, E.A.: Breast cancer screening in women at higher than average risk: recommendations from the ACR. J. Am. Coll. Radiol. **15**(3), 408–414 (2018)
2. Plana, M.N., et al.: Magnetic resonance imaging in the preoperative assessment of patients with primary breast cancer: systematic review of diagnostic accuracy and meta-analysis. Eur. Radiol. **22**(1), 26–38 (2012)
3. Song, H., Cui, X., Sun, F.: Tissue 3D segmentation and visualization on MRI. Int. J. Biomed. Imaging (2013). Article ID 859746
4. Fooladivanda, A., Shokouhi, S.B., Mosavi, M.R., Ahmadinejad, N.: Atlas-based automatic breast MRI segmentation using pectoral muscle and chest region model. In: ICBME (2014)
5. Raba, D., Oliver, A., Martí, J., Peracaula, M., Espunya, J.: Breast segmentation with pectoral muscle suppression on digital mammograms. In: Marques, J.S., Pérez de la Blanca, N., Pina, P. (eds.) IbPRIA 2005. LNCS, vol. 3523, pp. 471–478. Springer, Heidelberg (2005). https://doi.org/10.1007/11492542_58
6. Kannan, S.R., Ramathilagam, S., Sathya, A.: Robust fuzzy C-means in classifying breast tissue regions. In: ARTCom 2009, pp. 543–545 (2009)
7. Niukkanen, A., et al.: Quantitative volumetric K-means cluster segmentation of fibroglandular tissue and skin in breast MRI. J. Digit. Imaging **31**(4), 425–434 (2018)
8. Pathmanathan, P.: Predicting tumour location by simulating the deformation of the breast using nonlinear elasticity and the finite element method. Doctoral dissertation, Wolfson College University of Oxford (2006)
9. Nie, K., et al.: Development of a quantitative method for analysis of breast density based on three dimensional breast MRI. Med. Phys. **35**(12), 5253–5262 (2008)
10. Dalmış, M.U., et al.: Using deep learning to segment breast and fibroglandular tissue in MRI volumes. Med. Phys. **44**(2), 533–546 (2017)
11. Han, L., et al.: A nonlinear biomechanical model based registration method for aligning prone and supine MRI breast images. IEEE Trans. Med. Imaging **33**(3), 682–694 (2014)

12. Gubern-Merida, A., Kallenberg, M., Mann, R.M., Marti, R., Karssemeijer, N.: Breast segmentation and density estimation in breast MRI: a fully automatic framework. IEEE J. Biomed. Health Inform. **19**(1), 349–357 (2015)
13. Dempster, A.P., Laird, N.M., Rubin, D.B.: Maximum likelihood from incomplete data via the EM algorithm. J. Roy. Stat. Soc. B (Methodol.) **39**(1), 1–38 (1977)
14. Gudbjartsson, H., Patz, S.: Rician distribution of noisy MRI data. Magn. Reson. Med. **34**(6), 910–914 (1995)
15. Leys, C., Ley, C., Klein, O., Bernard, P., Licata, L.: Detecting outliers: do not use standard deviation around the mean, use absolute deviation around the median. J. Exp. Soc. Psychol. **49**(4), 764–766 (2013)
16. Boyd, S., Parikh, N., Chu, E., Peleato, B., Eckstein, J.: Distributed optimization and statistical learning via the alternating direction method of multipliers. Found. Trends Mach. Learn. **3**(1), 1–122 (2011)
17. Juntu, J., Sijbers, J., Van Dyck, D., Gielen, J.: Bias field correction for MRI images. In: Kurzyński, M., Puchała, E., Woźniak, M., Żołnierek, A. (eds.) Computer Recognition Systems. AINSC, vol. 30, pp. 543–551. Springer, Heidelberg (2005). https://doi.org/10.1007/3-540-32390-2_64
18. Mory, B., Ardon, R., Thiran, J.P.: Variational segmentation using fuzzy region competition and local non-parametric probability density functions. In: ICCV, pp. 1–8 (2007)
19. Lorentz, G.G.: Bernstein Polynomials. American Mathematical Society, Providence (2013)
20. Rudin, L.I., Osher, S., Fatemi, E.: Nonlinear total variation based noise removal algorithms. Physica D **60**(1–4), 259–268 (1992)
21. Chen, D.Q., Zhang, H., Cheng, L.Z.: A fast fixed point algorithm for total variation deblurring and segmentation. J. Math. Imaging Vis. **43**(3), 167–179 (2012)
22. Boyd, S., Vandenberghe, L.: Convex Optimization. Cambridge University Press, Cambridge (2004)

# Spatially-Coherent Segmentation Using Hierarchical Gaussian Mixture Reduction Based on Cauchy-Schwarz Divergence

Adama Nouboukpo and Mohand Said Allili[✉]

University of Quebec in Outaouais,
283 Boul Alexandre-Tache, Gatineau, QC J8X 3X7, Canada
{noua06,mohandsaid.allili}@uqo.ca

**Abstract.** Gaussian mixture models (GMM) are widely used for image segmentation. The bigger the number in the mixture, the higher will be the data likelihood. Unfortunately, too many GMM components leads to model overfitting and poor segmentation. Thus, there has been a growing interest in GMM reduction algorithms that rely on component fusion while preserving the structure of data. In this work, we present an algorithm based on a closed-form Cauchy-Schwarz divergence for GMM reduction. Contrarily to previous GMM reduction techniques which a single GMM, our approach can lead to multiple small GMMs describing more accurately the structure of the data. Experiments on image foreground segmentation demonstrate the effectiveness of our proposed model compared to state-of-art methods.

**Keywords:** Gaussian mixture models · Mixture reduction · Image segmentation · Cauchy-Schwarz divergence

## 1 Introduction

GMMs are semi-parametric density functions, which are represented as a weighted sum of Gaussian densities called components. They can practically approximate any density shape using a finite number of components. They are very useful for data clustering in particular for image segmentation where they have demonstrated a good performance [4,5]. Although using too many components increases the approximation accuracy, it often results in complex models which overfit data. To obtain less complex models, two approaches are used. The first approach (horizontal) generates multiple GMMs with different numbers of components, and choose the best one according an information theoretic criterion (e.g., AIC, BIC) [2,11]. The second approach (vertical), which is the interest of our work, starts from a GMM with a high number of components and reduce it to a less complex GMM by iteratively fusing the different components into Gaussians [8,13].

A simple method to reduce a GMM is to eliminate components that do not contribute much to the mixture. Alternatively, instead of deleting components

F. Karray et al. (Eds.): ICIAR 2019, LNCS 11662, pp. 388–396, 2019.
https://doi.org/10.1007/978-3-030-27202-9_35

of the GMM or re-estimating it, one could merge components while preserving the structure of the data [13]. The idea is to merge similar components that "belong together" in a clustering sense. Therefore, there is a need to formalize "component similarity". Among the used measures, Kullback-Leibler divergence (KLD) is the most popular [17]. However, there is no closed-form expression for the KLD between two GMMs [16]. Because of this limitation, several existing methods use an approximation of the KLD using sampling methods [13,14,17]. However, such approaches can be computationally expensive, especially when the dimensionality of the data is very high. On the other hand, mixture reduction is achieved by fusing two components at a time in the GMM into a single Gaussian. This can end up in the long run to bold components having large variance. In other words, merging two or more Gaussians is not necessarily a Gaussian-distributed as in the case, for example, in foreground image segmentation where both foreground (resp. background) regions are not necessarily Gaussian [3,5].

In this paper, we introduce a new technique for GMM reduction into one or multiple small GMMs describing the different structures of the data. More specifically, an initial GMM is reduced iteratively by clustering its components into separate small GMMs describing the structure of the data in a hierarchical way. To facilitate components clustering, we use the Cauchy-Schwarz divergence (CSD) which has a closed-form expression and its computational complexity varies linearly with the dimension of data. We apply our reduction algorithm to foreground segmentation in still images, namely in salient object and skin lesion segmentation. Comparison with state-of-the art methods have shown the performance of our method.

The rest of this paper is organized as follows: Sect. 2 briefly describes the theoretical background of our algorithm. Section 3 presents details of our proposed method for mixture reduction problem. Section 4 describes experimental results such as qualitative and quantitative results. We end the paper with a conclusion and future work perspectives.

## 2    Background

Given a random vector $x \in R^D$, we consider two GMMs with $K$ and $M$ their respective numbers of mixture components. Let $f(x)$ and $g(x)$ denote respectively their probability density functions (PDF) as follows:

$$f(x) = \sum_{k=1}^{K} \pi_k \mathcal{N}(x|\mu_k, \Sigma_k), \qquad g(x) = \sum_{m=1}^{M} \omega_m \mathcal{N}(x|\nu_m, \Lambda_m) \qquad (1)$$

where $(\pi_k, \mu_k, \Sigma_k)$, $k = 1, ..., K$ are the weights, mean vectors and covariance matrices of the Gaussians composing mixture $f$, and $(\omega_m, \nu_m, \Lambda_m)$, $m = 1, ..., M$, are the same parameters composing mixture $g$. $\mathcal{N}(x|\mu_k, \Sigma_k)$ and $\mathcal{N}(x|\nu_m, \Lambda_m)$ are the multivariate Gaussian distributions.

The Cauchy-Schwarz divergence is based on the Cauchy-Schwarz inequality for inner products, and it is formulated between $f$ and $g$ as follows [16]:

$$CSD(f,g) = -\log\left(\frac{\int f(x)g(x)dx}{\sqrt{\int f(x)^2 dx \int g(x)^2 dx}}\right) \tag{2}$$

It is clear that the term inside the parentheses takes its values in the interval $[0,1]$ with equality to 1 if and only if $f(x) = g(x)$, such that $CSD$ is always nonnegative and symmetric. The closed-form expression for CSD of a pair of GMMs can be derived using the Gaussian multiplication and identities, which forms the basic building block of (2). We obtain a closed-form expression for the CSD, which does not depend on $x$:

$$\begin{aligned}
CSD(f,g) = &-\log\left(\sum_{k=1}^{K}\sum_{m=1}^{M}\pi_k\omega_m\mathcal{N}(\mu_k|\nu_m,(\boldsymbol{\Sigma}_k+\boldsymbol{\Lambda}_m))\right) \\
&+\frac{1}{2}\log\left(\sum_{k=1}^{K}\sum_{k'=1}^{K}\pi_k\pi_{k'}\mathcal{N}(\mu_k|\mu_{k'},(\boldsymbol{\Sigma}_k+\boldsymbol{\Sigma}_{k'}))\right) \\
&+\frac{1}{2}\log\left(\sum_{m=1}^{M}\sum_{m'=1}^{M}\omega_m\omega_{m'}\mathcal{N}(\nu_m|\nu_{m'},(\boldsymbol{\Lambda}_k+\boldsymbol{\Lambda}_{m'}))\right)
\end{aligned} \tag{3}$$

This expression has computational complexity order of $O(K^2)$ and not integral computation is required as in the case of the KLD. Therefore, the CSD is chosen in this work because it can be computed in closed-form which results in a faster algorithm.

## 3    Proposed Mixture Reduction Method

The proposed method, coined CSGMR (Cauchy-Schwarz divergence for Gaussian mixture reduction), is formulated as follows. Let us consider a GMM with $K$ multivariate Gaussian densities of the form:

$$f(x|\boldsymbol{\Theta}) = \sum_{k=1}^{K}\pi_k\mathcal{N}(x|\mu_k,\boldsymbol{\Sigma}_k), \tag{4}$$

where $\mu_k, \boldsymbol{\Sigma}_k$ represent the mean vector and covariance matrix of the $k$th component, $\boldsymbol{\Theta} = \{\pi_k,\mu_k,\boldsymbol{\Sigma}_k\}_{k=1}^{K}$ is the set of all mixture parameters, with $\pi_k$ are the component weights that satisfy the constraints: $0 \leq \pi_k \leq 1$    and $\sum_{k=1}^{K}\pi_k = 1$. Generally, the Expectation-Maximization (EM) algorithm [9] based on the maximum likelihood estimation (MLE) is used to calculate the GMM parameters.

Given the mixture $f$ in (4), we wish to find a reduced mixture model $g$ $M$ having components ($M << K$) by collapsing the components of $f$ in those of $g$.

Note that a similar challenge has been addressed in [5] using finite mixtures of generalized Gaussians. However, the method is hard to generalize to multiple dimensions of data.

Contrarily to traditional mixture reduction methods which output a single mixture [8,13,14], our method outputs several mixture models describing different clusters in the structure of data with arbitrary dimension. This characteristic of our method will reveal its importance for clustering problems such as image segmentation, where data structure comprises several non-Gaussian groups. In addition, the reduction is carried out without causing a strong deviation from the structure of the original GMM one according to CSD measure. Suppose that the density of reduced model is:

$$g(x|\Phi) = \sum_{m=1}^{M} \omega_m p_m(x|\Psi_m), \tag{5}$$

where $p_m(x|\Psi_m) = \sum_{j=1}^{K_m} \pi_{jm} \mathcal{N}(x|\mu_{jm}, \Sigma_{jm})$, with $\Psi_m = \{\pi_{jm}, \mu_{jm}, \Sigma_{im}\}_{j=1}^{K_m}$ and $\Phi = \{\omega_m, \Psi_m\}_{m=1}^{M}$. The reduction is made in such a way that $\sum_{m=1}^{M} K_m <<$ $K$. Note that when $K_m = 1$, $m = 1, ..., M$, we are in the classical mixture reduction scheme where each reduced component in $g$ is a Gaussian, as proposed in [8,13].

## 3.1   Proposed Algorithm

Our mixture reduction method is similar to classical agglomerative clustering, where initial groups are Gaussian components which are iteratively merged into clusters. Therefore, the input of our algorithm is an initial mixture model $f(x|\Theta)$ having a large number of components, and the output is a reduced (super) mixture model $g(x|\Psi)$ composed of several small GMMs. For this purpose, we maintain *similarity matrix* indicating CSD distances between formed GMMs (clusters) at each merging iteration.

Let $f_1, f_2, ..., f_{N_c}$, with $M \leq N_c \leq K$, be intermediate models resulting from fusions of initial GMM components. A similarity matrix $S$ of size $N_c \times N_c$ is computed, where $S_{rs} = CSD(f_r, f_s)$, $\forall r \neq s$ and $r, s = 1, ..., N_c$. At each iteration of the reduction algorithm, we select the most similar groups to fuse, thus causing the smallest overall change in the initial mixture structure. More specifically, let $f_r$ and $f_s$ be two candidate models to be merged, where $K_r$ and $K_s$ are their number of components, respectively. To estimate the optimal number of components of their fusion, we use the Akaike (AIC) criterion [4] that will search the minimum of the following function:

$$K_{rs} = \underset{l \in [max(K_r, K_s), ..., K_r + K_s]}{argmin} \left\{ -\log(\Psi_l) + 2\lambda_l \right\}, \tag{6}$$

where $\log(\Psi_l)$ is the log-likelihood corresponding to a GMM model with the number of components $l$, and $\Psi_l$ is the MLE estimate. Finally, $\lambda_l$ is the number of the free parameters in that model. The following script summarizes our reduction algorithm:

---

**Algorithm 1. Proposed Algorithm: CSGMR**

---

**Input:** $f$: mixture of $K$ components
**Output:** $g$: mixture of $M$ mixtures ($M << K$)
1. Initialize the GMM $f$ and number of clusters $N_c \leftarrow K$;
2. Initialize the similarity matrix $S$;
3. **while** $N_c > M$ **do**
   | * Find the nearest pair of groups $(f_r, f_s)$ according to $S$;
   | * Merge $f_r$ and $f_s$ into $f_{rs}$ and remove $f_r$ and $f_s$;
   | * Estimate the number of components of $f_{rs}$ using AIC;
   | * Update $S$; $N_c \leftarrow N_c - 1$ ;
   **end**
4. Build the final GMM $g$ by the produced $M$ GMMs.

---

## 3.2 Foreground Image Segmentation

We apply the proposed method for foreground segmentation in natural and medical images (see illustration in Fig. 1). First, we generated an initial GMM by over-segmenting the image into superpixels using the SLIC method [1]. The superpixel itself is not enough to provide a robust image descriptor for segmentation, since the consistency of its neighborhood is not considered [10]. To take advantage of the superpixel structure and our method for segmentation, let $K$ be the number of produced superpixels. We model each superpixel as a multivariate Gaussian with parameters given by the mean vector and covariance matrix of the RGB color of its composing pixels. We then use our mixture reduction algorithm to form the foreground and background regions ($M = 2$).

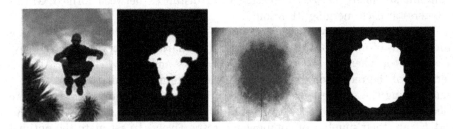

**Fig. 1.** Example of foreground segmentation.

To obtain compact regions for our segmentation, we enforce our reduction algorithm by imposing that two segments $S_i$, and $S_j$ can be merged together only if they are spatially adjacent. To this end, we construct and maintain a region adjacency graph $G$ in the clustering process, where the adjacency set of $S_i$ is denoted by $G_i$. Since our mixture reduction algorithm can output any number of clusters, we can tune the segmentation algorithm to produce any number of desired regions constituting the important structures of the image. For example, in binary segmentation where the objective is to segmentation the foreground from background, the output is $M = 2$.

## 4   Experiments and Results

We conducted several tests to assess the effectiveness and the usefulness of the proposed method. First, we compare the effectiveness of the proposed method against two of the best algorithms in the literature, namely COWA [6] and Runnalls [17]. We randomly generate a GMM with 10 components and 4 dimensions and search for an optimal reduced model comprising 5 components. We also conducted a binary classification of 20 Gaussians drawn from a sample of 3000 observations. As shown in Table 1, we can see that [17] has the lowest execution time followed by our method. However, our approach surpasses [17] and [6] in term of the reduction quality.

**Table 1.** Mixture simplification results.

|          | Execution time (sec) | Classification error |
|----------|----------------------|----------------------|
| COWA     | 0.0390               | 0.0710               |
| Runnalls | 0.0048               | 0.0033               |
| CSGMR    | 0.0054               | 0.0027               |

In order to illustrate the performance of the proposed method for image segmentation, we computed GMMs of different sizes ($K = 100, 125, 500$) for each

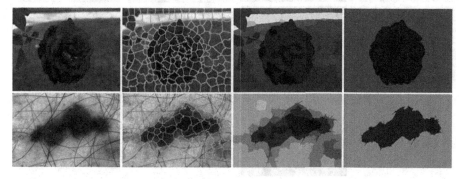

**Fig. 2.** Result of CSGMR on the ISIC and MSRA10K datasets: Original images (first column), initial superpixels (second column), reduction with ($M = 12$ top third column and $M = 6$ bottom third column), $M = 2$ (last column).

**Table 2.** Quantitative segmentation performance: (a) for ISIC and (b) for MSRA10K.

|     |           | [13]    | CSGMR   |
|-----|-----------|---------|---------|
| (a) | Accuracy  | 88.9326 | 97.0047 |
|     | Precision | 84.7651 | 97.0394 |
|     | Recall    | 83.1526 | 91.9662 |

|     |           | [13]    | CSGMR   |
|-----|-----------|---------|---------|
| (b) | Accuracy  | 92.9503 | 98.7359 |
|     | Precision | 94.0669 | 96.5222 |
|     | Recall    | 93.1526 | 95.9896 |

image and perform our mixture reduction algorithm. The experiments were performed using two different public datasets: ISIC dataset [15] and MSRA10K dataset [7]. All experiments were performed without any correction of the images. The visual results are shown in Fig. 2. In Fig. 2 (column two) with $K = 181$ and $K = 126$, the reduced mixture is, respectively, $M = 12$ and $K = 6$ (Fig. 2 column three). As presented in Fig. 2 (column 3), the foreground and the background are modeled by a mixture. In order to compare the results of the proposed method

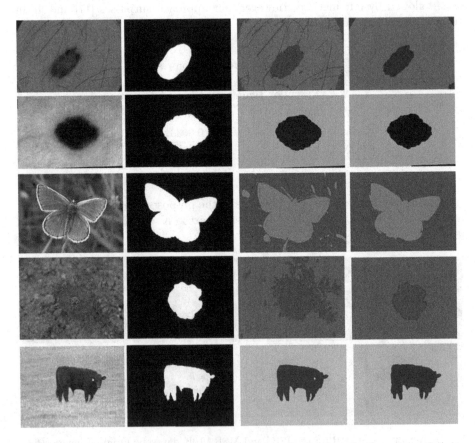

**Fig. 3.** Visual comparative results: Original images (first column), Ground-truth (second column), [12] result (third column) and CSGMR result (last column).

with [12], we focus our experiment in foreground and background detection i.e. $M = 2$ (see Fig. 3, column 3). The evaluation performance between our approach and [12] is conducted with 500 images in each dataset. The metrics used to quantify the segmentation result are recall, precision, accuracy. Note that higher values of these metrics indicate better results. The segmented image is the result of the reduced mixture. We can see that the images are segmented more correctly by using our proposed method. A quantitative comparative study between different methods is depicted in Table 2. It represents the average metrics for the 500 images selected from each dataset. According to these qualitative and quantitative results, obtained results with CSGMR are very encouraging and useful.

## 5   Conclusion

We have proposed an efficient GMM reduction algorithm based on CSD hierarchical clustering. Our method enables to quickly compute a compact version of an initial GMM to an another GMM constituted of non-Gaussian clusters. Experimental results on the simulated and image segmentation showed the effectiveness of the proposed technique with in comparison to other techniques. Note that our model can be extended easily into other exponential family distributions.

**Acknowledgment.** The authors would like to thank the Natural Sciences and Engineering Research Council of Canada (NSERC) for their support.

## References

1. Achanta, R., Shaji, A., et al.: SLIC superpixels compared to state-of-the-art superpixel methods. IEEE TPAMI **34**(11), 2274–2282 (2012)
2. Allili, M.S., Ziou, D., et al.: Image and video segmentation by combining unsupervised generalized Gaussian mixture modeling and feature selection. IEEE TCSVT **20**(10), 1373–1377 (2010)
3. Allili, M.S.: Effective object tracking by matching object and background models using active contours. In: IEEE ICIP, pp. 873–876 (2009)
4. Allili, M.S., Ziou, D.: Automatic colour-texture image segmentation using active contours. Int. J. Comput. Math. **84**(9), 1325–1338 (2007)
5. Boulmerka, A., Allili, M.S., et al.: A generalized multiclass histogram thresholding approach based on mixture modelling. PR **47**(3), 1330–1348 (2014)
6. Chen, H.D., Chang, K.C., Smith, C.: Constraint optimized weight adaptation for Gaussian mixture reduction. In: Signal Processing, Sensor Fusion, and Target Recognition, SPIE, vol. 7697 (2010)
7. Cheng, M.-M., Mitra, N.J., et al.: Global contrast based salient region detection. IEEE TPAMI **37**(3), 569–582 (2015)
8. Crouse, D.F., Willett, P., et al.: A look at Gaussian mixture reduction algorithms. In: IEEE International Conference on Information Fusion, pp. 1–8 (2011)
9. Dempster, A.P., Laird, N.M., et al.: Maximum likelihood from incomplete data via the EM algorithm. J. Roy. Stat. Soc. B **39**(1), 1–38 (1977)

10. Filali, I., Allili, M.S., et al.: Multi-scale salient object detection using graph ranking and global-local saliency refinement. Sig. Process. Image Commun. **47**, 380–401 (2016)
11. Figueiredo, M.T., Jain, A.K.: Unsupervised learning of finite mixture models. IEEE TPAMI **24**(3), 381–396 (2002)
12. Fu, Z., Wang, L.: Color image segmentation using Gaussian mixture model and EM algorithm. In: Wang, F.L., Lei, J., Lau, R.W.H., Zhang, J. (eds.) CMSP 2012. CCIS, vol. 346, pp. 61–66. Springer, Heidelberg (2012). https://doi.org/10.1007/978-3-642-35286-7_9
13. Goldberger, J., Roweis, S.T.: Hierarchical clustering of a mixture model. In: NIPS, pp. 505–512 (2005)
14. Hershey, J.R., Olsen, P.: Approximating the Kullback-Leibler divergence between Gaussian mixture models. In: IEEE ICASSP, pp. 317–320 (2007)
15. ISIC: The International Skin Imaging Collaboration. https://challenge2018.isic-archive.com/. Accessed 24 May 2019
16. Kampa, K., Hasanbelliu, E., Principe, J.: Closed-form Cauchy-Schwarz PDF divergence for mixture of Gaussians. In: IEEE IJCNN, pp. 2578–2585 (2011)
17. Runnalls, A.R.: Kullback-Leibler approach to Gaussian mixture reduction. IEEE TAES **43**(3), 989–999 (2007)

# Automatic Evaluation of Speech Therapy Exercises Based on Image Data

Zuzana Bílková[(✉)], Adam Novozámský, Adam Domínec, Šimon Greško,
Barbara Zitová, and Markéta Paroubková

The Czech Academy of Sciences, Institute of Information Theory and Automation,
Pod Vodárenskou věží 4, 182 08 Praha 8, Czech Republic
bilkova@utia.cas.cz

**Abstract.** The presented paper proposes a new method for unique automatic evaluation of speech therapy exercises, one part of the future software system for speech therapy support. The method is based on the detection of the lips and tongue movements, which will help to evaluate the quality of the exercise implementation. Four different types of exercises are introduced and the corresponding features, capturing the quality of the movements, are shown. The method was tested using manually annotated data and the proposed features were evaluated and analyzed. At the second part, the tongue detection is proposed based on the convolutional neural network approach and preliminary results were shown.

**Keywords:** Lip movement detection · Tongue segmentation ·
Speech therapy

## 1 Introduction

Automatic evaluation of speech therapy exercises is one of the focuses in our research to create a software system to support speech therapy for children and adults with inborn and acquired motor speech disorders. The system aims to improve articulation and a tongue motion based on individual treatment using exercises recommended by a therapist. The key component of the system is the evaluation of a tongue and lips motion based on image data from an ordinary web camera.

Existing applications only passively show exercises in the form of images, videos or text descriptions for the voice formulation but none of the available applications offers the possibility of an automatic assessment with commonly available cameras. The use of digital imaging techniques is new and enables the degree of interactivity where the treatment itself becomes more effective and a patient's return to normal life is accelerated. In addition, the methodology of language motion detection is also applicable in other areas, such as controlling various devices in quadriplegics, where existing solutions include special sensors that are stuck to the tongue.

Supported by TACR, grant No. TJ01000181, and the grant SVV–2017–260452.

F. Karray et al. (Eds.): ICIAR 2019, LNCS 11662, pp. 397–404, 2019.
https://doi.org/10.1007/978-3-030-27202-9_36

## 1.1   Related Work

To automatically evaluate the speech therapy exercises, tongue, its tip and lips motion must be detected. In the preliminary step a mouth must be located in the face image.

In the literature, there are several methods for face detection and detection of key facial features. Effective object detection proposed by Viola et al. [8] is a machine learning algorithm using Haar feature-based cascade classifiers. Widely used object detection method introduced in [2] by Dalal et al. is based on histogram of oriented gradients and support vector machines.

There are several methods for tongue segmentation. These methods are often used as the initial step for tongue diagnosis used in Chinese medicine. Zhang et al. [9] use tongue color, texture and geometry features to detect diabetes. HSI color space was used for tongue segmentation in [3,11]. Another common segmentation algorithm is the method of active contours, which is used in [6,10]. All of these methods are slow and they are not robust. They also suppose the tongue to be stucked out in only one position which is not sufficient to evaluate the complex tongue motion.

We have not found any paper concerning detection of the tip of the tongue which is a very complicated problem due to the self-similarity of the tongue tissue. Another part of the solution is the detection of lips, which can be often found in the voice activity detection systems, for example in [5], but there are no papers about the lips detection for speech therapy. A systematic review of studies on computer-based speech therapy systems or virtual speech therapists is presented in [1].

## 1.2   Speech Therapy Software

The proposed software system will offer an adjustable set of exercises recommended by an expert and its evaluation and it will also motivate the patients by incorporating an augmented reality, such as an augmented picture of a ladybug sitting on the nose tip when the tongue should be stucked out. The augmented reality is employed into the solution to increase understanding of the proper exercise movements. Moreover, the system will offer session archiving allowing the therapist to evaluate treatment progress and adjust its schedule.

The main part of the software evaluates the quality of the exercise implementation. Using the therapist expertise, we have distinguished three groups of exercises based on the information necessary for their evaluation. They work with tracking of the patient's lips, with the segmentation of the tongue and of the tongue tip detection, respectively. In the next Section we will focus on processing of images of mouth to obtain lips movement patterns and in the Sect. 3 the tongue segmentation and localization of its tip is discussed.

## 2   Evaluation of the Lips Exercises

The evaluation of exercises when the lips have to follow specified motion patterns is based on the lips detection and their tracking. In the preliminary step a patient's mouth is located in the face image. The proposed solution for detection of face parts uses Dlib library [4], based on an ensemble of regression trees that are trained to estimate the facial landmark positions directly from the pixel intensities. The Dlib library automatically detects 68 points in the face image in real-time allowing an easy detection of the mouth and the lips. The features are described in Table 1.

For the further processing, we focus on the lips and mouth location only, thus the image of a face is cropped according the position of selected points, as it is shown in Fig. 1. The cropped images are normalized with respect to their size and to the orientation between eyes. In order to evaluate the lips exercises we have proposed six features, derived from the positions of the detected lips points. They are illustrated in Fig. 1 by blue drawings and described in Table 1. They capture main movement patterns of the lips. In our tests, these features proved to be sufficient to evaluate the quality of the patient exercises, see Sect. 2.1.

For this paper, we selected four representative lip exercises to show how the features are used in the evaluation process. The exercises are *closed smile, open smile* and *crooked smile*, when only one mouth corner, left or right, is lifted.

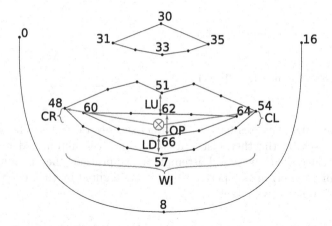

**Fig. 1.** Selection of key detected facial points and features for analysis of lips exercises. (Color figure online)

**Table 1.** Description of main features.

| Notation | Name | Description |
|---|---|---|
| CR | Corner - right | Vertical shift of the right corner with respect to the center |
| CL | Corner - left | Vertical shift of the left corner with respect to the center |
| LD | Lip - down | Height of the lower lip |
| LU | Lip - up | Height of the upper lip |
| OP | Open | Lips distance when mouth is open |
| WI | Wide | Horizontal distance of left and right corner |

Table 2 shows visualization of individual exercises with a formula for the corresponding feature calculation. If the exercise is executed correctly the values of the individual features are maximized. In the case of the closed smile both corners have to be lifted, therefore we control the minimum height of both corners, $\min(CL, CR)$, value -OP is maximized when the mouth is closed and finally the mouth widens when we smile, which captures the WI feature. The only difference in the open smile exercise is with the feature OP which controls the lips distance and here it should be maximized. In the case of the crooked smile, one of the corners is supposed to lift up and the other has to stay low and the mouth also widens, as it is shown in the last row of the table.

**Table 2.** Features used for evaluation of selected lips exercises.

| Name | Features Calculation | Visualization |
|---|---|---|
| Closed smile | $\min(CL, CR)$, -OP, WI | CR{ ⊗ OP }CL  WI |
| Open smile | $\min(CL, CR)$, OP, WI | CR{ ⊗ OP }CL  WI |
| Crooked smile - right | CR, -CL, WI | CR{ ⊗ }CL  WI |

The individual exercises have to be practised several times. The number of repetition is set by the therapist. Figure 2 shows the automated counting of smiles performed. The successful attempts are appraised (the green smile) and counted, while the erroneous performance is highlighted by the yellow icon and the count of smiles stays intact.

**Fig. 2.** Automated counting of smiles. (Color figure online)

## 2.1   Analysis of the Feature Performance

Testing of the method for the exercise evaluation based on the feature computation was realized using manually annotated data. The positions of lips points were detected manually and the proposed features were evaluated and plotted to see if they reflect the expected motion patterns. Figure 4 shows the values of the four features from Table 2 (in different colors) for the four chosen exercises. Each exercise is three times repeated. On the x axis values for acquired video frames are shown. We can see that the chosen features correctly capture the desired characteristics of the exercises, namely the high values for width and height of both corners and no significant change in the feature describing opening for the closed smile and similar expected behavior for the other exercises (Fig. 3).

**Fig. 3.** Feature bars representing the value of features of selected lips exercises.

Our tests demonstrate the validity of our solution for the evaluation of the speech therapy exercises.

## 3   Segmentation of the Tongue

The group of exercises based on the tongue and the tongue tip movements utilizes a segmentation of the tongue body and of its tip. For the speech therapy exercises we need to detect the tongue and its tip in real-time and in all their positions. Our solution is based on the convolutional neural network U-net [7] which proves to be sufficiently fast and robust. We use a single neural network to output both results - segmentation of the tongue and its tip - to achieve higher speed. The

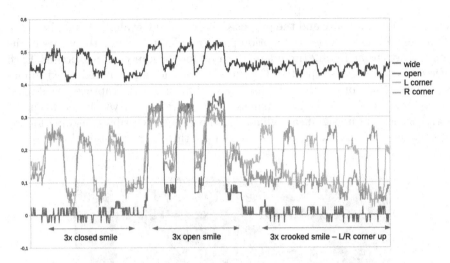

**Fig. 4.** Value of individual features in a video of performance of selected exercises.

output of the network has thus two frames - one is a mask for the tongue segmentation and the other is a mask for its tip. The network is trained on data we partially recorded and partially downloaded from the Internet with different quality to ensure robustness of our method with respect to the data quality.

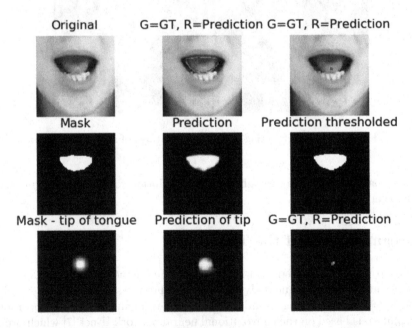

**Fig. 5.** Output of convolutional neural network Unet for segmentation of tongue and its tip. (Color figure online)

The data were manually annotated. We are still enlarging our database to provide bigger and more versatile training dataset.

The results of our current network based on U-net for segmentation of tongue and its tip is shown in Fig. 5. Green line and dot represent the ground truth - manually segmented tongue contour and the tip. The red lines are the prediction of the tongue contour. The red dots are the center of the mass of a mask predicted by the network, as shown in the middle column in the last row. We can see that the results correspond well to the ground truth even in the image where the whole tongue is in the mouth and the tip is hard to detect. However, to achieve required final robustness of the tongue detection method more testing and dataset collection creation is still needed.

## 4 Conclusion

The presented paper demonstrates the method for an automatic evaluation of speech therapy exercises. This is a part of the future software system for speech therapy support. The method is based on the detection of the lips and tongue movements and further evaluation of the quality of realized motion patterns, following the therapist recommendation. The efficiency of the method was demonstrated on the four different types of exercises, which were manually annotated and the proposed features evaluated and analyzed. Their discriminability has to be shown to be sufficient to be able to distinguish between correct and erroneous realization of an exercise. The tongue detection was proposed using the neural network approach and preliminary results were shown.

## References

1. Chen, Y.P.P., et al.: Systematic review of virtual speech therapists for speech disorders. Comput. Speech Lang. **37**, 98–128 (2016)
2. Dalal, N., Triggs, B.: Histograms of oriented gradients for human detection. In: International Conference on Computer Vision & Pattern Recognition (CVPR 2005), vol. 1, pp. 886–893. IEEE Computer Society (2005)
3. Du, J.q., Lu, Y.s., Zhu, M.f., Zhang, K., Ding, C.h.: A novel algorithm of color tongue image segmentation based on HSI. In: 2008 International Conference on BioMedical Engineering and Informatics, vol. 1, pp. 733–737. IEEE (2008)
4. Kazemi, V., Sullivan, J.: One millisecond face alignment with an ensemble of regression trees. In: Proceedings of the IEEE Conference on Computer Vision and Pattern Recognition, pp. 1867–1874 (2014)
5. Lopes, C.B., Gonçalves, A.L., Scharcanski, J., Jung, C.R.: Color-based lips extraction applied to voice activity detection. In: 2011 18th IEEE International Conference on Image Processing, pp. 1057–1060. IEEE (2011)
6. Pang, B., Zhang, D., Wang, K.: The bi-elliptical deformable contour and its application to automated tongue segmentation in Chinese medicine. IEEE Trans. Med. Imaging **24**(8), 946–956 (2005)
7. Ronneberger, O., Fischer, P., Brox, T.: U-Net: convolutional networks for biomedical image segmentation. In: Navab, N., Hornegger, J., Wells, W.M., Frangi, A.F. (eds.) MICCAI 2015. LNCS, vol. 9351, pp. 234–241. Springer, Cham (2015). https://doi.org/10.1007/978-3-319-24574-4_28

8. Viola, P., Jones, M., et al.: Rapid object detection using a boosted cascade of simple features. In: CVPR (1), vol. 1, pp. 511–518 (2001)

9. Zhang, B., Kumar, B.V., Zhang, D.: Detecting diabetes mellitus and nonproliferative diabetic retinopathy using tongue color, texture, and geometry features. IEEE Trans. Biomed. Eng. 61(2), 491–501 (2014)

10. Zhang, H., Zuo, W., Wang, K., Zhang, D.: A snake-based approach to automated segmentation of tongue image using polar edge detector. Int. J. Imaging Syst. Technol. 16(4), 103–112 (2006)

11. Zhongxu, Z., Aimin, W., Lansun, S.: The color tongue image segmentation based on mathematical morphology and his model. J. Beijing Polytech. Univ. 2 (1999)

# Signal Processing Techniques for Ultrasound Tissue Characterization and Imaging in Complex Biological Media

# Predicting Structural Properties of Cortical Bone by Combining Ultrasonic Attenuation and an Artificial Neural Network (ANN): 2-D FDTD Study

Kaustav Mohanty, Omid Yousefian, Yasamin Karbalaeisadegh, Micah Ulrich, and Marie Muller$^{(\boxtimes)}$

Department of Mechanical and Aerospace Engineering, NC State University, Raleigh, NC, USA
mmuller2@ncsu.edu

**Abstract.** The goal of this paper is to predict the micro-architectural parameters of cortical bone such as pore diameter $(\phi)$ and porosity (v) from ultrasound attenuation measurements using an artificial neural network (ANN). Slices from a 3-D CT scan of human femur are obtained. The micro-architectural parameters of porosity such as average pore size and porosity are calculated using image processing. When ultrasound waves propagate in porous structures, attenuation is observed due to scattering. Two-dimensional finite-difference time-domain simulations are carried out to obtain frequency dependent attenuation in those 2D structures. An artificial neural network (ANN) is then trained with the input feature vector as the frequency dependent attenuation and output as pore diameter $(\phi)$ and porosity (v). The ANN is composed of one input layer, 3 hidden layers and one output layer, all of which are fully connected. 340 attenuation data sets were acquired and trained over 2000 epochs with a batch size of 32. Data was split into train, validation and test. It was observed that the ANN predicted the micro-architectural parameters of the cortical bone with high accuracies and low losses with a minimum $R^2$ (goodness of fit) value of 0.95. ANN approaches could potentially help inform the solution of inverse-problems to retrieve bone porosity from ultrasound measurements. Ultimately, those inverse-problems could be used for the non-invasive diagnosis and monitoring of osteoporosis.

**Keywords:** Quantitative ultrasound · Multiple scattering · Cortical bone · Osteoporosis · Neural networks

## 1 Introduction

Aging has multiple complex effects one of which is progressive deterioration of the skeleton. Osteoporosis is defined as a bone mineral density (BMD) at least 2.5 standard deviations below the mean peak bone mass of a young healthy adult measured by dual – emission X-ray absorptiometry (DXA) [1, 2]. It affects the cortical as well as the trabecular bone. Although osteoporosis is defined by low bone mass, it is also associated with tissue degradation and altered micro-architecture, all contributing to deteriorated

© Springer Nature Switzerland AG 2019
F. Karray et al. (Eds.): ICIAR 2019, LNCS 11662, pp. 407–417, 2019.
https://doi.org/10.1007/978-3-030-27202-9_37

macroscopic mechanical properties [1, 3–5]. Because osteoporosis leads to higher mortality and reduction in life expectancy by 1.8 years [6–8], an early diagnosis of osteoporosis and the ability to monitor response to treatment is crucial. The current state of the art for the diagnosis of osteoporosis is Dual X-Ray Absorptiometry (DXA), which assesses BMD. Radiation exposure of DXA is low [9]. However, DXA only capture parts of the markers of osteoporosis and fails to describe changes in the microstructure of the porosity, now recognized as highly significant for the diagnosis of osteoporosis. BMD reports may trigger clinical decisions that results in therapeutic measures which are harmful for patients [10]. High resolution peripheral quantitative computed tomography (HR-pQCT) and magnetic resonance imaging (MRI) based techniques are also used for the characterization of bone. However the resolution of MRI is too low to capture the microstructure, and HR-pQCT is associated with high costs and radiation exposure making it unsuitable for large scale screening and monitoring response to treatment [11–13].

Ultrasound is an attractive alternative because it is low cost, widely accessible and non-ionizing. However, in highly heterogeneous biological tissues such as bone, traditional imaging methods fail. The impedance change between the bone matrix and the marrow is high (Reflection Coefficient = 0.44), and the inherent porous structure of bone introduces multiple scattering and aberrations. This makes ultrasound imaging of bone extremely challenging [14–16]. As an ultrasonic wave propagates through a complex porous structure such as bone, due to a large number of scattering events by the pores (in cortical bone) and the trabeculae (in trabecular bone), the micro-architectural properties of the porosity get stored in the backscattered ultrasound signals, which can be extracted using quantitative methods. A multitude of research studies has been done to assess the dependence of ultrasonic parameters on the micro-architectural properties of heterogeneous tissue such as cortical bone. Analysis of parameters such as frequency dependent attenuation, wave velocity (fast and slow), backscatter coefficient and diffusion constant has shown promise [17–25]. Various QUS methods have been developed to study how the speed of sound in bone relates to cortical thickness, macro mechanical properties such as Young's modulus, or micro-structural properties such as cortical density and porosity [26–34]. In cortical bone, which is the focus of the present study, Zheng et al. applied a spectral ratio method to estimate the normalized broadband ultrasound attenuation (nBUA) [35]. Yousefian et al. [36, 37] developed a phenomenological power law model to the ultrasonic attenuation data to characterize the cortical bone and potentially solve the inverse problem. The power law mode was associated with micro-architectural properties such as pore diameter ($\phi$) and pore density ($\rho$), both relevant to the diagnosis of osteoporosis. There is a strong need for proper modelling of ultrasound parameters such as frequency-dependent attenuation in cortical bone, and how they relate to the microstructure. When proper models are developed, the resolution of inverse problems can be sought in order to retrieve microstructural parameters from ultrasound data. However, due to the complexity of wave propagation in porous structures, developing these models is extremely challenging. Machine learning methods are currently being extensively used for clinical applications [38–41]. Clinical level classification accuracies of skin cancer and breast cancer are now achievable using Convolutional Neural Networks (CNN) [42]. Neural networks have the ability to identify patterns and relationships from complex data sets and predict outcomes [43, 44]. We propose to use machine learning methods as a guide to obtain information on the relevance of frequency-dependent attenuation to predict cortical micro-porosity. We envision that machine learning methods will inform modelling efforts by putting the spotlight on relationships between ultrasound parameters and microstructural parameters which are most relevant. We will then draw on this information to refine models of ultrasound propagation in cortical bone.

In this study, finite difference time domain (FDTD) simulations are conducted to calculate frequency dependent attenuation (1 MHz–8 MHz) in 2-D structures obtained from high resolution 3-D CT scans of the cortical bone (femur). An artificial neural network (ANN) is then trained over the acquired data set to predict micro-architectural parameters such as pore diameter ($\phi$) and porosity ($\nu$) from the simulated ultrasonic attenuation data.

## 2  Methodology

### 2.1  Images of Cortical Bone

2-D images were obtained from high resolution CT scans of a human femur, performed at the European Synchrotron Radiation Facility in Grenoble, France. Volumes with a 6.5 $\mu$m were obtained and 2-D planar cross sections were randomly taken. The 2-D cross sections were then normalized and binarized to obtain structures suitable for FDTD simulation as shown in Fig. 1. The white portion demarcates the pure bone domain whereas the black portion denotes the fluid filled pores. The porosity ($\nu$) was calculated by dividing the number of pixels associated with the fluid phase to the total number of pixels in the cross-section. To measure the average pore diameter, every single closed surface was labelled. The total number of labels provided the total number of pores. The surface area of these pores were then calculated and approximated to the area of a circle to obtain the equivalent pore diameter. FDTD simulations were carried out on 340 binarized samples with the pore diameter ($\phi$) and porosity ($\nu$) ranging from 27–115 $\mu$m and 0.01–0.2 respectively. Shown in Fig. 1 is a binarized 2-D map of the cortical bone for FDTD simulations.

### 2.2  FDTD Simulation

All simulations of ultrasonic wave propagation through these 2-D structures were carried out using SimSonic, an open source simulation software [29, 45]. The main propagating medium (white portion in Fig. 1) is assigned the properties of pure bone whereas the fluid filled pores are assigned properties of water. Both scattering and absorption contribute to the ultrasonic attenuation. However, in this paper we will only consider the ultrasonic attenuation because it reflects scattering, which is related to the microstructure. We choose this approximated approach as a first step, and because we propose to focus on the relationship between ultrasonic attenuation and micro-structural properties only, which we expect to be mostly influenced by scattering. Therefore, the absorption coefficient for the materials was set to 0 dB/cm/MHz. The assigned material

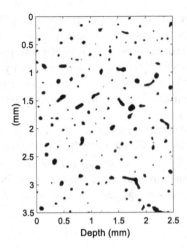

**Fig. 1.** Bone schematic geometry with φ = 50 and ν = 0.047

properties are summarized in Table 1. Simulations are carried out in 1 MHz frequency intervals in the frequency range of 1–8 MHz. The input signal (input pulse wave) is a Gaussian ultrasonic pulse with a −6 dB 20% bandwidth. Shown in Fig. 2 is the input signal in the time domain and frequency domain for a 3 MHz pulse.

**Table 1.** Material properties for FDTD simulations

| Solid Properties | Value | Fluid Properties | Value |
|---|---|---|---|
| Wave Speed $C_b$ (mm/μs) | 4 | Wave Speed $C_w$ (mm/μs) | 1.54 |
| Density $\rho_b$(g/ml) | 1.85 | Density $\rho_w$(g/ml) | 1.00 |
| $C_{11}$(GPa) | 29.6 | $C_{11}$(GPa) | 2.37 |
| $C_{22}$(GPa) | 29.6 | $C_{22}$(GPa) | 2.37 |
| $C_{12}$(GPa) | 17.6 | $C_{12}$(GPa) | 2.37 |
| $C_{66}$(GPa) | 6 | $C_{66}$(GPa) | 0.00 |

All simulations are carried out in 2-D with a grid step size of $\Delta x = \Delta y = 10$ μm (50 points per wavelength (PPW) for 8 MHz). The CFL number was set to 0.99 and the sampling time step $\Delta t$ was chosen as

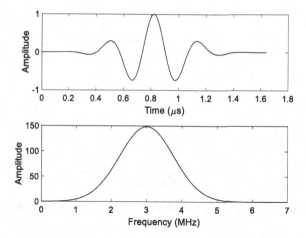

**Fig. 2.** MHz signal in time and frequency domain

$$\Delta t = 0.99 \frac{\Delta x}{\sqrt{d} c_{max}} \tag{1}$$

Where $c_{max}$ is 4 mm/μs and $d = 2$, since it is a 2-D simulation.

## 2.3 Attenuation Measurement: Time-Distance Matrix Approach (TDMA)

Plane ultrasonic waves are transmitted through the 2-D cortical bone structures using FDTD simulations. The transmitter size covers the entire simulation domain and is placed at 0 mm perpendicular to the depth axis (Fig. 1) to ensure plane wave propagation along the depth axis. Receivers are placed at 30 consecutive longitudinal positions along the sample in the direction of wave propagation. The receivers cover the entire length of the slab, hence recording the coherent, averaged wave. These receivers are set to record only the longitudinal waves propagating through the bone structure. Time domain signals are recorded in a time-distance matrix, s(t, x). The matrix is converted into the frequency domain, S(f, x). The frequency dependent attenuation is calculated as shown in Eq. 1 [19].

$$|S(f,x)| = e^{-\alpha(f)x} \tag{2}$$

The details of the methodology for determining the frequency dependent attenuation ($\alpha(f)$) can be found in the work done by Yousefian et al. [36].

Figure 3 shows an example of frequency dependent attenuation for two slabs of cortical bone with different porosities. It can be observed attenuation increases with frequency, and that an increase in porosity and in scatterer size, the attenuation due to scattering is enhanced.

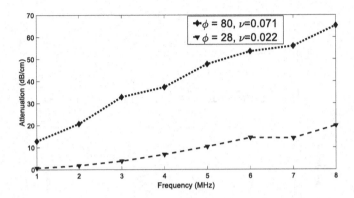

**Fig. 3.** Frequency dependent attenuation in two slabs of cortical bone

### 2.4  Neural Network Model

The ANN model built for this purpose consists of five fully connected layers, summarized in the schematic shown in Fig. 4. Figure 4 is a pictorial representation and does not indicate the actual number of neurons in each layer. The ANN is trained in a supervised manner. While training, the input is mapped to the desired output. The frequency dependent attenuation $\alpha(f)$ is treated as the input vector $\bar{X}$ whereas the pore diameter ($\phi$) and porosity ($\nu$) are treated as the output. The input vector $\bar{X}$ consists of 8 neurons, each neuron entailing the attenuation at a particular frequency (ranging from 1 MHz–8 MHz). The ReLu (rectified linear unit) activation function is used for the ANN regressor. The numbers of neurons is the hidden layers have been set as 24, 12 and 6. The model was compiled using a mean squared error (MSE) as the loss function and an adam optimizer. All the ANN modelling was done in the Python (3.6) API of TensorFlow (r1.10).

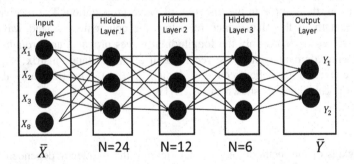

**Fig. 4.** Schematic of the ANN structure. The arrows depict connection between neurons

Once all the total FDTD data is acquired, it is split into training and test data (test size = 68 structures). Within the training set, another split is made for cross-validation (validation size = 55 structures). The ANN model is trained with the Adam optimizer.

For fine-tuning of hyper parameters, validation loss was monitored. The batch size while training were set to 32 samples and the ANN was trained over 2000 epochs. The total number of trainable parameters in the entire ANN was 608.

## 3  Results and Discussion

The validation losses and training losses of the ANN are shown in Fig. 5. The validation loss of the ANN model after 2000 epochs was found to be 0.02.

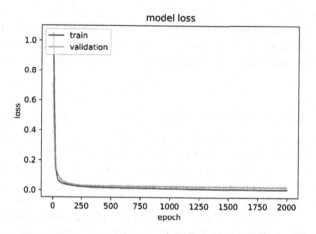

**Fig. 5.** Model losses

Once the training was completed, the training weights were used to predict the output on the test data. Shown in Fig. 6 is the comparison between the ANN predicted data and the actual data.

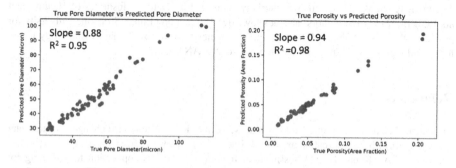

**Fig. 6.** Comparison between predicted data and true values

The x-axis depicts the true values whereas the y-axis depicts the values predicted by the ANN post training. An excellent agreement is found between the predicted values of porosity and average pore diameter and the true values. Normalized root mean square deviation (NRMSD) for the test data was found to be 0.073 and 0.094 for pore diameter ($\phi$) and porosity ($v$) respectively. The goodness of fit R2 were found to be 0.95 and 0.98 and the slopes of these linear fits were 0.94 and 0.88 for pore diameter ($\phi$) and porosity ($v$) respectively. These results show that it is possible to predict the micro-architectural parameters with high accuracy and low losses using an ANN. ANN has an extremely strong potential to predict quantitative information about the cortical bone from ultrasonic attenuation data. More importantly, these results demonstrate that the frequency-dependent attenuation is indeed an extremely relevant parameter for the assessment of cortical bone. With this knowledge, modelling efforts can be focused on this parameter, which could lead to the successful solution of inverse problems, for the non-invasive ultrasonic assessment of osteoporosis. Cortical bone is relevant to the diagnosis of osteoporosis. It is also a promising and convenient skeletal site for ultrasound-based modalities, due to the thin layer of soft tissue at the tibia.

# 4 Conclusion

2-D FDTD simulations were carried out on cortical bone structures obtained with high resolution Computed Tomography. Quantitative ultrasound methods were then applied to obtain the frequency dependent attenuation in the 1–8 MHz range. Using image processing, porosity ($v$) and pore diameter ($\phi$) were extracted. An ANN was used to map the input to the desired micro-structural properties of the cortical bone. The training was performed by minimizing the mean squared error. The trained model, taking the ultrasonic attenuation data as the input feature vector, then predicted these micro-architectural properties. There was excellent agreement between the true values and the predicted values. The ANN consistently predicted porosity ($v$) and pore diameter ($\phi$) with R2 values greater than 0.9. This proposed methodology of using an ANN to solve the inverse-problem for the cortical bone is evaluated on FDTD data and shows potential of extending it to experimental data also.

**Acknowledgement.** This work was partially supported by National Institutes of Health grant no. R03EB022743. The authors' also acknowledge Dr Quentin Grimal, Sorbonne University for providing the high resolution CT scans and Dr Maciej A. Mazurowski, Duke Radiology Dept., for consulting with us during the development of the ANN model.

# References

1. Chen, H., Zhou, X., Fujita, H., Onozuka, M., Kubo, K.Y.: Age-related changes in trabecular and cortical bone microstructure. Int. J. Endocrinol. **2013**, 9 (2013)
2. Kanis, J.A., Kanis, J.A.: Assessment of fracture risk and its application to screening for postmenopausal osteoporosis: synopsis of a WHO report. Osteoporos. Int. **4**, 368 (1994)
3. Yerramshetty, J., Akkus, O.: Changes in cortical bone mineral and microstructure with aging and osteoporosis. In: Silva, M. (eds.) Skeletal Aging and Osteoporosis. SMTEB, vol. 5, pp. 105–131. Springer, Heidelberg (2012). https://doi.org/10.1007/8415_2012_114

4. McCalden, R.W., McGlough, J.A., Barker, M.B., Court-Brown, C.M.: Age-related changes in the tensile properties of cortical bone. The relative importance of changes in porosity, mineralization and microstructure. J. Bone Jt. Surg. Ser. A 75(8), 1193–1205 (1993)
5. Schaffler, M.B., Burr, D.B.: Stiffness of compact bone: effects of porosity and density. J. Biomech. 21(1), 13–16 (1988)
6. Sornay-Rendu, E., Munoz, F., Duboeuf, F., Delmas, P.D.: Rate of forearm bone loss is associated with an increased risk of fracture independently of bone mass in postmenopausal women: the OFELY study. J. Bone Miner. Res. 20, 1929 (2005)
7. Braithwaite, R.S., Col, N.F., Wong, J.B.: Estimating hip fracture morbidity, mortality and costs. J. Am. Geriatr. Soc. 51, 364–370 (2003)
8. Schuit, S.C.E., et al.: Fracture incidence and association with bone mineral density in elderly men and women: the Rotterdam Study. Bone 34, 195 (2004)
9. Mazess, R., Chesnut, C.H., McClung, M., Genant, H.: Enhanced precision with dual-energy x-ray absorptiometry. Calcif. Tissue Int. 51, 14 (1992)
10. Lewiecki, E.M., Lane, N.E.: Common mistakes in the clinical use of bone mineral density testing. Nat. Clin. Pract. Rheumatol. 4, 667 (2008)
11. Boutroy, S., Bouxsein, M.L., Munoz, F., Delmas, P.D.: In vivo assessment of trabecular bone microarchitecture by high-resolution peripheral quantitative computed tomography. J. Clin. Endocrinol. Metabol. 90(12), 6508–6515 (2005)
12. Wehrli, F.W., Song, H.K., Saha, P.K., Wright, A.C.: Quantitative MRI for the assessment of bone structure and function. NMR Biomed. Int. J. Devoted Dev. Appl. Magn. Reson. Vivo 19, 731–764 (2006)
13. Link, T.M.: Osteoporosis imaging: state of the art and advanced. Radiology 263(1), 3–17 (2012)
14. Haïat, G., Lhémery, A., Renaud, F., Padilla, F., Laugier, P., Naili, S.: Velocity dispersion in trabecular bone: influence of multiple scattering and of absorption. J. Acoust. Soc. Am. 124, 4047 (2017)
15. Conoir, J.: Multiple scattering in a trabecular bone: influence of the marrow viscosity on the effective properties. J. Acoust. Soc. Am. 113, 2889–2892 (2003)
16. Litniewski, J., Wojcik, J., Nowicki, A.: Contribution of multiple scattering to the trabecular bone backscatter - dependence on porosity and frequency. In: 2012 IEEE International Ultrasonics Symposium, pp. 1–4 (2012)
17. Bennamane, A., Boutkedjirt, T.: Theoretical and experimental study of the ultrasonic attenuation in bovine cancellous bone. Appl. Acoust. 115, 50–60 (2017)
18. Karjalainen, J.P., Töyräs, J., Riekkinen, O., Hakulinen, M., Jurvelin, J.S.: Ultrasound backscatter imaging provides frequency-dependent information on structure, composition and mechanical properties of human trabecular bone. Ultrasound Med. Biol. 35, 1376 (2009)
19. Mézière, F., Muller, M., Bossy, E., Derode, A.: Measurements of ultrasound velocity and attenuation in numerical anisotropic porous media compared to Biot's and multiple scattering models. Ultrasonics 54(5), 1146–1154 (2014)
20. Anderson, C.C., Bauer, A.Q., Holland, M.R., Pakula, M., Laugier, P., Bretthorst, G.L.: Inverse problems in cancellous bone: estimation of the ultrasonic properties of fast and slow waves using Bayesian probability theory. J. Acoust. soc. Am. 128, 2940 (2010)
21. Padilla, F., Laugier, P.: Recent developments in trabecular bone characterization using ultrasound. Curr. Osteoporos. Rep. 3, 64 (2005)
22. Wear, K.A., et al.: Relationships of quantitative ultrasound parameters with cancellous bone microstructure in human calcaneus in vitro. J. Acoust. Sos. Am. 131, 1605 (2017)
23. Mohanty, K., Blackwell, J., Egan, T., Muller, M.: Characterization of the lung parenchyma using ultrasound multiple scattering. Ultrasound Med. Biol. 43(5), 993–1003 (2017)

24. Demi, L., Van Hoeve, W., Van Sloun, R.J.G., Soldati, G., Demi, M.: Determination of a potential quantitative measure of the state of the lung using lung ultrasound spectroscopy. Sci. Rep. **7**(1), 5–11 (2017)
25. Zhang, X., et al.: Lung ultrasound surface wave elastography, no. 1, pp. 4–6 (2016)
26. Moilanen, P., et al.: Ultrasonically determined thickness of long cortical bones: two-dimensional simulations of in vitro experiments. J. Acoust. Soc. Am. **122**, 1818 (2007)
27. Nicholson, P.H.F., Moilanen, P., Laugier, P., Timonen, J., Cheng, S., Talmant, M.: Ultrasonically determined thickness of long cortical bones: three-dimensional simulations of in vitro experiments. J. Acoust. Soc. Am. **122**, 2439 (2007)
28. Foiret, J., Minonzio, J.G., Chappard, C., Talmant, M., Laugier, P.: Combined estimation of thickness and velocities using ultrasound guided waves: a pioneering study on in vitro cortical bone samples. IEEE Trans. Ultrason. Ferroelectr. Freq. Control **61**(9), 1478–1488 (2014)
29. Bossy, E., Talmant, M., Laugier, P.: Three-dimensional simulations of ultrasonic axial transmission velocity measurement on cortical bone models. J. Acoust. Soc. Am. **115**(5 Pt 1), 2314–2324 (2004)
30. Mandarano-Filho, L.G., Bezuti, M.T., Mazzer, N., Barbieri, C.H.: Influence of cortical bone thickness on the ultrasound velocity. Acta Ortop. Bras. **20**(3), 184–190 (2012)
31. Rose, E.C., Hagenmüller, M., Jonas, I.E., Rahn, B.A.: Validation of speed of sound for the assessment of cortical bone maturity. Eur. J. Orthod. **27**, 190–195 (2005)
32. Bosisio, M.R., Talmant, M., Skalli, W., Laugier, P., Mitton, D.: Apparent Young's modulus of human radius using inverse finite-element method. J. Biomech. **40**(9), 2022–2028 (2007)
33. Sievänen, H., Cheng, S., Ollikainen, S., Uusi-Rasi, K.: Ultrasound velocity and cortical bone characteristics in vivo. Osteoporos. Int. **12**, 399 (2001)
34. Eneh, C.T.M., Jurvelin, J.S., Töyräs, J., Malo, M.K.H., Afara, I.O.: Porosity predicted from ultrasound backscatter using multivariate analysis can improve accuracy of cortical bone thickness assessment. J. Acoust. Soc. Am. **141**, 575 (2017)
35. Zheng, R., Le, L.H., Sacchi, M.D., Ta, D., Lou, E.: Spectral ratio method to estimate broadband ultrasound attenuation of cortical bones in vitro using multiple reflections. Phys. Med. Biol. **52**, 5855 (2007)
36. Yousefian, O., Karbalaeisadegh, Y., Banks, H.T., White, R.D., Muller, M.: The effect of pore size and density on ultrasonic attenuation in porous structures with mono-disperse random pore distribution: a two-dimensional in-silico study. J. Acoust. Soc. Am. **144**(2), 709–719 (2018)
37. Yousefian, O., White, R., Banks, H.T., Muller, M.: Ultrasonic attenuation spectroscopy and dispersion characteristics in cortical bone. In: IEEE International Ultrasonics Symposium, IUS (2017)
38. Geras, K.J., et al.: High-resolution breast cancer screening with multi-view deep convolutional neural networks, pp. 1–9 (2017)
39. Ribli, D., Horváth, A., Unger, Z., Pollner, P., Csabai, I.: Detecting and classifying lesions in mammograms with deep learning, pp. 1–7 (2018)
40. Kourou, K., Exarchos, T.P., Exarchos, K.P., Karamouzis, M.V., Fotiadis, D.I.: Machine learning applications in cancer prognosis and prediction. CSBJ **13**, 8–17 (2015)
41. Chen, J.H., Asch, S.M.: Machine learning and prediction in medicine — beyond the peak of inflated expectations. N. Engl. J. Med. **376**, 2507 (2017)
42. Esteva, A., et al.: Dermatologist-level classification of skin cancer with deep neural networks. Nature **542**, 115 (2017)
43. Zhou, B., Zhang, X.: Lung mass density analysis using deep neural network and lung ultrasound surface wave elastography. Ultrasonics **89**, 173–177 (2018)

44. Steele, A.J., Denaxas, S.C., Shah, A.D., Hemingway, H.: Machine learning models in electronic health records can outperform conventional survival models for predicting patient mortality in coronary artery disease. Plos One **13**, 1–20 (2018)
45. Bossy, E., Grimal, Q.: Numerical methods for ultrasonic bone characterization. In: Laugier, P., Haïat, G. (eds.) Bone Quantitative Ultrasound, pp. 181–228. Springer, Dordrecht (2011). https://doi.org/10.1007/978-94-007-0017-8_8

# B-line Detection and Localization by Means of Deep Learning: Preliminary In-vitro Results

Ruud J. G. van Sloun[1(✉)] and Libertario Demi[2(✉)]

[1] Faculty of Electrical Engineering, Eindhoven University of Technology,
Eindhoven, The Netherlands
r.j.g.vanslound@tue.nl
[2] Department of Information Engineering and Computer Science,
University of Trento, Trento, Italy
libertario.demi@unitn.it

**Abstract.** Lung ultrasound imaging is nowadays receiving growing attention. In fact, the analysis of specific artefactual patterns reveals important diagnostic information. A- and B-line artifacts are particularly important. A-lines are generally considered a sign of a healthy lung, while B-line artifacts correlate with a large variety of pathological conditions. B-lines have been found to indicate an increase in extravascular lung water, the presence of interstitial lung diseases, non-cardiogenic lung edema, interstitial pneumonia and lung contusion.

The capability to accurately and objectively detect and localize B-lines in a lung ultrasound video is therefore of great clinical interest. In this paper, we present a method aimed at supporting clinicians in the analysis of ultrasound videos by automatically detecting and localizing B-lines, in real-time. To this end, modern deep learning strategies have been used and a fully convolutional neural network has been trained to detect B-lines in B-mode images of dedicated ultrasound phantoms. Furthermore, neural attention maps have been calculated to visualize which components in the image triggered the network, thereby offering simultaneous weakly-supervised localization. An accuracy, sensitivity, specificity, negative and positive predictive value equal to 0.917, 0.915, 0.918, 0.950 and 0.864 were achieved in-vitro using data from dedicated lung-mimicking phantoms, respectively.

**Keywords:** Lung ultrasound · B-lines · Image analysis · Deep learning

## 1 Introduction

Due to the combined presence of air and soft tissue in the field of view, and due to the lack of signal processing techniques designed around the peculiarities of lung tissue, the application of ultrasound imaging to the diagnosis and monitoring of lung diseases nowadays still relies mainly on the analysis of imaging artifacts. Nevertheless, lung ultrasound imaging is receiving growing attention from both the clinical and technical world due to the great potential it carries in terms of the absence of ionizing radiation, the mobility of the equipment, and the real-time nature of this imaging modality. Of particular interest are several imaging-artifacts, e.g., A- and B-line artifacts [1–4].

© Springer Nature Switzerland AG 2019
F. Karray et al. (Eds.): ICIAR 2019, LNCS 11662, pp. 418–424, 2019.
https://doi.org/10.1007/978-3-030-27202-9_38

Alines can be described as hyper-echoic horizontal lines, which are normally displayed across the entire image and are parallel to the pleural-line. They represent the normal pattern of the lung, if pneumothorax is excluded. The presence of A-lines in the image is explained by the observation that a healthy lung, which can be seen as a cloud composed of closely packed 200–300 μ large air-bubbles (i.e. the alveoli), behaves practically as a perfect reflector to ultrasound waves [3, 4]. Consequently, when an ultrasound pulse transmitted by the probe reaches the pleura it is reflected many times between the probe and the pleura line before its amplitude is attenuated below the level necessary to be displayed in the image; which is due to the strong acoustic impendance miss-match between air and soft tissue. This phenomenon is then interpreted by the imaging system as the replication of the pleura line (the horizontal lines) at multiples of the actual depth of the pleura. Differently, B-line artifacts, defined as hyper-echoic vertical artifacts that originate from a point along the pleura-line and lie perpendicular to the latter, have been linked to an increase in extravascular lung water, interstitial lung diseases, non-cardiogenic lung edema, interstitial pneumonia and lung contusion [1–4]. All conditions in which the normal structure of the lung is modified, and where the size and spatial distribution of the air spaces are altered with respect to a healthy condition. In clinical practice, where the time to analyze the ultrasound videos is scarce, a tool able to support the clinicians in the task of identifying and localizing B-lines may be extremely helpful. In this work, we leverage modern deep learning strategies and train a fully convolutional neural network to perform this task on B-mode images of dedicated ultrasound lung-mimicking phantoms able to reproduce A- and B-lines artifacts [5]. Moreover, we calculate neural attention maps that enable the visualization of which components in the image triggered the network, thereby offering simultaneous localization. The proposed approach yielded an accuracy, sensitivity, specificity, negative and positive predictive value equal to 0.918, 0.904, 0.925, 0.945 and 0.873, respectively. Beyond its use for the purpose of clinical evaluation, this algorithm can also be applied as a data-filter. In fact, it could e.g. be utilized to select regions of interest in the ultrasound data that contain the most relevant information, thereby serving as a useful step prior to further quantitative signal processing of the ultrasound signals [5], consequently reducing the computational load of such operations.

## 2  Methods

### 2.1  Lung Mimicking Phantoms

Lung mimicking phantoms able to reproduce the typical A- and B-lines artifact (see Fig. 1) were used to facilitate generation of realistic ultrasound videos. These phantoms consisted of a cloud of air bubbles trapped in tissue mimicking material (gelatin). Two distinct phantom types were designed, employing two different populations of mono-disperse air-filled micro-bubbles, having a diameter equal to 170 and 80 μm, respectively. These bubble sizes were chosen to attain a cluster of air-bubbles, which were smaller in size than a normal alveolar sac, whose diameter is approximately 280 μm [6]. The mono-disperse micro-bubbles were generated using the MicroSphere Creator®

(Tide Microfluidics, Enschede, the Netherlands). Five phantoms were fabricated with each micro-bubble population [5].

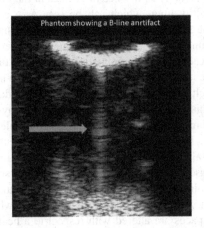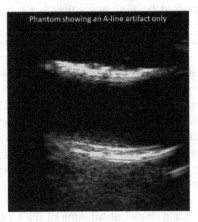

**Fig. 1.** Example of ultrasound images as obtained from the lung-mimicking phantoms and displaying a B-line artifact (left) and a A-line artifact (right) only. The B-line is indicated by the blue arrow. The image on the right clearly displays a replica (the deeper horizontal hyper echoic pattern) of the actual gel-air interface, i.e., an A-line. (Color figure online)

## 2.2   Ultrasound *in-vitro* Data

The ULA-OP [7] open research platform in combination with a LA533® (Esaote, Florence, Italy) linear-array probe were used to acquire B-mode ultrasound videos. A center frequency of 4.5 MHz and a 0.5-µs Gaussian pulse were employed for imaging. Ultrasound sweeps were obtained by manually operating the ultrasound probe, scanning the lung-mimicking phantom as to cover the entire bubble cloud (2 to 3 cm in diameter). Ten phantoms were scanned, and a total of 3162 ultrasound-video frames were stored for further analysis. Subsequently, video-frames were labeled as either 'B-line' or 'no B-line' by a clinical lung ultrasound expert with 20 years of experience. Four of these datasets where used as a hold-out test set for evaluation of detection performance. The accuracy, sensitivity and specificity are calculated on a frame-by-frame basis, by comparing the neural network outputs with the annotated labels. The presented metrics are evaluated on the test set, with the test set comprising four full acquisitions (sweeps).

## 2.3   Neural Network Architecture for B-line Detection

We designed a convolutional neural network (CNN) [8] consisting of 12 convolutional layers with a ReLU activation, each block of two such layers followed by a 2 × 2 max pool operation. ReLU activations were employed to introduce nonlinearity while mitigating vanishing gradients [9]. The resulting feature maps were then spatially average pooled to yield a single feature-vector representation per image. This feature vector served as the input of two fully-connected layers to yield logits that were followed by a Softmax function to assign (pseudo) probabilities to the two classes (B-line or no B-line present). An overview of the network architecture is given in Table 1. The use of global average pooling after the convolutional layers promotes learning of a set of explicit feature detectors of which the activations in the resulting feature maps relate directly to the two output classes via the subsequent fully connected layers. These feature maps, and their relation with the Softmax score for the positive class will then be used for localization, as described in Sect. 2.5.

**Table 1.** Neural network architecture.

| # | Type | Kerne | Activation | Output shape |
|---|------|-------|-----------|--------------|
| 1 | Convolutional | $3 \times 3$ | ReLU | (256, 256, 32) |
| 2 | Convolutional | $3 \times 3$ | ReLU | (256, 256, 32) |
| 3 | Max pooling | $2 \times 2$ | – | (128, 128, 32) |
| 4 | Convolutional | $3 \times 3$ | ReLU | (128, 128, 64) |
| 5 | Convolutional | $3 \times 3$ | ReLU | (128, 128, 64) |
| 6 | Max pooling | $2 \times 2$ | – | (64, 64, 64) |
| 7 | Convolutional | $3 \times 3$ | ReLU | (64, 64, 64) |
| 8 | Convolutional | $3 \times 3$ | ReLU | (64, 64, 64) |
| 9 | Max pooling | $2 \times 2$ | – | (32, 32, 64) |
| 10 | Convolutional | $3 \times 3$ | ReLU | (32, 32, 64) |
| 11 | Convolutional | $3 \times 3$ | ReLU | (32, 32, 64) |
| 12 | Max pooling | $2 \times 2$ | – | (16, 16, 64) |
| 13 | Convolutional | $3 \times 3$ | ReLU | (16, 16, 128) |
| 14 | Convolutional | $3 \times 3$ | ReLU | (16, 16, 128) |
| 15 | Max pooling | $2 \times 2$ | – | (8, 8, 128) |
| 16 | Convolutional | $3 \times 3$ | ReLU | (8, 8, 128) |
| 17 | Convolutional | $3 \times 3$ | ReLU | (8, 8, 128) |
| 18 | Global average pooling | $8 \times 8$ | – | 128 |
| 19 | Fully connected | – | ReLU | 256 |
| 20 | Fully connected | – | Softmax | 2 |

## 2.4    Training Strategy

A balanced training batch consisted of 32 randomly selected images with B-lines, and 32 others without, which were then subject to on-line data augmentation to achieve high data diversity during training, and thereby a network that is pseudo-invariant to specific manipulations. These manipulations included varying degrees of affine transformations, elastic warping, cropping, and blurring, and contrast distortion, as well as the addition of normally distributed white noise. We regularized the model by using dropout during training, with neurons dropped with a probability of 0.5 in dense layers, and a probability of 0.3 for the convolutional layers [10]. The neural network parameters were optimized to yield high log-likelihood using the Adam [11] solver with a learning rate of 1e−3, minimizing the cross-entropy between annotated labels and predictions.

### 2.5    Weakly-Supervised Localization by Class-Activation

To enable interpretation of CNN predictions by revealing regions in the image that trigger a specific classification decision, we resort to Class Activation Mapping (CAM). Since B-lines are local image phenomena, we here exploit CAM to perform weakly-supervised B-line localization directly from the class annotations, rather than e.g. through fully annotated segmentations. To this end, we use gradient-weighted CAM (grad-CAM) [12], and first compute the gradients of the positive class score with respect to each pixel from all image feature maps obtained at the last convolutional layer in the neural network. Their spatial averages reflect the importance of each such feature map for B-line detection, and are then used to construct a CAM for every input image: an importance-weighted combination of the corresponding CNN feature maps. We expect the feature maps to reflect specific visual patterns, with each pixel activated by the presence of such a pattern (e.g. the appearance of a B-line) within its receptive field [12].

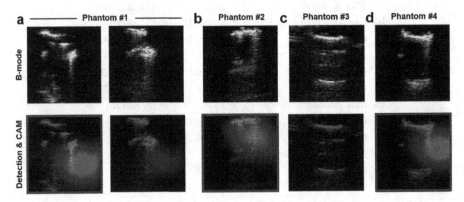

**Fig. 2.** (top) B-mode input data and (bottom) corresponding class activation maps (CAM) of B-line detection by the deep neural network for *in-vitro* acquisitions in 4 test phantoms (a–b). Blue boxes indicate detection. The heat maps provide information on the location of the B-line artifact in the frame. (Color figure online)

## 3    Results

Several illustrative B-mode images from four phantoms in the hold-out test set are given in Fig. 2. Qualitatively, detected B-lines are adequately localized through CAM. When B-lines are less prominent, e.g. when moving out of plane, activation maps also become less pronounced (Fig. 2a).

The overall frame-wise classification performance reached an accuracy, sensitivity and specificity of 0.917, 0.915, and 0.918, respectively. A notable negative predictive value of 0.950 was obtained.

## 4  Conclusion

Lung ultrasound imaging is nowadays an established tool used to evaluate the condition of the lung [2]. Despite this, there is still a lot to understand on the mechanism behind the artefactual patterns that appear in lung ultrasound images in the presence of an alteration of the lung structure. However, the identification and localization of such patterns (e.g. B-lines) already provides important clinical information.

In this paper, we present an image analysis method based on convolutional neural networks, which was developed to detect and localize B-lines in an ultrasound video. The method was tested on in-vitro data, with good results in terms of accuracy, sensitivity, specificity, negative and positive predictive value. Future work will include assessment of the proposed algorithm on clinical data.

Detecting and identifying regions of the images where a B-line artefact is present may not only serve visual inspection of the data, it can also aid the selection of a subset of data (region of interest) on which additional signal processing operations can be applied to extract additional, quantitative, information [5, 13, 14]. Specifically, this algorithm is in fact not designed to automatically count the amount of B-lines, but instead, to identify and localize (on which image line and until which depths) the part of the data from which the B-line artifact is reconstructed.

Moreover, future work will be focusing on characterization of the detected B-line artifact to enable adequate phenotyping of various lung pathologies [4].

While interesting, the main focus of this work was not to evaluate the influence of different network architectures on detection performance, but rather to show how gradient-based class activation mapping can be leveraged for weakly supervised localization of B-lines from merely the frame-based labels. A full optimization of the network architecture and hyperparameters would moreover be more meaningful when performed on a representative clinical dataset. We therefore consider this as future work.

**Acknowledgement.** The authors want to acknowledge M.D. Gino Soldati for the scoring of the ultrasound videos.

## References

1. Lichtenstein, D., et al.: The comet-tail artifact: an ultrasound sign of alveolar interstitial syndrome. Am. J. Respir. Crit. Care Med. **156**, 1640–1646 (1997)
2. Volpicelli, G., et al.: International Liaison Committee on Lung Ultrasound (ILC-LUS) for the International Consensus Conference on Lung Ultrasound (ICC-LUS). International evidence-based recommendations for point-of-care lung ultrasound. Intensive Care Med. **38**, 577–591 (2012)

3. Soldati, G., Demi, M., Inchingolo, R., Smargiassi, A., Demi, L.: On the physical basis of pulmonary sonographic interstitial syndrome. J. Ultrasound Med. (2016). http://doi.org/10.7863/ultra.15.08023

4. Soldati, G., Demi, M., Smargiassi, A., Inchingolo, R., Demi, L.: The role of ultrasound lung artefacts in the diagnosis of respiratory diseases. Expert Rev. Respir. Med. **13**, 163–172 (2018)

5. Demi, L., van de Hoeve, W., van Sloun, R.J.G., Soldati, G., Demi, M., et al.: Determination of a potential quantitative measure of the state of the lung using lung ultrasound spectroscopy. Sci. Rep. **7**, 12746 (2017)

6. Sagm, K., et al.: Characterization of normal and abnormal pulmonary surface by reflected ultrasound. Chest **74**, 29–33 (1978)

7. Boni, E., et al.: A reconfigurable and programmable FPGA based system for non-standard ultrasound methods. IEEE Trans. Ultrason. Ferroelectr. Freq. Control **59**, 1378–1385 (2012)

8. Krizhevsky, A., et al.: Imagenet classification with deep convolutional neural networks. In Advances in Neural Information Processing Systems, pp. 1097–1105 (2012)

9. LeCun, Y., et al.: Deep learning. Nature **521**(7553), 436–444 (2015)

10. Srivastava, N., et al.: Dropout: a simple way to prevent neural networks from overfitting. J. Mach. Learn. Res. **15**(1), 1929–1958 (2014)

11. Kingma, D.P., Ba, J.: Adam: a method for stochastic optimization. arXiv preprint arXiv: 1412.6980 (2014)

12. Selvaraju, R.R., et al.: Grad-cam: visual explanations from deep networks via gradient-based localization. In: IEEE International Conference on Computer Vision (ICCV), pp. 618–626 (2017)

13. Demi, L., Demi, M., Smargiassi, A., Inchinglo, R., Faita, F., Soldati, G.: Ultrasonography in lung pathologies: new perspective. Multidisc. Respir. Med. **9**, 27 (2014)

14. Mhanty, K., et al.: Characterization of the lung parenchyma using ultrasound multiple scattering. Ultrasound Med. Biol. **43**, 993–1003 (2017)

# Advances in Deep Learning

# Behavior-Based Compression
# for Convolutional Neural Networks

Koji Kamma[✉], Yuki Isoda, Sarimu Inoue, and Toshikazu Wada

Wakayama University, 930 Sakaedani, Wakayama-shi, Wakayama 640-8510, Japan
kanma@vrl.sys.wakayama-u.ac.jp
http://vrl.sys.wakayama-u.ac.jp/

**Abstract.** This paper presents a method for reducing the redundancy in both fully connected layers and convolutional layers of trained neural network models. The proposed method for fully connected layers consists of two steps, (1) Neuro-Coding: to encode the behavior of each neuron by a vector composed of its outputs corresponding to actual inputs and (2) Neuro-Unification: to unify the neurons having the similar behavioral vectors. Instead of just removing one of the similar neurons, the proposed method let the remaining neuron emulate the behavior of the removed one. Therefore, the proposed method can reduce the number of neurons with small sacrifice of accuracy without retraining. For convolutional layers, we propose Channel-Coding and Channel-Unification based on the same idea of Neuro-Coding and Neuro-Unification. In the convolutional layers, the behavior of each channel is encoded by its output feature maps, and channels with similar behaviors are unified. Through experiments with original and fine-tuned VGG16s, we confirmed that the proposed method performs better than the existing methods.

**Keywords:** Neuro-Coding · Neuro-Unification

## 1 Introduction

Deep neural networks (DNNs) have been showing dominant performances in the machine learning tasks. The key was the scale of the models. In fact, all the state-of-the-art models have a great number of parameters. Although, those models are too large for most of the applications where the models are desired. Therefore, it is important to make the DNN models smaller without degrading their performances.

A major approach for producing a small and accurate model is to compress a large pretrained model and retrain the compressed model to maintain the accuracy. Although, this retraining is a challenge, because it is computationally expensive, and one often needs cumbersome trials and errors for tuning hyperparameters.

The goal of this paper is to compress pretrained convolutional neural network (CNN) models while maintaining their accuracy to be as high as possible so that we need to retrain the models less frequently.

For fully connected layers, we propose a method consisting of two steps: (1) Neuro-Coding: to encode the behavior of each neuron and (2) Neuro-Unification: to unify the neurons which behave similarly. Each neuron outputs

© Springer Nature Switzerland AG 2019
F. Karray et al. (Eds.): ICIAR 2019, LNCS 11662, pp. 427–439, 2019.
https://doi.org/10.1007/978-3-030-27202-9_39

a scaler value corresponding to each input data. By recording those outputs, we create a behavioral vector for each neuron. If some neurons have similar behavioral vectors, we can unify those neurons, because they are redundant. Unifying a pair of neurons is, in other words, removing one of them and letting the remaining one emulate the behavior of the removed one by transferring the outgoing weights from the removed one to the remaining one, as we explain in Sect. 3. In this case, we can unify the neurons with small impact to the model accuracy.

For convolutional layers, we propose Channel-Coding and Channel-Unification based on the same idea. Channel-Coding encodes the channel-wise behavior and Channel-Unification unifies the channels with similar behaviors.

It is worth noting that compressing fully connected layers results in saving memory consumption and that compressing convolutional layers results in reducing the computational complexity required for inference. For instance, VGG16 [12] has about 90% of the parameters in fully connected layers, and the convolutional layers account for about 99% of the floating point operations. The proposed method can contribute to reducing both the memory consumption and the computational complexity.

We conducted some experiments with VGG16s on ImageNet. The results demonstrate that the proposed method can compress both the fully connected layers and the convolutional layers with small sacrifice of accuracy compared to the existing methods.

## 2    Related Works

We categorize the existing researches on DNN model compression into 5 groups: (1) Pruning, (2) Pruning with surgery, (3) Low-rank approximation, (4) Sparsification, and (5) Quantization.

The idea of pruning is to compute the saliency of each neuron or weight and to remove the least salient one. Optimal Brain Damage [7] is the pioneering pruning method which uses second derivative information of the cost function to calculate the saliency. There are also some other pruning methods for fully connected layers and/or convolutional layers [3,4,6,8,10,15].

Some pruning methods not only prunes but also executes "surgery" to compensate the impact of pruning so that the model needs to be retrained less frequently. Data-free Parameter Pruning [13] evaluates similarity of the neurons based on their incoming weights and "wires the similar neurons together". Optimal Brain Surgeon [5] is also a pruning method which executes surgery based on the Hessian of the cost function.

Xue et. al. suggested a method using low-rank approximation [14]. They apply singular value decomposition to large weight matrix, and approximate it by the product of small matrices by discarding the components with small singular values. This results in reducing the parameters with small sacrifice of accuracy. The drawback is that the number of weight matrices doubles and the model structure becomes more complicated.

The idea of sparsification is to make the weight matrices sparse by fine-tuning the models with L1 regularization. Liu et. al. suggested Sparse Convolutional

Neural Networks [9]. There are other methods to sparsify the weights such as [1]. Although, L1 regularization shifts the global minimum of the cost function and sacrifices accuracy.

Quantization is a different approach from the above 5 approaches. The methods in this group reduce the redundancy of each bitwise operation, e.g. changing the floating point precision from 32-bit to 8-bit. The methods proposed in [2,3] take this approach.

The proposed method in this paper belongs to "pruning with surgery" group. However, the way it executes the surgery is different from the existing methods. The proposed method can evaluate the behavioral similarity between the neurons or the channels accurately, which enables us to maintain high level of the accuracy while compressing the models.

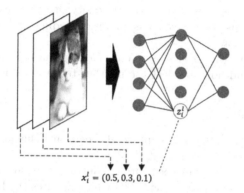

$$x_i^l = (0.5, 0.3, 0.1)$$

**Fig. 1.** The conceptual drawing of Neuro-Coding. When we input some samples to a neural network model, each neuron obtains a behavioral vector composed of their outputs.

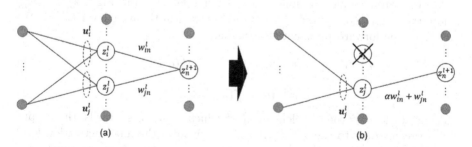

(a)  (b)

**Fig. 2.** Unification of neurons. (a) Initial state of the fully connected layers. (b) After merging $z_i^l$ into $z_j^l$. If the behavioral vectors of $z_i^l$ and $z_j^l$ are similar, we can unify them with small impact to the inner activation levels of the neurons in the next layer.

# 3    Compression for Fully Connected Layers

The steps of the proposed method are:

**Step1:** Prepare a pretrained model
**Step2:** Encode the behavior of each neuron by its outputs (Neuro-Coding)
**Step3:** Unify the neurons based on their behavioral similarity (Neuro-Unification)

Step3 should be repeated while the model is not small enough. It is worth noting that the behaviors of some neurons should change after some unifications. Therefore, repeating Step2 at certain intervals would enable us to compare the neuron behaviors more adequately, though it would require additional computational cost.

In practice, the model needs to be repeatedly retrained during the compression, because retraining the model should improve its performance. However, as one of our motivations is to reduce the necessity of retraining, we do not put retraining on the steps above. We focus on not degrading the model performance due to the compression.

We will explain the basics of Neuro-Coding and Neuro-Unification in Sects. 3.1 and 3.2 and how to select the neurons to be unified in Sect. 3.3.

## 3.1    Neuro-Coding

Neuro-Coding is a technique to capture the neuron behaviors. Figure 1 is the conceptual drawing. Let $\{z_1^l, \cdots, z_{N^l}^l\}$ be a set of the neurons in the $l^{th}$ layer. For a single input to the model, the neuron $z_i^l$ outputs a scalar value. By providing $D$ inputs, we can create a vector $\boldsymbol{x}_i^l \in \mathbb{R}^D$ which denotes the behavior of $z_i^l$. We call it a "behavioral vector".

## 3.2    Neuro-Unification

We begin with a simple example. We have a model shown in Fig. 2(a). Let $w_{in}^l$ denote the weight going from $z_i^l$ to the $n^{th}$ neuron in the next layer ($z_n^{l+1}$). We have the basic forward propagation formula:

$$y_n^{l+1}(d) = \cdots + x_i^l(d)w_{in}^l + \cdots + x_j^l(d)w_{jn}^l + \cdots, \tag{1}$$

$$x_n^{l+1}(d) = f(y_n^{l+1}(d)), \tag{2}$$

where $x_i^l(d)$ denotes the $d^{th}$ element of $\boldsymbol{x}_i^l$ which is, in other words, the output of $z_i^l$ corresponding to the $d^{th}$ input, $y_n^{l+1}(d)$ denotes the inner activation level of $z_n^{l+1}$ corresponding to the $d^{th}$ input, and $f$ denotes the activation function.

Assume that we have applied Neuro-Coding to the neurons in the $l^{th}$ layer and have obtained $\{\boldsymbol{x}_1^l, \cdots, \boldsymbol{x}_{N^l}^l\}$. If $\boldsymbol{x}_i^l = \alpha \boldsymbol{x}_j^l$ holds, we can unify $z_i^l$ and $z_j^l$ without affecting the inner activation levels of $\{z_1^{l+1}, \cdots, z_{N^{l+1}}^{l+1}\}$. As shown in Fig. 2(b), we can remove $z_i^l$ and update $w_{jn}^l$ as

$$w_{jn}^l := \alpha w_{in}^l + w_{jn}^l, \tag{3}$$

where := denotes assignment. Then, we can rewrite (1) as

$$y_n^{l+1}(d) = \cdots + x_j^l(d)(\alpha w_{in}^l + w_{jn}^l) + \cdots . \tag{4}$$

(1) and (4) are equivalent under the assumption that $x_i^l = \alpha x_j^l$, which means the inner activation level of $z_i^{l+1}$ is (and those of the other neurons in the $l+1^{th}$ layer are) preserved by letting $z_j^l$ emulate the behavior of $z_i^l$.

Next, we address the case of the neurons with linearly independent behavioral vectors. In this case, we cannot directly unify those neurons because the behavior of $z_i^l$ cannot be emulated by $z_j^l$. Therefore, we first approximate $x_i^l$ by a vector which is linearly dependent with $x_j^l$:

$$x_i^l \simeq \alpha x_j^l. \tag{5}$$

If we regard that $\alpha x_j^l$ is the behavioral vector of $z_i^l$, we can unify $z_i^l$ and $z_j^l$ by removing $z_i^l$ and updating the outgoing weights of $z_j^l$ in the same manner with (3).

Here is a question: How to determine $\alpha$? We should not significantly affect the inner activation levels of the neurons in the next layer. Thus, we have to simultaneously minimize the sum of squared error (SSE) of the inner activation levels of $\{z_1^{l+1}, \cdots, z_{N^{l+1}}^{l+1}\}$. In this case, the SSE, denoted by $S_{i,j}^{l+1}$, is given by

$$S_{i,j}^{l+1} = \sum_{n=1}^{N^{l+1}} \sum_{d=1}^{D} \left(\Delta y_n^{l+1}(d, i, j)\right)^2, \tag{6}$$

where $\Delta y_n^{l+1}(d, i, j)$ is the error of $y_n^{l+1}(d)$ caused by the unification:

$$\Delta y_n^{l+1}(d, i, j) = (\alpha x_j^l(d) - x_i^l(d))w_{in}^l. \tag{7}$$

Based on (6) and (7), $\alpha$ can be determined by solving the following:

$$\alpha_{i,j}^* = \underset{\alpha}{\operatorname{argmin}} \sum_{n=1}^{N^{l+1}} {w_{in}^l}^2 \sum_{d=1}^{D} (\alpha x_j^l(d) - x_i^l(d))^2. \tag{8}$$

We can omit $\sum_{n=1}^{N^{l+1}} {w_{in}^l}^2$ in (8) as it is a constant when $i$ is fixed. Moreover, we have the following definition:

$$\sum_{d=1}^{D} (\alpha x_j^l(d) - x_i^l(d))^2 = \|\alpha x_j^l - x_i^l\|^2. \tag{9}$$

Then, instead of (8), we have

$$\alpha_{i,j}^* = \underset{\alpha}{\operatorname{argmin}} \|\alpha x_j^l - x_i^l\|^2. \tag{10}$$

After all, we have to minimize the residual caused by approximating $x_i^l$ by $\alpha x_j^l$, which is equivalent to computing the orthogonal projection of $x_i^l$ onto $x_j^l$. Thus, we have

$$\alpha_{i,j}^* = \frac{{x_i^l}^T x_j^l}{\|x_j^l\|^2}. \tag{11}$$

If the approximation of $x_i^l$ is good enough, $z_j^l$ can emulate the major proportion of the behavior of $z_i^l$, and the impact to the propagation to the next layer is small.

### 3.3    Criteria for Selecting the Neurons to Be Unified

We already know how to unify a pair of neurons. Although, we have yet to know how to select the neurons to be unified when we have many possible neuron pairs.

When unifying the neurons in a layer, we should minimize the SSE of the inner activation levels of the neurons in the next layer. For this purpose, we define $r^l(i, j)$, the saliency of $(z_i^l, z_j^l)$ by the RHS of (6):

$$r^l(i, j) = \sum_{n=1}^{N^{l+1}} \sum_{d=1}^{D} \left( \Delta y_n^{l+1}(d, i, j) \right)^2 \tag{12}$$

By using (7), (9) and (11), we can rewrite (12) as

$$r^l(i, j) = \sum_{n=1}^{N^{l+1}} {w_{in}^l}^2 \left\| \frac{{x_i^l}^T x_j^l}{\|x_j^l\|^2} x_j^l - x_i^l \right\|^2 . \tag{13}$$

Note that we cannot ignore $\sum_{n=1}^{N^{l+1}} {w_{in}^l}^2$ here as it is not a constant before we fix $i$.

When we unify 2 or more pairs of neurons, how should we select the neuron pairs? For all the unifications that have happened in the $l^{th}$ layer, we have

$$S^{l+1} = \sum_{n=1}^{N^{l+1}} \sum_{d=1}^{D} \left( \sum_{(i,j) \in Z^l} \Delta y_n^{l+1}(d, i, j) \right)^2 , \tag{14}$$

where $Z^l$ denotes a set containing the tuples of indices of the unified neurons, e.g. $(i, j) \in Z^l$ means that $z_i^l$ has been merged into $z_j^l$. As (14) requires cumbersome computations, we use the following theorem for simplification.

**Theorem 1.** *Let $a_1, \cdots, a_N \in \mathbb{R}$. Then,*

$$\left( \sum_{i=1}^{N} a_i \right)^2 \leq N \sum_{i=1}^{N} a_i^2 . \tag{15}$$

*Proof.* Let $a_1, \cdots, a_N \in \mathbb{R}$ and $b_1, \cdots, b_N \in \mathbb{R}$. We have Cauchy-Schwarz inequality:

$$\left( \sum_{i=1}^{N} a_i b_i \right)^2 \leq \left( \sum_{i=1}^{N} a_i^2 \right) \left( \sum_{i=1}^{N} b_i^2 \right) . \tag{16}$$

Assign $b_i = 1$ for all $i$. Then,

$$\left( \sum_{i=1}^{N} a_i \right)^2 \leq N \sum_{i=1}^{N} a_i^2 . \tag{17}$$

Using Theorem 1 and (14), we get

$$S^{l+1} \leq q(Z^l) \sum_{(i,j)\in Z^l} \sum_{n=1}^{N^{l+1}} \sum_{d=1}^{D} \left( \Delta y_n^{l+1}(d,i,j) \right)^2, \tag{18}$$

where $q(Z^l)$ denotes the number of the elements in $Z^l$. We minimize this upper bound of $S^{l+1}$. Besides, the right side of (18) can be substituted using (12). Then, we get

$$\underset{Z^l}{\arg\min} \sum_{(i,j)\in Z^l} r^l(i,j) \quad \text{s.t.} \quad q(Z^l) = Q, \tag{19}$$

where $Q$ is a parameter we control. This is an combinatorial optimization problem.

Here, we introduce a constraint. Assume that $(i,j),(j,k) \in Z^l$. It means that we have merged $z_i^l$ into $z_j^l$, however, $z_j^l$ does not exist anymore as it has been merged into $z_k^l$. This is clearly an contradiction. Therefore, we cannot merge a neuron into $z_j^l$ if $\exists k, (j,k) \in Z^l$.

All that is left is to solve (19). We solve it in a greedy fashion. We select the neurons one by one based on the following cost function $C$ derived from (19).

$$C^l = \sum_{(i,j)\in Z^l} r^l(i,j). \tag{20}$$

# 4    Compression for Convolutional Layers

We propose Channel-Coding and Channel-Unification for compressing the convolutional layers. As some of the procedures of Channel-Coding and Channel-Unification are common with those of Neuro-Coding and Neuro-Unification, we focus on the different points in the following subsections.

## 4.1    Channel-Coding

Assume that the $l^{th}$ layer has $\nu^l$ channels and $\eta^l \times \eta^l$ width and height. Then, the output of each channel corresponding to $D$ inputs is a $D \times \eta^l \times \eta^l$ tensor. For channel-wize behavior comparison, we need to transform this tensor into a behavioral vector $x_i^l \in \mathbb{R}^{D\eta^{l^2}}$.

## 4.2    Channel-Unification

See Fig. 3. We first declare some notations. $K^l \in \mathbb{R}^{\nu^l \times \nu^{l+1} \times \tau \times \tau}$ denotes a convolutional kernel between the $l^{th}$ and the $l+1^{th}$ layers, where $\tau$ denotes the width and the height of the kernel under the assumption of a square-shaped kernel. The incoming and outgoing weights of channel $i$ in the $l^{th}$ layer are denoted by $\Psi_i^l \in \mathbb{R}^{\nu^{l-1} \times \tau \times \tau}$ and $\Omega_i^l \in \mathbb{R}^{\nu^{l+1} \times \tau \times \tau}$, respectively.

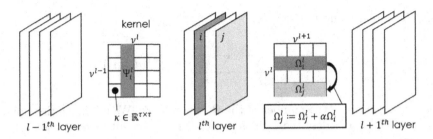

**Fig. 3.** Conceptual drawing of Channel-unification. When merging channel $i$ into channel $j$ in the $l^{th}$ layer, incoming weights and the outgoing weights of channel $i$ ($\Psi_i^l$ and $\Omega_i^l$) are removed, and the outgoing weights of channel $j$ ($\Omega_j^l$) are updated.

Let's think about merging channel $i$ into channel $j$ in the $l^{th}$ layer. We first need to encode their behaviors by $\boldsymbol{x}_i^l$ and $\boldsymbol{x}_j^l$, respectively. Second, assuming linear independence between those behavioral vectors, we need to approximate $\boldsymbol{x}_i^l$ by $\alpha \boldsymbol{x}_j^l$, where $\alpha$ is given by (11). Finally, we can delete the channel $i$, and update $\Omega_j^l$ as

$$\Omega_j^l := \alpha \Omega_i^l + \Omega_j^l. \tag{21}$$

## 5   Experiments

We apply the proposed method to original VGG16 and compare the performances with some existing methods. In addition, we conduct transfer-learning on VGG16 for a small-scale task, and try to compress this model in order to see how the proposed method works on a highly redundant model. In every experiment, we do not retrain the models during compression. We know that retraining must be done in the practical situations, although, we here want to evaluate how well the proposed method maintains the model performances while reducing the redundancy of the models.

### 5.1   Existing Methods for Comparison

We select 2 existing methods which are related to ours, Data-free Parameter Pruning (DPP) [13] and ORACLE Pruning (ORACLE) [10]. Both of the proposed method and DPP belong to "pruning with surgery" group, and ORACLE belongs to "pruning" group, as mentioned in Sect. 2.

**Data-Free Parameter Pruning.** DPP unifies the neurons with similar incoming weights. See Fig. 2(a). $\boldsymbol{u}_i^l$ denotes the incoming weights of $z_i^l$ including the bias term. If $\boldsymbol{u}_i^l \simeq \alpha \boldsymbol{u}_j^l$ and ReLU units are used in the $l^{th}$ layer, they remove $z_i^l$ and update the outgoing weights of $z_j^l$ in the same manner with (3).

**ORACLE Pruning.** ORACLE conducts channel-wise pruning for convolutional layers. ORACLE computes the saliency of each channel based on the derivative information of the cost function. For channel $i$ in the $l^{th}$ layer, the saliency is given as

$$\Theta_{l,i} = \frac{1}{D} \sum_{d=1}^{D} \left| \frac{1}{\eta^{l^2}} \sum_{j=1}^{\eta^{l^2}} \frac{\partial P}{\partial \chi_{i,j}^l(d)} \chi_{i,j}^l(d) \right|, \tag{22}$$

where $P$ denotes the cost function, and $\chi_{i,j}^l(d) \in \mathbb{R}^{\eta^{l^2}}$ denotes the $j^{th}$ element of a vectorized feature map corresponding to the $d^{th}$ input. They use some more tricks as well. See [10] for the detail.

ORACLE can be applied to fully connected layers as well. We just need to replace $\chi$s in (22) by $x$s.

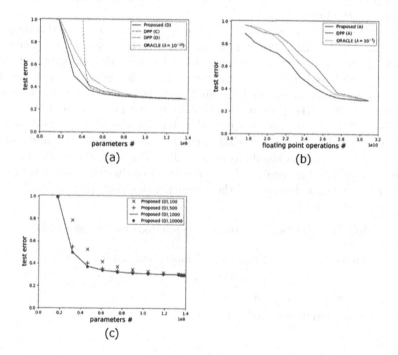

**Fig. 4.** Results for original VGG16: (a) comparison with the existing methods (fully connected layers), (b) comparison with existing methods (convolutional layers), (c) performance difference of the proposed method with respect to the number of data for Neuro-Coding.

## 5.2   Result for Fully Connected Layers

We conduct the experiments on original VGG16 supplied in torchvision package [11]. The target layers are FC-1 and FC-2.

We use ILSVRC2012 dataset. For encoding the neuron behaviors and/or computing the saliencies by the proposed method and ORACLE, we use 1,000 samples included in the training dataset (a random sample from each of 1,000 classes). For validation, we used the test dataset as is.

The proposed method and DPP cannot compare the saliencies across the layers. Thus, we execute those methods in several patterns. See Table 1. For example, in pettern (A), we first execute compression in FC1 until 25% of the neurons in FC1 are removed, then go on to FC2. Only for the last layer in each pattern, we keep compressing until only one neuron remains. For the proposed method and ORACLE, the computation of the saliencies is done once before the compression starts, and is not repeated. The other setups for ORACLE are the same with [10].

We observed that the performance of each method depends on the experimental setups. For simplicity and visibility of the figure, we pick up and show the best result(s) of each method. See Fig. 4(a). The performance is better if the curve goes in the lower side.

The performance of ORACLE was not as good as those of the proposed method and DPP. This is because the proposed method and DPP execute not only pruning but also surgeries. Though ORACLE looks theoretically sound as it uses the criteria based on the cost function of the model (cross entropy), iterative pruning without surgery results in a rapid degradation of the model accuracy.

The reason why the proposed method performs better than DPP is that DPP does not evaluate the influence of activation functions while ours does. The assumption behind DPP is that if the incoming weights of some neurons are similar, their outputs should also be similar. However, the similarity of the incoming weights of the neurons does not guarantee that their outputs are also similar due to the non-linearity of the activation functions such as ReLU.

**Table 1.** Execution patterns for the proposed method and DPP.

| Order | Neurons or channels removed in each layer | | |
|---|---|---|---|
| | 25% | 50% | 75% |
| From input side | (A) | (B) | (C) |
| From output side | (D) | (E) | (F) |

### 5.3   Result for Convolutional Layers

We conduct the experiments on the convolutional layers of VGG16. The compression targets are from Conv1-1 to Conv 5-3. We use the same dataset which we used in Sect. 5.2, and the same execution patterns in Table 1 for the proposed method and DPP.

We show the best result of each method on Fig. 4(b). Note that the horizontal axis represents the number of Floating Point Operations (FPOs). The proposed method shows much better performance than DPP and ORACLE.

In this case, ORACLE outperforms DPP. This should be because of the number of the target layers. ORACLE can compare the saliencies of the channels and select the least salient ones across the layers. On the other hand, DPP cannot compute the saliencies of the channel pairs across the layers, thus we compressed each layer by DPP in the fixed patterns. Further trials and errors in search for better patterns may improve the performance of DPP. Likewise, the proposed method may perform even better in other patterns.

## 5.4   Importance of Behavior Encoding

For evaluating how important it is to encode the neuron behaviors, we set the number of samples used for Neuro-Coding as 10,000, 1,000, 500 and 100, and applied Neuro-Unification to the fully connected layers of VGG16.

See Fig. 4(c). The trend is that the more samples are used for Neuro-Coding, the better the performance of Neuro-Unification is. It implies that when the number of samples for Neuro-Coding is not many enough, the neuron behaviors cannot be described well by the behavioral vectors, and the performance of Neuro-Unification becomes poor. Thus, it is crucial to use many data for Neuro-Coding enough to describe the neuron behaviors well.

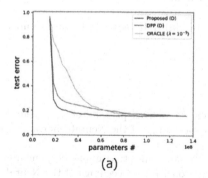
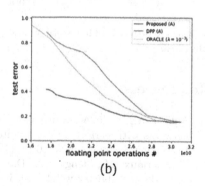

(a)                              (b)

**Fig. 5.** Results on fine-tuned VGG16: (a) The fully connected layers, (b) The convolutional layers. While the test error increased less than 1%, the proposed method reduced 68% of the parameters and 11% of the FPOs, respectively, even without retraining.

## 5.5   The Case of a Highly Redundant Model

We conducted transfer learning on VGG16 for classifying 31 dog breeds. We replaced 1,000 neurons in the output layer by 31 neurons, and fine-tuned only the fully connected layers for 100 epochs. We fed the training data in the minibatch of 100 and computed the gradients by SGD with cross entropy loss. The learning rate was 0.01, the momentum was 0.9 and the dropout rate was 0.5.

We used a subdataset of ILSVRC2012 dataset, containing 38,003 samples for training and 1,550 samples for test, which have "dog", "hound" or "husky" in the class names. For behavior encoding and computation of saliencies, we used 1,550 samples in the training dataset (50 randomly selected samples in each class). The rest of the experimental setups are the same with the ones in Sects. 5.2 and 5.3.

See Fig. 5. The proposed method performed much better for both the fully connected layers and the convolutional layers than the existing methods. The proposed method could reduce 68% of the parameters when the test error increased by less than 1%. For the convolutional layers, we could reduce the number of FPOs by about 11% with less than 1% increment in test error.

In this way, the proposed method can compress the model with small sacrifice of accuracy even without retraining when the model has lots of redundancy.

## 6   Conclusion

We proposed a method for compressing both fully connected layers and convolutional layers. The proposed method encodes the behaviors of the neurons or the channels by their outputs and unify the neurons or channels with similar behaviors, which enables to maintain the model performances in high level without retraining. On the experiments with original and fine-tuned VGG16s, the proposed methods performs much better than the existing methods, and the effectiveness of the proposed method is confirmed.

**Acknowlegement.** This work was supported by JSPS KAKENHI Grant Number 19K12020.

## References

1. Aghasi, A., Abdi, A., Nguyen, N., Romberg, J.: Convex pruning of deep neural networks with performance guarantee. In: Proceedings of the Neural Information Processing Systems, pp. 1–10 (2017)
2. Courbariaux, M., Bengiò, Y., David, J.P.: Binaryconnect: training deep neural networks with binary weights during propagations. In: Proceedings of the Neural Information Processing Systems, pp. 1–9 (2015)
3. Han, S., Mao, H., Dally, W.J.: Deep compression: compressing deep neural networks with pruning, trained quantization and huffman coding. In: Proceedings of the International Conference on Learning Representations, pp. 1–14 (2016)
4. Han, S., Pool, J., Tran, J., Dally, W.: Learning both weights and connections for efficient neural networks. In: Proceedings of the Neural Information Processing Systems, pp. 1–9 (2015)
5. Hassibi, B., Stork, D.G., Wolff, G.J.: Optimal brain surgeon and general network pruning. In: Proceedings of the International Conference on Neural Networks, pp. 293–299 (1993)
6. He, T., Fan, Y., Qian, Y., Tan, T., Yu, K.: Reshaping deep neural network for fast decoding by vertex-pruning. In: Proceedings of the International Conference on Acoustics, Speech and Signal Processing, pp. 245–249 (2014)
7. LeCun, Y., Denker, J.S., Solla, S.A.: Optimal brain damage. In: Proceedings of the Advances in Neural Information Processing Systems, pp. 598–605 (1989)

8. Li, H., Kadav, A., Durdanovic, I., Samet, H., Graf, H.P.: Pruning filters for efficient convnets. In: Proceedings of the International Conference on Learning Representations, pp. 1–13 (2017)
9. Liu, B., Wang, M., Foroosh, H., Tappen, M., Penksy, M.: Sparse convolutional neural networks. In: Proceedings of the Computer Vision and Pattern Recognition, pp. 806–814 (2015)
10. Molchanov, P., Tyree, S., Karras, T., Aila, T., Kautz, J.: Pruning convolutional neural networks for resource efficient inference. In: Proceedings of the International Conference on Learning Representations, pp. 1–17 (2017)
11. Paszke, A., et al. : Automatic differentiation in pytorch. In: NIPS-W (2017)
12. Simonyan, K., Zisserman, A.: Very deep convoolutional networks for large-scale image recognition. In: Proceedings of the International Conference on Learning Representations, pp. 1–14 (2015)
13. Srinivas, S., Babu, R.V.: Data-free parameter pruning for deep neural networks. In: Proceedings of the British Machine Vision Conference, no. 31, pp. 1–12 (2015)
14. Xue, J., Li, J., Gong, Y.: Restructuring of deep neural network acoustic models with singular value decomposition. In: Proceedings of the INTERSPEECH, pp. 2365–2369 (2013)
15. Yu, R., et al.: Pruning filters for efficient convnets. In: Proceedings of the Computer Vision and Pattern Recognition, pp. 9194–9203 (2018)

# Unsupervised Deep Shape from Template

Mohammad Ali Bagheri Orumi[1], M. Hadi Sepanj[1], Mahmoud Famouri[1],
Zohreh Azimifar[1(✉)], and Alexander Wong[2]

[1] School of Electrical and Computer Engineering, Shiraz University, Shiraz, Iran
{mohammad.ali.bagheri,mh.sepanj,mahmoud.famouri,
azimifar}@cse.shirazu.ac.ir
[2] Department of Systems Design Engineering, University of Waterloo,
Waterloo, ON N2L 3G1, Canada
a28wong@uwaterloo.ca

**Abstract.** This paper presents Unsupervised Deep Shape from Template (UDSfT), a novel method that leverages deep neural networks (DNNs) for reconstructing the 3D surface of an object using a single image. More specifically, the reconstruction of isometric deformable objects is achieved in the proposed UDSfT method via a DNN-based template-based framework. Unlike previous approaches that leverage supervised learning, the proposed UDSfT method leverages the notion of unsupervised learning to overcome this obstacle and provide real-time 3D reconstruction. More specifically, UDSfT achieves this via an unsupervised structure that leverages a combination of real-data and synthetic data. Experimental results show that the proposed UDSfT method outperforms the state-of-the-art Shape from Template methods in object 3D reconstruction.

**Keywords:** Deep learning · Depth estimation · Shape from Template

## 1 Introduction

Deformable object 3D reconstruction of RGB images and image sequences (video) is a desirable objective in computer vision. There are various applications which benefit from 3D reconstruction for example in robotics [2], medical imaging [11] etc. Since the depth information of an object is lost during the imaging process, reconstructing a 3D object in a sequence of images needs depth estimation of some pixels utilizing corresponding points between images which are extracted by descriptors. From the aspect of the object type, 3D reconstruction problem can be verified in two categories: rigid and non-rigid [14]. Despite the existence of prospering methods of 3D reconstruction, such as structure from motion [8], for rigid objects, deformable 3D reconstruction is still an unsolved problem. There are two main paradigms presented for non-rigid object 3D reconstruction known as non-rigid structure from motion (NRSfM) [4] and shape from template (SfT) [12]. SfT uses a single image and also a pre-defined template which demonstrates the information about shape and appearance of a known object. Usually, SfT procedure contains two major phases: (1) Finding corresponding points between the template and the image containing the deformed object. (2) 3D surface recovery utilizing the corresponding points.

F. Karray et al. (Eds.): ICIAR 2019, LNCS 11662, pp. 440–451, 2019.
https://doi.org/10.1007/978-3-030-27202-9_40

Subsequent to the success of the Deep Neural Networks (DNN) methodology, specially CNNs, in the computer vision applications such as object detection [9], classification [16] and depth estimation [5], some DNN SfT methods have been proposed lately [7]. These methods are designed to learn the warp function between the input image and the 3D template based on training data. Despite the effectiveness of the mentioned methods, they suffer from a salient limitation. They are in need of ground-truth for training phase which is arduous to provide or even sometimes impossible to obtain for real data.

In this paper, an unsupervised deep SfT (UDSfT) is proposed to confront with the mentioned limitation above, the first (to the best of our knowledge) unsupervised deep SfT method based on deep convolutional networks. This proposed method has several features which distinguish it from previous works which are pointed out in the following.

UDSfT proposes a novel approach for SfT which is trained with supervised synthetic data without any essential training with real data. This property of UDSfT makes this method needless to any ground-truth on the real data which is a dominating feature. It is dense, i.e. it is capable of generating scads of points in the 3D reconstruction phase. It is a robust method that encounters most of SfT challenges such as occlusion (internal and external), illumination changes and smooth object rotation.

This paper is organized as follows. A brief overview of the related literature is provided in Sect. 2. The proposed UDSfT approach is introduced and discussed in detail in Sect. 3. Experimental results and discussion are presented in Sect. 4, and conclusions are drawn in Sect. 5.

## 2  Related Work

This section reviews some SfT methods and some of their desired details. Specifically, the non-DNN SfT methods are discussed, and then the recently proposed DNN SfT method is studied.

### 2.1  Non-DNN SfT

Since the 3D reconstruction of a non-rigid surface is one of the desirable goals in computer vision, there are lots of methods proposed for this purpose. SfT [3] is a monocular surface reconstruction method which is proposed to represent the deformation of a non-rigid surface. As long as there are a variety of different deformed surfaces that have the same projection, the procedure of reconstruction of a deformable object is an ill-posed problem. Hence, in order to resolve this dubiety, it is common in the literature to consider the *Isometry* assumption as a constraint for the deformable object reconstruction [13].

In [12], Ngo et al. propose a sophisticated template based 3D reconstruction method which is based on utilizing Laplacian meshes in the reconstruction phase. They have used a linear system to recover the 3D shape which considers a linear combination for a subset of vertex coordinates of a mesh. Despite the excellent performance of this method, there are some limitations which are discussed in the following. Since they have considered a triangular mesh and applied constraints on all of the edges of the mesh, the constraint numbers are quite high, and as a sequence to that the computation load gets complicated.

On the contrary of frequent use of global warp function for SfT purpose, [6] proposes an isometric SfT approach which uses the corresponding keypoints between the deformed image and template to estimate the depth of objects locally. This method uses both the local texture and the neighboring matches to estimate local warp function which is represented by an affine transformation. In spite of the noticeable improvement in running time by Famouri et al., their method is not yet usable in real-time applications because there is still a bottleneck in finding corresponding keypoints time.

### 2.2   DNN SfT

In recent years, computer vision has been significantly improved with the emergence of the DNNs. Recently, some DNN based methods have been proposed to solve the monocular non-rigid 3D reconstruction problems. These methods have outperformed the state of the art methods of this field both in run-time and precision criteria.

To the best of our knowledge, *Hybrid Deformation Model network* (a.k.a., HDM-net) [7] is the very first approach which solves the SfT problem with the aid of DNNs. [7] proposes an auto-encoder network capable of learning the warp function which maps the input image to the 3D deformation parameters of the template. In contrast to previous works (non-DNNs) which required intense computations and a time-consuming procedure to provide a dense-reconstructed 3D surface, HDM-net results in a dense-surface with a lower cost of computation and also no need for multiple frames which is one the advantages of HDM-net. It should be noticed that HDM-net is a supervised method. This fact results in a crucial requirement for ground truth in training procedure which is sometimes impossible to be provided in the real data.

## 3   Proposed Method

As discussed in the previous sections, the majority of the non-DNN 3D reconstruction methods are not implementable in real-time due to the massive load of the required computation. Despite emerging DNN methods which solved the irrational time-consumption problem of the antecedent works, a new challenge manifested. These methods suffer from a critical requirement for the labeled real-data which is sometimes intricate to be provided.

This work proposes UDSfT method which is a novel DNN based method for the SfT procedure. UDSfT is an unsupervised approach which removes the existence-obligation of the real-data labels through training the proposed network with labeled synthetic data and applying the obtained trained network on the real data.

### 3.1   Problem Formulation

Figure 1 shows the geometrical model of UDSfT. In this configuration, it is assumed that the 3D template of the surface is known and is represented by $T_{3D} \subset \mathbb{R}^3$. The 2D template is also known and similarly represented by $T_{2D} \subset \mathbb{R}^2$ which describes both the appearance and texture of $T_{3D}$. It is noticeable that there is a one-to-one mapping between $T_{3D}$ and $T_{2D}$ denoted by $\Delta : T_{2D} \longmapsto T_{3D}$. The image of isometric deformed surface is denoted by $I \subset \mathbb{R}^2$ which is known and is considered as an input to the method.

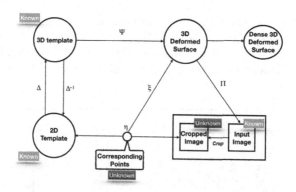

**Fig. 1.** Geometrical Model of UDSfT.

The main goal is to reconstruct the 3D shape of the surface from $I$ which results in an output $S \subset \mathbb{R}^3$. The 3D deformed surface $S$ is obtained by performing $\Psi : T_{3D} \longmapsto S$ isometric deformation map on the original 3D template $T_{3D}$. $\Pi$ is a projection function which maps every 3D point of $S$ to its corresponding point on the $I$ i.e. $\mathbb{R}^3 \longmapsto \mathbb{R}^2$. The unknown warp function $\eta$ is responsible for producing the corresponding points between the input image and $T_{2D}$ while the unknown function $\xi$ learns the transformation parameters from $\mathbb{R}^2$ to $\mathbb{R}^3$.

### 3.2   Network Architecture

UDSfT is a DNN method consist of four blocks which every block solves a sub-problem of the 3D reconstruction objective. One of the most significant reasons for dividing the 3D reconstruction problem into different sub-problems is that as experiments demonstrate such compartmentalization grants UDSfT the ability to function without any particular supervision on real-data. This kind of approach also helps UDSfT to be interpretative by a human since every block has a vivid certain duty. It is noticeable that these blocks are collaborating in a cascade layout. The first block is *Cropper* which is responsible for detecting the desired surface in the input image. The next block is *CPM* (Corresponding Points Matching) which is responsible for finding the specified points between the input image and $T_{2D}$. Actually, the two remaining blocks, *VPE* (Volumetric Position Estimator) and *Interpolator*, are in charge of recovering the 3D points utilizing apriori processed 2D outputs of the previous blocks. The Interpolator block is employed to satisfy the purpose of obtaining a dense reconstruction.

The remainder of this section verifies the details of UDSfT method, the arrangement of the blocks and how they cooperate to fulfill the objective.

**Cropper.** UDSfT utilizes the cropper block in order to homogenize the synthetic data and real-data by means of cropping the desired surface in both. In fact, after performing the cropper, all the image contents except the desired surface itself vanish which alleviates the CPM block duty to find the corresponding points by concentrating on the surface per se. This block gets $I$ as the input and generates a binary image with the same size utilizing the auto-encoder and residual networks structure. The architecture of the cropper block is shown in the Fig. 2.

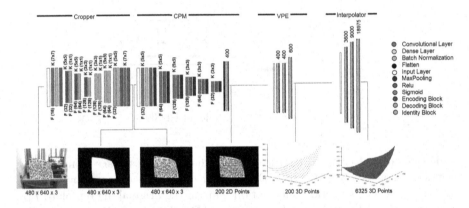

**Fig. 2.** Structure of proposed UDSfT. As it is shown in the image the structure is consisted of four blocks. Each block's desired input and output sample are brought in the figure.

The output binary mask demonstrates the surface position by assigning the 1's to the pixels which are reckoned as elements of the surface and 0's to the background pixels. By pixel-wise multiplication of the mentioned output mask in $I$, a cropped surface image ($I_c$) is obtained i.e.

$$\mathcal{B} = Cropper(I, W_c), \quad I_c = I \circ \mathcal{B} \tag{1}$$

where $W_c$, $\mathcal{B}$ and $\circ$ denotes the network weights matrix, the output binary mask and the Hadamard pixel by pixel multiplication symbol, respectively.

It is noticeable that, w.r.t. the nature of convolutional NNs it is probable that the DNN lose some beneficial information in the forward path. In order to solve this detriment, the cropper block utilizes the residual network structure to make the DNN remember that information which results in an improvement in the procedure. The structure of residual blocks used in the UDSfT networks are illustrated in Fig. 3.

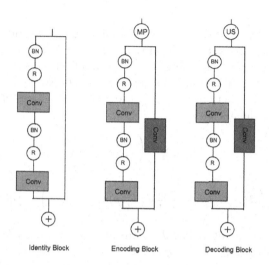

**Fig. 3.** Structure of residual blocks used in UDSfT method. (BN: Batch Normalization, R: Relu)

**CPM.** As mentioned in Sect. 1, the majority of the SfT methods contains two main steps. The CPM block used in UDSfT is the equivalent of the first phase of SfT. According to traditional non-DNN SfT methods [6] which endeavours to find some corresponding points between input image and the template, CPM leverages those specified 2D points which cover the whole surface. These lattice-formed points are informative knowledge which are capable of representing the raw input image. Hence, UDSfT uses this kind of information to substitute the raw image and the 2D points set. This process helps the UDSfT operates without any particular supervision for the real-data.

The main goal of CPM is to find some specified lattice points in the image which are predefined in the training phase of the CPM block. As shown in Fig. 2 CPM consists of convolutional and dense layers which estimate corresponding points between $I_c$ and $T_{2D}$.

$$P_{2D}(X, Y) = CPM(I_c, W_{CPM}) \tag{2}$$

where $P_{2D}(., .)$ and $W_{CPM}$ demonstrate the set of 2D positions of corresponding points and the network weights matrix, respectively.

Due to the nature of the convolutional layers, CPM generates the result by a local viewpoint while the dense layers bring the global viewpoint to the CPM block. It is noticeable that CPM operates the regression for a limited number of pre-defined points. As verified in [1] with the growth of the number of pre-defined points, the accuracy of the CPM drops. In addition, a dense output of the CPM results in a time-consuming VPE block. In order to solve this deficiency, UDSfT utilizes an interpolator block to generate a dense output.

**VPE.** The VPE block of the UDSfT is mimicking the second step of the SfT methods mentioned in Sect. 1. Usually, the non-DNN SfT methods utilizes a closed form solution in order to find the transformation function between the 2D corresponding points and the 3D deformed surface. For example, it is shown in [3] that the closed form function $\xi$ which is brought in the following, is responsible for reconstructing the 3D surface.

$$\xi(p) = \text{sqrt}\left( J_\Delta^\mathsf{T}(p) J_\Delta(p) \right.$$

$$\left( J_\eta^\mathsf{T}(p) J_\eta(p) - \frac{1}{||\hat{\eta}(p)||_2^2} J_\eta^\mathsf{T}(p) \eta(p)^\mathsf{T} J_\eta(p) \right)^{-1} \right) \hat{\eta}(p) \tag{3}$$

where $p$ is a corresponding point, $J(.)$ indicates the Jacobian operator and $\hat{\eta}$ is the homogeneous presentation of $\eta$ i.e.,

$$\hat{\eta} \propto \begin{bmatrix} \eta \\ 1 \end{bmatrix} \tag{4}$$

On the other hand, DNN based methods approach the SfT procedure from a different aspect of view. They attempt to obtain the depth of the pixels directly from the raw image itself instead of acquiring the depth from the corresponding 2D points.

One of the most significant features of DNN methodology is the capability of learning the linear, non-linear and highly non-linear functions. Considering this fact alongside the knowledge of existing closed form functions which are utilized to reconstruct the 3D surfaces, the UDSfT method proposes a novel approach with a different aspect of view. The VPE block which is illustrated in Fig. 2, learns the transformation function between the 2D points and the 3D deformed surface which is also demonstrated as $\xi$ in Fig. 1.

**Interpolator.** After performing 3D reconstruction process in VPE block a deformed surface is generated as the result. The noticeable point about the generated deformed surface is that it contains a limited amount of points. As it is obvious a more dense estimated deformed surface gives better results in the 3D reconstruction process. For this purpose, UDSfT utilizes an interpolator block after the VPE block to make the 3D reconstruction result dense. The interpolator block receives the output of the VPE block as its input and interpolates the existing points in order to produce more points for the deformed surface. This action results in a dense deformed surface. Separating the interpolator block from the rest of blocks causes the whole process load of the method decrease. Also this causes the rest of the blocks confront with a simpler problem with lesser amount of points which results in a better performance of the whole method. As another benefit of separating the interpolator block it can be mentioned that since the input is obtained from the VPE block, the interpolator block is capable of learning the previous block errors and noises. Hence, the dense points are also refined and the amount of noise in the results is reduced. The interpolator block is illustrated in Fig. 2.

### 3.3    Training

In this section, the training procedure details of the Cropper block, CPM block, VPE block and the Interpolator block is discussed.

The cropper is the first block which is trained in the UDSfT procedure. This block uses ADAM [10] optimization with learning rate equal to $10^{-4}$ and parameters set as $\beta_1 = \beta_2 = 0.9$. The cropper is trained with batches with size equal to 9 and uses mean square error as the loss function as brought in the following.

$$\mathcal{L}_{Cropper} = \frac{1}{N} \sum_{i=1}^{N} ||\hat{\mathcal{B}}^i - \mathcal{B}^i||^2 \tag{5}$$

where $N = hwb_s$, $h$, $w$ are the height and width of the image and $b_s$ is the batch size. $\mathcal{B}$ is also defined in Sect. 3.2 and $\mathcal{B}^i$ presents the $i^{th}$ pixel of the mask.

The CPM is the next block to be trained which consists of two parts. In order to construct the first part which is responsible for extracting the input features, an Undercomplete Auto-Encoder Network (UAEN) is employed. UAEN receives an image as its input and reproduces the same image as the output. This procedure causes the encoder part of UAEN learns some features which are capable of reconstructing the input image. This means that those features are reach enough and have significant information within. Hence, a freezed form of the encoder part of the UAEN is used as the first part of the CPM block without considering the decoder part of the UAEN. The second part which is responsible for 2D position estimation of the corresponding points, is built from a sequence of convolutional layers followed by a fully connected layer. It should be noticed that the second part is not trained solitary, it is trained after combining with the freezed encoder part as a single network. The loss function used in both parts is the mean square error. Further information about CPM and its implementation procedure details are available in [1].

The forthcoming block is VPE which is trained with synthetic data described in Sect. 4. Afterwards, VPE is fine-tuned using the outputs of CPM block as its input. VPE also uses ADAM optimization with learning rate equal to $10^{-2}$ and its loss function is brought in the following.

$$\mathcal{L}_{VPE} = \frac{1}{M} \sum_{i=1}^{M} \left| \hat{T_{3D}}^i - T_{3D}^i \right| \tag{6}$$

where $M$ is the number of corresponding points multiplied into the batch size, $|.|$ indicates the mathematical absolute operator and $T_{3D}^i$ represents the voxels position of $i^{th}$ corresponding point which is in $(X, Y, Z)$ form.

Since Interpolator block has an analogous training settings to the VPE block, further expositions about this block are relinquished.

## 4   Experimental Results and Discussions

In this section, the performance of the proposed UDSfT method is evaluated utilizing both the real data and synthetic data. In this paper, the Kinect_paper data-set which is provided by Varol et al. [15] is used as the real data-set while the procedure of generating synthetic data-set is discussed in the following.

**Data-Set.** As it is prevalent in the DNN area, these methods require abundant amount of data. Since the DNN-based SfT methods have emerged recently in the field, there are no admissible public data-set of this kind available. Therefore, we have designed and generated an appropriate data-set to show the performance of the UDSfT. The generated data-set is used for the training UDSfT network blocks which consists of the following parts. *Images of the deformed surface, Binary masks, 2D coordinates, 3D coordinates* and *Dense 3D coordinates.*

The template used for generating the data-set is adopted from the Kinect_paper data-set. As the very first step for generating the data-set, a lattice formed set of points ($T_{2D}$ which contains 200 points) is considered on the template which demonstrates the predefined point coordinates for the networks in order to find the correspondence between them and the input deformed image ($I_{480 \times 640}$). The 3D template ($T_{3D}$ which contains 200 points) is also obtained by presenting the homogeneous form of the 2D template which the depth of the pixels are estimated according to the camera intrinsic parameters which are known. A Dense 3D template is also generated with 6,325 points constructing the lattice scattered uniformly on the template. In addition, a binary mask ($T_{Mask}$) is generated which has the same size as the template and is designed to indicate the desired surface placement in the image. Every corresponding pixels which belongs to the surface has a value equal to 1 in the binary mask while 0 means that the pixel is not a subset of the surface.

The next step in data-set generation procedure is performing a various set of deformations on the previously obtained parameters. The deformations utilized in this work consist of cylindrical deformation, slight rotation and transition alongside uniformly random depth shifts. A random combination of these deformations is performed on the template, $T_{2D}$, $T_{3D}$, dense form of $T_{3D}$ and $T_{Mask}$ in order to generate an element for the data-set.

As the result 10,000 elements are generated (each element consists of two images and three set of points) which are randomly divided into three parts. 70% of the results are assigned to the training, 15% to the test and 15% to the validation procedure. A visual sample of one element of the synthetic data-set is illustrated in the Fig. 4.

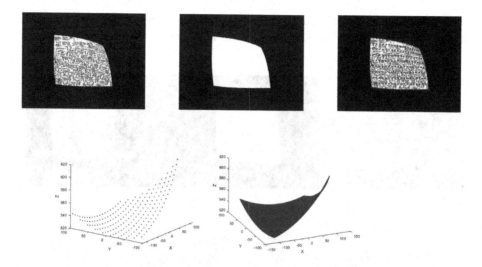

**Fig. 4.** Visual sample of one element of the synthetic data-set.

## 4.1 Results on Synthetic and Real Data

UDSfT is evaluated in terms of 3D reconstruction while the corresponding point matching results are brought in [1]. The results are compared against the DNN-based state-of-the-art method HDM-Net [7]. Also, there are a set of comparisons between UDSfT and the Non-DNN approaches such as Fast-SfT [6]. It is noticeable that the comparisons occur according to the ability of each method in terms of the type of the data-set, for example HDM-net is proposed for synthetic data hence, it is not fair to be validated and compared with other methods on the real-data. The numerical results are demonstrated in the Table 1.

**Table 1.** Evaluation results of UDSfT on real and synthetic data-set in comparison with other methods alongside their processing time. Note that, unlike other tested methods, the proposed UDSfT is the first unsupervised approach in literature.

| Method | AVG Error-Real data | AVG Error-synthetic data | Time (ms) |
|---|---|---|---|
| SfT [12] | 5.20 mm | - | 2432 |
| Fast-SfT [6] | 6.58 mm | - | 854 |
| HDM-net [7] | - | 8.16 mm | 571 |
| **UDSfT** | **6.46 mm** | **1.37 mm** | **626** |

As it can be inferred from the Table 1, UDSfT outperforms the HDM-net. Although the 3D reconstruction error of Ngo et al. method in real-data is better than UDSfT, it is obvious that UDSfT outperforms it in terms of time consumption.

Figure 5 illustrates the qualitative results for the UDSfT. The image demonstrates the input of the UDSfT and output of each block of the UDSfT.

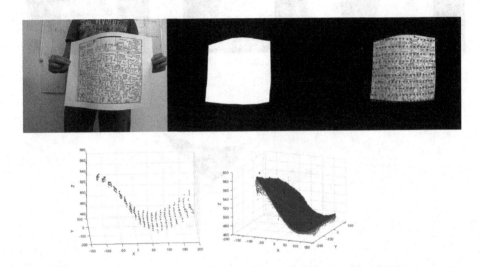

**Fig. 5.** Input and output of UDSfT. The first row shows the UDSfT input image, Cropper output and CPM output (blue points on the surface) respectively. The second row shows VPE output and Interpolator output (red points are the UDSfT result while the blue points are ground-truth). (Color figure online)

## 5    Conclusion

This paper has presented UDSfT, the first unsupervised, dense, real-time solution to the SfT problem. UDSfT employs a self-supervised concept in order to alleviate the crucial urge for supervision in the 3D reconstruction area. UDSfT is a DNN-based method with a high accuracy capable of operating in real-time which makes it quite useful in a wide range of applications. In the future the authors aim to improve the results by utilizing the attention networks in order to increase the attention on the template.

## References

1. Bagheri, M., Famouri, M., Azimifar, Z., Nazemi, A.: Deep learning-based corresponding points fast matching. In: International Conference on Pattern Recognition and Artificial Intelligence, pp. 256–260 (2018)
2. Banerjee, D., Yu, K., Aggarwal, G.: Robotic arm based 3D reconstruction test automation. IEEE Access **6**, 7206–7213 (2018)
3. Bartoli, A., Gérard, Y., Chadebecq, F., Collins, T., Pizarro, D.: Shape-from-template. IEEE Trans. Pattern Anal. Mach. Intell. **37**(10), 2099–2118 (2015)

4. Chhatkuli, A., Pizarro, D., Collins, T., Bartoli, A.: Inextensible non-rigid structure-from-motion by second-order cone programming. IEEE Trans. Pattern Anal. Mach. Intell. **40**(10), 2428–2441 (2018)

5. Eigen, D., Fergus, R.: Predicting depth, surface normals and semantic labels with a common multi-scale convolutional architecture. In: Proceedings of the IEEE International Conference on Computer Vision, pp. 2650–2658 (2015)

6. Famouri, M., Bartoli, A., Azimifar, Z.: Fast shape-from-template using local features. Machi. Vis. Appl. **29**(1), 73–93 (2018)

7. Golyanik, V., Shimada, S., Varanasi, K., Stricker, D.: HDM-net: monocular non-rigid 3D reconstruction with learned deformation model. In: Bourdot, P., Cobb, S., Interrante, V., Kato, H., Stricker, D. (eds.) EuroVR 2018. LNCS, vol. 11162, pp. 51–72. Springer, Cham (2018). https://doi.org/10.1007/978-3-030-01790-3_4

8. Hartley, R., Zisserman, A.: Multiple View Geometry in Computer Vision. Cambridge University Press, Cambridge (2003)

9. Kang, K., et al.: T-CNN: tubelets with convolutional neural networks for object detection from videos. IEEE Trans. Circ. Syst. Video Technol. **28**(10), 2896–2907 (2018)

10. Kingma, D.P., Ba, J.: Adam: A method for stochastic optimization. arXiv preprint arXiv:1412.6980 (2014)

11. Liu, J., et al.: 3D feature constrained reconstruction for low-dose CT imaging. IEEE Trans. Circ. Syst. Video Technol. **28**(5), 1232–1247 (2018)

12. Ngo, D.T., Östlund, J., Fua, P.: Template-based monocular 3D shape recovery using laplacian meshes. IEEE Trans. Pattern Anal. Mach. Intell. **38**(1), 172–187 (2016)

13. Östlund, J., Varol, A., Ngo, D.T., Fua, P.: Laplacian meshes for monocular 3D shape recovery. In: Fitzgibbon, A., Lazebnik, S., Perona, P., Sato, Y., Schmid, C. (eds.) ECCV 2012. LNCS, vol. 7574, pp. 412–425. Springer, Heidelberg (2012). https://doi.org/10.1007/978-3-642-33712-3_30

14. Szeliski, R.: Computer Vision: Algorithms and Applications. Springer Science & Business Media (2010)

15. Varol, A., Shaji, A., Salzmann, M., Fua, P.: Monocular 3D reconstruction of locally textured surfaces. IEEE Trans. Patt. Anal. Mach. Intell. **34**(6), 1118–1130 (2012)

16. Zhang, C., et al.: A hybrid MLP-CNN classifier for very fine resolution remotely sensedimage classification. ISPRS J. Photogramm. Remote Sens. **140**, 133–144 (2018)

# Strategies for Improving Single-Head Continual Learning Performance

Alaa El Khatib$^{(\boxtimes)}$ and Fakhri Karray

University of Waterloo, Waterloo, ON, Canada
{alaa.elkhatib,karray}@uwaterloo.ca

**Abstract.** Catastrophic forgetting has long been seen as the main obstacle to building continual learning models. We argue in this paper that an equally challenging characteristic of the continual learning framework is that data are never completely available at the same time, making it difficult to learn joint conditional distributions over them. This is most evident in the usually large gap between single-head and multi-head performance of continual learning models. We propose in this paper two strategies to improve performance of continual learning models, particularly in the single-head framework and for image classification tasks. First, we argue that learning multiple binary classifiers, rather than a single multi-class classifier, for each presentation of data is more consistent with the single-head framework. Moreover, we argue that auxiliary, unlabelled data can be used in tandem with this approach to slow the decay in performance of these binary classifiers over time.

**Keywords:** Continual learning · Catastrophic forgetting

## 1 Introduction

Continual learning refers to a framework of machine learning in which models are to learn tasks sequentially. These models are expected to accumulate knowledge over time, such that newly acquired knowledge does not undo previous learning. This framework more closely resembles the learning process of intelligent beings, including humans, and is thus seen as a potential path toward building models capable of artificial general intelligence (AGI) [1,2].

By contrast, the commonly used framework for machine learning entails optimizing a model to perform a single task, with no regard to forgetting or potential subsequent learning. Over the past decade, many breakthroughs have been achieved within this framework, in computer vision, natural language, and other applications. It is nowadays possible to train models that can surpass human performance on various narrowly defined tasks within this framework. On the other hand, machine learning models continue to be poor accumulators of knowledge, and are significantly outperformed by humans in the continual learning arena.

The challenging nature of the continual learning framework has long been attributed to the so-called *catastrophic forgetting* phenomenon: the steep degradation in a model's performance on a task once it is subsequently trained on

© Springer Nature Switzerland AG 2019
F. Karray et al. (Eds.): ICIAR 2019, LNCS 11662, pp. 452–460, 2019.
https://doi.org/10.1007/978-3-030-27202-9_41

another. Considering that learning a subsequent task means modifying a model's parameters—and hence, undoing any preceding optimization—it is rather unsurprising that neural networks "forget" previous skills when they acquire new ones.

Most of the research effort in continual learning has focused primarily on ways to counter catastrophic forgetting and, in so doing, retain knowledge in a model's parameters over multiple optimizations with different objectives. Various approaches have been proposed over the years, including parameter regularization strategies, rehearsal and pseudo-rehearsal, and network growing.

We argue in this paper that, in being mainly focused on countering catastrophic forgetting, continual learning research has neglected what we see as a more detrimental issue facing continual learning—performance of single-head models. Continual learning models are usually presented in one of two settings: multi-head and single-head, with the latter's performance usually being much worse. [4] We look more closely at the source of performance degradation in single-head models and propose two strategies to remedy it. We show that the commonly used softmax cross entropy loss is not well aligned with the single-head framework. Instead we propose using multiple binary cross entropy losses. We argue that, coupled with auxiliary unlabelled data, this leads to single-head models that are more robust to the addition of new classes during future learning.

The rest of this paper is organized as follows. We review related work on continual learning and countering catastrophic forgetting in Sect. 2. We present the proposed approach in Sect. 3 and experimental results in Sect. 4. Finally, we conclude the paper in Sect. 5.

## 2 Related Work

### 2.1 Countering Catastrophic Forgetting

Continual learning has been approached in the literature almost always from the point of view of countering catastrophic forgetting. To tackle the issue, researchers have proposed a number of methods, which can roughly be grouped into three categories: (1) rehearsal and pseudo-rehearsal, (2) network growing, and (3) regularization approaches.

Rehearsal-based approaches generally counter forgetting by periodically retraining continual learning models on previously learned data [5,6]. The approach, hence, requires that training data be stored and accumulated for all learned tasks. Pseudo-rehearsal approaches attempt to circumvent the memory requirement of rehearsal by using surrogate data, generated on the spot, in place of training data from previous training periods [7,8].

The second category of approaches to countering forgetting includes methods that gradually increase the number of parameters of the model as it learns more tasks. Thus, previously optimized parameters may be frozen, and newly acquired knowledge is absorbed in the newly added parameters [9,10].

Finally, a large number of approaches proposed to counter catastrophic forgetting use some form of regularization to slow down learning on "important" parameters. The recently proposed elastic weight consolidation (EWC) is one such approach [2]. EWC estimates the importance of model parameters to previously learned tasks using fisher information matrix and scales a per-parameter L2 penalty by the estimated importance.

## 2.2 Single-Head vs. Multi-Head

The literature on continual learning does not dedicate much attention to the single-head vs. multi-head question. In most cases, models are evaluated in either of the settings without explicit reasoning. In other cases, researchers argue that reporting results in the multi-head setting is justified by the fact that it is often significantly more feasible to predict the task from which an input sample is drawn than to classify it into one of the classes of that task. Some researchers, on the other hand, have argued, correctly in our view, that reporting results in the multi-head setting paints an overly optimistic picture for the performance of continual learning models, compared to single-head performance, and that it is not always straightforward to distinguish between tasks without external input [4].

## 3  Proposed Approach

Before presenting the proposed strategies, we introduce the following terminology to simplify our presentation.

- A *learning experience* is the process of presenting a set of training data to the model and the corresponding optimization of the model's parameters. Each learning experience derives from a different, possibly mutually exclusive, dataset. The subset of classes present in the training data of one experience is also different from, and possibly mutually exclusive with, the subset present in another.
- An *episode* is a sequence of learning experiences.
- A *task* encapsulates a set of classes among which a model should learn to discriminate. When evaluating a model on a task, no external information is given to the model that would allow it to narrow down the subset of classes from which a test image comes. On the other hand, when evaluating a model's performance on a set of tasks, the model is told the task (and hence which subset of classes) from which each test image is drawn. In terms of network architecture, each task corresponds to a different output *head* (a subset of output units grouped together). The subset of classes corresponding to each task (or head) can be expanded over time. We provide this definition to remove any ambiguities when discussing single-head and multi-head settings.

To give a concrete example, consider a model that learns the 10 classes of MNIST [11] in a continual learning framework, 2 classes at a time. In both single-head and multi-head settings, this corresponds to an *episode* of 5 *learning experiences*. In the single-head setting, all the 5 learning experiences are over the same task (call it, for example, *mnist-0*), hence there is only one output *head*. The output units in this head however are expanded with each new learning experience: with the first experience, the *mnist-0* head contains 2 units, corresponding to classes 0 and 1; by the $5^{th}$ experience, it contains 10 units, corresponding to the 10 classes. In each learning experience, the model is presented with data from 2 classes only, but is evaluated on data drawn from all the classes in the *mnist-0* head. By contrast, in the multi-head setting, the model eventually contains 5 heads, each with 2 output units. With each presented image, the model is told which head to use (by the end, this increases the probability of correctly guessing the class of an image randomly from $\frac{1}{10}$ in the single-head setting to $\frac{1}{2}$ in the multi-head setting).

## 3.1  Binary vs. Multi-class Classification Loss

We focus in this work on image classification tasks, where the objective is to train a model to learn to predict class $y \in \mathcal{C}$ given an image $\mathbf{x}$. The cost function often used here is the cross entropy or the multi-class negative log-likelihood:

$$L(\theta) = -\frac{1}{N} \sum_{i=1}^{N} \log p_\theta(y_i|\mathbf{x}_i), \qquad (1)$$

where $N$ is the number of training samples and $y_i$ is the true class of $\mathbf{x}_i$. Note that here the model probability distribution $p_\theta$ is a softmax distribution over all the classes present in the current learning experience:

$$p_\theta(y|\mathbf{x}) = \frac{e^{z_y}}{\sum_{j \in \mathcal{C}} e^{z_j}}. \qquad (2)$$

We argue here that this cost function is not an appropriate choice for the loss in the single-head setting. This function drives the output of the unit corresponding to the correct class to be higher than the output of the other units in the learning experience. Ideally, the optimization should drive the model distribution toward the one-hot encoded ground truth. In practice, however, the resulting distribution has higher entropy, even for correctly classified inputs. For example, a high-accuracy model on a 4-class classification problem may correctly predict a probability distribution $[0.25, 0.25, 0.3, 0.2]$ for a sample from class 2 (out of classes 0–3). While this may not affect performance in a multi-head setting, it does have the potential to degrade performance in the single-head setting.

Consider, for example, that in a subsequent learning experience this same model learns another 4 classes, 4–7, using the same cost function. When evaluating this model with samples drawn from classes 0–7, the predicted class of the model is the maximum output across all output units in the output head. This would be a reasonable prediction strategy had the model been trained to minimize a single negative log-likelihood for all 8 classes. However, with model being trained with 2 learning experiences, one for classes 0–3 and another for 4–7, this is no longer the case. This is because units 0–3 have been optimized to output values that make sense *relative to outputs from other units in the same learning experience*. The same is true for units 4–7. Now, presented with a test sample, say from class 2, the output of the units from the first learning experience may be $[0.2, 0.2, 0.32, 0.28]$ and the output of the units from the second learning experience may be $[0.35, 0.25, 0.25, 0.15]$. The maximum taken across the units of the first learning experience corresponds to the correct class. Taken across all classes, however, it is wrong.

This example illustrates the weakness of optimizing the output of units only relative to other units in the same learning experience. What is the alternative, though? Optimization relative to all units in the head is not possible in the continual learning framework.

We conjecture that optimizing separate binary classifiers for each class in a learning experience leads to predictions better suited to an expanding single-head that can be extended with additional classes over time. Taken on its own, a binary classifier is optimized to output a high probability for a correct sample and a low probability for any other sample. Of course, the samples seen in the training set of a learning experience are still limited to a subset of classes from the total in the head. And so, one could argue that the binary classifier is still making relative predictions just as the softmax classifier. Our experiments, however, suggest this is not the case, especially when coupled with unlabelled auxiliary data, as we discuss in the next section.

To train a binary classifier for a unit, we binarize the labels of the samples in the corresponding learning experience. In optimization, we jointly minimize multiple binary cross entropy cost functions, one for each unit in the learning experience:

$$L(\theta) = \sum_{u=1}^{R} L_u, \tag{3}$$

where R is the number of units in the learning experience and

$$L_u = -\frac{1}{N} \sum_{i=1}^{N} \log p_\theta(y_i^{(u)} | \mathbf{x}_i). \tag{4}$$

$p_\theta$ here is a binary distribution over $y^{(u)}$, where $y^{(u)} = 1$ for a sample from class $u$ and 0 otherwise.

## 3.2   Using Auxiliary Unlabelled Data

In order to arrive at more general binary classifiers for each class (i.e., classifiers that will not significantly deteriorate when faced with samples drawn from outside the classes they was trained with), we propose augmenting the training sets for all learning experiences with additional data. Ideally, one would want to have training data for all classes that will eventually be added to an output head present for all learning experiences. But that is not feasible in the continual learning framework. We instead propose to use unlabelled data.

Unlabelled data is cheap to obtain. For a robot navigating an environment, for example, unlabelled images can be randomly sampled from its surroundings. In web-connected applications, random data can be scraped from the internet.

We augment the training set for each learning experience with random unlabelled data. To train a binary classifier, these data samples are given negative labels. This assumption may not always hold. However, for many applications, such as image classification, the probability of a randomly sampled image to be positive for any class is so low that the resulting data contamination, if any, ends up being negligible.

### 3.3   Anticipatory Regularization

We combine the above strategies with our previously proposed approach, anticipatory regularization [3]. We proposed anticipatory regularization as a way to counter catastrophic forgetting that, in contrast to other regularization solutions to forgetting that attempt to penalize departure from learned parameters, is forward-looking. In short, we augment a normal classification network, such as a convolutional net, with a decoder branch and penalize reconstruction error. This drives the network toward learning representations that are more general, and thus possibly useful for future tasks. This, consequently, reduces the need to modify network parameters significantly with future learning.

## 4   Experiments

In this section, we present our experimental results. We begin by a comparison of multi-head and single-head continual learning settings. In both settings, we train a convolutional neural network (CNN) on CIFAR100 [12] incrementally. We present results for different episode configurations. In the baseline episode, there is a single learning experience with all 100 classes. We also use episodes with 2 50-class experiences, 5 20-class experiences, 10 10-class experiences, 20 5-class experiences, and 50 2-class experiences. These episode configurations are designed to show how the multi-head and single-head settings affect performance in scenarios ranging from a large number of small learning experiences to a single large learning experience.

Figures 1 and 2 show results in the multi-head and single-head settings, respectively. We note a number of observations from these two figures. First, generally, multi-head performance is significantly better than single-head performance. Second, using multi-head performance as a measure of forgetting can be misleading: as Fig. 1 shows, performance for the baseline episode (where there is no continual learning or forgetting) is worse than all other episodes. In fact, as the number of learning experiences increases, the final average accuracy on all tasks in the episode increases. Which is counter-intuitive, as one would expect the larger number of learning experiences to bring about more forgetting. The reason behind this, of course, is that a as the number of learning experiences in an episode increases, the difficulty of each individual task decreases, which raises the average performance overall. Table 1 illustrates this point more clearly. The table shows the final average accuracy in each case vs. the accuracy of a random guessing model.

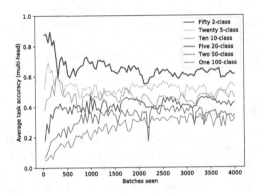

**Fig. 1.** Average accuracy on CIFAR100 for different multi-head episode configurations.

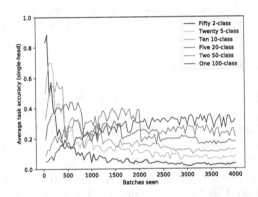

**Fig. 2.** Average accuracy on CIFAR100 for different single-head episode configurations.

Another observation we note from these results is that the degradation in performance that can be ascribed to catastrophic forgetting is significantly less than that can be ascribed to the single-head setting. This highlights the importance of learning to recognize classes in a way that is robust to the addition of classes over time. This is what we sought to address with the proposed strategies.

Figure 3 shows the result of our proposed approach in the single-head setting. Each learning experience is drawn from 6 classes from the classes of CIFAR100 and STL10 [13]. By the end of the episode, the model is evaluated with data from the 10 classes of STL10 and the first 30 classes of CIFAR100 (a 40-class classification task). Unlabelled auxiliary data are drawn from the unlabelled dataset of STL10. We augment each learning experience with 2000 unlabelled samples.

The results show that the proposed strategies improve single-head performance significantly (by about 10%). We note that this is remarkable in view of the fact that none of the strategies proposed work to counter catastrophic forgetting explicitly.

**Table 1.** Final average accuracy on CIFAR100 for different multi-head and single-head episode configurations.

| Episode | Multi-head | | | Single-head | | |
|---|---|---|---|---|---|---|
| | Trained | Random | $\Delta$ | Trained | Random | $\Delta$ |
| Two 50-class | 34.8% | 2.00% | 32.8% | 20.9% | 1.00% | 19.9% |
| Five 20-class | 43.0% | 5.00% | 38.0% | 18.1% | 1.00% | 17.1% |
| Ten 10-class | 45.8% | 10.0% | 35.8% | 12.9% | 1.00% | 11.9% |
| Twenty 5-class | 53.0% | 20.0% | 33.0% | 8.61% | 1.00% | 7.61% |
| Fifty 2-class | 61.4% | 50.0% | 11.4% | 3.45% | 1.00% | 2.98% |
| One 100-class | - | - | - | 32.5% | 1.00% | 31.5% |

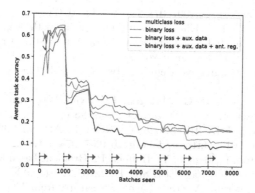

**Fig. 3.** Average accuracy on CIFAR100 and STL10 in the single-head setting using the proposed strategies. Arrows correspond to transitions in learning experiences.

## 5   Conclusion

We propose in this paper strategies for improving the performance of continual learning models. Specifically, we focus on performance in the single-head setting. We show that by a combination of a loss function more suited to this learning framework, the use of auxiliary unlabelled data, and the use of anticipatory regularization, we are able to achieve a significant improvement in the single-head average accuracy. We also show a comparison between multi-head and single-head evaluation settings, and argue that the performance degradation brought about by catastrophic forgetting is smaller than that caused by the inability of a single-head model to distinguish between classes learned in different learning experiences.

# References

1. Hasselmo, M.: Avoiding catastrophic forgetting. Trends Cogn. Sci. **21**(6), 407–408 (2017)
2. Kirkpatrick, J., et al.: Overcoming catastrophic forgetting in neural nets. Proc. Nat. Acad. Sci. **114**(13), 3521–3526 (2017)
3. El Khatib, A., Karray, F.: Preempting catastrophic forgetting in continual learning model by anticipatory regularization. In: Proceedings of International Joint Conference on Neural Networks (IJCNN), Budapest (2019). (Accepted, not yet published)
4. Chaudhry, A., Dokania, P.K., Ajanthan, T., Torr, P.H.S.: Riemannian walk for incremental learning: understanding forgetting and intransigence. In: Ferrari, V., Hebert, M., Sminchisescu, C., Weiss, Y. (eds.) ECCV 2018. LNCS, vol. 11215, pp. 556–572. Springer, Cham (2018). https://doi.org/10.1007/978-3-030-01252-6_33
5. Robins, A.: Catastrophic forgetting in neural networks: the role of rehearsal mechanisms. In: Proceedings of The First New Zealand International Two-Stream Conference on Artificial Neural Networks and Expert Systems (1993)
6. Ratcliff, R.: Connectionist models of recognition memory: constraints imposed by learning and forgetting functions. Psychol. Rev. **92**(2), 285–308 (1990)
7. Li, Z., Hoiem, D.: Learning without forgetting. In: Leibe, B., Matas, J., Sebe, N., Welling, M. (eds.) ECCV 2016. LNCS, vol. 9908, pp. 614–629. Springer, Cham (2016). https://doi.org/10.1007/978-3-319-46493-0_37
8. Shin, H., Lee, J., Kim, J., Kim, J.: Continual learning with deep generative replay. In: Guyon, I., et al. (eds.) Advances in Neural Information Processing Systems, vol. 30, pp. 2990–2999. Curran Associates Inc. (2017)
9. Rusu., A., et al.: Progressive Neural Networks. CoRR (2016). http://arxiv.org/abs/1606.04671
10. Terekhov, A.V., Montone, G., O'Regan, J.K.: Knowledge transfer in deep block-modular neural networks. In: Wilson, S.P., Verschure, P.F.M.J., Mura, A., Prescott, T.J. (eds.) LIVINGMACHINES 2015. LNCS (LNAI), vol. 9222, pp. 268–279. Springer, Cham (2015). https://doi.org/10.1007/978-3-319-22979-9_27
11. LeCun, Y., Bottou, L., Bengio, Y., Haffner, P.: Gradient-based learning applied to document recognition. Proc. IEEE **86**(11), 2278–2324 (1998)
12. Krizhevsky, A.: Learning Multiple Layers of Features from Tiny Images. Technical report (2009)
13. Coates, A., Lee, H., Ng, A.: An analysis of single layer networks in unsupervised feature learning. In: Proceedings of AISTATS (2011)

# Affine Variational Autoencoders

Rene Bidart[1,2(✉)] and Alexander Wong[1,2]

[1] Waterloo Artificial Intelligence Institute, Waterloo, ON, Canada
[2] University of Waterloo, Waterloo, ON, Canada
{rbbidart,a28wong}@uwaterloo.ca

**Abstract.** Variational autoencoders (VAEs) have in recent years become one of the most powerful approaches to learning useful latent representations of data in an unsupervised manner. However, a major challenge with VAEs is that they have tremendous difficulty in generalizing to data that deviate from the training set (e.g., perturbed image variants). Normally data augmentation is leveraged to overcome this limitation; however, this is not only computational expensive but also necessitates the construction of more complex models. In this study, we introduce the notion of affine variational autoencoders (AVAEs), which extends upon the conventional VAE architecture through the introduction of affine layers. More specifically, within the AVAE architecture an affine layer perturbs the input image prior to the encoder, and a second affine layer performs an inverse perturbation to the output of the decoder. The parameters of the affine layers are learned to enable the AVAE to encode images at canonical perturbations, resulting in a better reconstruction and a disentangled latent space without the need for data augmentation or the use of more complex models. Experimental results demonstrate the efficacy of the proposed VAE architecture for generalizing to images in the MNIST validation set under affine perturbations without the need for data augmentation, demonstrating significantly reduced loss when compared to conventional VAEs.

**Keywords:** Deep learning · Variational autoencoders ·
Image generation · Perturbation

## 1 Introduction

Variational Autoencoders (VAE) [7] are generative models that can encode an data into a latent representation, as well as decoding back into data in the original domain. In recently years, VAEs have emerged into one of the most popular approaches to learning useful latent representations of images, and have been demonstrated its usefulness for tackling a wide variety of problems including image compression and generation (one of its most popular uses), music generation [14], creating dense representations for reinforcement learning [5], and even the creation of chemicals [3].

Supported by NSERC and the Canada Research Chairs program.

F. Karray et al. (Eds.): ICIAR 2019, LNCS 11662, pp. 461–472, 2019.
https://doi.org/10.1007/978-3-030-27202-9_42

One of the biggest challenges when leveraging VAEs is that they have tremendous difficulty in generalizing to data seen outside of the training set. For example, VAEs perform poorly for reconstructing images that have been perturbed, even by simple transformations. One of the most common approaches for mitigating this challenge is to leverage data augmentation, where a VAE is trained on data that has been randomly perturbed, thus improving the ability of the VAE to generalize to some pre-specified set of transformations. Unfortunately, not only is this approach computationally expensive but we also demonstrated that it necessitates an increase in model complexity in Sect. 4.2.

In addition, the use of data augmentation to compensate for the generalization capabilities of VAEs under perturbations is intuitively unappealing, especially since humans can easily understand objects regardless of their orientation. Motivated to tackle this generalization challenge, there has been extensive work in creating models that generalize across various orientations, ranging from the use of learned transforms to some canonical orientation [6] to the design of architectures that are equivariant to a specific transform [1].

In this study, we propose an alternative to the aforementioned approaches, which we will referred to as Affine Variational AutoEncoders (AVAEs). In the AVAE architecture, which extends upon the conventional VAE architecture through the introduction of affine layers. More specifically, an affine layer is integrated before the encoder to perturb the image to the canonical perturbation the network was trained on, thus enabling this perturbation to be encoded using the VAE and augment the latent space with the affine transform parameters, $\alpha$. For decoding, the latent space is sampled, and a second affine layer is integrated after the decoder to perform an inverse affine transform to produce the final output. The parameters of the affine layers are learned such that the resulting transform minimizes the loss of the VAE, and thus optimizing $\alpha$ to reduce this loss.

In a VAE, the latent encoding of an image is not necessarily disentangled, meaning that the individual variables do not have any semantically meaningful interpretation. Because it is desirable to have a representation that explicitly encodes semantically meaningful properties, there has been extensive work on the topic of learning disentangled representations [9,10,13,16] for a variety of properties, such as orientation, color or lighting. Another benefit of the approach proposed in this study is that the AVAE automatically disentangles the perturbation of an image from its latent representation.

In addition to VAEs, other deep generative models for images exist, such as generative adversarial networks [4] where the model learns to generate samples by forcing them to be indistinguishable from real images, and flow based generative models, where the distribution of images is explicitly learned through a sequence of invertible transforms from the image to a latent distribution [2]. We have chosen VAEs in this study because their encoder - decoder structure allows for both image generation and image compression into a latent representation, while their relatively simple structure allows more of a focus on the core goal of creating an architecture that has strong generalization capabilities and robustness under affine perturbations.

This paper is organized as follows. First, background and related work is discussed in Sect. 2. The proposed Affine Variational Autoencoder (AVAE) is described in detail in Sect. 3. Finally, the experimental setup and experimental results are discussed in Sect. 4.

## 2 Background and Related Work

In this section, we review various methods for improving the generalization capabilities of generative models and for learning disentangled representations. We also briefly explain equivariance and why it is useful, as well as review the concept of VAE.

### 2.1 Variational Auto Encoder

Variational autoencoders [7] (VAE) are generative models where it is assumed that the data, $X = \{x\}_{i=1}^{n}$ are generated from latent variables. An encoder and decoder network are simultaneously trained, where the encoder models the posterior distribution of latent variables $z$, given an image $x$ as $q_\phi(z|x)$, and a decoder that gives the probability of data (in this case, an image) conditioned on a latent variable $p_\rho$. It is assumed that the latent variables are independent standard normal, and that the generator will produce the mean of a $k \times k$ dimensional isotropic multivariate normal distribution, with the variance fixed as 1.

$$L_{VAE} = -E_{z \sim q_\phi}[log p_\rho(x|z)] + KL(q_\phi(z|x)||p_\rho(z))] \tag{1}$$

The objective of the VAE is to maximize the evidence lower bound shown in Eq. 1. To create this model, we use neural networks to approximate both $p$ and $q$. Because $q$ outputs the parameters for a normal distribution it is easy to compute the KL divergence $KL(q_\phi(z|x)||p_\rho(z))]$. To compute $-E_{z \sim q_\phi}[log p_\rho(x|z)]$, we will sample a single $z$ value from $q$, assuming that it is a good approximation of $p(z|x)$.

This entire network is differentiable, so can be trained with stochastic gradient descent, using the loss function shown in Eq. 1, where for each image we encode it into the parameters of a normal distribution, sample $z$ from this distribution, and then decode this to get $p(x|z)$.

### 2.2 Equivariance

Many recent developments in computer vision leverage the concept of convolutional layers, which is very powerful in that it encodes translation symmetry, enforced through weight sharing. This means that convolutional layers are equivariant under translations, but this is not true for other properties we may want symmetry for, such as scaling, rotations, and shear [1].

In general, equivariance is the property that a function commutes with some transformation, in this case translation. Formally, a function $f : X \mapsto Y$ is equivariant under a set of transforms $T$ if:

$$f(T(x)) = T'(f(x)) \tag{2}$$

In this study, we approach the problem of ensuring equivariance by explicitly undoing the transformation $T$ using $T^{-1}$. Assuming the encoder (excluding the affine layer) is shown as $q$, the affine transform is $t^{-1}$, and the latent representation is $z$ we apply:

$$f(t(x)) = q(t^{-1}(t(x))) = [q(x), \alpha] = t'([(q(x), 0]) = t'([(q(t^{-1}(x)), 0]) = t'(f(x)) \tag{3}$$

Here the $\alpha$ indicates the learned parameters from $t^{-1}$, and we use square brackets [] to explicitly indicate that learned transform parameters are appended to the latent space, $z$ after $t^{-1}$ is applied. $t'$ is the affine transform in the latent space, or simply the composition of the affine transform parameters with the existing parameters, $\alpha$. The application of $t^{-1}$ ensures that the encoder $q$ will act equivalently for all transforms $t$, and because the transform parameters, $\alpha$ is preserved, this transform commutes with the function by applying $t'$ directly to $\alpha$. This is based on the assumption that we can compute $t^{-1}$ using the process described in Sect. 3.2.

## 2.3  Generalizing to Affine Transforms and Disentangled Representations

There have been many attempts to learn representations that are robust under a set of transformations for uses such as image classification, compression, and generation. In addition, it is a goal to encode these transforms in an explicit way in the latent space, resulting in a more interpretable model.

Spatial Transformer Networks (STN) [6] apply an affine transform to the input image, transforming it to some canonical orientation. This can be described in terms of three components:

1. **Localization Network**: This is a neural network taking an image as input, and outputting the affine transformation parameters, $\alpha \in \mathbb{R}^6$ to be applied to this image.
2. **Sampling Grid**: Given a transform, the grid of coordinates in the input image associated with each pixel in the output image
3. **Image sampling**: Given the grid, use bilinear sampling to apply it to the input image.

This is differentiable, so it can be trained using stochastic gradient descent along with the rest of the network. The limitation with the use of STNs is that they approximate the best transform based on the localization network, and are not guaranteed to output the best transform, because if the STN network produces incorrect parameters, there is no process for the model to go back and update the transform.

More generally, there has been research on learning disentangled representations where semantically relevant variables are explicit in the latent space [13]. In general these are not limited to affine transforms, and include variations such a lighting, color, or physical attributes like shape. One approach is based on semi-supervised learning, where images are generated based on both a latent variable and some relevant factor of variation, which are assumed to be independent [9]. For face generation, disentangling shape and appearance was tackled through the synthesis of appearance on a template followed by a deformation [16]. Other work divides the latent space into explicit and implicit factors of variation, and training process of varying only one factor while fixing the others is used to enforce the disentangled latent space [10]. These methods all require supervised inputs, where they are labeled based on some factor of variation.

Other work has created networks that are equivariant to one specific factor of variation, for example, constructing deep convolutional neural networks that are equivariant to rotation and reflection [1]. While this is an interesting method, adding more factors of variation in this way increases the complexity dramatically, so is difficult to scale. Another approach to ensure deep convolutional neural networks are invariant to arbitrary affine transforms is to add a layer that applies a random affine transform to the feature map, forcing the model to output the same classification regardless of the orientation of the image [15], but additional methods are needed to get a disentangled representation based on this approach.

Another approach uses a transform invariant autoencoder and an inference model to infer transform parameters. The transformation invariance is achieved by using a cost function that allows the restored input to match any transformed image, rather than the exact input image [11]. Our method simplifies their approach, as we do not force the VAE to encode an image at any orientation, we learn the transform parameter first, then encode the image. Also, the use of a VAE allows sampling images, which is not possible with their autoencoder.

The proposed AVAE does not require explicit labels, and also does not require an increase in model complexity by forcing a single model to represent all possible perturbation of an image. As such, the proposed AVAE enables the learning of a generative model that is equivariant to affine perturbations without the need for forcing equivariance via model size expansion and data augmentation.

## 3 Affine Variational Autoencoders

The proposed Affine Variational Autoencoders (AVAE) extends upon the conventional VAE architecture with the introduction of two affine layers. More specifically, the input of the architecture is fed into the first affine layer, which performs an affine transform on the input before passing it into an encoder for latent space representation. The output of the decoder in the AVAE architecture is fed into a second affine layer, which performs an inverse affine transform to the output of the decoder to produce the final output. The parameters of the affine layers are learned such that the resulting AVAE can effectively encode input images at canonical perturbations, resulting in a better reconstruction, and a disentangled latent space without the need for data augmentation. In this section we will described the details of the proposed AVAE (Fig. 1).

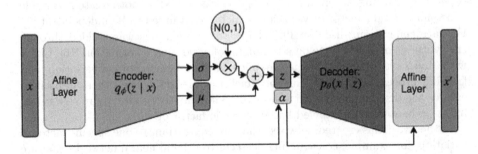

**Fig. 1.** Proposed Affine Variational AutoEncoder (AVAE) architecture. The AVAE architecture extends upon the conventional VAE architecture with the introduction of two affine layers. The first affine layer performs a learned affine transform to the input image, parameterized by α. This is encoded and decoded by the encoder and decoder, respectively, and finally the second affine layer performs a learned inverse transform to produce the final output.

## 3.1   Affine Transforms

The key concept introduced in the proposed AVAE architecture is the introduction of two affine layers on top of the VAE architecture. Unlike the spatial transformer network architecture, the proposed AVAE architecture does not output the parameters of the transform through a localization network. As a result, each affine layer in the AVAE consists of two parts: (i) a sampling grid, where the grid of coordinates in the input associated with each pixel in the output is determined for a given transform, and (ii) image sampling, where bilinear sampling is applied to the input given the derived grid.

More specifically, the affine layers in the AVAE architecture both take an affine transform as input, parameterized by an $3x3$ affine transform matrix, $\alpha$.

$$\alpha = \begin{bmatrix} \alpha_1 & \alpha_2 & \alpha_3 \\ \alpha_4 & \alpha_5 & \alpha_6 \\ \alpha_7 & \alpha_8 & \alpha_9 \end{bmatrix} \tag{4}$$

For example, in the case of rotational perturbations, the resulting transform can be represented as:

$$\alpha = \begin{bmatrix} cos(\theta) & sin(\theta) & 0 \\ -sin(\theta) & cos(\theta) & 0 \\ 0 & 0 & 1 \end{bmatrix} \tag{5}$$

The key difference between the two affine layers in the AVAE is that the first affine layer performs an affine transform on the input directly based on $\alpha$, while the second affine layer performs an affine transform on the input based on the inverse of $\alpha$.

## 3.2   Optimization and Training

Given an input image $x$, the objective of a conventional VAE is to learn a representation, $z = q_\phi(x)$ such that the loss, $L_{VAE}$ is minimized, or that the decoded image $x' = p_\rho(z)$ is as close as possible to $x$, and that the latent representation $z$ is distributed as $N(0, 1)$, as indicated in Sect. 2.1. In the proposed AVAE, the addition of the affine layers allows us to optimize the transform, $A(x) = x_A$, such that the loss of $p_\rho(q_\rho(x_A))$ is minimized.

More specifically, in the proposed AVAE, to encode an image we must learn $\alpha$ that minimizes the VAE loss in order to find the optimal affine transformation to apply to the input image. Therefore, we can formulate this as the following optimization problem:

$$\alpha = \operatorname*{argmin}_{\alpha} \left\{ L_{VAE}[A^{-1}(p_\rho(q_\phi(A(x))))] \right\} \tag{6}$$

where $A$ refers to the first affine layer, $A^{-1}$ refers to the second affine layer, both taking $\alpha$ as parameters. Note that the VAE parameters $q_\phi, p_\rho$ remain unchanged during this process.

The parameters of the affine layers can be learned using any optimization method, but most notably because this is a differentiable function, it is possible to optimize using gradient descent on $\alpha$.

Training of the proposed AVAE is done identically to the process of training a conventional VAE, as outlined in Sect. 2.1. The affine layers can either be trained or can be totally ignored during this training process (and derived as a post processing stage). As such, it is possible to take any conventional VAE architecture and transform it to an AVAE architecture by adding these affine layers.

## 4   Experiments

In this section, we will demonstrate the efficacy of the proposed AVAE architecture for improving generalization capabilities for images under affine perturbations.

## 4.1   Dataset

For these experiments we leverage the MNIST dataset. MNIST is particular useful for illustrating the efficacy of perturbation robustness in generative models since all digits come in a standard orientation, and as such enables the generation of test images with defined affine perturbations for evaluation of generalization performance.

## 4.2   Implementation

All experiments were implemented using Pytorch [12], and trained using a Nvidia 1080Ti GPU. Optimization was done using the Adam Optimizer [8], with the learning rate set to 0.001, and the weight decay set to 0.0005. The MNIST dataset was normalized by mean and standard deviation, but otherwise no other preprocessing was used.

## 4.3   Experiment 1: Generalization Under Rotational Perturbations

VAEs are only good at encoding data into a latent representation when they were trained on that type of data. While a VAE can easily encode and generate examples of digits, the model is unable to generalize to rotated digits unless it was explicitly trained on this data. In the first experiment, we explore quantitatively the generalization of VAEs under perturbation via a comprehensive analysis under different rotational perturbations.

As shown in Fig. 2(a), the performance of a conventional VAE architecture decreases as they are forced to encode images that deviate from the training set, in this case in the form of a rotation. The loss reaches a maximum around 100 degrees, with it decreasing after this. This is because many digits look similar when vertically flipped, like 1 or 8, so models can effectively reconstruct those with a 180° rotation. Figure 2(b) visually shows the inability of the VAE to encode and decode images after they have been rotated.

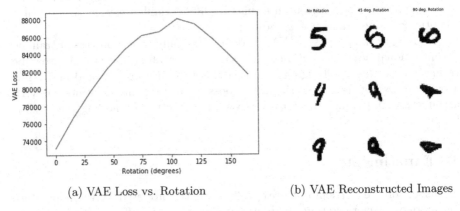

(a) VAE Loss vs. Rotation              (b) VAE Reconstructed Images

**Fig. 2. (a)**: Average loss of a VAE over the MNIST validation set while varying rotational perturbation. Model was trained without data augmentation, so does not generalize well to novel orientations as the input image deviates from the training set. **(b)**: Examples of reconstructed images from a VAE trained on MNIST with no rotation, 45°. rotation, and 90° rotation. It can be clearly observed that the quality of the reconstructed images degrade significantly under rotation.

## 4.4   Experiment 2: Limitations of Data Augmentation

One approach to create a generative model that is able to generalize well is to ensure they are trained to see all possible perturbations of these input images. This is known as data augmentation, and involves pre-specifying a set of transforms that are considered acceptable inputs to the model, so the model should generalize to this set of transforms. In the second experiment, we explore quantitatively the generalization of VAEs trained via data augmentation under perturbation via a comprehensive analysis under different rotational perturbations.

By training VAEs with an identical architecture on both a rotation-augmented dataset and a dataset without rotation data augmentation, we can see that for any given loss the model trained with a rotation-augmented dataset will require a significantly larger latent size. This is shown in Fig. 3. This could be partially avoided through the use of a more complex model, but reinforces the assertion that it is expensive to make a VAE generalize well to perturbations via data augmentation.

## 4.5   Experiment 3: Performance of Affine Variational Autoencoders

The proposed AVAE architecture allows for generative models that are more robust to perturbations without the added expense of training on augmented data. In the third experiment, we explore quantitatively the generalization of the proposed AVAE architecture under perturbation via a comprehensive analysis under different affine transforms such as rotational perturbations and shear perturbations.

**Comprehensive Analysis over Rotational Perturbations.** First, we perform a comprehensive analysis to evaluate the generalization of the performance of the AVAE against rotational perturbations. As shown in Fig. 3(b), which shows the loss when using a conventional VAE architecture vs. the proposed AVAE architecture, it can be clearly observed that the loss when using AVAE is significantly reduced across all rotational perturbations. The unusual shape of the loss of the proposed AVAE is due to distortions in the image stemming from the rotation, and resampling of the image at a new orientation. These are relatively largest when the rotation is diagonal (45 or 135°), and do not appear when it is a multiple of a 90° rotation.

Figure 4 shows specific examples of the poor reconstruction performance of the conventional VAE architecture when generalizing to rotation perturbations, while the proposed AVAE architecture performs well under such perturbations. Overall this indicates that by leveraging the proposed AVAE architecture, one can construct generative models that can generalize well to images under perturbations.

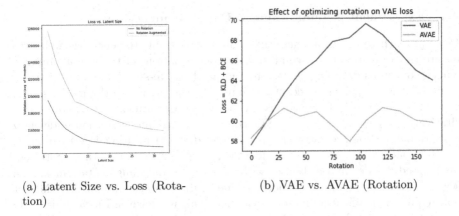

(a) Latent Size vs. Loss (Rotation)

(b) VAE vs. AVAE (Rotation)

**Fig. 3.** (a): Comparison of the loss associated with VAEs trained on data with and without rotation augmentation. The rotation augmented model requires a larger latent size to get comparable loss. (b): Loss with VAE architecture vs. AVAE architecture. Loss is significantly reduced in the proposed AVAE architecture across all rotations.

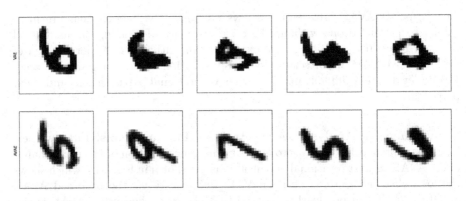

**Fig. 4.** Examples of reconstructed images using conventional VAE architecture (top row) and the proposed AVAE architecture (bottom row) under rotational perturbations.

**Comprehensive Analysis over Shear Perturbations.** Next, we perform a comprehensive analysis to evaluate the generalization of the performance of the AVAE against shear perturbations. As shown in Fig. 5, it can be observed that there is a clear improvement in the performance of the proposed AVAE architecture compared to the conventional VAE architecture across most shear perturbations. The improvements of AVAE over VAE is not as significant as in the case of rotational perturbations due to the fact that the conventional VAE architecture tends to generalize better to shear perturbations than rotational perturbations.

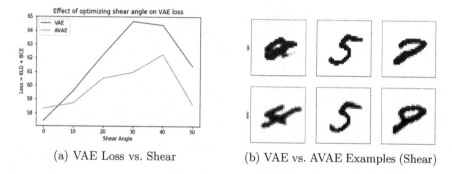

(a) VAE Loss vs. Shear              (b) VAE vs. AVAE Examples (Shear)

**Fig. 5. (a)**: Comparison of the performance of the VAE and AVE under shear perturbations of various angles. AVAE shows overall improved performance compared to the
VAE. **(b)**: Examples of reconstructed images using conventional VAE architecture (top
row) and the proposed AVAE architecture (bottom row) under shear perturbations.

## 5  Conclusion and Future Work

In this work, we introduce an alternative method to ensure equivariance to
affine perturbations in the form of the proposed affine variational autoencoders
(AVAE). In the proposed AVAE architecture, affine layers are introduced into the
architecture to enable an affine transform prior to encoding and an inverse affine
transform after the decoding, with the parameters of the affine layers learned.
Experimental results show that the proposed AVAE architecture can achieve
good encoding performance even under different affine perturbations without
the need for data augmentation. We motivate the proposed AVAE approach by
showing the limitations of VAEs in encoding data under various affine perturbations, as well as that data augmentation has some limitations solving this issue
due to increased model complexity or latent size required to encode a variety of
affine perturbations such as rotational and shear perturbations.

Currently, the AVAE presented in this study is limited because it must be
trained on a set of images of a fixed perturbation in order to get the maximum
performance gains in terms of encoding an image as efficiently as possible. A
useful extension would be to investigate training on images without a fixed perturbation, by simultaneously optimizing the transform and the encoder for a
batch of images. Given some constraint on the latent variable size, it could be
possible to perturb all images to the same perturbation, as this would result in
the greatest representation capacity for a given latent size.

## References

1. Cohen, T., Welling, M.: Group equivariant convolutional networks. In: International Conference on Machine Learning, pp. 2990–2999 (2016)
2. Dinh, L., Krueger, D., Bengio, Y.: Nice: non-linear independent components estimation. arXiv preprint arXiv:1410.8516 (2014)

3. Gómez-Bombarelli, R., et al.: Automatic chemical design using a data-driven continuous representation of molecules. ACS Cent. Sci. **4**(2), 268–276 (2018)
4. Goodfellow, I., et al.: Generative adversarial nets. In: Advances in Neural Information Processing Systems, pp. 2672–2680 (2014)
5. Ha, D., Schmidhuber, J.: World models. arXiv preprint arXiv:1803.10122 (2018)
6. Jaderberg, M., Simonyan, K., Zisserman, A., Kavukcuoglu, K.: Spatial transformer networks. CoRR abs/1506.02025 (2015). http://arxiv.org/abs/1506.02025
7. Kingma, D.P., Welling, M.: Auto-Encoding Variational Bayes. ArXiv e-prints, December 2013
8. Kingma, D.P., Ba, J.: Adam: a method for stochastic optimization. arXiv preprint arXiv:1412.6980 (2014)
9. Kingma, D.P., Mohamed, S., Rezende, D.J., Welling, M.: Semi-supervised learning with deep generative models. In: Advances in Neural Information Processing Systems, pp. 3581–3589 (2014)
10. Kulkarni, T.D., Whitney, W.F., Kohli, P., Tenenbaum, J.: Deep convolutional inverse graphics network. In: Advances in Neural Information Processing Systems, pp. 2539–2547 (2015)
11. Matsuo, T., Fukuhara, H., Shimada, N.: Transform invariant auto-encoder. In: 2017 IEEE/RSJ International Conference on Intelligent Robots and Systems (IROS), pp. 2359–2364. IEEE (2017)
12. Paszke, A., et al.: Automatic Differentiation in Pytorch (2017)
13. Ridgeway, K.: A survey of inductive biases for factorial representation-learning. arXiv preprint arXiv:1612.05299 (2016)
14. Roberts, A., Engel, J., Raffel, C., Hawthorne, C., Eck, D.: A hierarchical latent vector model for learning long-term structure in music. arXiv preprint arXiv:1803.05428 (2018)
15. Shen, X., Tian, X., He, A., Sun, S., Tao, D.: Transform-invariant convolutional neural networks for image classification and search. In: Proceedings of the 24th ACM International Conference on Multimedia, pp. 1345–1354. ACM (2016)
16. Shu, Z., Sahasrabudhe, M., Alp Güler, R., Samaras, D., Paragios, N., Kokkinos, I.: Deforming autoencoders: unsupervised disentangling of shape and appearance. In: Ferrari, V., Hebert, M., Sminchisescu, C., Weiss, Y. (eds.) ECCV 2018. LNCS, vol. 11214, pp. 664–680. Springer, Cham (2018). https://doi.org/10.1007/978-3-030-01249-6_40

# Author Index

Printed in the United States
By Bookmasters